THE COMPLETE ILLUSTRATED STITCH ENCYCLOPEDIA

THE COMPLETE ILLUSTRATED STITCH ENCYCLOPEDIA

Crafter's Choice®
New York

Designed and edited by Eaglemoss Publications Ltd

Based on *Needlecraft Magic*

Photographic credits: (front cover) Alan Duns (tl,c,br); Coral Mula (tr,bl);
(back cover) Edward J Allwright (cr);
Maria Diaz (bl); Alan Duns (br); Coral Mula (cl)

First published in North America in 2001 by
Crafter's Choice®
1271 Avenue of the Americas
New York, NY 10020

ISBN 0-965-019650

Printed in the United States of America

Contents

Introduction

For hundreds of years, embroiderers have used needle and thread to create beautiful designs on fabric and canvas, and have passed their skills down the generations, adding new techniques and patterns. *The Complete Illustrated Stitch Encyclopedia* is a comprehensive guide to this creative craft, packed with hundreds of stitches and useful skills. Encompassing designs and techniques from both the past and the present, this informative encyclopedia will help you to become a confident stitcher and develop your own style.

How to Use This Book

Clear color photographs and illustrated step-by-step instructions show you how to work more than 250 stitches and perfect a wide range of techniques. Each technique is explained in simple stages with advice from the experts to help you achieve flawless results. Once you have mastered the stitches and techniques, you can test your skills by making the beautiful projects featured. For easy reference, the encyclopedia is divided into five chapters:

Before You Start gives vital information on basic materials and techniques, such as choosing and preparing threads and fabrics, using a hoop, following a chart, and transferring designs.

Embroidery Stitch Library explains how to work a variety of stitches, from old favorites, such as counted cross stitch and satin stitch, to the more advanced, including shisha and blackwork. Complete with valuable information on the best threads and fabrics to use, there is a fascinating collection of projects, such as comfy slippers for children, a pretty floral lampshade, and stylish table linen.

Needlepoint Stitch Library features numerous stitches to work on canvas, from simple tent stitches to the more complex textured stitches. A colorful collection of fun-to-make designs includes a maple leaf pincushion, a Peruvian-inspired bag, a medieval-style cushion, and an attractive cushion cover influenced by a Turkish kilim.

Special Techniques comprises traditional needlecrafts, from pulled thread work to ribbon embroidery, Hardanger, and Bargello. Items to make include a traditional Florentine footstool cover and an elegant contemporary rug.

Finishing and Making Up gives essential information on how to present your embroidery, such as straightening distorted canvases and framing pictures.

The Complete Illustrated Stitch Encyclopedia will teach you exciting new skills as you make beautiful gifts to delight family and friends, and decorative items to furnish your home. This practical and easy-to-use encyclopedia invites you to share a time-honored craft that has brought pleasure and satisfaction to stitchers across the world. Enjoy!

Chapter I
Before You Start

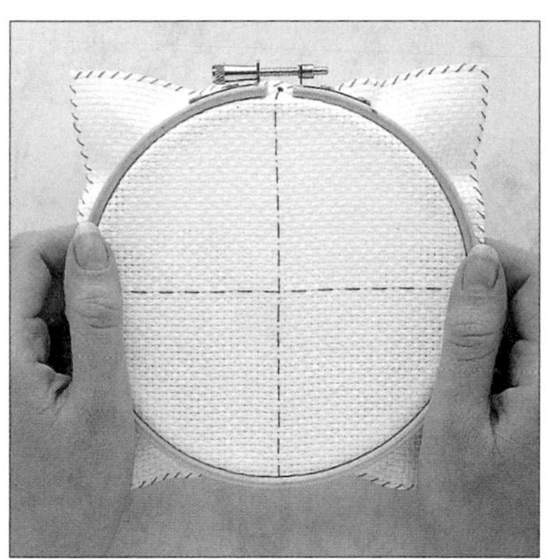

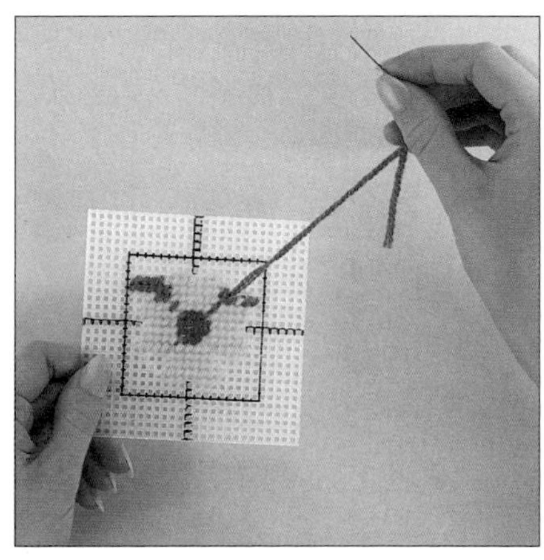

Handling threads

There's a huge choice of threads available for embroidery and needlepoint, each with its own special qualities. They fall into two groups—divisible threads and non-divisible threads. Divisible threads can be separated or combined to make thinner or thicker threads. You can also use several lengths of some non-divisible threads together for a bulky look.

Before starting a project, cut the threads into manageable lengths of no more than 12–16 in. (30–40 cm). To keep them neat and prevent tangling, store them in either a store-bought or homemade organizer (see page 10).

Tapestry yarn is a hardwearing, twisted thread which cannot be divided. Small skeins are available in a wide range of colors. Large skeins for background areas come in a restricted color range.

Brilliant cutwork and embroidery thread is a non-divisible thread available in quite a few colors. It is often used for blackwork and monograms.

Metallic threads are available in a limited number of shades. They are effective for highlighting stitches in other threads and can also be used on their own.

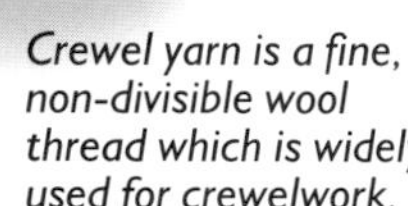

Crewel yarn is a fine, non-divisible wool thread which is widely used for crewelwork.

Embroidery floss is made up of six strands which can be divided and recombined to give whatever thickness you require.

Danish flower thread is a fine, non-divisible thread with a matte finish. It is used for counted thread embroidery, particularly counted cross stitch.

Ribbon comes in many different colors, widths, and materials.

Matte embroidery cotton is a heavy, twisted thread with a matte finish. It works well on fairly coarse fabric and cannot be divided.

Machine embroidery threads are available in a wide variety of colors. They may be glossy or metallic, and some are space-dyed with stripes. They are non-divisible.

Silk is usually reserved for luxury fabrics such as silk. This divisible thread should be used in short lengths only, as it snags and wears thin quickly.

Persian yarn consists of three fine, loosely twisted strands which you can divide and then recombine.

Pearl cotton is a shiny twisted thread available in three weights (3, 5, and 8), and a range of solid and shaded colors. It cannot be divided.

Storing threads on a card

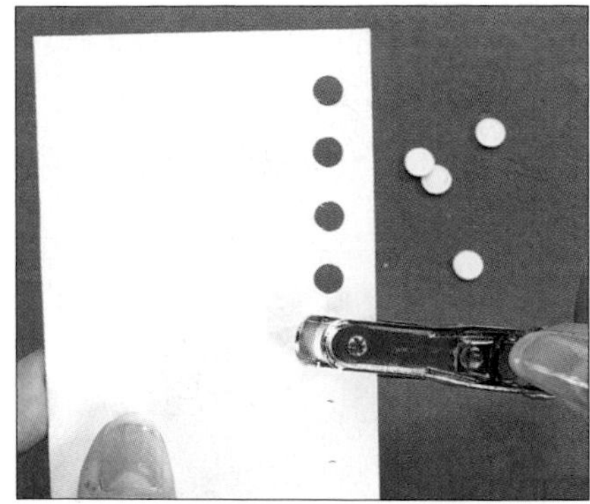

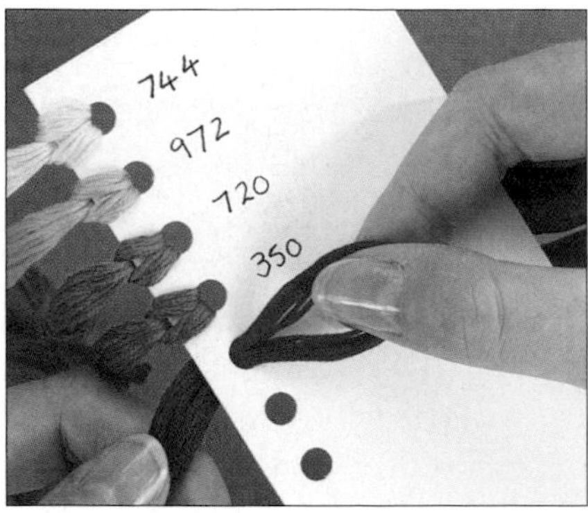

1 Cut a strip of card 10 x 4 in. (25 x 10 cm). Use a single hole punch to make a row of holes about 3/8 in. (1 cm) apart, along one long edge.

2 Loop the threads through the holes and pass the ends through, as though making a fringe. Write the shade number beside each hole.

For long-term storage, split each type of thread into color groups such as reds, greens, yellows, and blues and keep each group in its own labeled box.

Storing threads in a braid

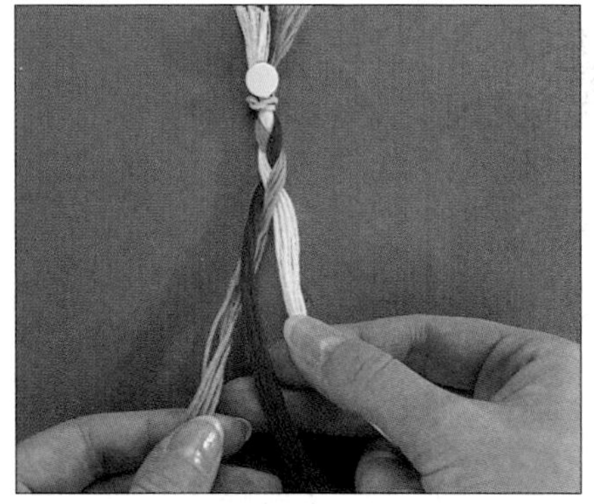

1 Hold three bunches of threads together at one end with a rubber band. Pin them to a firm surface, then braid them together loosely.

2 To remove a single strand of thread, hold the thread braid in one hand and use the other hand to pull the thread downward gently.

Dividing and combining embroidery floss

For a smooth finish to your work, always divide embroidery floss into separate strands before you start stitching, even if you are using all six strands. Then recombine the required number of strands.

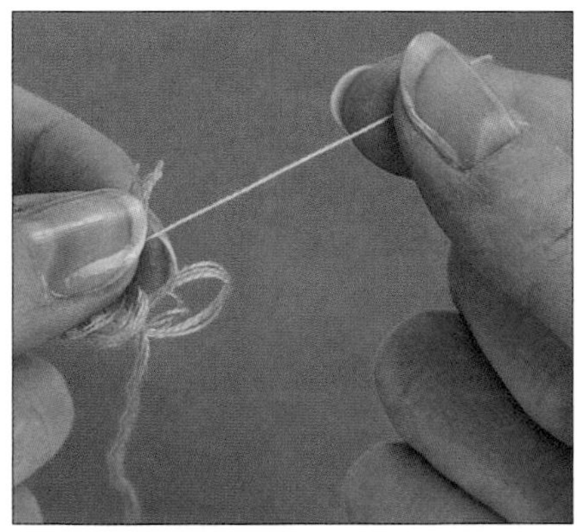

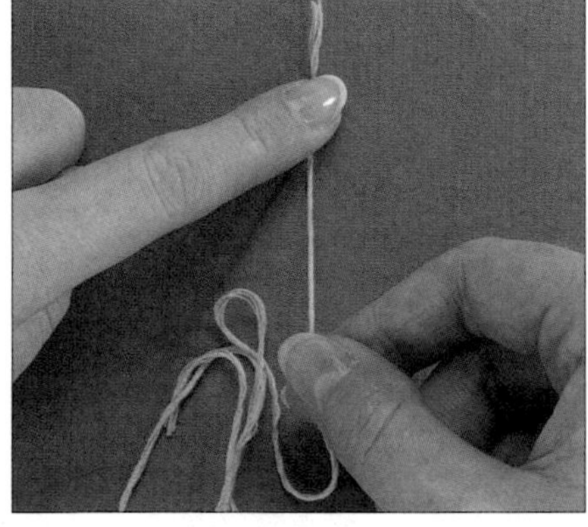

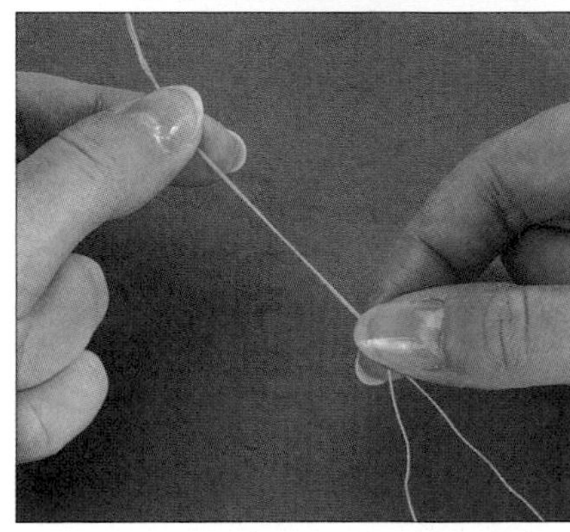

1 Cut a 15 in. (38 cm) length of floss. Firmly grasp the top of the floss length in one hand. Then use the other hand to pull up one strand.

2 Smooth out the remaining bunched strands. Repeat these two steps to withdraw more individual strands, as required.

3 To combine strands, hold two strands with the tops level. Smooth them along the length—don't twist them. Add more strands one by one.

Fabric guide

Embroidery fabrics fall into two groups—evenweaves and non-evenweaves. Evenweave fabric has an equal number of horizontal (weft) and vertical (warp) threads to every 1 in. (2.5 cm). This number is called the count; the higher the count, the finer the weave. Evenweave fabric is used for counted thread techniques, such as cross stitch, blackwork, and drawn-thread work.

Non-evenweave fabric includes a great variety of fabrics in which the thread count is *not* equal in both directions. These fabrics are used for surface, or free-style embroidery and for appliqué and cutwork.

Department stores stock the most popular fabrics, but a wider range is available from needlecraft stores. Use the best-quality fabric you can afford, to ensure that your work will last for many years.

Evenweave fabrics

Single evenweave fabric is woven with single threads. Linen is the traditional fiber used for single evenweave, but it is sometimes blended with cotton or other fibers. All-cotton, cotton-synthetic, and all-synthetic evenweaves are also available. Most single evenweaves fall in the 20-30-count range. The color range is fairly limited—white, cream, and natural being by far the most common. **Hardanger fabric** is woven from double threads—pure cotton or cotton-viscose—and is usually 22-count. It is used for cross stitch, traditional Norwegian Hardanger embroidery, and other counted thread techniques. In addition to white, it comes in several other colors. **Aida** (pronounced "aid-a") is the most popular fabric for counted cross stitch, and is woven from blocks of threads. Aida is usually 100% cotton, and comes in a range of colors and counts, 11- and 14-count being among the most common. Variations on the basic aida fabric include a "rustic" style, which has a homespun texture; a "damask" type, made from a cotton-rayon blend, which has a soft sheen; and a kind that has a grid of blue threads woven through it to serve as a guide to positioning stitches—these are pulled out once the embroidery is worked. **Bands** are made of aida fabric or evenweave linen. They can be decorated and then applied to towels, tablecloths, and bed linens. They are sold by the yard (meter) in a range of widths, colors, and edgings.

Other evenweave fabrics

Perforated paper has a 14-count grid of holes. Popular for counted thread work, it can be trimmed close to the stitching without fraying.

Vinyl-Weave™, a washable and tear-resistant plastic material, is used for counted cross stitch. It is available in small cream-colored sheets.

Damask/aida fabric has woven designs, such as flowers and foliage, interspersed with areas of aida which can be used for counted thread techniques.

Non-evenweave fabrics

This huge category includes fabrics with a plain weave (the simplest kind, also used for evenweave) and other weaves such as twill, satin, and velvet. Some of the plain weaves, such as gingham, have a regular woven pattern which can be used for counted cross stitch, but most of these fabrics are used for other kinds of embroidery and for appliqué. Several manufacturers produce non-evenweave fabrics specially designed for embroidery, usually woven from linen, cotton, or a cotton-synthetic blend and generally restricted to neutral colors. Some decorator fabrics are suitable for embroidery. Firmly woven cottons, such as **lawn** and **poplin**, are useful multipurpose fabrics. **Wool** can be decorated with surface embroidery. **Silk**, the most luxurious of all the embroidery fabrics, comes in a range of weights, from fine to heavy.

Stabilizing fabrics

Water-soluble fabric is a thin plastic film used to stabilize delicate fabrics for machine embroidery. Two layers are stretched over the embroidery fabric; the film dissolves when immersed in water.

Tear-away embroidery backing is a non-woven material which is basted to the wrong side of the fabric to stabilize it for hand or machine embroidery. On completion, the backing is carefully torn or cut away from around the embroidered motif.

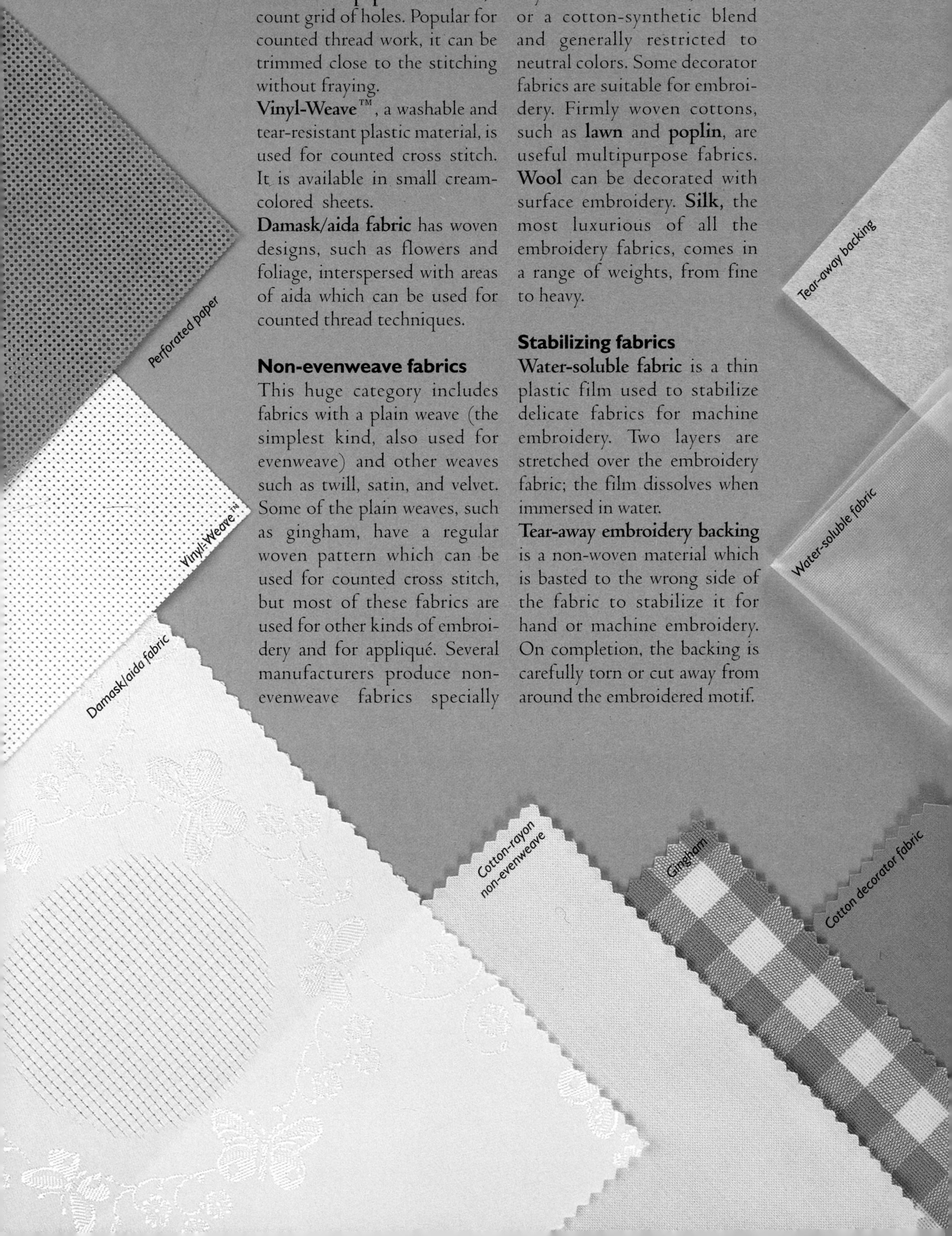

Transferring designs

There are many ways of transferring embroidery designs to fabric. The method you should choose depends mainly on the type of fabric, the type of design, and the time it will take to complete the embroidery.

For all methods, except basting, make sure that your embroidery covers the design lines, just in case you cannot remove the marks completely. Always test the chosen method on a scrap of fabric first.

Dressmaker's carbon paper is suitable for transferring designs onto smooth, washable fabrics in light to medium colors. Choose carbon paper in a color close to your fabric shade. Take care not to lean on the paper or you could leave smudges on the fabric.

Transfer pencils are useful for transferring both large and small designs onto smooth, washable fabrics. The fabric must be paler than the pencil color. For the best results, keep the pencil sharp.

Air-erasable marking pens are suitable for rough and smooth fabrics, including those that are not washable. However, the marks fade quickly, so use them only for designs that will take just a short time to complete. This method is best suited to pale fabrics, on which the marks will be visible.

Water-soluble marking pens can be used on both rough and smooth washable fabrics. They, too, are best suited to fairly pale fabrics for visibility.

Dressmaker's chalk works best on smooth fabrics in any color. It brushes off easily, so it should be used only for small designs that can be completed quickly.

Basting can be used to mark out designs on any fabric in any color.

The pricking method is a traditional method of transferring designs, suitable for any fabric. The powder brushes off easily, so the design outlines are usually reinforced with a marker pen.

Using dressmaker's carbon paper

1 Trace your design onto tracing paper with an ordinary pencil. Lay out your fabric right side up, and pin or tape the tracing on top. Slip a piece of dressmaker's carbon, carbon side down, in between.

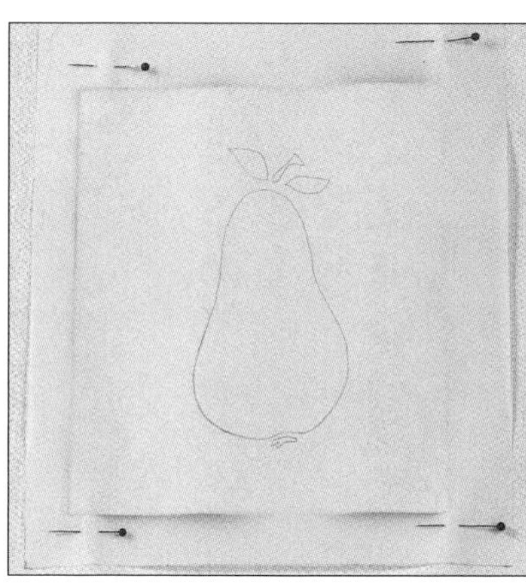

2 Firmly trace over the pencil lines with a pencil or tracing wheel. Check that the design has transferred to the fabric, and go over the lines, if need be. Wash out the transfer marks after working the embroidery.

Using a transfer pencil

1 Trace your design onto tracing paper with an ordinary pencil. Turn over the tracing, and go over the lines with the transfer pencil.

2 Lay out your fabric right side up, and lay the tracing, transfer side down, on top. Press with a medium-hot iron to transfer the design. Wash out the transfer marks after working the embroidery.

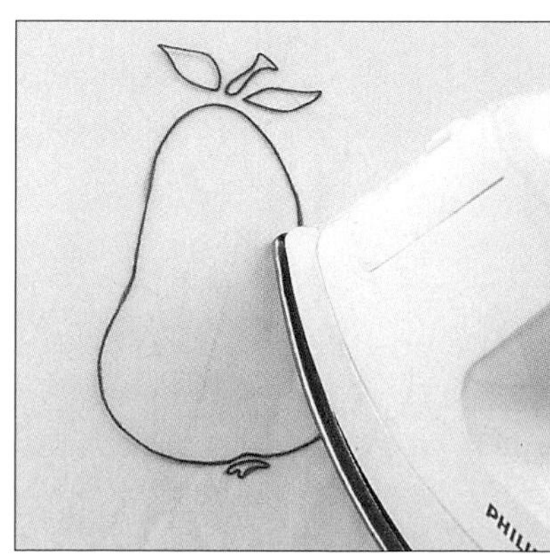

Using fabric markers and dressmaker's chalk

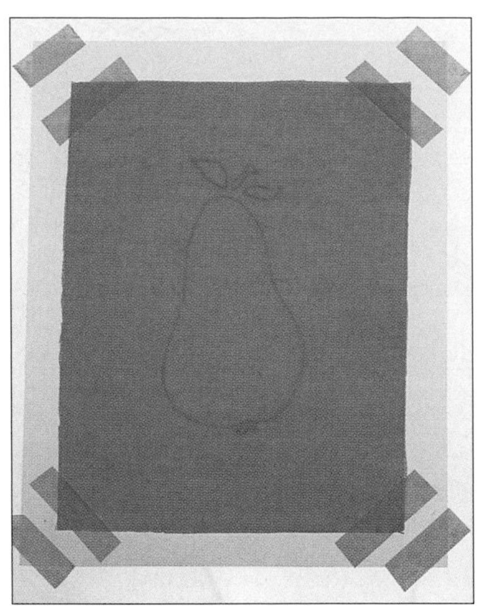

1 Trace the design with an ordinary pencil. Tape the tracing onto a sunny window, and tape the fabric, right side up, on top. Alternatively, lay the tracing and fabric on a piece of glass placed over a lamp.

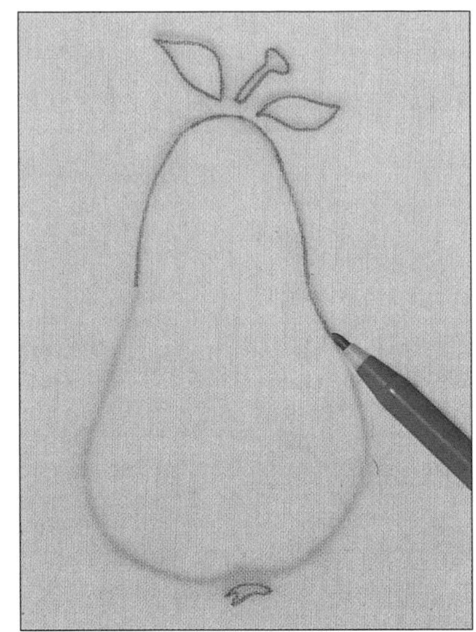

2 Trace the design onto the fabric with a marker pen or dressmaker's chalk. Marks made with an air-erasable marker will fade with time, and chalk will brush off. Use water to remove marks made with a water-soluble marker.

Basting

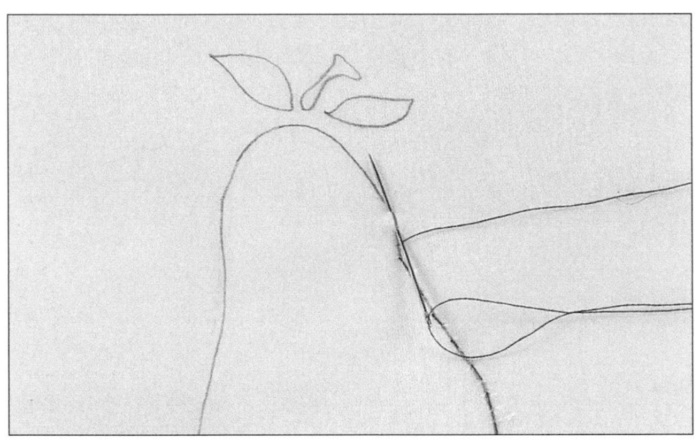

1 Trace the design with an ordinary pencil. Lay out the fabric, right side up, then position the tracing on top. Baste over the lines with sewing thread, using a color that contrasts with the fabric.

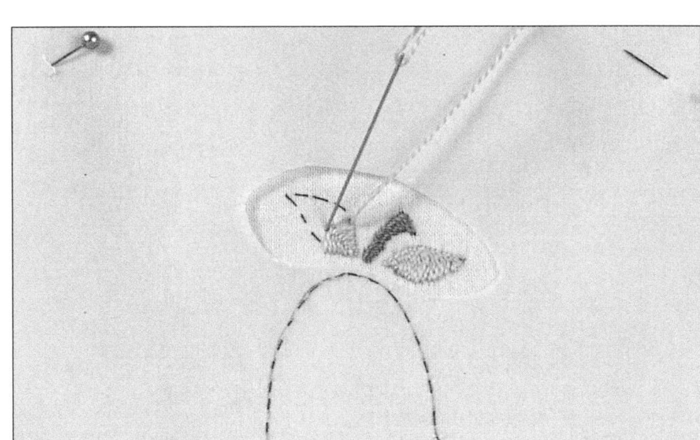

2 Tear away the tracing over the area of the design you wish to work first. Either cover the basting with embroidery or remove it as you go along. When the design is complete, remove any remaining visible basting threads.

The pricking method

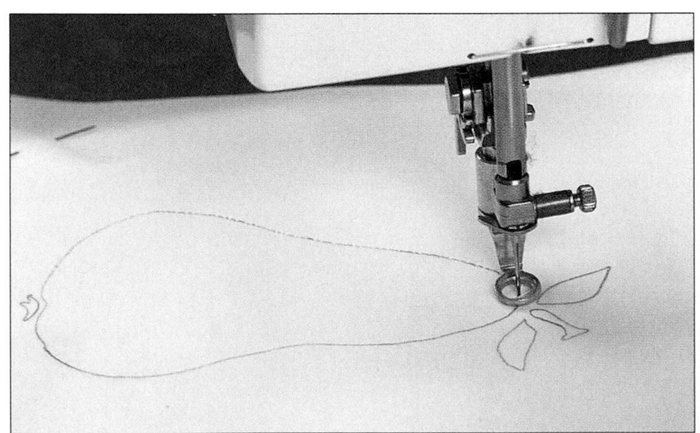

1 Trace your design and pin the tracing to a scrap of fabric. Set the sewing machine, unthreaded, to a long straight stitch. Fit an embroidery foot, if you have one, then stitch along the design lines to mark the paper. Alternatively, use a needle stuck into a cork.

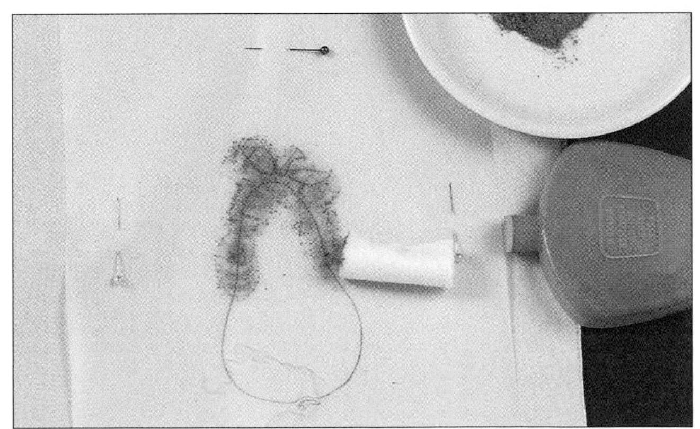

2 Remove the backing fabric, then pin the tracing to the fabric to be embroidered. Roll up a scrap of felt, dip it into pounce powder, and then rub it over the tracing. Take off the tracing and brush off any excess powder. If you wish, use a marker pen to join up the dotted outline.

Counted cross stitch

The appeal of counted cross stitch is that you can recreate a design exactly and achieve perfect results. The designs are worked from charts printed on squared paper, each square representing one cross stitch. The stitches are worked on evenweave fabric which has easily countable threads that form a grid, like the squares on the chart.

Fabrics, threads, and needles

Most cross stitch embroidery is worked on evenweave fabric (see page 11). The simplest evenweave to use is aida cloth, because each stitch is worked over one thread intersection, and the gaps between these are easy to see.

When you work on single evenweave, you need to count threads, as you will be working over two or more. However, with practice you will find these fairly easy to count, provided the count is not exceptionally high.

You can use many types of thread for counted cross stitch. However, the most versatile is cotton/embroidery floss. You can separate it into different numbers of strands to suit the fabric count, and it comes in a range of colors. Only work with lengths of up to 15 in. (38 cm), to avoid tangles.

Unlike surface embroidery—for which a sharp-pointed crewel or (larger) chenille needle is normally required—counted cross stitch is worked using a tapestry needle. This has a blunt point and so will slip between the fabric threads without splitting them.

Getting started

Before you start to stitch, cut the fabric at least 2 in. (5 cm) larger all around than the motif, and overcast the edges or cover them with masking tape to prevent fraying. Mark the center with basting, as shown below.

You'll find it easier to work the stitching if you use an embroidery frame of some kind—either a hoop (see page 16) or a rectangular frame (see page 20). This will make it easier to count the threads and to stitch with an even tension.

22-count
18-count
14-count
11-count
8-count

Aida has blocks of threads which are easy to see and count. Popular counts are 11, with 11 thread blocks per inch (2.5 cm) and 14, with 14 thread blocks per inch (2.5 cm).

Embroidery floss has six strands which you split and then recombine to suit the fabric and the design. Unless stated otherwise, use two strands on 14-count fabric and three on coarser 11-count.

Preparing the fabric

1 Cut the fabric at least 2 in. (5 cm) larger all around than the motif. Overcast the raw edges by hand, or zigzag-stitch all around.

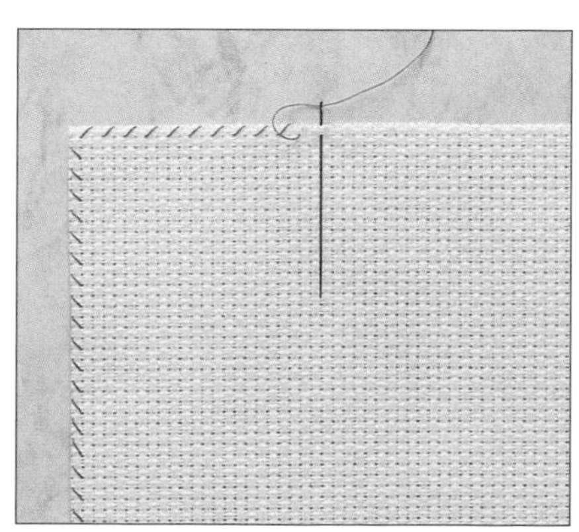

2 Fold the fabric into quarters. Unfold it and work a line of basting along each fold. The point at which the basting lines cross each other marks the center of the fabric.

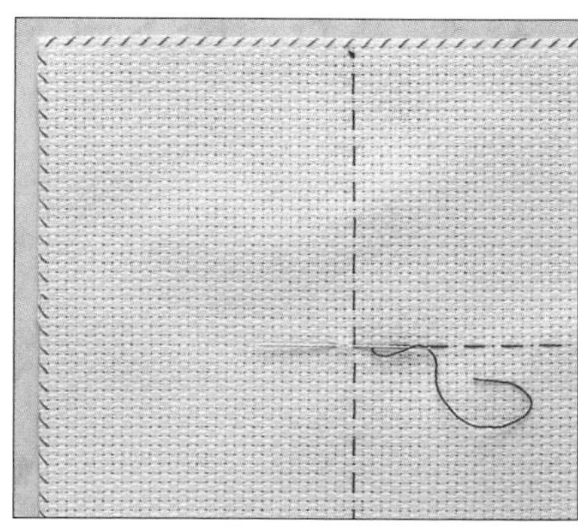

Mounting the fabric in a hoop

You'll always get better results if you use an embroidery hoop. It holds the fabric taut, so you stitch more evenly, and it reduces fabric distortion.

Embroidery hoops consist of an inner ring which fits inside an adjustable outer ring. They are made of wood or plastic and range in size from 4 to 12 in. (10 to 30 cm) in diameter. Choose a hoop that's large enough to fit the project; for larger pieces, move the fabric around in the hoop as you finish each section, taking care not to damage the stitching.

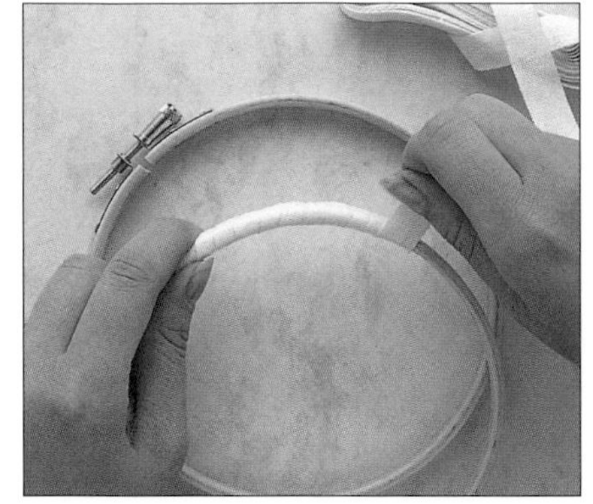

1 To prevent the fabric from slipping, bind the smaller ring with cotton tape. Secure the end with a few stitches.

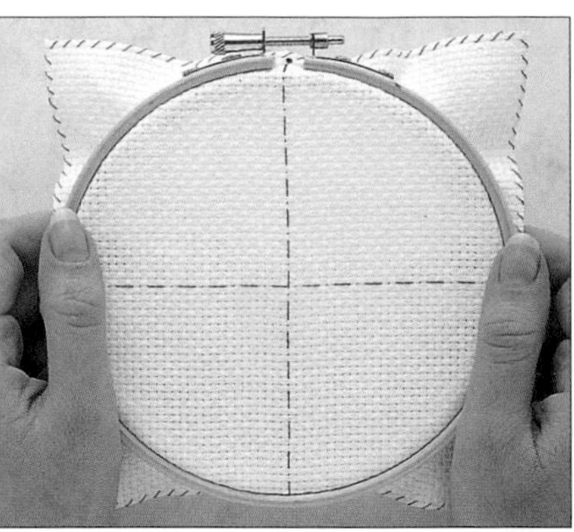

2 Center the fabric over the smaller ring. Ease the larger ring in place, making sure the fabric is taut and even. Tighten the screw on the outer ring.

Using counted cross stitch charts

Using a counted cross stitch chart is just a matter of matching the squares on the chart with the grid of threads on your evenweave fabric. This book uses two types of chart: color and black and white. On each type, one filled square represents one stitch.

Color symbol charts (see below) show each stitch as a symbol drawn in a square of the appropriate color. The key (below right) shows which color thread to use for each symbol and the number of skeins required.

Black and white charts show each stitch as a symbol.

Small symbols or **colored triangles** on some charts show fractional, or three-quarter, stitches.

Heavy lines indicate outlines and special details. These are usually worked in backstitch, added after the cross stitch is complete.

Arrows at the center of each edge enable you to find the center of the design so that you can relate it to the center of the fabric. To find the center, join the arrows with a pencil and ruler. Always start stitching in the center, working outward from the center of the design, to prevent distortion.

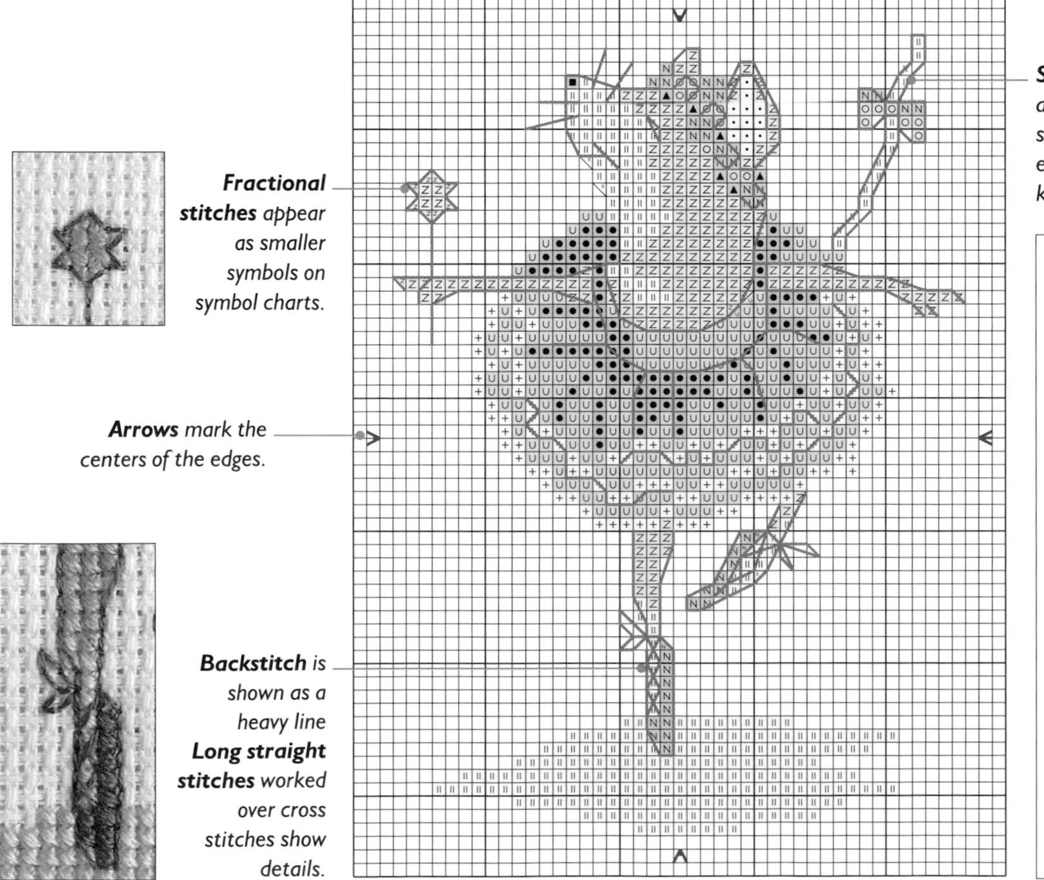

Symbols *Each colored square with a symbol indicates a single cross stitch. The correct thread color for each symbol is shown in the color key below.*

COLOR KEY

COLORS	SKEINS
● 322 Dark blue	1
■ 434 Dark brown	1
Z 437 Golden brown	1
II 739 Light golden brown	1
+ 775 Light blue	1
▲ 987 Green	1
N 3687 Dark pink	1
O 3688 Pink	1
· 3689 Light pink	1
U 3755 Blue	1

Backstitch—use one strand Dark brown 434

Waste canvas

Using waste canvas makes it possible to stitch your favorite cross stitch motifs on anything from T-shirts and towels to curtains and bedspreads no matter what fabric they're made of.

Waste canvas is an evenweave, mesh-like fabric, woven from threads stiffened with starch. It's very easy to use—you simply baste it over the area you want to embroider and then work the design through the canvas onto the fabric, using the mesh as a stitching guide.

Colored threads are woven into the canvas at regular intervals to make it easy to place the design. The mesh is formed from pairs of threads—when you stitch, treat each pair as a single thread, and insert the needle through the large holes that are between the thread intersections. When you have finished stitching, use a small amount of water to dampen the waste canvas to soften the starch, then pull out the threads one by one, to leave a perfectly stitched design on your main fabric.

Waste canvas is sold by the yard or in pre-cut pieces. It comes in a range of mesh sizes, from 8 pairs of threads per inch (2.5 cm), to 16 pairs of threads per inch (2.5 cm). If you can't find waste canvas in the mesh size you need, you can use a ordinary single thread or Penelope canvas instead. Don't try to use interlock canvas as the threads will be difficult to remove.

For stitching, use a crewel or chenille needle instead of the usual tapestry needle—the sharp point will penetrate the fabric weave more easily. Take care not to split the canvas threads.

Using waste canvas

1 Cut a piece of waste canvas at least 1 in. (2.5 cm) larger all around than the finished design. Pin the canvas in position on the right side of the fabric, making sure that the fabric grain lines up with the canvas mesh.

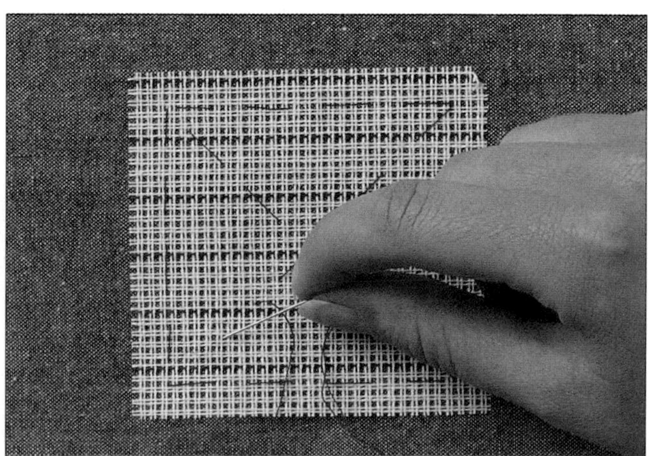

2 Using thread in a contrasting color, baste around the edge of the canvas and from corner to corner. For a large piece, add more basting to hold the canvas flat. On stretchy fabrics, secure the canvas with masking tape.

3 Work the design, stitching through both the canvas and the fabric. Hold the needle at a right angle to the surface, and take it through the exact center of each hole.

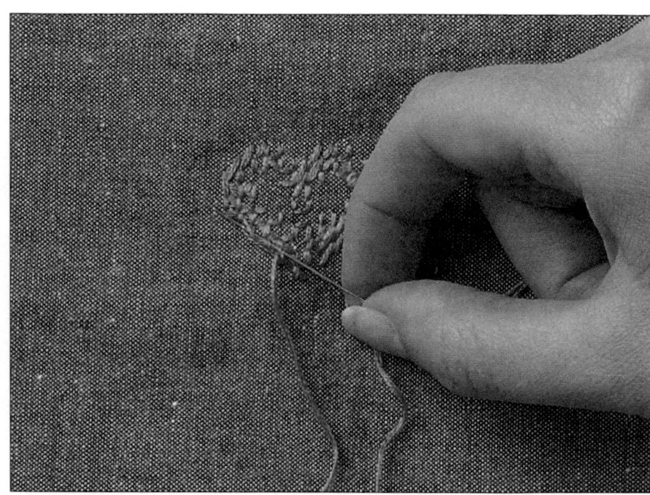

4 Make sure that the thread ends are carefully secured on the wrong side of the work; otherwise they may pull loose when you remove the canvas threads.

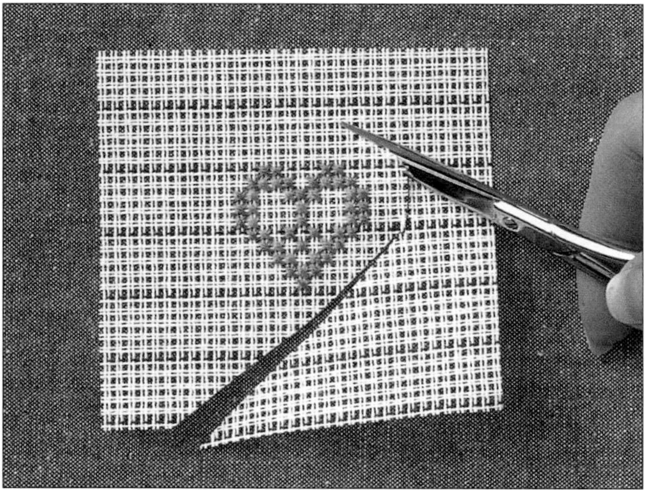

5 When the design is complete, remove the basting threads. Then use small, sharp scissors to trim the waste canvas close to the design, leaving two or three double threads of canvas all around the embroidery.

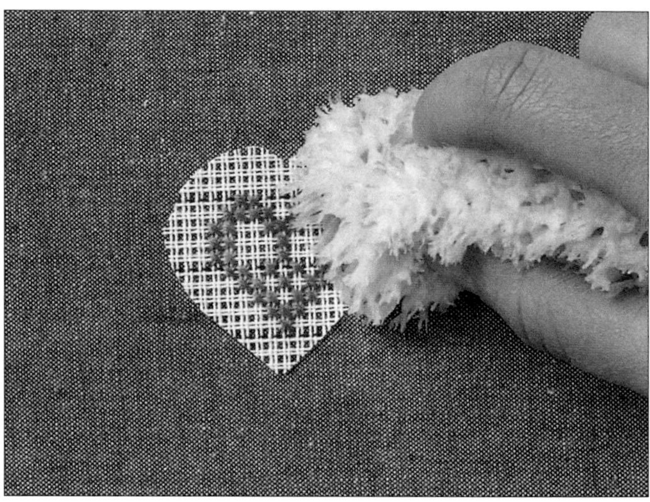

6 Using a damp sponge or absorbent cotton, moisten the work very slightly to dissolve the starch holding the canvas threads together. Use only a little water, as the starch could glue the canvas to the embroidery threads.

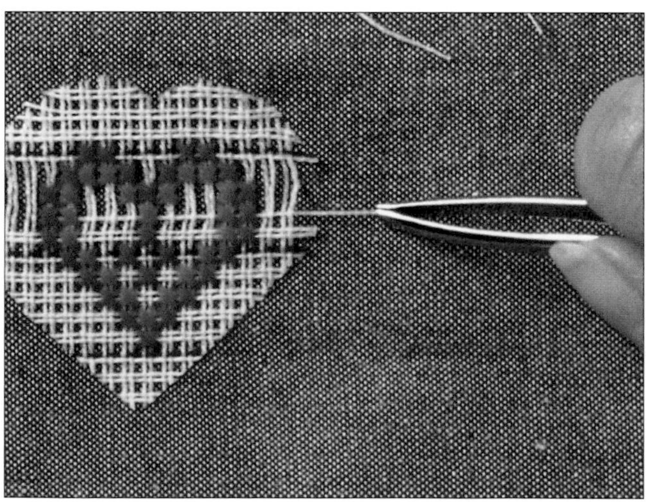

7 Using tweezers, pull out the canvas threads one by one. Remove all the threads lying in one direction first, then turn the work and pull out the threads lying the other way. Pull the threads straight out—don't pull at an angle—and hold the opposite edge firmly at all times.

Messy motifs

Motifs stitched with waste canvas can look messy if the stitches are placed inaccurately. When two stitches share the same hole, make sure the needle enters the fabric below in exactly the same place each time. Use a stabbing motion, taking the needle down through the canvas and fabric, then up again.

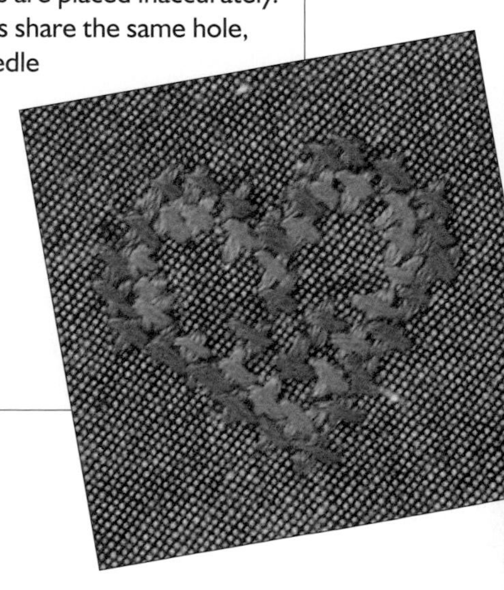

Starting needlepoint

Needlepoint—also known as canvaswork or canvas embroidery—is the art of stitching designs onto canvas or a stiffened, open-weave fabric, covering it fully. The grid of holes makes it easy to follow a chart and form stitches of exactly the same size.

Tapestry needles are best for canvas, as their blunt points won't split the canvas threads.

Types of canvas

Needlepoint canvas is made from evenly woven cotton or linen and also from rigid plastic. Fabric canvas comes in two basic types, mono and Penelope.

Mono canvas has evenly spaced single threads with all the holes the same size. The threads are sometimes interlocked to make the canvas more stable.

Penelope canvas has pairs of threads that create a grid of small and larger holes. Stitch into the small holes to work finer details.

Plastic canvas is used when a firm base is needed, or for three-dimensional items.

Getting ready to stitch

If you are using a chart, work from the center of the design so that you can count the canvas threads from a central point. Before you start, mark the chart center with a ruler and pencil. Mark the center of the canvas with basting (see page 20.)

Check that the needle is the right size for your thread and that it passes easily through the canvas holes. Also, check that the thread covers the canvas well. Use lengths of thread no more than 20 in. (50 cm) long; or it may become fluffy.

Using frames

On needlepoint pieces up to about 6 in. (15 cm) square, you can work with the canvas in your hand. On larger pieces, a frame will help you to work even stitches and prevents canvas distortion.

One of the most popular threads for needlepoint is tapestry yarn, a 4-ply yarn used on 10- or 12-mesh canvas. Persian yarn is a 3-ply yarn, while strands of crewel yarn, a 2-ply yarn, can be combined as required to cover the canvas. Matte embroidery cotton is also sometimes used.

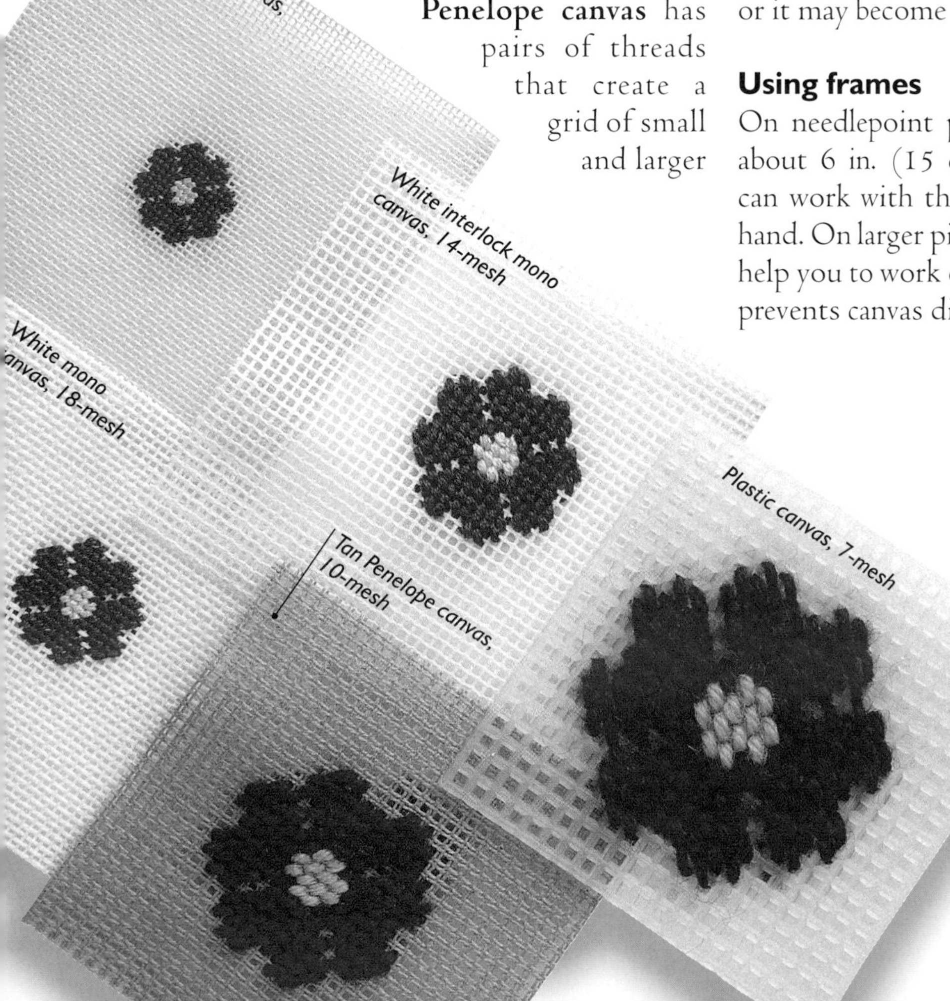

Canvas is graded by mesh count. For example, 10-mesh canvas has ten threads to 1 in. (2.5 cm). The higher the mesh count, the finer the canvas, and the smaller the stitched motif.

This design was stitched on 10-mesh Penelope canvas using tapestry yarn and a size 18 tapestry needle.

Preparing the canvas

1 Cut the canvas at least 2 in. (5 cm) larger all around than the area to be stitched. Mark the center of each edge. Baste between opposite marks with contrasting sewing thread to mark the center of the canvas.

2 Bind the edges of the canvas with masking tape. This will help to prevent the canvas from fraying and will prevent your embroidery yarn from catching on the canvas.

Using an adjustable scroll frame

1 Dismantle the frame. Bind the sides of the canvas with masking tape. Turn under 3/8 in. (1 cm) on the top edge. Using heavy-duty thread, overcast to the webbing on one roller. Overcast the lower edge to the other roller.

2 Assemble the frame. Using heavy-duty thread and a chenille needle, lace the sides of the canvas to the sides of the frame, knotting the thread securely at the top and bottom. Tighten the rollers so that the canvas is quite taut.

3 For long pieces of work, stitch the design from the top down. As you complete each section, cut the lacing, wind the work around the top roller, then re-lace the sides.

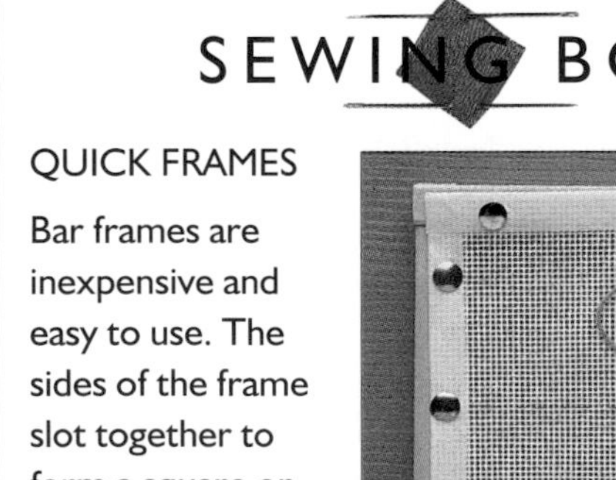

SEWING BOX

QUICK FRAMES

Bar frames are inexpensive and easy to use. The sides of the frame slot together to form a square or rectangle. Use thumbtacks or staples to attach the canvas.

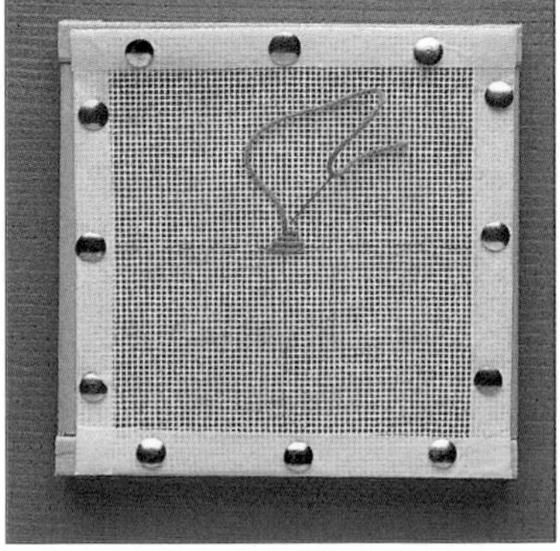

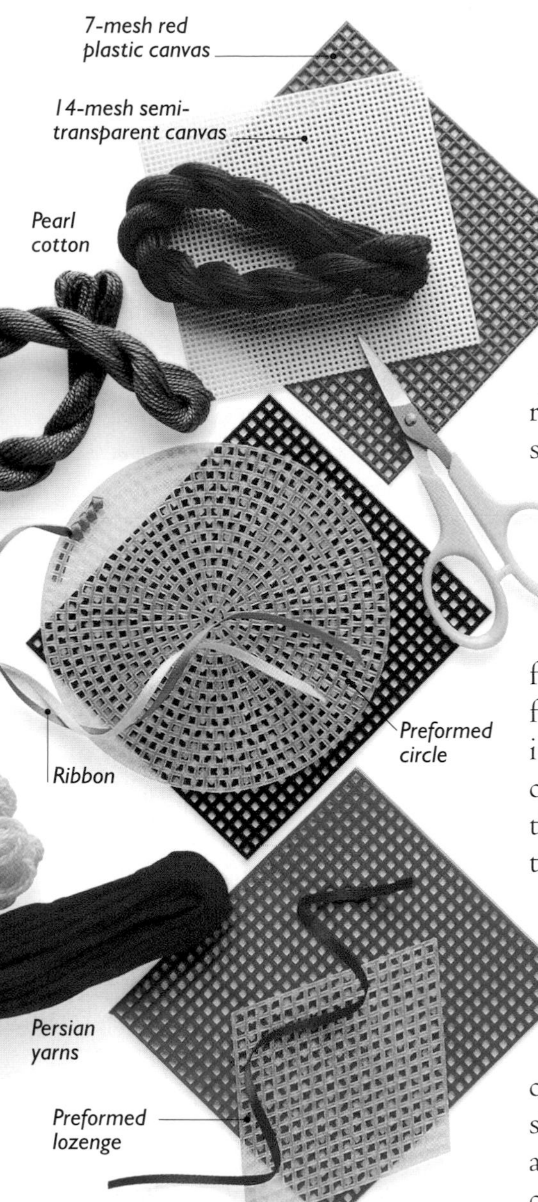

Plastic canvas

Plastic canvas is the newest material for needlepoint, and it opens up all sorts of possibilities. It consists of a plastic sheet, punched with a regular grid of holes, which you stitch in exactly the same way as any ordinary canvas. Plastic canvas is easy to handle—the mesh doesn't distort, so there's no need to use a frame, and the edges don't fray. It is quite rigid, so it is ideal for making mats or hanging items such as earrings. It can be cut and shaped to make useful three-dimensional objects such as trinket boxes. It can also be used as a backing to stiffen other embroidered fabrics.

Types of plastic canvas

The most widely available plastic canvas is 7-mesh. It comes in sheets of semitransparent plastic and opaque, colored plastic. You can also buy semitransparent, preformed shapes, to make into objects such as coasters, bags, and Christmas tree decorations. The finer 10- and 14-mesh plastic canvas, sold in small semitransparent sheets, is less widely available.

Using plastic canvas

Threads Use any thread that you would normally use on ordinary canvas, or try a more unusual thread, such as narrow ribbon.

Stitches Tent stitch is most often used for plastic canvas, but most other stitches work equally well, including diagonal satin stitch and cross stitch.

Joining and finishing If pieces are to be edged or joined (instead of framed) stitch them leaving one row of unworked holes around the edges. Use either overcasting or braided cross stitch to finish the edge or to join two pieces together. Overcasting is the easier of the two stitches, although braided cross stitch gives an attractive plaited finish.

Cutting and stitching plastic canvas

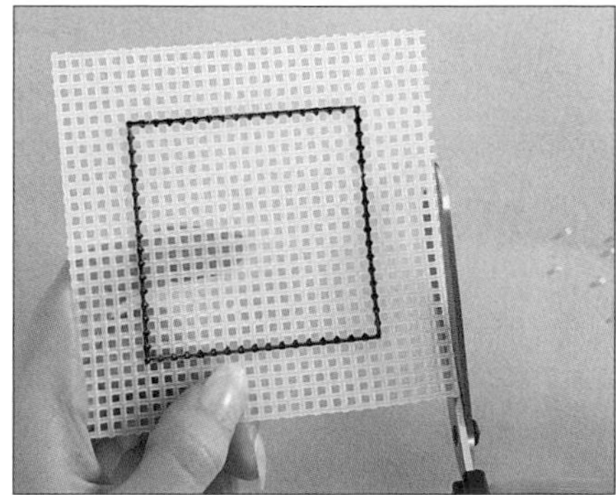

1 Mark out the shapes with a permanent marker—the ink from ordinary pens will rub off. Cut out, leaving a margin of at least five holes all around. Trim off the bumps of plastic protruding along the edges.

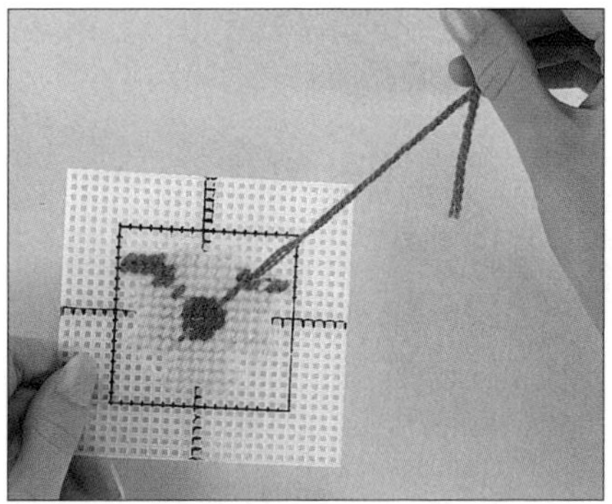

2 Using a ruler and permanent marker, measure and mark the center of each edge. Join each pair of opposite marks to find the center. Stitch the design, working outward from the center of the canvas.

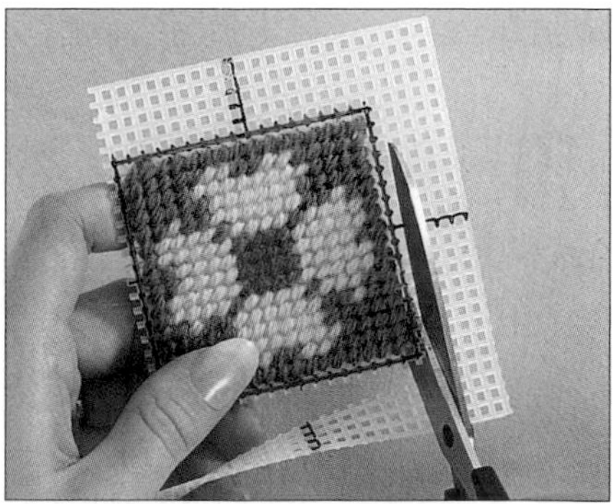

3 When the design is complete, trim the plastic canvas to size. For pieces that will be edged or joined, leave one row of unworked holes all around the stitching. For pieces that will be framed, leave at least five holes.

Edging plastic canvas with overcasting

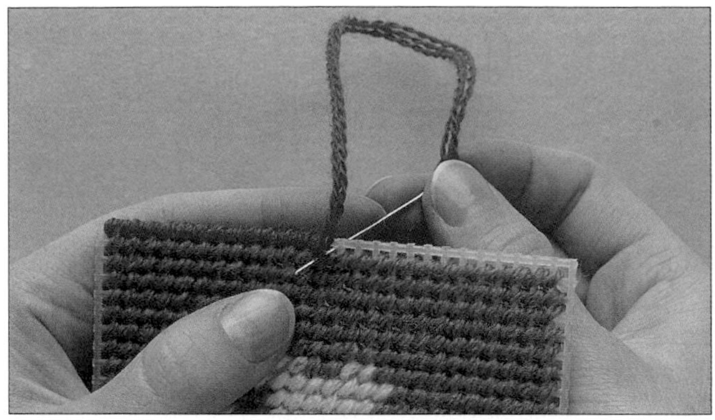

1 Work overcasting from left to right. Bring the needle out to the front at your starting point. Bring the needle out to the front again one hole to the right, pulling the thread through so that it lies over the edge of the canvas. Continue in this way.

2 When you reach an inside corner, work one stitch into the corner hole. For an outside corner, work two or three stitches into the corner hole, so that the thread covers the corner. Take care not to force too many stitches through the corner hole, or you may tear the plastic mesh.

Edging plastic canvas with braided cross stitch

1 Work braided cross stitch from left to right. Bring the needle to the front through the first hole. Take the thread over the edge of the plastic canvas, and bring the needle through to the front through the third hole. Then bring the needle to the front through the first hole again.

2 To start the second stitch, bring the needle to the front through the fourth hole. Take the thread to the back, then bring it out to the front again through the second hole. Continue like this, using the fifth and third holes for the next stitch, then the sixth and fourth holes, and so on.

Joining plastic canvas

Place the two pieces together with the wrong sides facing and edges and holes aligned. Secure the thread on the wrong side of one piece, close to your starting point. Working from the right side, overcast the two edges together as shown, taking the needle through both pieces in one movement. Alternatively, use braided cross stitch.

Making a hinge for a box lid

Edge both pieces with overcasting or braided cross stitch (see above). Secure a length of matching thread on the wrong side of one piece, close to where the hinge is required. Holding the pieces edge to edge, take a stitch between them. Work six more closely spaced stitches, then fasten off the thread end securely.

Chapter 2
Embroidery Stitch Library

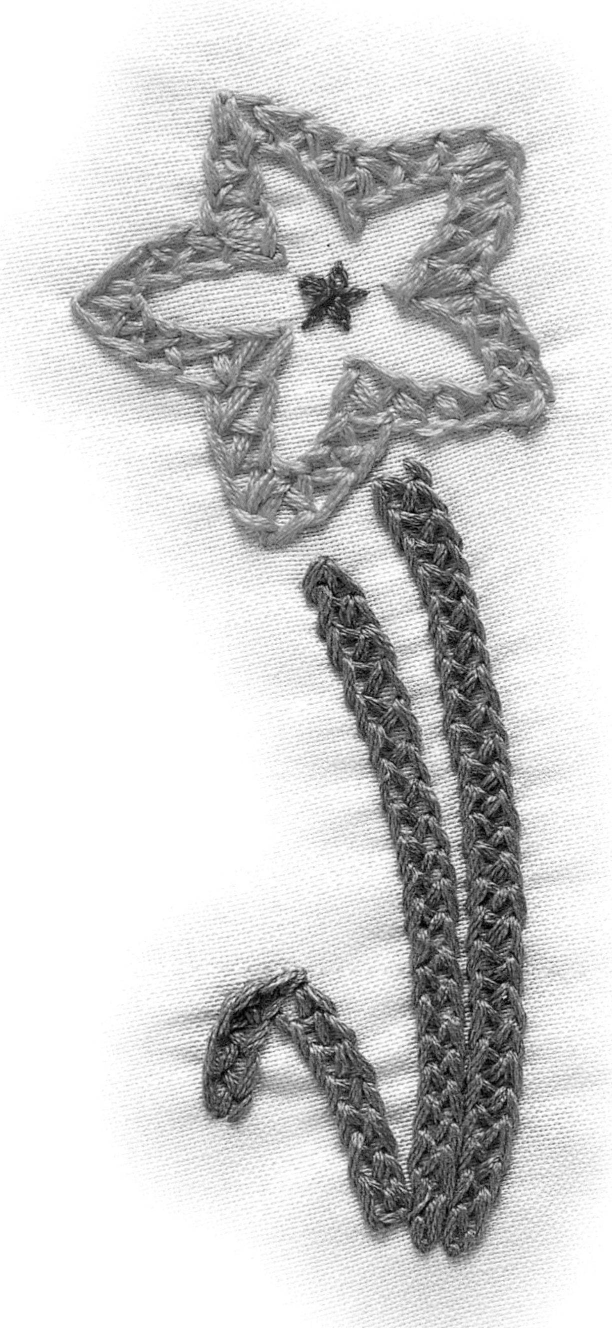

Easy straight stitches

Straight stitches are very simple to work and can be used in many different types of counted and free embroidery.

Basic straight stitch is worked as a single stitch and can be used to create texture, fill shapes, and suggest basic daisy-type flowers.

The other stitches shown here are all line stitches. They can be used alone for linear designs, to outline shapes, and to add detail to designs using other stitches.

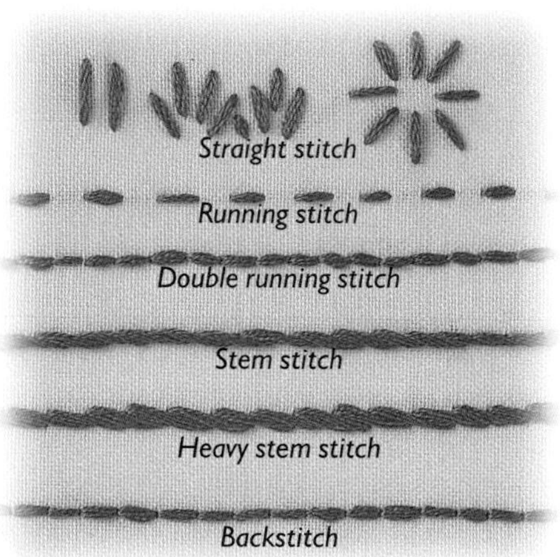

Running stitch makes a broken line suitable for fine outlines.

Double running stitch looks very similar to backstitch but forms a slightly lighter line.

Stem stitch makes a slightly raised, solid line and is ideal for curved lines, such as stems and tendrils in floral designs. It can also be used to fill in shapes.

Backstitch makes a fine, slightly raised line for outlines and details, especially in cross stitch.

Securing the starting thread

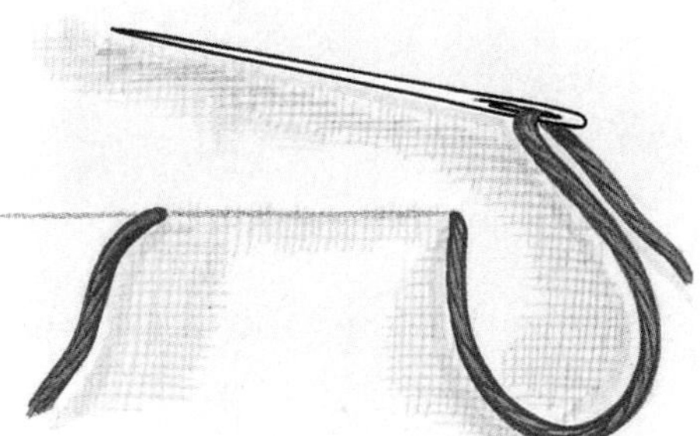

1 Take the needle to the back of the fabric, a little way from your starting point. Leave a short tail of thread at the front. Bring the needle to the front at your starting point.

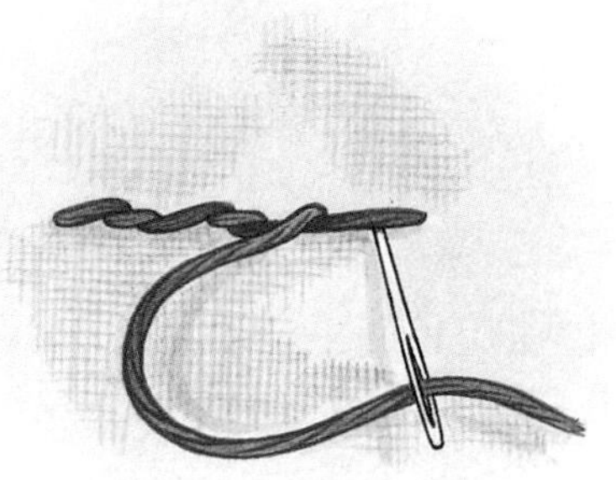

2 As you work along the line, stitch over the thread at the back to secure it. Then pull the loose thread end through to the back and snip it off close to the surface.

Fastening off

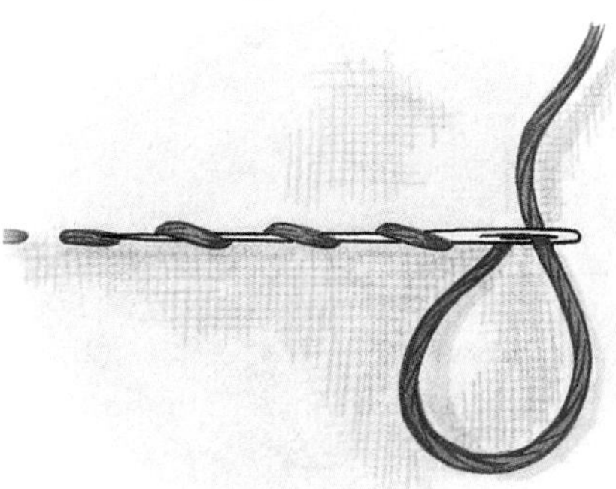

To secure the thread end when you have finished, take the needle to the back of the fabric. Weave the thread into the back of several stitches and trim it off close to the surface.

Working basic straight stitch

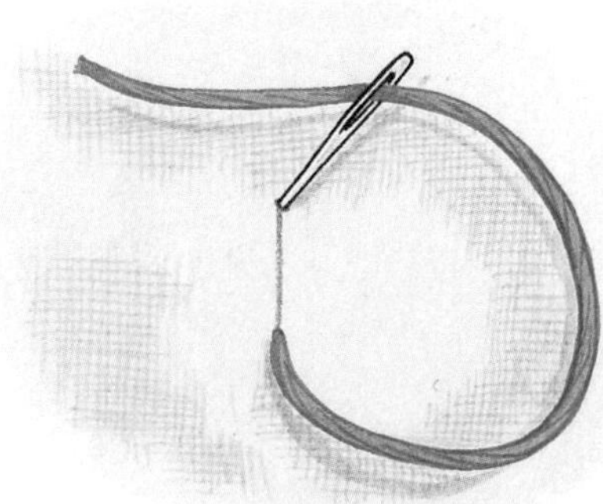

To work an individual straight stitch, bring the needle out to the front. Push it through to the wrong side to make a single stitch of the required length.

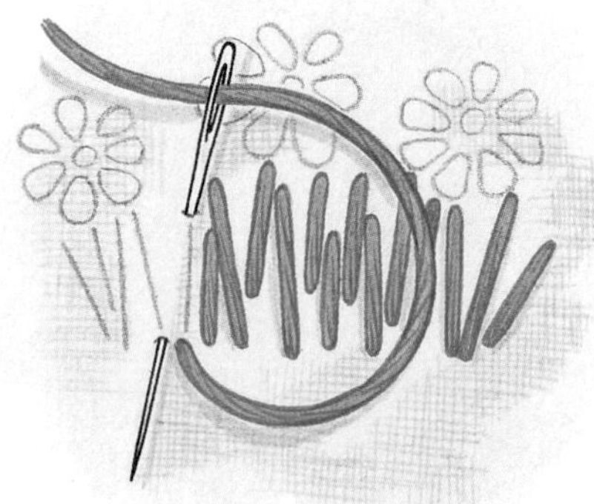

To work a cluster of straight stitches, work individual straight stitches of varying lengths and in different directions according to the design.

To create a simple straight-stitch flower, make as many straight stitches as desired, working outward from a central circle or oval.

Working running stitch

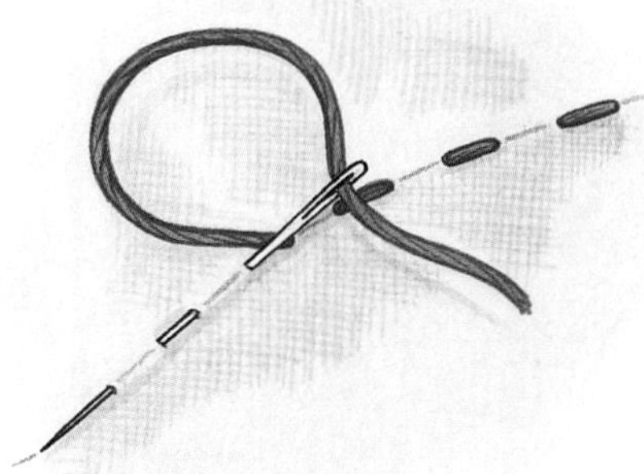

Bring the needle out to the front at your starting point. Pass the needle in and out of the fabric along the stitching line. Work several stitches at a time if work is unframed, keeping the length and tension even.

Double running stitch

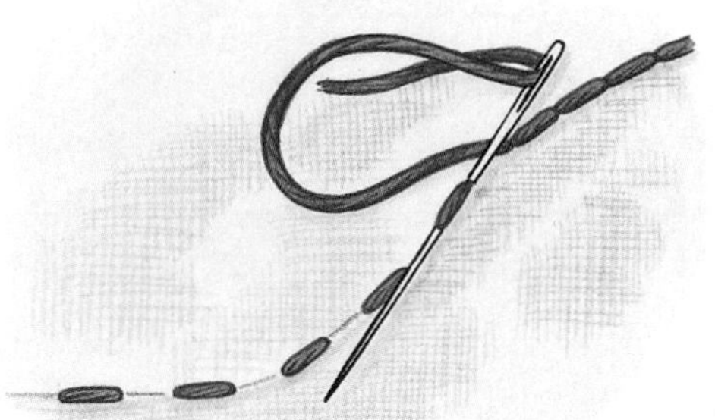

Work a row of evenly spaced running stitches along the stitching line, including any offshoot stitches. Turn the work around. Work another set of running stitches, filling in the spaces left by the first and using the same holes.

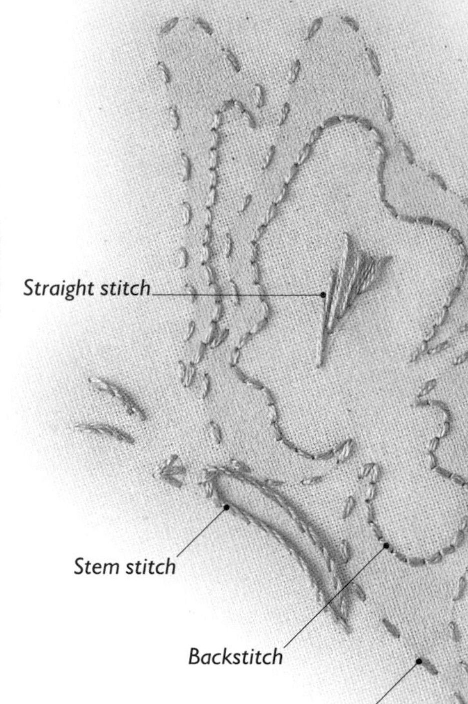

Working stem stitch

1 Work upward, keeping the working thread to the right of the needle. Bring the needle out to the front and insert it a little way from your starting point. Bring it out again, half a stitch length back.

2 Insert the needle half a stitch length from the end of the previous stitch. Bring it out at the end of the previous stitch, through the same hole in the fabric. Continue in this way.

For a heavy stem-stitch line, angle the needle slightly as you insert it, and work smaller stitches.

Working backstitch

1 Working from right to left, bring the needle out to the front one stitch length from your starting point. Insert the needle at your starting point and bring it out again, two stitch lengths away.

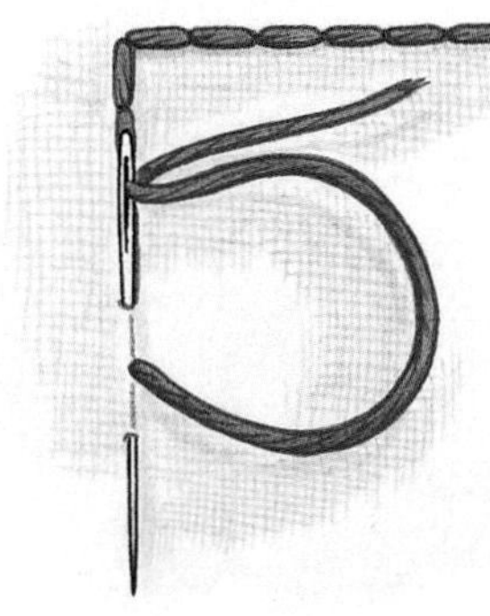

2 Pull the thread through to leave a single stitch at the front. Then repeat step **1**, inserting the needle in the hole at the end of the previous stitch. Continue in this way, keeping all the stitches the same length.

Ragged stems
Stem stitch looks ragged and untidy when the stitches are too long and the needle is not inserted along the center of the line to make each stitch. Keep the stitches small, and make them all the same length to ensure a smoothly stitched line.

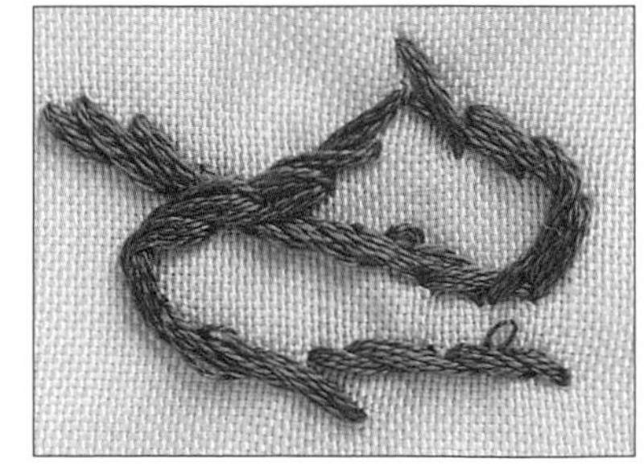

Satin stitches

This popular and versatile filling stitch covers shapes with a smooth, satiny surface. You can use the various forms of satin stitch to fill large and small areas and to create subtle shading effects.

The technique is simple, and it's well worth practicing to achieve perfect results. Make sure that your stitches are no more than ½ in. (12 mm) long, and place the needle precisely for an evenly stitched edge. Always use an embroidery hoop or frame to keep the tension even. *Note to left-handed readers:* The stitches in this book are shown as if worked flat, without a frame, and by a right-handed person. If you "stab" the needle (as required with a frame), you can work in any comfortable or convenient direction.

Basic satin stitch consists of straight stitches worked close together in parallel lines. With its clear outlines, it fills both rounded and pointed shapes, as well as narrow borders. To enhance its satinlike sheen, use a glossy thread, such as embroidery floss. You can also vary the direction of the stitches to give the effect of light and shade.

Encroaching satin stitch is used to cover large areas. It is worked in staggered rows which blend into each other without an obvious join, avoiding the need for over-long stitches.

Padded satin stitch is worked over a base of other stitches, such as running stitch, stem stitch, or chain stitch, to create a slightly raised area of stitches.

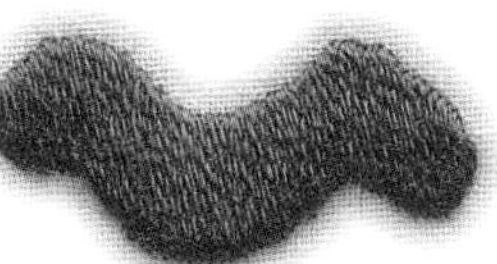

Basic satin stitch

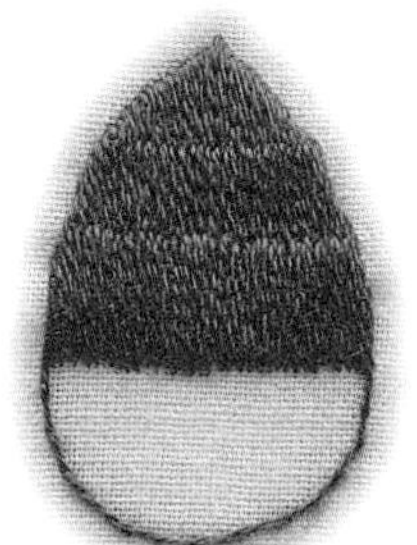

Encroaching satin stitch

Padded satin stitch

Starting and fastening off satin stitch

When you have finished satin-stitching a motif, always secure the thread ends and trim them off before working the next motif. Don't trail the thread across the back of the work to start another motif—it may show through as a shadow on your finished work, especially on lightweight or pale fabric.

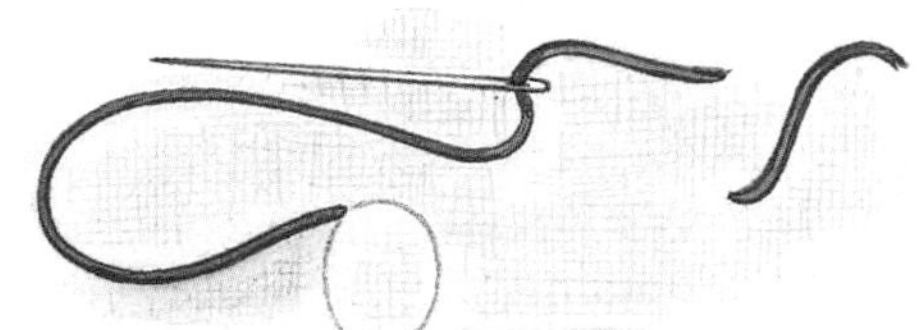

1 A little way from your starting point, take the needle through to the back of the fabric, leaving approximately a 3 in. (8 cm) tail of thread on the right side. Bring the needle out to the front again at your starting point on the edge of the motif.

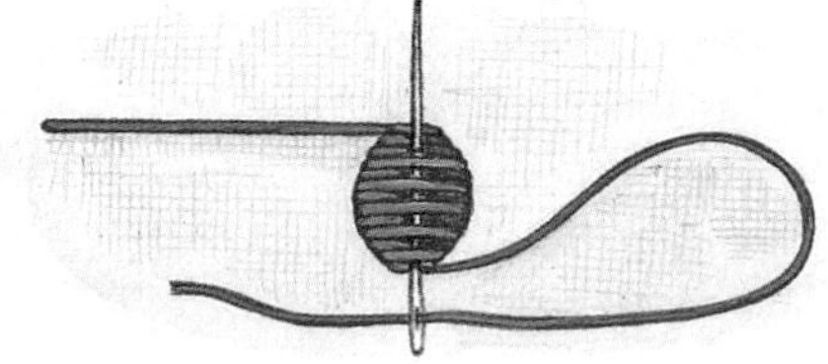

2 When you have filled in the motif, take the thread through to the back. Weave it into the back of your stitching, and trim it off close to the surface. Then pull the first thread end to the wrong side, weave it in, and trim it off in the same way.

Filling a rounded shape with basic satin stitch

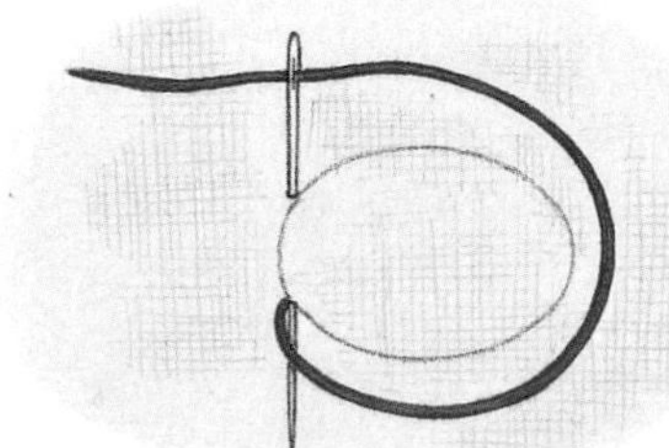

1 Bring the needle out at the front of the fabric at the edge of the shape. Insert the needle at the opposite edge, and bring it out again next to where you started.

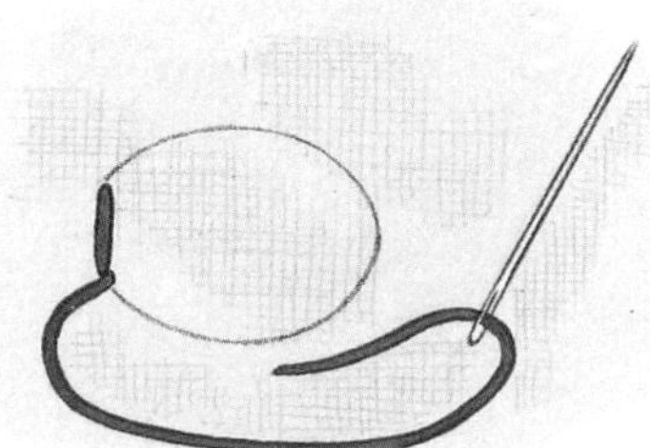

2 Pull the thread through gently, so that it runs straight between the marked lines without wavering; it should lie smoothly against the surface of the fabric, without puckering it.

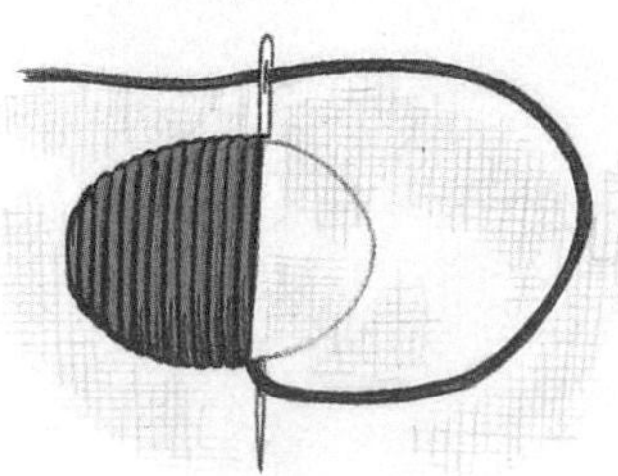

3 Repeat steps **1–2**, keeping the stitches parallel and close together so that they lie neatly and evenly on the surface of the fabric.

Filling a pointed shape with basic satin stitch

1 Bring out the needle at the tip of the point, and make a short stitch along the outline.

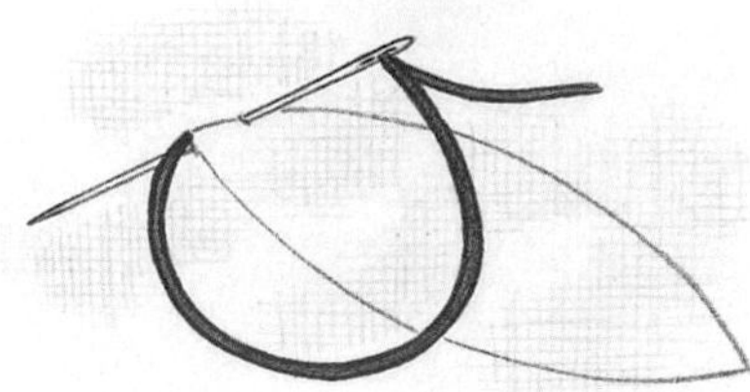

2 Fill in the shape with satin stitches, graduating the length of the stitches to fit the shape.

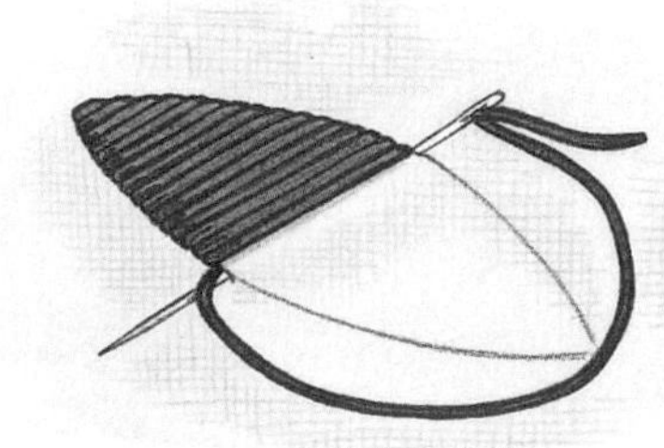

Working a basic satin-stitched line

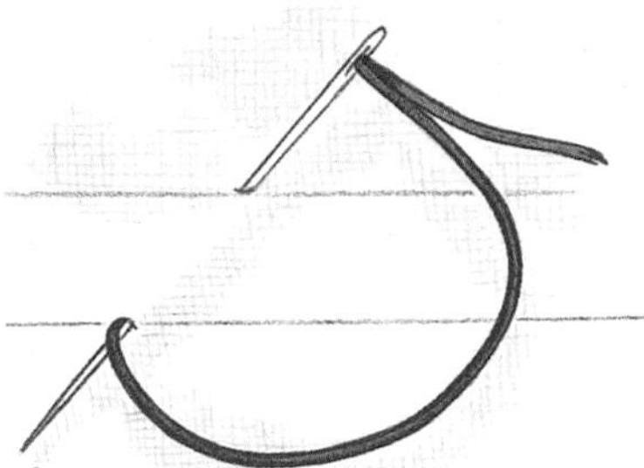

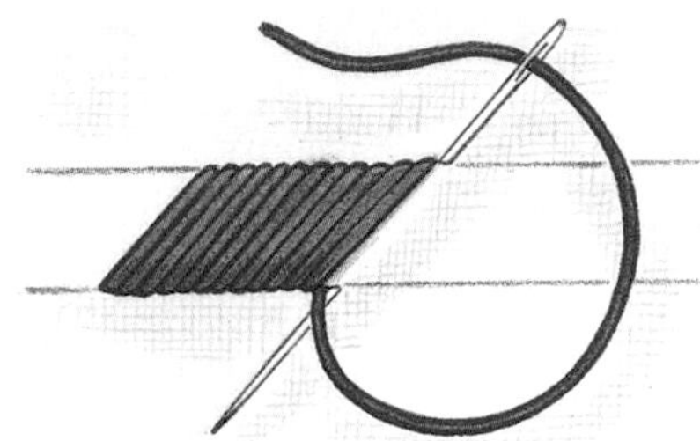

1 Bring the needle out at the front of the fabric at the lower marked line. Take the thread upward and insert the needle on the top row, at a 45-degree angle to the marked line; bring it out again next to where you started.

2 Work parallel, closely spaced stitches along the row, keeping them at exactly the same angle and placing the needle precisely on the marked lines to create even edges.

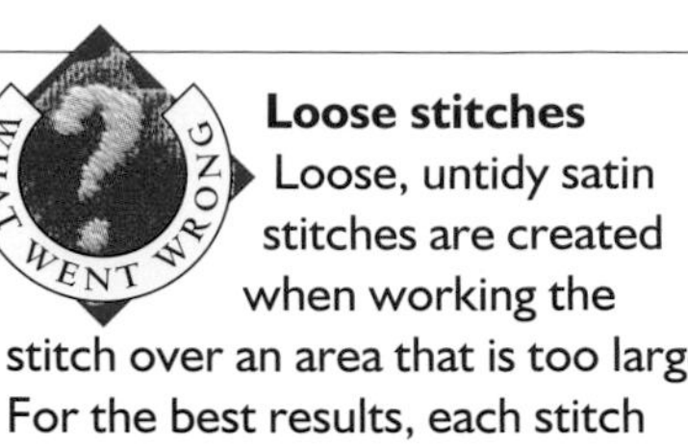

Loose stitches
Loose, untidy satin stitches are created when working the stitch over an area that is too large. For the best results, each stitch should be no more than ⅜–½ in. (10-12 mm) long. For large areas use encroaching satin stitch, worked in manageable rows.

Working encroaching satin stitch

1 Start stitching at the top of the shape to be filled. Work a row of vertical satin stitches across the shape, aligning the bases of the stitches.

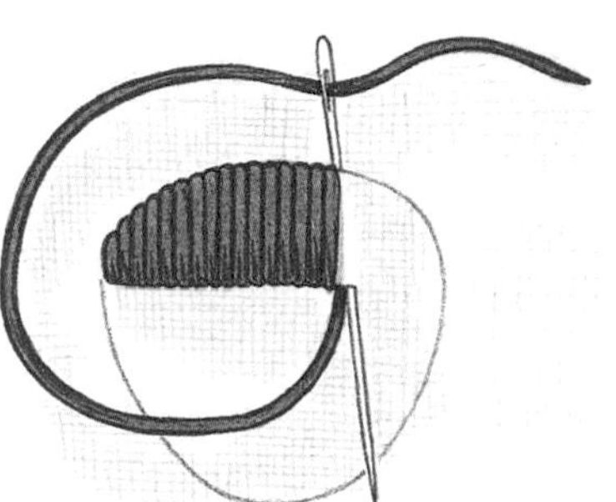

2 Carry the thread under the stitches at the back to work the next row in the same direction. Place the top of each stitch between bases of two stitches in row above. Repeat to work subsequent rows.

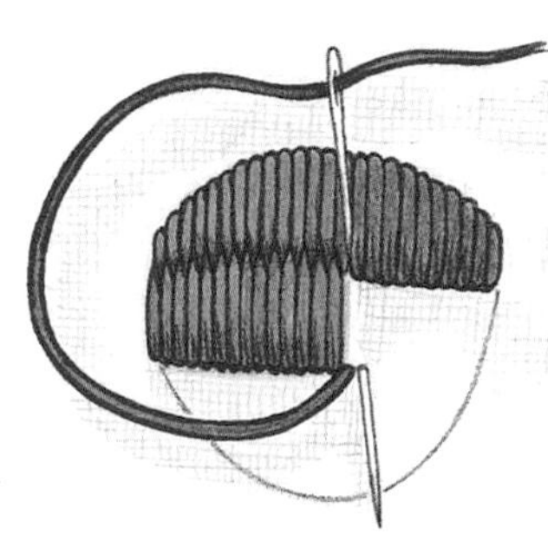

Working padded satin stitch

1 Work small running stitches around the edge of the shape to be filled, then work more small stitches inside the shape to create a foundation.

2 Work basic satin stitch, as shown on page 27, over the foundation to create a raised effect.

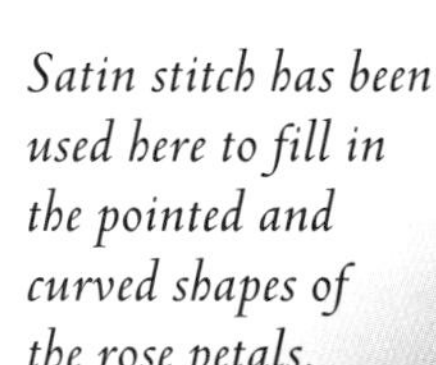

Satin stitch has been used here to fill in the pointed and curved shapes of the rose petals.

Once you've mastered basic satin stitch and its variations, you can add extra definition to motifs with a variety of padded effects. In the simplest version of padded satin stitch, the satin stitches are worked over a seed-stitched base (see page 35). The techniques shown here use a range of methods and materials to achieve interesting raised effects.

All the stitches create a smooth, solidly stitched surface and are ideal for narrow shapes such as stems, leaves, and flower petals. Split larger shapes into smaller, narrower areas and work each one separately, so that the long edges of neighboring rows just touch.

When working any of these stitches, remember that the smooth surface is enhanced by using light-reflecting threads such as embroidery floss or pearl cotton. Always mount your fabric in a hoop or frame to avoid fabric distortion and to keep the stitches even. For details on ordinary padded satin stitch, see page 28.

Satin stitch worked over a split-stitch outline has a subtle raised effect around the edges.

Self-padded satin stitch has a somewhat more raised finish than ordinary padded satin stitch. This effect is achieved by working two, three, or more layers of satin stitch over the shape.

Felt-padded satin stitch has a highly raised finish, giving motifs an almost three-dimensional look. The motif is padded with felt before it is satin-stitched—you can use one or more layers of felt, depending on the effect you want.

Satin stitch worked over cord or string looks very good when used for stems, tendrils, scrolls, and whorls. The cord or string is stitched to the fabric then covered with short, straight or diagonal satin stitches.

Satin stitch worked over a split-stitch outline

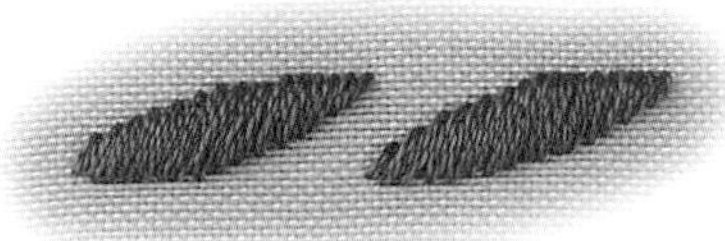

Self-padded satin stitch

Felt-padded satin stitch

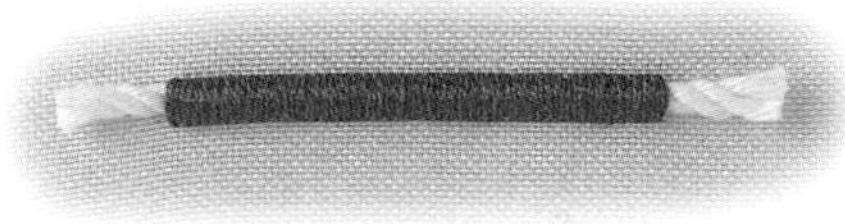

Satin stitch worked over cord

Working satin stitch over a split-stitch outline

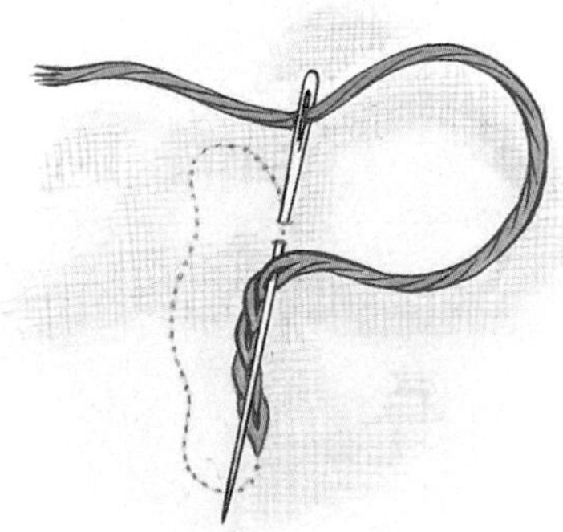

1 Outline the shape with split stitch. To start, make a small straight stitch, then bring the needle to the front again halfway along the stitch you've just made, splitting the thread with the needle. Continue in this way to complete the outline.

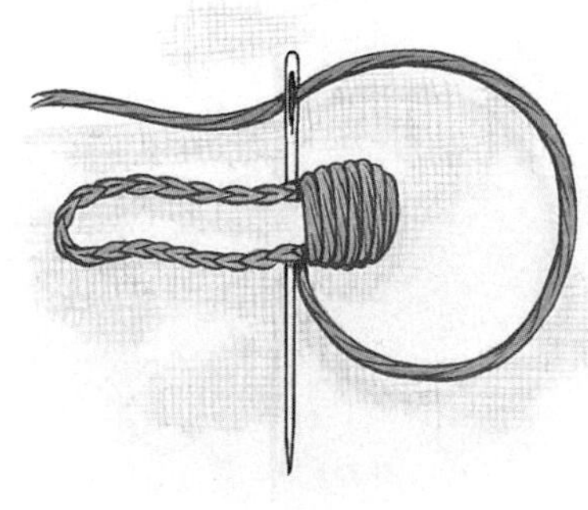

2 Bring the thread to the front again outside the split-stitched outline. Fill the shape with straight or diagonal satin stitches, working over both the shape and the outline.

Lumpy padding

Felt-padded satin stitch can look lumpy if the felt pieces are cut too large. For a smooth finish, they need to be carefully graded. Cut the top layer slightly smaller all around than the shape to be filled, and each under layer correspondingly smaller than the layer above.

Working self-padded satin stitch

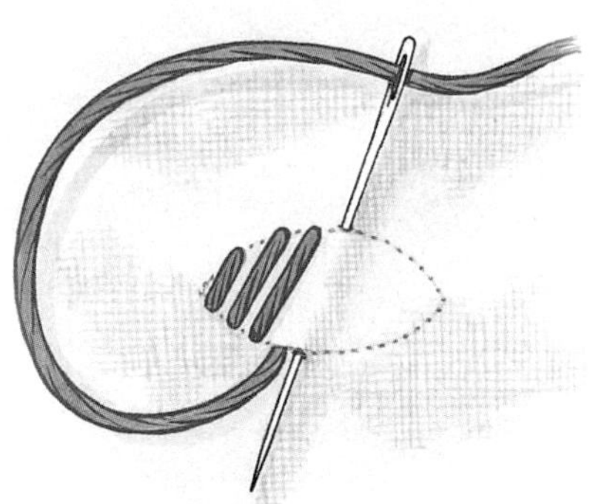

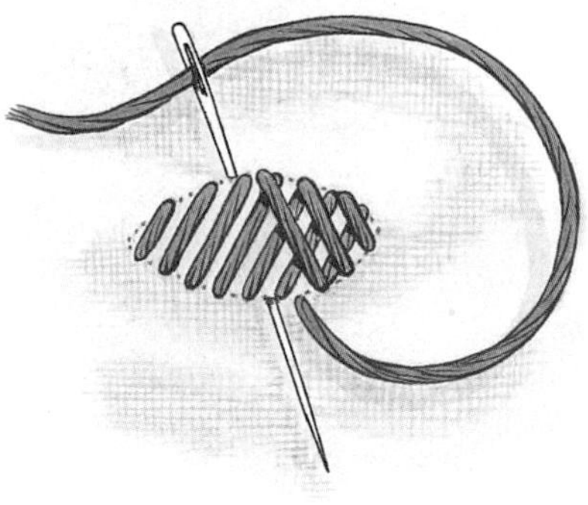

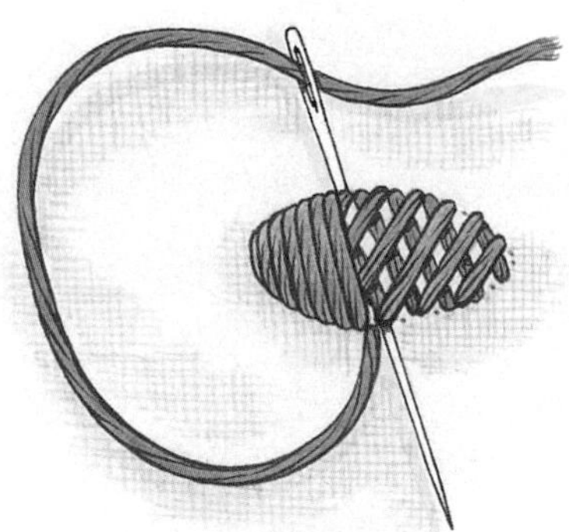

1 Bring the needle to the front at one side of the shape, just inside the marked outline. Fill the shape with diagonal satin stitches; work them fairly close together, but not as closely as usual for basic satin stitch.

2 Satin-stitch across the shape again, as in step 1, but this time slant the stitches in the opposite direction. If you wish, add more rows of padding, slanting each row in the opposite direction from the one below.

3 Work the final layer of satin stitches over the padding. Work straight or diagonal stitches close together as for basic satin stitch. Slant diagonal stitches in the opposite direction from the top row of padding stitches.

Working felt-padded satin stitch

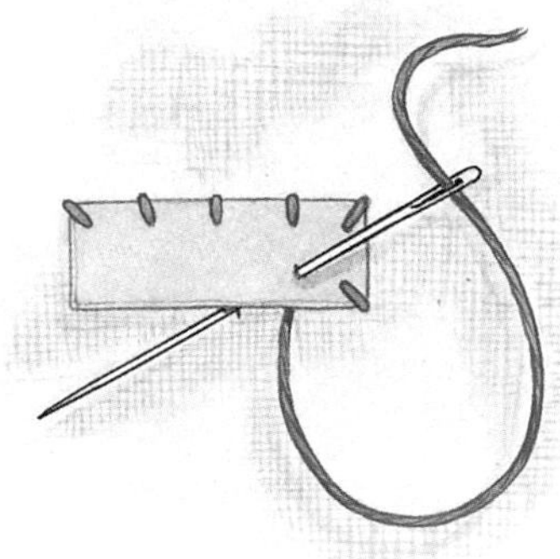

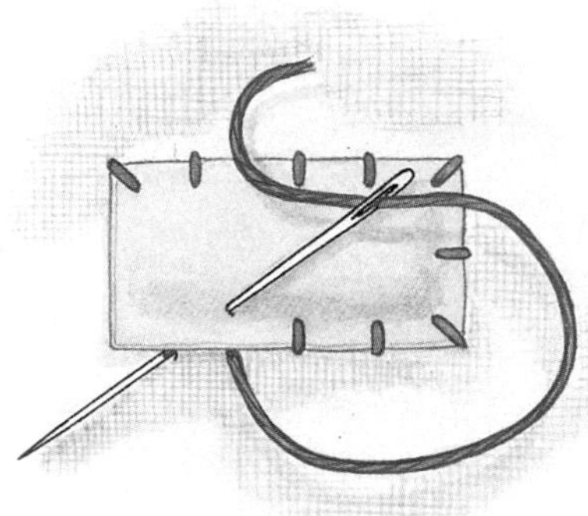

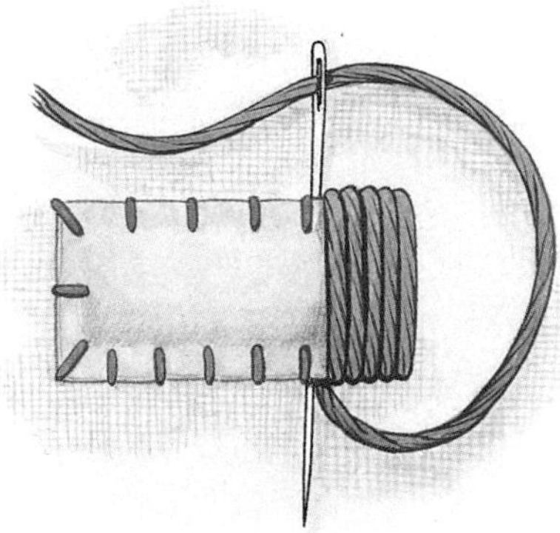

1 Draw one, two, or more shapes on the felt, making each one slightly smaller than the one before. Cut out the shapes with sharp scissors. Stitch the smallest shape to the fabric with small, straight stitches.

2 Center the next-largest shape over the first, and stitch it down in the same way. Repeat to stitch any remaining shapes over the top.

3 Work straight or diagonal satin stitches over the padding. Work the stitches close together so the padding is completely covered.

Working satin stitches over cord or string

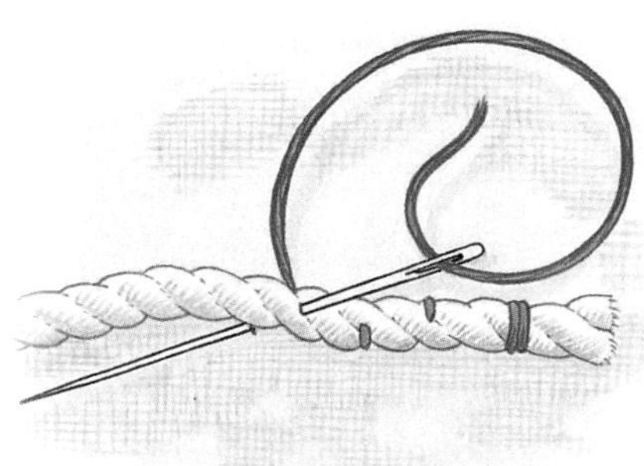

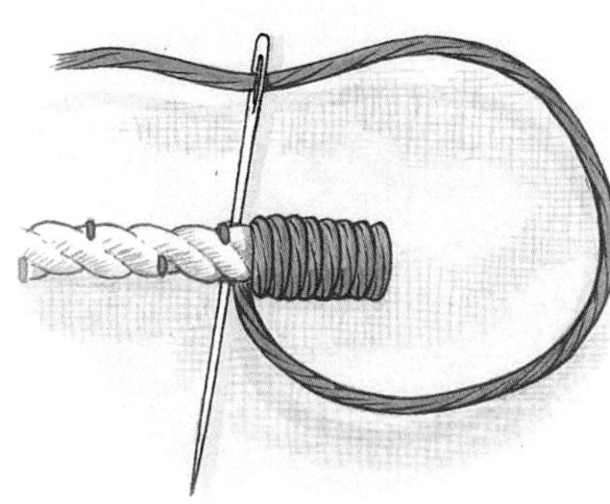

1 Cut the cord or string to size. Stitch it to the fabric with sewing threads, taking the stitches through the cord or string alternately from side to side. Trim any loose strands from the ends of the cord or string.

2 Satin-stitch across the cord or string, either at a right angle to the cord or string or on the diagonal. Arrange the satin stitches close together so the padding is completely covered by the stitching.

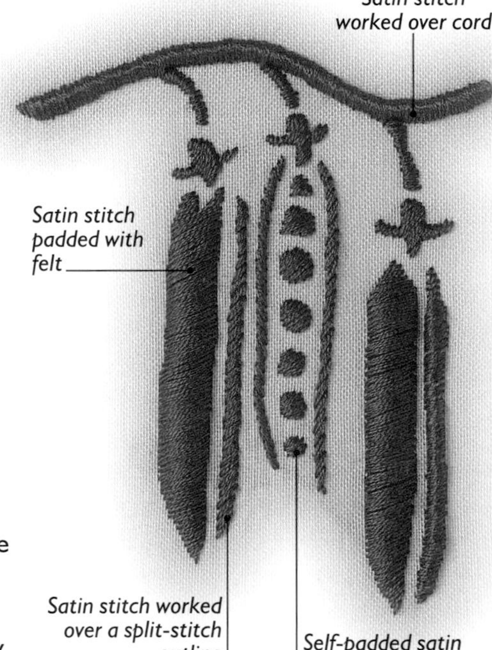

Solid filling stitches

Solid filling stitches create solid areas of embroidery in a single color or shaded colors.

Choose a thread that covers the fabric well. For a glossy effect, choose embroidery floss; for softly shaded long and short stitch, choose crewel wool. Always use an embroidery frame to help keep the stitches even.

Brick stitch gives an interesting surface texture with a woven look. It is generally used to fill large areas in a single color, but you can also use it for shaded effects.

Surface satin stitch (also called laid work) looks like basic satin stitch but it is more economical with thread. Long stitches are often held in place with other decorative stitches.

Long and short stitch is a popular stitch for creating shaded areas of color. It takes its name from the foundation row of long and short stitches, which gives a solid outline. The subsequent rows create irregular lines, allowing you to blend different thread colors for subtle and naturalistic effects. Enhance the naturalistic effect by changing the stitch direction.

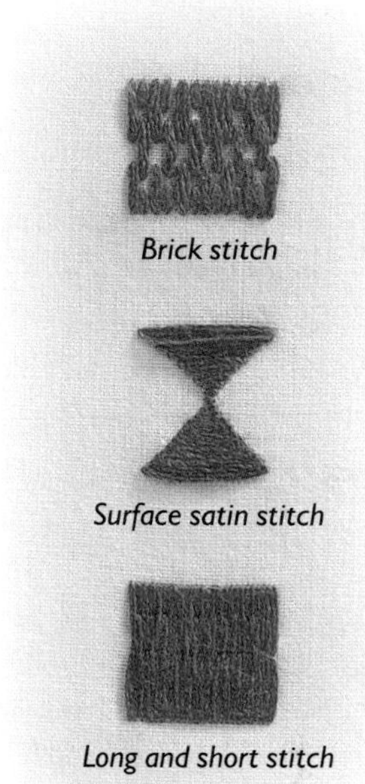
Brick stitch

Surface satin stitch

Long and short stitch

Working brick stitch

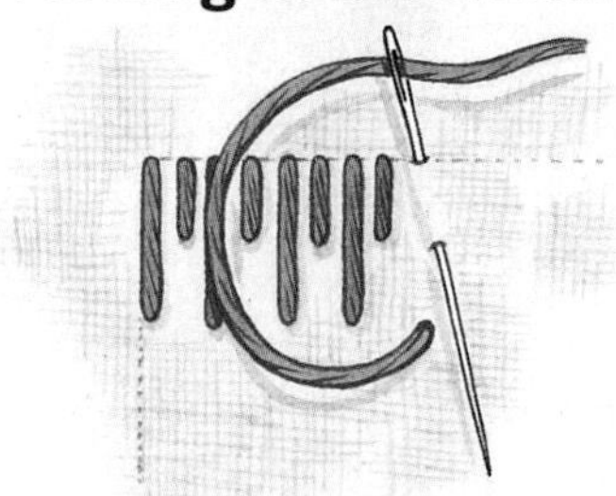

1 Work the first row from left to right. Make alternate long and short stitches along the top edge of the shape to be filled. Make the short stitches half the length of the long stitches.

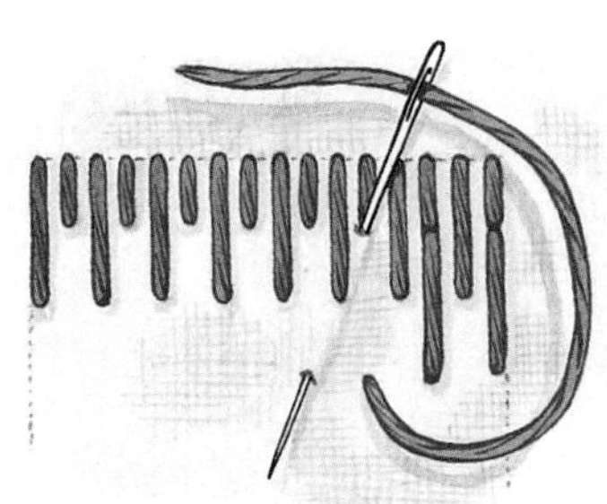

2 Work the second row from right to left, filling in the spaces with vertical straight stitches. Make all the stitches the same length as the long stitches in the previous row.

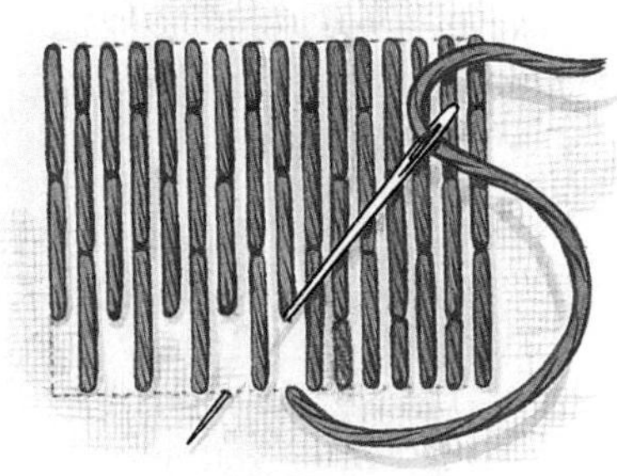

3 Continue working alternately from left to right and right to left, keeping the stitches even to form a bricklike pattern. On the last row fill in the spaces with short stitches.

Working surface satin stitch

1 Bring the thread to the front and work a stitch straight across the shape with a stabbing motion. Bring the needle out again as close as possible to the end of the first stitch.

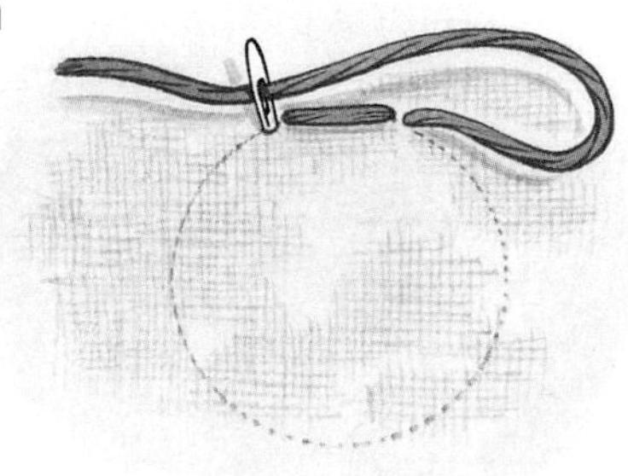

2 Insert the needle into the fabric straight across the shape in the opposite direction to form the next satin stitch. Repeat these two steps to fill the shape.

Alternatively, space the stitches slightly farther apart and fill in with a second sequence of stitches.

Working long and short stitch

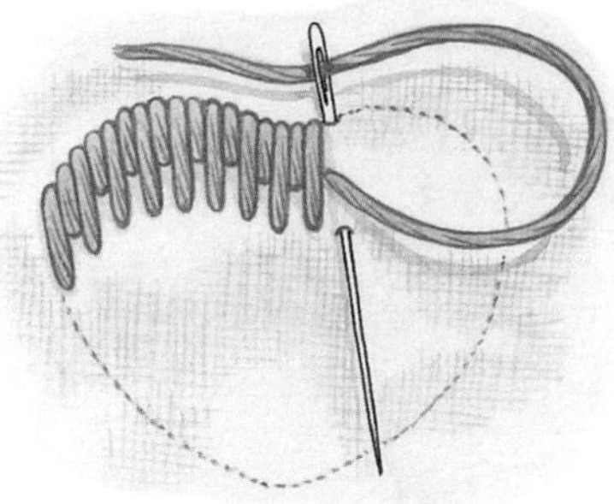

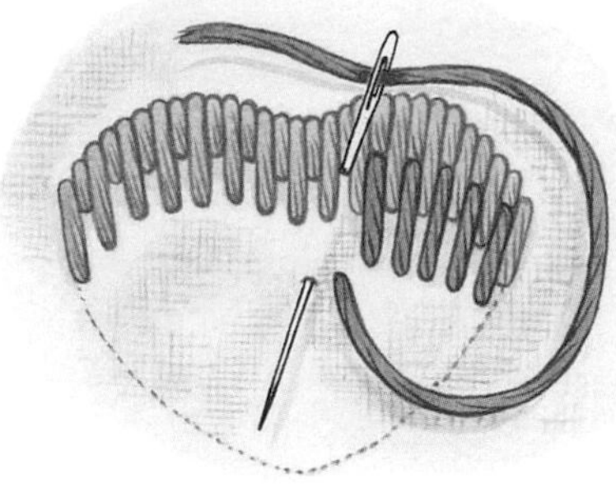

1 Work the foundation row in alternate long and short stitches, working from left to right and following the outline of the shape to be filled. Work the stitches close together.

2 Work the second row from right to left, filling in the spaces left by the first row and keeping the stitches all the same length.

3 Work subsequent rows alternately from left to right and right to left, keeping all the stitches the same length, as in step **2**. Change thread color as you work for a subtle blended effect, and work stitches closely so no background fabric shows.

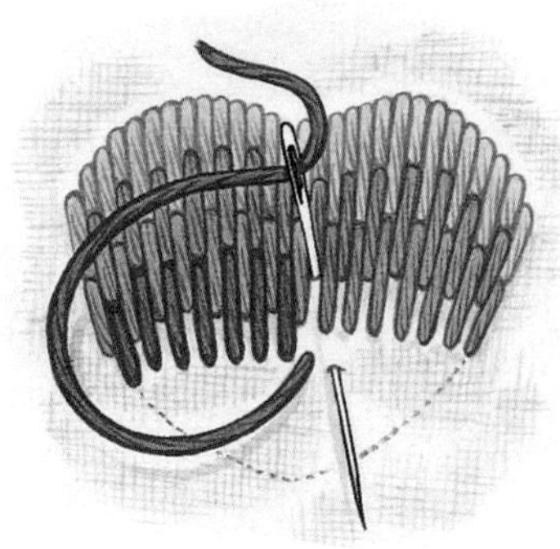

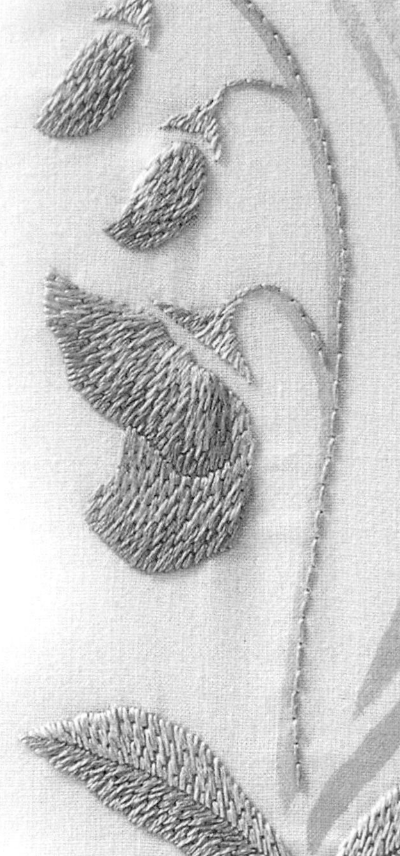

Long and short stitch in graduated shades suggests the delicate coloring of sweet peas.

Changing the direction of long and short stitch

The direction in which long and short stitch is worked is very important in creating the right shaded effect within a design.

When working a flower design, fill each petal with stitches worked from base to tip for a natural-looking blend of colors. The first row of stitches can be fanned out for a radiating effect within each petal.

WHAT WENT WRONG

Poor shading
Colors that contrast too strongly produce visible dividing lines between each change of thread. For a subtle shaded effect, choose colors that are close in tone, and work each new color into the spaces left by the previous row so that they blend well.

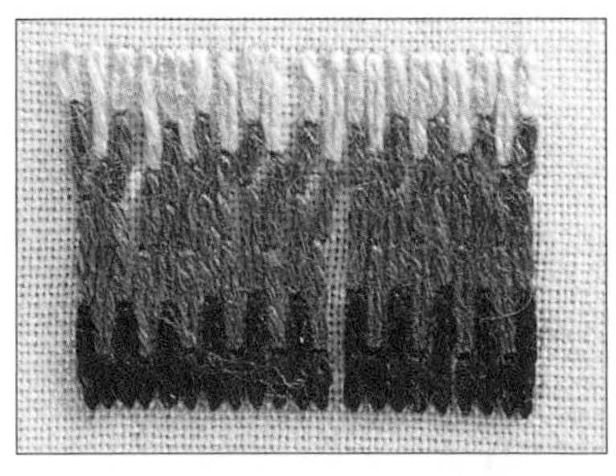

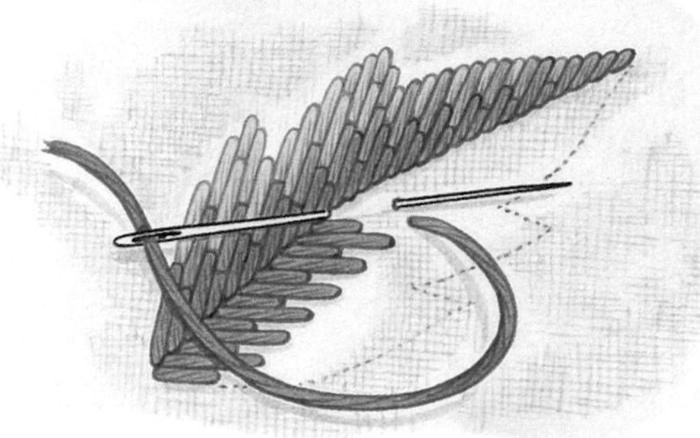

To create natural shading on a leaf, slant the stitches in opposite directions on each side of the central vein and use two or three shades of green.

Fishbone stitch and the variations described below are overlapping straight stitches which are closely worked to create a solid filling. They are used mainly to cover small, narrow shapes, such as leaves and flower petals. You can also use them to fill large and irregular shapes, by working multiple rows of stitches, butted up together.

When you are working an individual motif, use a sharp pencil or an air-erasable or water-soluble marking pen to draw a line through the center of the shape to provide a stitching guide. To work rows of stitches, draw parallel lines across the shape to keep the rows an even width. The stitches look untidy when they are too long, so keep them fairly short.

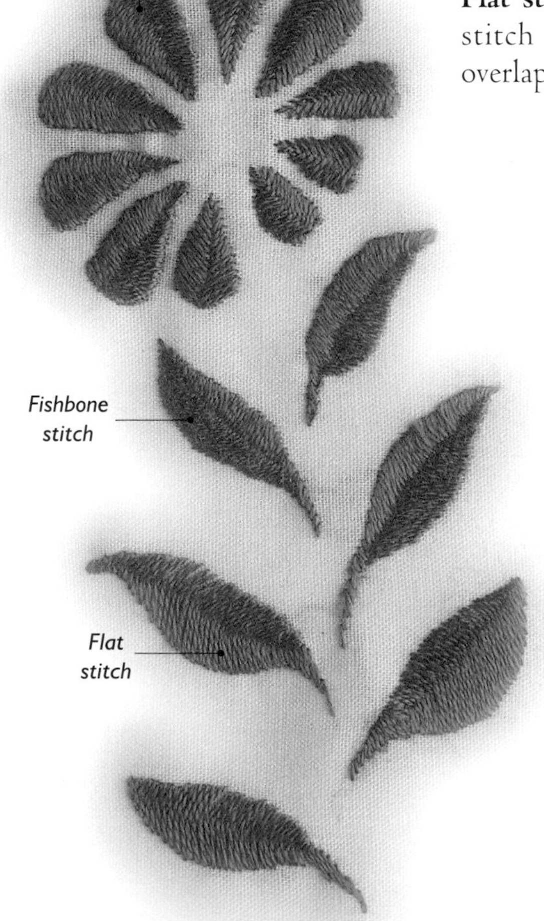

Light-reflecting threads, such as embroidery floss or pearl cotton, are ideal for these stitches, as they enhance the smoothness of the surface and reveal the different directions of the stitches. The stitches look equally effective worked in a single color or a shaded thread. Work the stitches very close together to cover the background fabric completely. Always mount the fabric in a frame to help keep the tension even and avoid distortion.

Fishbone stitch gives a smooth surface with a neat division down the center of the shape where the stitches overlap. The decorative line produced is similar to the main vein on a leaf.

Raised fishbone stitch gives a more woven finish, with a three-dimensional look.

Flat stitch is similar to fishbone stitch with less sharply angled overlapping stitches.

Fishbone stitch

Raised fishbone stitch

Flat stitch

Starting and finishing stitching

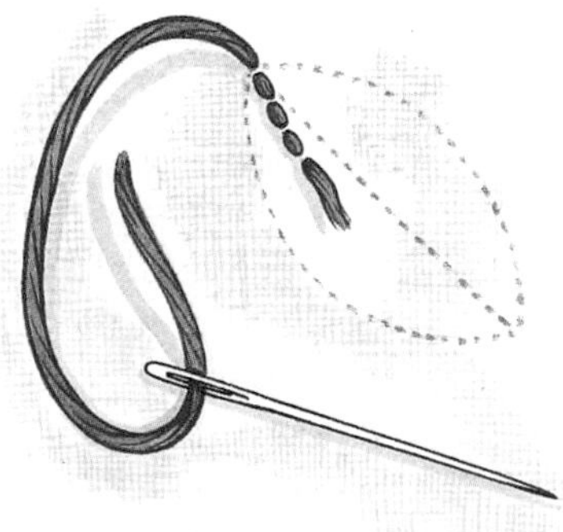

1 Anchor the thread close to the top of the shape with two or three small stitches. Take the thread to the back, and bring it to the front at your starting point.

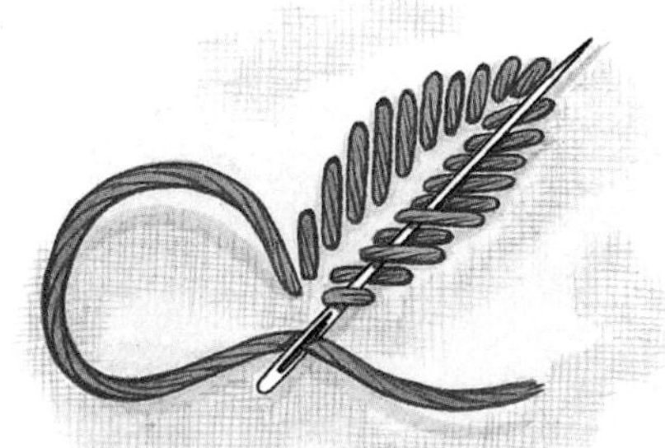

2 When the shape is completed, take the thread to the back and secure the end by darning it into the last few stitches worked.

Working fishbone stitch

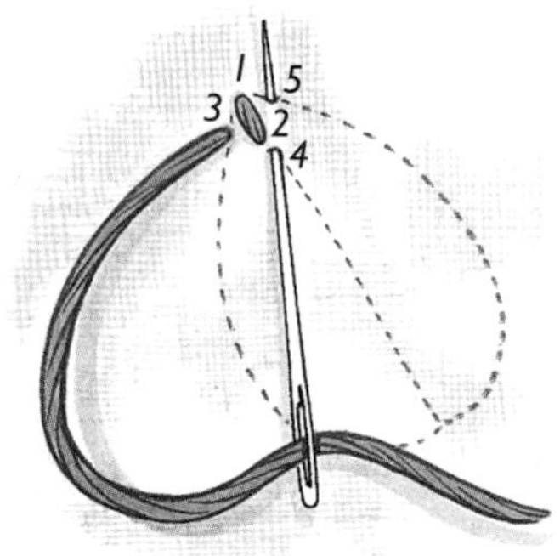

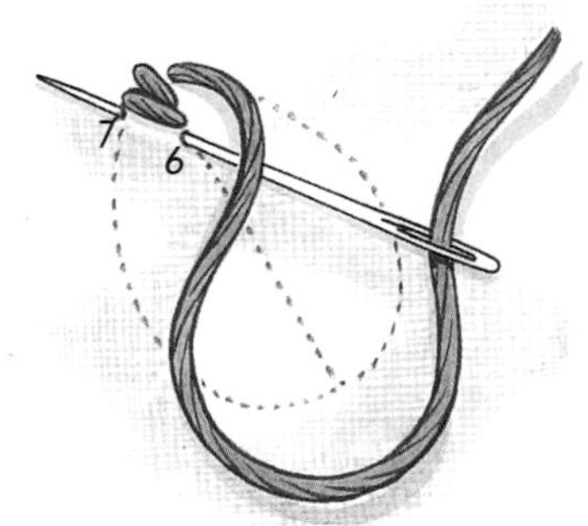

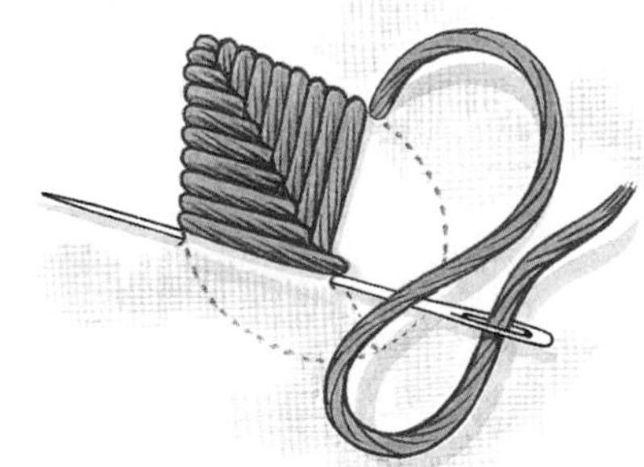

1 Bring the needle out at 1 and make a short, straight stitch downward to 2. Bring the needle through at 3. Insert it slightly to the right of the center line at 4. Then bring the needle through on the right-hand edge of the shape at 5.

2 Insert the needle slightly to the left of the center line at 6. Bring it out at 7 on the left-hand edge, just below the previous stitch.

3 Continue working from side to side in the same way until the shape is filled. Take the thread through to the back and secure it.

Working raised fishbone stitch

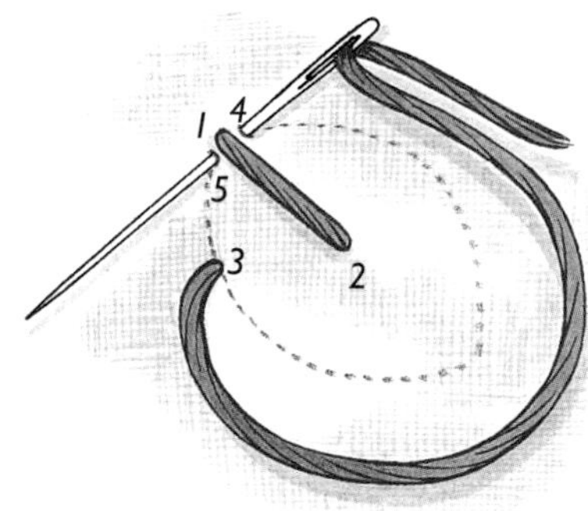

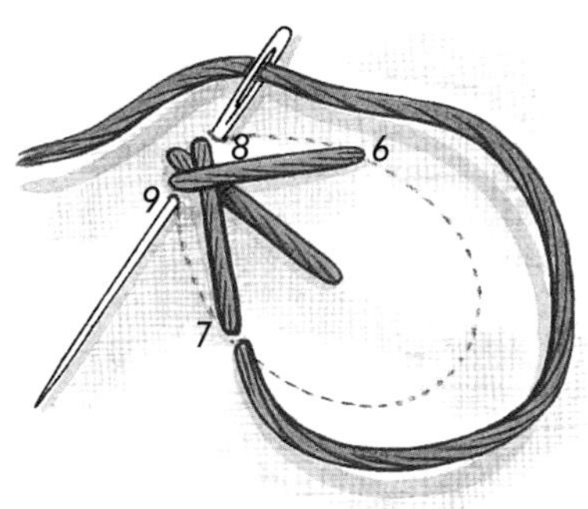

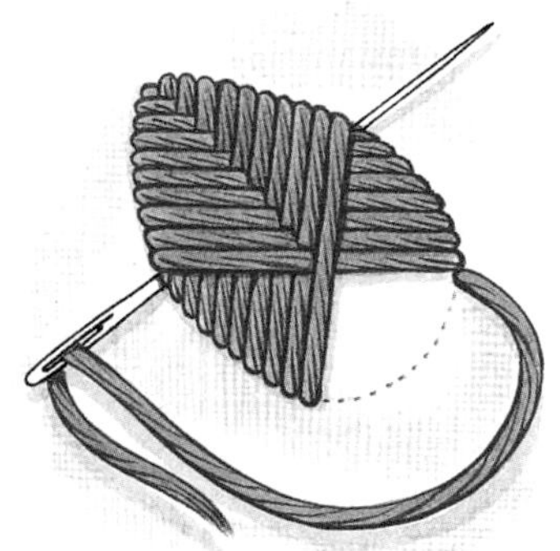

1 Bring the needle out at 1 and insert it at 2. Bring the needle through at the left-hand edge at 3. Insert the needle just to the right of your starting point at 4, and bring it out at 5.

2 Insert the needle at the right-hand edge at 6 and bring it to the front at 7. Make a short horizontal stitch just below the first, from 8 to 9.

3 Continue working in this way to cover the shape. Take the thread to the back and secure it.

Working flat stitch

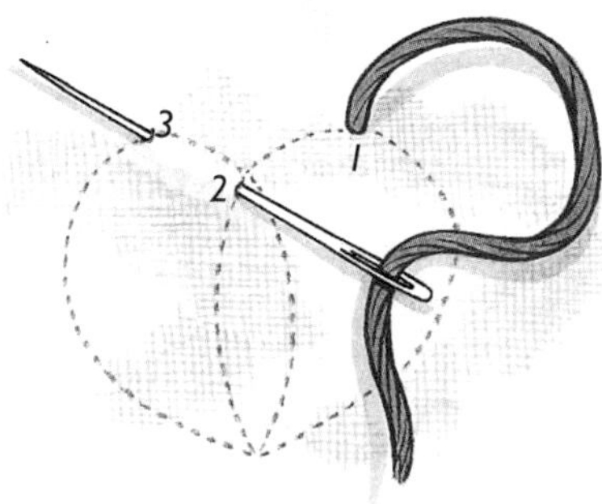

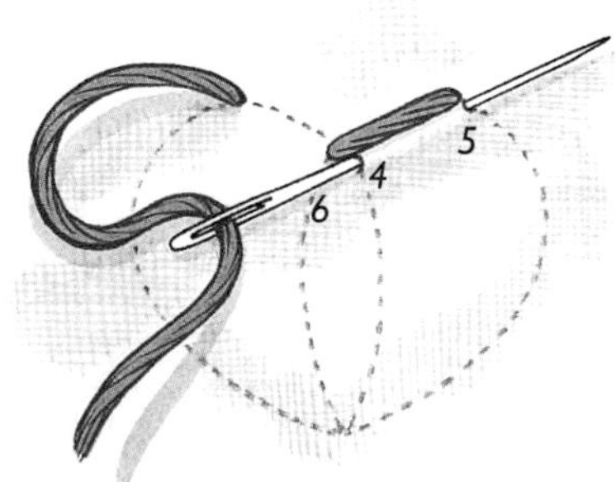

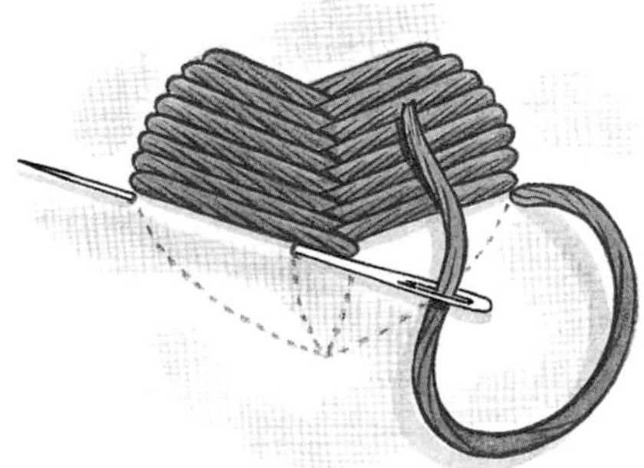

1 Mark a double line down the center of the shape. Bring the needle out at 1, insert it at 2, and bring it out on the left-hand edge at 3.

2 Take the needle to the back at 4 and bring it out on the right-hand edge at 5. Insert the needle again on the left-hand central line at 6.

3 Continue in this way, working the overlapping stitches from side to the side, angling them less steeply than for fishbone stitch.

Open filling stitches

Open filling stitches are used to fill a shape, while allowing some of the background to show through. They can be scattered at random or worked in more formal arrangements. They make pretty borders when positioned side by side in neat symmetrical rows.

Seed stitch, or seeding, can be worked in pairs or clusters, or it can be scattered randomly across a shape—this technique is called powdering. You can vary the effect by changing the direction of the stitches and the spacing.

Sheaf filling stitch looks like tiny bundles of wheat and makes an attractive light filling. When working widely spaced stitches, fasten off the thread after completing each one, and rejoin it in the appropriate place to continue.

Leaf stitch is useful for filling small shapes, such as leaves and petals. The stitches, which are worked upward from bottom to top, overlap to create a plaited strip down the center of the shape. When working a leaf-stitch border, make all the stitches the same length for a straight edge or vary the lengths for a wavy outline.

Open fishbone stitch, which is worked from top to bottom, has overlapped stitches, giving a more open look. Working backstitch or split stitch around a shape filled with either open fishbone or leaf stitch defines the outline (see pages 26 and 29).

Seed stitch

Sheaf filling stitch

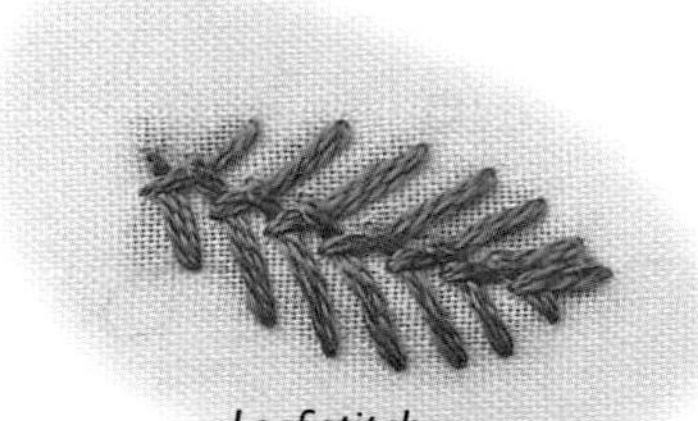
Leaf stitch

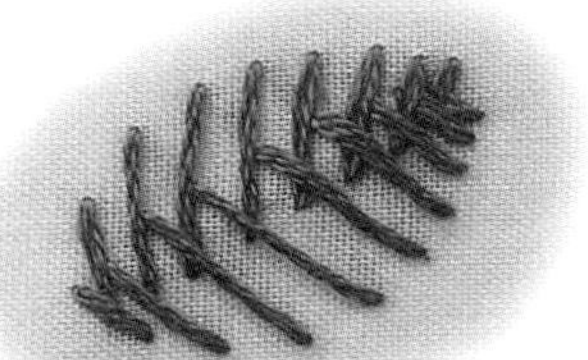
Open fishbone stitch

Starting and fastening off

Insert the needle close to your starting point, leaving a 2 in. (5 cm) tail of thread on the right side, close to the position of the first stitch. Work the filling stitch to fill the shape. To finish, take the thread to the back and darn it through the back of the last few stitches. Secure the next thread length in the same way.

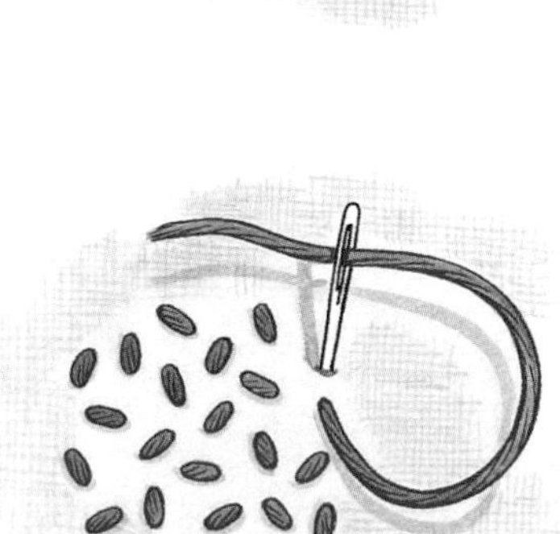

Working seed stitch

Work tiny straight stitches in pairs, scattering them over the fabric at different angles.

Alternatively, scatter single straight stitches randomly for a lighter look.

WHAT WENT WRONG

Pucker problem

When working open filling stitches, it's easy to pull the thread too taut, causing the fabric to pucker and the stitches to distort. To avoid this problem, mount the work in an embroidery frame, and make sure that the thread lies smoothly against the back of the fabric at all times.

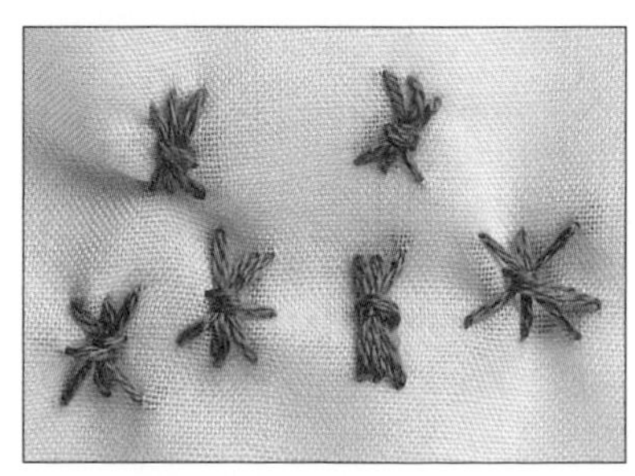

Working sheaf filling stitch

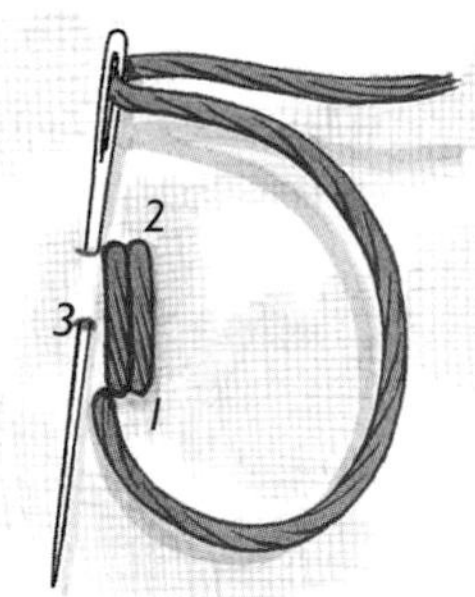

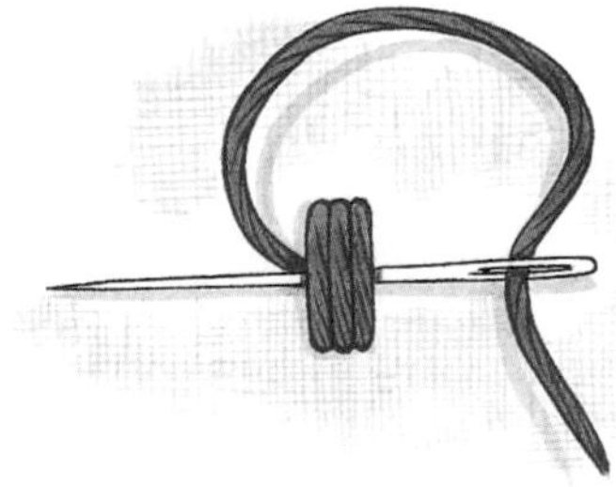

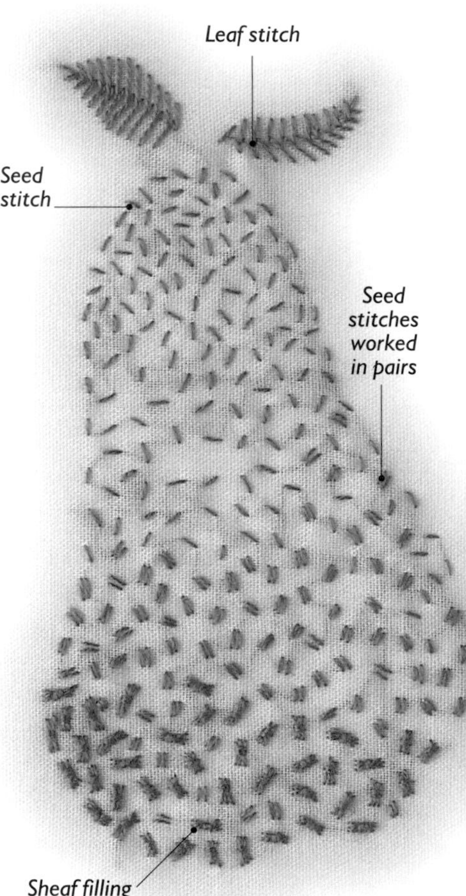

1 Bring the thread to the front and work a vertical satin stitch from 1 to 2. Work two more satin stitches to the left of the first, then bring the needle point through at 3.

2 Pull the thread through. Take the needle over the satin stitch group and back under, without entering the fabric. Pull the thread slightly to bunch the satin stitches in the center.

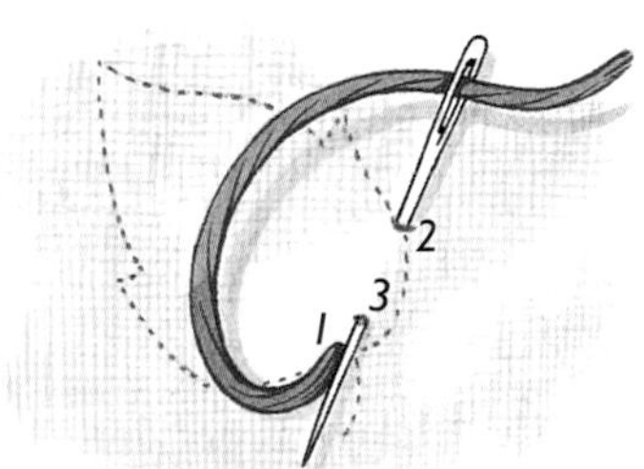

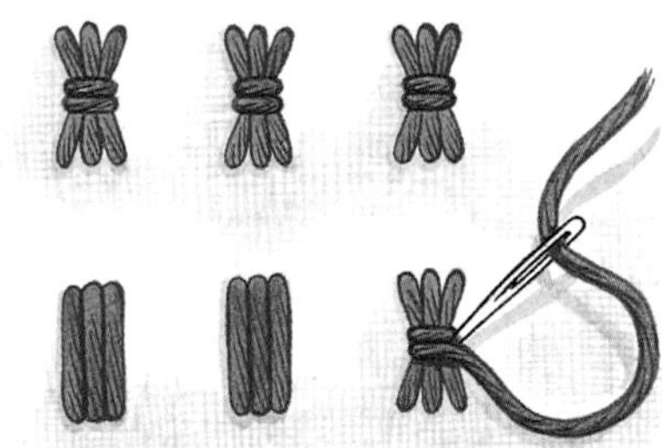

3 Take the needle over the satin stitches again, then take it through the fabric behind the group.

4 To work sheaf stitch in two colors, work all the satin stitch groups over the shape first, then work the tying stitches in a second color.

Working leaf stitch

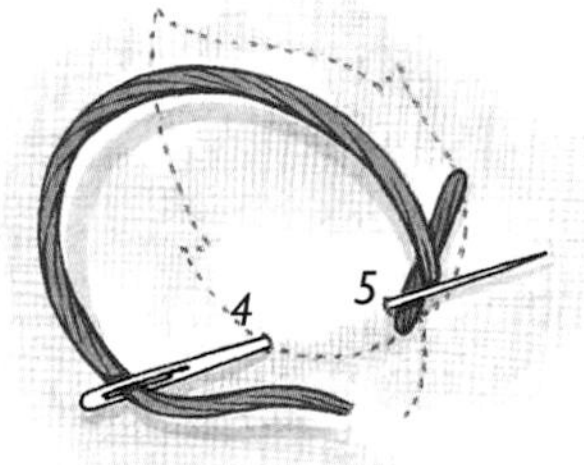

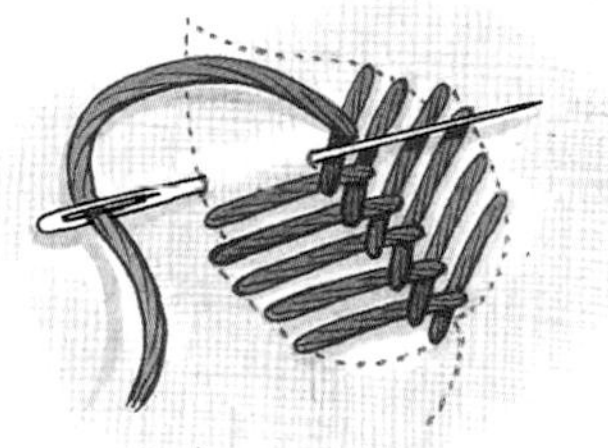

1 Bring the needle to the front on the left edge of the shape at 1. Make a slanting stitch to the right-hand edge at 2. Bring the needle to the front near the center at 3.

2 Make a slanting stitch to the left-hand edge at 4 and bring the needle through to the front at 5, ready to start the next stitch.

3 Continue working in the same way, inserting the needle alternately to the left and right edges and bringing it out near the center.

Working open fishbone stitch

1 Mark two lines within the shape to keep the stitches even. Bring the needle to the front at 1 and take a slanting stitch to the right-hand edge at 2. Bring the needle out at 3 and take it to the back at 4. Bring it to the front at 5.

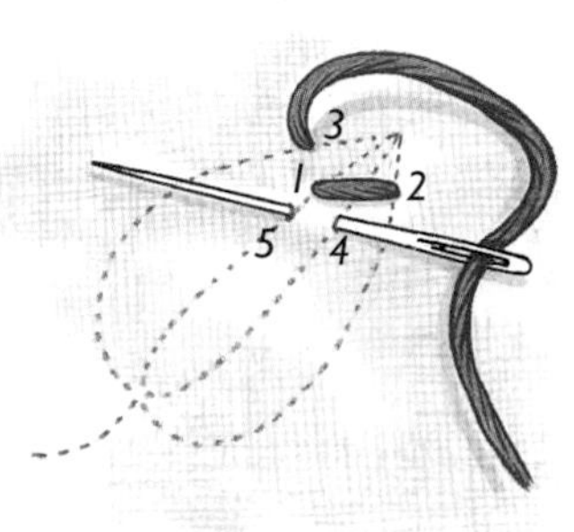

2 Continue working slanted stitches alternately from side to side until the shape is filled.

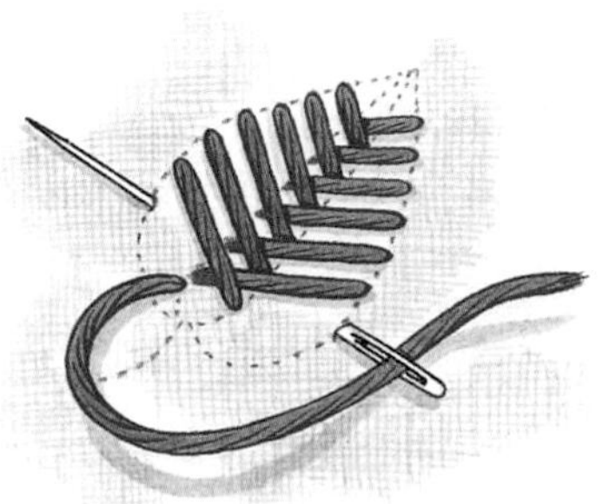

The four types of open filling stitch described here are very versatile and look equally attractive on evenweave and non-evenweave fabrics. They consist of straight or slanting stitches, or a combination of both, and are all quite simple to work.

On evenweave fabrics they can be used to fill backgrounds or shapes with perfectly spaced geometric patterns, while on other fabrics, you can create a free, less regimented arrangement. If you prefer a neater, more regular look on a non-evenweave embroidery fabric, mark a series of tiny, evenly spaced dots on the fabric first, with a water-soluble or an air-erasable marking pen to guide the positioning of your stitches.

To start and fasten off any of these stitches, refer to page 25.

Darning stitch is a variation of basic running stitch in which the stitches are longer, with just a small piece of fabric picked up between each one. You can vary the position of the darning stitches or add a second or third color to create a wide variety of interesting geometric patterns. This stitch is traditionally used in Eastern Europe and the Greek Islands to make wide, decorative borders on clothes and household linens. For information on running stitch, see page 26.

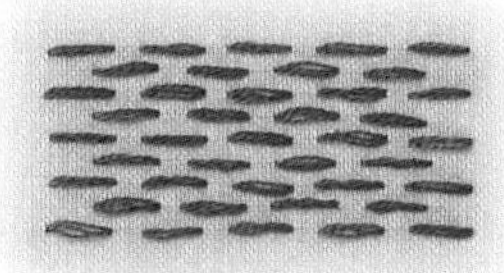

Darning stitch

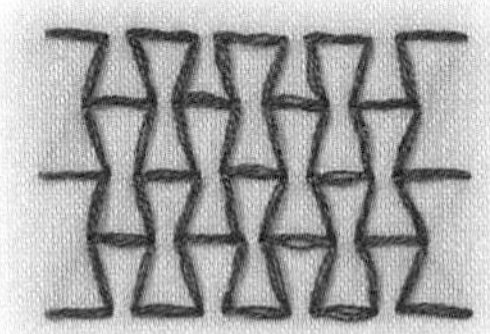

Japanese darning stitch

Arrowhead stitch

Bosnia stitch

Japanese darning stitch is another attractive variation of darning stitch. It is worked over two journeys and can be stitched in two, three, or more contrasting thread colors to give a more decorative effect.

Arrowhead stitch makes a pretty zigzag pattern across the fabric. For an allover filling, it can be worked in vertical rows with the tips of the stitches touching. Alternatively, individual arrowheads can be scattered at random across the fabric.

Bosnia stitch produces a delicate filling or wide border. It combines both upright and diagonal stitches and is worked in horizontal rows over two journeys. On traditional Bosnian embroideries, rows of this stitch are sometimes interlaced with a contrasting thread.

Working darning stitch

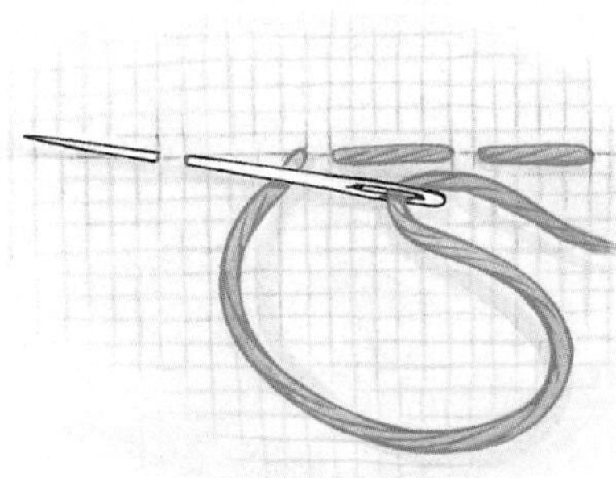

1 Bring the thread through to the right side at the top, right-hand corner of the shape. Work a horizontal row of running stitches across the shape, picking up a tiny piece of fabric between each stitch.

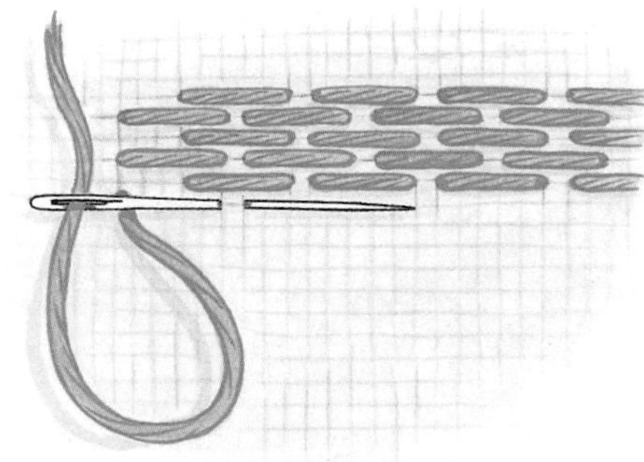

2 At the end of the row, turn and work back in the opposite direction, just below the previous row. Arrange the stitches so that they alternate with those on the previous row. Repeat step **2** to fill the shape.

Working Japanese darning stitch

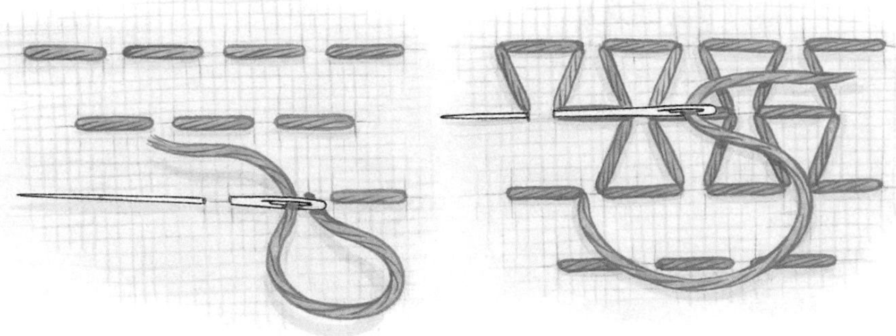

1 Bring the needle to the front at the top of the shape. Work spaced horizontal rows of darning stitch over the shape to be filled. Space the stitches and rows evenly and arrange the stitches alternately on the rows.

2 Bring the thread through at the right of the second row, and work a series of slanting stitches to join the first two rows, taking the needle in and out of the holes made by the darning stitches. Repeat step **2** over the shape, working each joining row separately.

Working arrowhead stitch

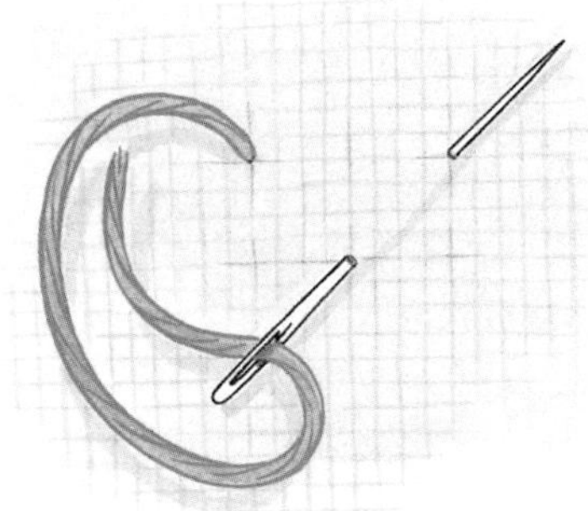

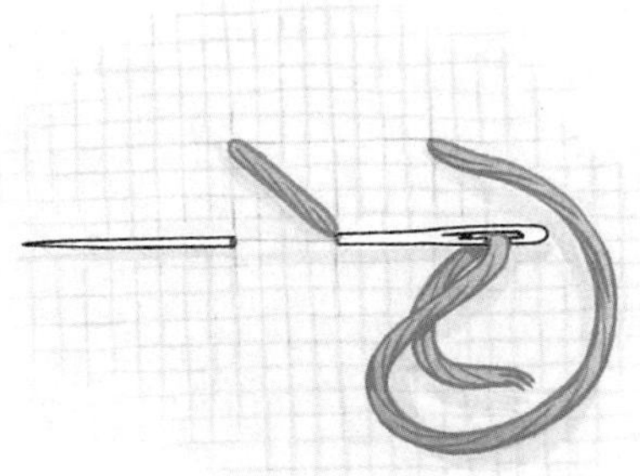

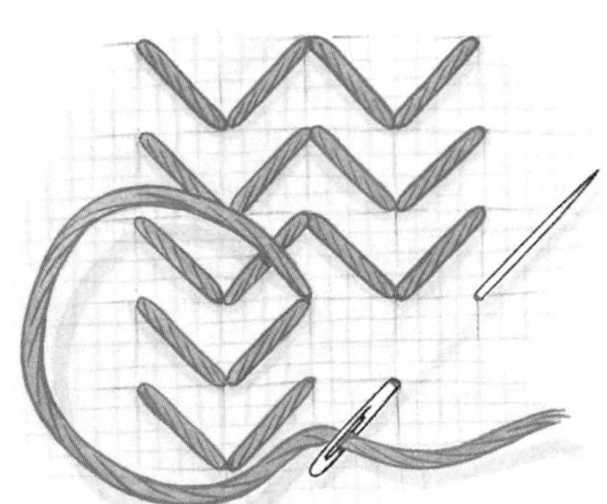

1 Bring the needle to the front at the top left-hand corner of the shape. Insert the needle lower down to the right and bring it through to the right, level with the point where it first emerged, to make the first half of the arrowhead.

2 Insert the needle into the base of the first stitch, then bring it out to the left, below the top of the first stitch. Pull the thread through to complete the first arrowhead. Work the next arrowhead directly below the first, and continue in this way down to the bottom of the shape.

3 Work the second and subsequent rows to the right of the first row, spacing the stitches evenly and making sure that all the arrowheads touch at the tips of the stitches.

Working Bosnia stitch

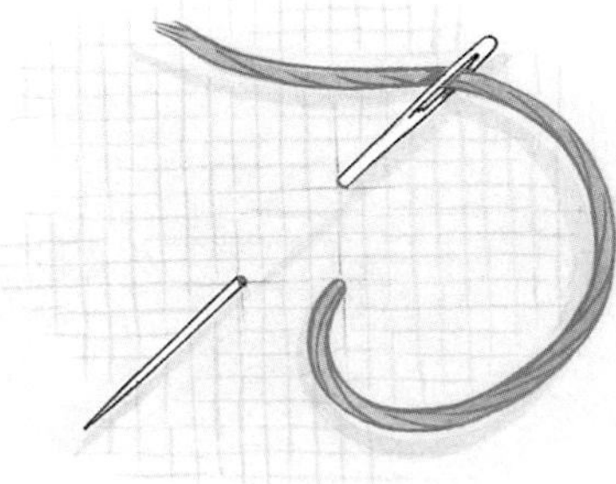

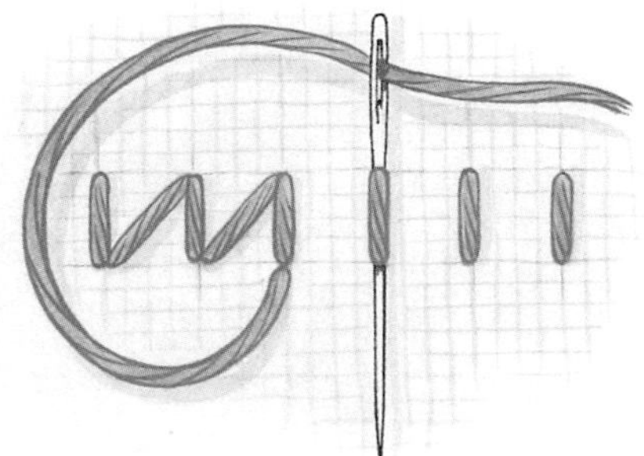

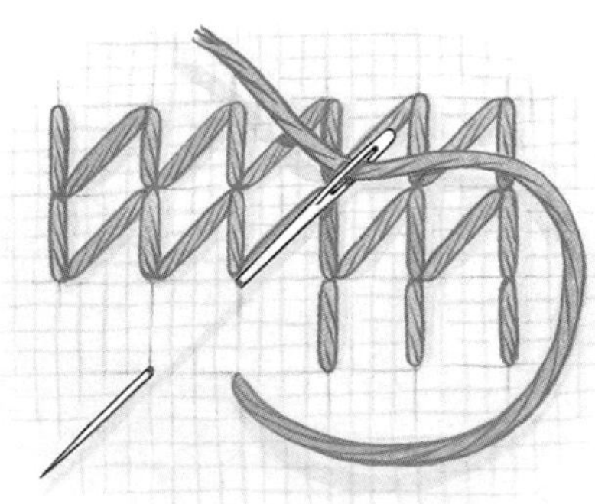

1 Bring the thread to the front at the top right-hand corner of the shape. Insert the needle a short distance above and bring it through level with the point where it first emerged and a short distance away to the left.

2 Repeat to make a horizontal row of identical evenly spaced, upright stitches. At the end of the row, turn and fill in the spaces between the uprights with a row of slanting stitches worked from left to right.

3 Continue in this way to fill the shape, arranging the rows directly below one another so that the upright stitches create vertical lines.

Border stitches

The border stitches shown here are easy to work and make decorative lines on non-evenweave fabrics. All the stitches make fairly narrow rows —they can all be used in straight lines, and two of them, split stitch and fern stitch, follow curves well.

When using these simple border stitches, you can vary your threads to create different effects—experiment by stitching with embroidery floss, soft crewel or tapestry yarn, metallic gold thread, or a shiny, brightly colored rayon.

When working these stitches, to make sure that the stitches in each line are level, draw guide lines on the fabric with a water-soluble or air-erasable marking pen.

To start and fasten off any of the border stitches, refer to page 25.

Fern stitch makes a pretty, branched line which looks somewhat like the fronds of a fern. It is often used to embroider foliage and for decorating leaf and flower shapes.

Fern stitch

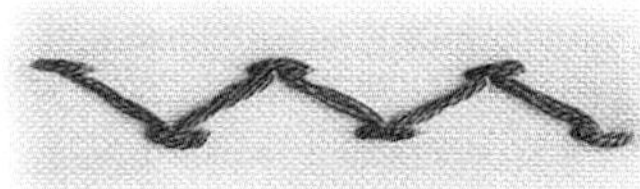

Chevron stitch

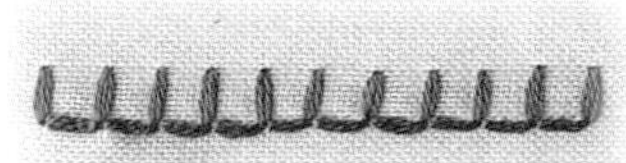

Paris stitch

Split stitch

Chevron stitch is worked between two parallel lines in a way similar to herringbone stitch (see page 49) and it makes an attractive zigzag line. Chevron stitch is also used in smocking, across the tiny folds of gathered fabric, to make both diamond and surface honeycomb patterns.

Paris stitch makes a neat line with branched stitches along the upper edge. When working this stitch on a loosely woven fabric, you can pull the working thread taut as you stitch to make a pattern of tiny holes between the stitches. (See pulled thread work, page 245.)

Split stitch is formed by the needle splitting the embroidery thread as the stitches are worked, and it produces a flat, narrow line. It is a stitch that has been used both as an outline stitch and as a solid filling since medieval times, in particular to embroider church vestments and wall hangings.

Working fern stitch

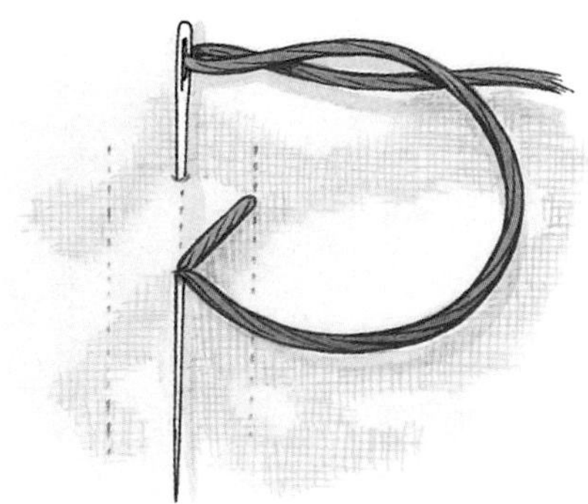

1 Draw three evenly spaced vertical guide lines on the fabric. Bring the needle out to the front, close to the top of the row. Work a group of three straight stitches of identical length at angles to each other and sharing the same base hole.

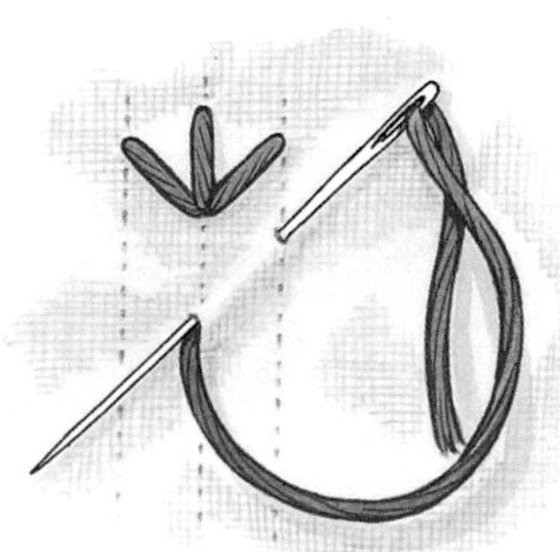

2 After working the third stitch of the top group, bring the needle through an equal distance down the line, ready to work the next stitch. Work all the following groups in the same way; make the right-hand stitch first, and bring the needle through at the base of this stitch.

3 Work the left-hand stitch of the group in the same way, and then work the center stitch, bringing the needle through an equal distance down the line to work the next group. Repeat steps **2** and **3** along the row.

Working chevron stitch

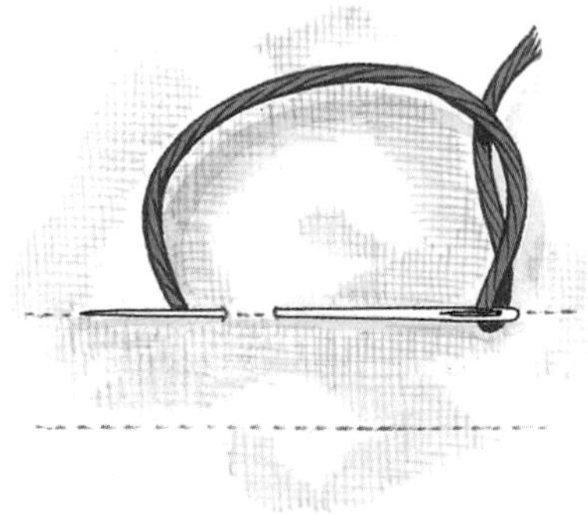

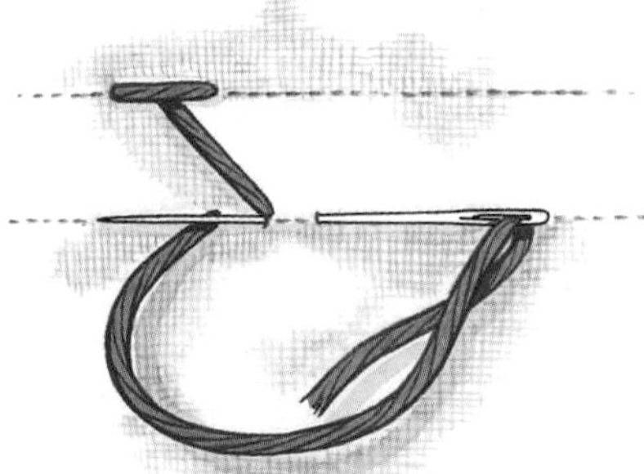

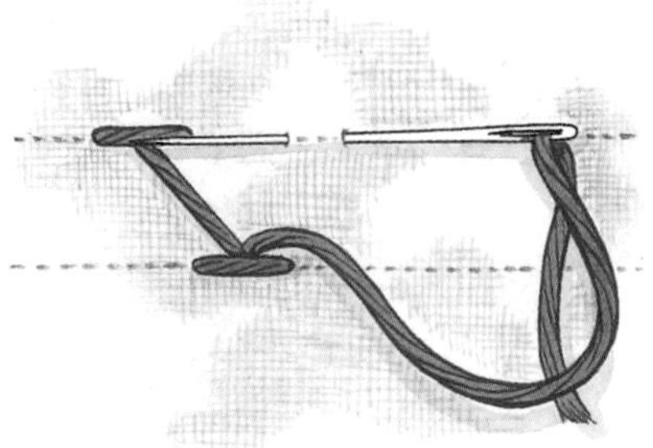

1 Draw two horizontal guide lines on the fabric. Start on the top guide line at the left of the row. Make a short straight stitch, and bring the needle out to the front at the center of the stitch.

2 Take a diagonal stitch across to the lower guide line, then make a second straight stitch along this line. Bring the needle out to the front at the center of the straight stitch.

3 Take a second diagonal stitch across to the top guide line, and make an identical short straight stitch; repeat steps **2** and **3** along the row.

Working Paris stitch

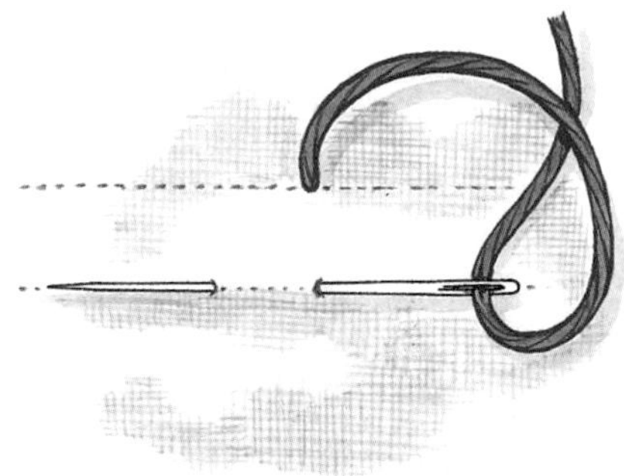

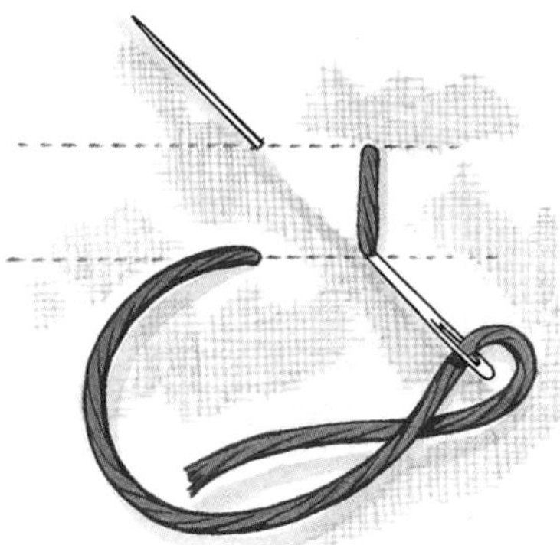

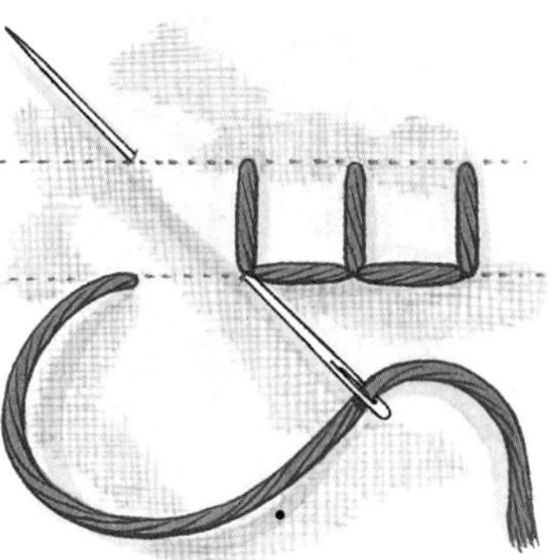

1 Start at the top, near the right-hand end of the row. Work a short straight stitch downward at a right angle to the line, bringing the needle through an equal distance along the line.

2 Insert the needle at the base of the first stitch, and bring it out to the front on the top line above the left-hand end of the preceding stitch.

3 Repeat steps **1** and **2** along the row, making sure that the stitches are level.

Working split stitch

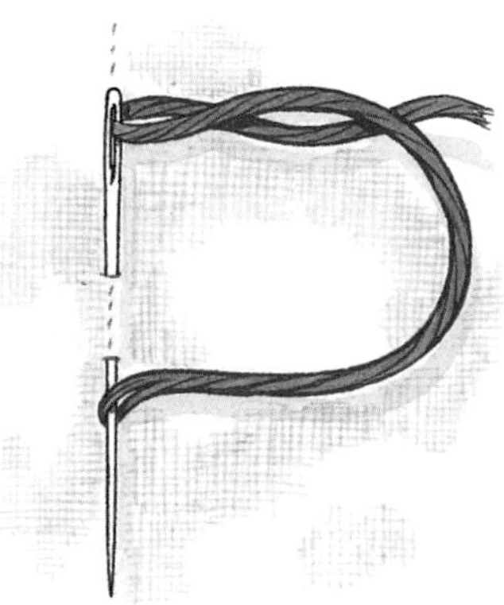

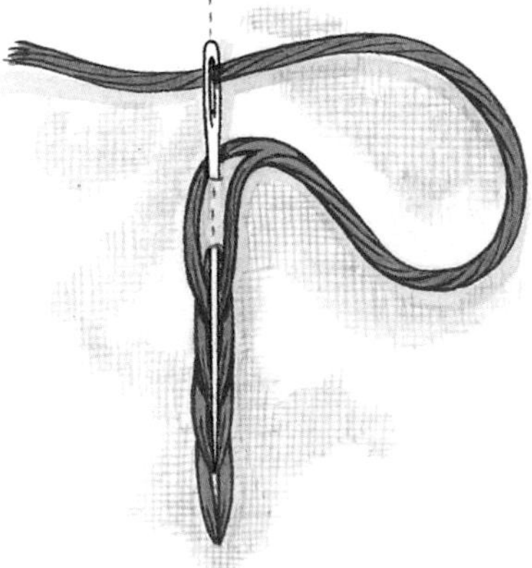

1 Start at the bottom of the line. Make a stitch upward along the line, and bring the point of the needle back through both the fabric and the working thread, about halfway along the stitch.

2 Continue working upward along the line, working each stitch with a forward and backward motion and splitting it with the point of the needle.

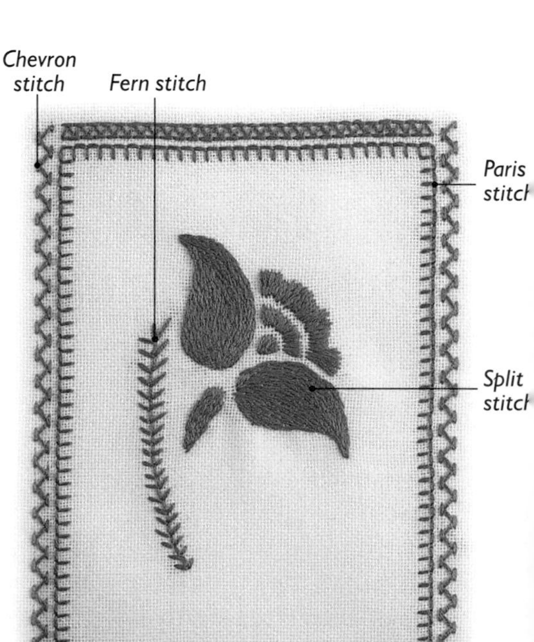

Isolated stitches

The stitches in this section create textured accents and splashes of color, and are used to create contrasting highlights on the fabric background or over a smoothly stitched surface.

The stitches are very versatile. You can scatter them over a shape at random, arrange them in groups in a more regular way, or work them individually. You can also make a heavily textured filling by working arrowheads and crow's feet close together.

Try working these stitches in a thick thread to contrast with the weight of thread used for the main stitching; rounded threads, such as pearl cotton or brilliant cut-work and embroidery threads, are ideal, as they help the stitches to stand out well.

To keep the stitches neat, draw an outline of the shape on the fabric with a water-soluble or air-erasable marking pen, and stretch the fabric in an embroidery frame.

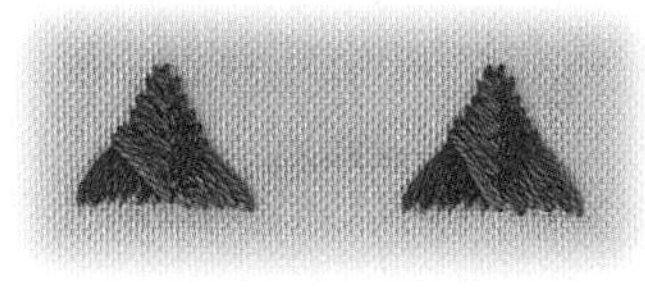

Arrowhead

Crow's foot

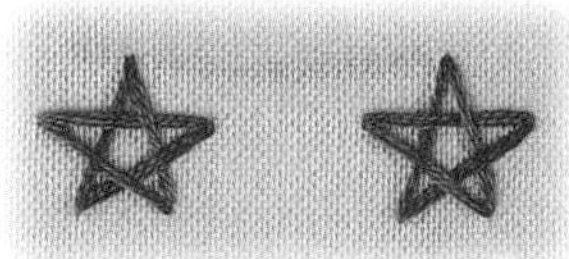

Star darn

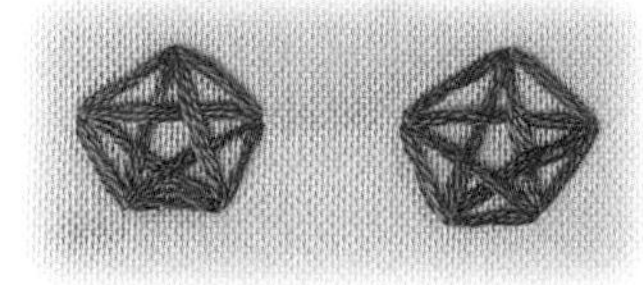

Framed star darn

To start and fasten off the stitches in this section, refer to page 77.

Arrowheads are very decorative, densely worked surface stitches, also used in tailoring (at the ends of pockets, for example). The shape is filled with slanting stitches. The arrowhead is based on an equilateral triangle, in which all three sides are the same length.

Crow's foot is similar to an arrowhead, but the stitches point downward.

Star darn creates an open, five-pointed star. The stitches at the back of the fabric are directly underneath stitches at the front, so that no thread shadows show through on the right side.

Framed star darn is a variation of star darn with a frame of straight stitches around the star.

Working an arrowhead

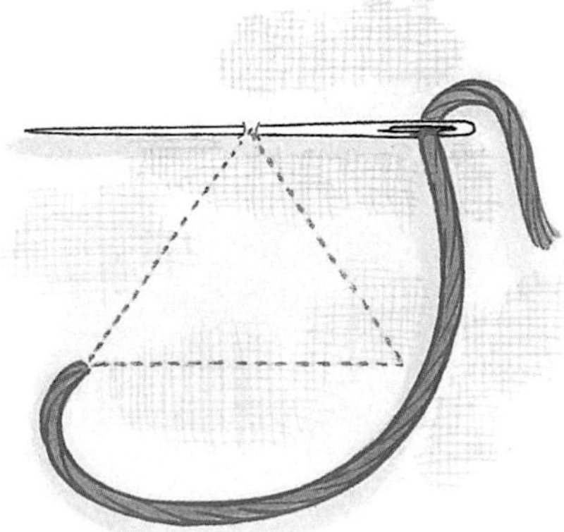

1 Mark an equilateral triangle pointing upward on the fabric, and start at the bottom left-hand corner. Make a short stitch from right to left into the top corner.

2 Make a long stitch from right to left along the bottom of the triangle. Make a second stitch at the top corner, below and a little wider than the first stitch, then make a stitch along the bottom, as shown.

3 Continue in this way, alternating stitches at the top and bottom of the triangle until it is filled with overlapping stitches. Work the stitches close together so that the fabric is completely covered.

Working a crow's foot

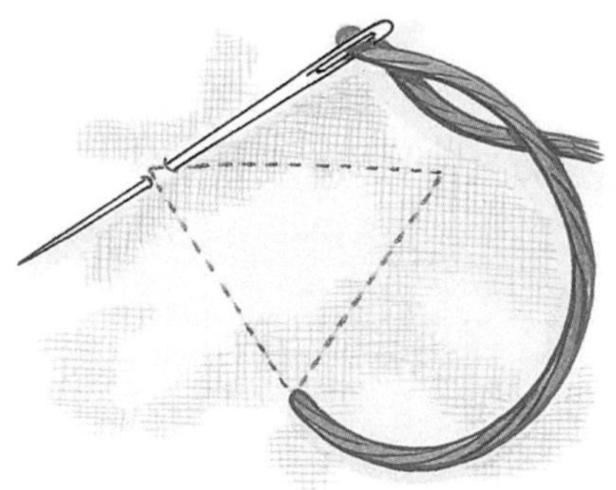

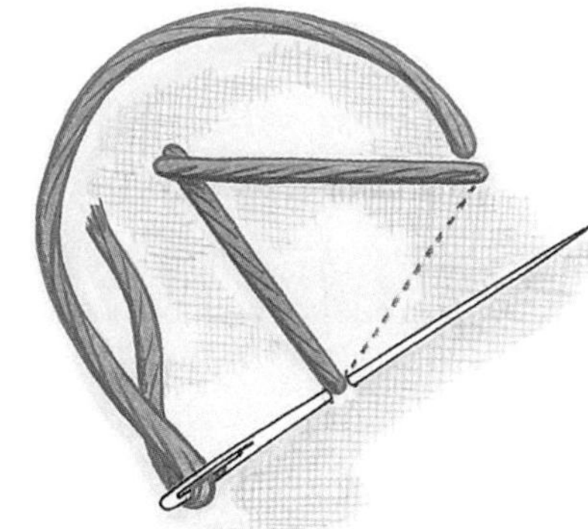

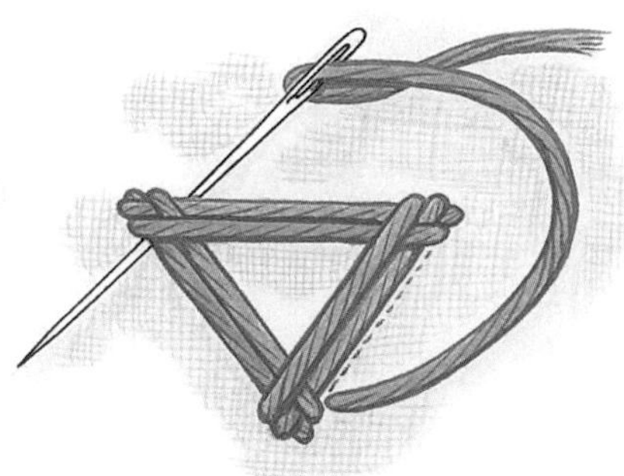

1 Mark an equilateral triangle pointing downward on the fabric, and start slightly to the right of the bottom corner. Make a short stitch from right to left at the top left-hand corner, and pull the thread through.

2 Make a similar stitch from right to left at the top right-hand corner. Make a similar stitch at the bottom, but work the stitch from left to right. Bring the needle out slightly above and to the right of your starting point.

3 Continue in this way, taking a stitch along each side of the triangle in turn until the shape is filled with overlapping stitches. Work the stitches close together so that the fabric is completely covered.

Working a star darn

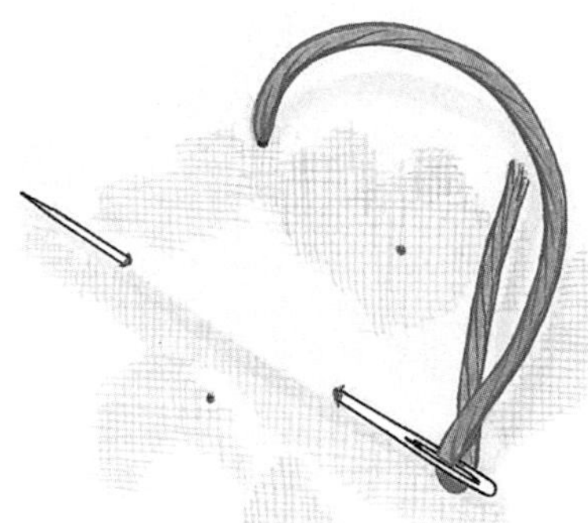

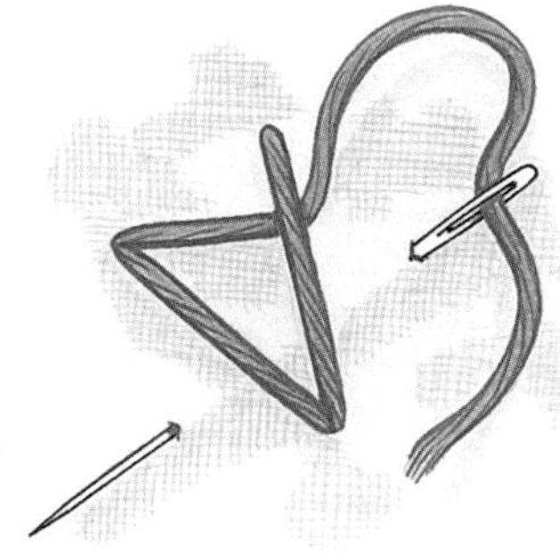

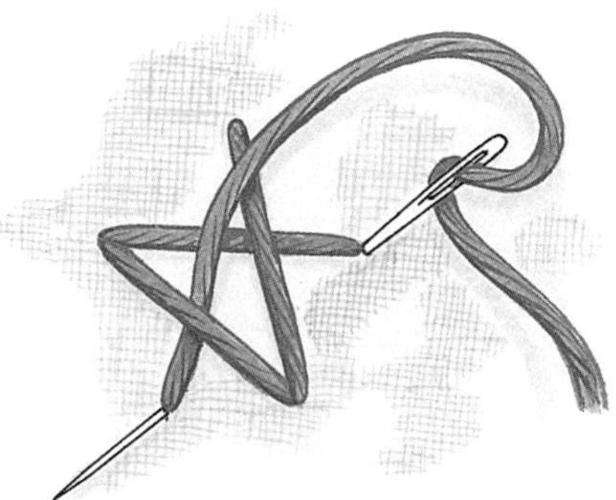

1 Mark the five points of the star on the fabric, and bring the needle out at the top point. Insert the needle at the bottom right-hand point, and bring it out at the top left-hand point.

2 Insert the needle at the bottom right-hand point, and bring it out at the top left point again. Insert it at the top right, taking the working thread under the first stitch. Bring it out at the bottom left.

3 Insert the needle at the top right again, taking the thread under the nearest stitch, and bring it out at the bottom left. To finish, insert the needle at the top point, slipping it under the horizontal stitch.

Working a framed star darn

Work an ordinary star darn, but do not fasten off the thread end when the star is complete. Instead, bring the thread out at an adjacent point and work a framework of five stitches to join the points of the star.

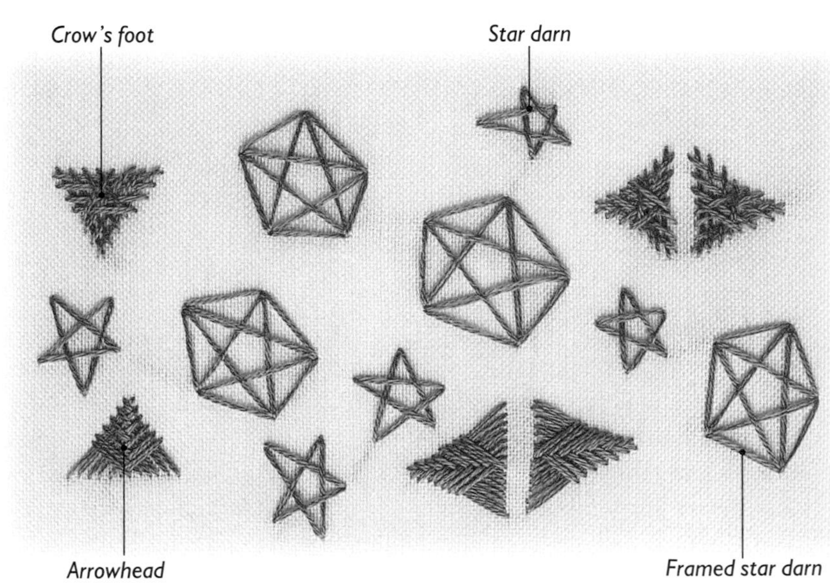

Cross stitches

Cross stitch forms a diagonal cross on the front of the fabric; each cross is composed of two diagonal stitches worked one on top of the other. It is one of the easiest embroidery stitches to learn and use.

Cross stitch front

Counted cross stitch is worked from charts on special even-weave fabrics (see page 11), on which the threads are easy to see and count, so that even beginners can produce stitches of a uniform size and shape.

You can use rows of cross stitches to form blocks of color, or you can work individual stitches. Always make sure that all the lower stitches slant one way and all the upper stitches slant the other way for a neat finish.

Two other stitches are often shown on charts. **Fractional stitches (three-quarter stitches)** are a variation of normal cross stitch; they consist of a full diagonal and a half diagonal stitch. A single three-quarter stitch fills half the space of a full cross stitch, while a double three-quarter stitch takes up the space of a full cross stitch. These stitches are used to create smoother outlines around curved shapes and to add details. They are shown on counted cross stitch charts as either a small symbol or a colored triangle.

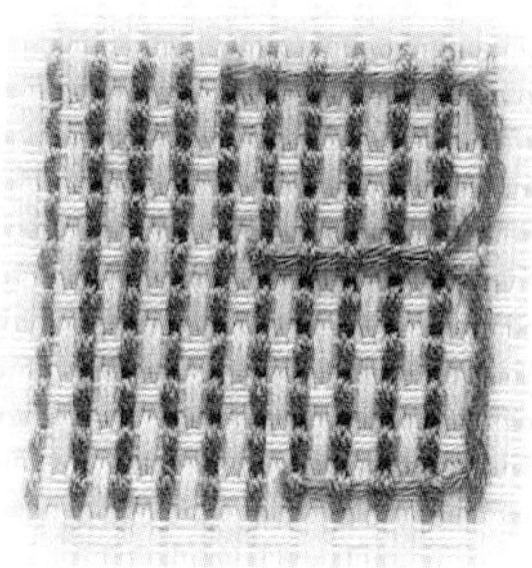
Cross stitch back

Backstitch is used to create outlines around blocks of cross stitch and to add linear details. It is shown on charts as a heavy line.

Starting and fastening off

For a professional finish, always weave the loose ends of the thread into the the back of the work. Don't tie a knot in the thread—the knot will make a lump on the right side and may eventually work loose, so that your stitching unravels.

1 Close to your starting point, take the needle through to the back of the fabric, leaving a 2 in. (5 cm) thread end at the front. You will secure this later, when you have finished stitching the length of thread.

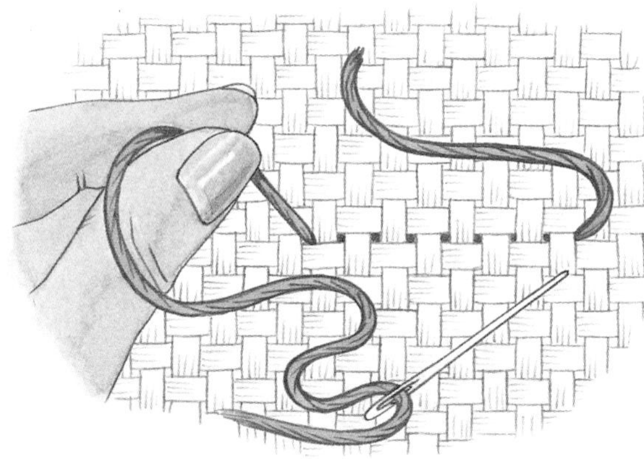

2 When you have about 2 in. (5 cm) of thread left, or you've finished the color block, take the needle through to the back and darn the thread end under several stitches. Then pull the loose thread end at the start of your stitching through to the back and darn it in.

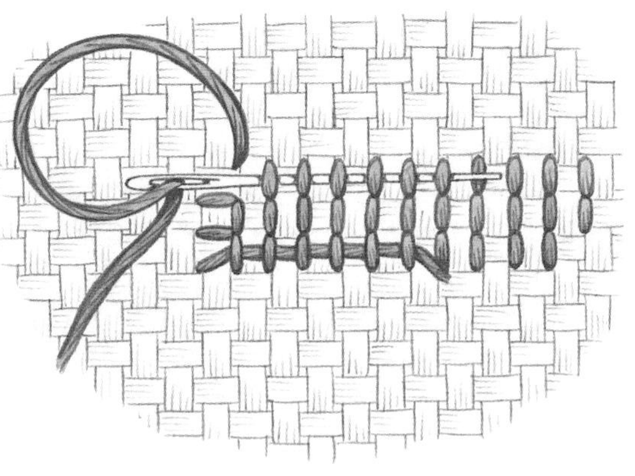

COMPLETING A COLOR AREA

Always fasten off the thread after completing each stitched area. Don't be tempted to carry a length of thread between two stitched areas on the wrong side. It will show through to the right side and spoil your work.

Joining in a new thread

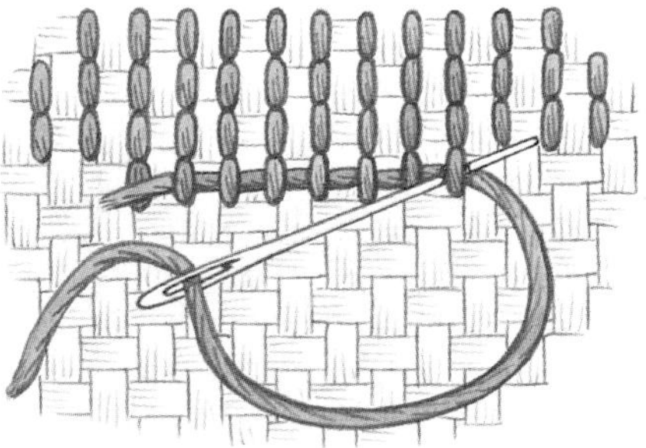

On the back of the fabric, run the new length of thread under the back of several stitches close to where you are working. Then take a small backstitch over the last stitch, and bring the needle out in the correct place at the front of the fabric.

Working individual counted cross stitches

On aida cloth, take the needle down one hole and to the right of where it emerged. Pull the thread through. Bring the needle out one hole to the left, and insert it one hole up and one to the right.

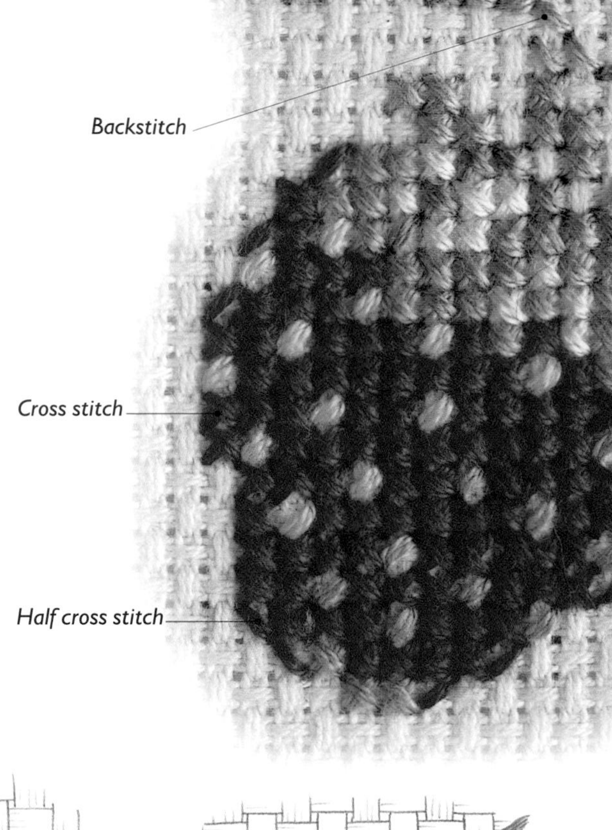

Working a row of counted cross stitch

Each row of counted cross stitch is worked in two journeys. It does not matter which direction you start stitching, so long as all the lower stitches slant one way and all the top stitches the other.

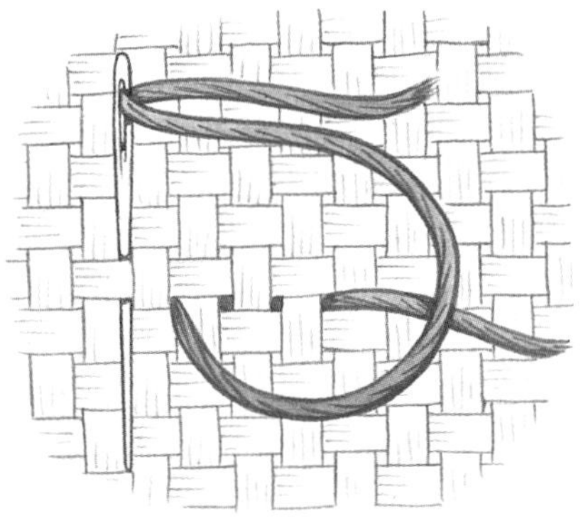

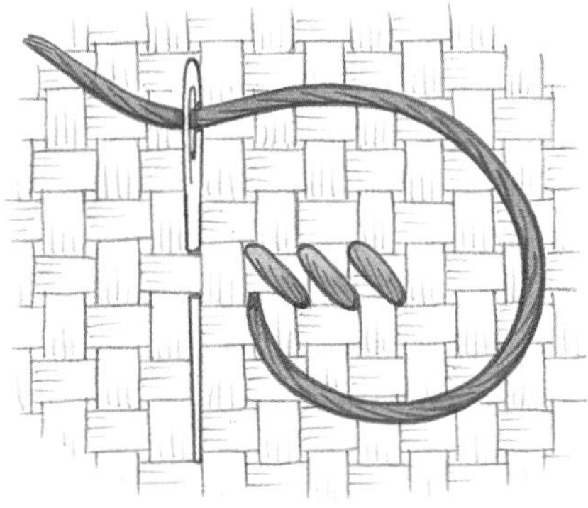

1 Bring the needle out to the front at the start of the work—this will usually be at the center of the design. To start working from right to left, insert the needle one hole up and one hole to the left, to make a diagonal stitch, and bring it out one hole down.

2 Insert the needle one hole up and one hole to the left, then bring it out one hole down. Continue working like this to form a row of upward diagonal stitches.

3 To complete the crosses, work back from left to right. Bring the needle out directly below the top of the last diagonal. Insert it one hole up and one to the right and bring it out one hole down. Continue like this to the end of the row.

Working fractional (three-quarter) stitches

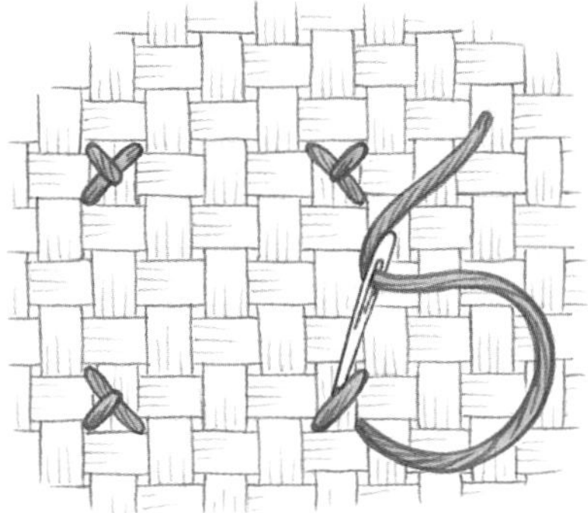

Single three-quarter stitch
This fills half the space of one whole cross stitch. Work a full-sized diagonal. Bring the needle out at the corner of the fabric block, then take it down in the center, over the full diagonal.

Double three-quarter stitch
This fills the space of one whole cross stitch. Work two three-quarter stitches back to back; the full diagonals share the same holes and the half stitches share the same center point.

Working backstitch

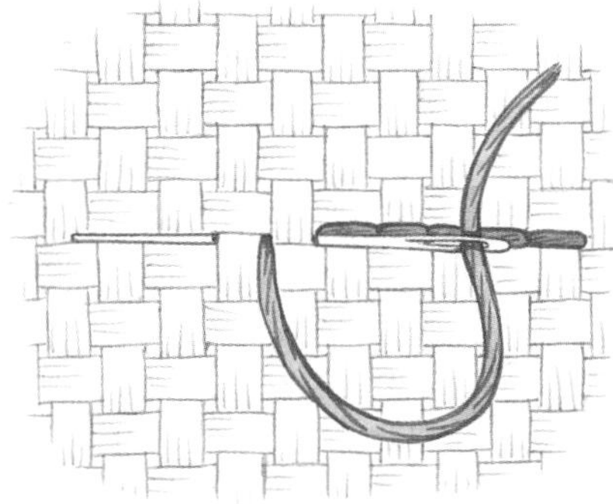

Bring the needle out on the right side of the fabric and take a backward stitch, horizontally, vertically, or diagonally. Bring the needle out again, one stitch length from the start of the first stitch. Continue in this way.

Two-sided cross stitch

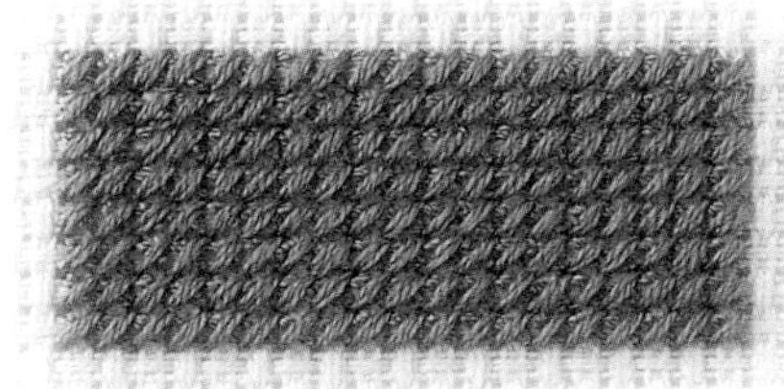
Alternate cross stitch

Half cross stitch

One reason for the popularity of cross stitch is its versatility. Merely by working only one half of the stitch, for example, you can produce a textural contrast with the rest of the stitching. By choosing a different method of working the stitch, you can make the work reversible, so that cross stitches appear on both sides of the fabric. This is especially desirable on semitransparent fabrics, where the vertical lines made by the usual method would show through to the right side. Here, two alternative methods are shown.

To start and fasten off these stitches, see page 43.

Two-sided cross stitch entails four journeys to complete a row. Note that the last, right-handed stitch of the row disregards the principle of slanting the stitches uniformly, but this is not particularly noticeable.

Alternate cross stitch also entails four journeys to complete a row, but all the lower stitches are completed before the crossing stitches are worked. Like two-sided cross stitch, it uses up more thread than ordinary cross stitch.

Half cross stitch is simply a half-worked cross stitch. It's used with full cross stitches to create a thinner stitch texture. Usually, half cross stitches should slant from bottom left to top right, regardless of the direction of the top diagonals of adjacent full cross stitches. However, you can vary this rule for a less formal effect.

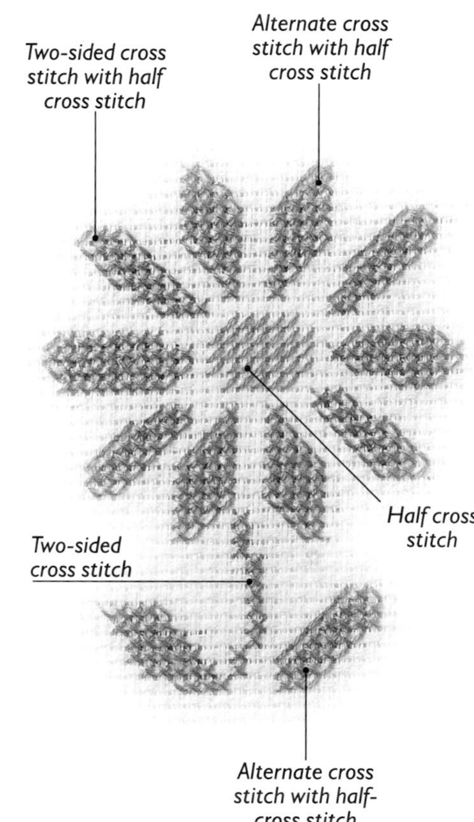

Working two-sided cross stitch

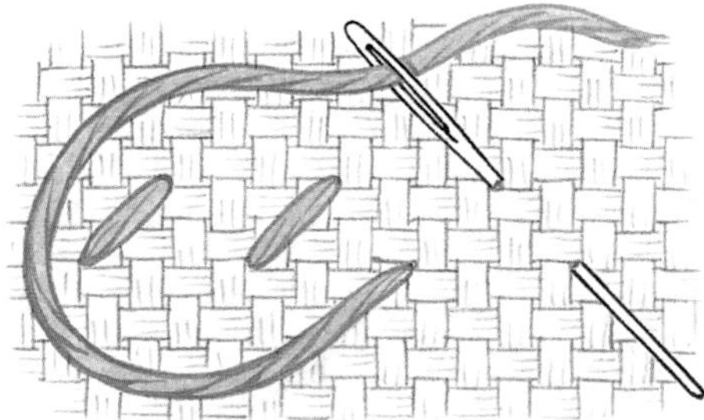

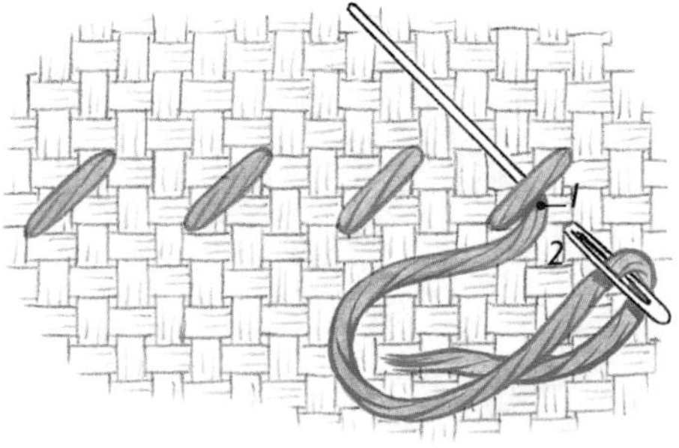

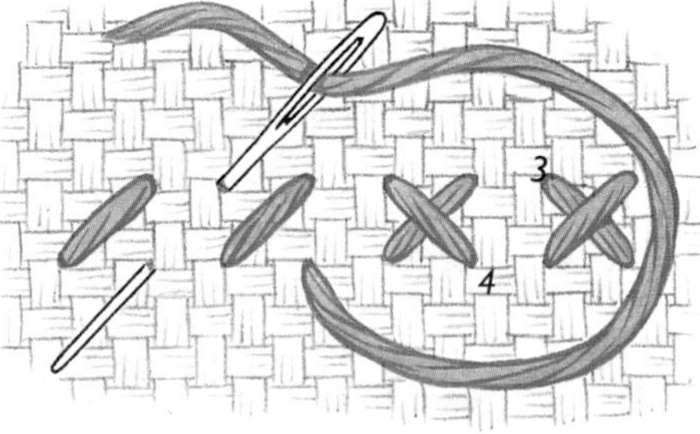

1 Working from left to right and over pairs of aida blocks, work evenly spaced diagonal stitches slanting from bottom left to top right and covering alternate pairs of blocks.

2 At the end of the row, bring the needle through at 1 at the center of the last diagonal stitch. Insert it at 2, and bring it through at 1 again under the slanting stitch.

3 Insert the needle at 3 and bring it out again at 4. Then work back along the row, from right to left, making diagonal stitches to complete the cross stitches.

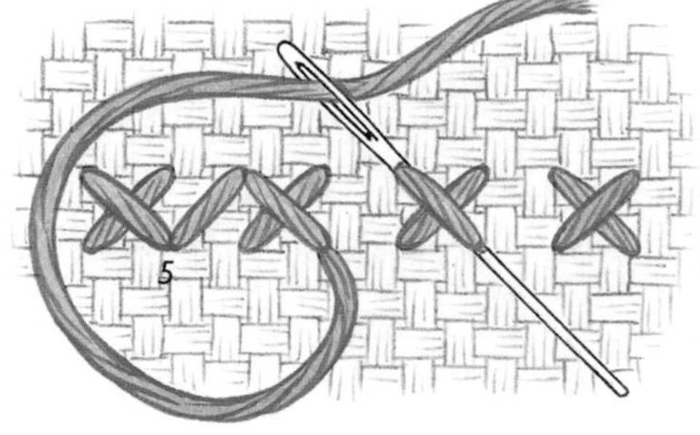

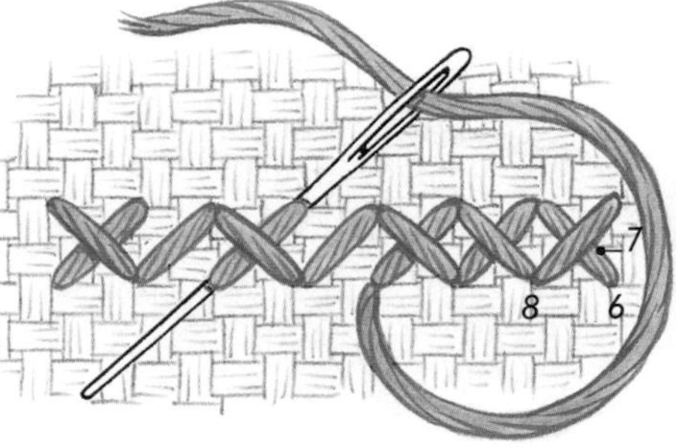

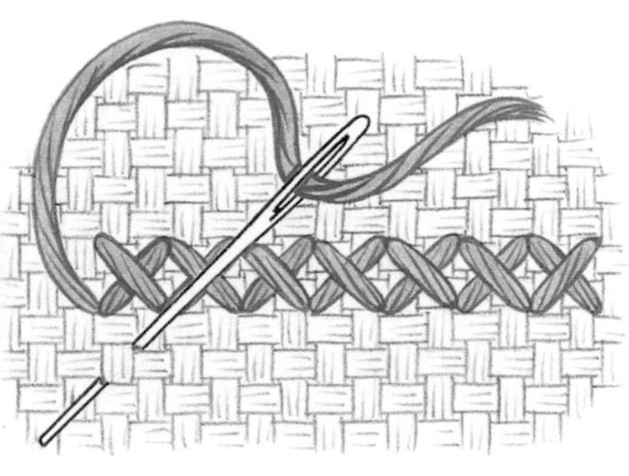

4 Work back across the row: bring the needle up at 5, at the point where the thread emerged previously; pull the thread through. Continue as in step 1 to the end of the row.

5 At the end of the row, bring the needle out at the bottom right of the last cross at 6. Insert it at the center of the cross at 7 and bring it out again at the bottom left of the cross at 8. Pull the thread through, and work back along the row from right to left to complete the crosses.

6 Start the second and subsequent rows by making a half stitch, bringing the thread through in the correct position to work the first stitch. Take care to secure the thread ends neatly to avoid spoiling the neatness of the wrong side.

Working alternate cross stitch

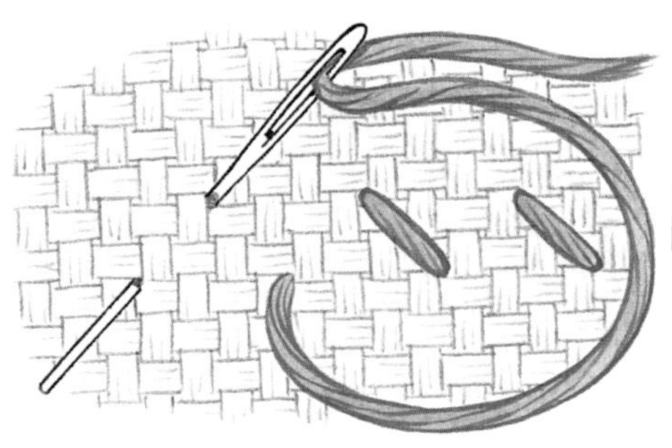

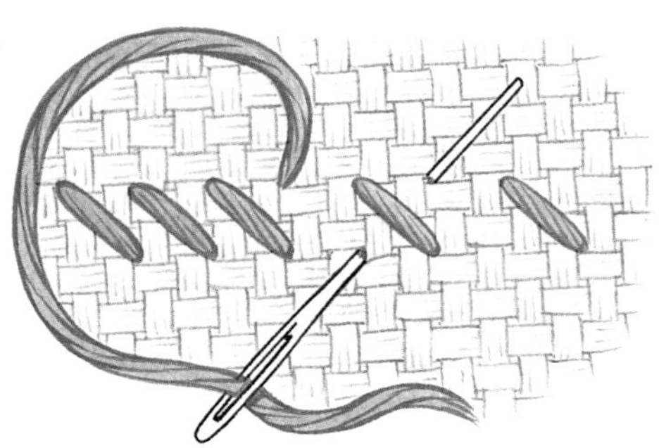

1 Work a row of evenly spaced diagonal stitches over alternate pairs of aida blocks; work from right to left, and slant the stitches from bottom right to top left.

2 Work from left to right, making diagonal stitches between the alternate stitches to complete the row.

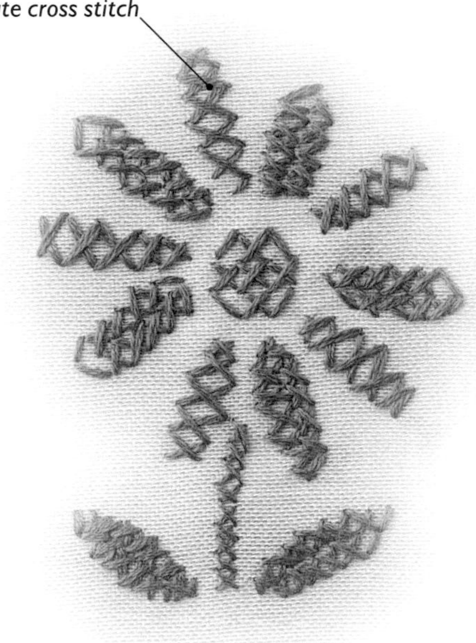

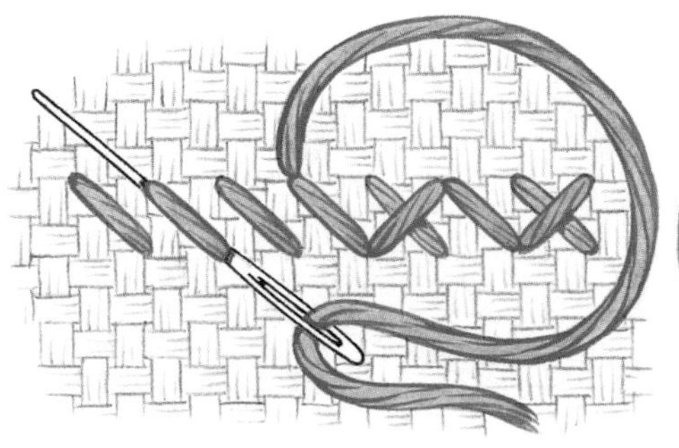

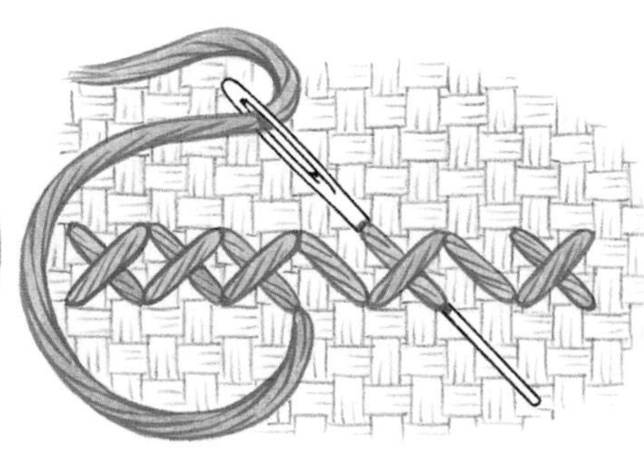

3 Work from right to left, working a row of alternate diagonal stitches slanting from top right to bottom left to complete alternate crosses.

4 Working from left to right, complete the remaining crosses. Work the next and subsequent rows below the first previous row until the block of stitching is complete.

Working half cross stitch

Working from left to right, make a row of diagonal stitches slanting from bottom left to top right.

If you enjoy working basic cross stitch, why not add these two variations to your repertoire? One is a vertically/horizontally-aligned stitch with an Oriental flavor; the other, an ingenious way of using cross stitch to add monograms or other motifs to household linens. Both should be worked on even-weave fabrics.

Chinese cross stitch, a variation of upright cross stitch (see page 51), consists of rectangular blocks of two vertical stitches and a long horizontal stitch. The blocks are arranged with a half drop to make a wavy line. Chinese cross stitch can also be used in pulled thread work (see page 245), in which the stitches are pulled tightly to create a pattern of holes in a loosely woven fabric.

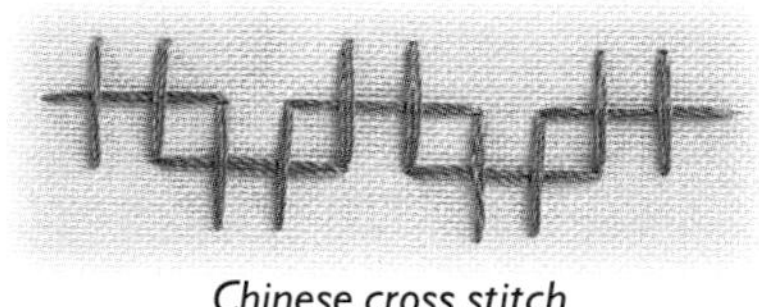

Chinese cross stitch

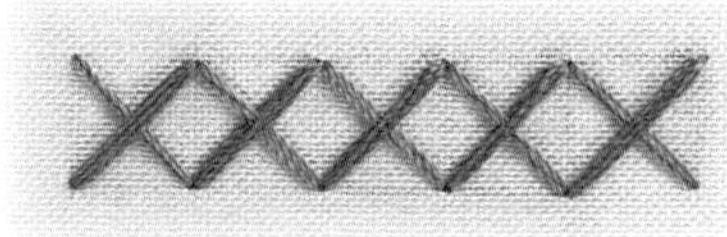

Marking cross stitch (front)

Marking cross stitch (back)

Marking cross stitch, a variation of basic cross stitch, is reversible—each complete stitch forms a cross on the front of the fabric and a square of straight stitches on the back. You can use it to work monograms and borders on items of household linen in which both sides of the item will be seen. It's also ideal for semi-transparent fabrics such as voile, organdy and fine linen—the straight stitches on the wrong side show through to create a rather shadowy pattern. Work marking cross stitch downward in rows, and remember that you may have to make occasional re-crosses in order to complete the squares on the reverse. Marking cross stitch uses up more thread than ordinary cross stitch.

Working Chinese cross stitch

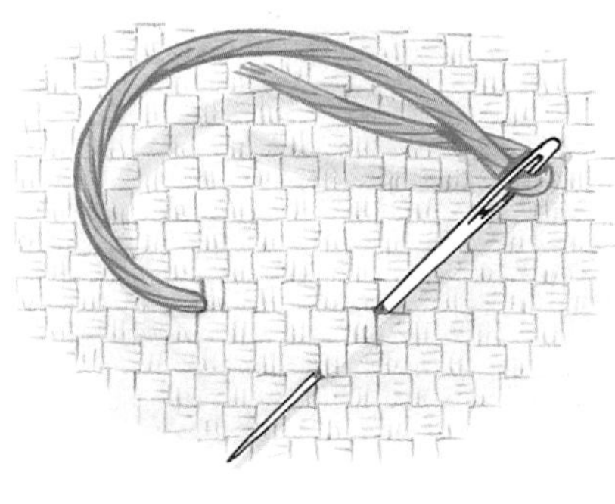

1 In this example (on aida), horizontal stitches cover six blocks, vertical stitches four. Make a horizontal stitch from left to right; bring the needle up two blocks down and to the left.

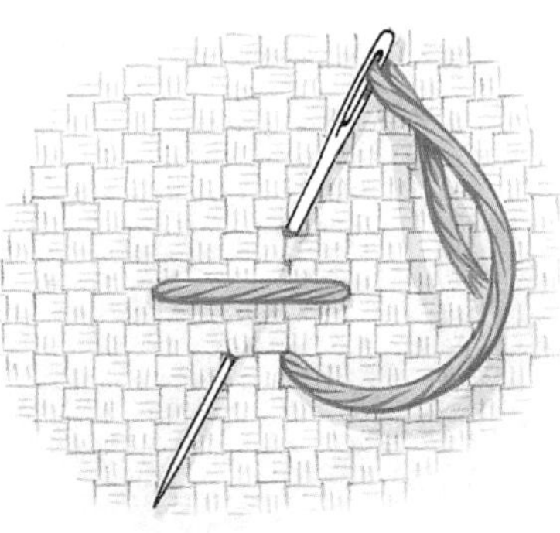

2 Make a vertical stitch,over four blocks, then bring the needle up two blocks to the left of the first one.

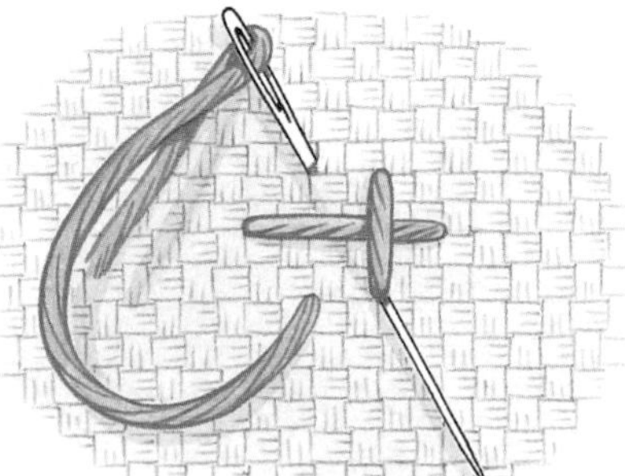

3 Make a second vertical stitch, and bring the needle up at the bottom of the first one, thus completing the first Chinese cross.

4 The second cross is worked a half-drop below the first, the third on the original level, and so on, producing a wavy line. Repeat the rows as desired.

Working marking cross stitch

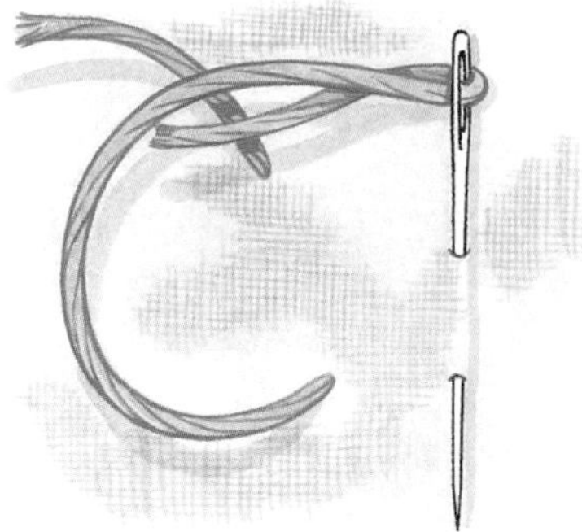

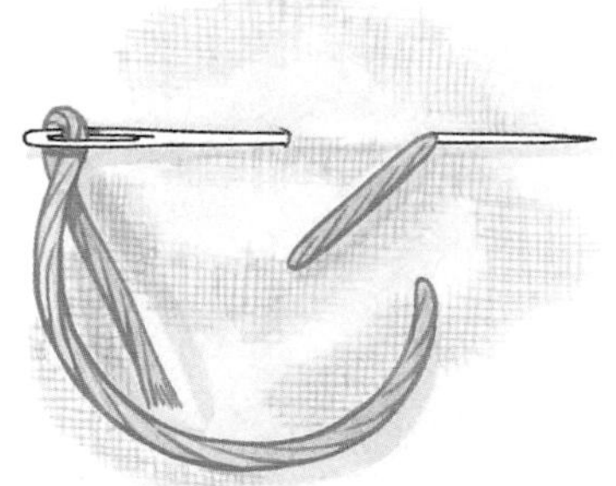

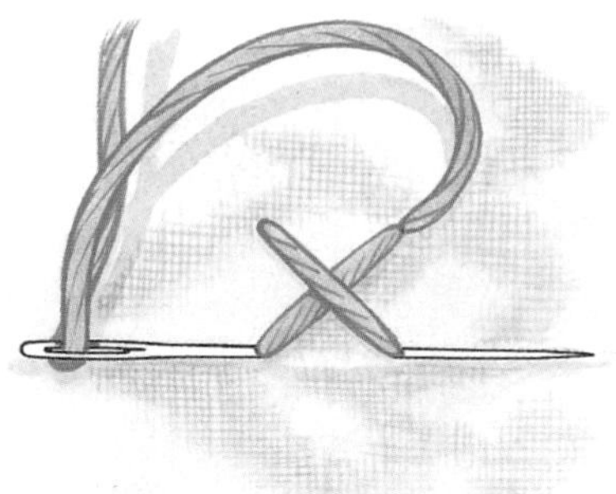

1 Work downward, following the stitch sequence carefully. Start at the bottom left corner of the square block the first cross will cover. Work the first diagonal, inserting the needle at the top right of the block and bringing it out at the bottom corner.

2 Pull the thread through. Work the second diagonal of the first cross, inserting the needle along the top edge of the block and bringing it out at the top right corner.

3 Work another diagonal over the first by inserting the needle at the bottom left. Bring the needle out at the bottom right corner, and pull the thread through to complete the first cross.

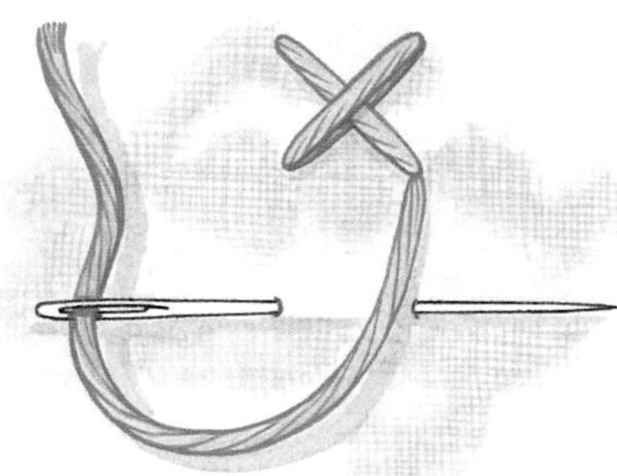

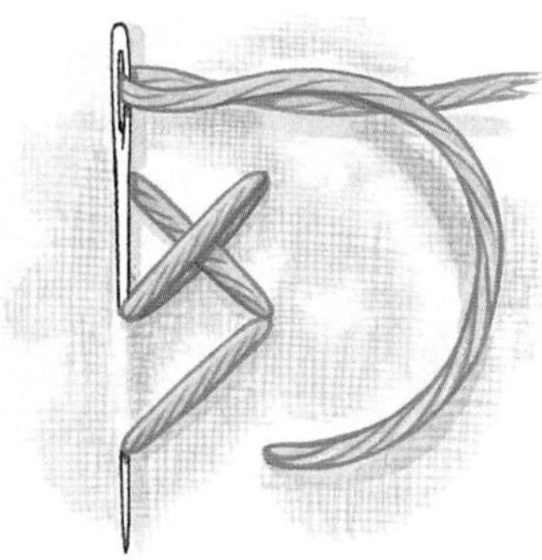

4 Work the first diagonal of the second and subsequent crosses in the same row by inserting the needle at the bottom left of the block. Bring it out at the bottom right.

5 Pull the thread through and work the second diagonal of the same cross by inserting the needle at the top left of the block. Bring it out at the bottom left.

6 Work another diagonal over the first diagonal of the same cross by inserting the needle at the top right of the block. Bring it out at the bottom right and pull the thread through to complete the cross. Repeat from step **4** along the row.

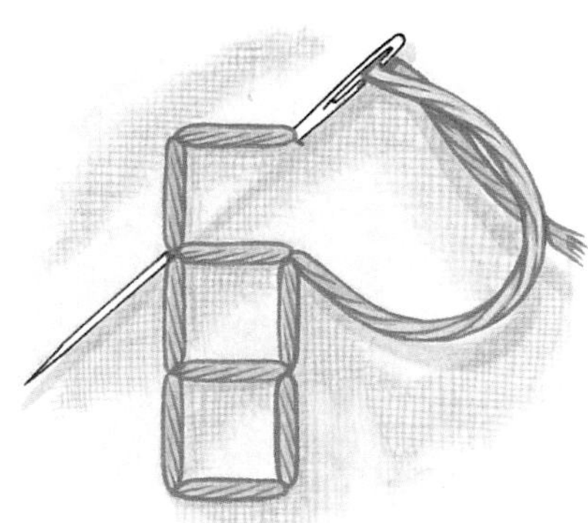

7 At the end of the row, turn the fabric over. Re-thread the needle with the thread end that was left at the beginning, and take a diagonal stitch under the square block to complete the first square of straight stitches. Pull the thread through and secure the end.

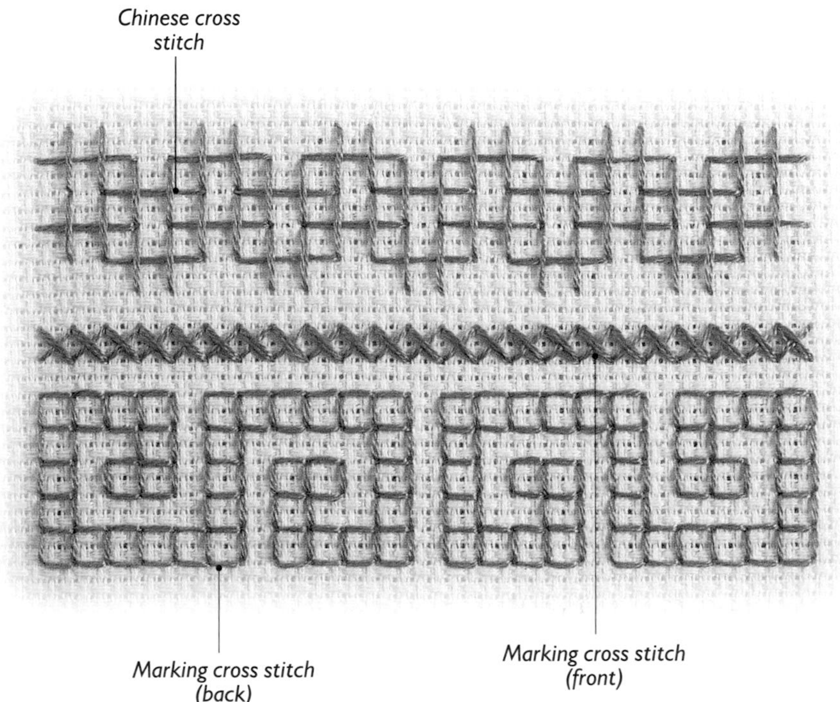

Herringbone stitches

Herringbone stitch and its many variations are versatile stitches with a zigzag or crisscross effect. Use them for linear designs and borders, and to give an open effect when filling in large areas of embroidery. They are equally at home on evenweave and non-evenweave fabrics.

For a neat finish, try to make all the stitches the same length, and slant the arms of the crosses at the same angle all the way along the row. On non-evenweave fabric, mark the stitching line with parallel rows of basting, or draw guide lines with a marking pen. When embroidering on evenweave fabric, use the fabric threads as a stitching guide.

Basic herringbone stitch makes a lightweight zigzag line. You can work the stitches more closely for a crisscross effect.

Double herringbone stitch gives a heavier line. It consists of a base row of basic herringbone stitch, with a second row worked over the top. You can use a second color for the top row for a decorative effect.

Woven double herringbone stitch is a little more intricate than double herringbone stitch. When working the top row, you pass the thread under and over the stitches on the first row to give a woven effect.

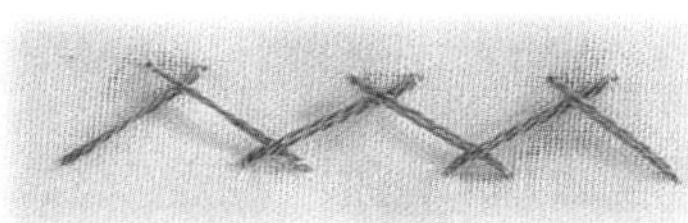

Basic herringbone stitch

Double herringbone stitch

Woven double herringbone stitch

Starting and fastening off herringbone stitch

1 To start, leave a 2–4 in. (5–10 cm) tail of thread at the front to the left of your starting point. Work two or three running stitches, then bring the thread to the front at your starting point.

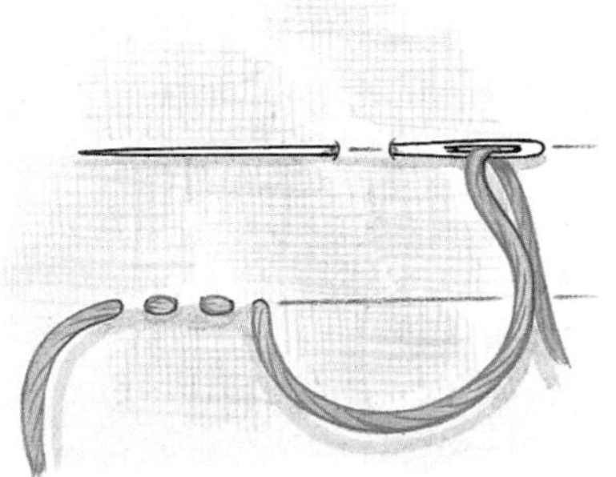

2 To finish, take the needle to the back and darn in the thread end under several stitches. Return to the beginning of the row and pull out the running stitches. Darn in the thread end at the back.

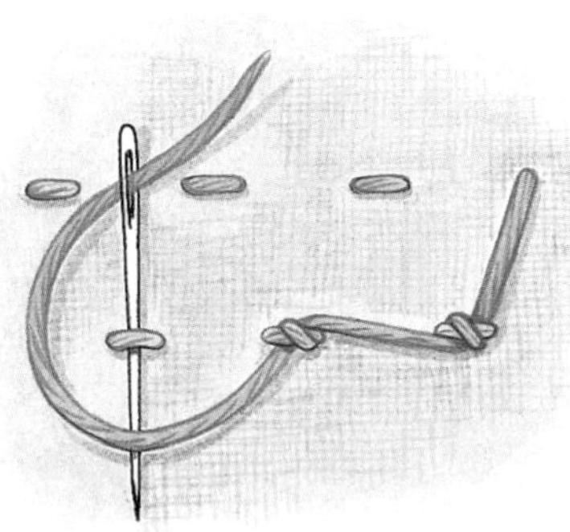

Working basic herringbone stitch

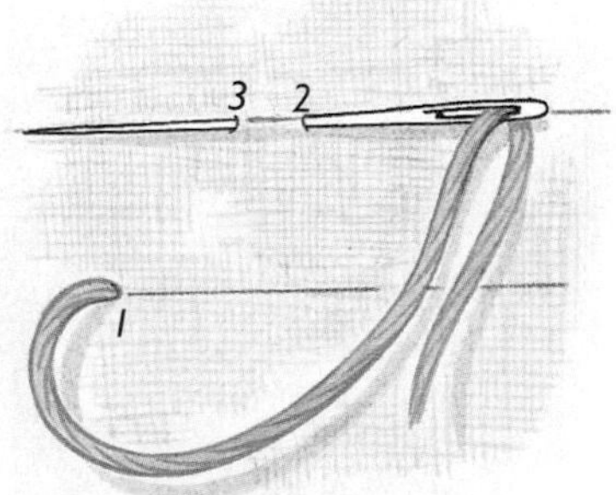

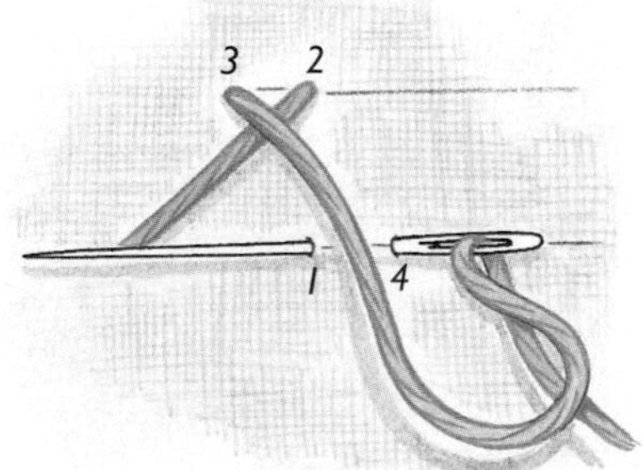

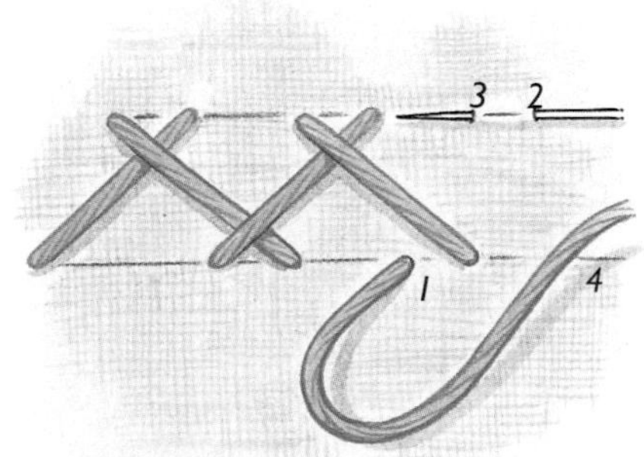

1 Bring the thread to the front of the fabric at the left-hand edge of the lower line at 1. Make a slanting stitch to the top right, inserting the needle at 2. Bring the needle to the front again a short distance to the left at 3.

2 To complete the first cross, make a slanting stitch toward the lower line, inserting the needle at 4. Bring the needle to the front at 1, directly below 2, ready to work the second cross.

3 Repeat the 1, 2, 3, 4 sequence along the row, making sure you keep the spacing and the length of the individual crosses perfectly even all the way along the row.

Working herringbone stitch variations on evenweave

When stitching on an evenweave fabric such as aida or linen, work herringbone stitch in the same way as basic herringbone stitch. You can vary the spacing of both the slanting and horizontal stitches to achieve different effects.

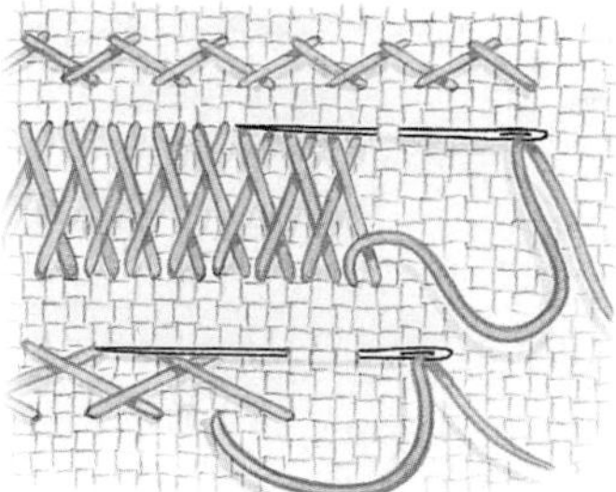

Working double herringbone stitch

Work a row of basic herringbone stitch. Then, use the same or a contrasting thread color to work a second row over the first. Arrange the crosses neatly to fill the spaces left by the first row.

Working woven double herringbone stitch

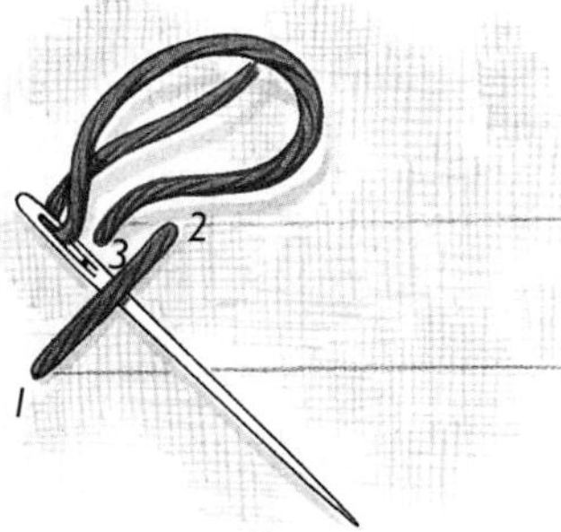

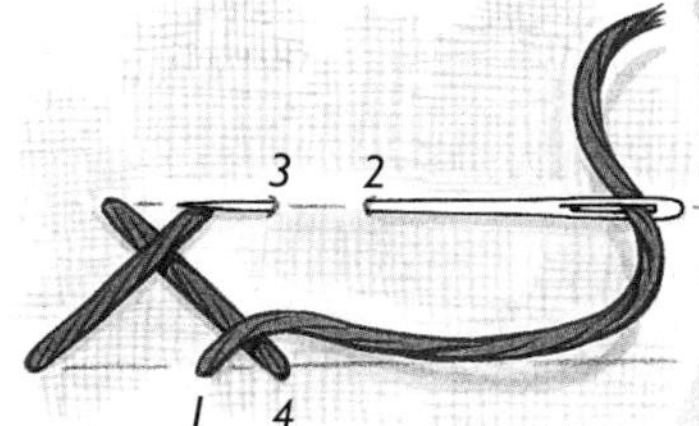

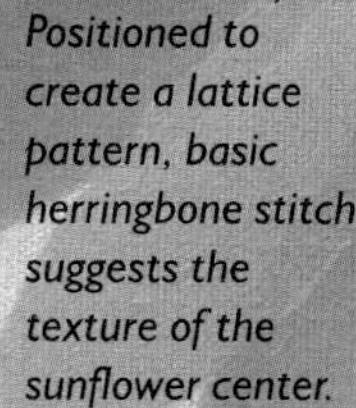

Positioned to create a lattice pattern, basic herringbone stitch suggests the texture of the sunflower center.

1 Make the first half of the cross as in **basic herringbone stitch**, step **1**, on page 49. To complete the cross, make a slanting stitch toward the lower line, taking the thread under the first slanting arm.

2 Insert the needle at 4 and bring it out at 1 in the usual way. Continue in this way along the row, making sure that the needle slips under the first slanting arm of each cross.

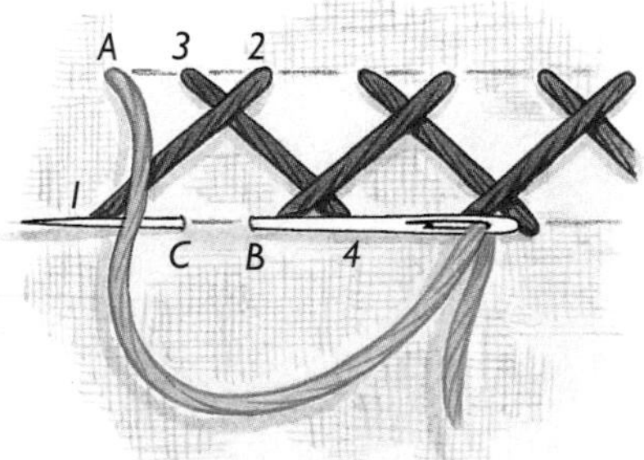

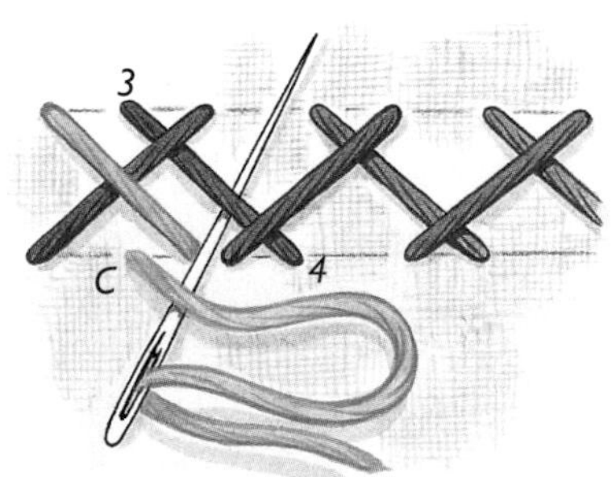

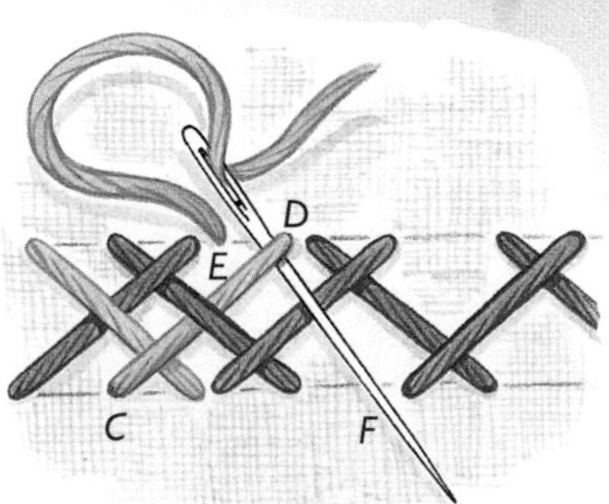

3 To work the second row, bring the second thread to the front on the top line at A, directly above 1. Make a slanting stitch to the lower line, inserting the needle at B. Bring the needle to the front at C.

4 Slip the needle under the second slanting arm of the first cross on the previous row, and gently pull the thread through.

5 Insert the needle at D and bring it to the front at E. Then slip the needle under the slanting arm C–D. Insert the needle at F to complete the first stitch on the second row. Continue in this way, repeating the sequence from C to F.

Open filling stitches

Open filling stitches are a good way of filling a shape with texture and color while allowing some of the fabric to show through. You can work them close together to give a dense, highly worked effect or, in a technique called powdering, you can space them farther apart to make a light filling.

The stitches are usually worked at random across the shape to be filled, but they can also be arranged in rows to form a variety of neat, regular patterns.

To work open filling stitches randomly, make the first stitch fairly close to the edge of the shape to be filled. Work the next stitch a short distance away. Keep stitching in this way to fill the shape.

When working parallel rows of open filling stitches on a non-evenweave fabric, mark a series of tiny, regularly spaced dots on the fabric with a water-soluble marking pen to help you position the stitches. When working on evenweave fabric, count the fabric threads or blocks to space the stitches.

Upright cross stitch (also known as St. George cross stitch) is a very simple stitch which can be worked at random on non-evenweave embroidery fabrics or in neat rows on evenweave fabrics.

Star filling stitch is a star-shaped stitch which can be worked using up to three different threads. It consists of an upright cross stitch which is topped with a diagonal cross stitch and a smaller cross stitch.

Ermine filling stitch resembles ermine tails when it is worked in black thread on white fabric.

Upright cross stitch

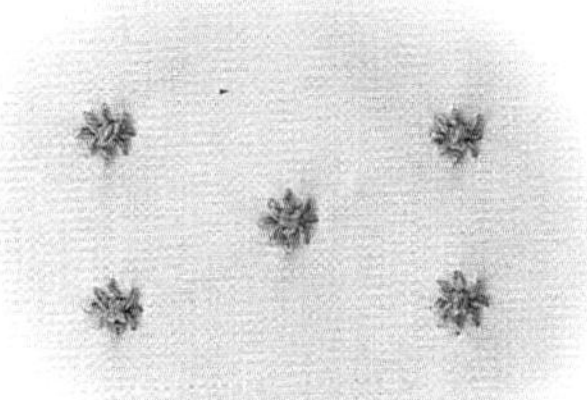

Star filling stitch

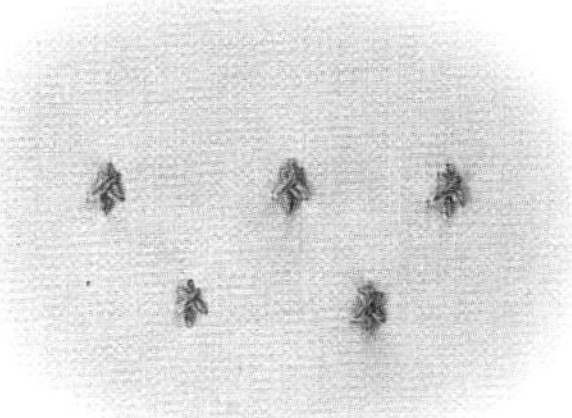

Ermine filling stitch

Starting and fastening off

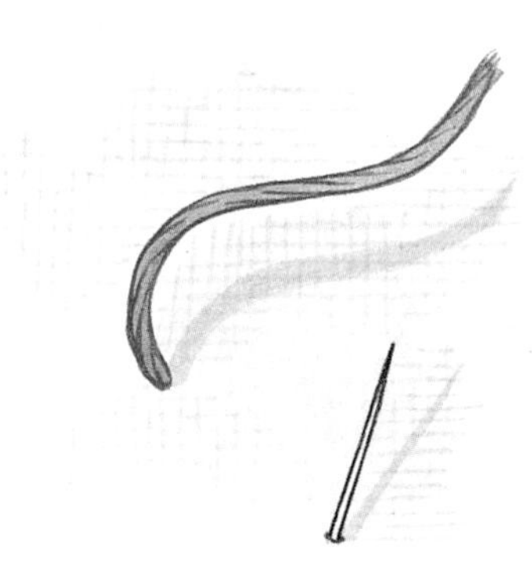

1 To begin working an open filling stitch, take the needle through to the back, close to your starting point. Leave a 2 in. (5 cm) tail of thread at the front. Then bring the needle out to the front at the starting point.

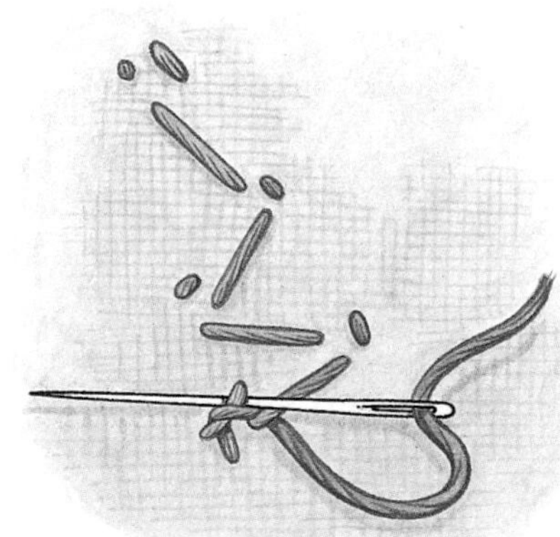

2 To secure the thread end when you have finished, take the needle to the back, darn the thread end through the back of the last stitch, and trim it off. Return to the beginning of the stitching, pull the tail of thread through to the back and darn the end under the first stitch as before.

3 To join in a new thread, darn the end through the back of the previously worked stitch, as before. Bring the needle out to the front and continue stitching.

Working upright cross stitch

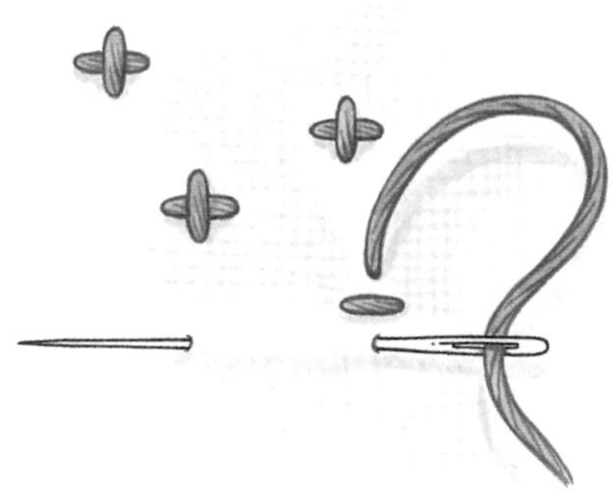

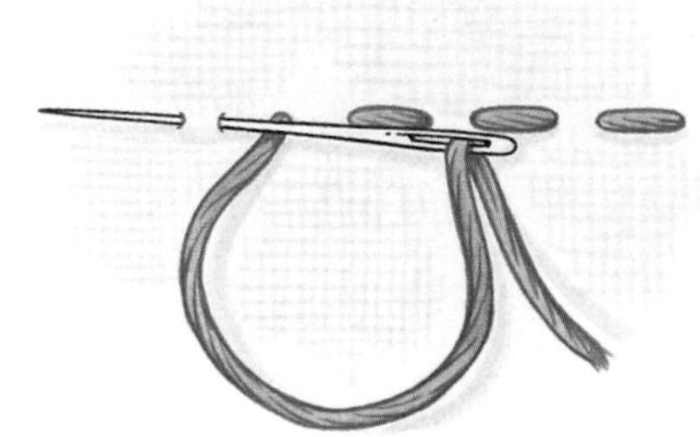

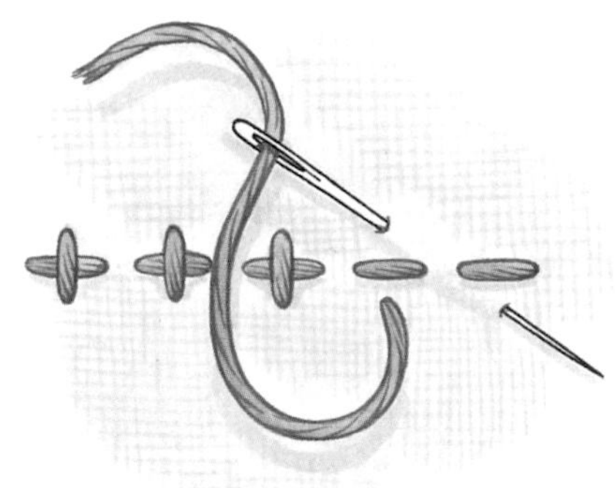

On non-evenweave fabric, work each stitch individually. Work a short horizontal stitch, then cross it with a vertical stitch of the same size. Continue in this way across the shape.

1 On evenweave fabric, begin by working a row of evenly spaced horizontal stitches from right to left.

2 Then cross the stitches with vertical stitches. Repeat this sequence to fill the shape.

Working star filling stitch

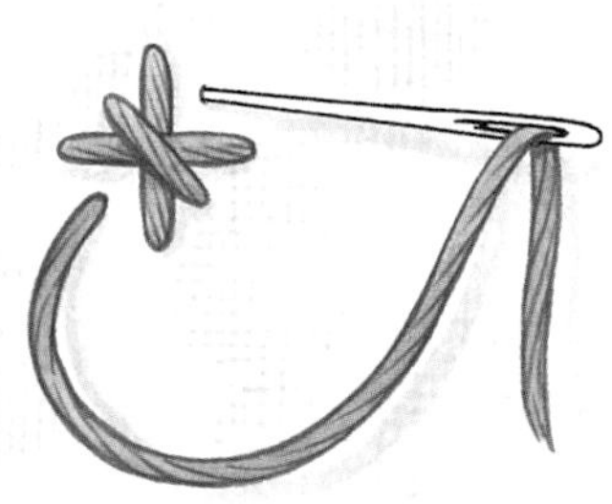

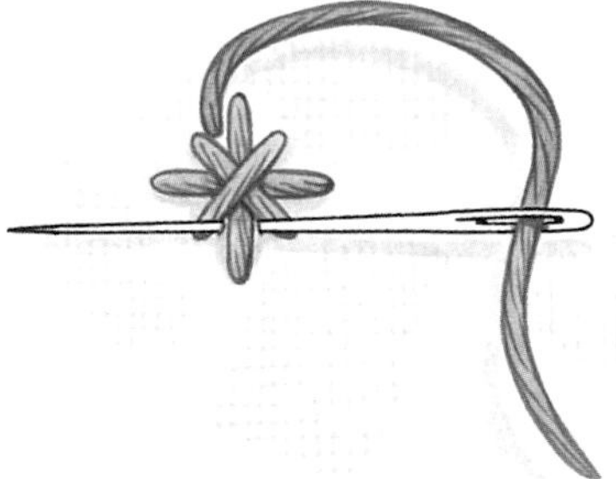

1 Work a large upright cross stitch, as shown above. Then work an ordinary cross stitch over the top. Make both crosses the same size.

2 Work a tiny ordinary cross stitch over the top of the large crosses to anchor them.

WHAT WENT WRONG

Tension too tight
Untidy areas of open filling stitches are caused when the thread is pulled too tightly. For a neat finish, try to make all the stitches the same size, and keep the tension of the thread constant as you move from stitch to stitch.

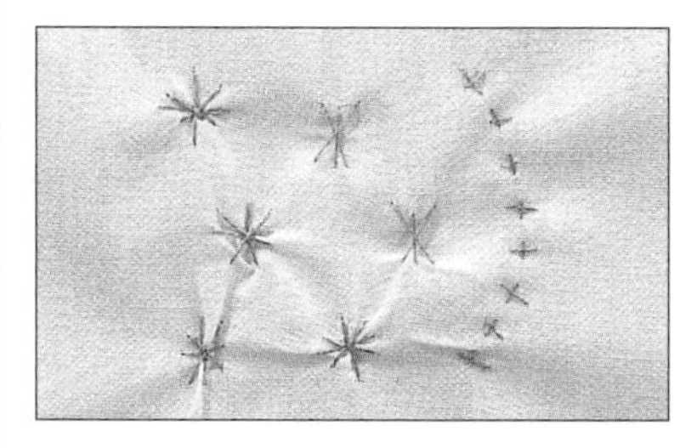

To work star filling stitch in more than one color and/or weight of thread, work each type of cross in a separate journey. Work all the upright crosses first, change your thread, then work the large ordinary crosses. To finish, work the small ordinary crosses in your third thread.

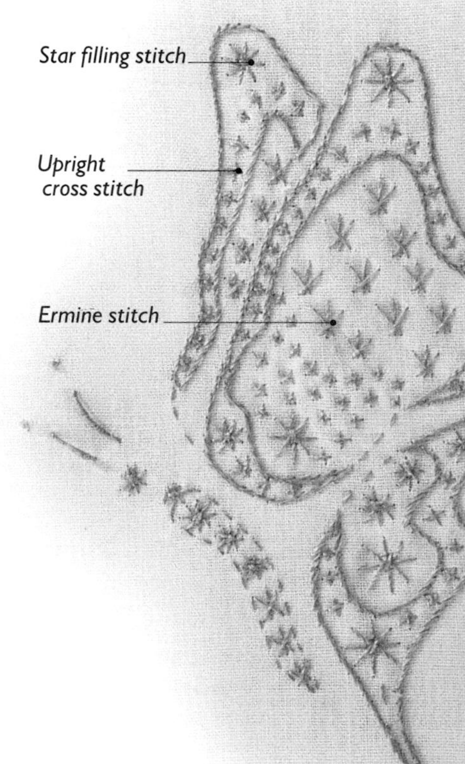

Working ermine filling stitch

Work a long vertical stitch, then add an elongated ordinary cross stitch. Make the cross narrower at the base than the top, and position it so that the lower tip of the vertical stitch shows below the cross.

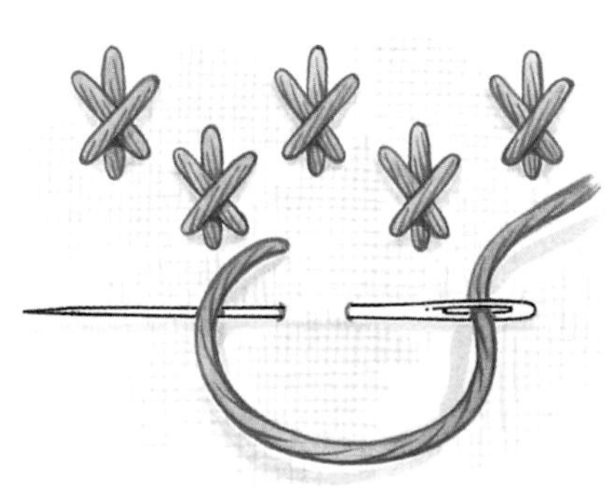

The open filling stitches shown here are ideal for filling backgrounds and rectangular and square shapes. You can arrange the individual stitches close together to create a dense, solidly stitched filling or space them out for a more delicate effect.

Before starting to work any of these stitches on non-evenweave fabric, make a series of tiny, regularly spaced dots on the fabric, using either a water-soluble marking pen or a sharp pencil to mark the position of the individual stitches. On evenweave fabrics, simply count the threads or aida blocks to space the stitches evenly.

To start and fasten off any of these stitches, refer to page 43.

Spaced cross stitch filling creates a spacious network over the fabric when worked in evenly spaced rows. Space the stitches widely apart, or arrange them close together so that the corner of each cross touches to form a grid pattern.

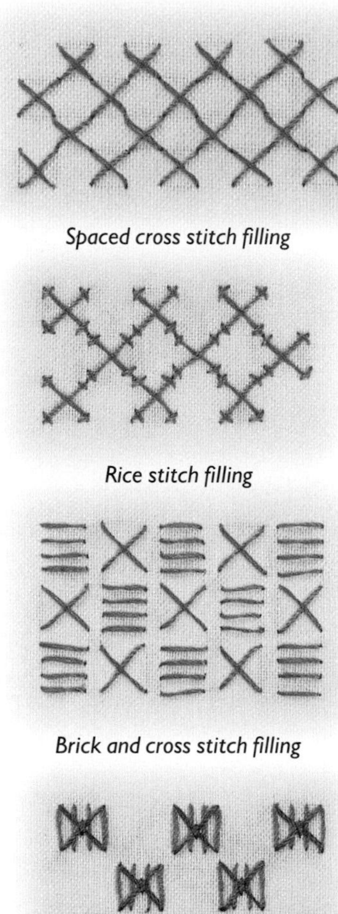

Spaced cross stitch filling

Rice stitch filling

Brick and cross stitch filling

Chessboard stitch filling

Rice stitch filling is very similar to spaced cross stitch filling, but the arms of each cross are overstitched with a short diagonal, using the same or a contrasting thread color.

Brick and cross stitch filling is a variation of spaced cross stitch filling in which the spaces between the crosses are filled with blocks of widely spaced horizontal straight stitches, creating a checkerboard effect. You can work a simple variation of this stitch by alternating square blocks of three straight stitches with upright cross stitch; for details on upright cross stitch, see page 52.

Chessboard stitch filling produces a highly decorative pattern which is usually worked in two different thread colors. Square blocks of four upright straight stitches are worked on one journey, then these are covered by a large cross stitch, anchored in the center with a short vertical stitch.

Working spaced cross stitch filling

1 Bring the thread to the front at the top of the shape. Work a horizontal row of regularly spaced individual cross stitches across the fabric.

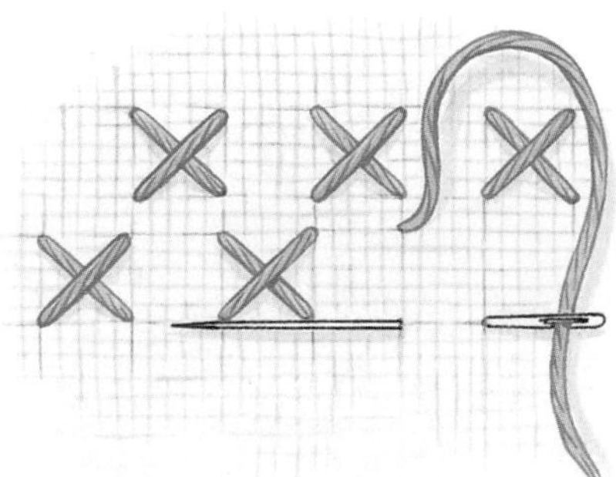

2 Work the second row in the opposite direction; position the crosses below the spaces on the first row, as shown, or position them so that the corners touch. Continue in this way to fill the shape.

Uneven stitching
Unevenly spaced cross stitch filling has an untidy look. To ensure evenly spaced stitches on non-evenweave fabrics, always mark the position of the stitches first, with tiny, evenly spaced dots.

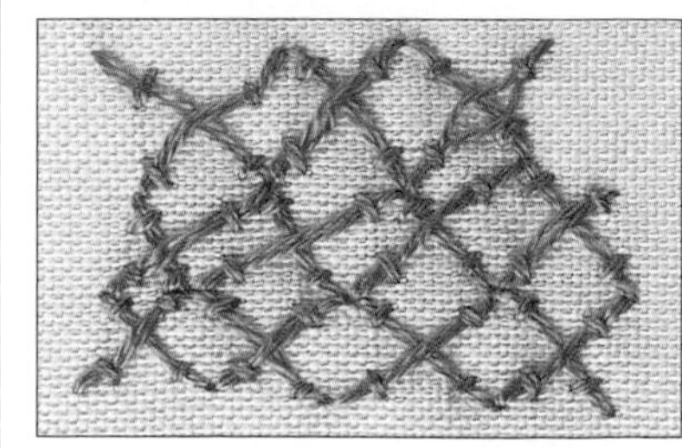

Working rice stitch filling

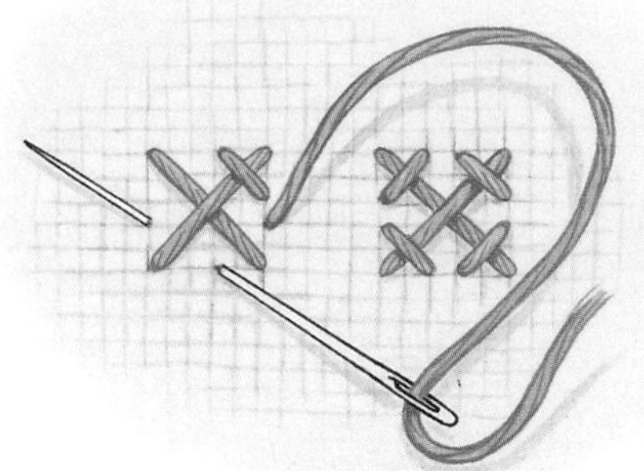

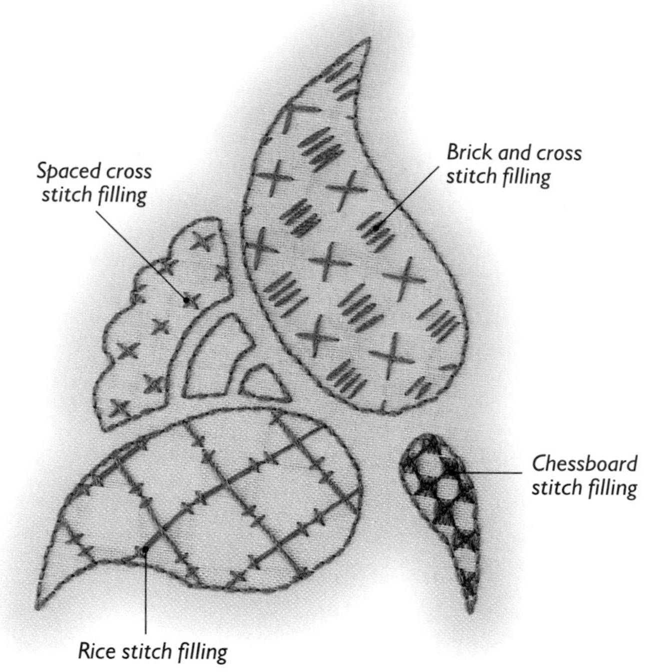

1 Secure the thread and bring it through at the top of the shape. Work a cross stitch; then, in the same or a contrasting thread, make a short diagonal stitch over each arm of the cross to make a rice stitch. Repeat across the fabric to make a row of regularly spaced stitches—make the spaces the same size as the stitches.

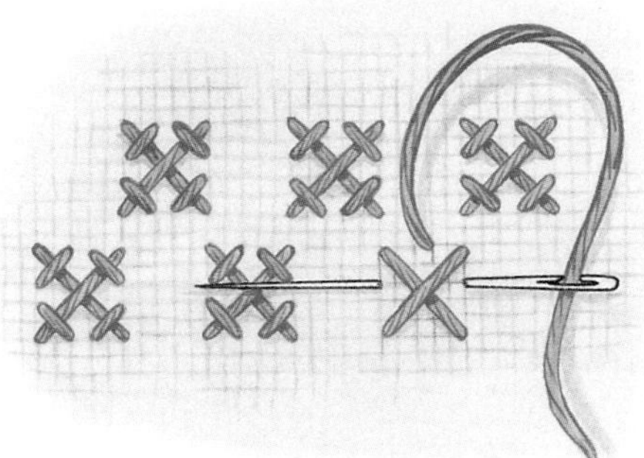

2 Work the second row of stitches in the opposite direction to the first row, spacing the rice stitches on this row so that they fit neatly below the spaces left on the first row. Repeat these two rows to fill the shape.

Working brick and cross stitch filling

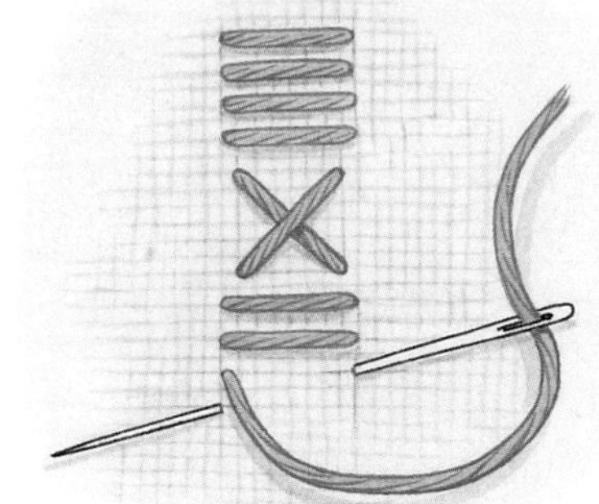

1 Bring the thread out to the front at the top of the shape. Work a vertical row of square blocks of four horizontal straight stitches alternating with large cross stitches, making sure that the straight stitch blocks and the cross stitches are evenly spaced.

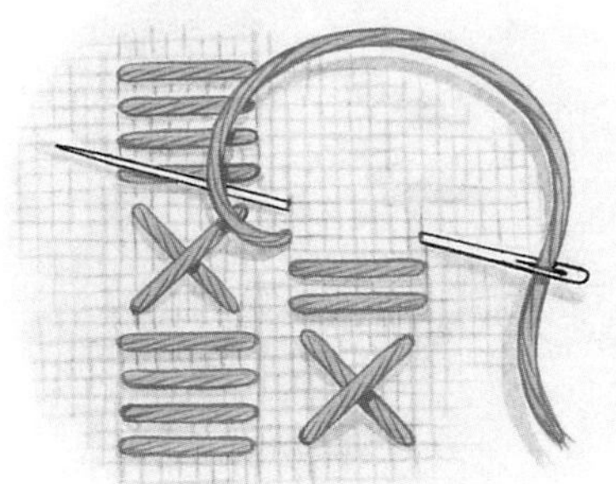

2 Work the second row of stitches in the opposite direction, alternating the components on this row so the stitches form a checked brick and cross pattern. Repeat these two rows to fill the shape.

Working chessboard stitch filling

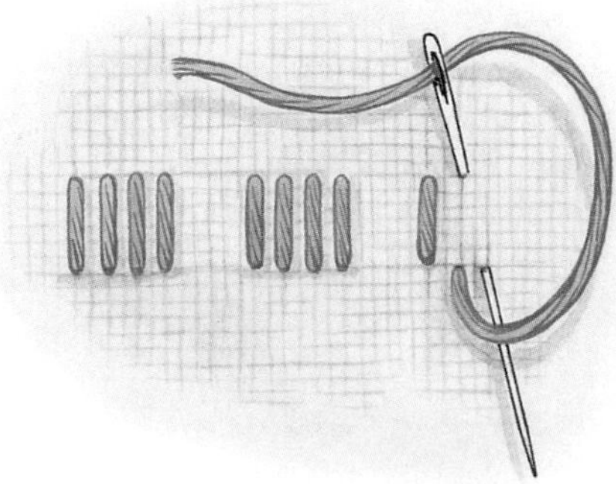

1 Secure the first color and bring it through at the top of the shape. Work a horizontal row of regularly spaced square blocks of four vertical straight stitches across the fabric.

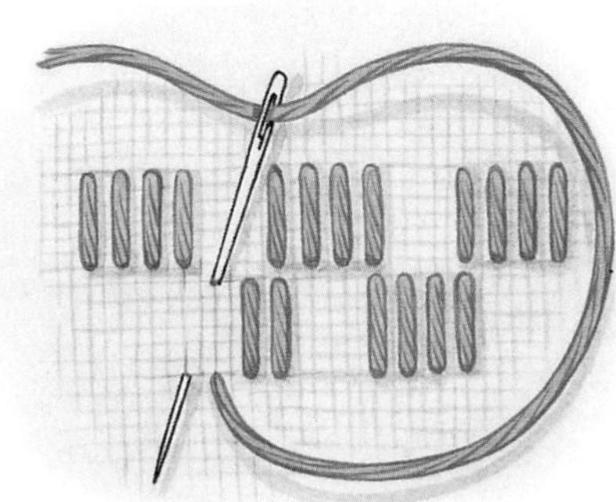

2 Work the second row of straight stitch blocks in the opposite direction to the first, spacing the blocks so they fit neatly below the spaces left on the first row. Repeat these two rows to fill the shape.

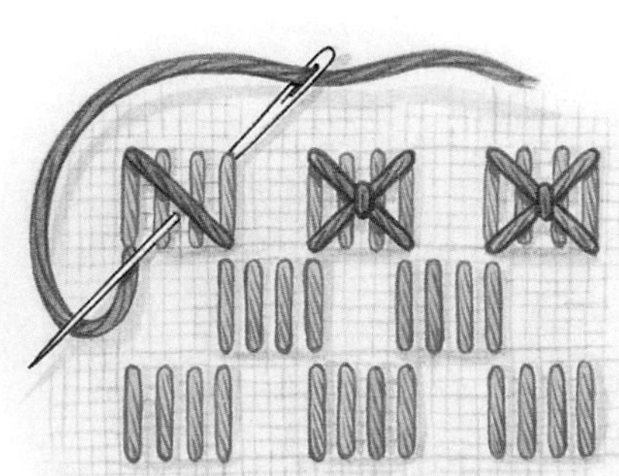

3 Bring the second thread color to the front at the top of the shape. Work a cross stitch over each block of straight stitches, anchoring the center of the cross with a short vertical stitch before moving on to the next block.

Crossed border stitches

The three stitches described below are all variations of ordinary cross stitch. In the same way as with cross stitch, all these stitches benefit from being worked on a fabric with an even weave to help keep the stitches neat, of identical size, and evenly spaced. When working on non-evenweave fabric, use a water-soluble or an air-erasable marking pen to mark guide lines on the fabric to help keep your stitching even.

All of these stitches can be worked in a straight line to create a border or used to fill large or irregular shapes by arranging multiple rows so that the edges of adjacent rows touch. Make all the rows the same width for a formal effect or vary them to fill the shape in a more random way.

When working these stitches, it is a good idea to mount your fabric in a frame to prevent fabric distortion.

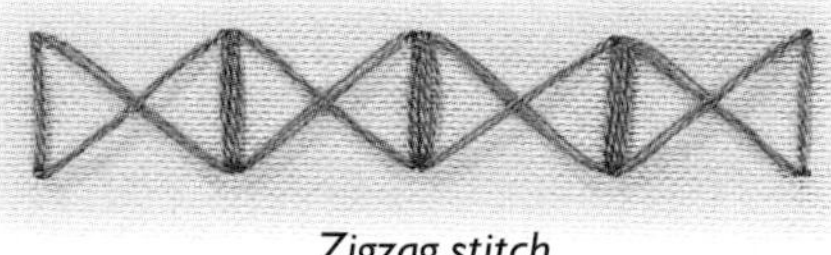
Zigzag stitch

Belgian cross stitch

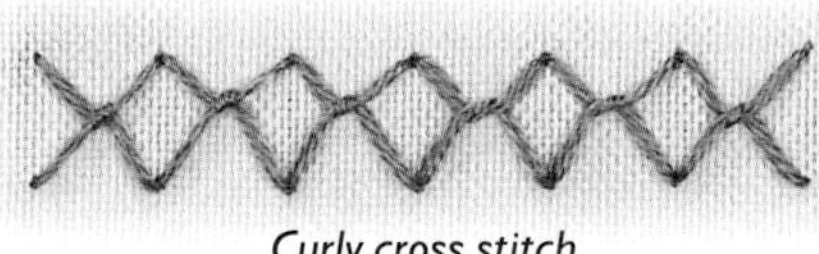
Curly cross stitch

To start and fasten off any of these stitches, see page 49.

Zigzag stitch is the simplest to work of the stitches in this section. Complete each row over two journeys to make a delicate geometric pattern. Try working it on evenweave between two rows of short, even satin stitch.

Belgian cross stitch is worked in one journey, and the row is formed by repeating a sequence of overlapping diagonal stitches.

Curly cross stitch is a textured variation of ordinary cross stitch. It is worked in rows over two horizontal journeys. It can be worked solidly, so that all the rows touch, or spaced out in a checkerboard fashion.

Working zigzag stitch

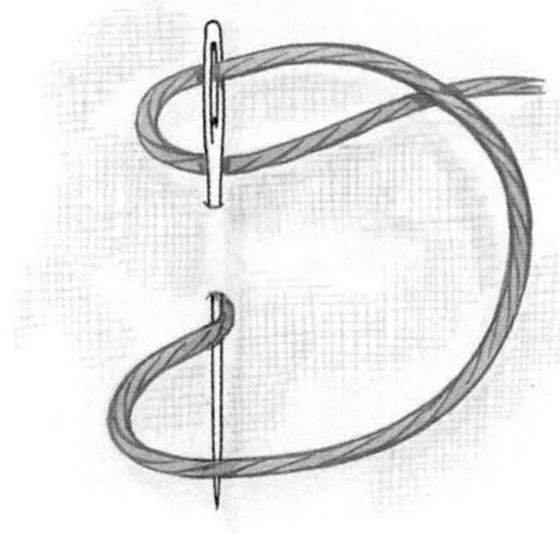

1 Bring the needle to the front of the fabric at the bottom right of the row. Make a short vertical stitch across the row, bringing the needle out at the point where it originally emerged.

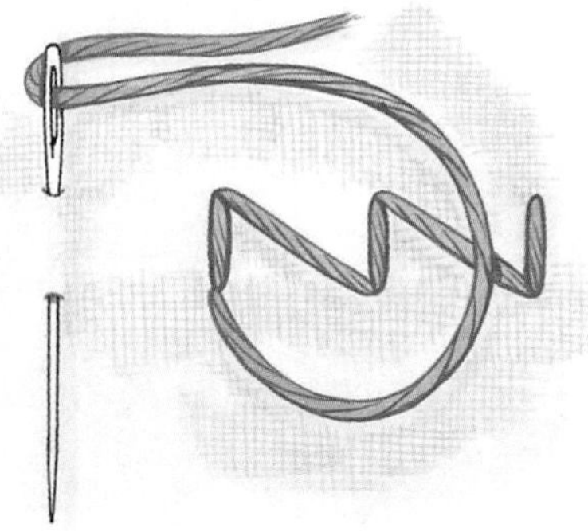

2 Complete the zigzag by inserting the needle at the top of the row a short distance to the left. Bring it out level with your starting point, ready to work the next vertical stitch. Continue in this way along the row, alternating vertical and diagonal stitches.

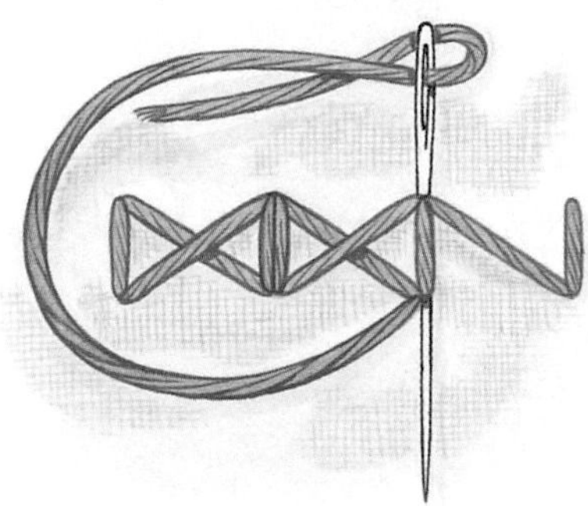

3 At the end of the row, work an identical set of vertical and diagonal stitches from left to right so that they share the same holes in the fabric as those on the first row.

Working Belgian cross stitch

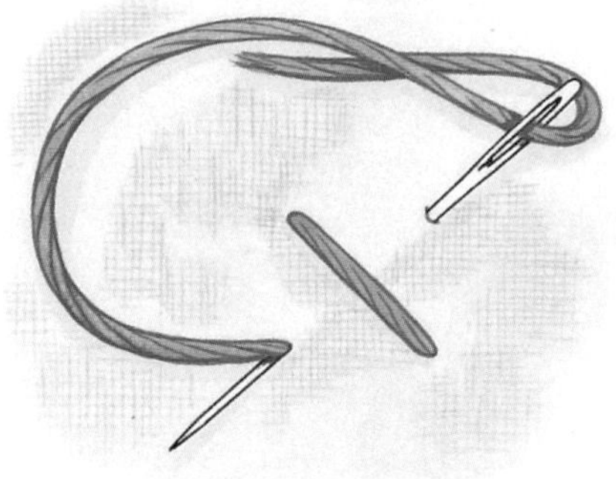

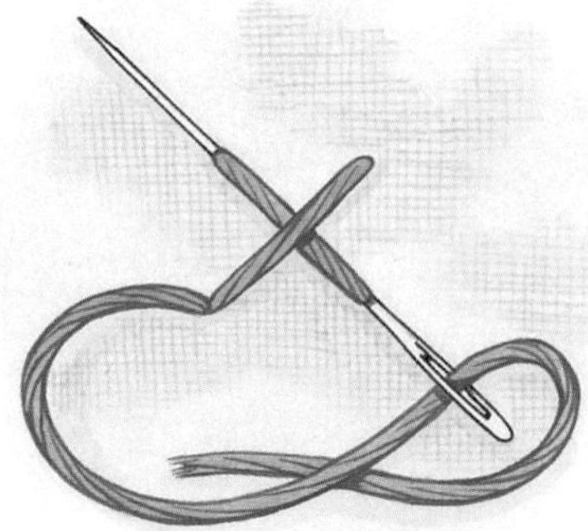

1 Bring the needle to the front at the top left of the row. Work two diagonal stitches to make a large cross, bringing the needle to the front at the bottom left-hand corner of the cross.

2 Insert the needle at the bottom right of the cross to make a horizontal stitch. Bring the needle out at the top left.

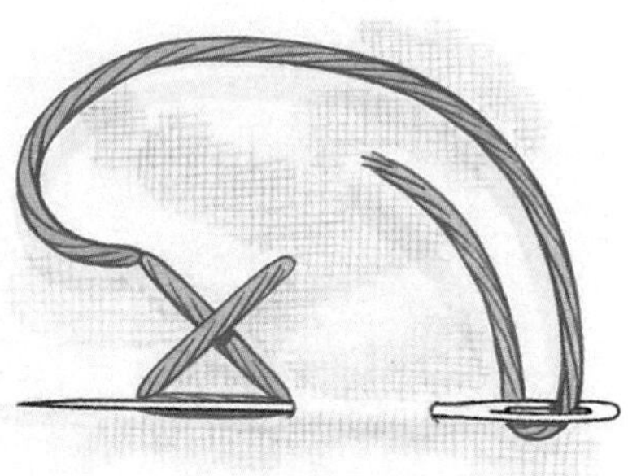

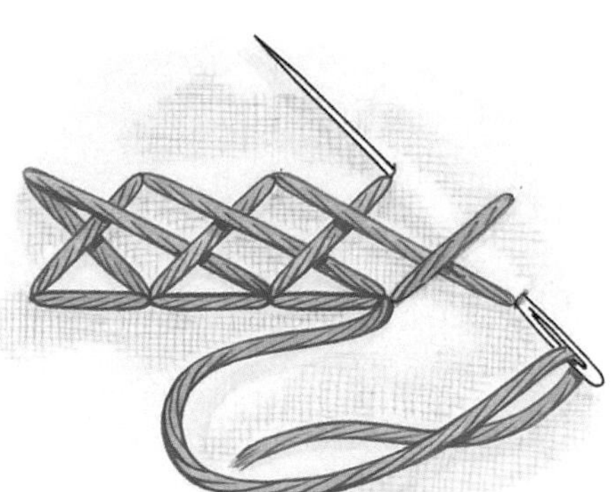

3 Insert the needle a short distance to the right of the base of the cross to make a long diagonal stitch. Bring the needle out at the bottom right of the cross to complete the first sequence.

4 Repeat the sequence of stitches along the row, omitting the first stitch of the cross with every repeat and spacing the stitches evenly.

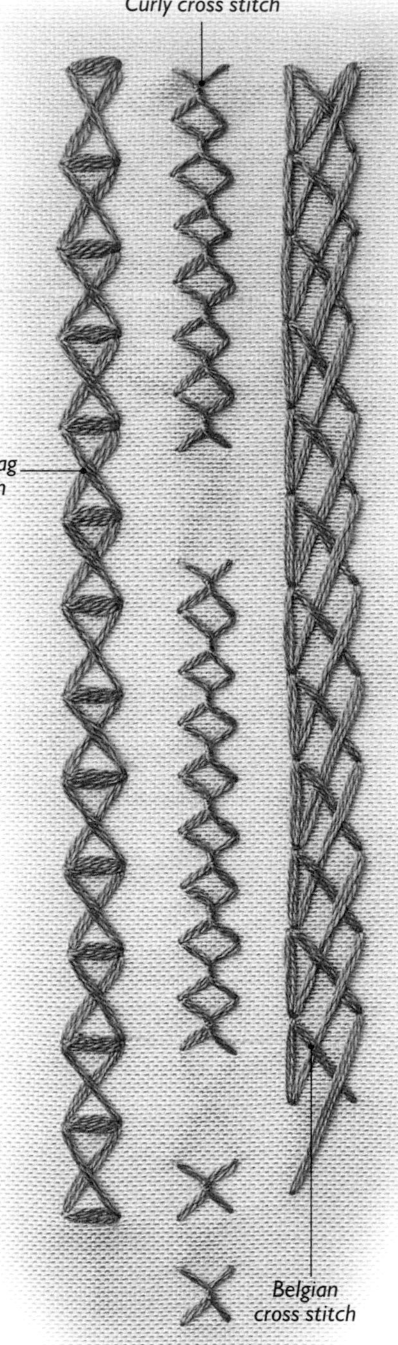

Working curly cross stitch

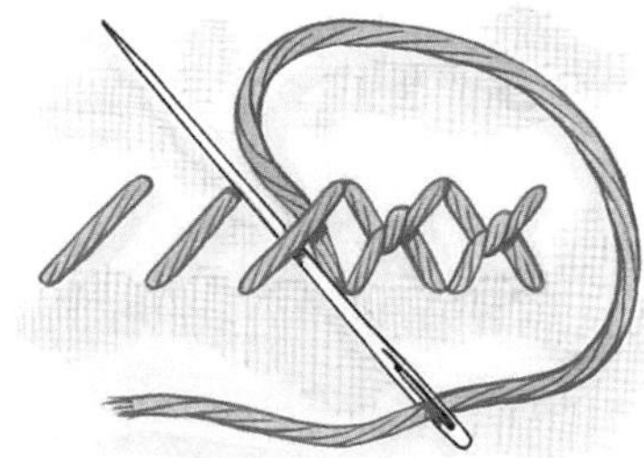

1 Work from left to right to make a row of diagonal stitches slanting from bottom left to top right. Turn and bring the needle through at the bottom right-hand corner of the row as if to complete a cross, but slip the needle under the diagonal stitch.

2 Pull the thread through, then slip the needle under the diagonal stitch again. Pull the thread through gently to tighten, and then insert the needle at the top left-hand corner to complete the cross and bring it through ready to make the next stitch. Repeat along the row.

Blanket stitches

Blanket stitch, or buttonhole stitch, is a versatile looped stitch with many variations. It is used for surface embroidery, to edge appliqué, and as a decorative finish for hems. It can be worked in straight or curved lines.

When working blanket stitch always fasten off the thread well to prevent it from unraveling. For surface embroidery, weave the loose thread into the back, as in method A. If you are finishing a fabric edge, use method B.

Always work from left to right, pulling the needle through the fabric toward you. For a neat finish the stitches need to be of a uniform size. To help, you can use an erasable marking pen to draw guide lines on the fabric.

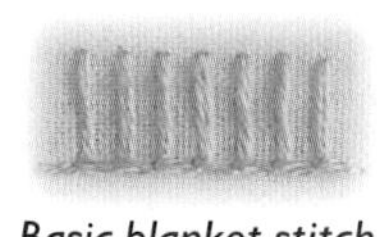

Basic blanket stitch

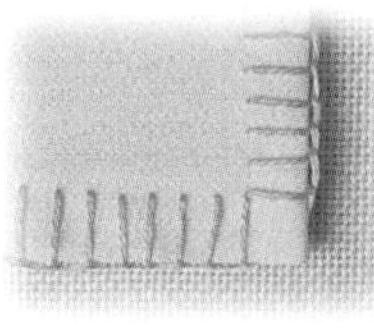

Blanket stitch on a fabric edge

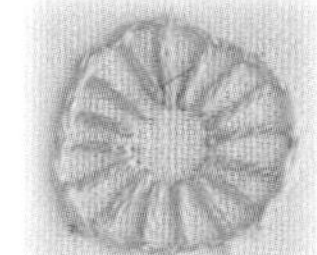

Basic blanket stitch worked in a circle

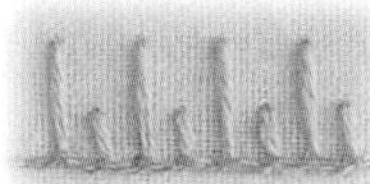

Long and short blanket stitch

Basic blanket stitch used to edge appliqué

Pyramid blanket stitch

Basic blanket stitch consists of evenly spaced interlaced, angular loops. When the stitch is worked as an edging, the lower part of each loop sits on the fabric edge.

Long and short blanket stitch has evenly spaced, alternate long and short uprights.

Pyramid blanket stitch has uprights graduated in length to form a neat pyramid shape.

Securing the thread

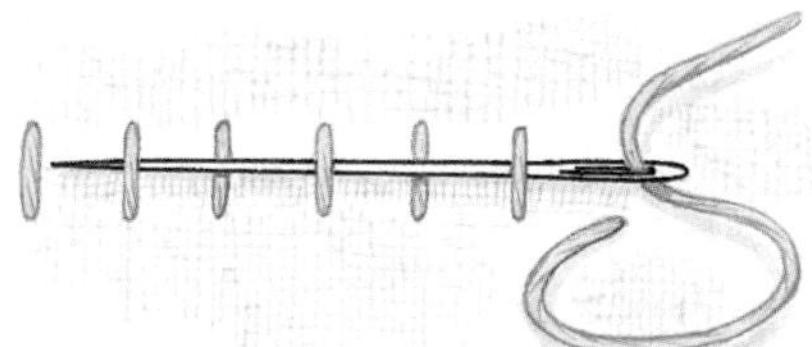

Method A Bring the needle through to the front at your starting point, leaving a short tail of thread at the back. Work a few stitches, then turn the fabric over and weave the loose thread into the back of the stitches. To finish, fasten off the thread in the same way.

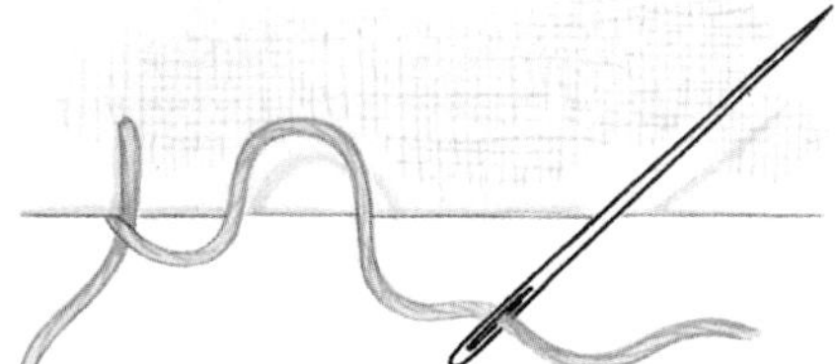

1 **Method B** Use this method for edging appliqué and fabric edges. To start, insert the needle at the top edge of the stitching line, leaving a tail of thread at the front. Take the working thread over the loose thread, ready to work the next stitch.

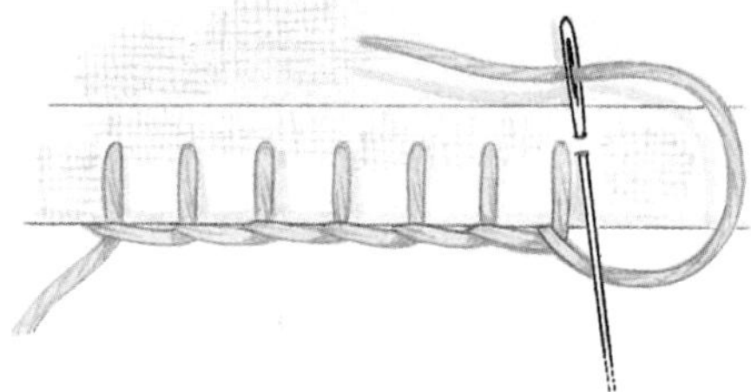

2 Work the row of stitches, then take the thread to the back. Make two or three tiny stitches on top of each other, next to the last upright, taking the needle through the background fabric only. Fasten off the thread at the start in the same way.

Working blanket stitch for surface embroidery

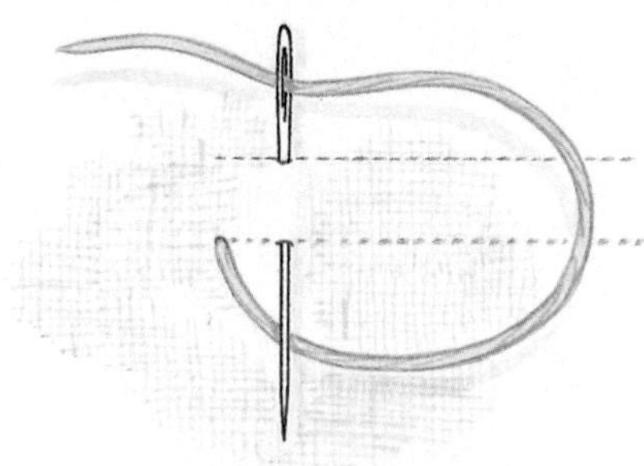

1 Bring the needle to the front on the lower line and insert it at the top, a little way to the right. Bring it out directly below, keeping the thread under the tip of the needle.

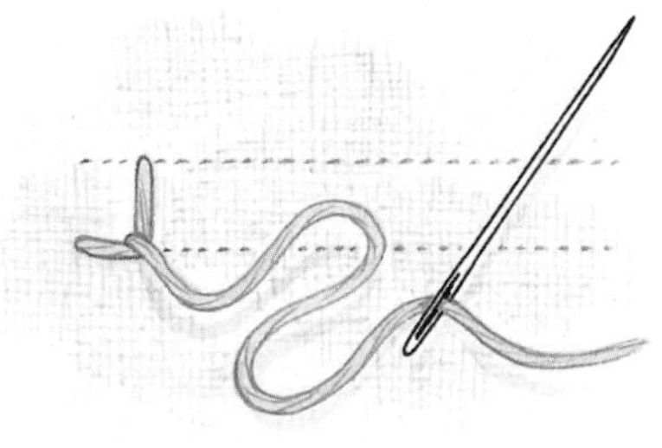

2 Pull the thread through the fabric, over the top of the working thread. Gently pull the thread to form a firm loop at the lower line.

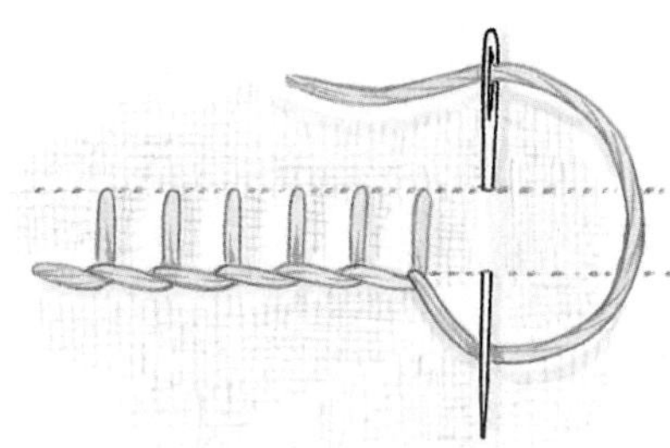

3 Continue working in this way, spacing the upright stitches evenly and making them all the same height.

Working blanket stitch around a curved shape

1 Work blanket stitches around the shape, with the loops on the outside and the uprights facing toward the center.

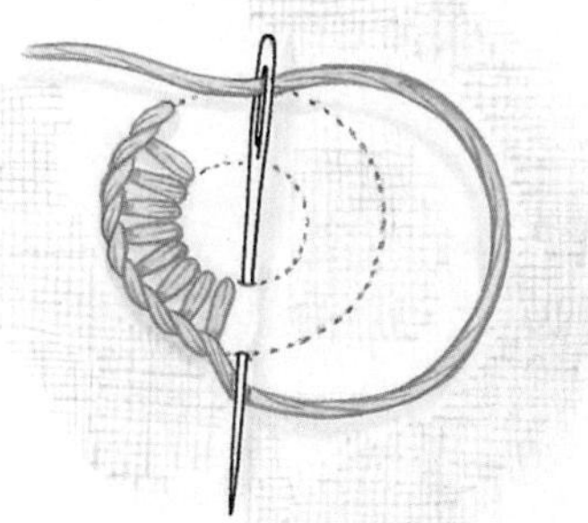

2 When you have stitched all around, work the last upright. Take the needle back through the fabric at the point where it originally emerged.

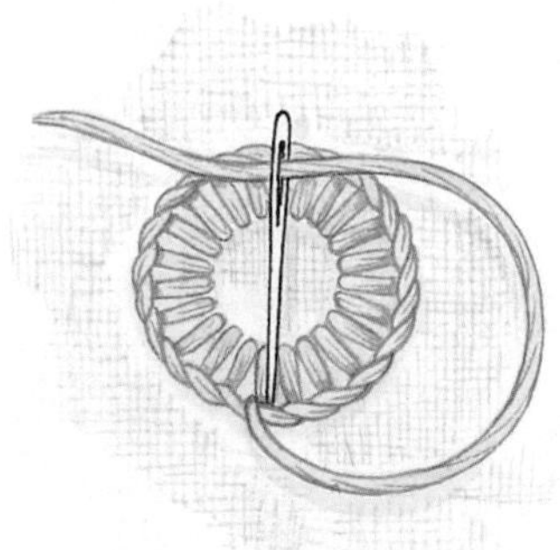

Working blanket stitch as an edging for appliqué

Baste or fuse the fabric shape in place. Blanket-stitch around the edge, keeping the stitches you are working toward you. Work the top of the uprights through both fabrics and bring the needle out to the front just outside the edge of the shape, through the background fabric only.

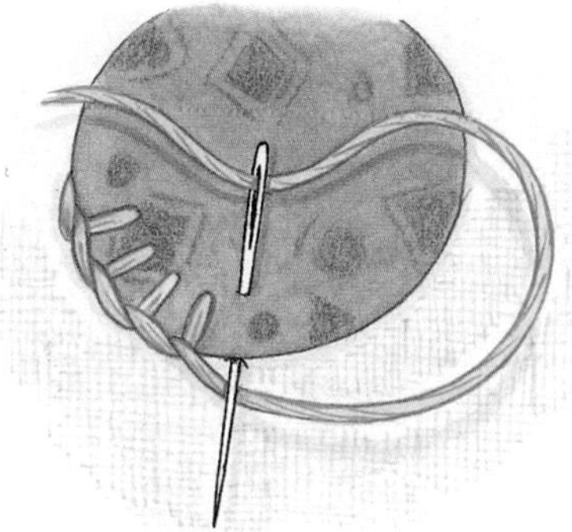

WHAT WENT WRONG

Messy stitches
Untidy blanket stitch is the result of working unevenly spaced and sized stitches. Try to keep the stitches of an even length and space them out at equal intervals along the row.

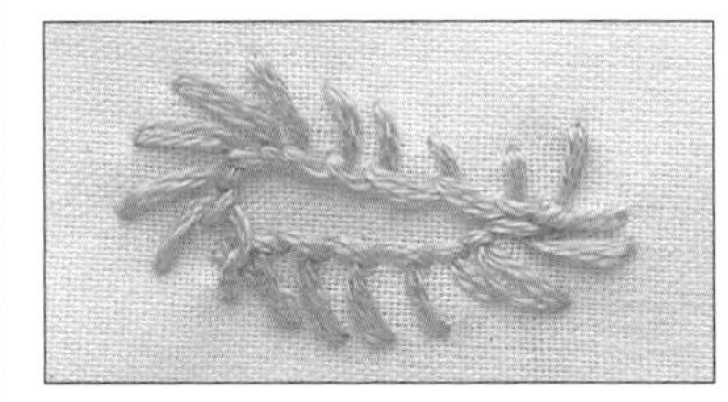

Finishing a fabric edge

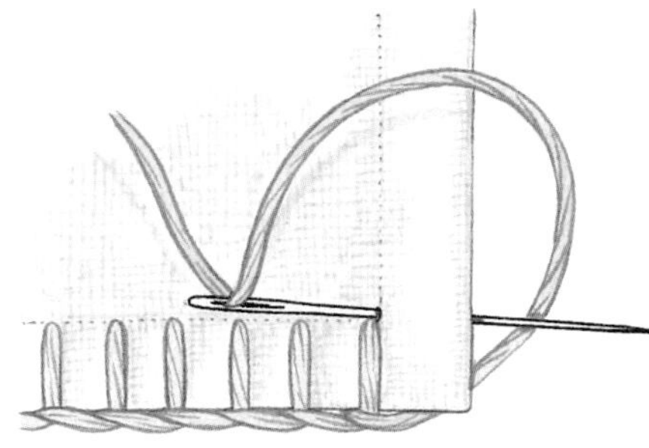

Work blanket stitch along the fabric edge, positioning the loops on the edge of the fabric. To turn a corner, stitch up to the corner, then insert the needle at the same point as the last upright. Bring it out at the perpendicular edge, carrying the thread under the fabric.

Blanket stitch makes a decorative finish for appliqué shapes.

Working long and short blanket stitch

Work in the same way as ordinary blanket stitch, but stitch alternately long and short uprights.

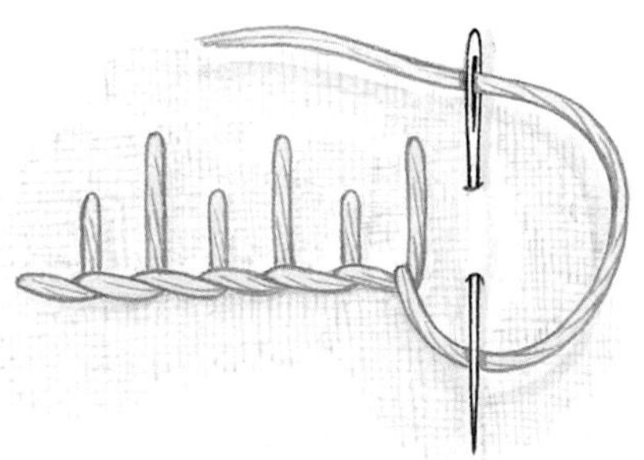

Working pyramid blanket stitch

Work in the same way as ordinary blanket stitch, but graduate the length of the uprights so they form neat pyramid shapes.

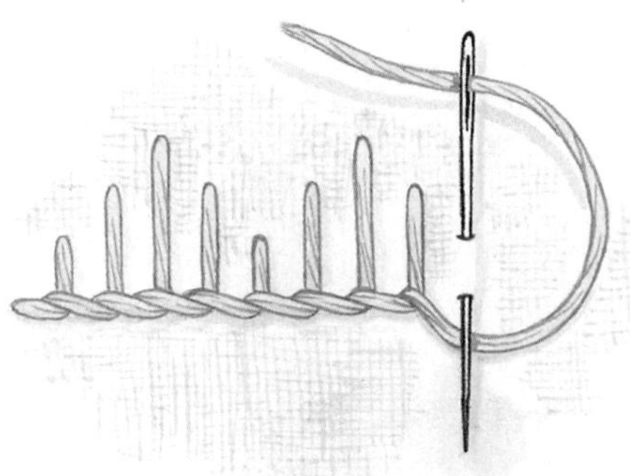

When blanket stitch is worked close together, producing a thicker effect, it is usually called buttonhole stitch. Whatever name is used, these looped stitches, in all their varied forms, are among the most useful in the embroiderer's repertoire.

The secret of working the stitches in this section is to match the size of the stitches with the weight of the thread. Very small buttonhole stitches worked with a heavy embroidery thread tend to look bulky and distorted; in contrast, very large buttonhole stitches worked in a thin thread have a spidery appearance, and the loops do not retain their shape.

Variations of the two basic stitches are numerous; some, such as closed buttonhole stitch, can be worked around quite intricate curves, while others, including double buttonhole stitch, look best when they are worked in a straight line.

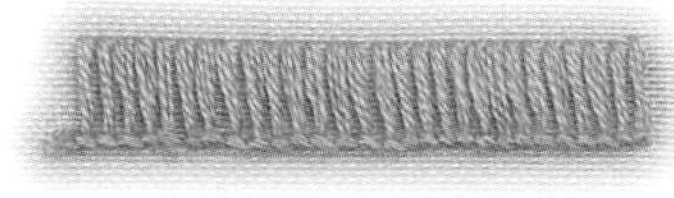

Buttonhole stitch

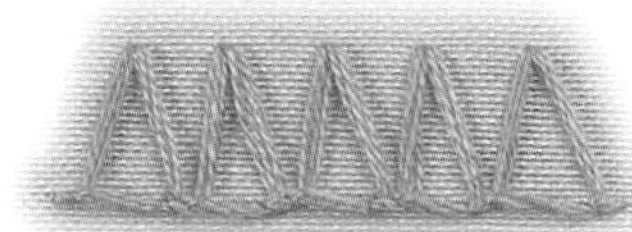

Closed buttonhole stitch

Crossed buttonhole stitch

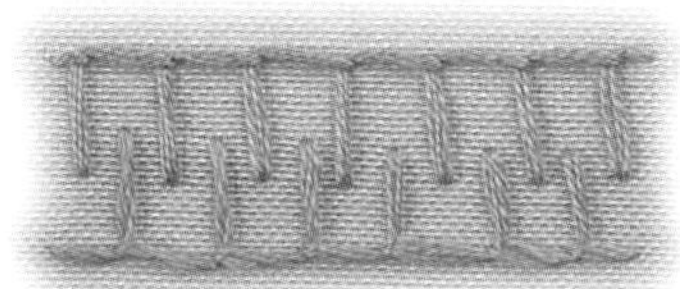

Double buttonhole stitch

To start and fasten off any of the stitches in this section, refer to page 57. Instructions for working basic blanket stitch are given on the same page.

Buttonhole stitch is used for surface embroidery and as the main stitch in cutwork, such as Richelieu work, a form of cutwork in which the open areas are crossed by buttonhole-stitched bars.

Closed buttonhole stitch is highly decorative and can be used instead of blanket stitch to make attractive edgings for hems.

Crossed buttonhole stitch can be used in single rows for borders or in multiple rows as a filling.

Double buttonhole stitch is a useful stitch for creating fillings and wide borders.

Working buttonhole stitch

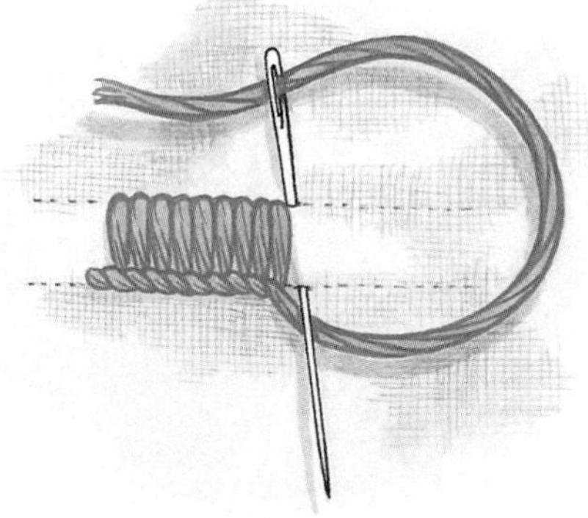

1 Mark two parallel lines on the fabric. Bring the needle out at the bottom left. Insert the needle directly above on the top line and bring it out on the bottom line a little way to the right, with the thread under the point. Repeat along the row, spacing the stitches close together.

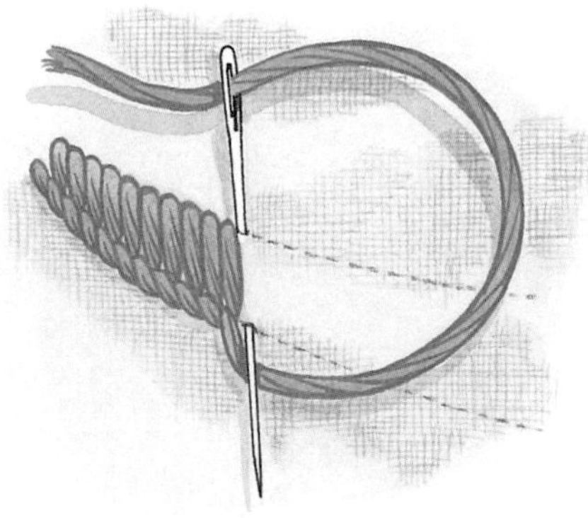

2 For a neat, flat finish along a curved edge, follow step **1** (left) but lengthen the stitches at the center of the curve and shorten them at the end of the curve.

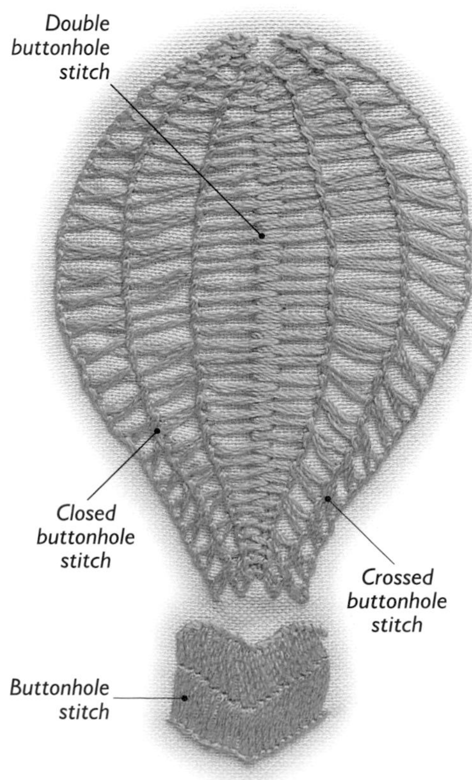

Working closed buttonhole stitch

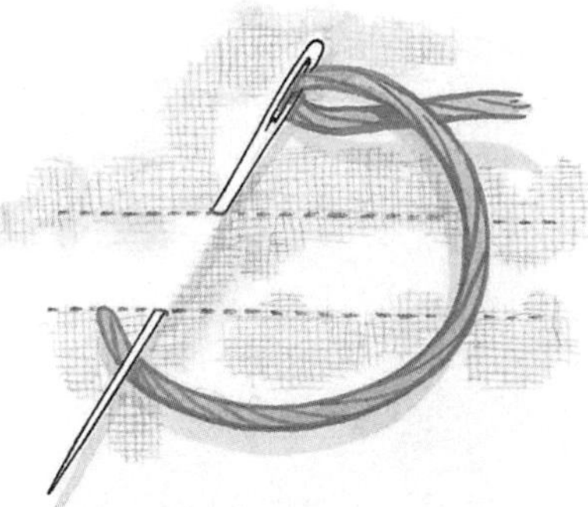

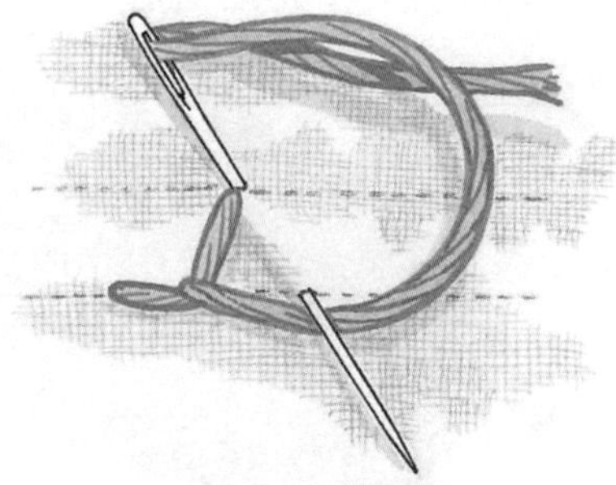

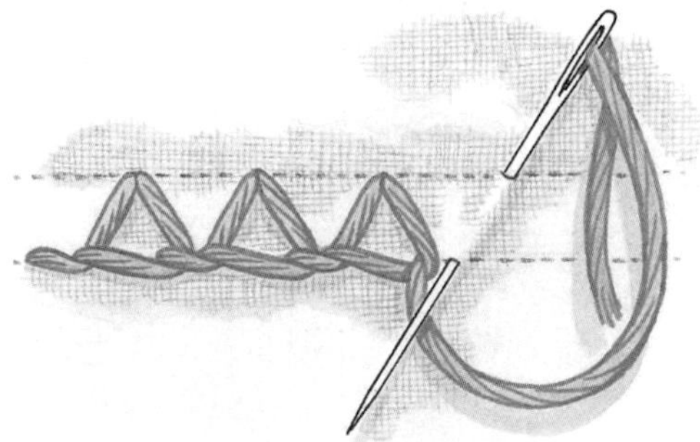

1 Mark two parallel lines on the fabric and start at the bottom left. Insert the needle on the top line and bring it out on the bottom line, slanting to the left as shown, with the thread under the point of the needle.

2 Pull the thread through gently. Insert the needle at the top of the previous stitch, and make another stitch slanting to the right, creating a triangle shape.

3 Pull the thread through gently to complete the first closed buttonhole stitch, making sure the thread is under the point of the needle. Repeat along the row, spacing the stitches evenly.

Working crossed buttonhole stitch

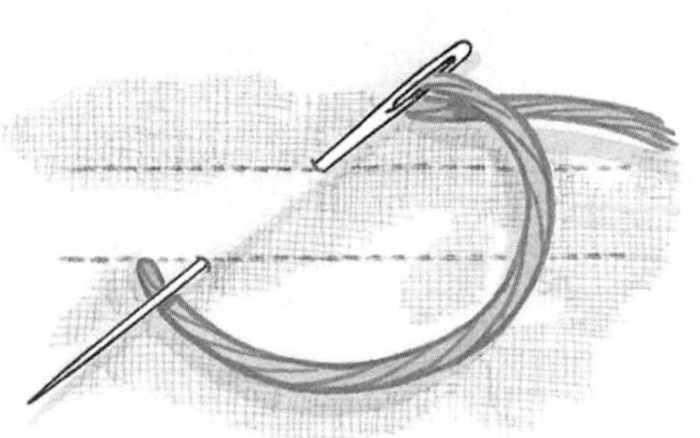

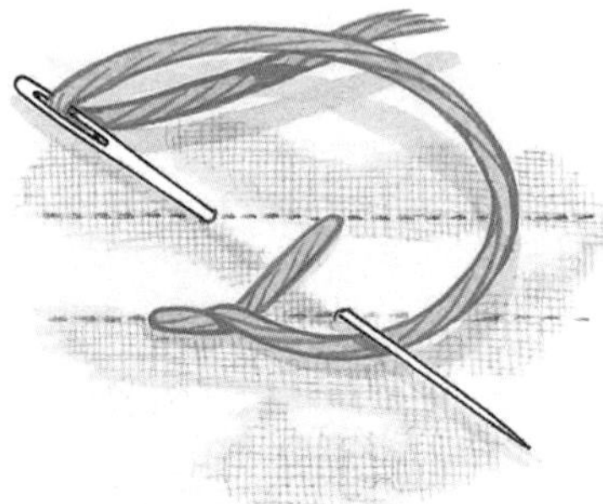

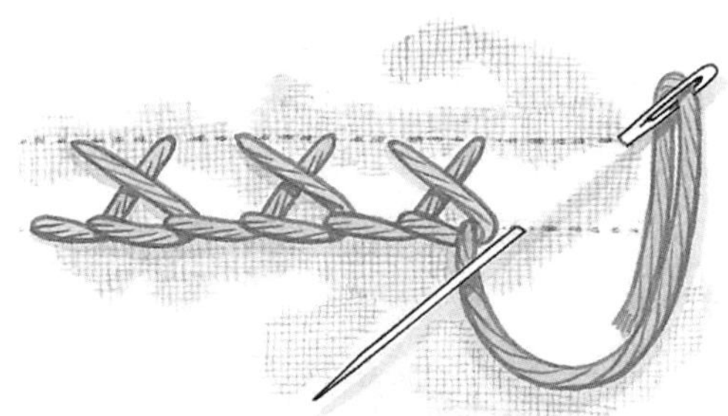

1 Mark two parallel lines on your fabric; start at the bottom left. Insert the needle to the right on the top line and bring it out on the bottom line, slanting to the left. Make sure the working thread is under the point.

2 Insert the needle on the top line to the left of the previous stitch. Bring it out on the bottom line below the top of the first stitch, with the working thread under the point.

3 Pull the needle through gently to complete the first crossed buttonhole stitch. Continue in this way to complete the row, spacing the stitches evenly.

Working double buttonhole stitch

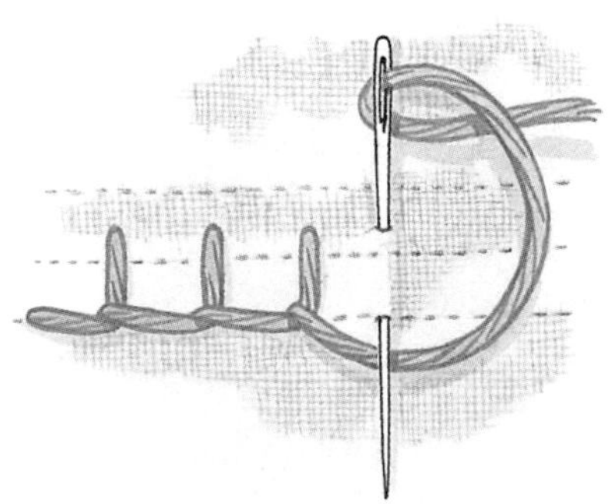

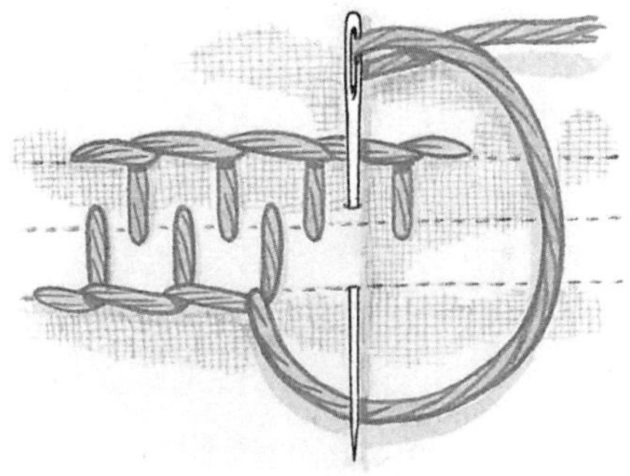

1 Mark three parallel lines on the fabric; start at the bottom left. Work a row of widely spaced blanket stitches along the bottom line, with the tips of the stitches slightly over the center line.

2 Rotate the fabric 180 degrees. Work a second row of identical blanket stitches below the first; arrange them so that the tips of the stitches on this row fit neatly into the spaces between the tips of the stitches on the first row.

Rough stitches
To avoid a rough, gappy finish when you are working buttonhole stitch, always insert the needle and bring it out again exactly on the drawn guide lines, and position the upright stitches very close together.

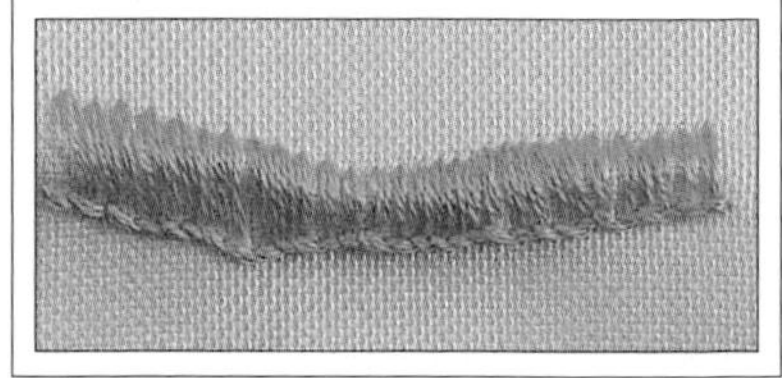

Chain stitches

Chain stitch is one of the oldest embroidery stitches in existence. It has many variations—some are worked in a similar way to the basic chain, but the chains may be twisted or spaced in a different way.

Basic chain stitch resembles links in a chain and can be used on curves or straight lines. It is slightly raised and is popular for crewel work.

Lazy daisy stitch is also called detached chain stitch. It is an isolated stitch which is frequently worked radiating outward in a circle to give the impression of petals clustered in a flower head.

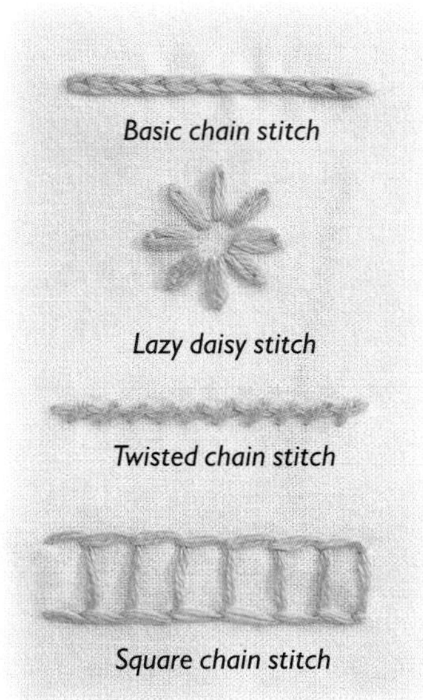

Twisted chain stitch makes an attractive, textured line which looks complicated but is easy to work. **Square chain stitch**, also known as open chain stitch or ladder stitch, makes a flat, wide line. When working this stitch, mark two parallel lines on the fabric with a water-soluble marking pen to help keep the stitches of identical width.

You can vary the effect of any of these stitches by using different embroidery threads. For example, using a round, twisted thread such as pearl cotton for twisted chain stitch will give a raised effect.

Starting and finishing chain stitch

1 To start, take the needle to the back, close to the top of the stitching line, leaving a 2 in. (5 cm) tail of thread at the front. At the end of the row, take a short straight stitch over the last thread loop.

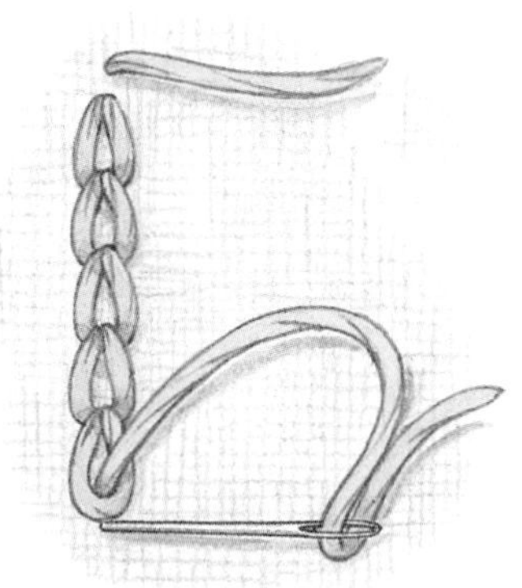

2 Darn the thread end into the last few stitches at the back of the work. Return to the beginning of the row, pull the tail of thread to the wrong side, and darn the end under the back of the first few stitches in the same way.

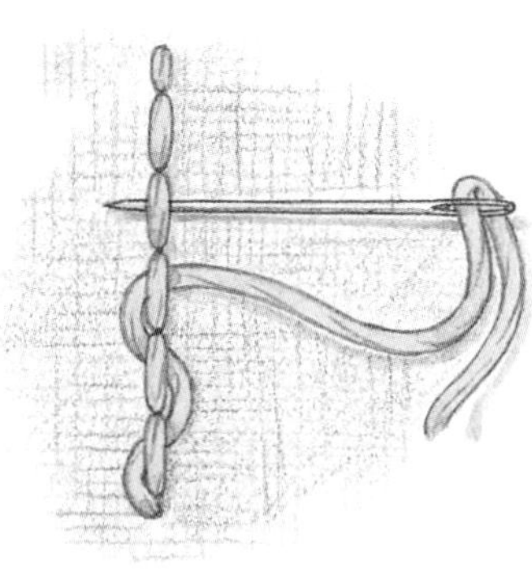

Working chain stitch

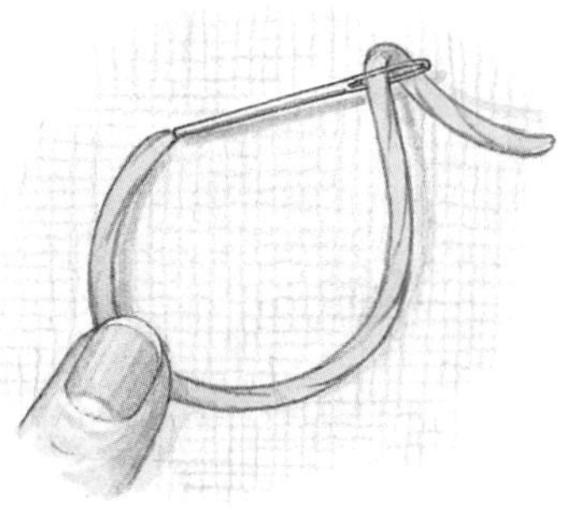

1 Work downward along a single stitching line. Bring the thread through to the front at the top of the stitching line. Form the working thread into a loop, and, holding the loop in place with your thumb, re-insert the needle in the same hole.

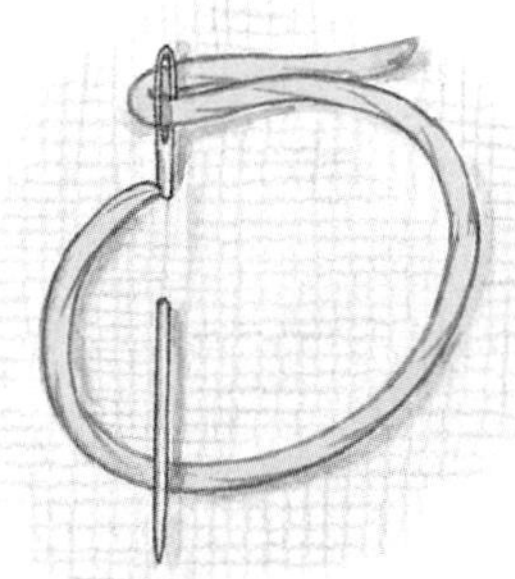

2 Still holding the thread loop with your thumb, bring the point of the needle to the front, a stitch length away from the starting point. With the loop of thread under the needle, pull the needle through to make the first chain.

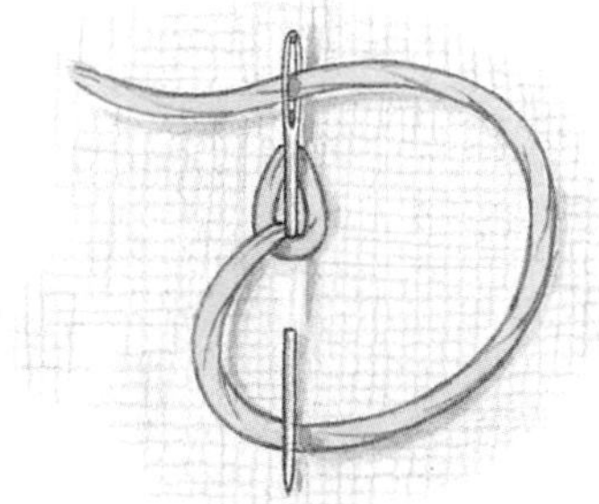

3 Form a loop of thread and insert the needle beside the emerging thread. Bring the point of the needle out a stitch length away, and pull it through over the working thread to make the second chain. Continue in this way.

Working lazy daisy stitch

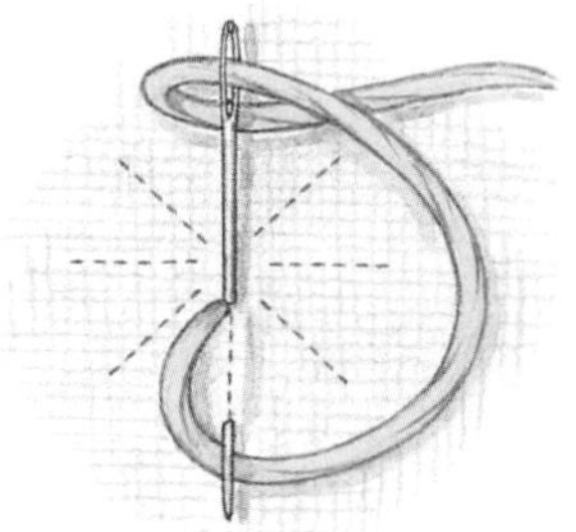

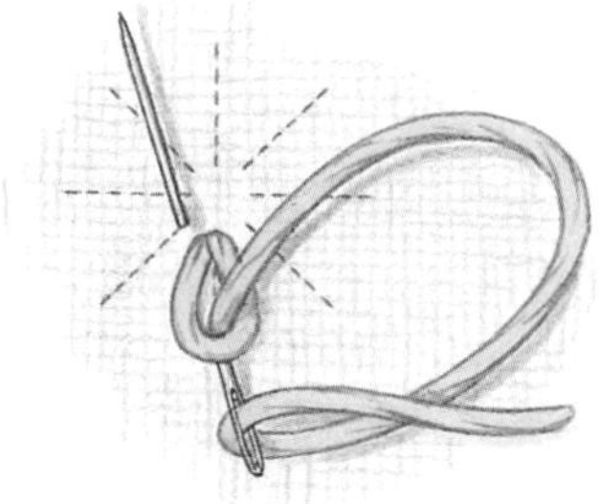

1 Bring the needle through to the front of the fabric. Insert the needle beside the emerging thread, and bring it out to the front again, a stitch length away, looping the working thread under the point of the needle.

2 Pull the thread so that the loop lies flat. Make a short straight stitch over the loop to anchor it. Bring the needle out to the front, ready to begin the next stitch.

Working twisted chain stitch

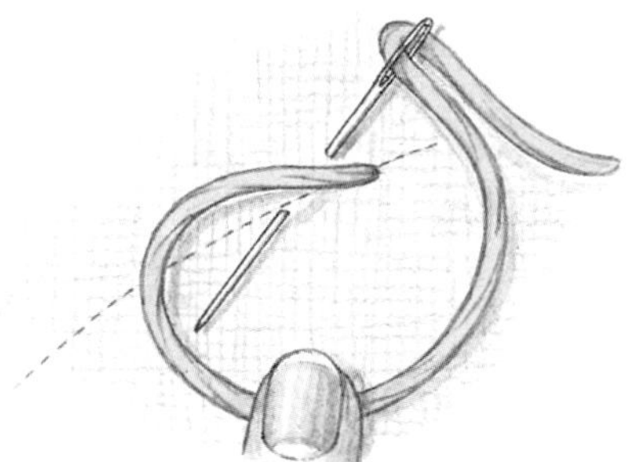

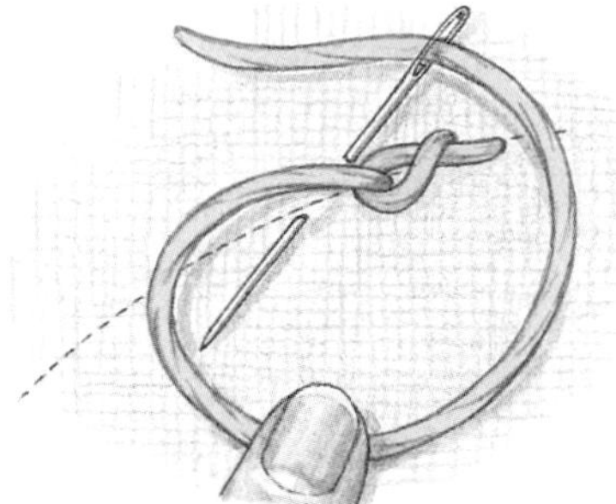

1 Working downward, bring the needle and thread through to the front of the fabric on the stitching line. Holding the thread down with your thumb to make a loop, take a small slanting stitch across the line.

2 Keeping the thread loop under the needle, pull the needle through to make a twisted chain. Holding the thread down, take another slanting stitch across the design line. Continue in this way along the line.

Working square chain stitch

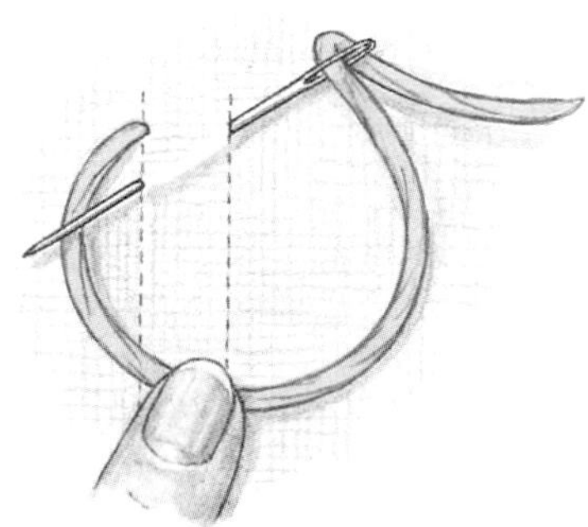

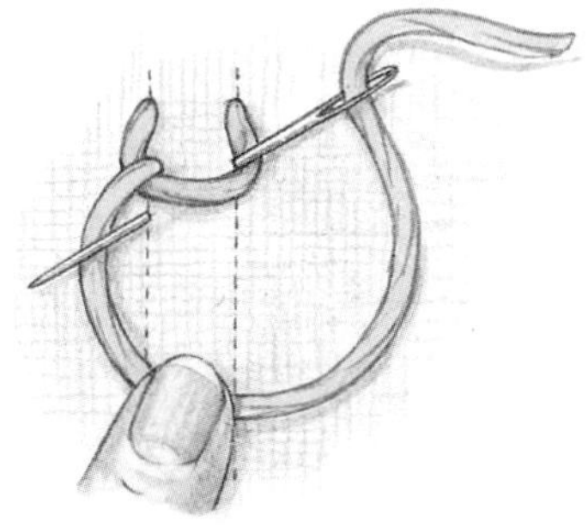

1 Work downward between two parallel stitching lines. Bring the needle to the front at the top of the left-hand line. Insert the needle at the top of the right-hand line, and bring the point out a stitch length below where the thread first emerged. Loop the thread under the needle, then pull the needle through to form the first stitch.

2 Insert the point of the needle into the right-hand line, level with the emerging thread. Bring the point of the needle out on the left-hand line a short distance below the emerging thread. Loop the thread under the needle, and pull the needle through. Continue in this way.

WHAT WENT WRONG

Messy stitches

Untidy chain stitch is usually the result of either working stitches of unequal length or working them with an uneven tension. For a neat finish, try to make all the stitches of identical length, and keep the tension of the thread loops the same right along the row.

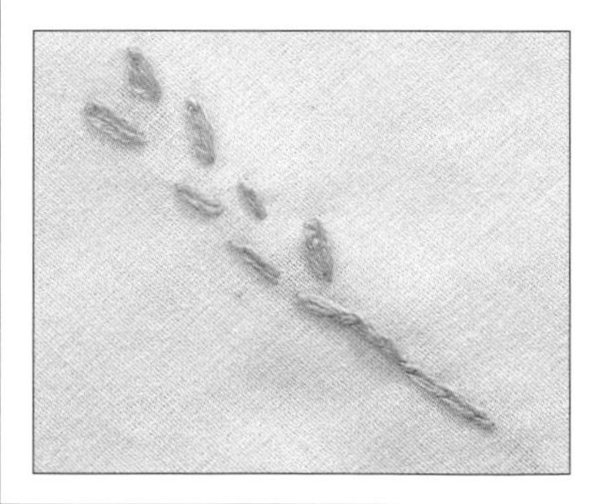

The three chain stitch variations shown here all produce an intricate, wide line, which is ideal for borders. To help keep the stitches the same width, draw parallel guide lines on your fabric with a water- or air-erasable marking pen. To enhance the crisp character of these stitches, use a cotton thread, such as floss or pearl cotton.

For details on basic chain stitch and variations such as lazy daisy stitch, refer to pages 61 and 62.

Double chain stitch is a favorite in Indian embroideries. It makes an attractive, plaited line.

Crested chain stitch, or Spanish coral stitch, combines chain stitch and coral stitch to make an intricate openwork ladder. For details on coral stitch, refer to page 81.

Feathered chain stitch, also known as chained feather stitch, makes a zigzag line with knotted points. It is useful for delicate borders and can also be worked in multiple rows to fill a shape with texture.

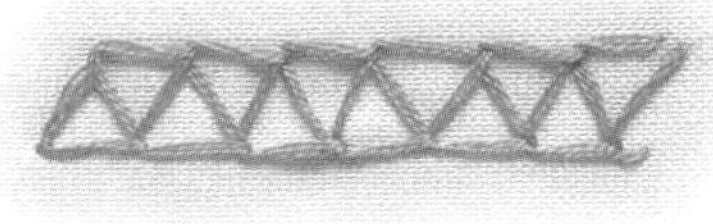

Double chain stitch

Crested chain stitch

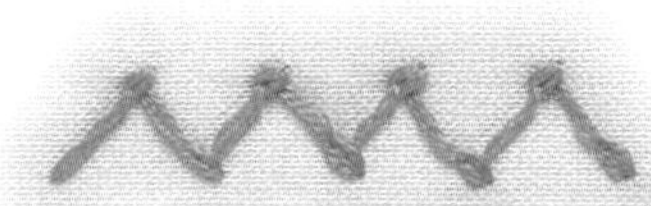

Feathered chain stitch

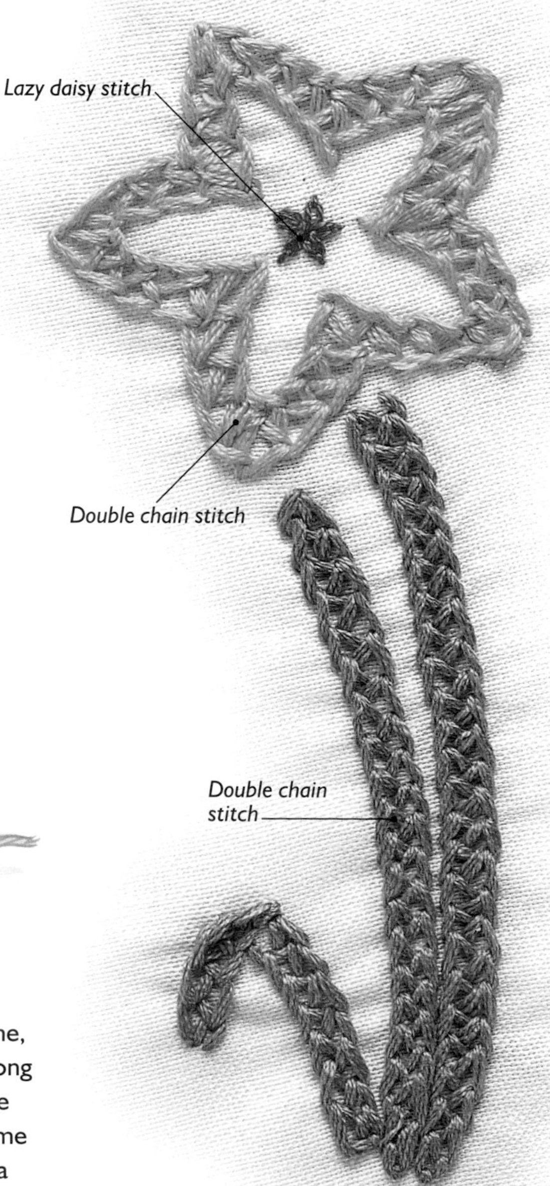

Working double chain stitch

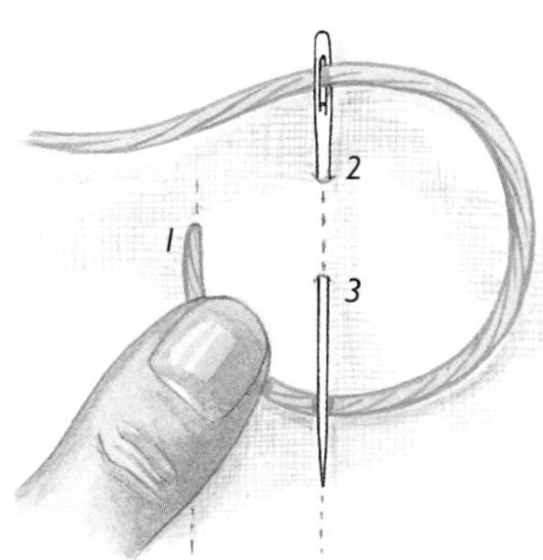

1 Draw parallel guide lines on the fabric. Bring the needle out at 1 just below the top of the left-hand guide line. Insert it at 2 at the top of the guide line, and bring it out at 3. Hold the thread under the needle with your thumb, and pull the needle through to make the first stitch.

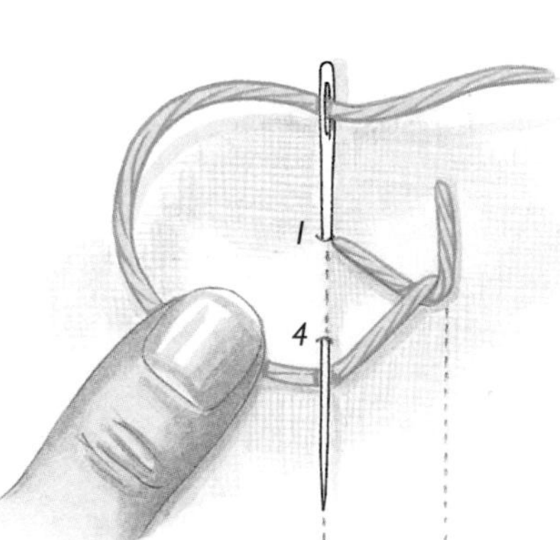

2 Insert the needle on the left-hand line at 1 again and let it emerge at 4. Hold the thread below the needle with your thumb, and pull the needle through to make the second stitch.

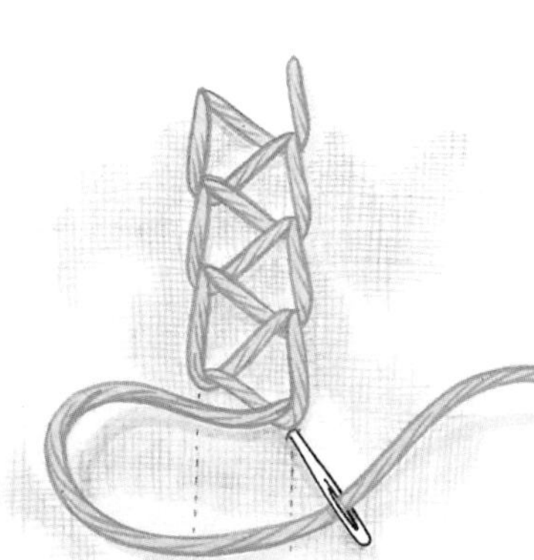

3 Repeat steps **1–2** along the line, making stitches alternately along the right-hand and left-hand guide lines. Make all the stitches the same length. Secure the last loop with a short straight stitch, as shown.

Double chain stitch

Crested chain stitch

Feathered chain stitch

Working crested chain stitch

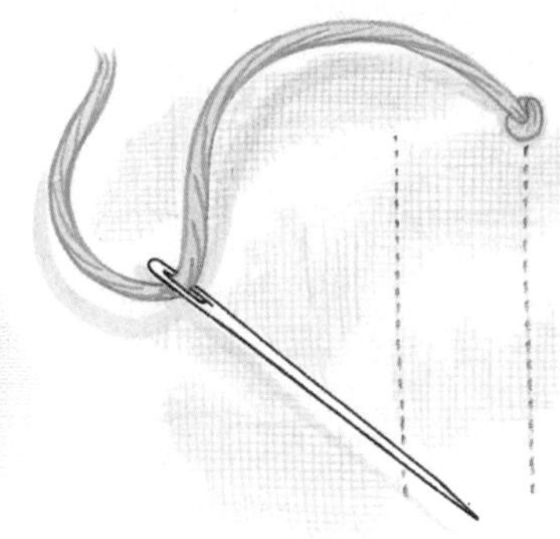

1 Bring the thread out at the top of the right-hand guide line. Make a small basic chain stitch, and pull the needle and thread through to make a small knot on the fabric.

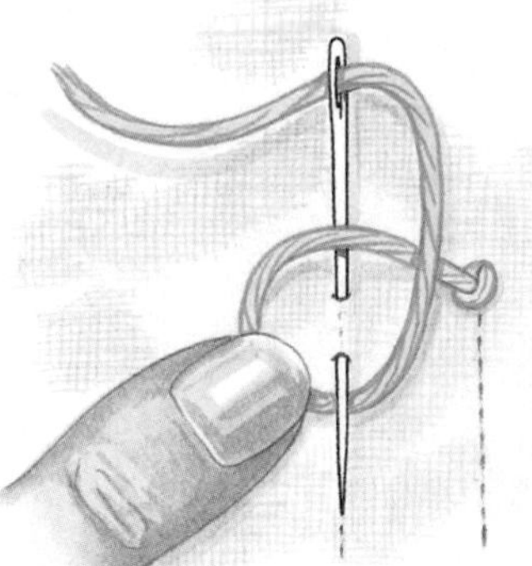

2 Carry the thread over to the left-hand line and make a loop. Holding the loop down with your thumb, insert the needle just below the top of the guide line. Bring the point out a short distance below, passing the needle under and over the working thread.

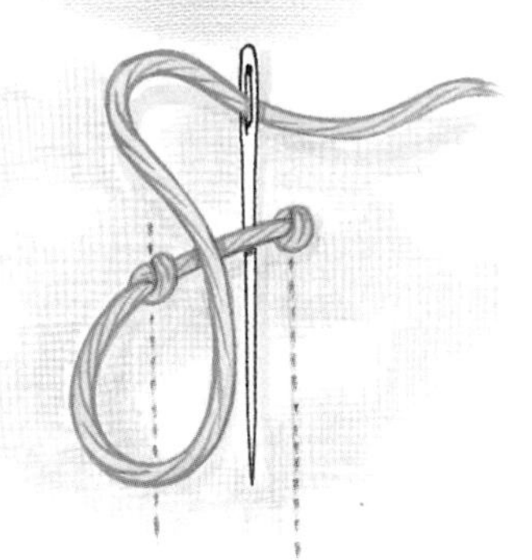

3 Carefully pull the thread through to form a coral stitch. Slip the needle downward under the diagonal stitch just made, without piercing the background fabric, and pull the thread through, ready to work the next stitch.

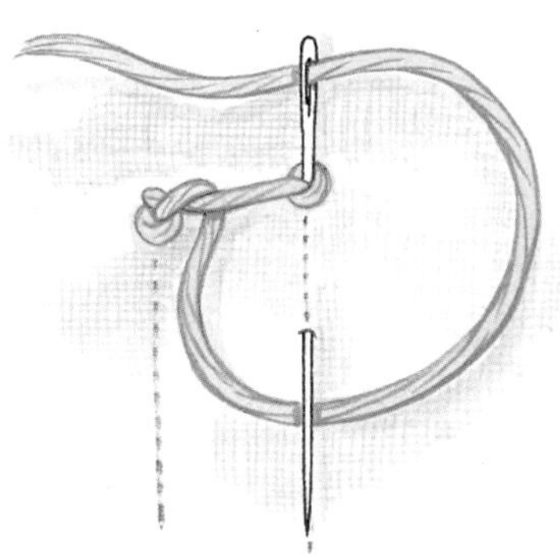

4 Insert the needle on the right-hand guide line through the first chain stitch. Bring the point out a short distance below. With the working thread under the point, pull the needle through to make a large chain stitch.

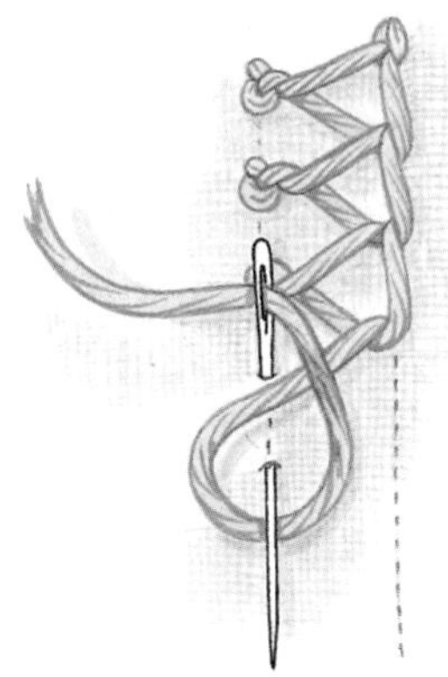

5 Repeat steps **2–4** along the row, making coral stitches on the left and large chain stitches on the right. Take care to slip the needle under the diagonal stitch each time you move from left to right across the row.

Working feathered chain stitch

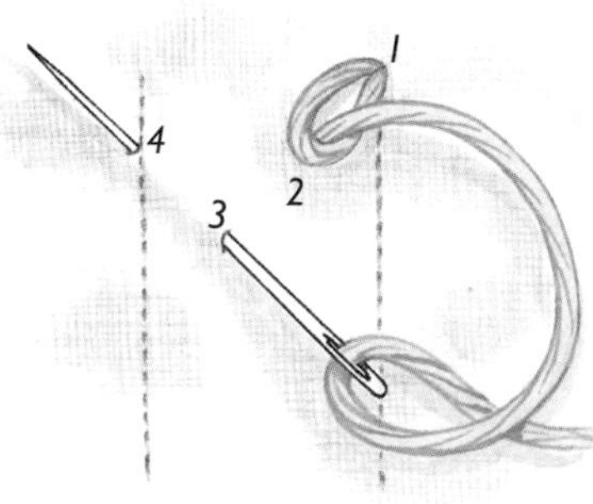

1 Bring the needle out at 1 at the top of the right-hand guide line. Insert it close to 1, bring it out at an angle at 2, and pull the thread through to make a chain stitch. Insert the needle at 3 and bring out at 4 on left-hand guide line.

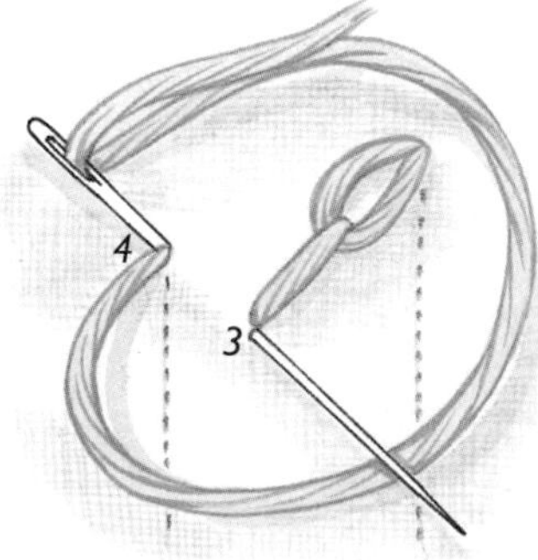

2 Insert the needle close to 4 again and bring it out at 3, over the working thread, to make a second chain stitch. Try to keep the alternating slants of the chain stitches consistent along the row.

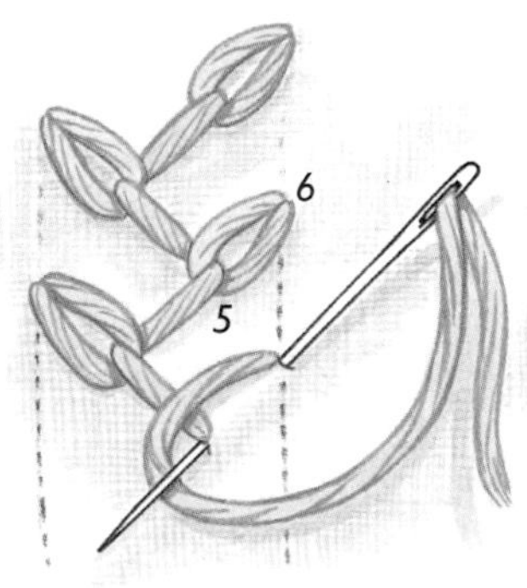

3 Insert the needle at 5 and bring it out again at 6, along the right-hand guide line. Continue in this way down the row, working chain stitches alternately from side to side.

The first two chain stitch variations in this section create bold lines and can follow intricate patterns with ease. The third stitch is a two-color variation which is fun to work, and the fourth makes a decorative line suitable for a border.

All the stitches are worked downward in a way similar to chain stitch. You can vary the effects by changing your thread for example, using embroidery floss will create a flatter, less three-dimensional line than the same stitch worked in a twisted thread like pearl cotton.

To start and fasten off any of the stitches shown in this section, refer to page 61.

Heavy chain stitch is a quick and easy variation of basic chain stitch, and it is often used in Asian Indian embroideries—it makes a heavy, almost corded line.

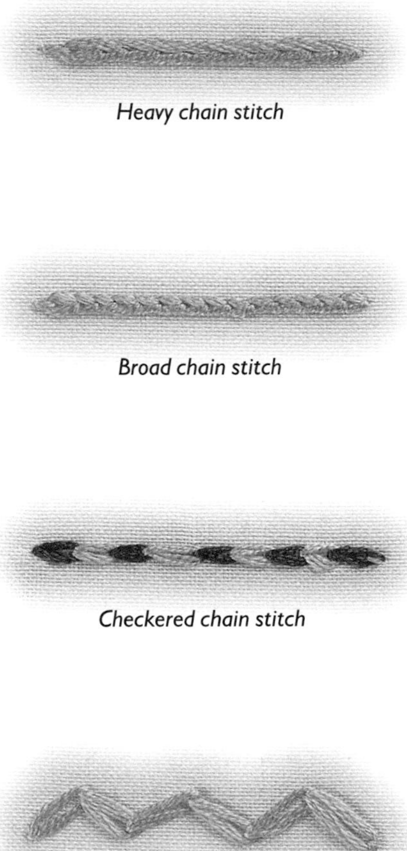

Heavy chain stitch

Broad chain stitch

Checkered chain stitch

Zigzag chain stitch

Broad chain stitch is worked in a similar way, and it makes a wide, strongly defined line which is also useful as an outline stitch.

Checkered chain stitch, also known as magic chain stitch, is worked in two contrasting thread colors. They are threaded into the needle together, but only one is used at a time. The stitches are worked using alternate colors, as shown here; or you can work two or three stitches in one thread then change to the other.

Zigzag chain stitch creates a zigzag line which can be worked in rows to fill a shape with texture. Unlike the other three stitches, this stitch is best worked in a straight line. When working this stitch, as either a line stitch or a filling, mark parallel guide lines on your fabric with a water-soluble marking pen to help keep the stitches of identical width.

Working heavy chain stitch

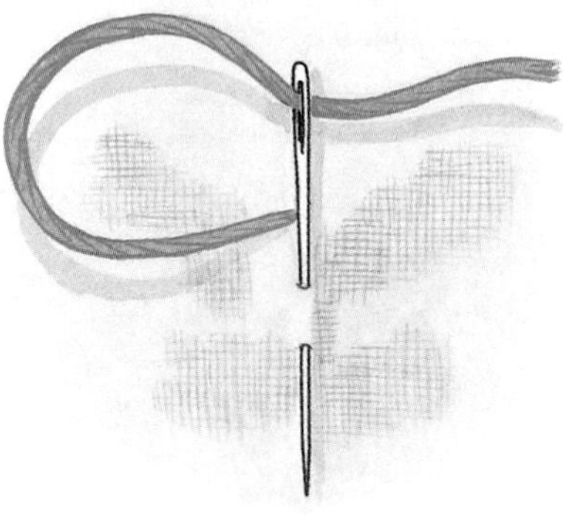

1 Start a short distance from the top of the row. Insert the needle slightly lower down to make a vertical straight stitch, bringing out the point a little farther down the row.

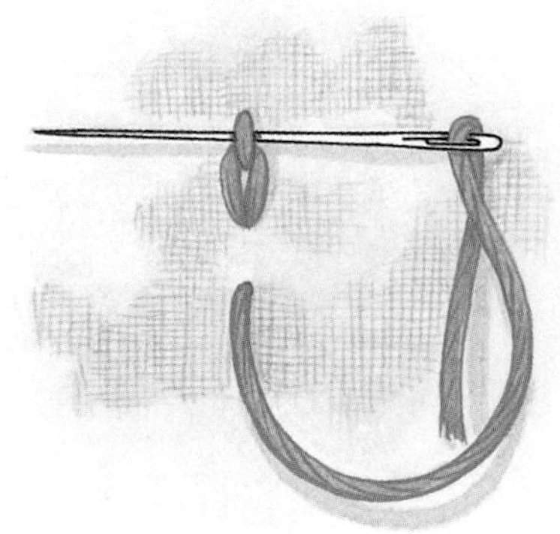

2 Slip the needle under the vertical stitch, and take it back down where it emerged. Pull the thread through to make the first chain loop. Work the second chain loop just below the first one, again slipping the needle under the vertical stitch.

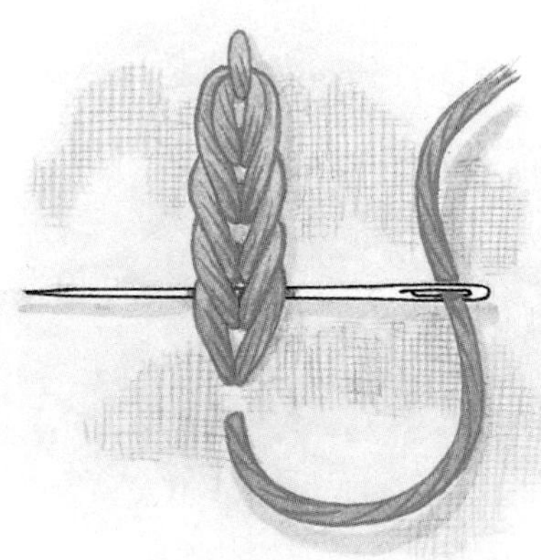

3 Position subsequent chain loops at regular intervals along the row, slipping the needle under the two previous chain loops without picking up any fabric.

Working broad chain stitch

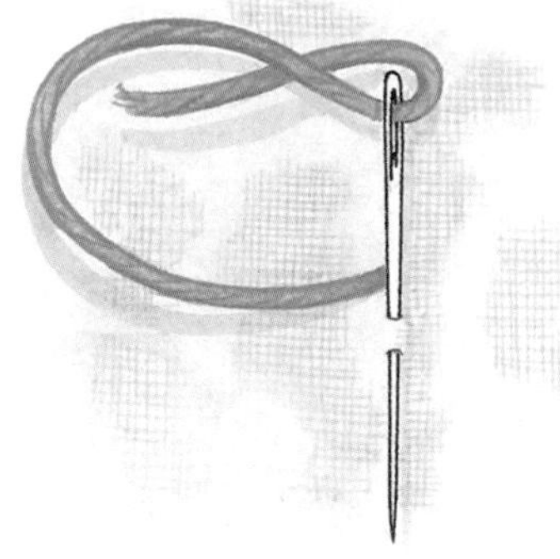

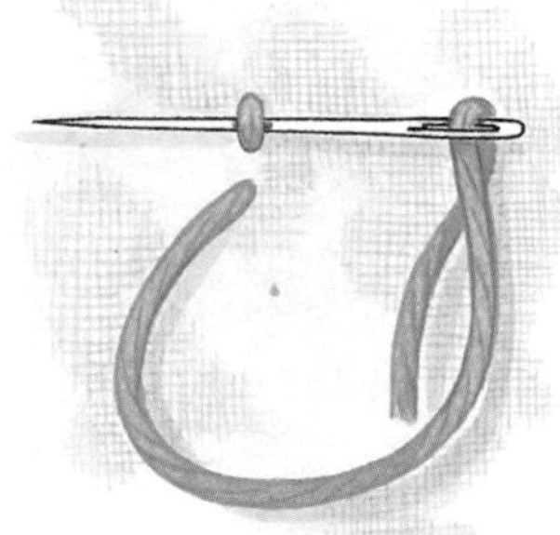

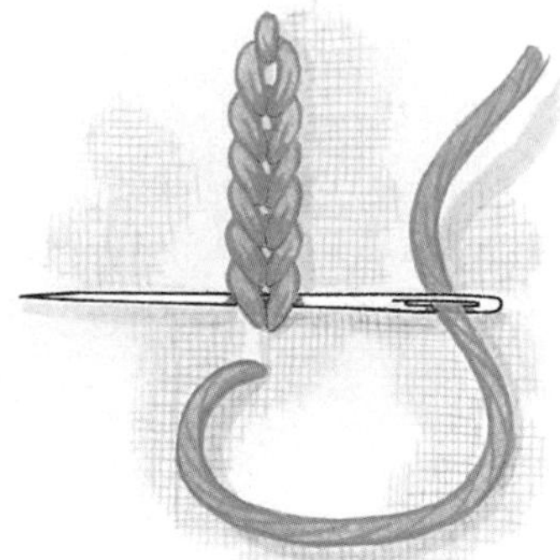

1 Start a short distance below the top of the row. Insert the needle slightly lower down to make a shorter straight stitch than for heavy chain stitch. Bring the needle out just below this stitch.

2 Pull the thread through. Slip the needle under the vertical stitch and insert it again where it last emerged. Pull the thread through to make a chain loop, but allow the loop to lie fairly loosely on the fabric.

3 Work subsequent chain loops directly below the first one. Space the loops quite close together, and slip the needle under the previous chain loop each time, taking care not to pick up any of the fabric.

Working checkered chain stitch

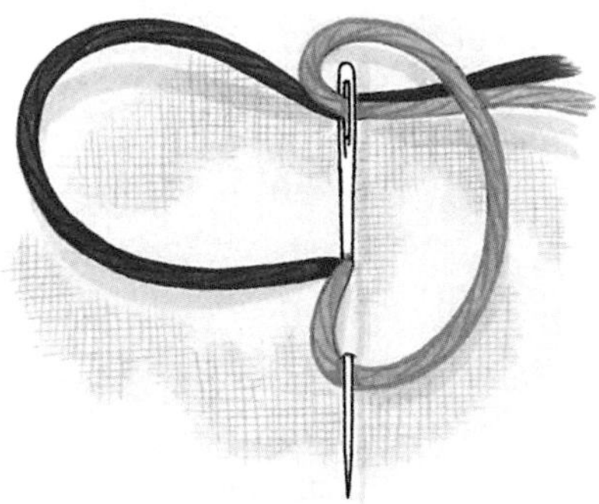

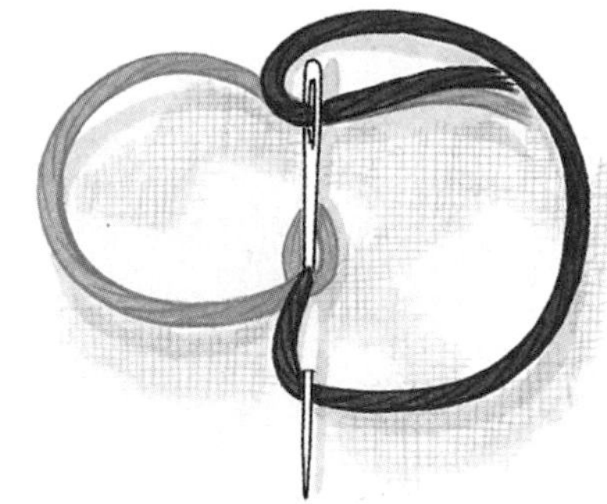

1 With two thread colors in the needle, start at the top of the row. Work a chain stitch in the first color, keeping the second thread above the needle point. Pull both the threads through to complete the first stitch.

2 Work a second chain stitch, but this time reverse the position of the threads so you make a stitch using the second color. Continue in this way down the row, alternating the colors.

Checkered chain stitch

Heavy chain stitch

Broad chain stitch

Zigzag chain stitch

Working zigzag chain stitch

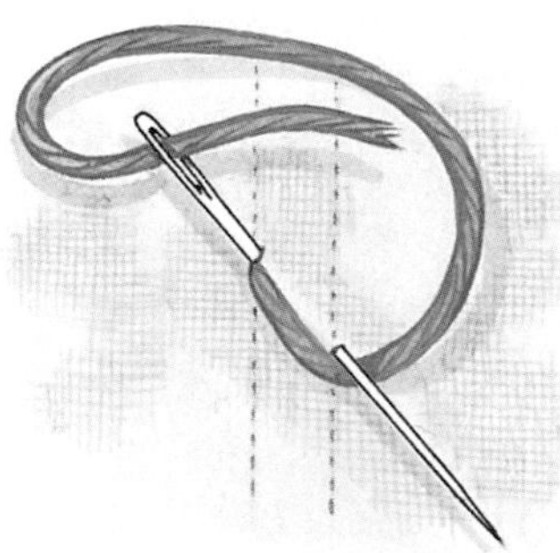

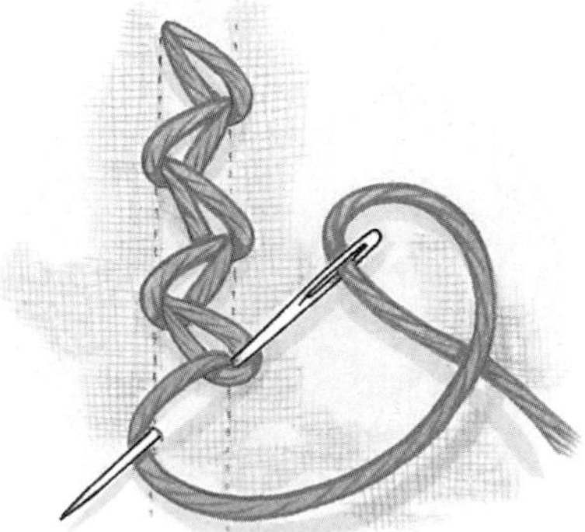

1 Mark two parallel guide lines on the fabric. Start at the top of the left-hand line. Insert the needle at an angle so that the tip emerges along the right-hand line. Pull the thread through to make a chain stitch.

2 Make a second chain stitch, slanting in the opposite direction to the first stitch. Continue in this way down the row, working chain stitches alternately from side to side.

Feather- & fly stitches

Featherstitch and its variations are attractive looped stitches which make delicate feathery lines. They are worked in individual rows to make narrow borders and in multiple rows to create deeper borders and fillings.

Fly stitches produce a distinctive "Y" shape. They, too, can be arranged in rows to make borders. They also look effective worked individually as an open filling stitch or scattered in the sky of a landscape to resemble a flight of distant birds. Alternatively, try lengthening the tail of fly stitches and working them randomly over the fabric, overlapping each other, to suggest grasses in a meadow—perhaps using different weights of thread.

The more complex stitches in this section look more effective when worked regularly, as shown. Experiment to find the best weight of thread to bring out the character of the stitch.

To work these stitches, leave a 2 in. (5 cm) tail of thread on the front, close to your starting point. Work the row of stitches, then take the thread to the back and darn the end into the last few stitches. Return to the beginning of the row, pull the thread tail to the back, and darn it under a few stitches. Where appropriate, mark stitching guide lines on your fabric with an air-erasable pen.

Featherstitch makes a pretty, rather narrow line. It is used for surface embroidery, for smocking, and to embellish crazy patchwork.

Double featherstitch makes a wide, branching line and is often used to decorate babies' and children's clothes.

Maidenhair stitch makes a delicate, fernlike line which looks equally attractive worked on a small or large scale.

Fly stitch creates a "Y" shape. As an extra decorative touch, work a French knot in the center of the "V," using a contrasting color.

Plaited fly stitch consists of elongated fly stitches overlapped to create a pretty plaited line.

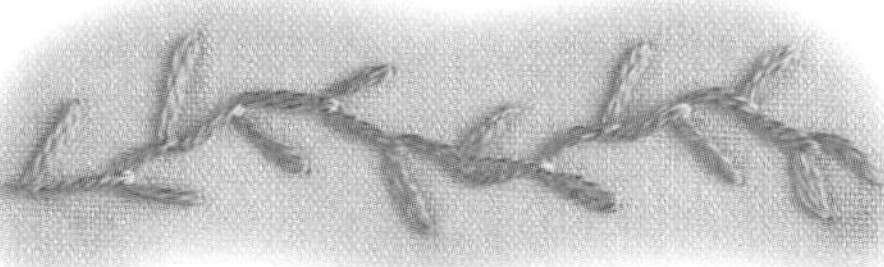

Featherstitch

Double featherstitch

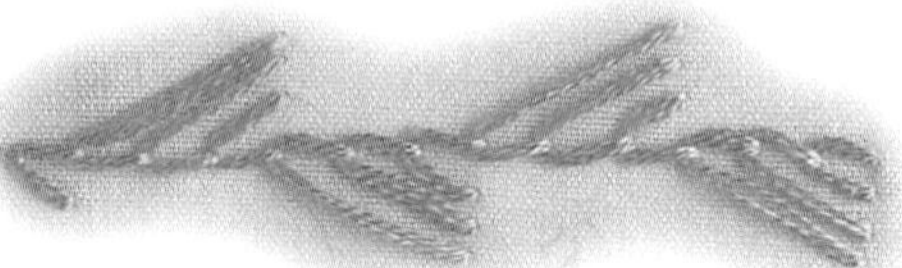

Maidenhair stitch

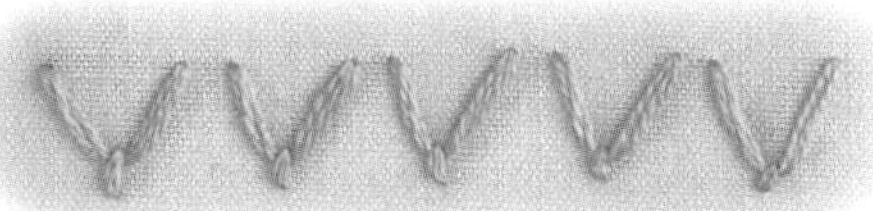

Fly stitch

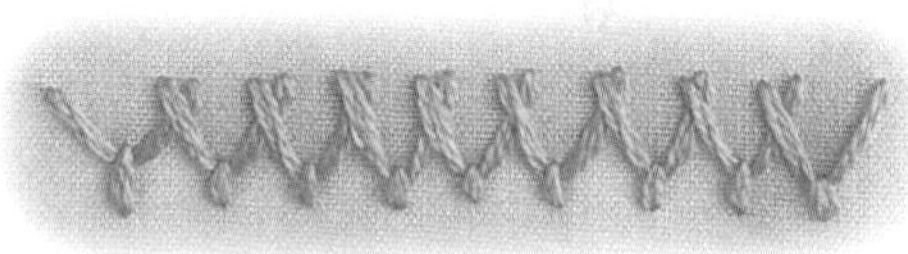

Plaited fly stitch

Working featherstitch

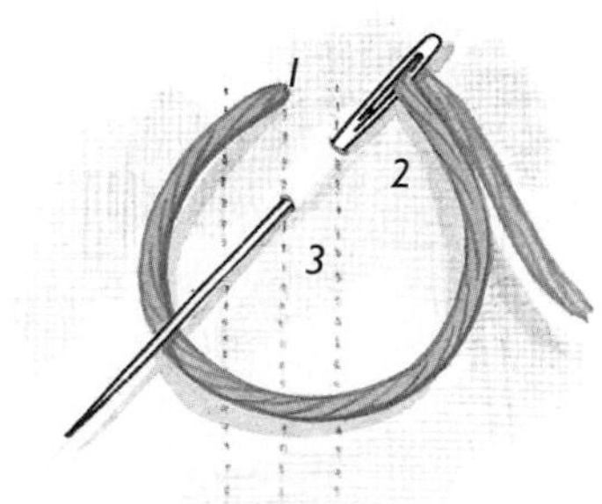

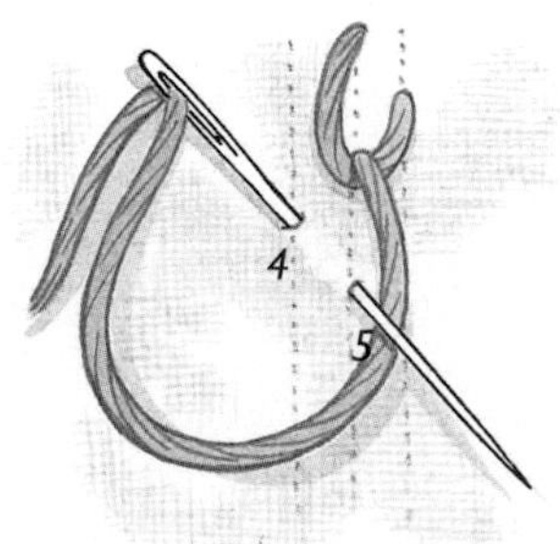

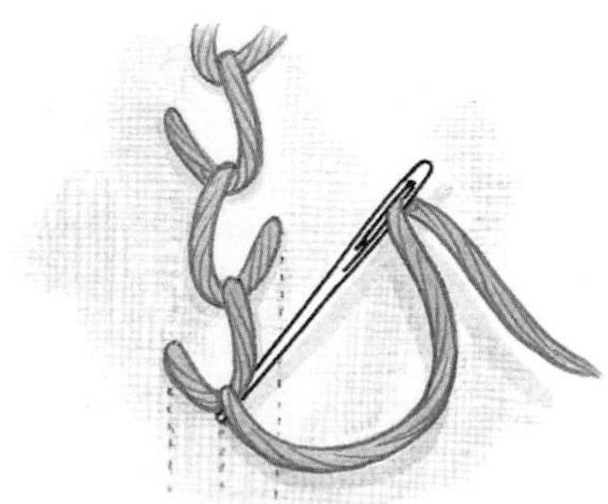

1 Mark three parallel vertical lines on your fabric. Bring the needle to the front at 1 and insert it at 2. Bring the needle to the front at 3, over the working thread. Pull the needle through to complete the first stitch.

2 Insert the needle lower down on the left-hand line at 4, then bring it out to the front on the center line at 5, over the working thread. Pull the needle through to complete the second stitch.

3 Repeat steps **1–2**, alternating the looped stitches to the left and to the right of the center line. At the end of the row, make a small vertical stitch over the last loop, and secure the thread.

Working double featherstitch

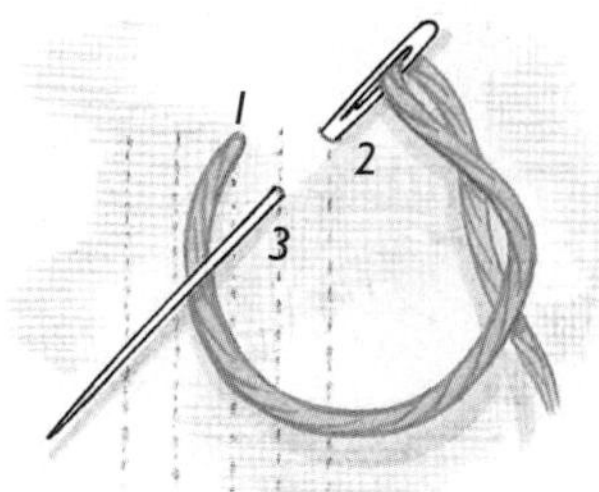

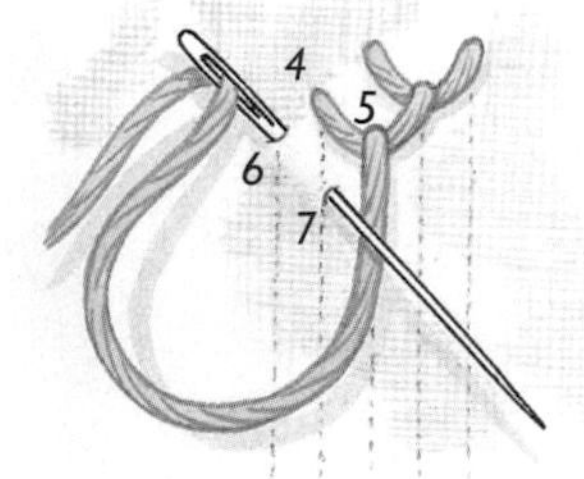

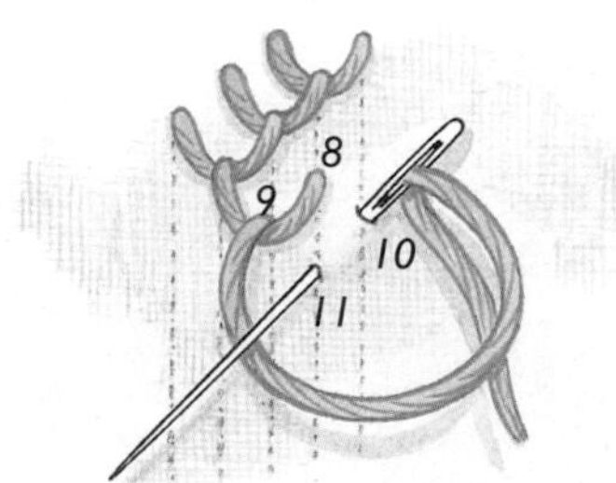

1 Mark five parallel vertical lines on your fabric. Bring the needle to the front at 1. Insert it on the right-hand line at 2, and bring it to the front at 3, over the working thread.

2 Following the number sequence, make two more featherstitches diagonally to the left of the first stitch, making each one exactly the same size. This completes the first set of stitches.

3 Working in the opposite direction toward the right-hand line, make two more featherstitches, arranging them diagonally below the first set of stitches.

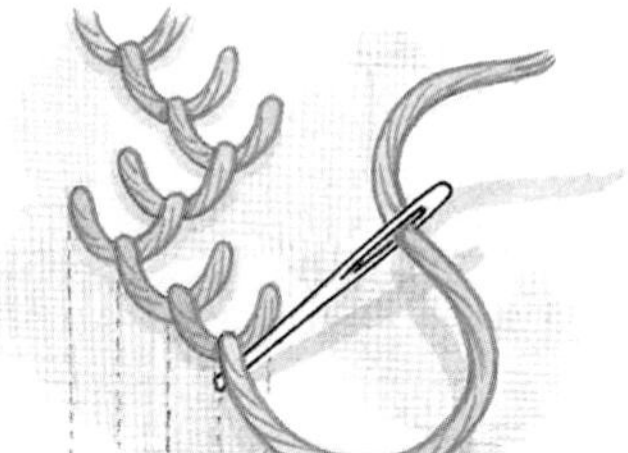

4 Continue in this way along the row, making pairs of stitches alternately to the left and to the right. At the end of the row, make a small vertical stitch over the last loop to secure the thread.

Working maidenhair stitch

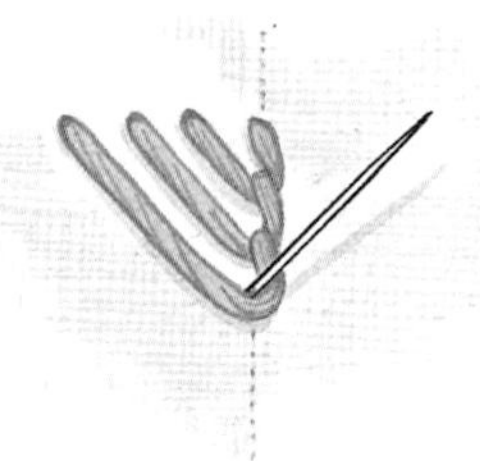

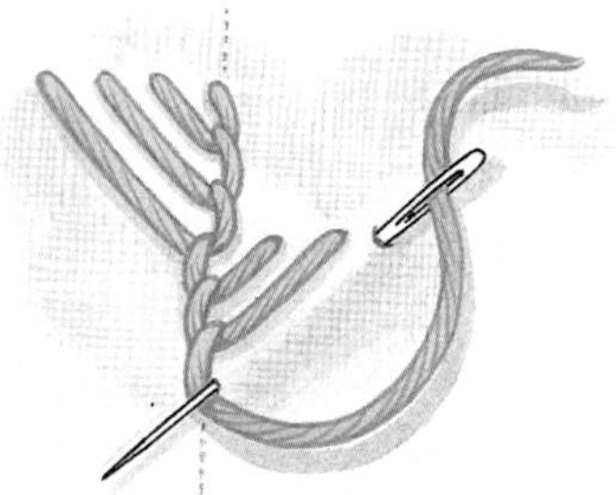

1 Mark a vertical line on the fabric. Bring the needle to the front at the top of the line and work three feather-stitches to the left of the line. Graduate the lengths so that the tops align.

2 Work a second group of three stitches below the first, positioning them to the right of the line. Continue in this way.

Working fly stitch

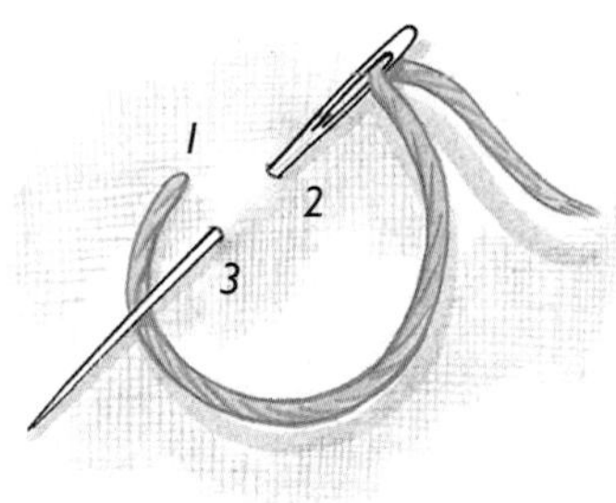

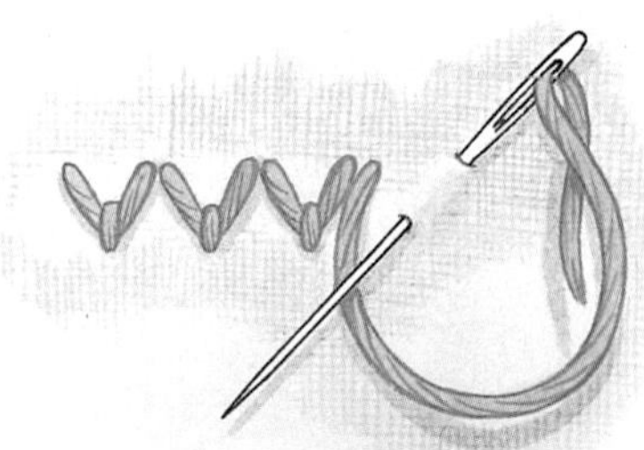

1 Bring the needle to the front at 1. Insert it to the right at 2. Bring the needle out over the working thread at 3.

2 Pull the needle through and make a vertical stitch over the loop to anchor it to the fabric.

3 To make a horizontal row of fly stitches, bring the needle to the front at the top right of the first stitch and repeat steps **1–2** along the row.

Working plaited fly stitch

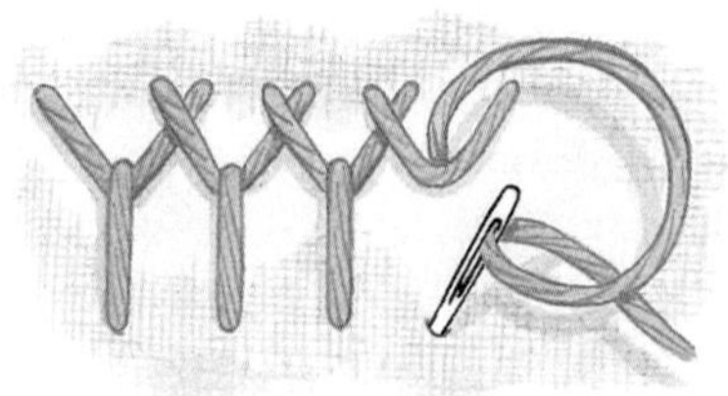

Work a row of fly stitches with elongated tails, arranging the stitches so that each new stitch slightly overlaps the previous one.

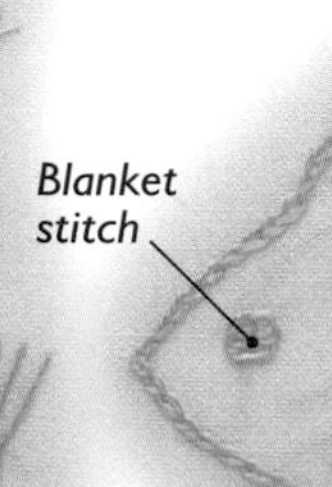

Featherstitches form one of the main "families" of embroidery stitches as do chain stitch and cross stitch. Here are four more featherstitches to add to those you have already learned.

Looped stitches can look more complicated to work than they are in practice, and one of the secrets of working any of these stitches correctly is to match the size of the stitches with the weight of the thread being used. Untidy looped stitches are usually the result of pulling the thread too tightly when working the stitches. Practice makes perfect when it comes to keeping the tension of your stitching correct.

Closed featherstitch makes a wide, lacy line and is worked between two parallel guide lines. It is best worked in a straight line. Besides being used for surface embroidery, closed featherstitch is also used as a couching stitch to attach groups of threads or narrow ribbon.

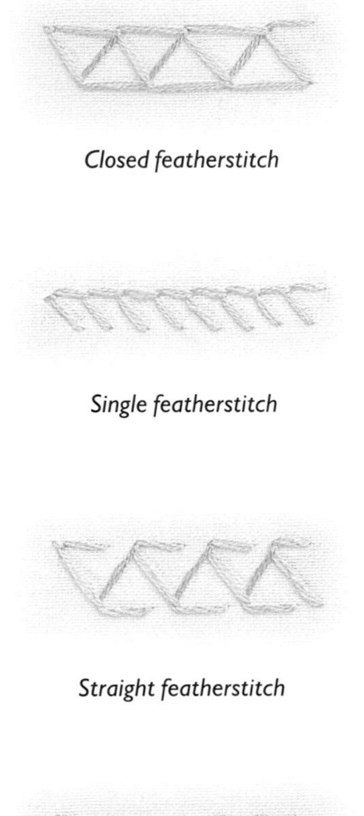

Closed featherstitch

Single featherstitch

Straight featherstitch

Spanish knotted featherstitch

Single featherstitch is a simple variation of ordinary featherstitch, but here the "feathers" are made along only one side of the row, which makes this stitch look plainer. It makes a pretty, rather narrow line and can be used in straight lines or to follow a gentle curve, with the looped edge on either the outside or inside of the curve.

Straight featherstitch has an angularity and sense of movement that would make it suitable for Native American-style embroidery. Try it along the edge of a wooden shawl, worked in Persian wool.

Spanish knotted featherstitch is the most complex stitch in the family and makes a wide, plaited line best worked in a straight line.

For more information on other featherstitches, refer to page 67.

Working closed featherstitch

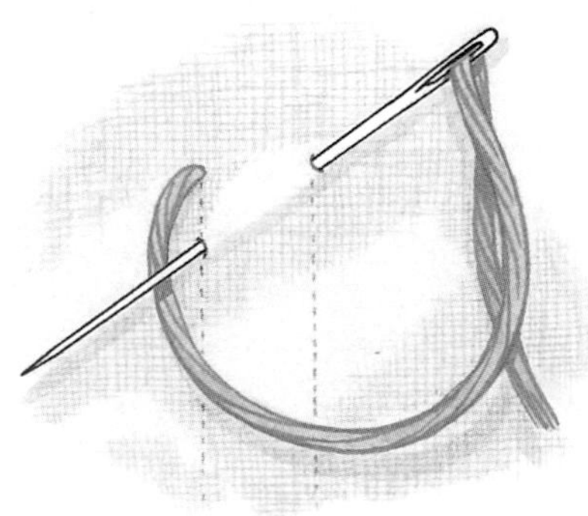

1 Mark two parallel guide lines on your fabric. Start at the top of the left-hand line. Insert the needle at the same height on the right-hand line and bring it through a short distance below along the left-hand line, with the thread under the needle point.

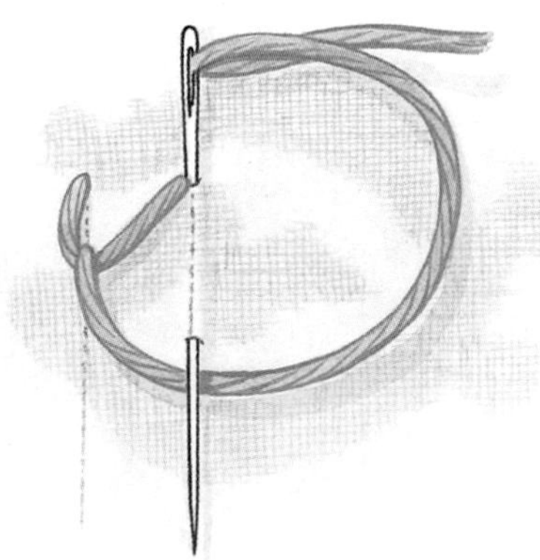

2 Pull the thread through. Insert the needle at the top of the right-hand line and bring it out farther down the line. Pull the thread through to complete the first stitch.

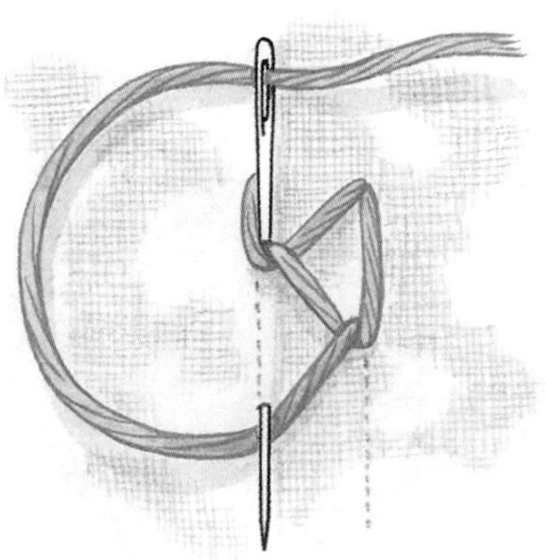

3 Insert the needle again on the left-hand line at the point where it emerged at the beginning of the previous stitch, and bring it out farther down the same line. Pull the thread through to complete the second closed featherstitch. Repeat steps **2** and **3** along the line.

Single featherstitch

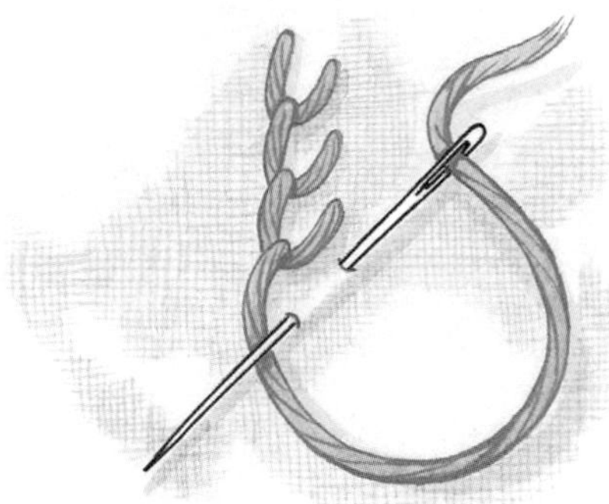

Start at the top of the row. Insert the needle to the right, and bring it out at an angle over the working thread to form a looped stitch. Repeat down the row, arranging the loops at the right-hand side of the line.

Straight featherstitch

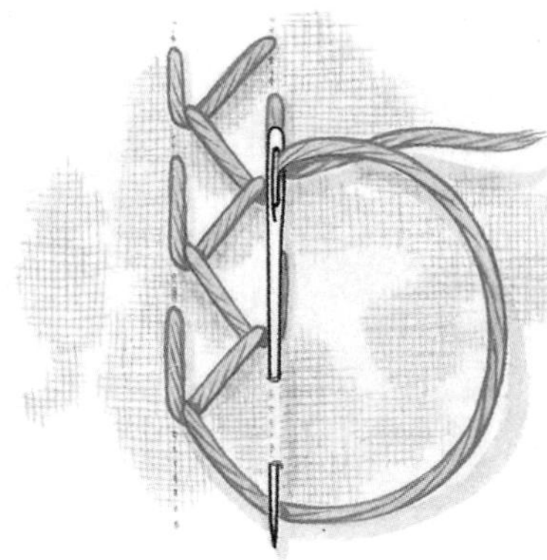

Work in the same way as for closed featherstitch, on page 69, but make each vertical stitch slightly shorter to leave gaps along the outer edges of the row.

WHAT WENT WRONG

Neat stitching
When working single featherstitch make sure the thread is not pulled too tightly during stitching, as this will create puckering. Also, stitch length and spacing are very important for a neat finish.

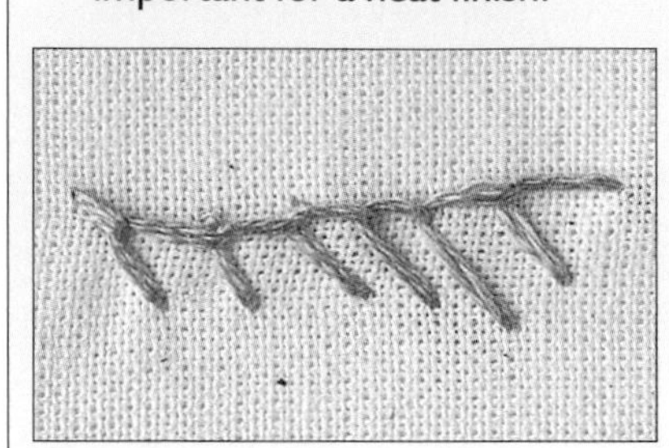

Working Spanish knotted featherstitch

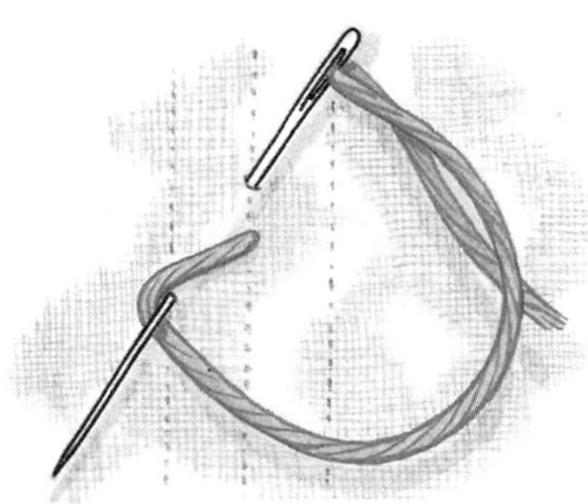

1 Mark three parallel guide lines on your fabric. Start near the top of the center line. Hold the thread down along the left-hand line with your thumb, insert the needle slightly higher up the center line, and bring it out at an angle along the left-hand line. Loop the thread over the needle point and pull it through.

2 Insert the needle between the two previous stitches along the center line and bring it out lower down on the right-hand line. Loop the thread over and under the needle point and pull the needle through to complete the preparatory stage.

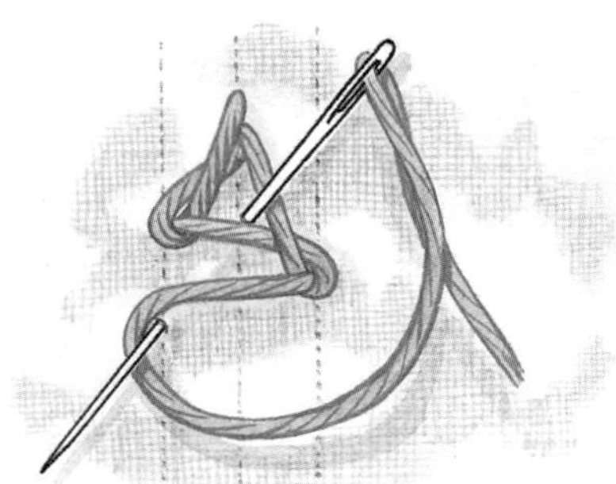

3 Insert the needle just above the point where the line is crossed by the previous stitch, and bring it out lower down on the left-hand line. Loop the thread over and under the needle and pull the needle through.

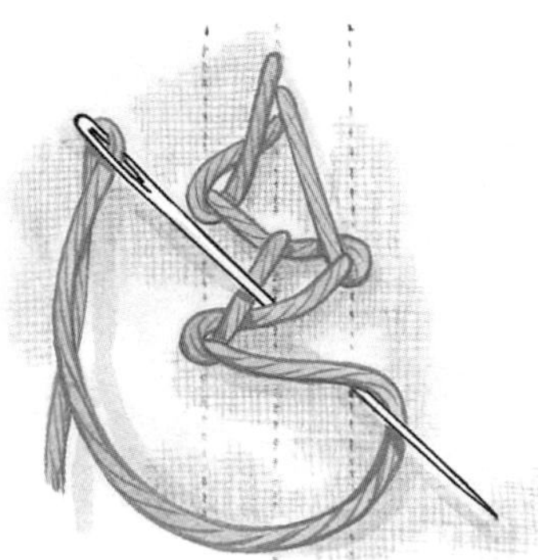

4 Insert the needle lower on the center line and bring it out lower down on the right-hand line. Loop the thread over and under the needle point and pull the needle through to complete the second stitch. Repeat steps **3** and **4** along the row.

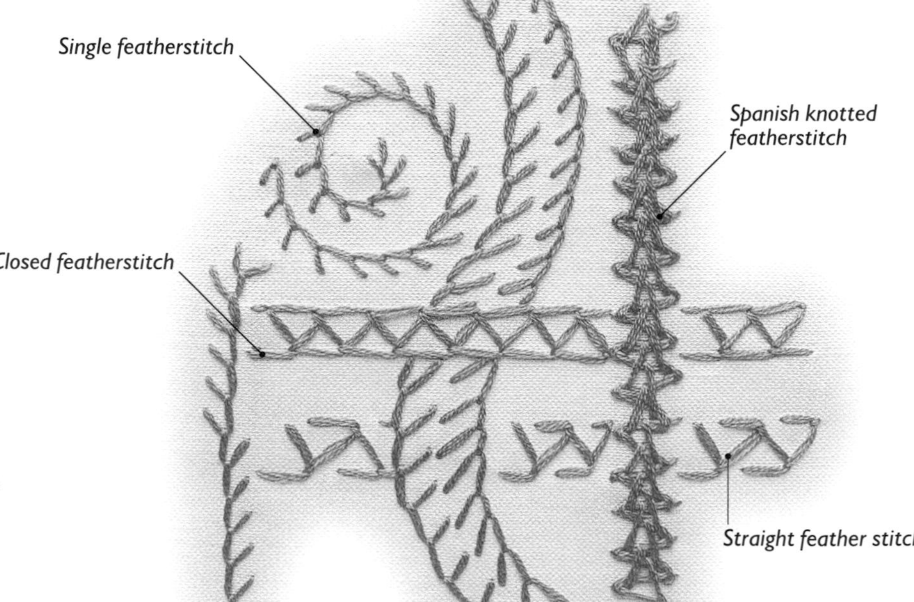

Cretan stitches

Cretan stitch and its variations originated in Crete, where they are still used to decorate traditional garments, as well as household linens. They create pretty borders with an open, plaited finish, and they can be worked more closely to fill small, narrow shapes, such as leaves and flower petals.

To help keep the stitches evenly spaced, use basting or an air or water-soluble marking pen to mark guide lines along the center of the row.

At the beginning of the row, secure the thread with a few running stitches; when you've finished, weave the thread end into the back of the work, then remove the running stitches at the beginning and weave in the thread in the same way.

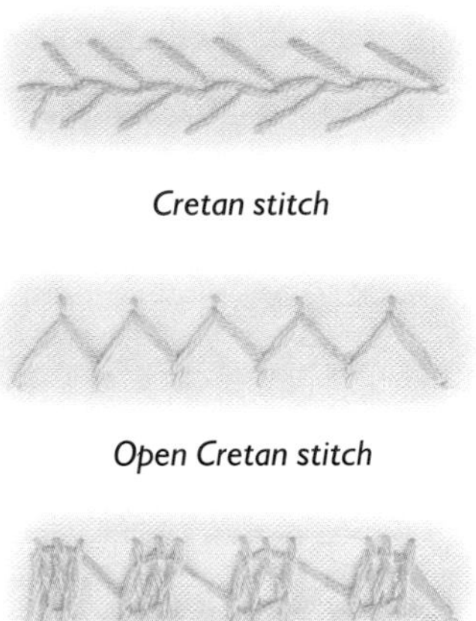

Cretan stitch

Open Cretan stitch

Scottish Cretan stitch

Cretan stitch creates a smooth surface with a central plaited line.

Open Cretan stitch forms a light, open zigzag which can be used for straight lines and gentle curves.

Scottish Cretan stitch is an elaborate version of open Cretan stitch. It is used only in straight lines and is not suitable for filling shapes.

Filling a shape with Cretan stitch

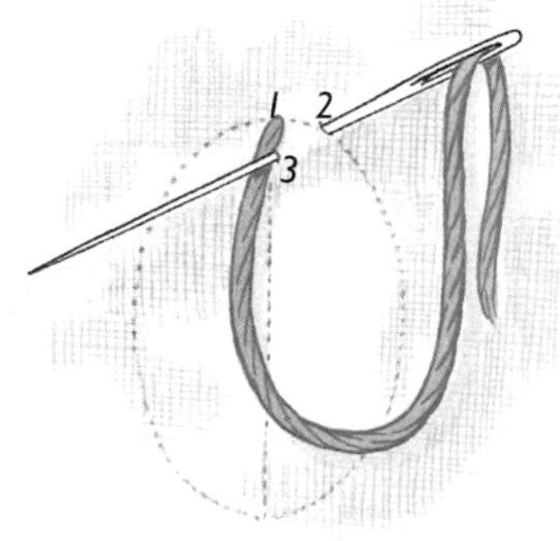

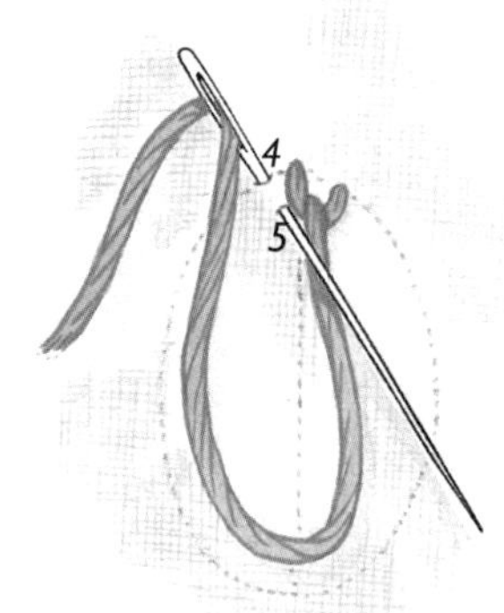

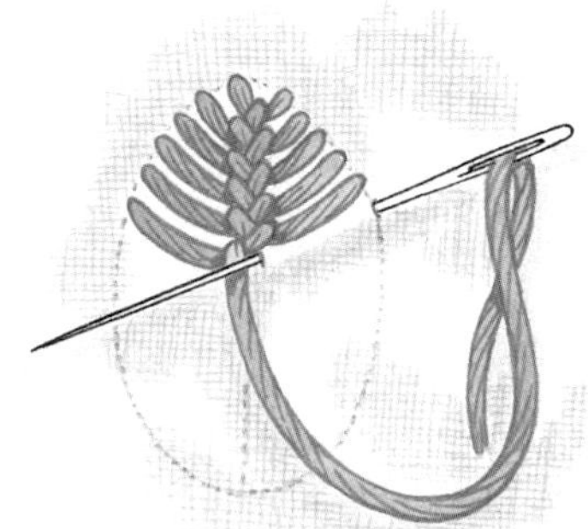

1 Draw a guide line down the center of the shape. Bring the needle out at 1 at the center top. Insert it at 2 at the right-hand edge, and bring it out at 3, just right of the center. Loop the working thread under the point.

2 Pull the thread through. Insert the needle at the left-hand edge of the shape at 4, and bring it out at 5, just left of the center, with the working thread under the point. Pull the thread through to complete the second stitch.

3 Continue in this way, alternating the stitches from side to side of the shape to create the central plait. Space the stitches as shown, or work them more closely together.

Working Cretan stitch in a straight line

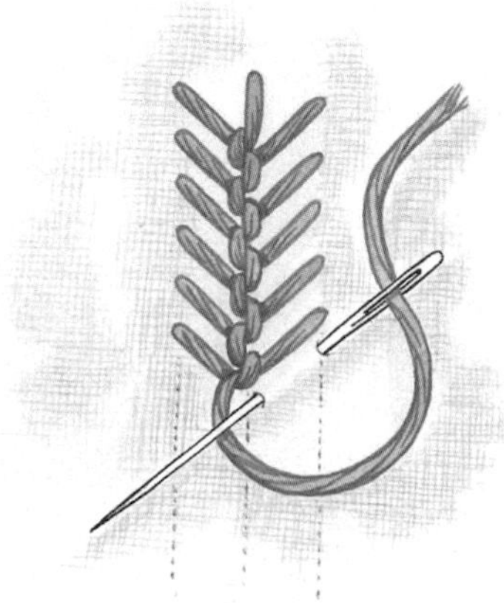

Mark three parallel guide lines on the fabric. Work downward, as shown for Cretan stitch (above), alternating the stitches from side to side as if you were filling a shape. Space the stitches evenly as shown to create an open, plaited effect.

WHAT WENT WRONG

Untidy borders

Cretan stitch borders with irregular edges and unevenly spaced stitches have a rough, unfinished look. Before you start stitching, mark guide lines on the fabric, and mount it in an embroidery frame to keep the thread tension even.

Working open Cretan stitch

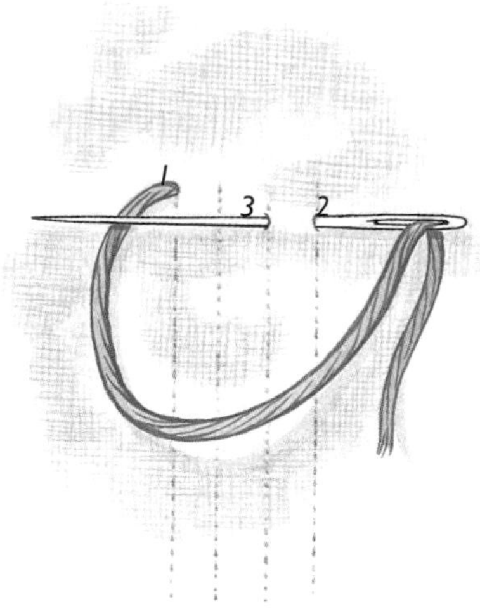

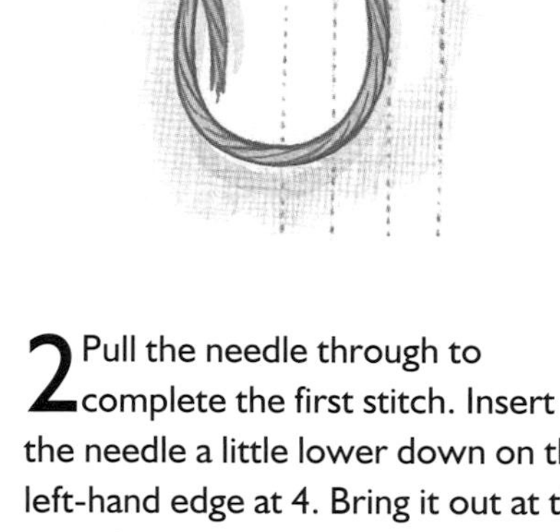

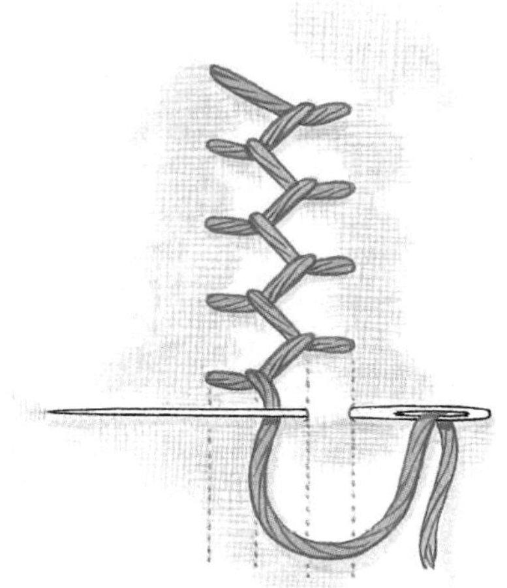

1 Mark the width of the row with two guide lines. Draw two lines between these to divide the space into three. Bring the needle through at the top left at 1. Insert it slightly lower down at the right-hand edge at 2 and bring it out at the same level on the next line at 3. Loop the working thread under the point.

2 Pull the needle through to complete the first stitch. Insert the needle a little lower down on the left-hand edge at 4. Bring it out at the same level on the next guide line at 5 and loop the thread under the point. Pull the thread through.

3 Continue in this way, working alternately from side to side of the shape. Space the stitches evenly down the row to create a light, zigzag line.

Working Scottish Cretan stitch

1 Bring the needle through at the top left and work a block of five closely worked, open Cretan stitches as shown above. Slip the needle upward under the left-hand stitches without picking up any fabric; pull the thread through. Then slip it under the right-hand stitches.

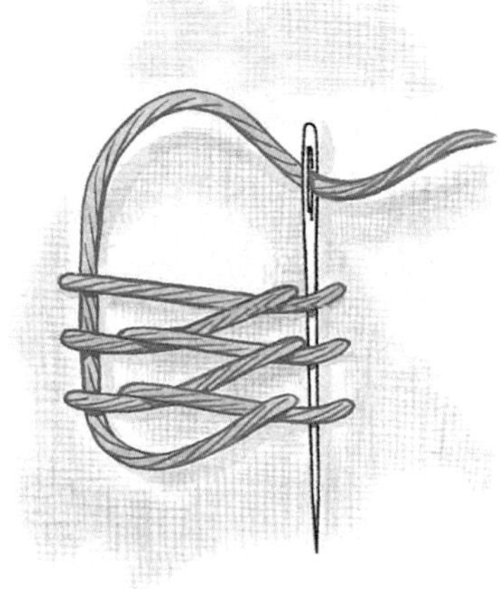

2 Pull the thread through, adjusting the tension so that the threading is quite tight but does not distort the block. Make a second block a short distance below the first. Repeat down the row, spacing the blocks evenly. At the end of the row, take the thread to the wrong side and fasten off.

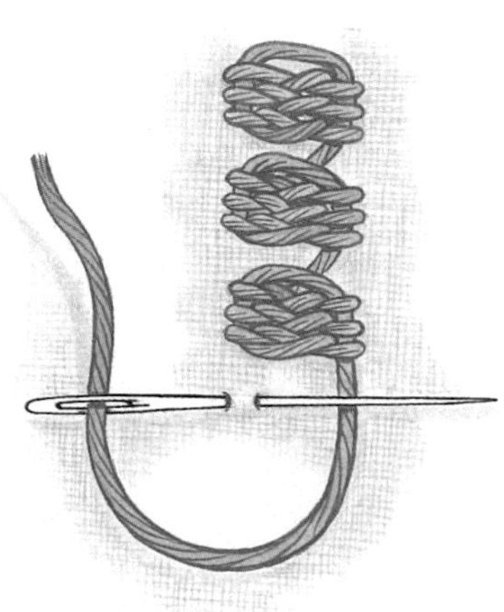

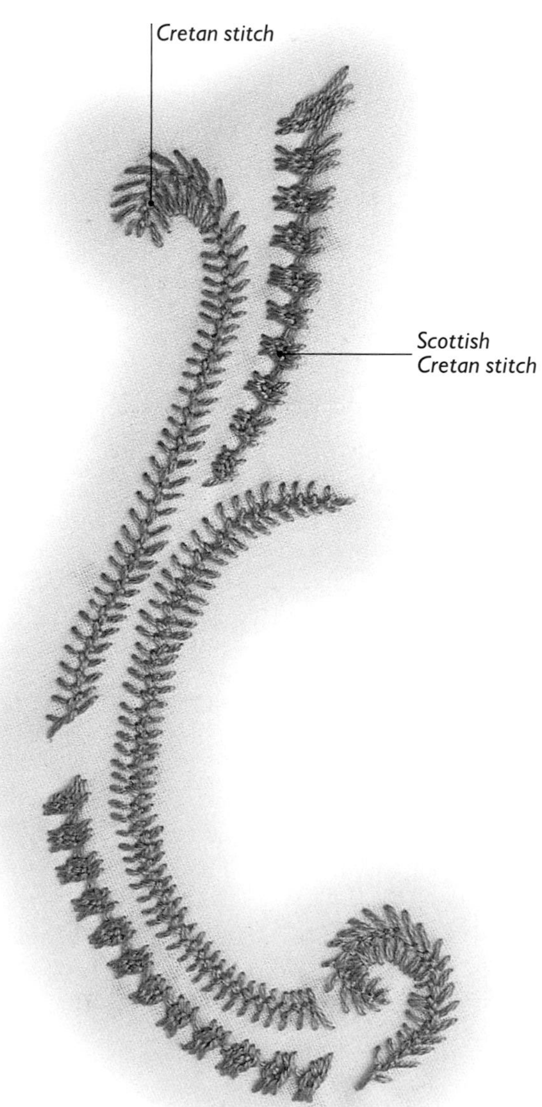

Open filling stitches

The looped stitches in this section are all variations of fly stitch and are used as open filling stitches. All the variations look more complicated to work than they are in practice, and the secret of working any of these stitches correctly is to work them neatly, evenly, and of identical size across the shape.

A great deal of the effectiveness of these filling stitches lies in the interplay between the fabric, the thread, and the stitch structure. A balance of scale is important. For example, stitches worked small-scale in a fine thread would look insignificant on a coarse linen fabric. Choose, instead, a no. 3 pearl cotton or Persian wool, and make the stitches relatively large. To check the fabric-thread-stitch balance, view the work from different distances and in different kinds of lighting. Experiment to find the best combination.

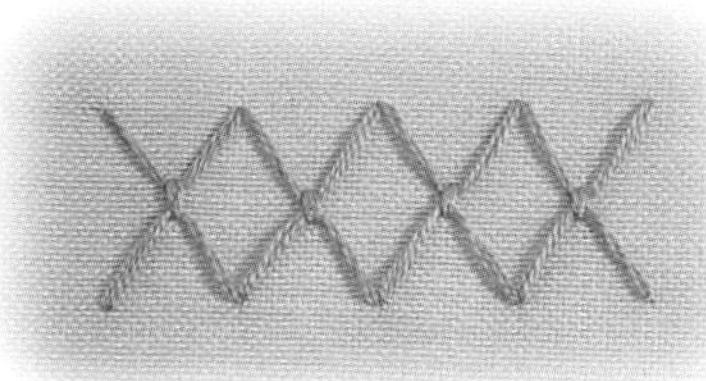

Fly stitch filling

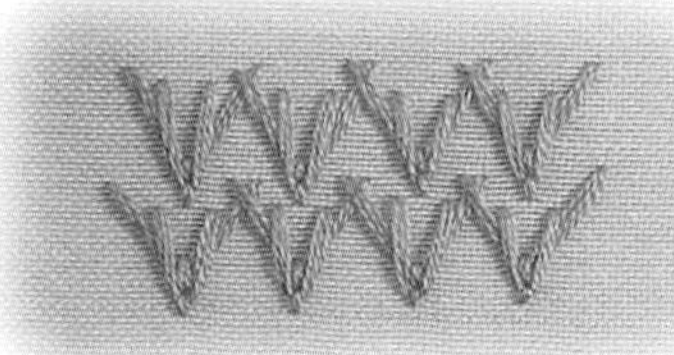

Double fly stitch

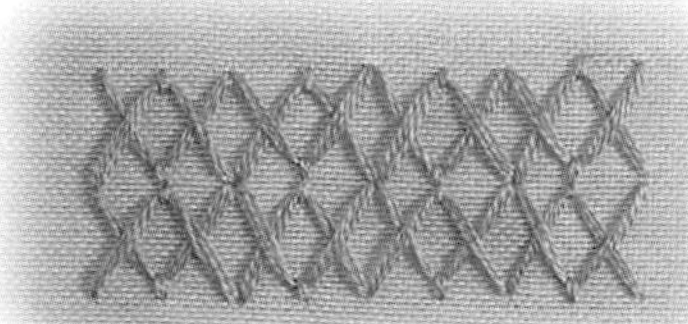

Reversed fly stitch

For details on working fly stitch, refer to page 67.

To start and fasten off any of the stitches featured in this section, refer to page 61.

Fly stitch filling creates a pretty net effect, as the tails of two adjoining rows of stitches share the same holes.

Double fly stitch is a more complex variation in which two different sizes of stitch are arranged in vertical rows with the tips of the larger stitches overlapping. This creates a delicate feathered effect.

Reversed fly stitch creates neat diamond patterns. This stitch has two identically sized stitches placed one on top of the other with one facing downward and the other facing upward. The stitches are repeated in vertical rows to create the filling.

Working fly stitch filling

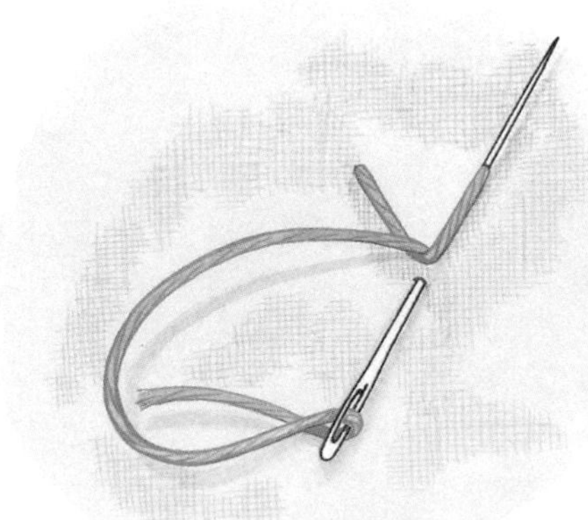

1 Starting at the top left, make a basic fly stitch with a short tail. Bring the needle to the front at the top of the right of the "Y," ready to work the next stitch. Work a row of identical stitches.

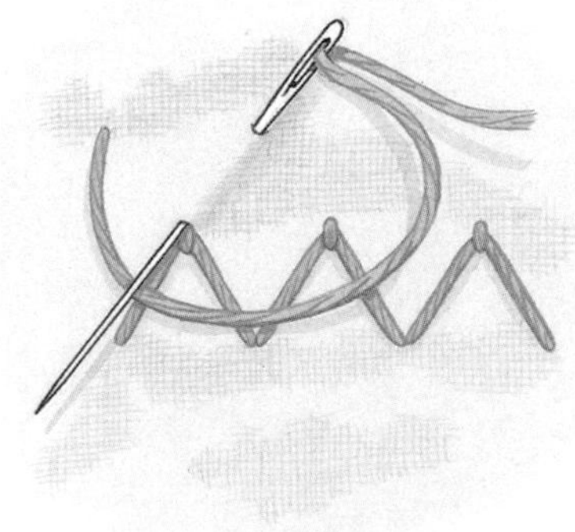

2 Turn the fabric at the end of the row, and work another row of stitches directly above the first, so the points of the stitches on the second row share the same holes as those worked on the first row.

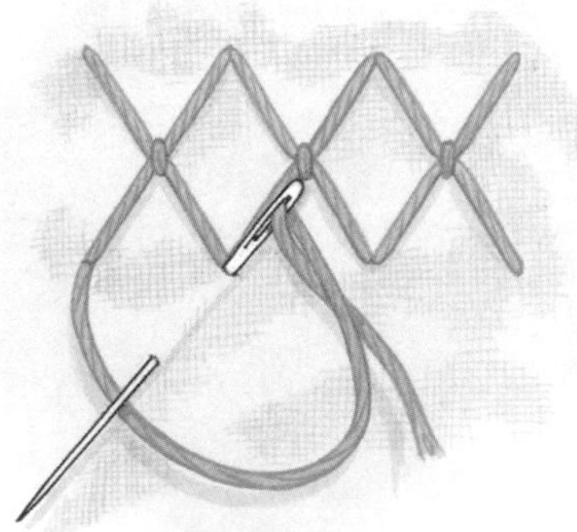

3 Turn the fabric at the end of the row, and work the next row of stitches directly below the previous row. Repeat these two rows until the shape is filled.

Working double fly stitch

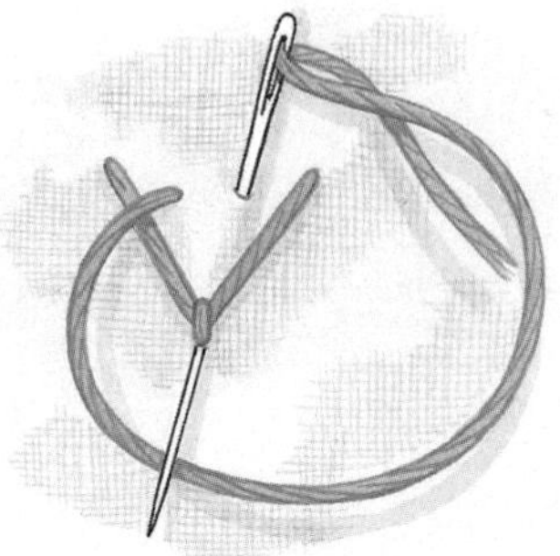

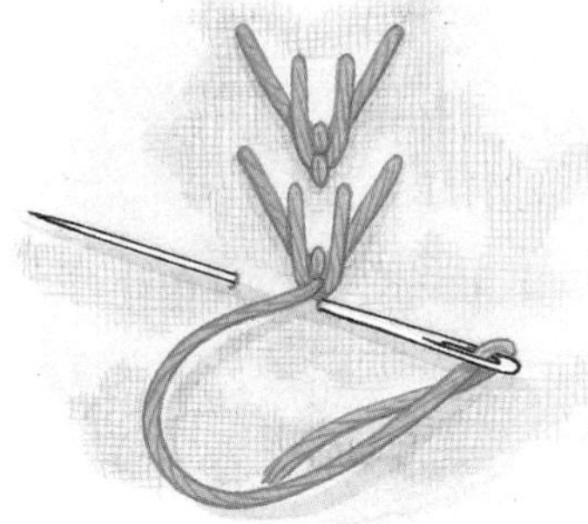

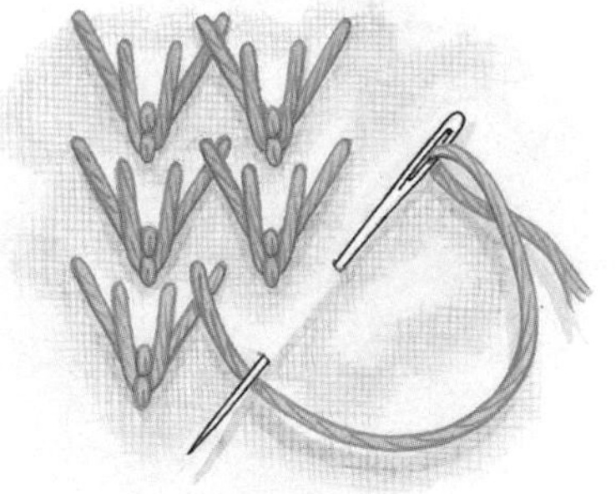

1 Make a fly stitch with a short tail. Bring the needle out inside the left-hand arm of the "Y," as shown. Make a narrow fly stitch over the first stitch so that the top of the tail shares the same hole as the base of the previous tail.

2 Bring the needle out to the left of the top of the tail, and repeat step **1** to make a vertical row of double fly stitches. Fasten the thread at the end of the row and rejoin it at the top, ready to work the next row.

3 Work another row of double fly stitch, but this time arrange the larger fly stitches so the left-hand tips of the "Y" overlap the right-hand tips of the larger fly stitches on the previous row. Work in vertical rows until the shape is filled.

Working reversed fly stitch

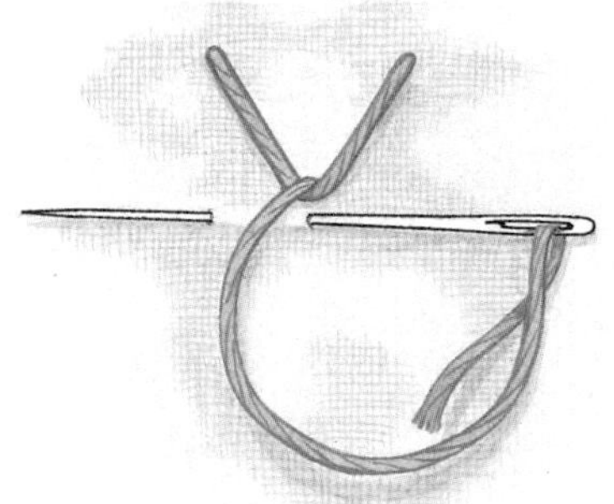

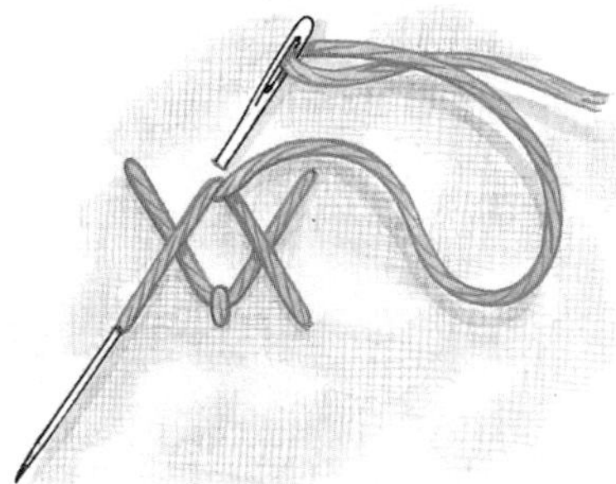

1 Starting at the top left of the fabric, make a basic fly stitch with a short tail. Bring the needle out level with the base of the tail, directly under the left-hand tip of the first stitch.

2 Work a fly stitch upside down over the first stitch to make a rectangular block. Bring the needle out at the bottom left-hand corner of the block, ready to make the next reversed fly stitch.

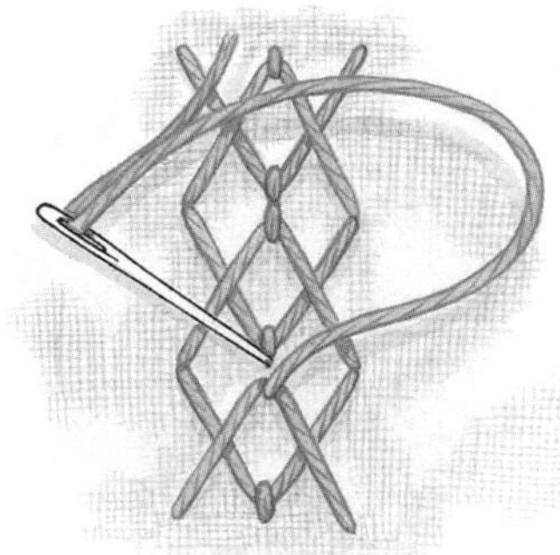

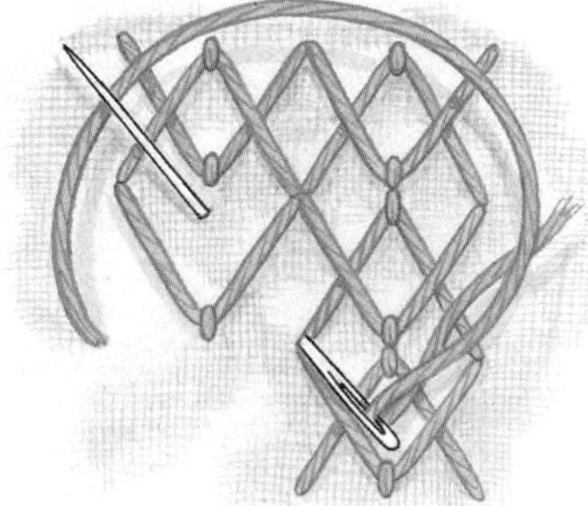

3 Repeat steps **1** and **2** to make a vertical row of reversed fly stitch, arranging the stitches so the tips and tails of the "Y" shapes share common holes in the fabric. Turn the fabric at the end of the row.

4 Work another row of reversed fly stitch, but this time arrange the large fly stitches so the tips of the "Y" shapes share common holes with those on the previous row. Work in vertical rows until the shape is filled.

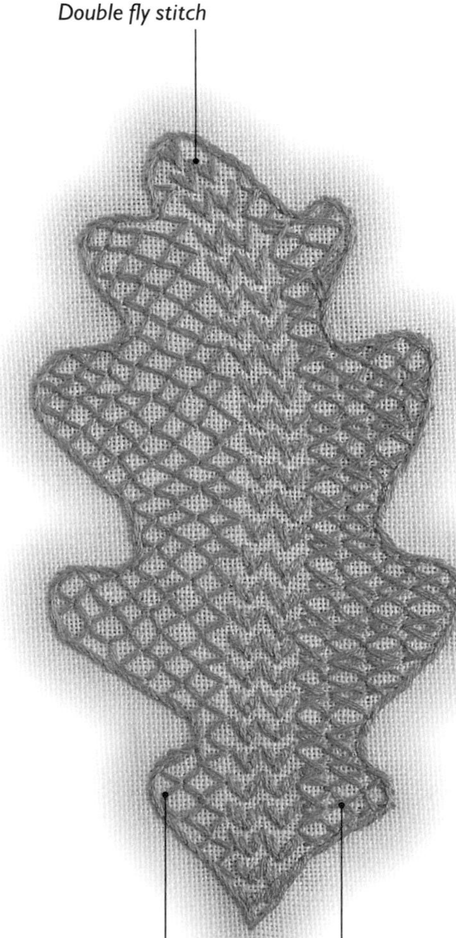

Pile stitches

Pile stitches produce an attractive three-dimensional pile which provides an appealing contrast with smoothly stitched areas of embroidery. They can be worked in a single band to make an interesting border or in multiple rows as a solid filling. They are particularly effective when used to suggest pistils and stamens in floral designs.

You can use any type of thread to work pile stitches, but a soft, wool thread, such as Persian, tapestry, or crewel yarn, will give the thickest, most luxuriant pile. Choose a closely woven, even- or non-evenweave, to work on.

When working straight rows, mark guide lines on your fabric with an air-erasable marking pen. Slip a pencil or knitting needle through the loops as you work them to make sure they are of identical size.

After working the area in your chosen stitch, carefully cut the loops with a small pair of sharp scissors to form the pile. As an alternative, leave the loops intact for a smoother effect.

Turkey stitch produces closely worked rows of firm, plush pile.

Velvet stitch creates more loosely tufted thread layers topped with cross stitch.

Turkey work, cut

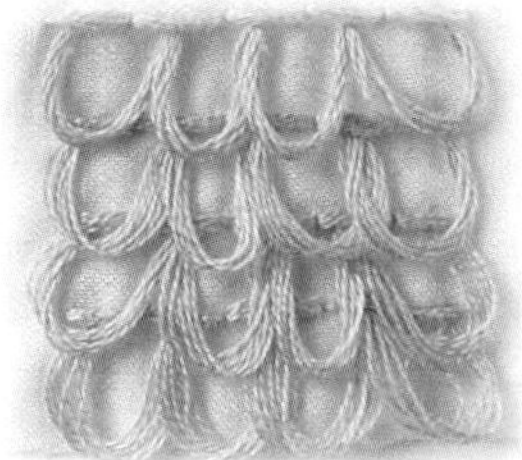

Turkey work, uncut

Velvet stitch, cut

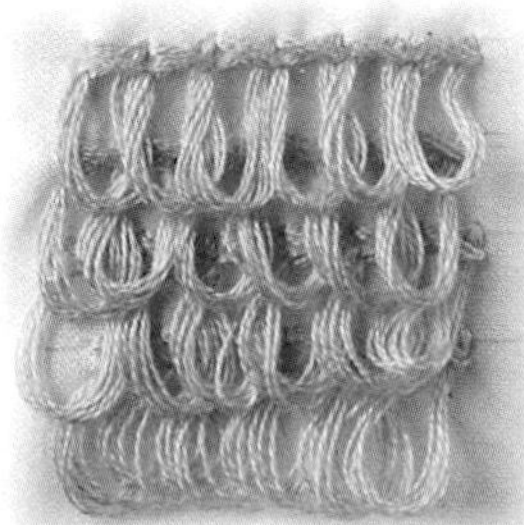

Velvet stitch, uncut

Turkey work

1 Take the needle to the back at the bottom left of the shape to be filled (1), and bring it out to the left at 2, leaving a ¾ in. (2 cm) tail of thread at the front. With the working thread above the needle, make a horizontal stitch to the right at 3. Bring the needle to the front again at 1 and pull the thread through.

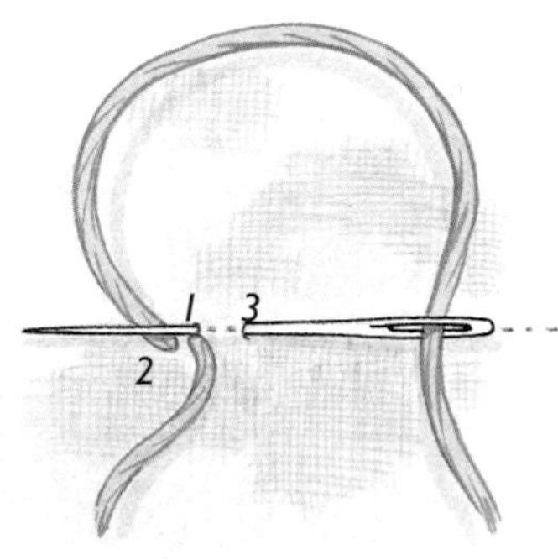

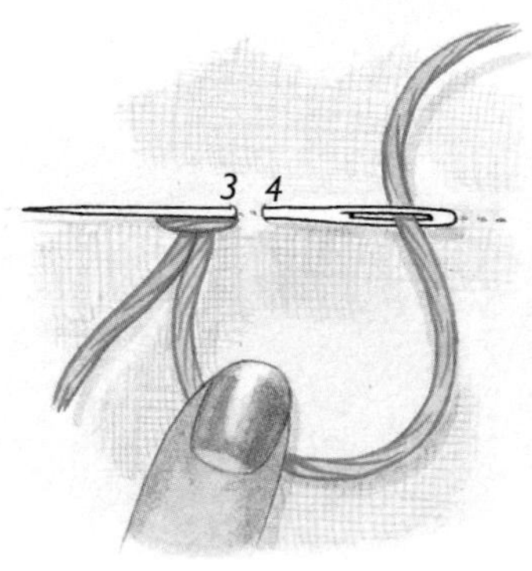

2 With the working thread below the needle, make a short horizontal stitch from 4 to 3. Pull the needle through gently, holding down the working thread so that it forms a small loop below the line of stitching.

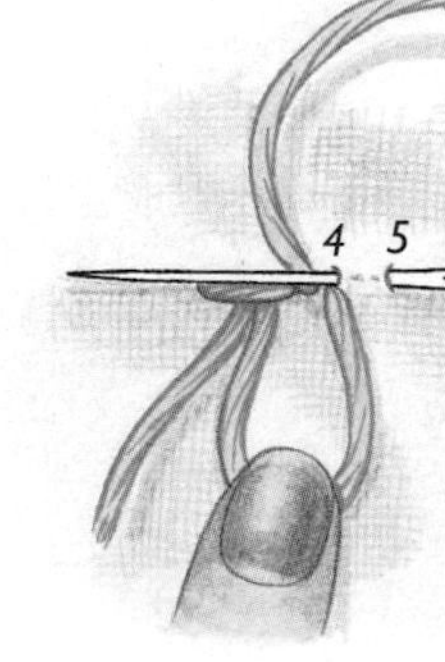

3 With the working thread above the needle, make another short stitch from 5 to 4. Pull the needle through to complete the stitch.

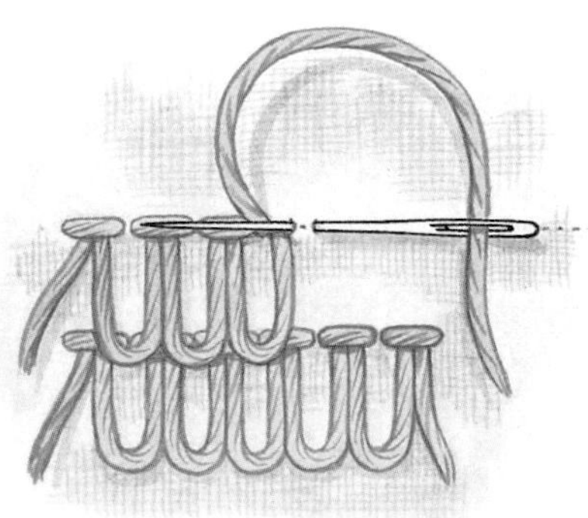

4 Repeat steps **2** and **3**. At the end of the row, take the thread to the back and fasten it off. Work the next row above the first row, following steps **1–3**. When the shape is filled, use a small pair of scissors to cut the loops, if desired.

Working velvet stitch

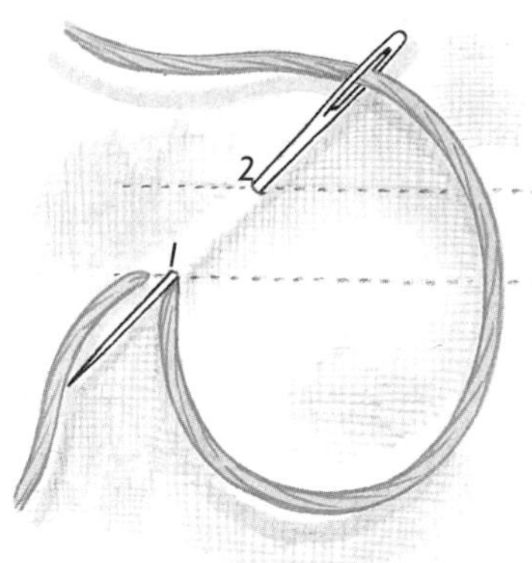

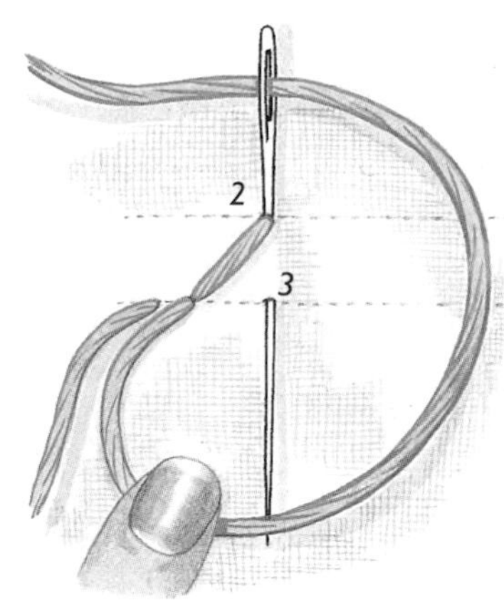

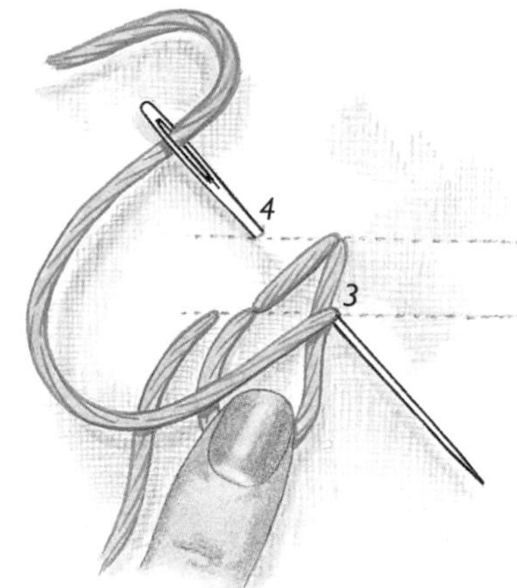

1 Take the needle to the back at the bottom left of the fabric, close to the starting point, leaving a 2 in. (5 cm) tail. Bring the needle to the front at 1 and make a short diagonal stitch to 2. Bring the needle back to the front at 1.

2 Holding the working thread down in a small loop, make a short vertical stitch from 2 to 3 and pull the thread through, keeping the loop above the needle.

3 Make a diagonal stitch from 3 to 4, taking the thread over the first diagonal and the loop. Bring the needle out at 3 again to complete the cross and to anchor the loop.

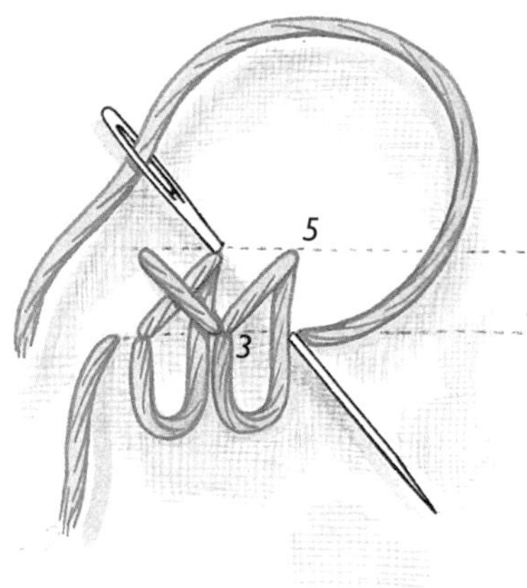

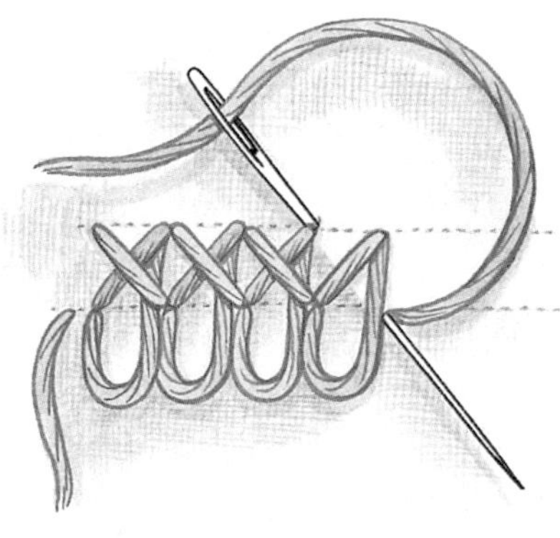

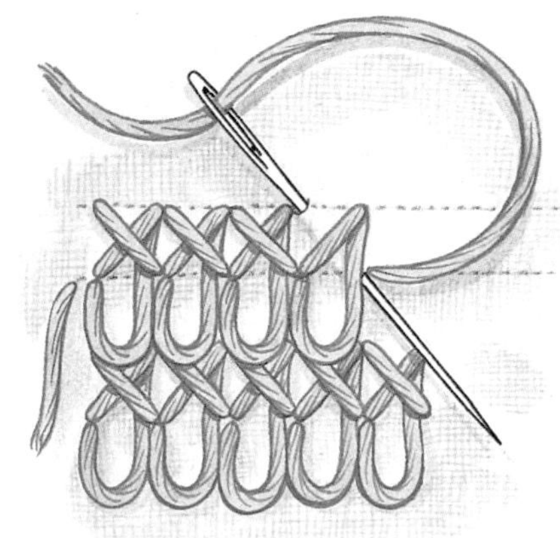

4 To work the next stitch, make a diagonal stitch from 3 to 5 and bring the needle out to the front again at 3. Repeat steps **2–4**, making sure that the second loop is the same length as the first one.

5 Continue in this way. At the end of the row, take the thread through to the wrong side and fasten it off. Return to the start of the row, take the thread tail to the back and darn it under several stitches.

6 Work the next and subsequent rows above the first, following steps **1–5**. When the shape is filled, cut the loops if desired.

WHAT WENT WRONG

Messy pile
Pile worked on loosely woven fabric may unravel as individual stitches work loose. To prevent this, work pile stitches on closely woven fabric so they are held securely in place. Alternatively, spread a thin layer of craft glue on the wrong side of the stitching and allow it to dry before cutting the loops.

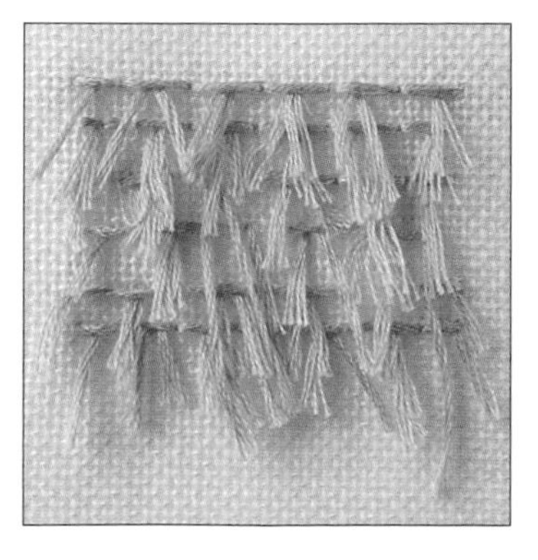

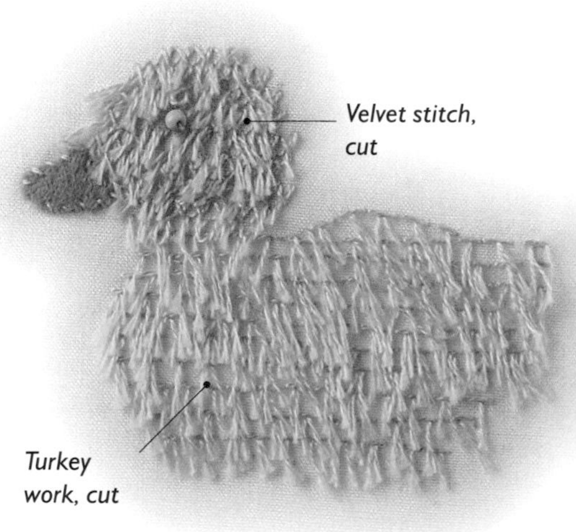

Isolated knots

French, Chinese, and bullion knots are isolated knotted stitches which are used to add texture and details or to fill in small areas. They can be a little tricky to master, so it's worth practicing them to achieve the perfect knot.

The size of the individual stitches and the effect produced can be varied by working with different threads. For example, pearl cotton or Persian yarn gives a more raised effect than embroidery floss.

French knots are small, circular knotted stitches which stand out from the fabric. They are used alone or in small groups to highlight a particular feature of a design, such as an eye or a flower center, often using a thicker thread than is used for the surrounding embroidery. French knots can also be lightly scattered over a shape to add color and texture, or worked close together to fill a shape with dense, knotted stitching.

Chinese knots are used in the same way as French knots, but are slightly flatter and easier to work.

Bullion knots form knotted coils of thread on the surface of the fabric and look somewhat like tiny caterpillars. Use them to accentuate parts of a design, or work several together to form a raised rose shape. They can be used as a light or heavy filling. When working bullion knots, choose a chenille needle, which is relatively thick and makes a correspondingly plump coil of thread.

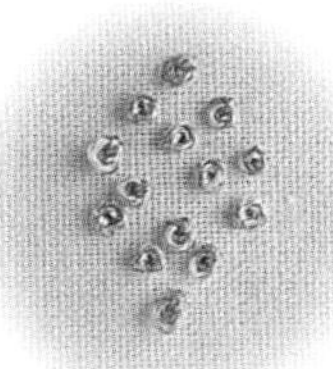

French knots

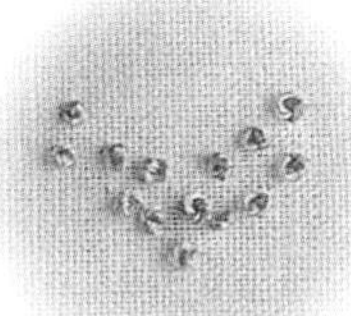

Chinese knots

Bullion knots

Starting and fastening off knotted stitches

When you are working individual knots or widely spaced knots, fasten off the thread after each knot. When working groups of closely spaced knots, you can carry the thread across the back of the fabric between knots, instead of fastening it off after every stitch.

To start, work two or three tiny stitches at the back of the fabric, positioning them where they will be covered by the embroidery stitch. To finish, fasten off the thread in the same way, directly beneath the knot. Trim the thread close to the fabric.

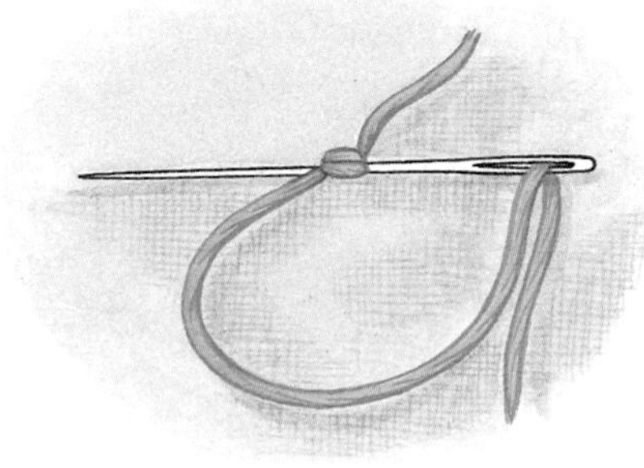

Working a French knot

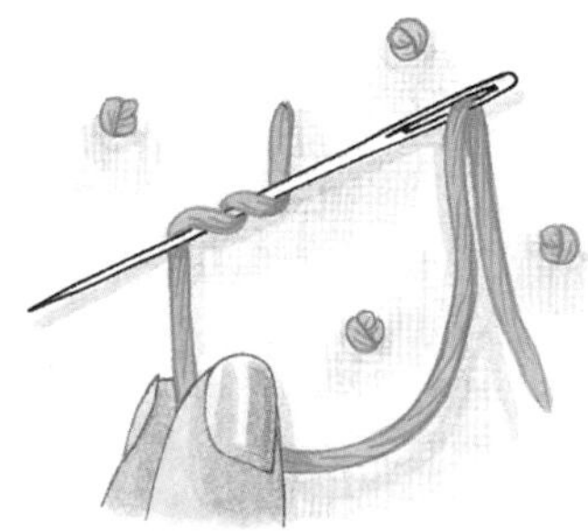

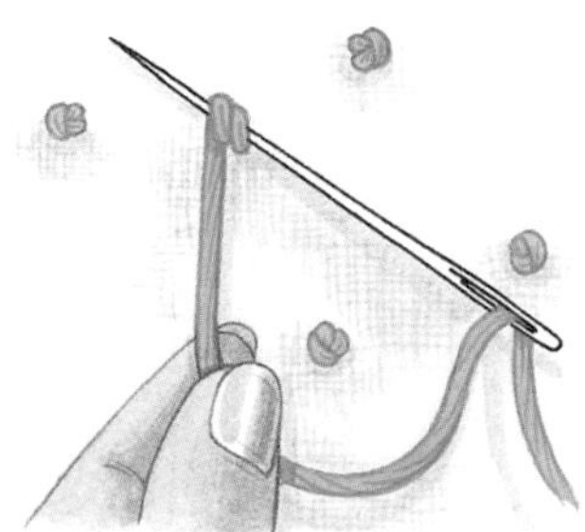

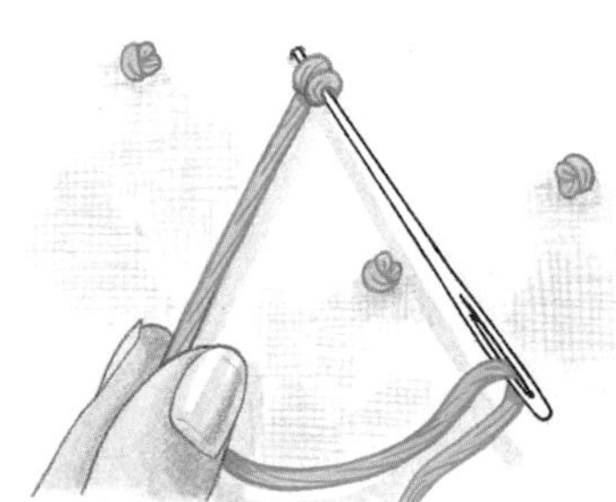

1 Bring the thread through to the front of the fabric. Holding the thread taut with one hand, wrap it twice around the needle.

2 Pull the thread gently to tighten the twists around the needle. Don't overtighten the twists, or you will find it difficult to slide the needle through in the next step.

3 Still holding the thread taut with one hand, insert the needle into the fabric close to the point where it originally emerged. Pull the needle and thread through to the back, leaving a loose knot at the front.

Working a Chinese knot

Bring the thread through to the front. Make a loose loop of thread around the needle, and insert the point into the fabric close to where it emerged. Tighten the thread, hold the loop down on the fabric with one thumb, and pull the needle through to complete the knot.

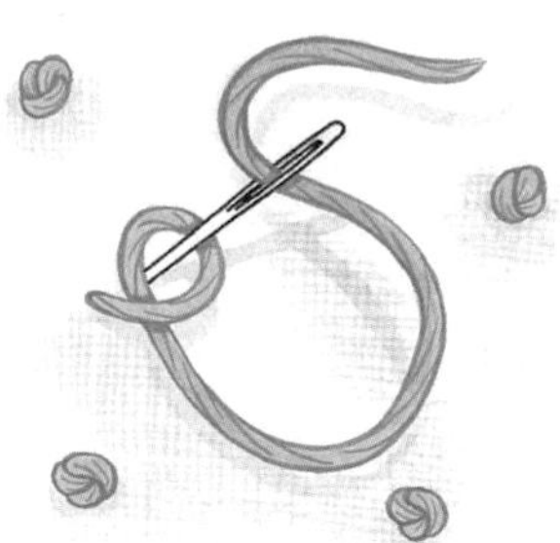

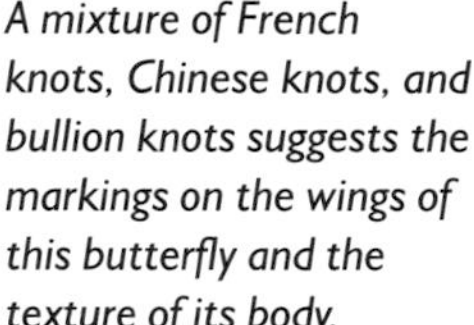

A mixture of French knots, Chinese knots, and bullion knots suggests the markings on the wings of this butterfly and the texture of its body.

Messy bullion knots

Untidy bullion knots are often the result of twisting the working thread too tightly around the needle; overtightening the thread makes it difficult to pull the needle through evenly without distorting the twists. You may need to practice this stage several times before you get the best tension for your thread.

Working a bullion knot

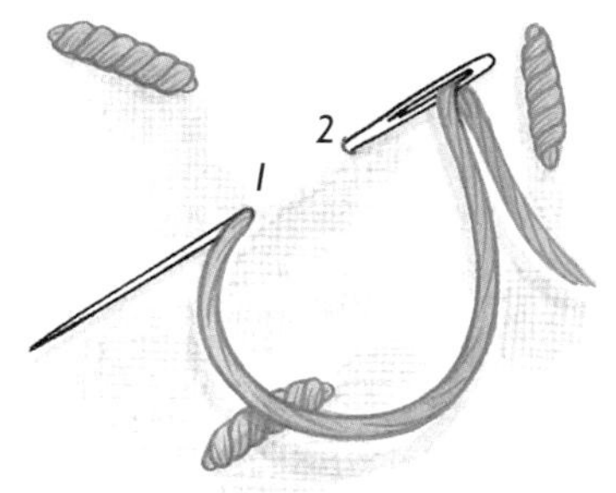

1 Bring the needle through to the front (1). Insert the point of the needle a short way back (2), and bring the needle to the front again where it originally emerged (1). Don't pull the thread through.

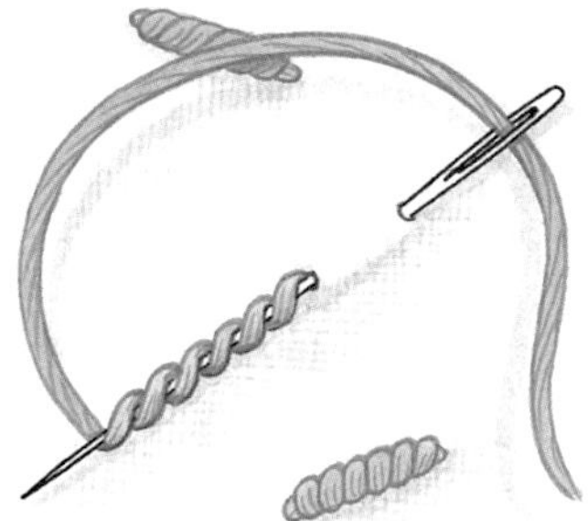

2 Holding the working thread taut with one hand, wrap it around the needle point five to seven times to make a coil of twists.

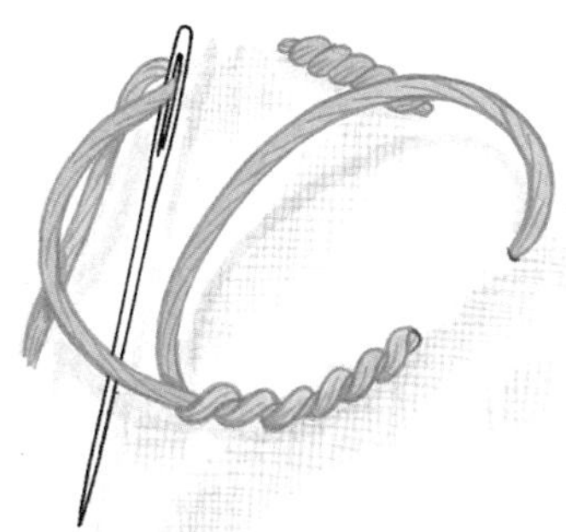

3 Carefully pull the needle through both the fabric and the twists on the needle, taking care not to distort the twists. This stage may take some practice to perfect.

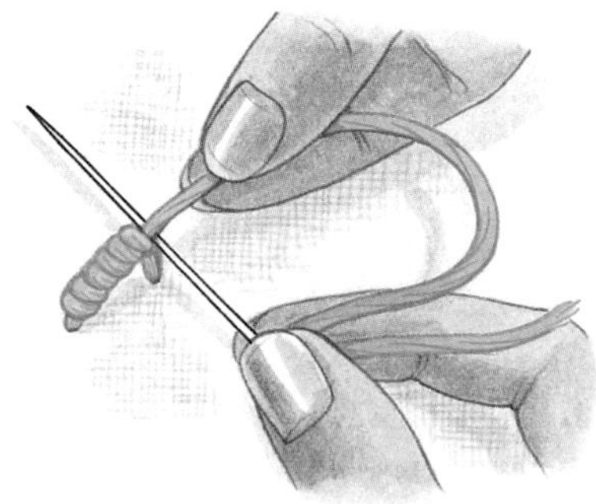

4 Gently pull the thread back so that the coil of twists lies flat on the fabric. Then tighten the thread and use the point of the needle to pack the twists together evenly.

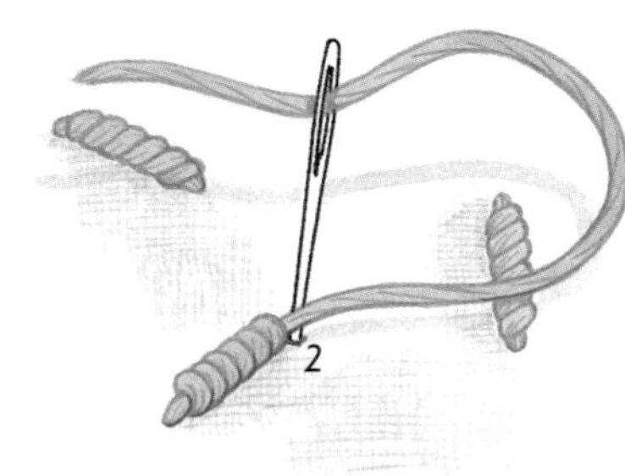

5 To finish the knot, take the needle and thread back through the fabric at position 2.

The stitches featured here can be worked individually or clustered in small groups to highlight specific sections of a design, such as the center of a flower. They can also be lightly scattered over a shape to add color and texture, or worked close together to fill a shape with dense, highly textured stitching. They are particularly effective when worked in a thick thread, such as pearl cotton, and combine well with a knotted outline stitch such as coral stitch (see page 81). To start and finish any of the stitches featured here, refer to page 77.

Knot stitch is an upright cross, with a small knot at the intersection. For details on cross stitch, see page 45.

Cross and twist stitch consists of a cross with an upright leg and a small twisted knot at the center.

Square bosses are cross stitches with overstitched arms for added interest and texture. The name derives from the raised ornaments found at the intersection of ribs in Gothic architecture.

Danish knots are small, highly textured knots. They are easy to work on both evenweave and non-evenweave fabrics.

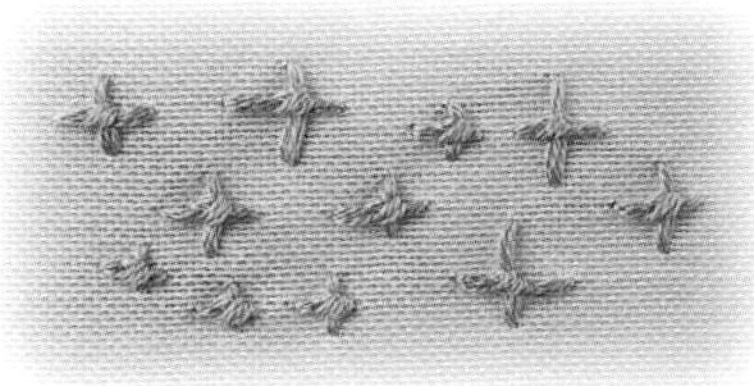

Knot stitch

Cross and twist stitch

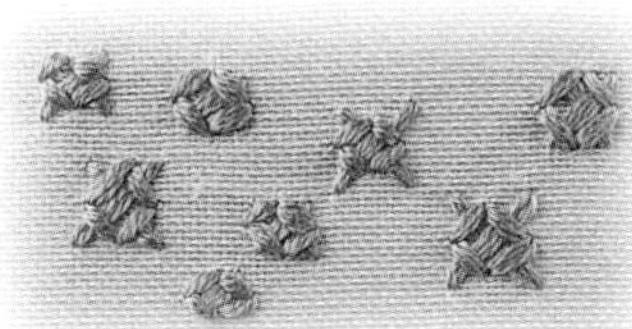

Square bosses

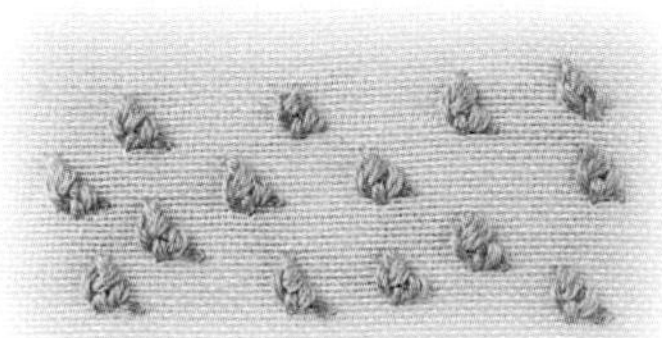

Danish knots

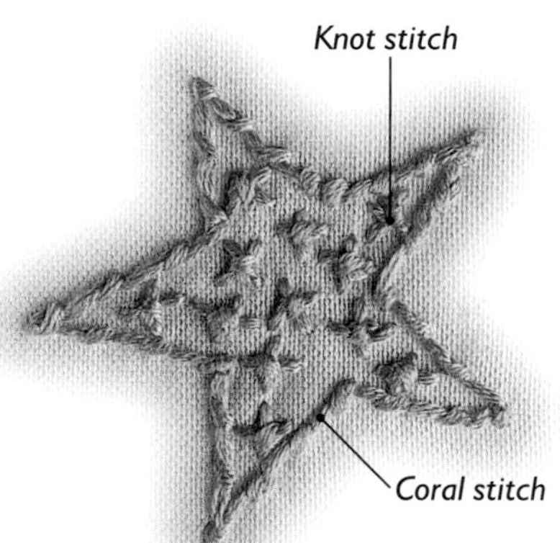

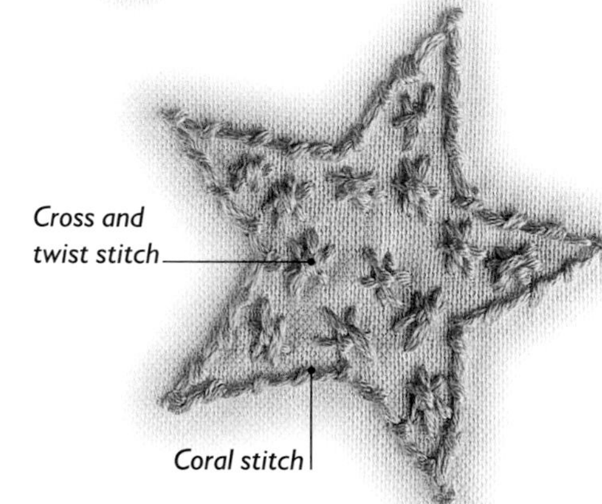

Working knot stitch

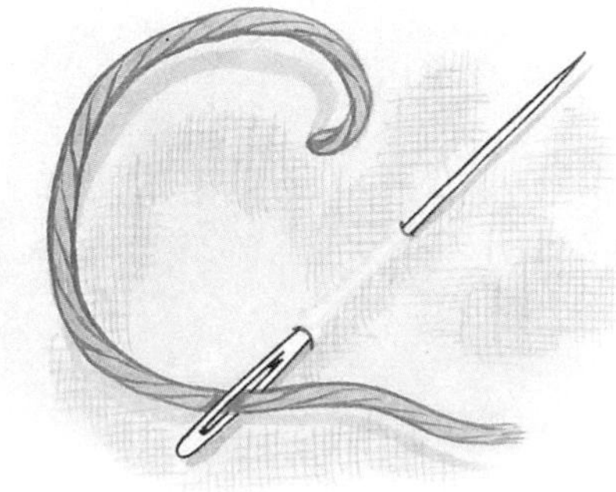

1 Bring the needle to the front and make a vertical stitch downward. Bring the needle through to the right of the vertical stitch, as if you were going to make an upright cross stitch.

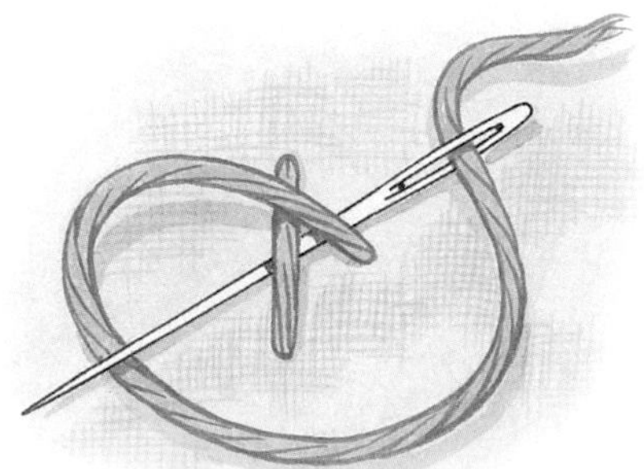

2 Take the working thread across the vertical stitch. Slip the needle under the working thread and the vertical stitch, without picking up the fabric. Then loop the working thread under the needle point.

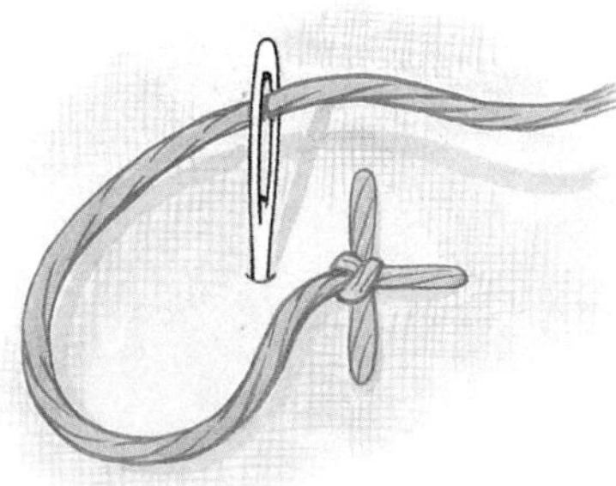

3 Carefully tighten the working thread to make a knot. Insert the needle into the fabric at the left of the knot to complete the cross.

Working cross and twist stitch

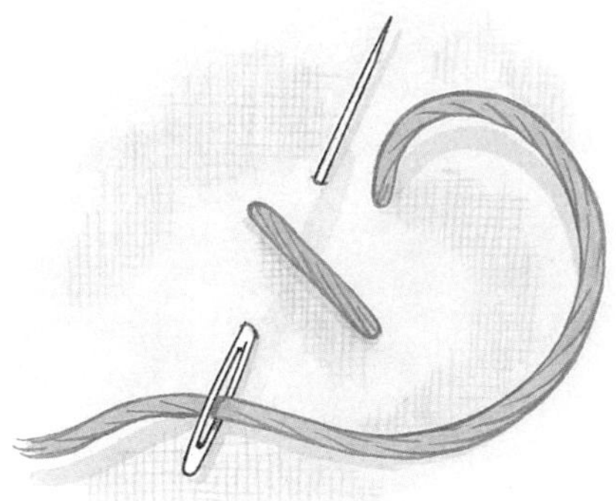

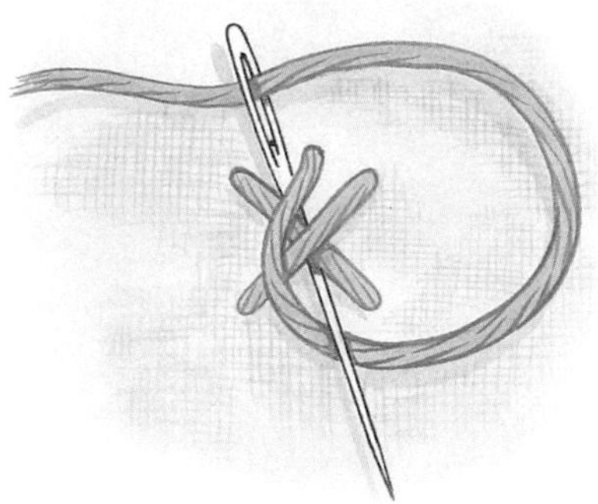

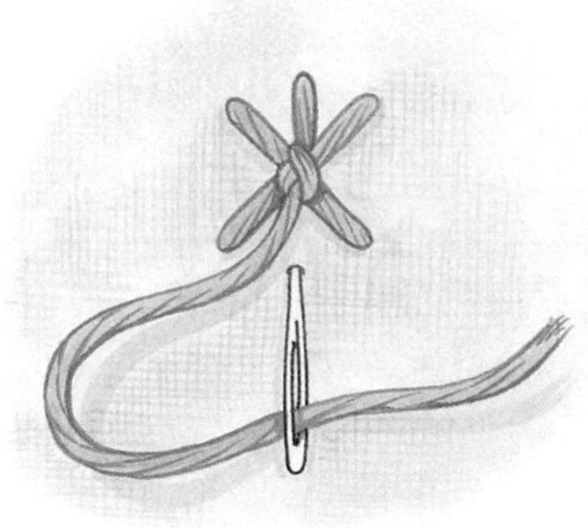

1 Bring the needle to the front and work an ordinary cross stitch. Bring the needle to the front a little way above the center top of the cross.

2 Take the needle under the working thread and the cross stitch, without picking up any fabric. Then loop the working thread under the needle point.

3 Tighten the working thread to make a twisted knot. Insert the needle just below the center bottom of the cross to complete the stitch.

Working a square boss

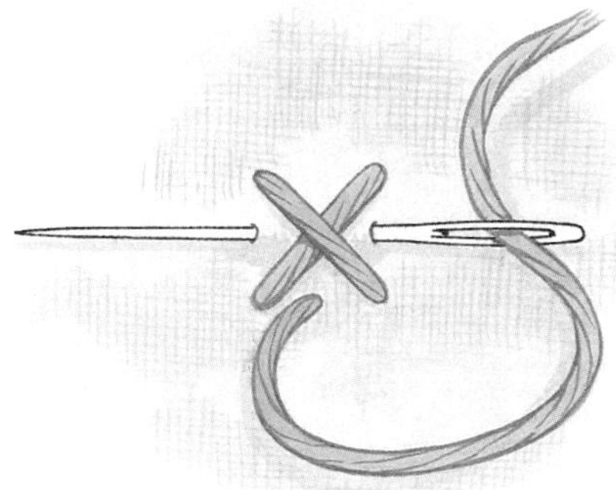

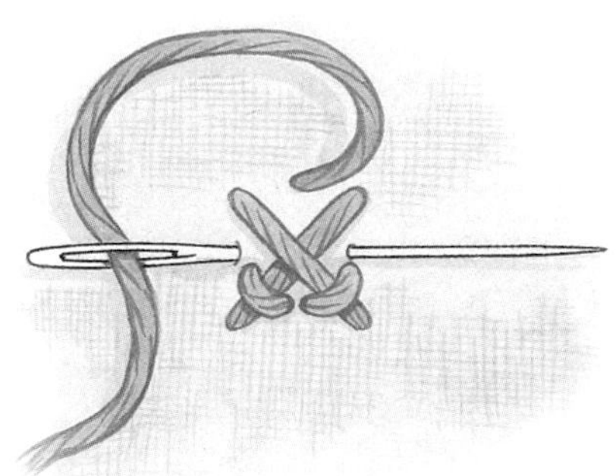

1 Bring the needle to the front and work an ordinary cross stitch. Bring the needle through at the center bottom of the cross. Insert it at the center right to work a stitch over the bottom right arm of the cross. Bring the needle and thread through at the center left of the cross.

2 Make a stitch over the left arm of the cross, and bring the needle to the front at the center top. Pull the thread through and make a stitch over the top left arm. Bring the needle to the front at the center right.

3 Pull the thread through and make a stitch over the top right arm of the cross, taking the needle and thread to the back at the center top.

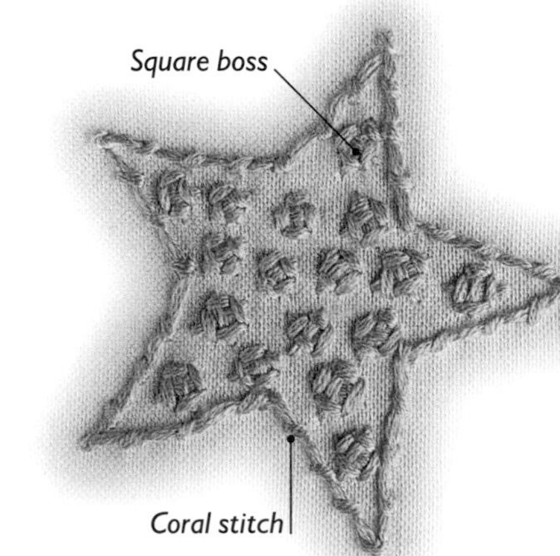

Working a Danish knot

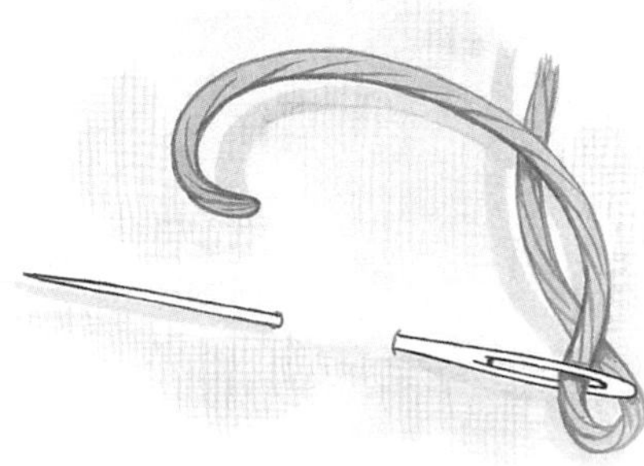

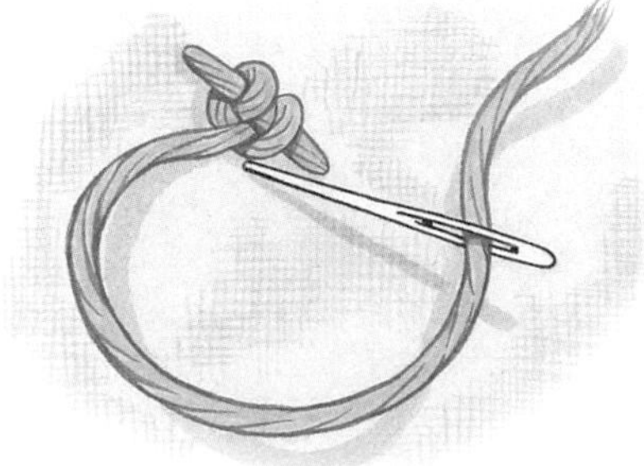

1 Bring the needle to the front of the fabric and make a short, diagonal stitch slanting from top left to bottom right. Bring the needle through below the center of the diagonal stitch.

2 Loop the working thread twice over the diagonal stitch without picking up any fabric. Tighten the loops. Take the needle to the back, close to where it last emerged.

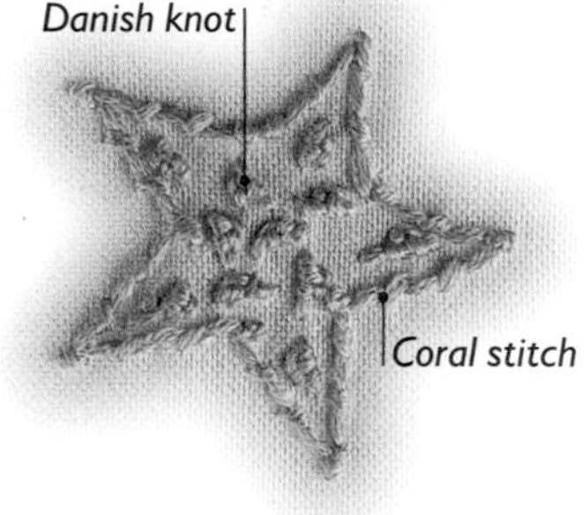

Outline stitches

The knotted outline stitches shown here are used mainly to create textured outlines and borders, but they can also be worked in closely arranged, straight or curving rows to make pretty fillings. They can be used to fill a circle, for example, by working outward from the center in a tight spiral.

You can achieve a variety of effects with different threads. Pearl cotton, for example, makes the knots stand out more boldly than embroidery floss. For a neat, even finish, mark guide lines on the fabric with an air-erasable marking pen.

Coral stitch makes a pretty outline punctuated with tiny knots. Use it to follow intricate curves and details and to stitch branches and twiggy areas of naturalistic designs.

Double knot stitch makes a decorative line with plump knots which stand out from the fabric like a row of beads.

Portuguese knot stitch makes a heavy, twisted line which resembles a length of knotted rope.

Scroll stitch makes a slightly stepped, knotted line, perfect for ornate designs with lots of twists and turns.

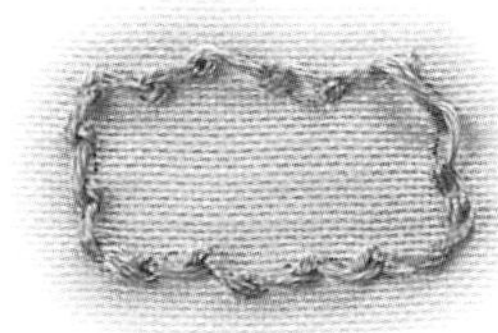

Coral stitch

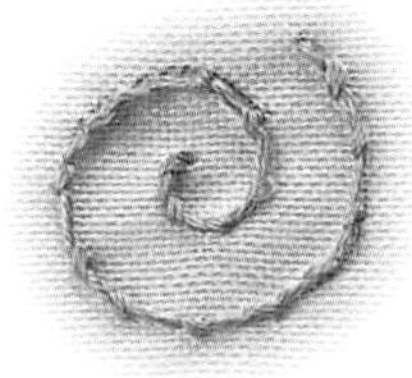

Double knot stitch

Portuguese knot stitch

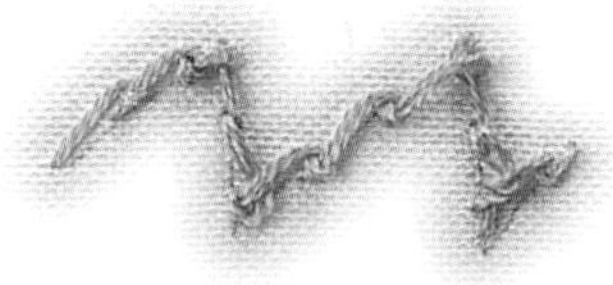

Scroll stitch

Starting and fastening off

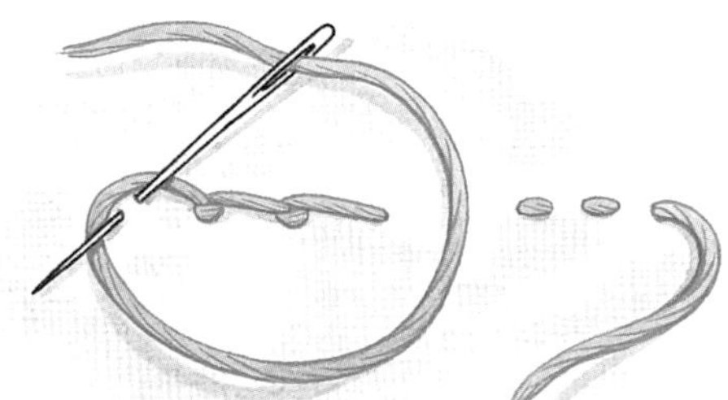

1 Leave a 2–4 in. (5–10 cm) tail of thread at the front, close to your starting point. Work two or three running stitches outside the row to anchor the thread temporarily. Work the knotted stitches, then take the needle to the back.

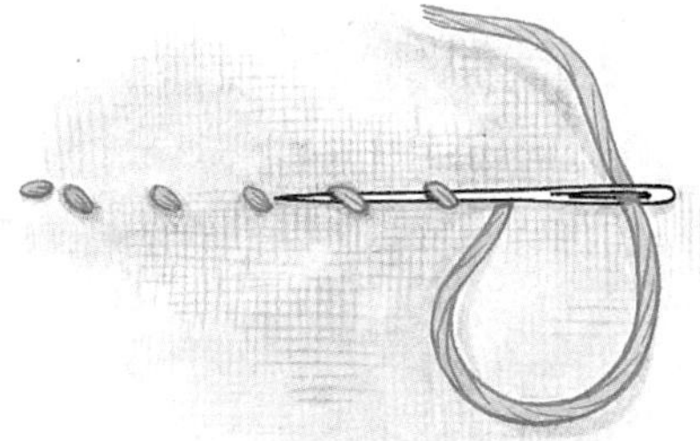

2 Darn the thread end under the last few stitches you have worked. Return to the start of the row, remove the running stitches, and pull the thread tail through to the back. Darn the end under the first few stitches.

Working coral stitch

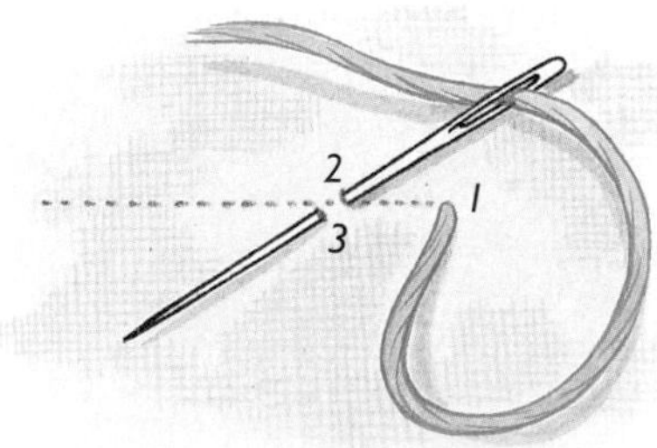

1 Work from right to left. Bring the needle to the front at the right-hand end of your guide line at 1. Make a tiny diagonal stitch from 2 to 3, picking up just a tiny section of fabric. Do not pull the needle through.

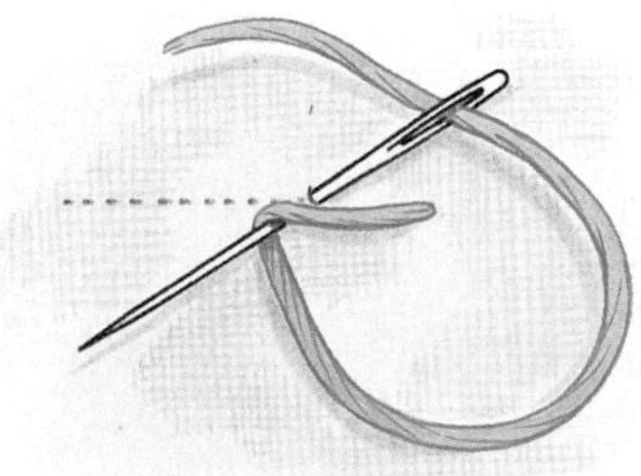

2 Loop the working thread over and under the needle. Gently pull the thread through to secure the stitch and form a small knot.

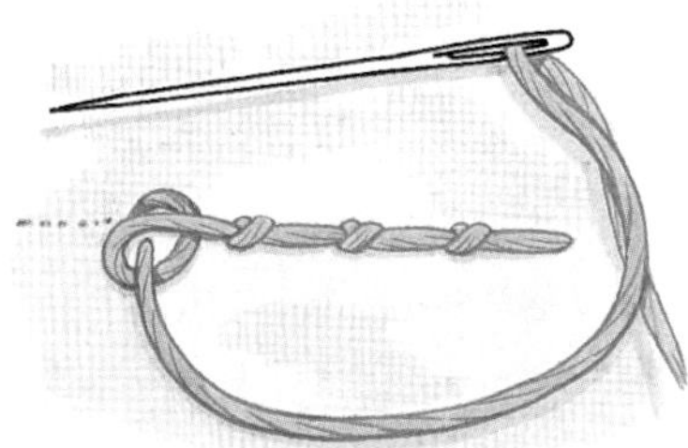

3 Continue in this way along the line, making tiny diagonal stitches and looping the thread around the needle. Space the knots evenly or at random.

Working double knot stitch

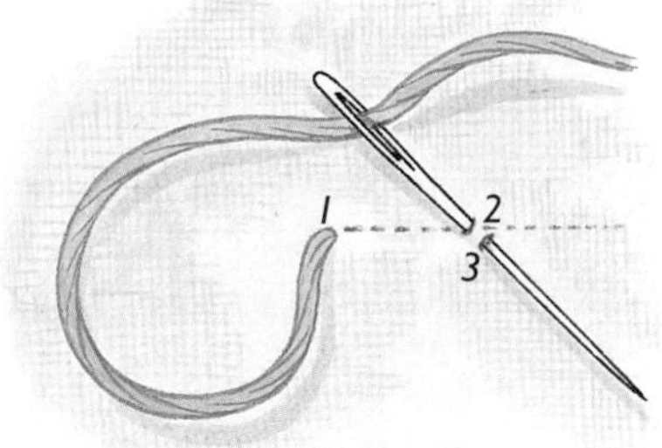

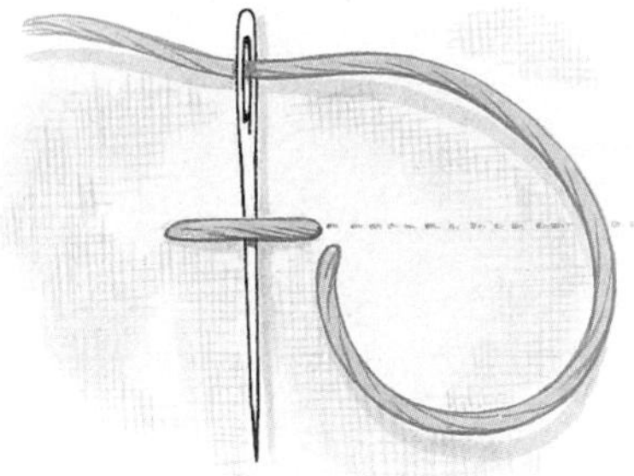

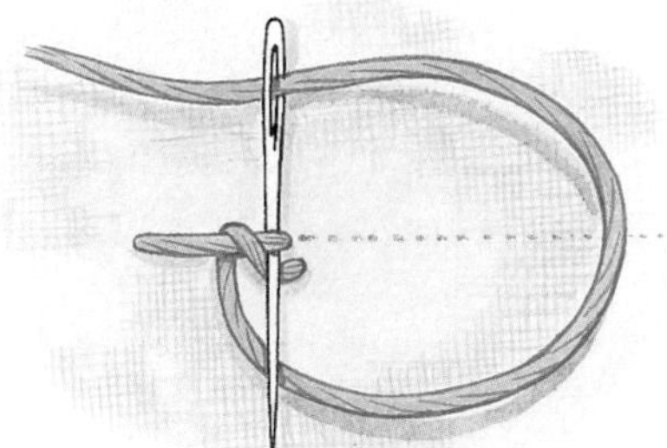

1 Work from left to right. Bring the needle to the front at 1. Make a short straight stitch, and insert the needle at 2. Bring the needle out at 3, and pull the thread through.

2 Take the needle under the straight stitch, as shown, without entering the fabric, and pull the thread through loosely.

3 Take the needle under the straight stitch again and over the working thread as shown. Pull the thread through to complete the first knot. Continue in this way along the line.

Working Portuguese knot stitch

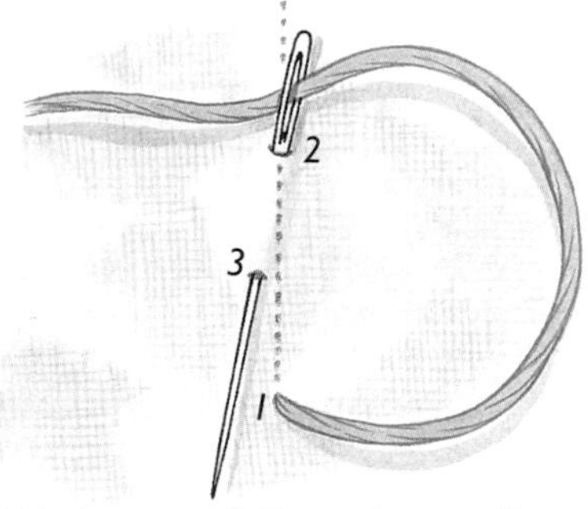

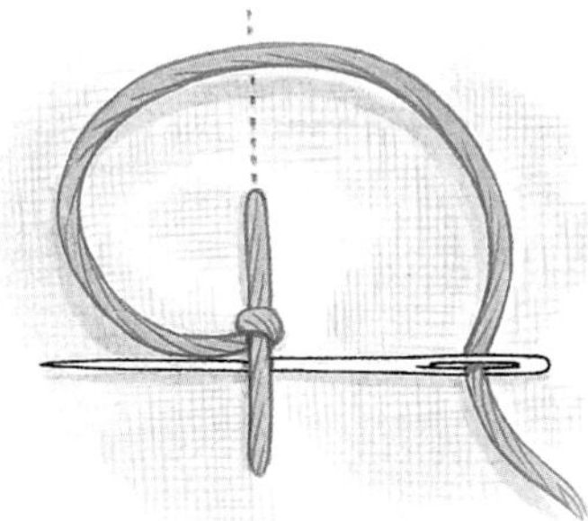

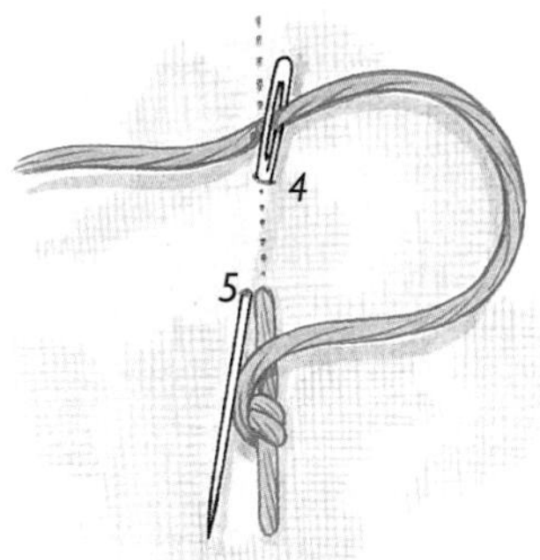

1 Work upward. Bring the needle to the front at the bottom of the guide line at 1. Insert it at 2 and bring it out again at 3, halfway between 1 and 2 and just to the left of the guide line.

2 Take the needle under the straight stitch from right to left, without entering the fabric. Pull gently to tighten the tying stitch. Work a second tying stitch directly below the first.

3 Insert the needle at 4 and bring it to the front at 5, just to the left of the top of the first stitch.

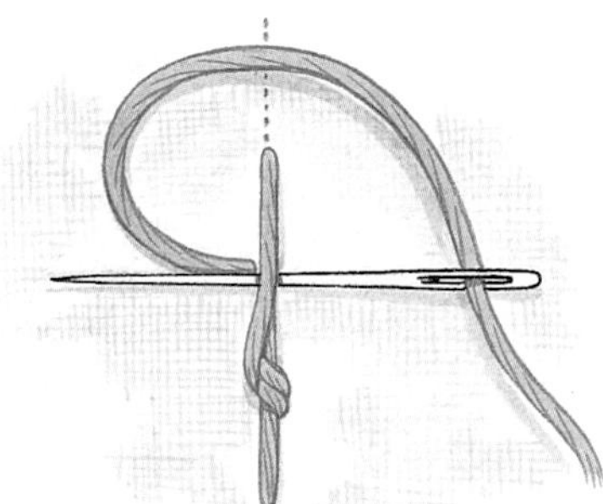

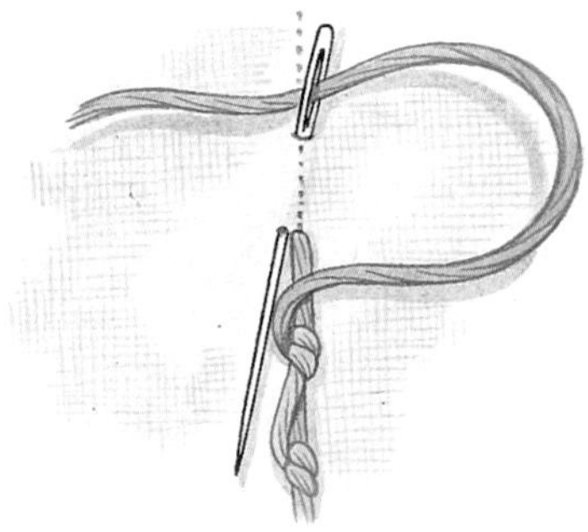

4 Make two tying stitches as before, but take the needle under both the first and second vertical straight stitches.

5 Repeat steps **3–4** along the line, keeping the vertical stitches all the same length to space the knots evenly.

Working scroll stitch

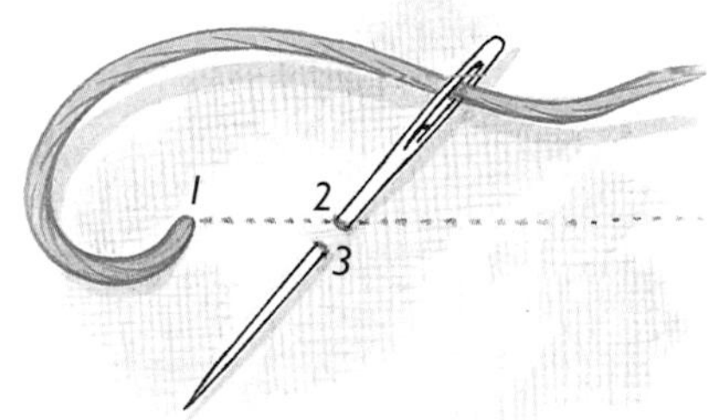

1 Work from left to right. Bring the needle to the front at 1. Make a diagonal straight stitch, inserting the needle at 2 and bringing it out at 3.

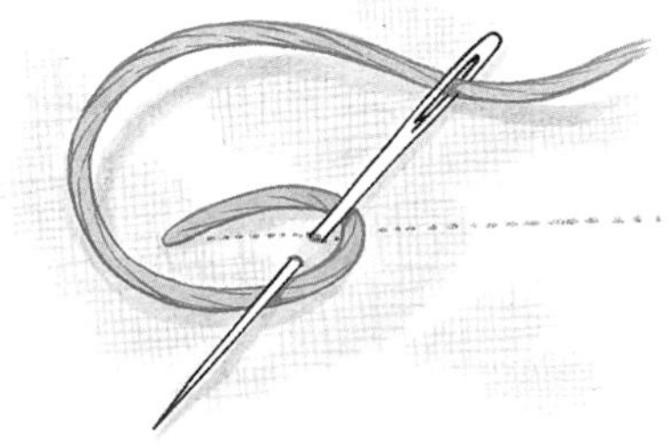

2 Loop the working thread round the needle. Tighten the thread, then pull the needle through to complete the first knot. Repeat along the line.

Knotted band stitches

The knotted stitches described below make wide, intricate bands. They are normally worked for borders but can also be used for filling narrow shapes. The stitches are easy to master, but take a bit of practice to be worked evenly.

When working on evenweave fabric, count the threads or fabric blocks to keep the rows straight and the stitches of identical size. On non-evenweave fabric, mark parallel lines with a fabric marking pen.

Knotted pearl stitch produces a wide, rather open band with a knotted surface. It is worked sideways and can be used in a straight line or to follow gentle curves.

Ladder stitch is worked downward and makes a straight, closely worked band with knotted edges. You can thread matching or contrasting ribbon through the rungs for a more decorative effect.

Knotted buttonhole stitch is a variation of blanket stitch (see page 57). It can be worked in a circle, with the vertical stitches worked outside or inside the curve. It can also be worked in rows to fill a shape. For a delicate border, work two rows of knotted buttonhole stitch close together with the looped edges facing each other and the vertical stitches fanning out at each side. You can graduate the lengths of the vertical stitches or make them all the same length.

Tailor's buttonhole stitch is another variation of blanket stitch. It makes a strong, durable edge, so it's useful for finishing raw fabric edges. It can also be used as a heavyweight filling stitch; for the best results, mount the fabric in a frame to minimize distortion.

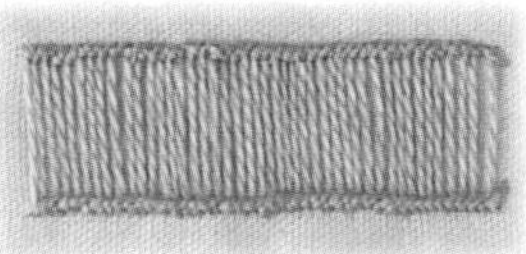

Ladder stitch

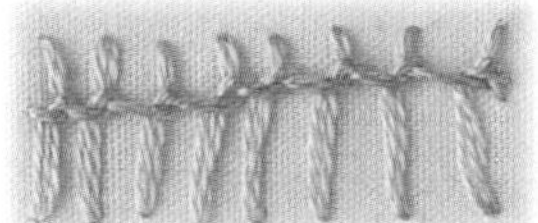

Knotted pearl stitch

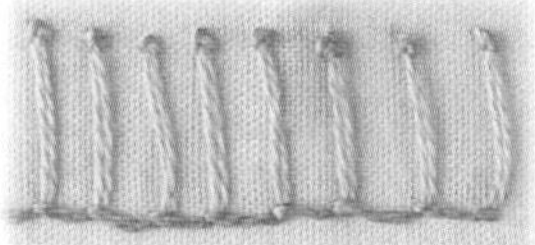

Knotted buttonhole stitch

Tailor's buttonhole stitch

Starting and fastening off stitching

1 Leave a 4 in. (10 cm) tail of thread on the front of the fabric. Anchor the thread with two or three running stitches.

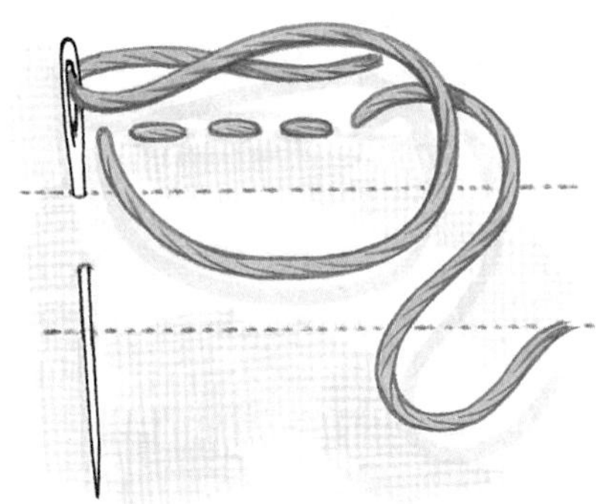

2 Work the stitches and fasten off the thread end by taking the needle through to the back and darning in the end under several stitches. Return to the beginning, pull out the running stitches and pull the tail of thread through to the back. Darn the thread end under the first few stitches you worked.

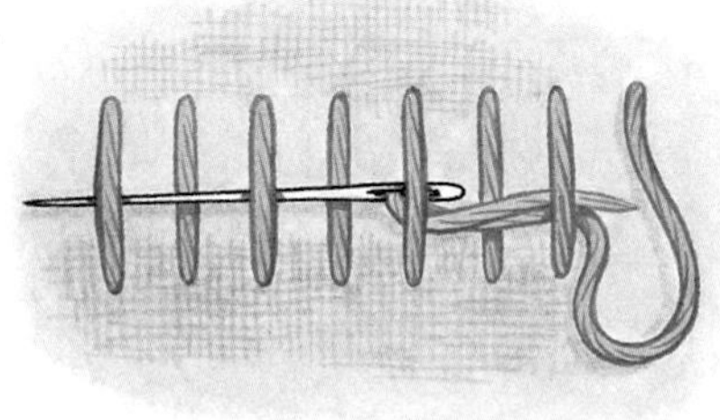

Working knotted pearl stitch

1 Work from right to left. Make a short vertical stitch at the right-hand side, then bring the needle up below it at 1. Take the needle under the stitch and the working thread, and insert it at 2. Pull the thread to tighten the loop into a knot. Bring the needle out at 3.

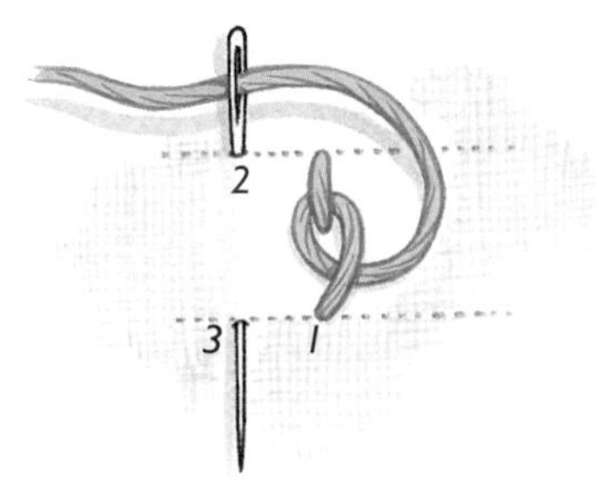

2 Loop the thread over and under the stitch, and insert the needle into the fabric at 4. Pull the thread to tighten the loop into a knot. Continue working in this way.

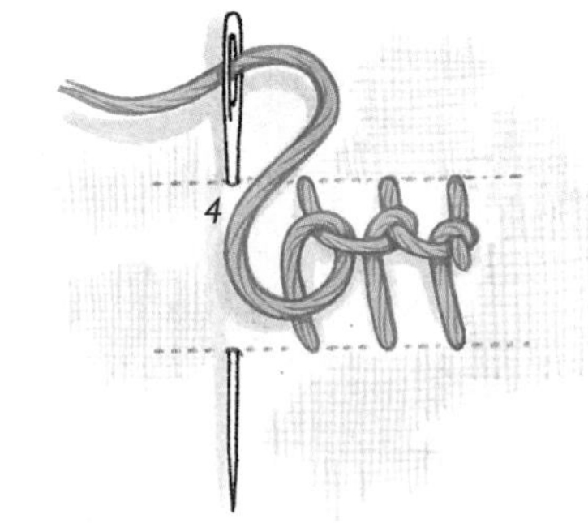

Working ladder stitch

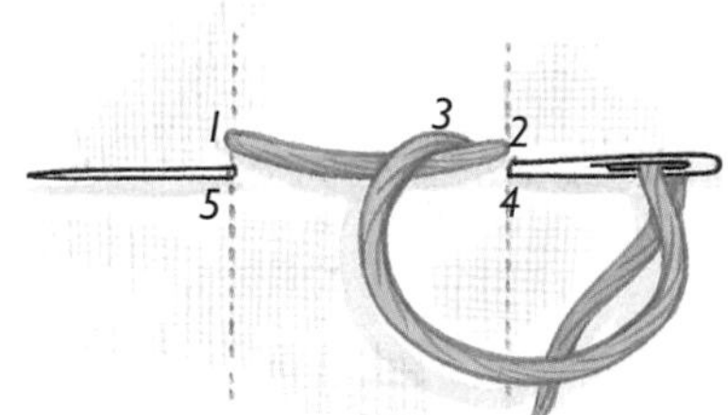

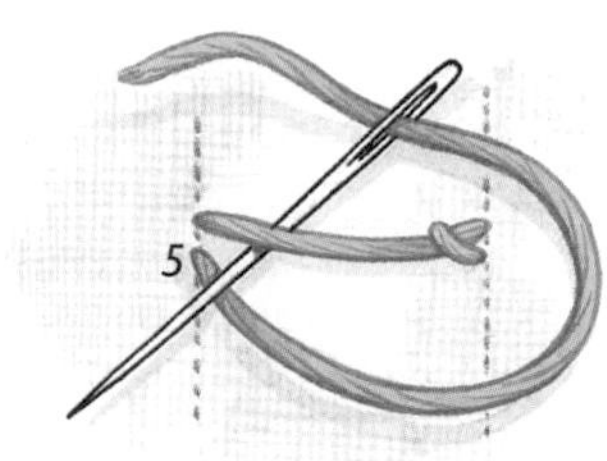

1 Bring the needle out to the front at 1 and insert it again at 2 to make the first rung of the ladder. Bring the needle out to the front at 3 and insert it at 4. Bring the needle out at 5.

2 Take the point of the needle under the left-hand end of the first rung, and bring it out over the working thread, without entering the fabric. Pull the thread through gently to make a small knot at the left-hand edge of the rung.

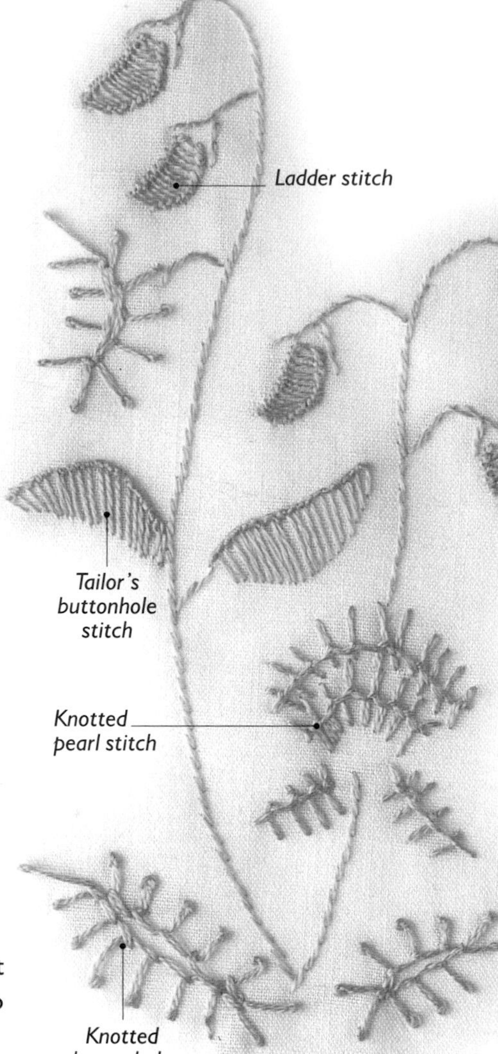

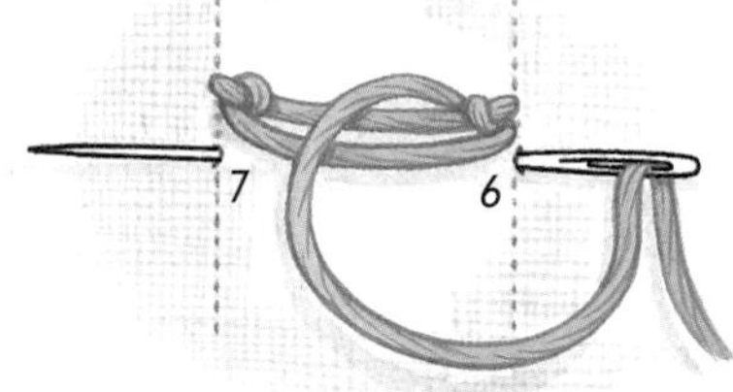

3 Without allowing the needle to enter the fabric, make another knot at the right-hand end of the rung by sliding the needle from right to left behind the right-hand knot. This also makes a second rung.

4 Pull the thread through and insert the needle at 6. Come through to the front at 7. Repeat step **3** at the left-hand side of the fabric to make a knot over the second rung. Repeat steps **3** and **4** alternately to complete the band.

Working knotted buttonhole stitch

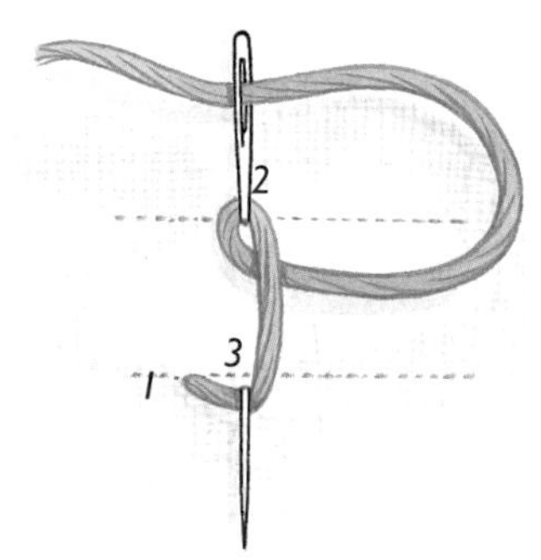

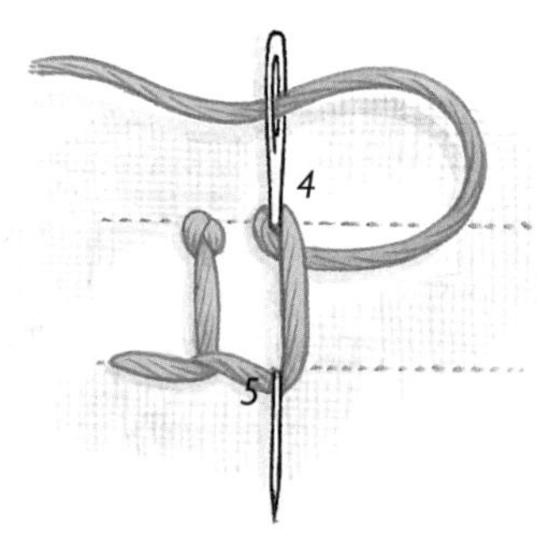

1 Work from left to right. Come out to the front at 1, make a loop with the thread, and hold it in place on the top line. Insert the needle through the loop at 2 and bring it out to the front over the working thread at 3.

2 Pull the thread to form a knot. Begin the next stitch by making another loop on the top line. Holding the loop in place, insert the needle through the loop at 4 and come out to the front over the working thread at 5. Continue in this way.

Working tailor's buttonhole stitch

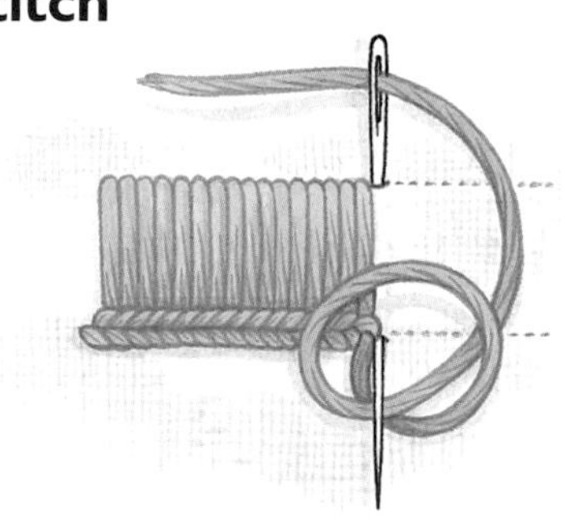

Work tailor's buttonhole stitch from left to right in a similar way to blanket stitch. Insert the needle at the top and bring it out directly below, keeping the thread under the needle. Wind the thread round the needle point, tighten the loop, then pull the needle through to complete the stitch. Work the stitches closely together, so that the knots lie next to each other, making a strong, tightly stitched edge.

Knotted border stitches

The knotted border stitches described in this section make intricate lines which add interesting textural detail to embroidered designs.

When working any type of knotted stitch, it is useful to hold the part of the stitch with the knot down firmly on the background fabric with one thumb while you gently pull the working thread through with your other hand. To start and fasten off the thread, refer to page 81.

When you are working on non-evenweave fabrics, always mark the position of the rows first with basting or a water-soluble or air-erasable marking pen. For zigzag coral stitch and diamond stitch, mark two parallel vertical lines; for Basque knot stitch mark a single horizontal line. On evenweave fabrics, count the threads or the fabric blocks to help keep the rows straight and the stitches of identical size.

Zigzag coral stitch

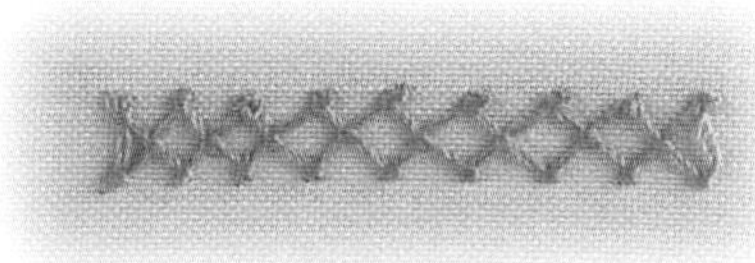

Diamond stitch

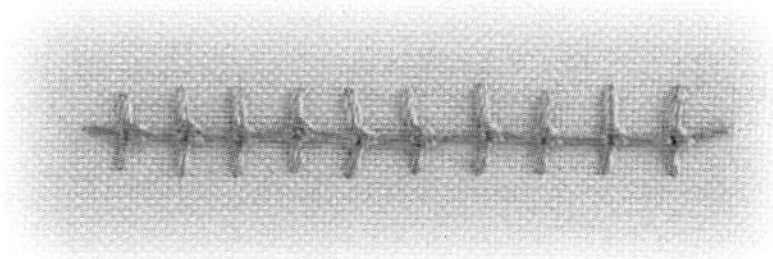

Basque knot stitch

Zigzag coral stitch makes a wide, decorative line. It's an easy variation of coral stitch and can be used only to work straight lines and very gradual curves. For details on coral stitch, see page 81.

Diamond stitch combines knots and straight stitches to make an interesting, textured border pattern resembling a row of diamonds. Try it around the edge of a placemat.

Basque knot stitch has a neat, spiky character and can be used individually to add texture and detail, in single rows to create neat borders, or in multiple rows to fill a shape.

Working zigzag coral stitch

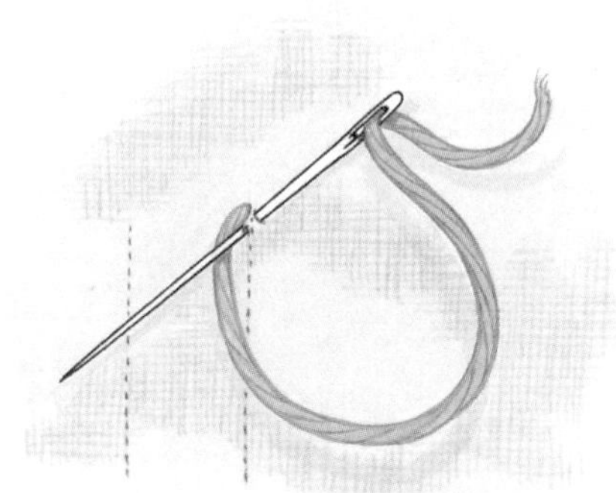

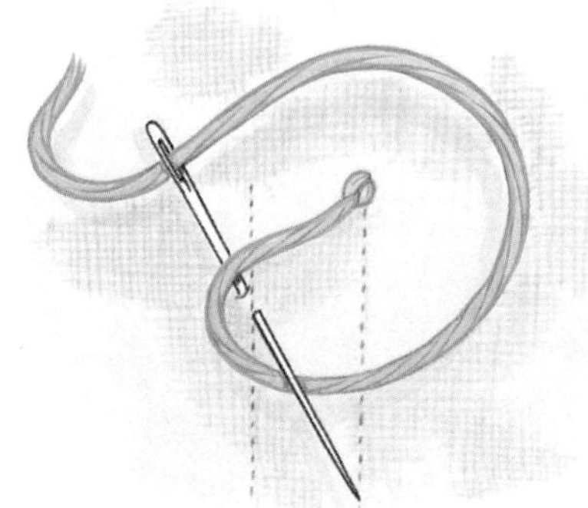

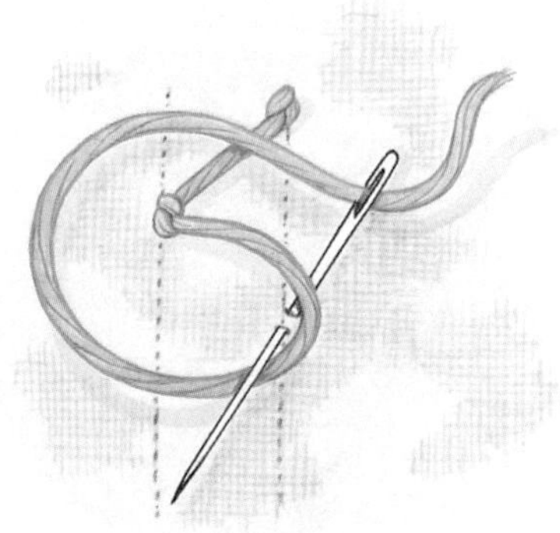

1 Mark two parallel lines on the fabric. Bring the needle to the front at the top of the right-hand guide line and work a coral stitch, as shown on page 81.

2 Carry the thread diagonally over to the left-hand guide line. Pick up a tiny section of fabric and loop the thread over, then under the needle as shown. Pull the needle through.

3 Carry the thread diagonally across to the right-hand guide line, insert the needle, and pick up a tiny section of fabric. Loop the thread over, then under the needle. Pull the needle through. Repeat steps **2–3** down the row, working alternately to the right and left to make a zigzag line.

Working diamond stitch

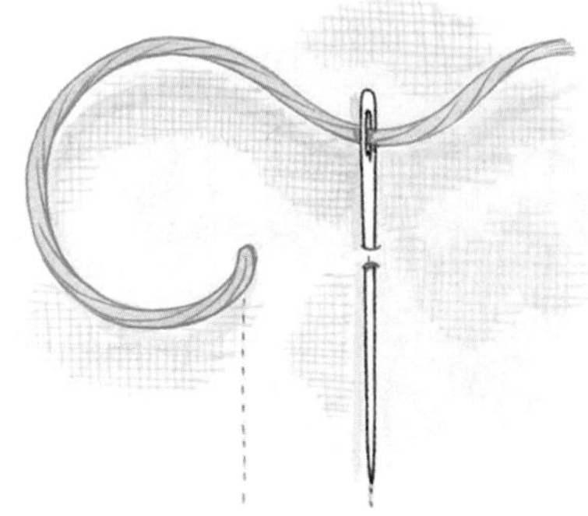

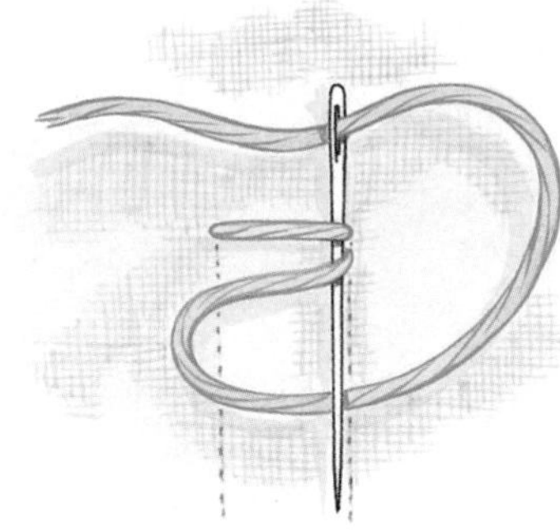

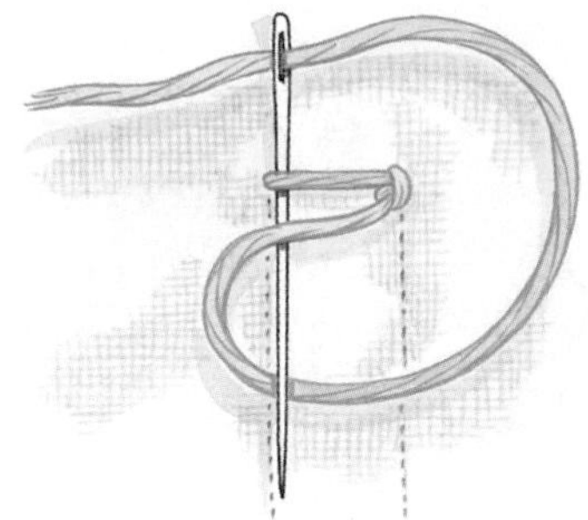

1 Mark two parallel guide lines on the fabric. Bring the needle to the front at the top left. Make a horizontal stitch across to the right-hand guide line, and bring the needle out just below the first stitch.

2 Slip the point of the needle under the horizontal stitch. Loop the working thread over, then under the needle point, and pull the needle through to make a small knot.

3 Take the thread across to the left-hand guide line, and make another knot in the same way. Insert the needle just below the knot, and bring it out again a short distance below.

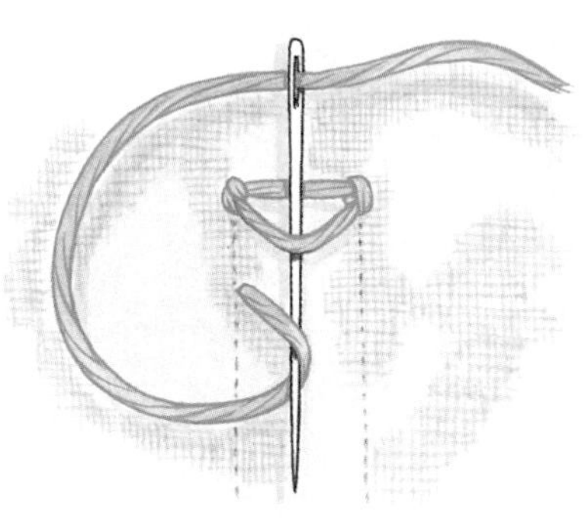

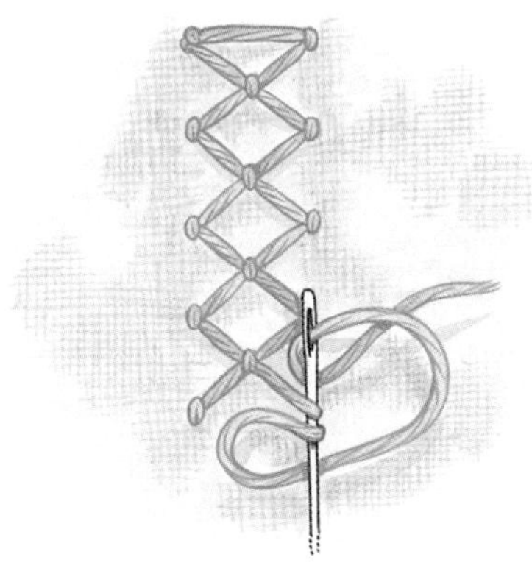

4 Take the needle under the second horizontal stitch. Loop the working thread over, then under the point again. Pull the thread through to make a knot, pulling down the horizontal stitch so that it makes a V shape.

5 Insert the needle on the right-hand guide line at the same level as the stitch on the left, and bring it out just below; then repeat steps **2–4** down the row to make a diamond pattern.

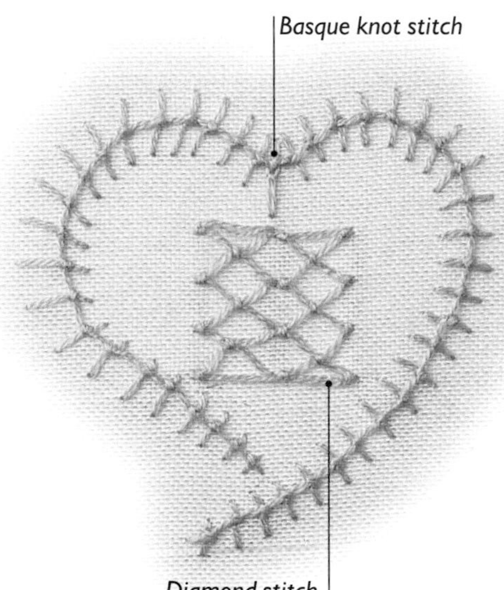

Working Basque knot stitch

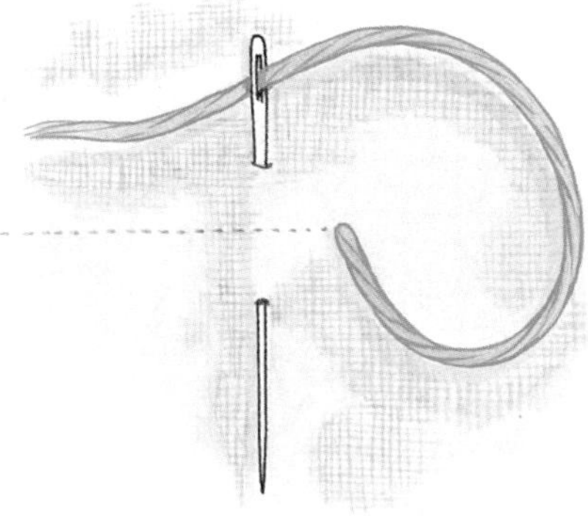

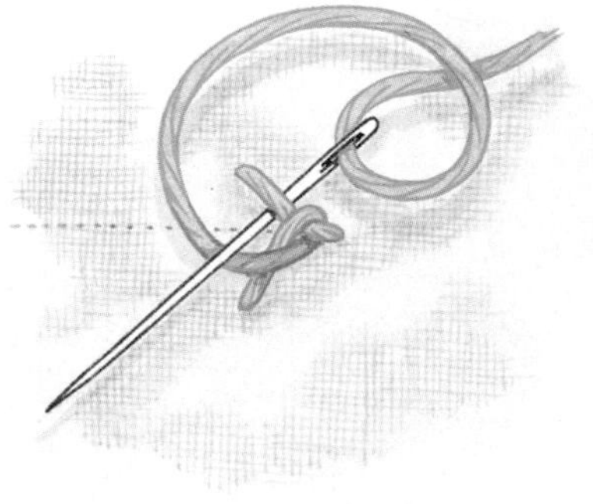

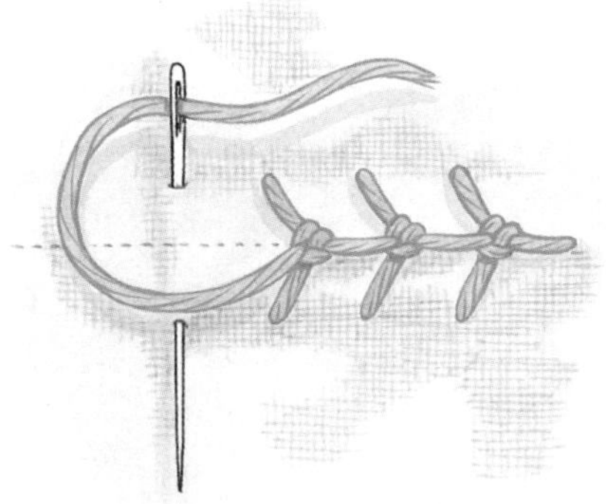

1 Mark a horizontal guide line on the fabric. Bring the needle to the front at the right-hand end. Insert the needle above the line and bring it out below the line. Pull the thread through gently to make a loose diagonal stitch.

2 Loop the working thread twice over the diagonal stitch without going through the fabric. Holding the loops down with your thumb, pull the thread through and center the knot along the guide line.

3 Continue in this way along the row, making the diagonal stitches very loose so that you can center the knots over the guide line.

Couching

Couching involves laying a decorative thread on the fabric and stitching it in place with a second thread. It is often used in metal thread embroidery and in working designs with threads that are too thick, delicate, or textured to sew through the fabric. The technique is versatile—you can use it for outlines and linear designs, and to fill small or large shapes.

The thread that is laid down is called the laid thread. Various threads can be used: metallic threads, cords, string (which is covered by the stitches) are some examples.

For the couching thread, use a fine, fairly strong, smooth thread, such as silk sewing thread or two or three strands of embroidery floss. It can match or contrast with the color of the laid thread.

Mark the position of the couching on the fabric with basting or a marking pen, and mount the fabric in a frame to prevent puckering. For linear designs, mark each line, then work the couching on top. For solidly couched areas, mark just the position of the first row of couching. Work this, then use it as a foundation row for the remaining rows.

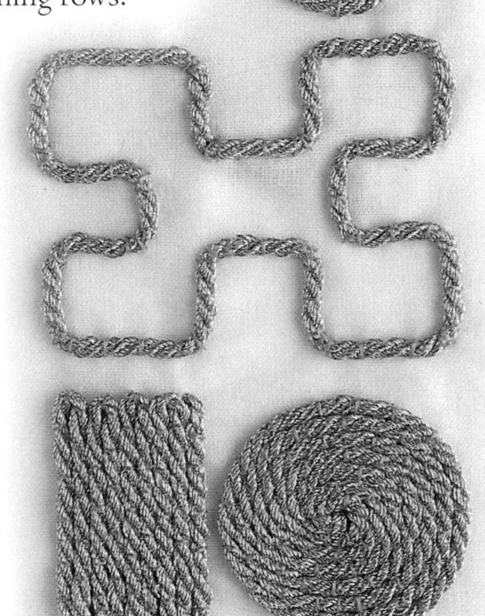

Starting off couching

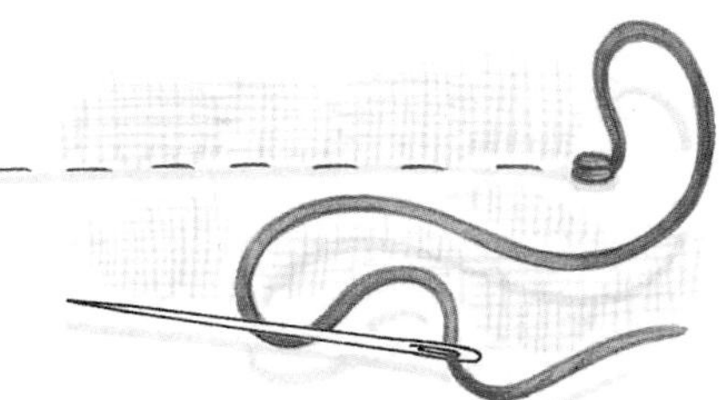

1 Start at the right-hand end of the couching line. Secure the couching thread first with two or three backstitches, placing them where they will be covered by the laid thread. Leave a 2 in. (5 cm) tail of thread at the back of the fabric.

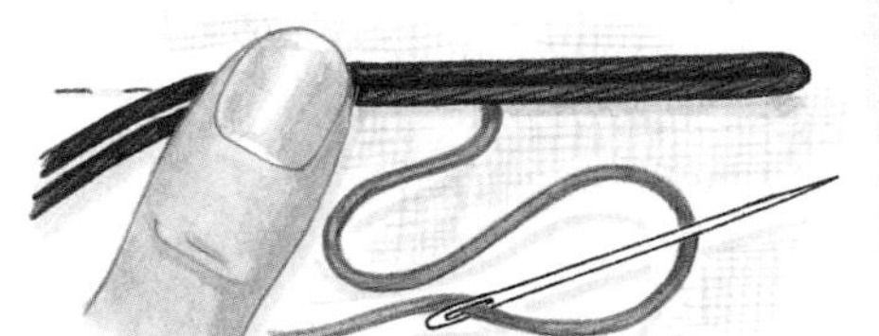

2 Place the laid thread on the fabric, leaving an extra 2 in. (5 cm) at the start of the couching line. Hold the laid thread in place with one thumb.

Fastening off couching

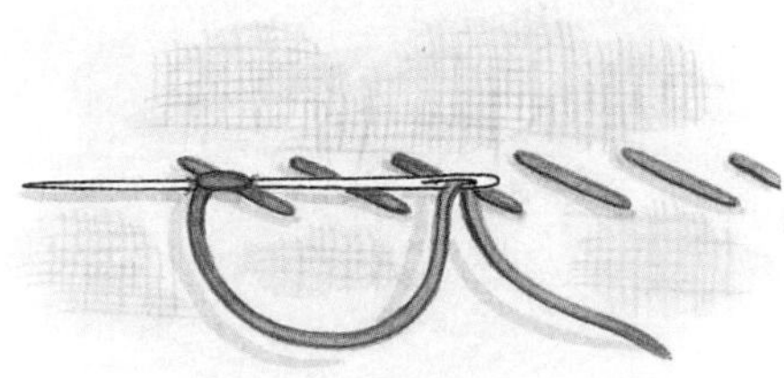

To fasten off the couching thread, take it to the back of the fabric. Secure it with a few stitches beneath the laid thread. Leave a 2 in. (5 cm) tail of couching thread. Then cut off the laid thread, leaving a 2 in. (5 cm) tail.

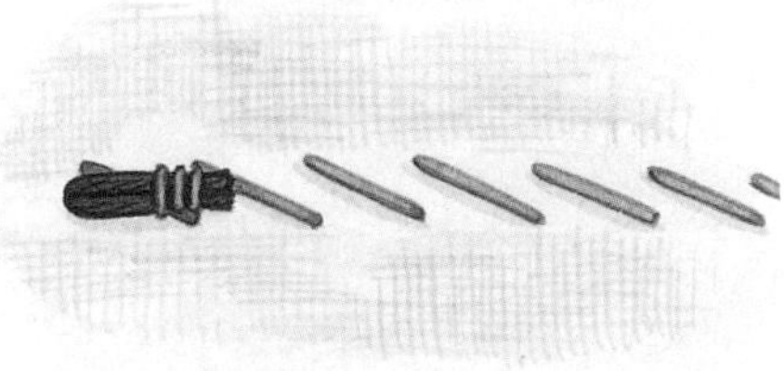

To secure a fine or medium-weight laid thread, thread the end through a chenille needle and gently take it through to the back of the fabric. At the back, fold the end over the row of stitching, then secure it with a few stitches, using the couching thread.

To secure a thick laid thread, make a small hole in the fabric with a large needle or the point of a stiletto. Wrap tape around the end of the laid thread, poke it carefully through the hole, and pull it to the back. Secure as for a fine or medium-weight thread.

Working basic couching

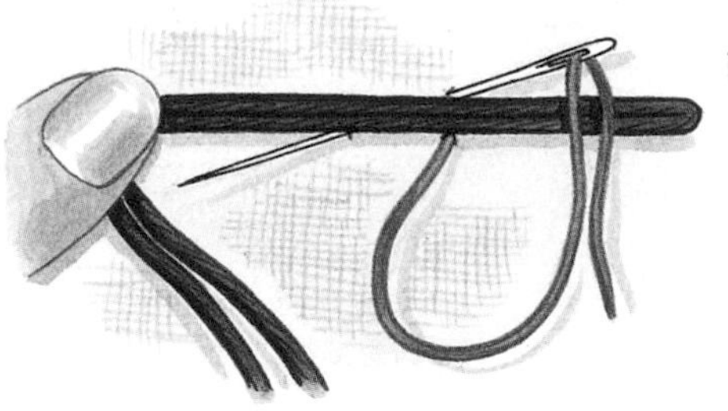

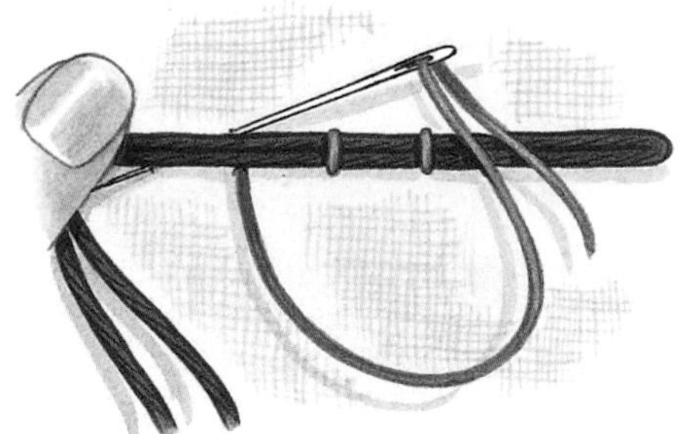

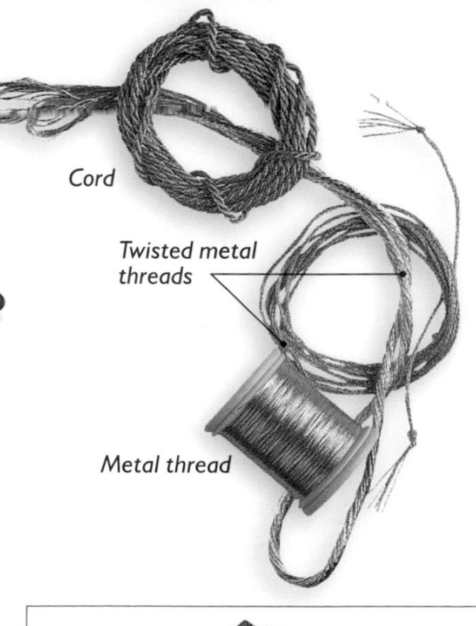

1 If you are using two strands of laid thread, fold a single length in half and position it on the fabric with the strands side by side. Bring the couching thread to the front, just below the laid thread. Make a tiny vertical stitch over the laid thread. Bring the needle to the front again a short distance to the left.

2 Continue making vertical stitches over the laid thread until it is anchored to the fabric along its length. Space the stitches evenly.

SEWING BOX

USING METALLIC THREADS

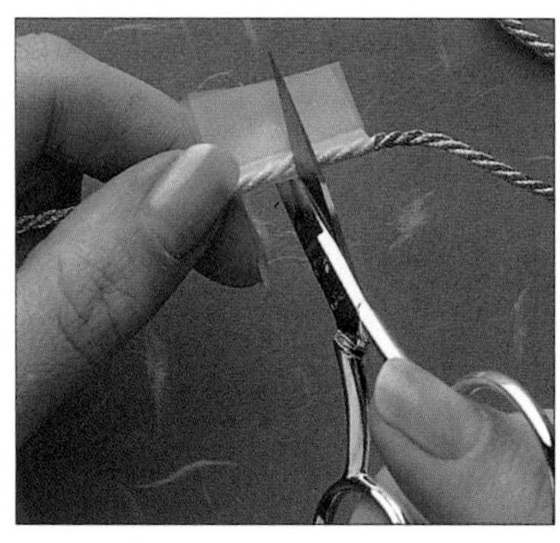

Metallic threads can split and fray easily, so handle them carefully. Wrapping tape around the ends helps to prevent the ends from unraveling. Before cutting the thread, simply wrap tape around it where you wish to cut it. Cut through the middle of the tape, so that each end of the thread is wrapped in a narrow strip of tape.

Working a corner

When using a single thread, turn the laid thread at right angles at the corner. Secure it at the corner with three closely spaced stitches, fanning them out around the corner.

When using a double thread, turn the laid thread at right angles at the corner. Secure with two closely spaced stitches, then make a third, short stitch over the outer thread only.

Working couching as a filling

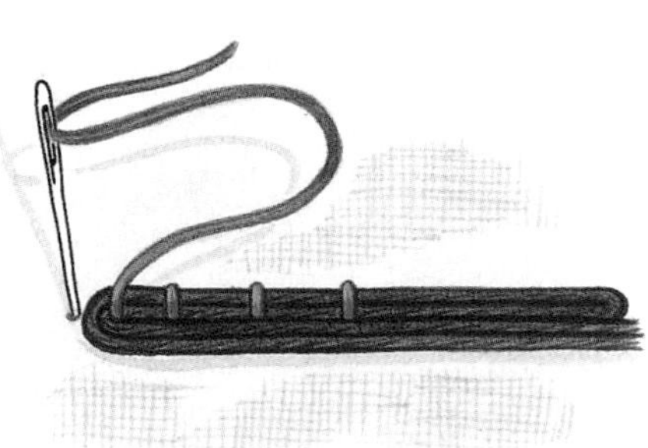

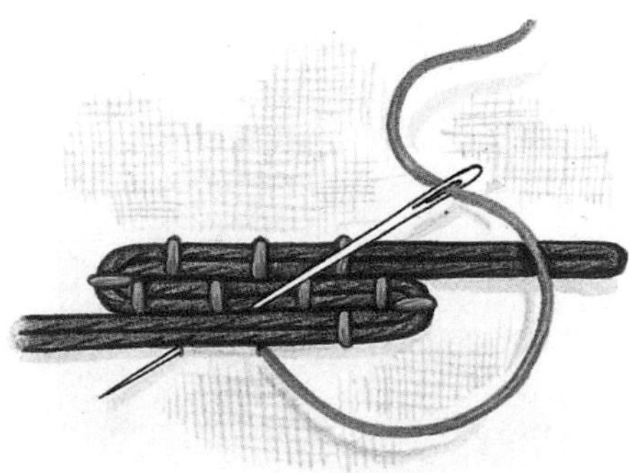

1 Work the first row from right to left, as in **Basic couching** (page 87). At the end of the row, turn the laid threads in the opposite direction. Make a horizontal stitch to secure the threads at the turning point.

2 Turn the work upside down, and work the second row from right to left across the shape. Place the couching stitches between the couching stitches on the previous row. At the end of the row, turn and secure the laid thread as in step 1.

3 Turn the work the right way around again, and work the third row, lining up the couching stitches with the couching stitches in the first row. Continue in this way until you have filled in the shape.

Couching usually involves stitching a thick thread in place with a thinner one, but the couching stitches shown here use just one thread. They are all worked in two movements: first a long stitch is laid across the shape, then it is tied down on the return journey.

All of the stitches create an attractive solid filling, suitable for both small shapes and large backgrounds. Where necessary, use an air-erasable marking pen to mark out guide lines on the fabric.

Romanian couching produces a smoothly stitched flat surface tied down with long slanted stitches to keep the laid stitches even.

Bokhara couching gives a similarly smooth surface but with a more pronounced pattern.

New England laid stitch is used mainly to fill long, narrow shapes and borders. To fill large areas, position multiple rows of stitches with the edges touching. It is very economical to work, as most of the thread stays on the top of the fabric.

Colcha stitch creates a rough, almost woven surface which looks particularly effective when worked in crewel or Persian yarn.

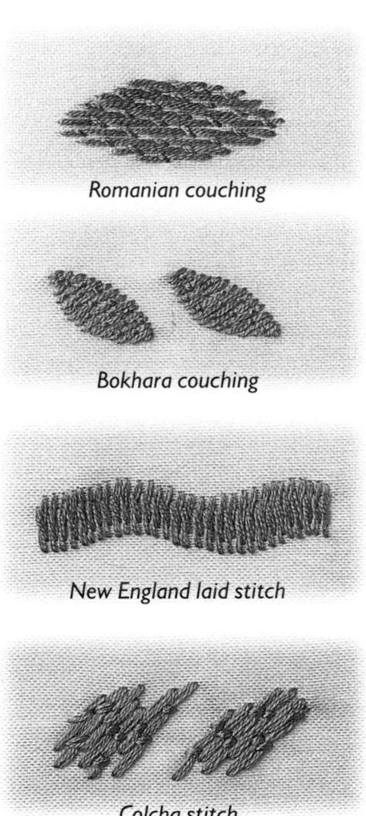

Romanian couching

Bokhara couching

New England laid stitch

Colcha stitch

Working Romanian couching

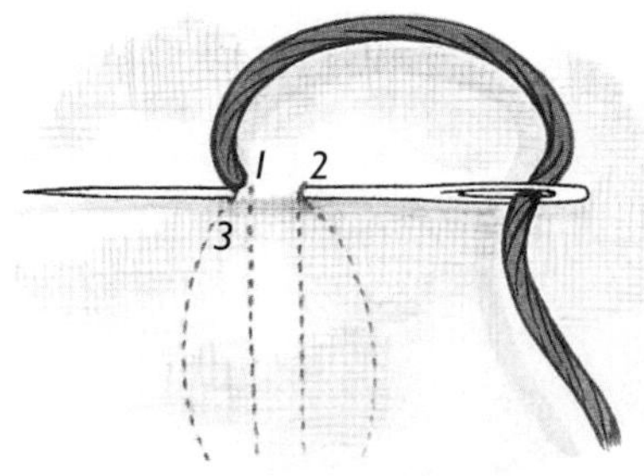

1 For narrow, rounded shapes, mark parallel guide lines down the center of the area to be filled. Bring the thread to the front at 1 and make a short straight stitch to 2. Bring the needle through to the front again at 3.

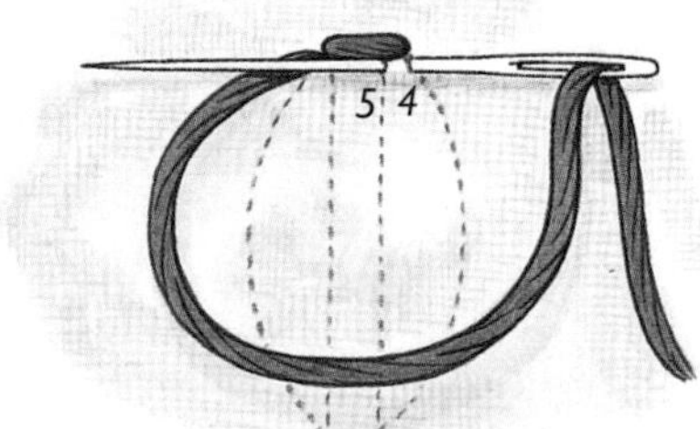

2 Make a long stitch across the shape, inserting the needle at 4 and bringing the point through on the right-hand guide line at 5. Keeping the working thread under the needle, pull the needle through.

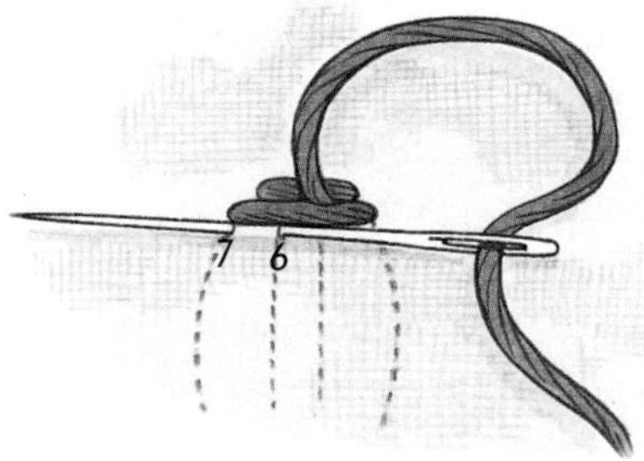

3 Make a slanted stitch over the laid thread to tie it down on the fabric, inserting the needle on the left-hand guide line at 6 and bringing it out at the left-hand edge of the shape at 7.

4 Repeat step **2** to position the next laid thread below the previous one, then repeat step **3** to tie it down. Continue in this way, arranging the tying-down stitches in a neat line down the center of the shape.

To fill large areas, bring the needle through to the front at the top left-hand edge of the shape. Take a long stitch to the opposite edge, and bring the needle through, just below and to the left of the end of the laid thread. Working from right to left, tie down the laid thread with evenly spaced slanted stitches. Continue in this way to fill the shape.

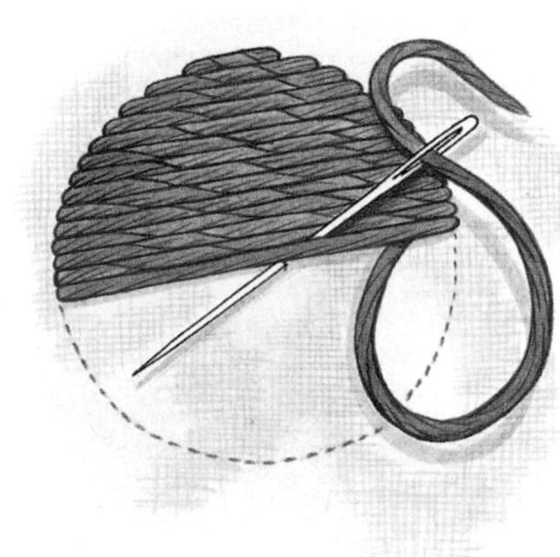

Working Bokhara couching

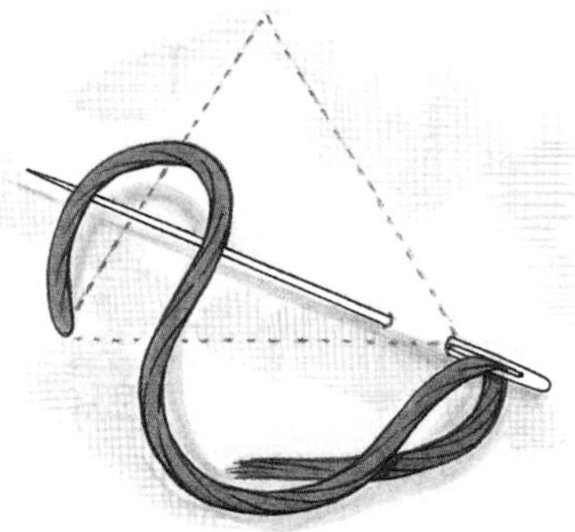

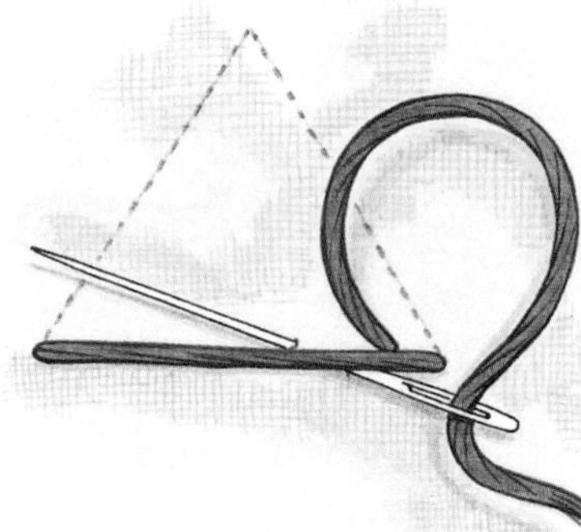

1 Bring the needle through to the front at the bottom left-hand edge of the shape, and insert it at the bottom right-hand edge. Bring the needle out just above and to the left.

2 Insert the needle below the laid thread to make a short diagonal tying-down stitch. Bring the needle out a short distance away to the left, at the top of the laid thread.

3 Repeat step **2** along the length of the laid thread, placing the tying-down stitches at regular intervals along the thread. At the left-hand edge, bring the needle through, ready to lay the next thread above the first.

4 Repeat steps **1–3** until the shape is filled, making sure that the laid threads are placed close together to cover the fabric completely. Place the tying-down stitches on each row slightly to the right of those on the previous row to make neat lines.

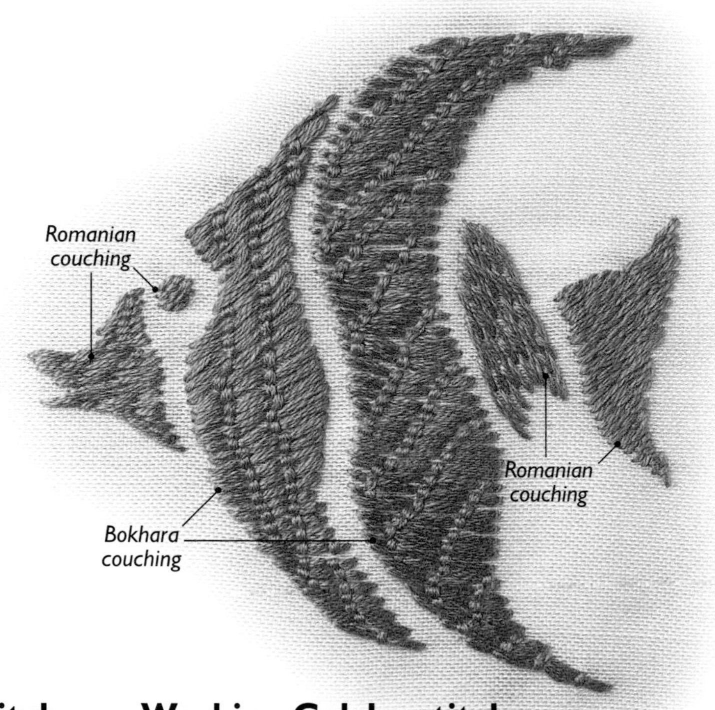

Working New England laid stitch

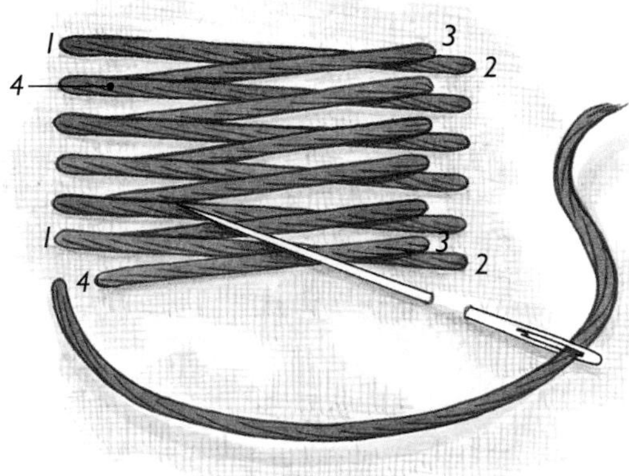

Bring the needle through at 1 and make a long slanted stitch to 2. Bring the needle through just above the first stitch at 3. Make a long slanted stitch toward the left-hand edge, inserting the needle at 4 and bringing it out below the left-hand edge of the first stitch. Repeat the sequence 1–4 to fill the shape.

Working Colcha stitch

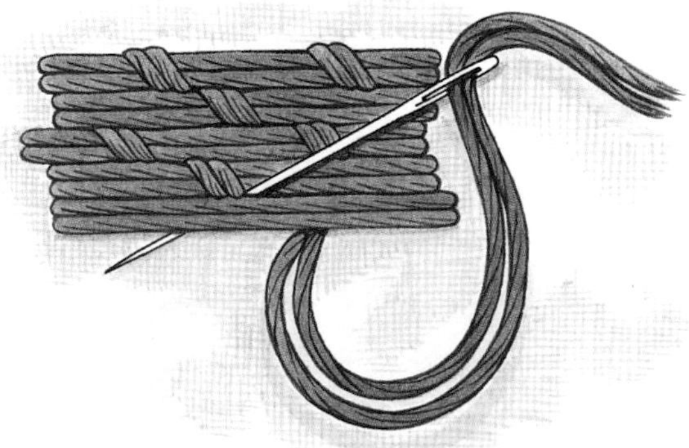

Using two threads in the needle at the same time, work a long stitch across the shape from left to right. Then bring the needle to the front, below and just to the left of the end of the laid thread; working along the thread, tie it down at regular intervals. Repeat to fill the shape.

Blackwork patterns

Blackwork is a fascinating form of counted thread embroidery that uses simple straight stitches to build up patterns. The patterns, which are often geometric, are repeated to fill large or small areas and to add texture to pictorial designs. The typical contrast in weight and density of the different patterns is achieved by varying the number of stitches used to create each pattern and by using threads of different thicknesses.

This form of embroidery is usually worked in black thread on white or cream evenweave fabric, but the patterns can look just as effective in colored threads. The easiest fabric to use is 14-count aida. With a little practice, you can move on to finer fabrics. Cotton or silk embroidery floss, brilliant cutwork and embroidery cotton, pearl cotton, and ordinary sewing thread are all suitable. Use a size 24 tapestry needle for 14-count aida and a size 26 tapestry needle for 28-count evenweave. In order to get the correct stitch tension, always mount the fabric in an embroidery frame.

Building up patterns

Most blackwork patterns consist of an outline and a filling. The most common outline stitch is double running stitch (see page 26.) The fillings use stitches such as backstitch, cross stitch, and running stitch.

Repeated patterns are usually built up in journeys; you work part of the pattern on the outward journey and fill in the gaps on the return. The two patterns featured here are both worked in this way.

Pattern one is suitable for small areas. It is worked fairly densely in backstitch and cross stitch.

Pattern two is worked in running stitch and backstitch, and makes a lightweight filling for larger areas.

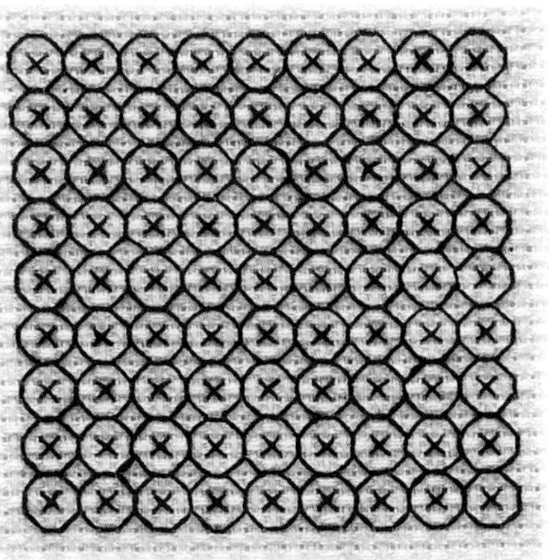

Pattern one

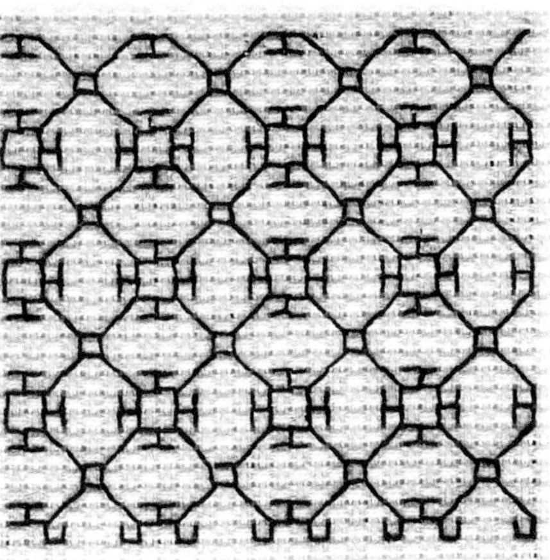

Pattern two

Marking the fabric center

Fold the fabric in half both ways and crease lightly. In contrasting thread, baste along the creases. The basting lines cross at the center of the fabric. Remove the basting when the stitching is complete.

Starting and fastening off

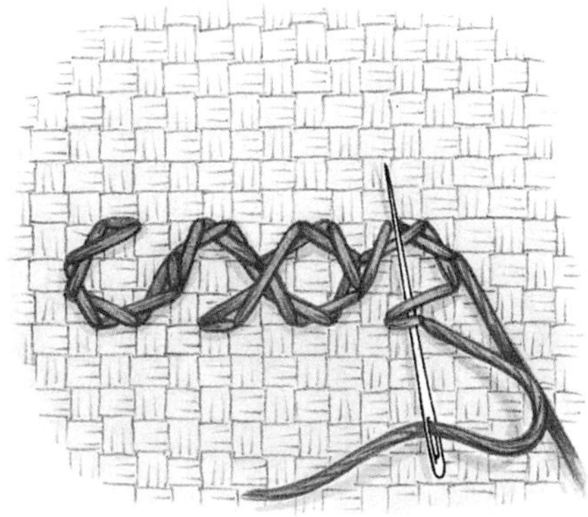

1 Knot the end of the thread. About 3 in. (8 cm) from the starting point, take the needle to the back, leaving the knot at the front of the fabric. Bring the needle out to the front at the starting point.

2 When you have about 3 in. (8 cm) of thread left, or you've finished the pattern, take the needle to the back and darn the end under several stitches. Then snip off the knot at the start of your stitching, pull the loose thread to the back, and darn it in.

Working pattern one

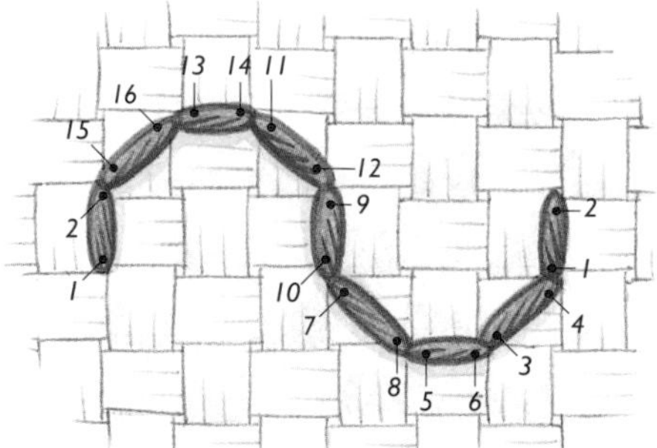

1 Bring the needle to the front at 1 (right), and insert it at 2. Continue in this way, following the sequence 3–16, to backstitch two halves of the first pair of octagons. Repeat the sequence 1–16 to the left-hand edge of the space.

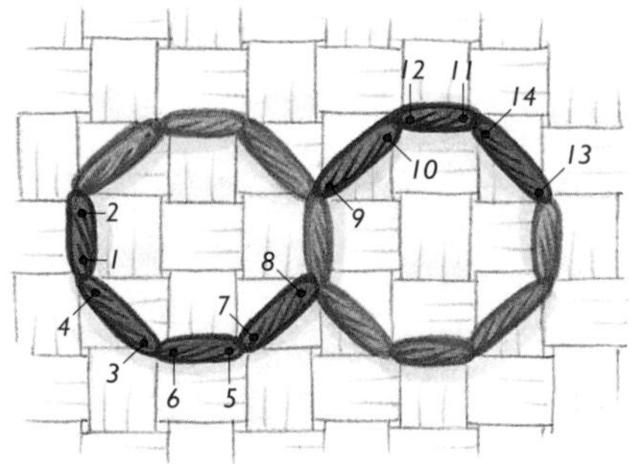

2 Start the return journey at the left-hand edge of the design area. Follow the sequence 1–14 (shown in purple) to complete the first two octagons.

PRISTINE FINISH

Everyone makes mistakes, and sometimes stitches are worked where a space should have been left. A fine fuzz can be left on the surface of the fabric when stitches are pulled out. This can be removed by pressing tape onto the fabric. The thread ends will adhere to the tape, leaving the fabric clear.

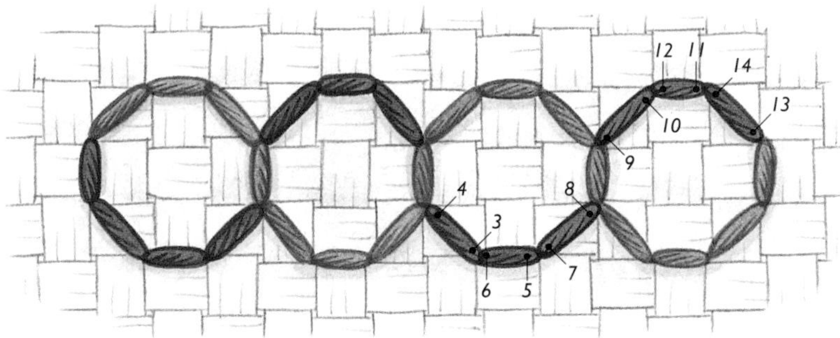

3 Follow the sequence 3–14 to complete the journey across the design area. The bases of the stitched octagons form the top of the octagons on the following row, so, on subsequent rows, omit stitches 13–14 on outward journeys and stitches 11–12 on return journeys.

4 Work a cross stitch in the center of each octagon. Take care to be consistent in slanting the top and bottom stitches.

Working pattern two

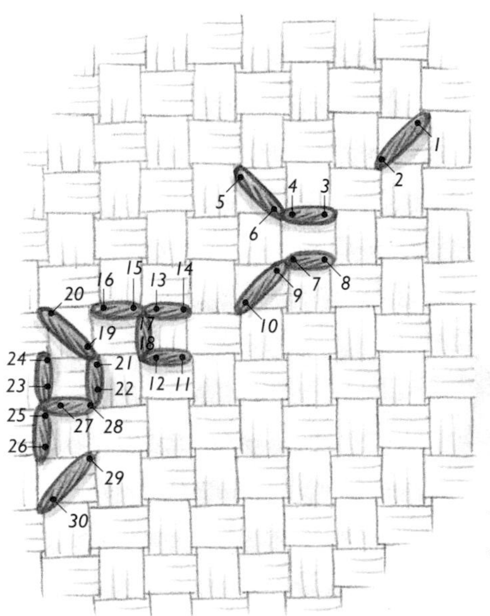

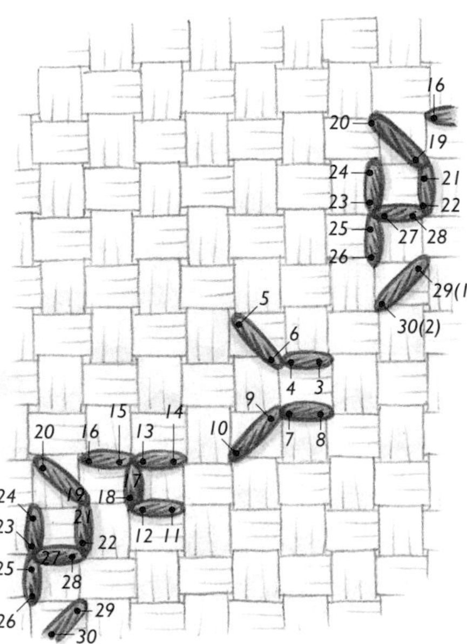

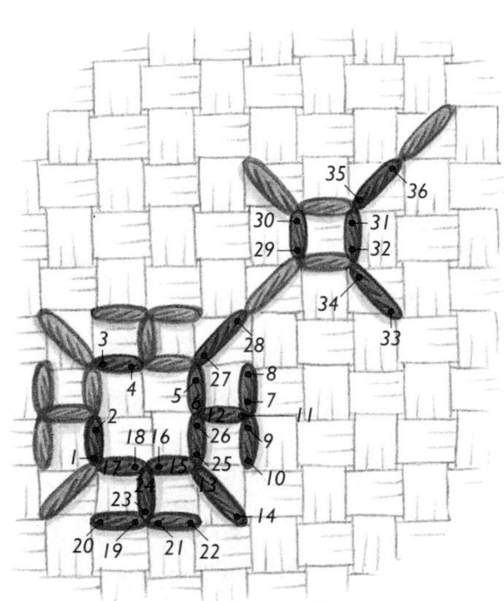

1 Follow the sequence 1–30 (shown in pink) to partially work the first motif. The pattern is worked diagonally from top right to bottom left.

2 The sequence 29–30 repeats the sequence 1–2. Continue to repeat the sequence 1–30 until you reach the bottom left of the design area.

3 To work the second journey, follow the sequence 1–36 (shown in purple). Repeat the sequence to fill in the gaps left on the outward journey.

Originally blackwork was used almost exclusively to decorate clothing. Many 16th-century portraits of ladies and gentlemen show linen collars or sleeves richly embellished with blackwork patterns. Today, these rediscovered patterns are more often used to decorate household linens or to make attractive pictures or wall hangings.

Mount your fabric in a frame and always work from the center out; it's much easier to fill in partial patterns around an irregular shape as you reach the edges than to start with part repeats. For more details on blackwork and instructions for patterns one and two, refer to pages 91 and 92.

Pattern collection

The four patterns shown here are used to provide variations of tone and density in a design.

Patterns three and five are lightly stitched, which makes them ideal for delicate subjects and for covering large areas quickly.

Patterns four and six are much more densely worked, providing shade, contrast, and weight.

Pattern three

Pattern four

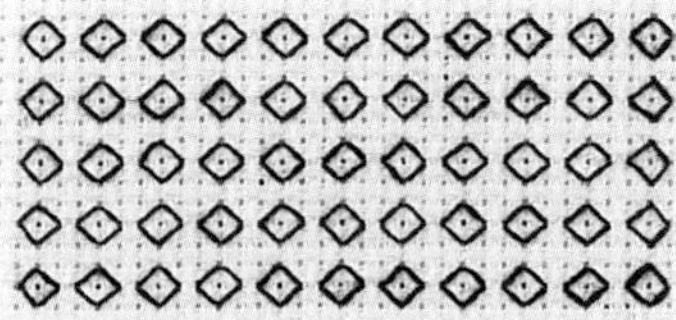

Pattern five

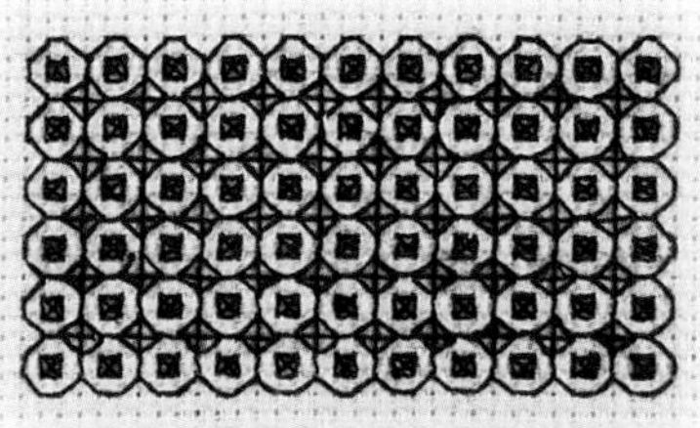

Pattern six

Working pattern three

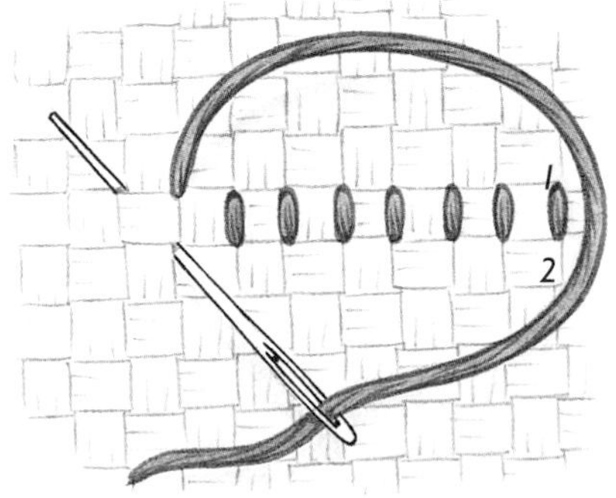

1 Work from right to left. Bring the needle to the front at 1, and insert it at 2. Continue in this way, working small vertical straight stitches over one fabric block, until you reach the left-hand edge of the design area.

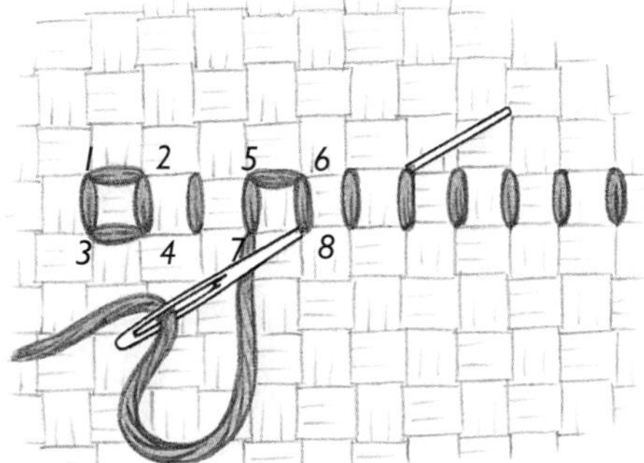

2 Work from left to right. Work horizontal stitches over one fabric block as shown, following the sequence 1–8. Continue in this way until you reach the right-hand edge of the area to be filled.

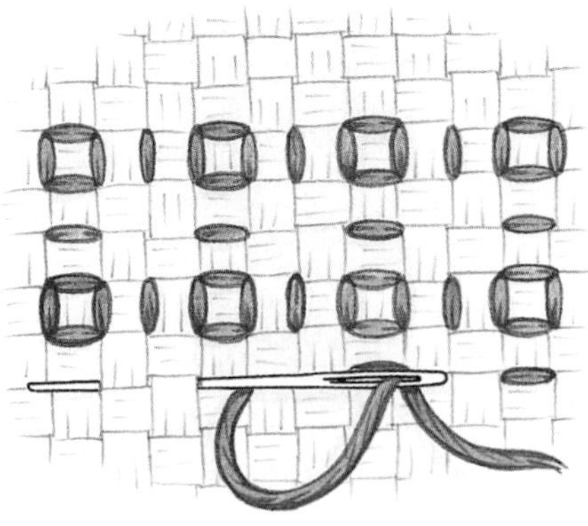

3 Work from right to left. Work small horizontal stitches below the base of the squares, as shown, to complete the pattern. Continue in this way to fill the design area, positioning subsequent blocks of stitches directly below the first.

Working pattern four

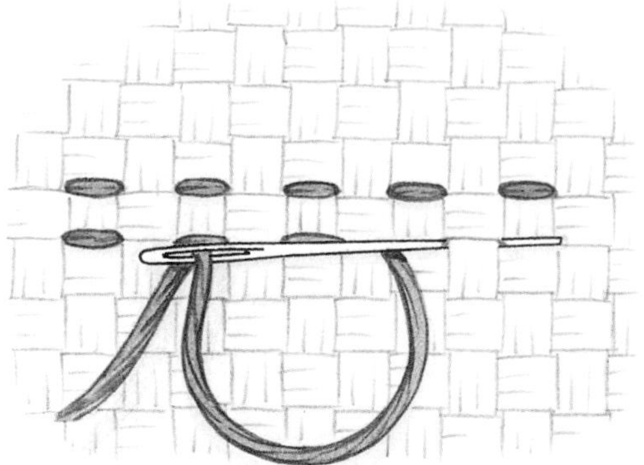

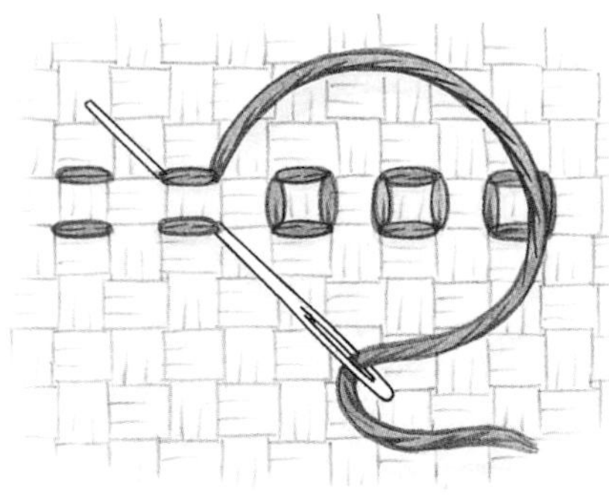

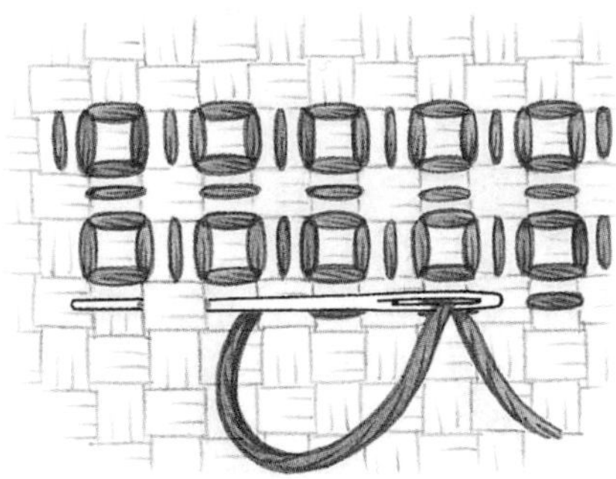

1 Working from right to left, work small horizontal stitches to the left-hand edge of the shape. Then, working from left to right, work a second row of small horizontal stitches under the first, as shown.

2 Work from right to left. Work small vertical stitches to form squares from the rows of horizontal stitches.

3 Working from left to right, make a vertical stitch between each square; then, working from right to left, make a horizontal stitch below each square, centering each stitch across a fabric block.

Working pattern five

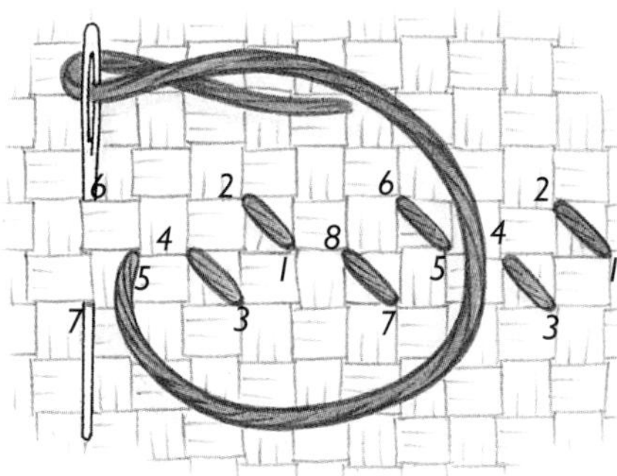

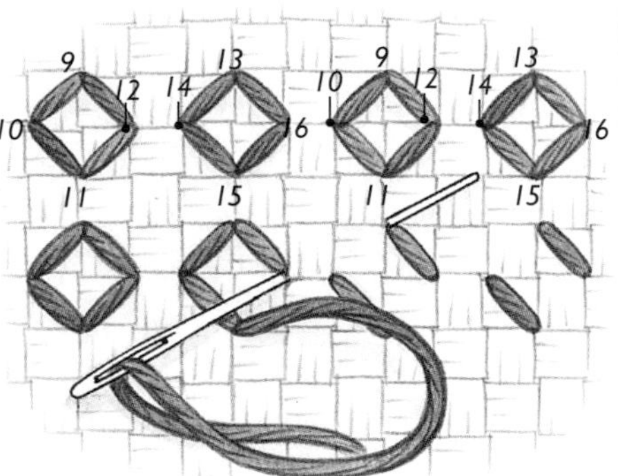

1 Work from right to left. Make four small diagonal stitches following the sequence 1–8. Continue to the left-hand edge of the shape.

2 Work from left to right. Make four diagonal stitches, following the sequence 9–16. Continue in this way to form diamond shapes across the fabric. Work subsequent rows beneath the first, leaving one unworked fabric block between each row.

SEWING BOX

TONAL VALUES

When deciding which areas of a design should be light or dark, you may find a newspaper very helpful. Various sizes of newsprint can give a variety of tones. Headlines suggest large, bold patterns, while solid print can suggest small repeats. Tear pieces of newsprint into the appropriate shapes and lay them on the design to help you decide where to position the various dark and light patterns.

Working pattern six

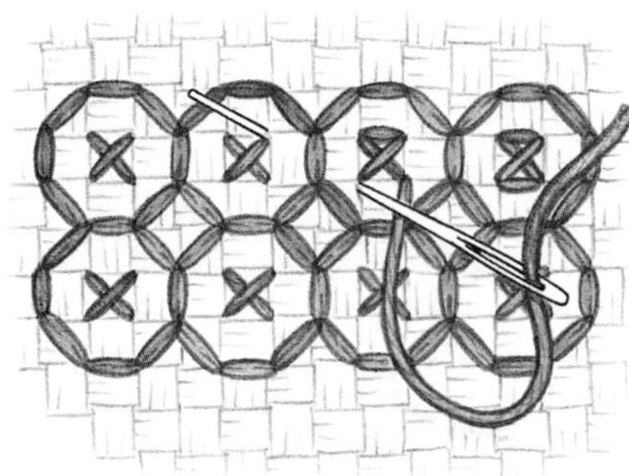

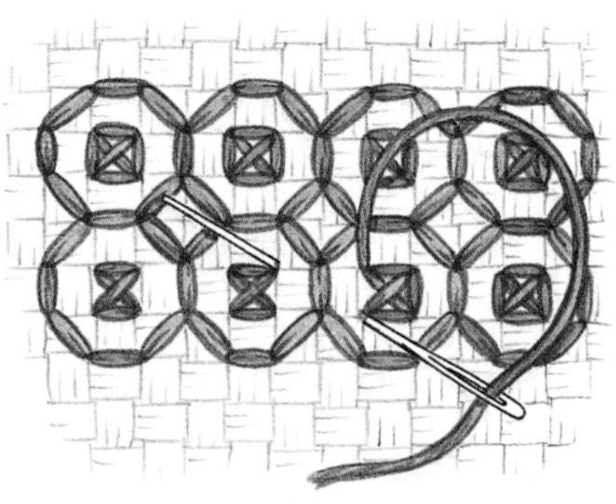

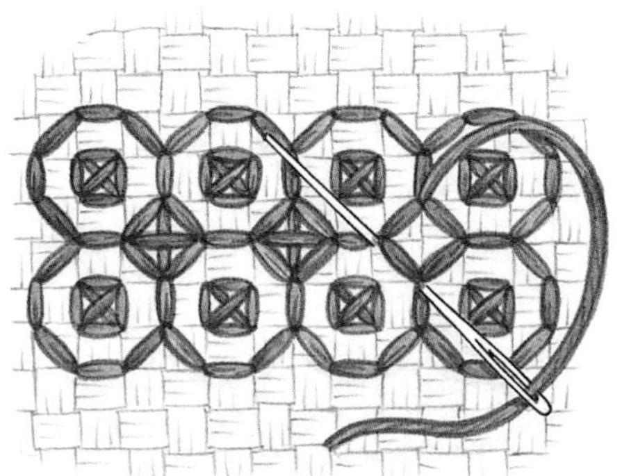

1 First fill the shape with Pattern one (see page 92). Add horizontal stitches across the top and base of each cross stitch.

2 Work small vertical stitches to the left and right of the cross stitches to form squares around them.

3 To complete the pattern, work small vertical and horizontal stitches to form crosses inside the diamond shapes between octagons.

Blackwork patterns are very versatile and can be used to add extra depth and tone to other forms of counted thread work. For added variety, designs can be worked at an angle: work the stitches diagonally across the fabric blocks in the usual sequence.

Pattern collection

The patterns shown here are based on the square and the star and produce a fairly dense texture. **Patterns seven and eight** give a light effect and are made up of squares and diagonal stitches. **Pattern nine** alternates stars and squares and provides greater density than patterns seven and eight. **Pattern ten** is fairly heavyweight and links stars with a series of straight and diagonal stitches.

For more blackwork patterns, see pages 91–94.

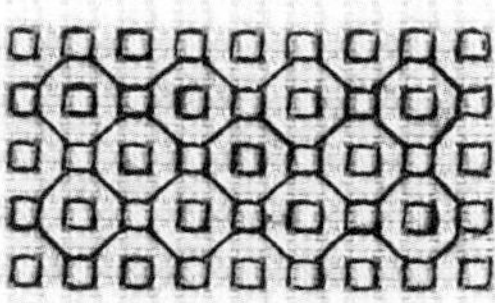

Pattern seven

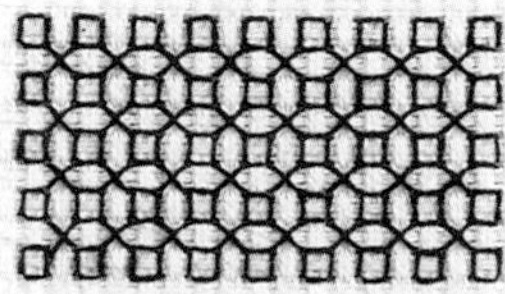

Pattern eight

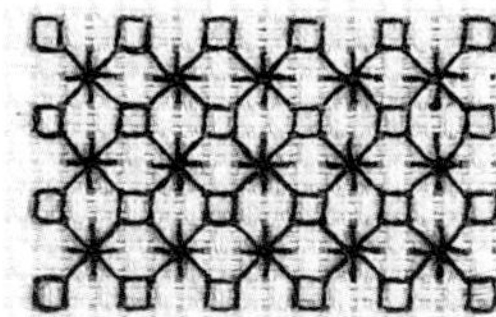

Pattern nine

Pattern ten

Pattern seven worked diagonally

Working pattern seven

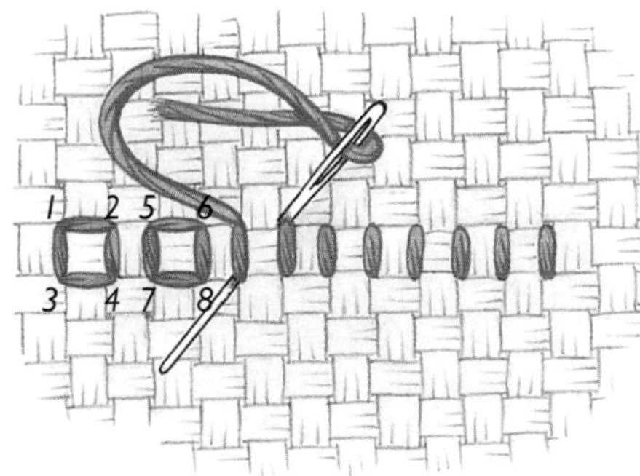

1 Working from right to left, make a row of upright stitches over one fabric block as in step **1** of Pattern three (see page 93). Join with horizontal stitches to form squares, following the sequence 1–8. Repeat to fill the shape, placing the rows one block apart.

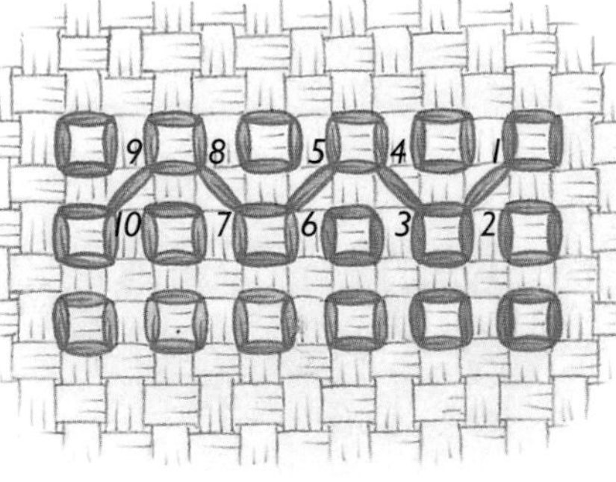

2 Rejoin the thread near the top right of the shape, and join the first two rows of squares with diagonal stitches following the sequence 1–10.

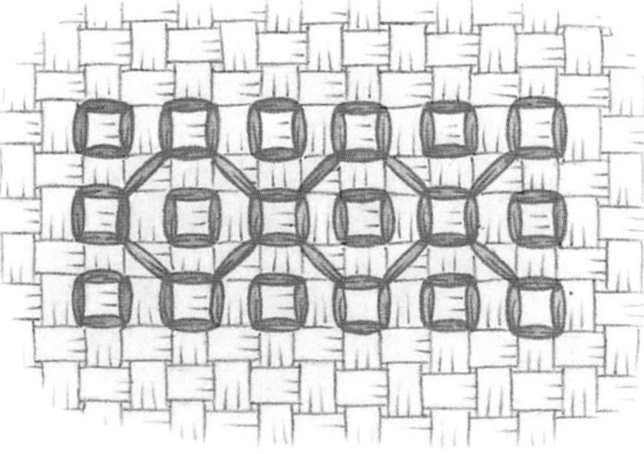

3 Turn at the end of the row and join the second and third row of squares in the same way, but this time slant the stitches to complete the lozenge shapes. Repeat these two rows to fill the shape.

Working pattern eight

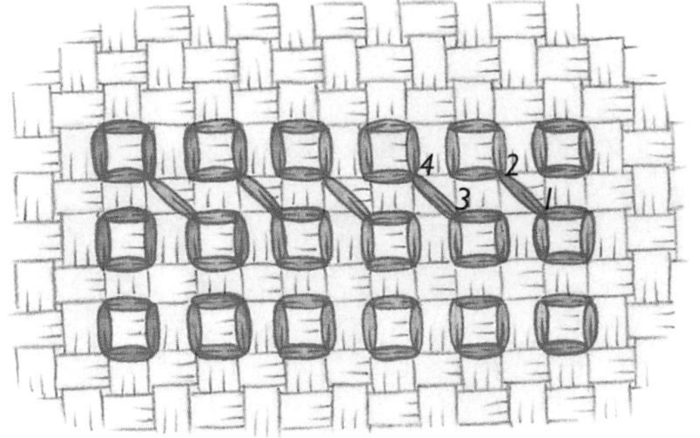

1 Fill the shape with squares as in step **1** on page 95. Starting near the top right, join the first two rows of squares with diagonal stitches following the sequence 1–4.

2 Turn at the end of the row. Work diagonal stitches crossing those previously made and following the sequence 5–8. Repeat these two rows to fill the shape.

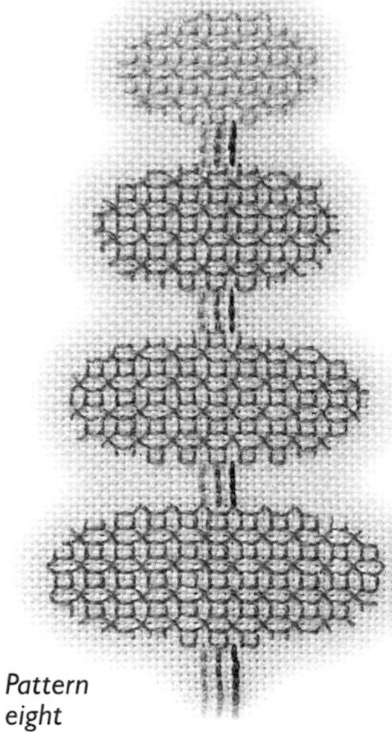
Pattern eight

Working pattern nine

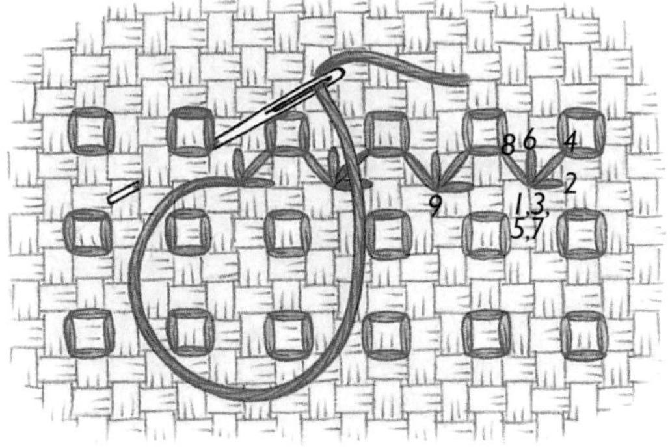

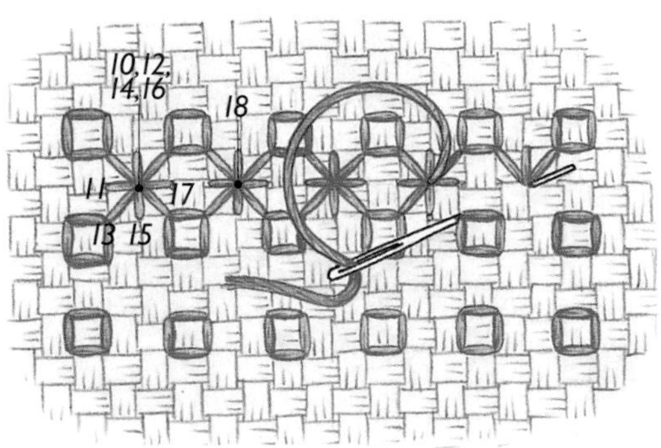

1 Work squares as in step **1** on page 95, but space them two blocks apart. Starting at the top right, work straight and diagonal stitches, following the sequence 1–9. Note that four stitches share the same hole.

2 Turn at the end of the row, and follow the sequence 10–18 to complete the star shapes. Repeat these two rows to fill the shape. Remember that in each sequence four stitches share the same hole.

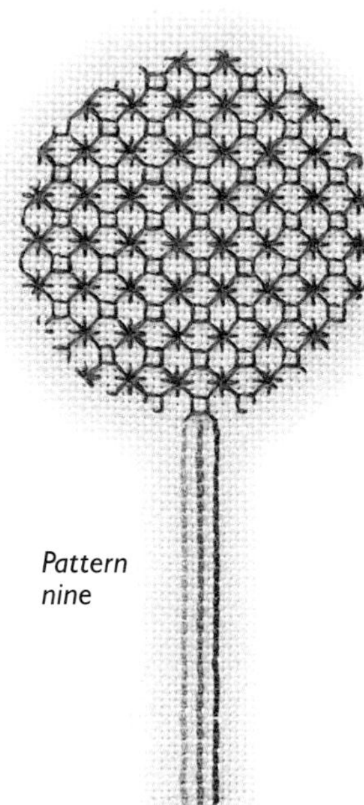
Pattern nine

Working pattern ten

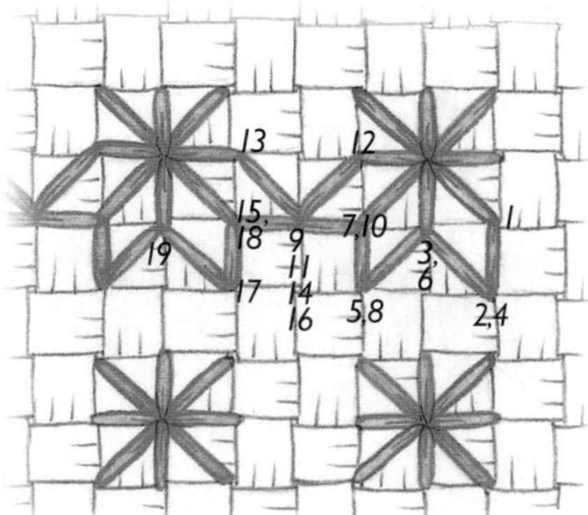

1 Make rows of stars as in pattern 9 (above), but position the stars and rows two blocks apart. Work straight and diagonal stitches below the first row, following the sequence 1–19. Some stitches share the same hole.

2 Turn at the end of the row. Work straight and diagonal stitches as before to finish the pattern between the first two rows of stars. Repeat these two rows to fill the shape.

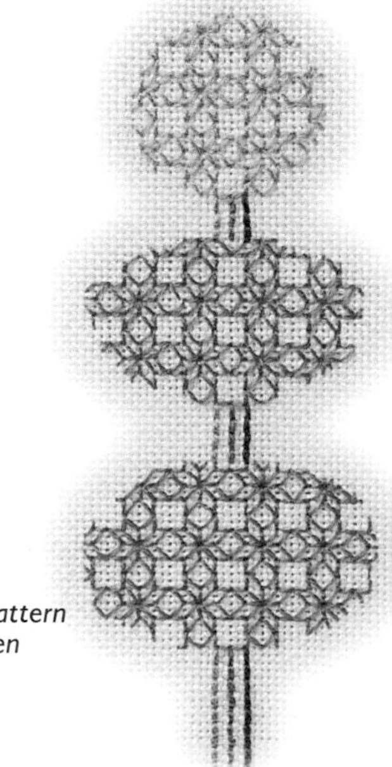
Pattern ten

Shisha stitches

A traditional Indian handicraft, Shisha embroidery is used to stitch tiny round mirrors or pieces of tin onto fabric. A framework of stitches secures the mirror, and an embroidered border hides the rough edges. The exotic patterns produced can be used to give a colorful ethnic look to clothes, home furnishings, and accessories.

Shisha mirrors are sold by specialist needlework suppliers; alternatively, use large sequins or paillettes with a hole near the edge, which can be covered by the embroidered border.

Any embroidery thread can be used for Shisha work, but embroidery floss is the most versatile, as the number of strands can be varied to suit the size of the mirror or sequin. Metallic threads also work well. Use the same thread to work both the framework and the border; you may need to use one length of thread for the framework and a second length to complete the border. Try to avoid breaking off and rejoining the border thread—the finished embroidery will look much neater without breaks.

Shisha stitch 1

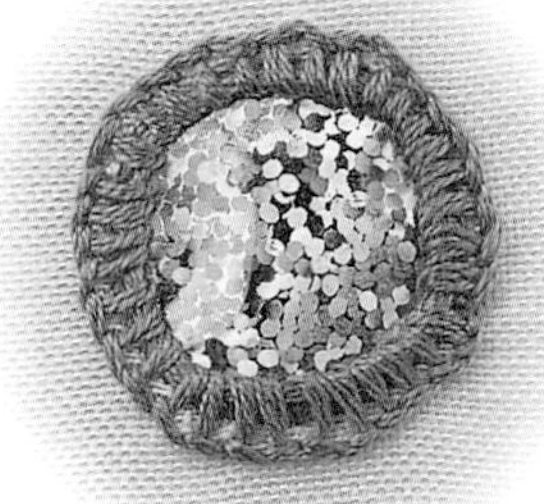

Shisha stitch 2

Shisha stitch 3

Shisha stitch 1 is a modern American variation which leaves the framework uncovered to form part of the decoration. The edges of the mirror remain visible, so use either mirrors with a smooth edge or sequins.

Shisha stitch 2 has a simple framework which is covered with a plain border of blanket stitch (see page 57).

Shisha stitch 3 is the traditional method of securing mirrors to fabric with a snug framework of straight stitches, and it takes a little practice to perfect.

Starting and ending

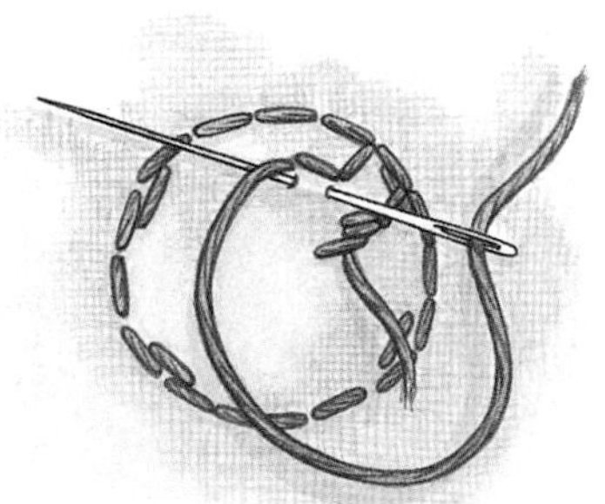

To start, anchor the thread with three tiny straight stitches, positioned so that they will be covered by the mirror. After working the embroidery, fasten off the thread with three straight stitches on the back of the fabric, directly beneath the mirror.

Working Shisha stitch 1

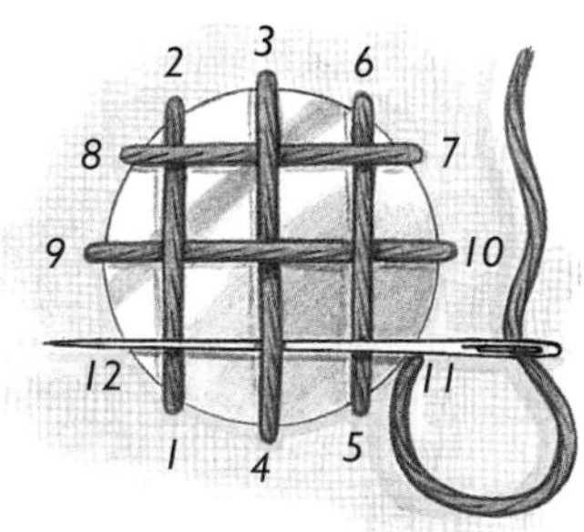

1 Bring the needle to the front at 1 and make three vertical stitches across the mirror, following the sequence 2–6. Then make three horizontal stitches, weaving them through the previous stitches and following the sequence 7–12.

2 Bring the needle to the front, close to the edge of the mirror, and work basic chain stitches (see page 61) on the fabric around the mirror. Space the stitches evenly, and work them as close to the mirror as possible.

Working Shisha stitch 2

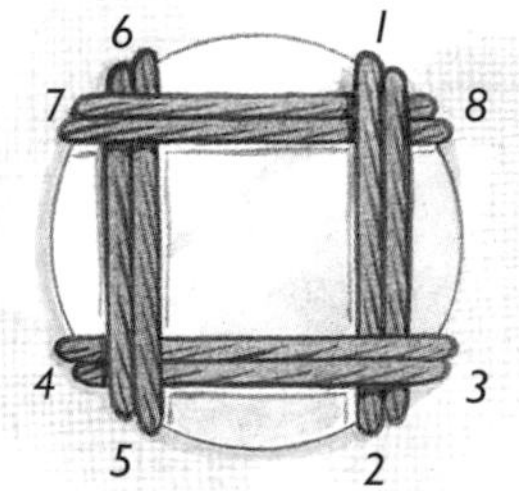

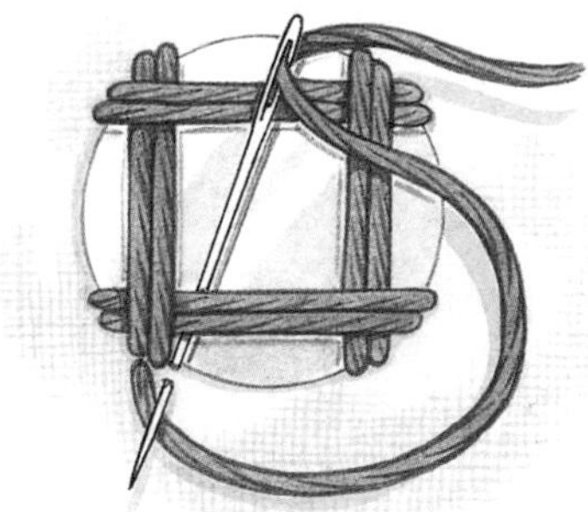

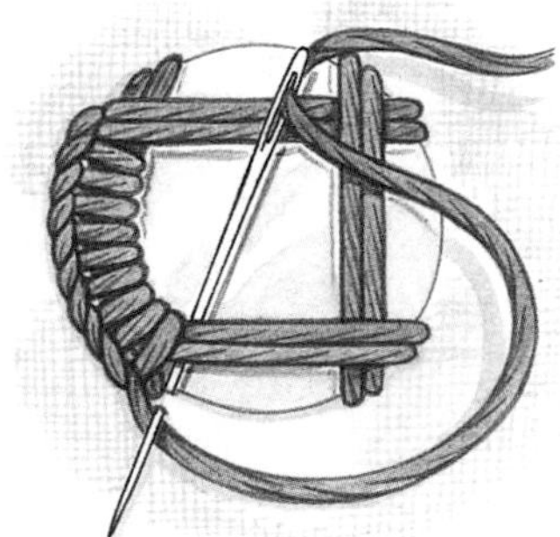

1 Bring the needle to the front at 1, and work four straight stitches, following the sequence 2–8, to make a square framework. Be careful to take the thread from 7–8 under the stitch 1–2. Bring the needle through at 1 again, and repeat with a second set of stitches inside the first.

2 Bring the needle to the front, close to the edge of the mirror, and take it over and under the framework. Pick up a tiny piece of fabric at the edge of the mirror, and pull the needle through over the working thread.

3 Continue in this way, working in a counterclockwise direction around the mirror; take the needle over and under pairs of framework threads with every stitch, and work the stitches close together to cover the edge of the mirror completely.

Working Shisha stitch 3

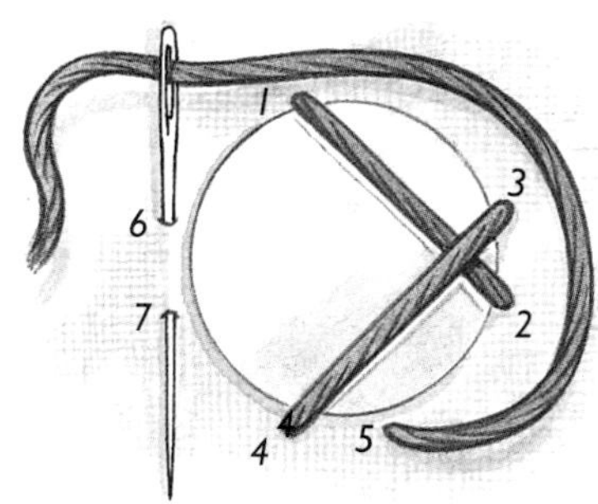

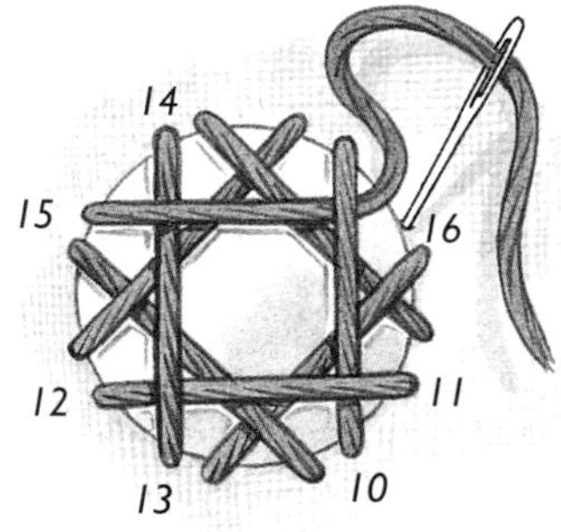

1 Bring the thread to the front at the top of the mirror at 1. Holding the mirror down on the fabric with your free thumb, work the first three stitches of the framework, following the sequence 2–7.

2 Slip the needle under the first stitch of the framework, then insert it at 8 to complete the diamond-shaped bottom framework. Bring the needle to the front at 9, ready to work the top square framework.

3 Take the needle across the mirror, insert it at 10, and bring it to the front at 11. Follow the sequence 12–16 to complete the top framework.

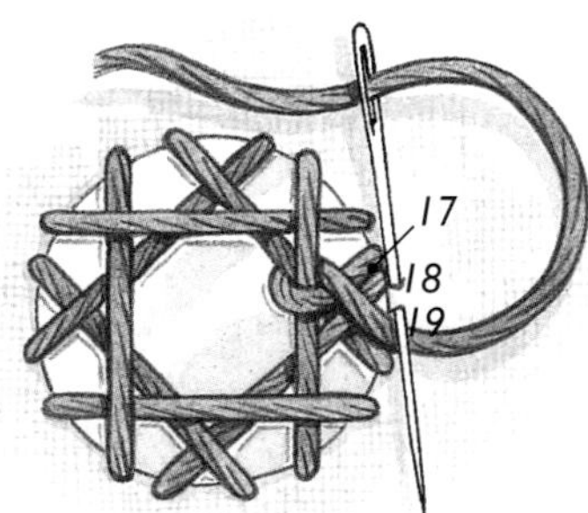

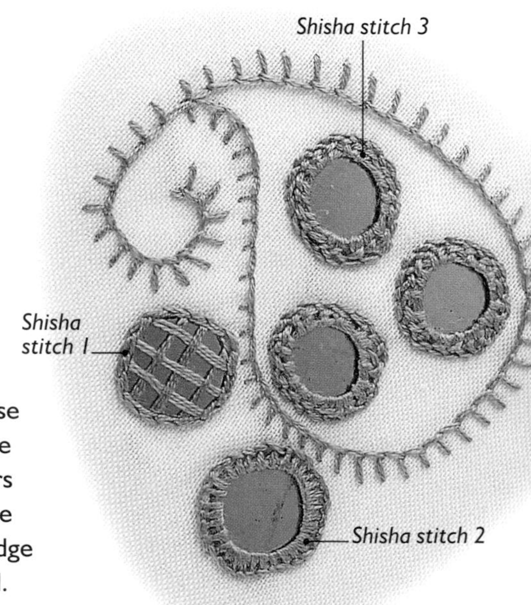

4 Bring the needle to the front at 17. Take it over and under the framework where the vertical and diagonal stitches intersect. Insert the needle at 18, and bring it to the front again at 19, keeping the working thread under the needle. Pull the thread through.

5 Repeat step **4**, working clockwise around the mirror and taking the working thread over and under pairs of threads with every stitch. Arrange the stitches close together so the edge of the mirror is completely covered.

Easy whipped stitches

Whipped stitches create a very decorative effect, particularly when they are worked in two colors. Ideal for outlines, they can also be repeated across a shape to make a light filling.

There are many types of whipped stitches, but they all have one thing in common: each has a foundation row of a basic stitch, such as running or chain stitch, which is then whipped over with a second thread. In the majority of cases, the second thread does not enter the fabric. Use a crewel or chenille needle to work the foundation row. For the whipping, use a tapestry needle to avoid splitting the foundation stitches.

You can vary the look of these stitches by using different threads for the whipping; pearl cotton, for example, gives a raised, rope-like effect, while embroidery floss produces a flatter, wider line. You can also use metallic threads that are too heavy or fragile to stitch directly into the fabric. As a general rule, choose a slightly thicker thread for the whipping stitches, so that they stand out well from the background fabric.

Whipped running stitch, also known as cordonnet stitch, makes a narrow, loosely twisted line.

Whipped backstitch makes a neat, slightly raised line.

Whipped stem stitch makes a light-textured line, like fine cord.

Whipped chain stitch makes a wider, very decorative line.

Whipped satin stitch is used both as a wide line stitch and as a solid filling for narrow shapes, such as leaves. In this case, the whipping stitches are worked into the fabric, so work them with a sharp-pointed embroidery needle.

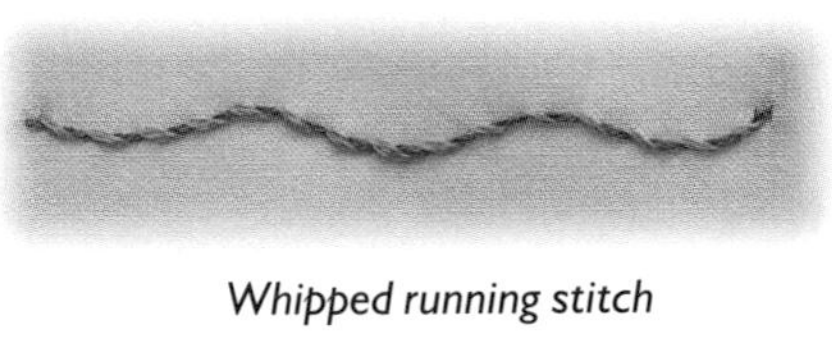

Whipped running stitch

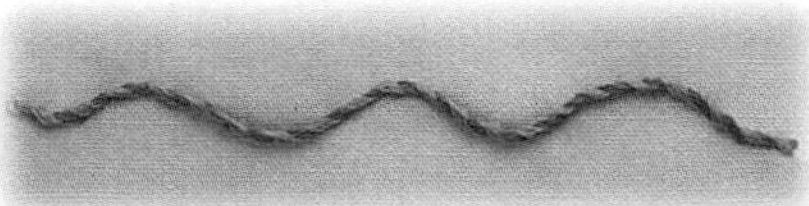

Whipped backstitch

Whipped stem stitch

Whipped chain stitch

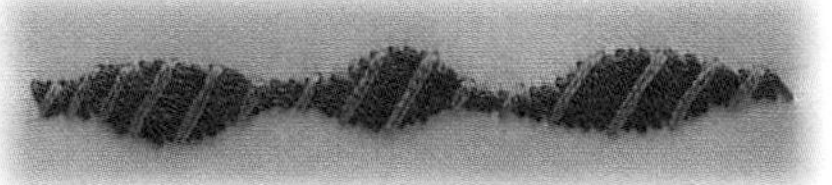

Whipped satin stitch

Starting and fastening off

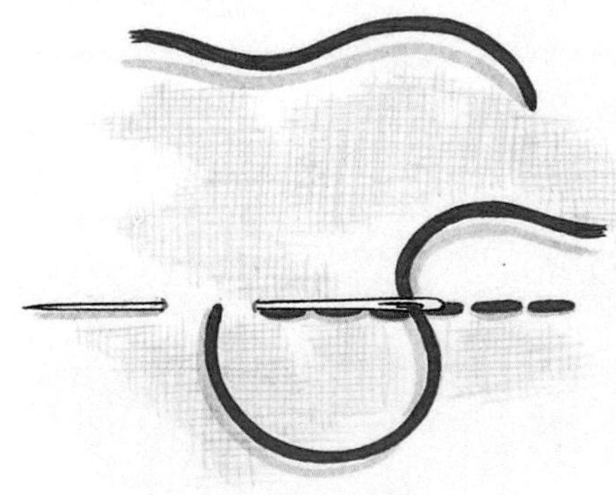

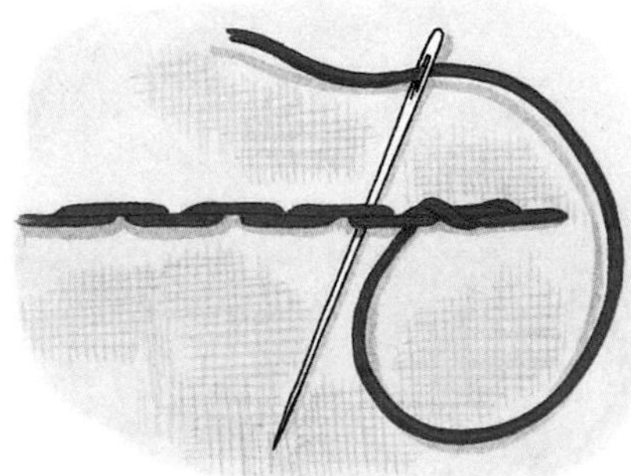

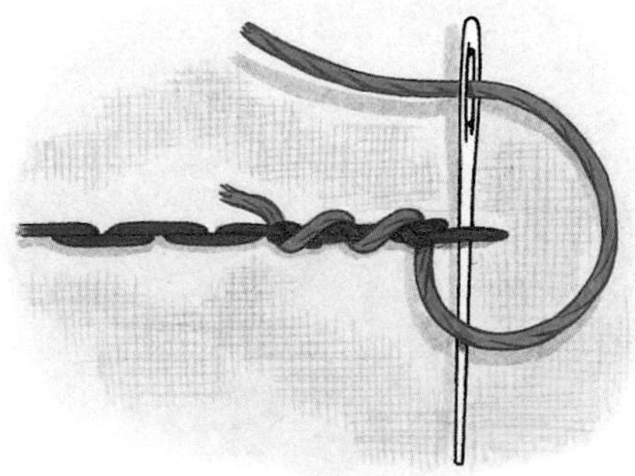

1 To start the foundation row, leave a 2 in. (5 cm) tail of thread on the front of the fabric, close to your starting point. Stitch the foundation row.

2 At the end of the row, take the thread to the back and darn it into the last few stitches. Return to the beginning of the row, pull the thread tail through to the back, and darn the end under the first few stitches.

3 To secure the beginning of the whipping thread, darn it into the back of the first few stitches of the foundation row. Bring the thread to the front and work the whipping stitches. To secure the end of the thread, darn it into the back of several foundation stitches in the same way.

Working whipped running stitch

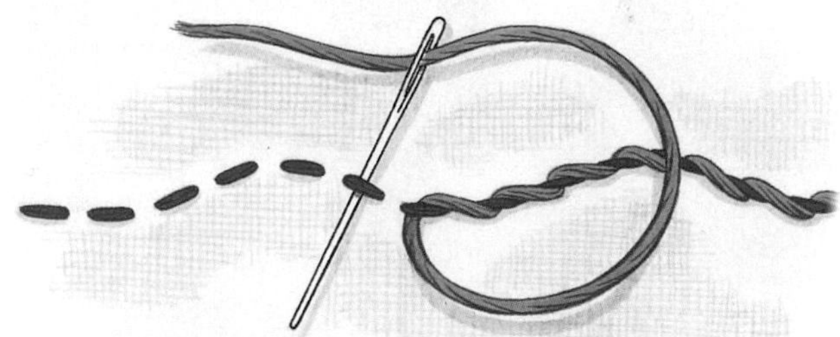

1 Work a foundation row of running stitch (see page 26). Make the stitches closer together than usual.

2 Using a tapestry needle, bring the whipping thread to the front at the beginning of the foundation row. Whip the thread over and under the running stitches without going through the fabric.

Working whipped backstitch

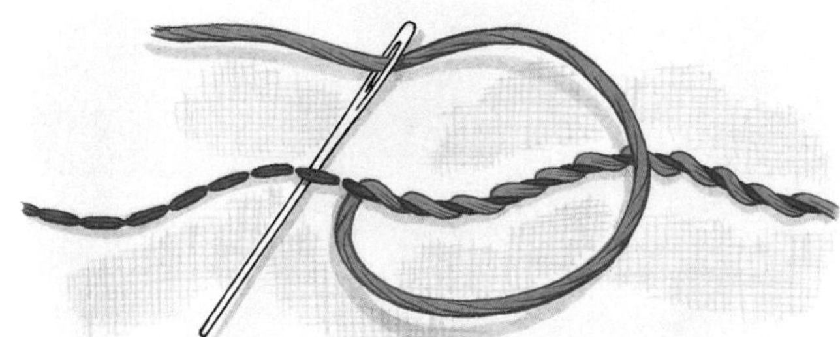

1 Work a row of backstitch (see page 26), making the backstitches a little larger than usual.

2 Using a tapestry needle, bring the whipping thread to the front at the beginning of the foundation row. Whip the thread over and under the backstitches without going through the fabric.

Working whipped stem stitch

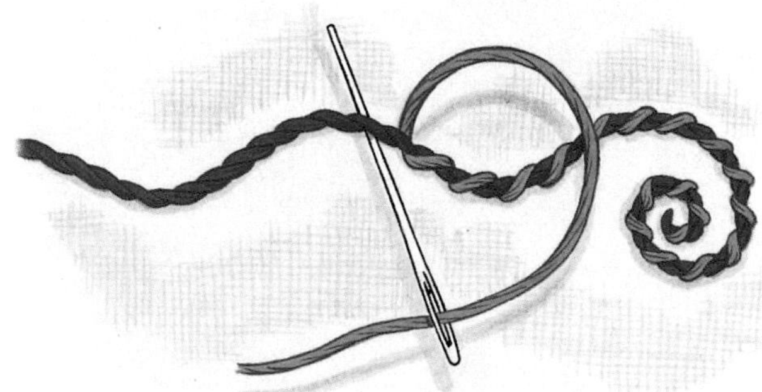

1 Work a row of stem stitch (see page 26). Make the stitches larger than usual.

2 Using a tapestry needle, bring the whipping thread to the front at the start of the foundation row. Whip the thread over and under the stem stitches without going through the fabric.

Working whipped chain stitch

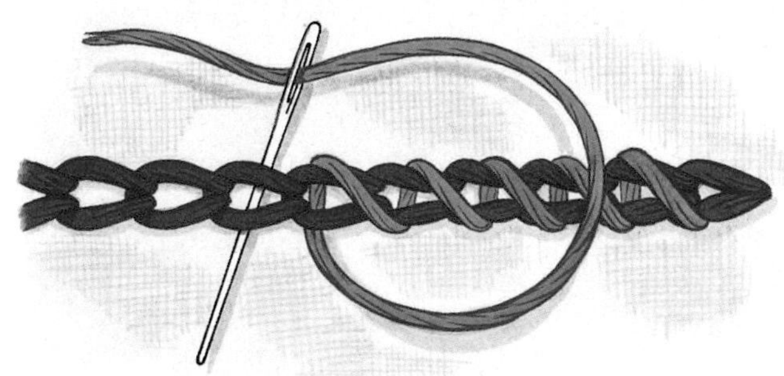

1 Work a row of chain stitch (see page 61). Turn the fabric around so that the start of the row is on the right.

2 Using a tapestry needle, bring the whipping thread to the front at the start of the row. Whip over and under the row, without going through the fabric.

Working whipped satin stitch

Work satin stitch to fill the shape (see page 28). Using a crewel or chenille needle, bring the whipping thread to the front at the top of the shape. Work the whipping stitches at right angles to the satin stitches. Space them slightly apart, inserting the needle close to the edge of the satin stitching.

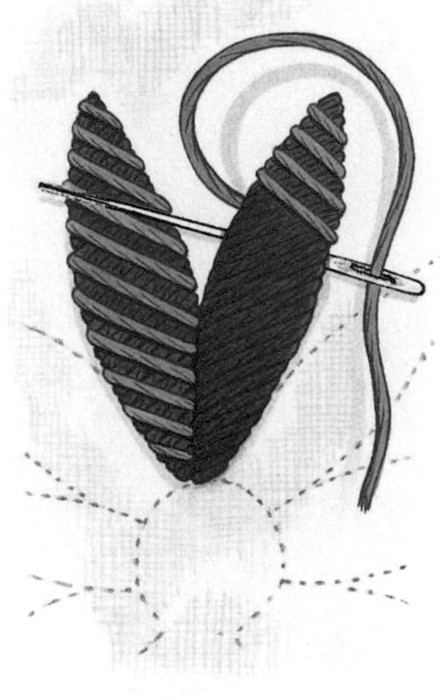

Laced border stitches

Laced stitches create a very decorative effect, as they are worked in two or more thread colors. A simple foundation row in the first color is embellished with a second color of thread, which is laced or knotted over the top, without entering the fabric. Some stitches use a third color.

The stitches shown here are usually thought of as wide border stitches, but they can also be used for fillings by working several rows close together.

When working these stitches in straight rows, mark guide lines with a water-soluble or air-erasable marking pen. To start and fasten off any of these stitches, refer to page 99. You should use an embroidery needle to work the foundation row and a tapestry needle to add the ornamentation.

Tied herringbone stitch and the more flowing **threaded herringbone stitch** (also known as interlaced herringbone) are both very easy to work. The first gives a pretty knotted band; the second has a softer, woven feel.

Interlaced chain stitch makes a decorative line in three thread colors, while **raised chain band** gives a more open line with a knotted central band.

Checkered chain band gives a plaited effect. It's rather complex: two different threads are woven alternately through a row of straight stitches.

Working tied herringbone stitch

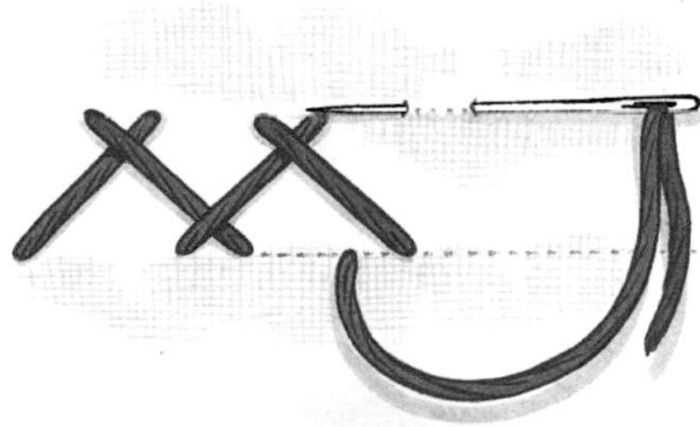

1 Bring the embroidery needle to the front at the bottom left, and work a row of herringbone stitch, as shown on page 49. Fasten off the thread securely.

2 Thread a tapestry needle with a second thread and bring it to the front at the bottom right-hand end of the row. Work coral stitches (see page 81) over the herringbone intersections.

Tied herringbone stitch

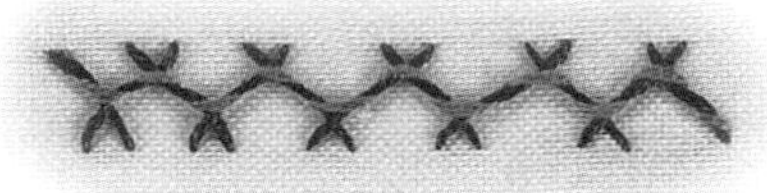

Threaded herringbone stitch

Interlaced chain stitch

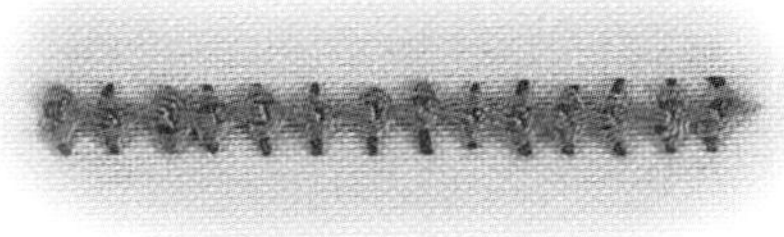

Raised chain band

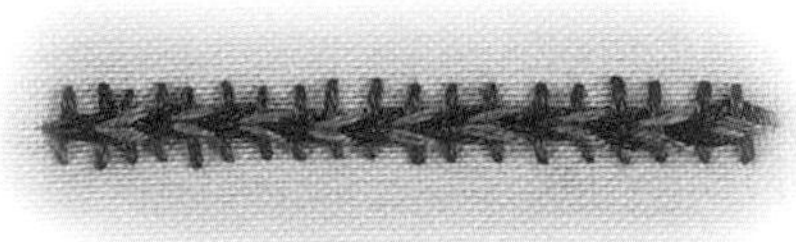

Checkered chain band

Working threaded herringbone stitch

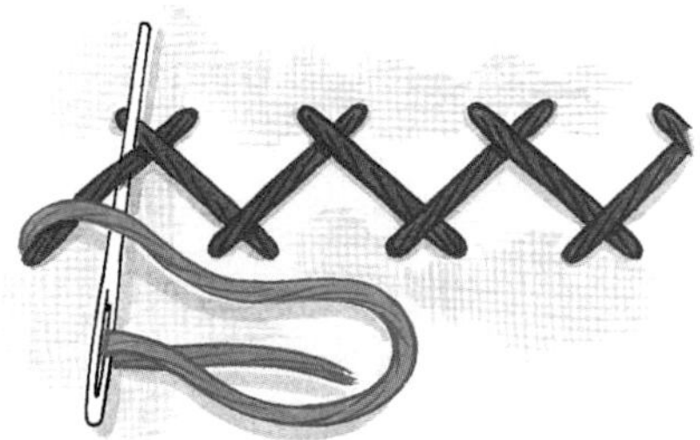

1 Work a row of herringbone stitch, as in step 1 (above). Thread a tapestry needle with a contrasting thread, and bring it to the front just above the base of the first stitch. Slip the needle upward beneath the first diagonal stitch as shown.

2 Pull the thread through, then slip the needle downward beneath the second diagonal stitch. Repeat along the row. Take the thread to the back and fasten it off.

Working Interlaced chain stitch

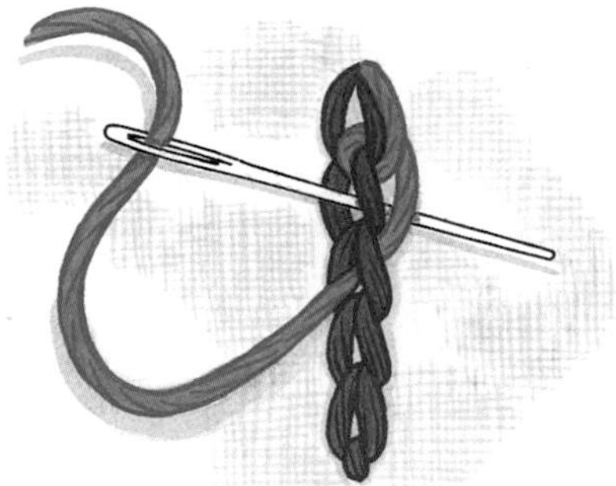

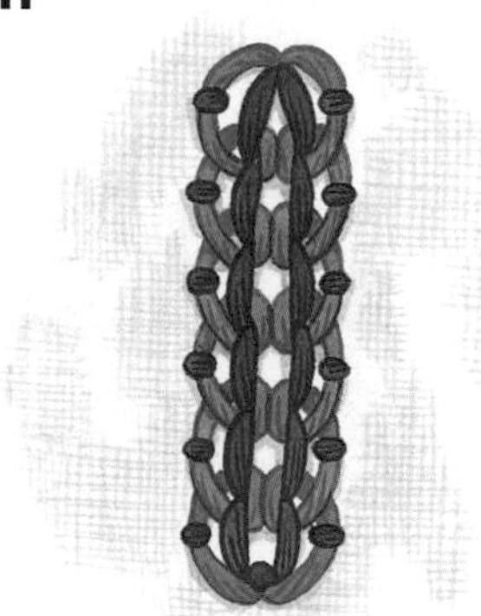

1 Work a vertical row of fairly large chain stitches. Thread a tapestry needle with a second thread, and bring it to the front at the top. Take the needle under the second chain stitch and back up through the first. Then take it under the third chain stitch and back up through the second.

2 Continue in this way down the right-hand side of the chain, keeping the loops quite loose. Lace the left side of the chain in the same way. Thread a tapestry needle with a third thread, and work tiny horizontal straight stitches at regular intervals to anchor each whipped loop.

Working raised chain band

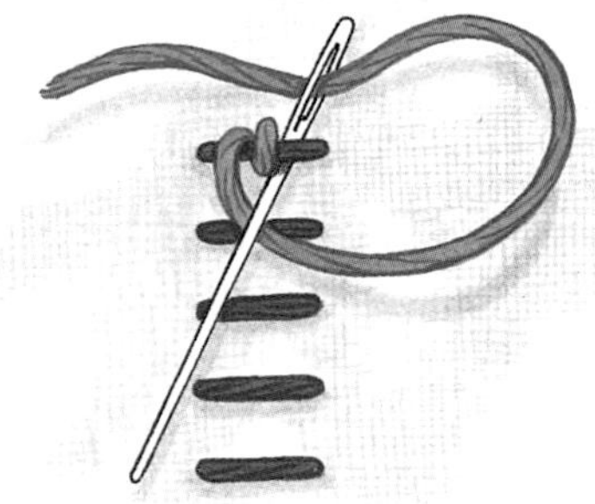

1 Work a vertical row of straight stitches. Thread a tapestry needle with a second thread, and bring it to the front at the top. Take it under the first stitch and pull the thread through.

2 Slip the needle under the first stitch, just right of the center, keeping the working thread under the needle. Pull the thread through, leaving a loop below the straight stitch.

3 Repeat these two movements along the row, following steps **1–2**. Take the thread through to the back and fasten it off securely.

Working checkered chain band

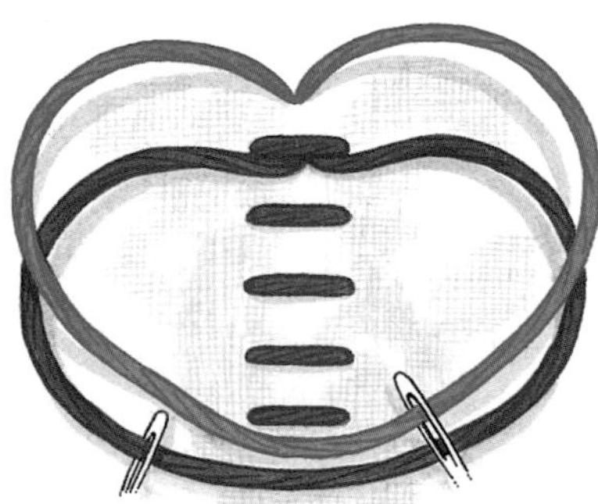

1 Work a vertical row of straight stitches as in step **1** of raised chain band. Thread two tapestry needles with contrasting threads, doubling the thread in each. Bring the first thread out above the top stitch and the second out below the stitch.

2 Take the first needle over the first straight stitch, looping the first thread around the second thread. Then take the needle under the second straight stitch and through the second thread loop, as shown.

3 Take the second needle over the second straight stitch, looping the second thread around the first thread. Then take it under the third straight stitch and through the first thread loop. Continue in this way. Take the threads to the back and fasten them off.

Spider's web stitches

Spider's web stitches, also known as woven wheels, are used in free and ribbon embroidery to create heavily textured surfaces. Worked individually, they make effective flower centers and add bold splashes of color to geometric designs.

The three stitches featured here are all constructed in the same way: a framework of straight stitches (spokes) is laced with a thicker thread. The lacing thread enters the fabric only at the beginning and end of the lacing.

Work the framework with an embroidery needle and a plain, smooth thread such as embroidery floss or pearl cotton; use a thicker thread or ribbon with a tapestry needle for the lacing.

For a neat finish, mark the shape of the spider's web—a circle or oval—on the fabric. Use an embroidery frame and space the foundation stitches across the shape as evenly as possible.

To secure the framework thread, anchor it with two or three tiny stitches in the center of the space to be covered by the spider's web. Anchor the lacing thread by weaving it into the back of the foundation stitches.

Spider's web, or woven wheel, has an odd number of foundation stitches. There are usually five or seven, but more or fewer can be used. The lacing thread is woven over and under the spokes.

Ribbed spider's web, or ribbed wheel, has an even number of spokes—usually eight or twelve—with a laced spiral of backstitches.

Stem stitch spider's web, or stem stitch wheel, is similar to the ribbed but has stem-stitch lacing.

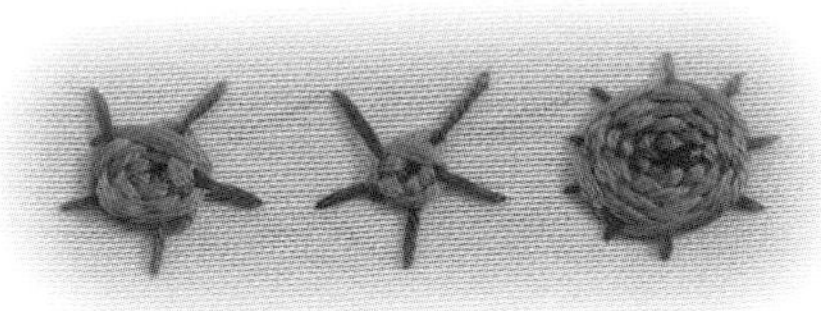

Spider's web stitch

Ribbed spider's web stitch

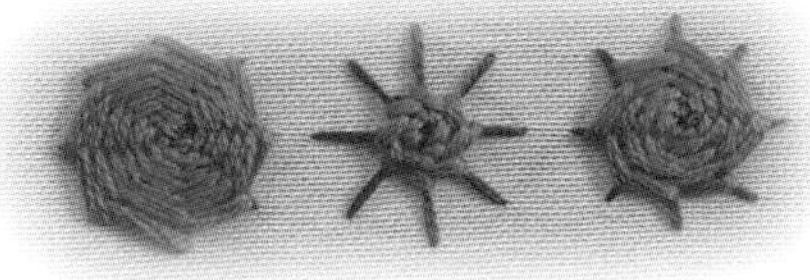

Stem stitch spider's web

Working spider's web stitch

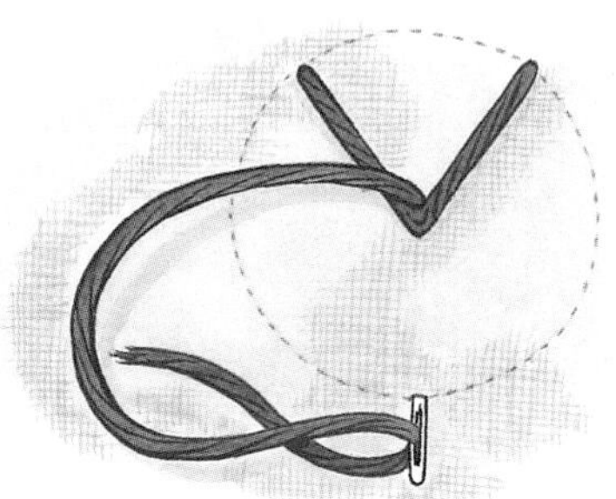

1 For a small, five-spoke framework, bring the needle to the front at the edge of the shape. Work a fly stitch with a long anchoring stitch, to make three spokes.

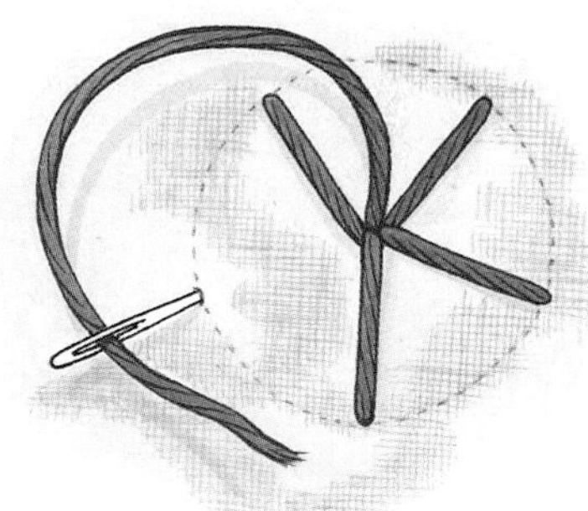

2 Bring the needle to the front again at the center of the fly stitch. Make two straight stitches to complete the framework.

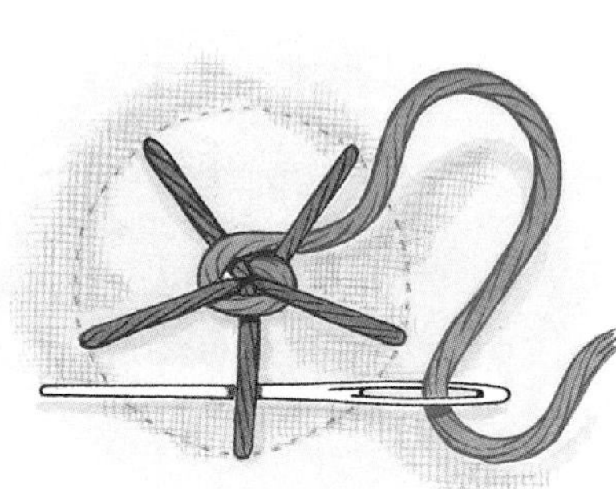

3 Using a tapestry needle, bring the lacing thread to the front at the center. Working outward in a spiral, weave the thread over and under the spokes until the web is the desired size. Take the thread to the back at the edge of the shape.

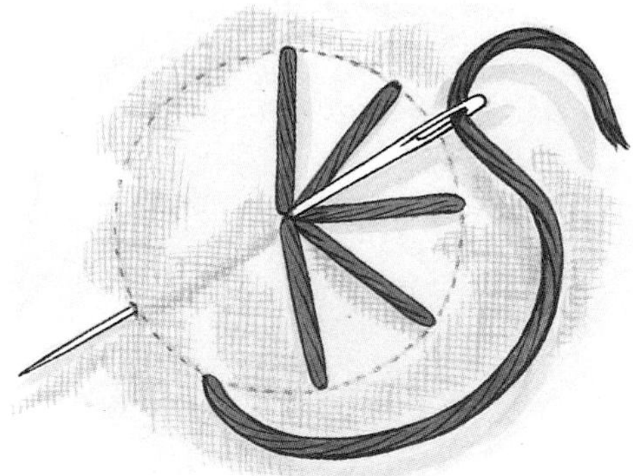

For a larger framework with more spokes, work an odd number of straight stitches radiating out from the center. Work the lacing following step **3**.

Working ribbed spider's web stitch

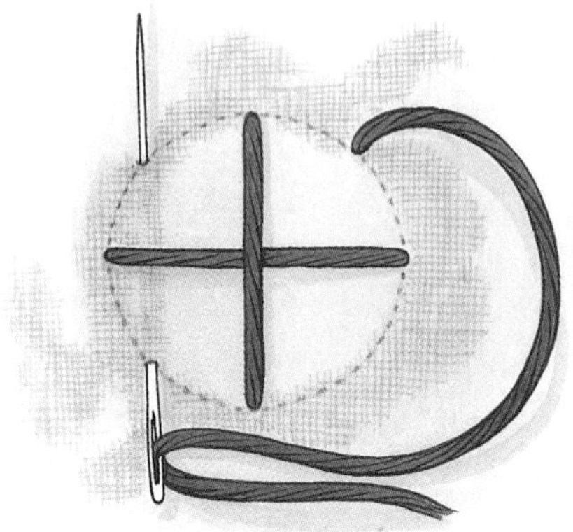

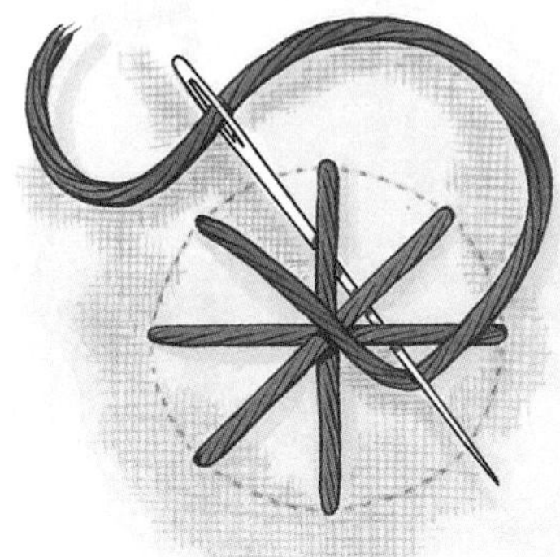

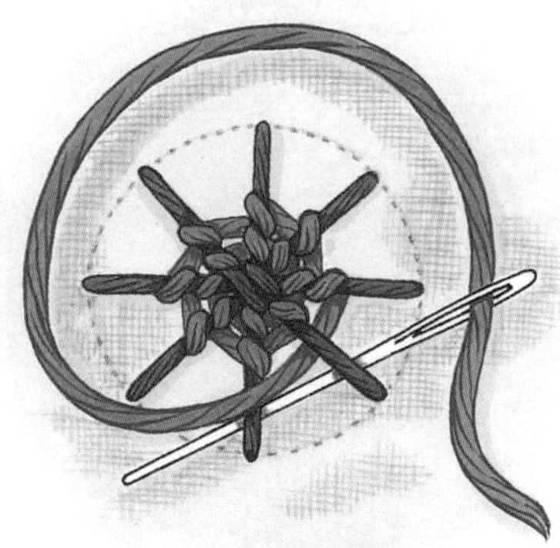

1 Bring the needle to the front at the edge of the shape. Work three straight stitches from edge to edge, crossing at the center. Bring the needle to the front at the edge, ready to work the fourth crossing stitch.

2 Take the needle over and under the center of the three previously worked stitches and loop the working thread under the point. Pull the thread gently to make a knot. Complete the fourth stitch.

3 Using a tapestry needle, bring the lacing thread through at the center of the web. Working outward in a spiral, make a series of backstitches over individual spokes until the web is the desired size. Take the thread to the back at the edge of the shape.

A ribbed spider's web worked over 12 spokes, complete with dangling spider, creates a richly textured embroidered motif.

To work ribbed spider's web stitch with a larger framework, work an uneven number of straight stitches across the shape. Follow step **2** to make the last stitch, and step **3** to lace the framework.

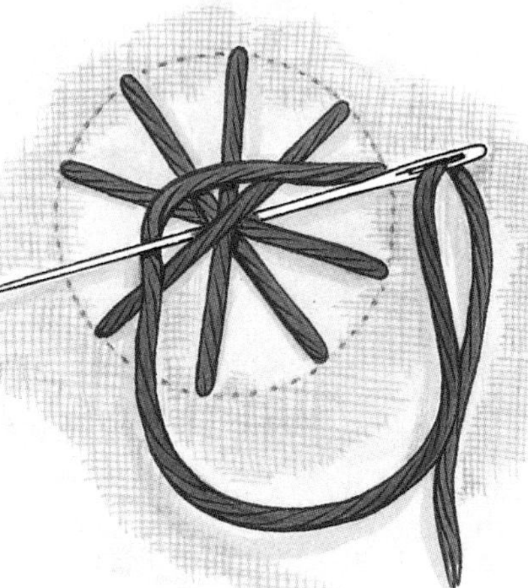

Working stem stitch spider's web

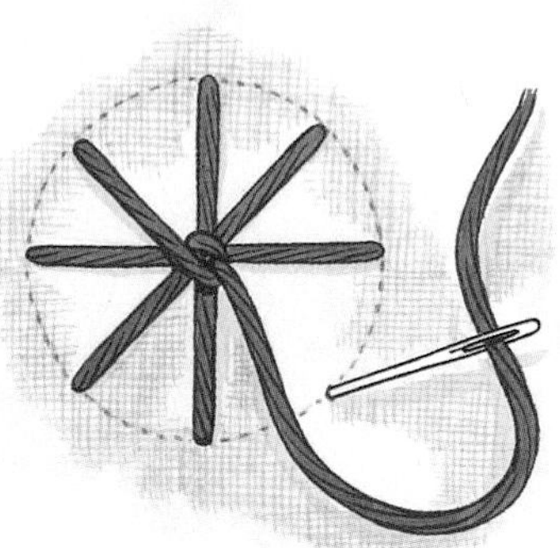

1 Work the framework to the desired size, with an even number of spokes, following the steps for Ribbed spider's web stitch.

2 Using a tapestry needle, bring the lacing thread to the front at the center of the web. Work stem stitches outwards in a spiral, going forward over two spokes and back under one spoke until the web is the desired size.

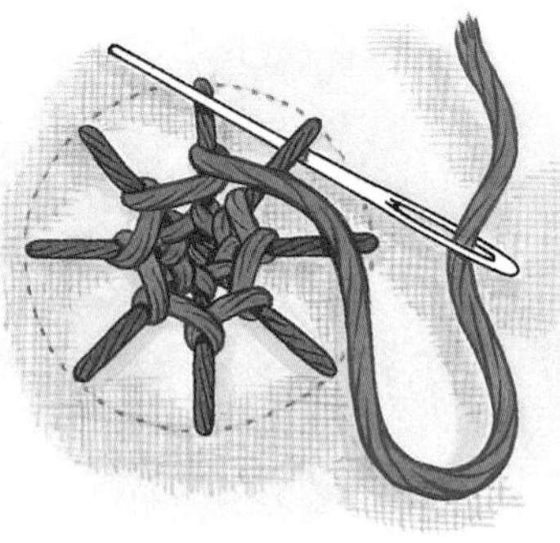

Mock smocking stitches

Mock smocking is very decorative, and it's deceptively simple to work. It resembles true smocking, but is worked on flat evenweave instead of gathered non-evenweave fabric. On clothing, it can be used to decorate yokes, bodices, and cuffs; it also looks good on household items such as tablecloths, napkins, and placemats.

Mock smocking stitches are all made in the same way: a foundation of spaced cross stitches is worked first, then a second thread is laced through the cross stitches.

The lacing thread enters the fabric only at the beginning and end of the row, so use a tapestry needle for the lacing so as to avoid snagging the fabric.

Any evenweave fabric is suitable for mock smocking. One of the most suitable fabrics is 14-count damask aida; this has a pretty sheen which shows off the stitching well. Mock smocking stitches can be used on non-evenweave fabric, but the finished result may be somewhat disappointing, as the effect depends on perfectly even stitches.

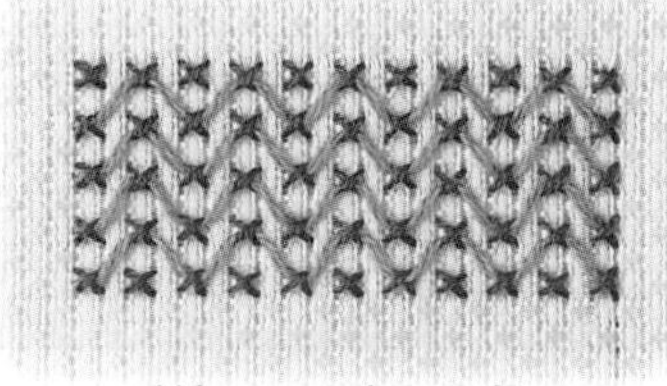

Waves mock smocking

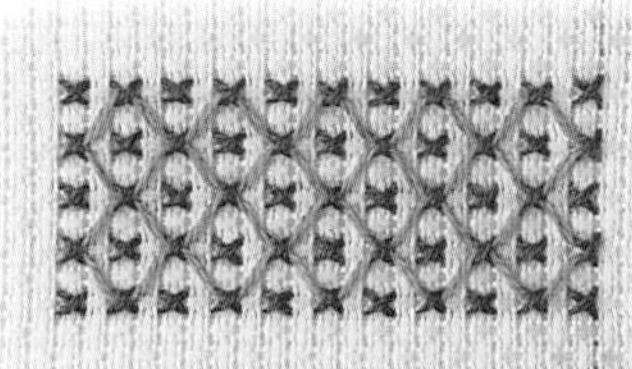

Trellis mock smocking

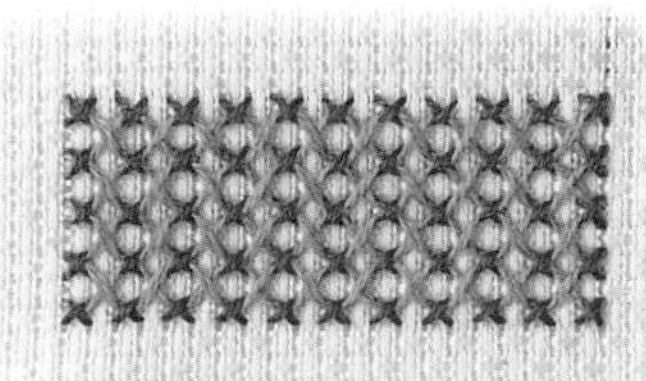

Honeycomb mock smocking

Work all the stitches shown here over at least three foundation rows, and make sure that each foundation row has an odd number of stitches so that the laced patterns can be finished neatly.

To start and fasten off any of the stitches below and overleaf, see page 99.

Waves mock smocking is a simple stitch to work and creates neat rows of wavelike zigzags.

Trellis mock smocking makes a laced trellis pattern which works particularly well over a large area.

Honeycomb mock smocking looks best when two different colors are used for the lacing.

Waves mock smocking

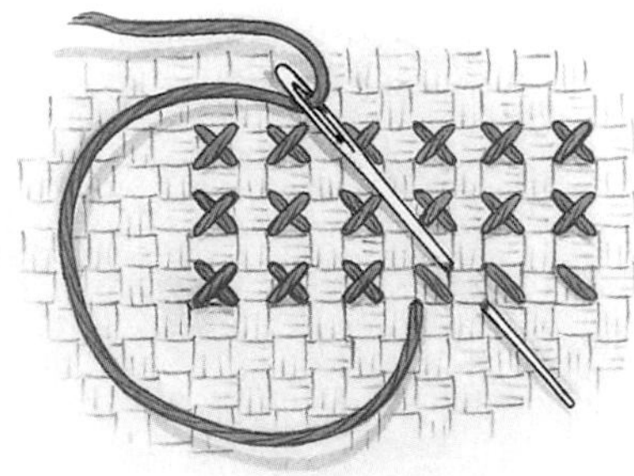

1 Work a foundation row of an odd number of cross stitches. Make each stitch over one fabric block and leave one fabric block between each stitch. Work a second row, one fabric block below the first, placing the crosses directly below the crosses on the first row. Continue in this way to work at least three foundation rows.

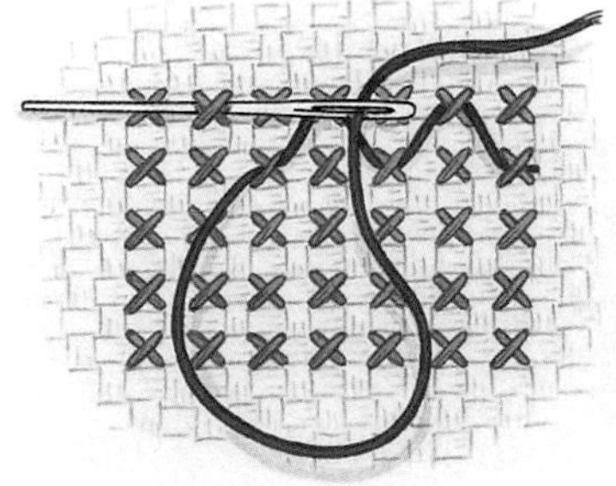

2 Bring the lacing thread out at the edge of the right-hand cross on the second foundation row. Slip the needle under the cross, pull the thread through, then slip the needle under the second cross on the first row and pull the thread through again. Continue in this way.

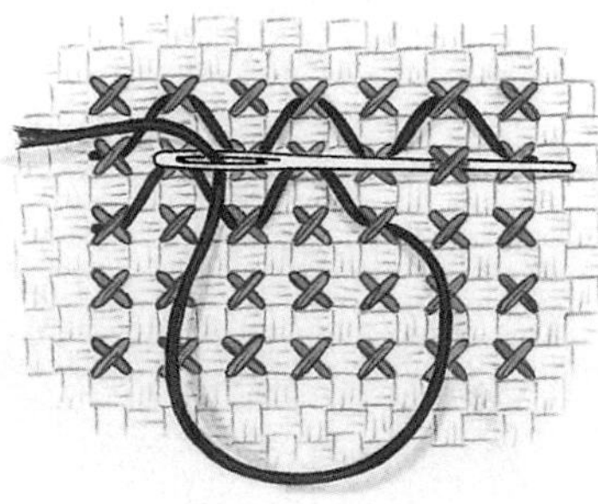

3 Insert the needle at the edge of the last cross on the second row. Bring it out to the front at the left-hand end of the next row down. Repeat the lacing in the opposite direction, this time lacing alternate stitches on rows two and three. Continue in this way to lace the remaining foundation rows.

Trellis mock smocking

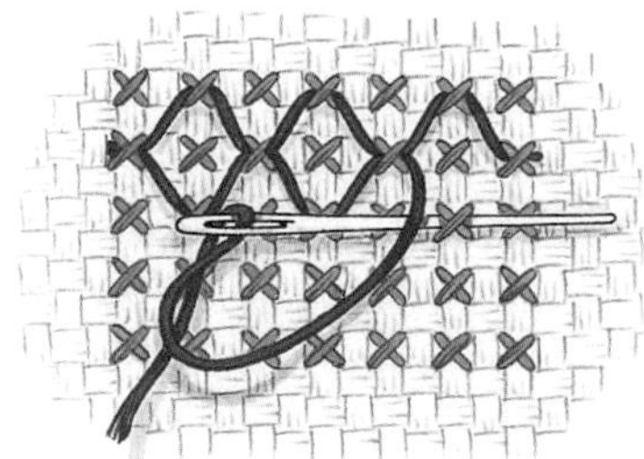

1 Work the foundation and the first lacing row, as for Waves (page 105). Insert the needle at the edge of the last cross, and bring it out just below. Work a second row of lacing from left to right to make a series of diamonds.

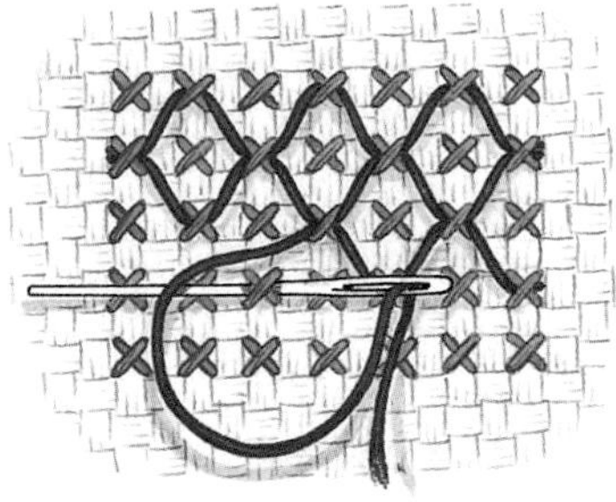

2 At the end of the row, insert the needle just below the point where it emerged on the first row. Bring it out to the front again, two crosses below. Repeat the lacing from right to left, this time lacing alternate stitches on rows four and three. Continue in this way.

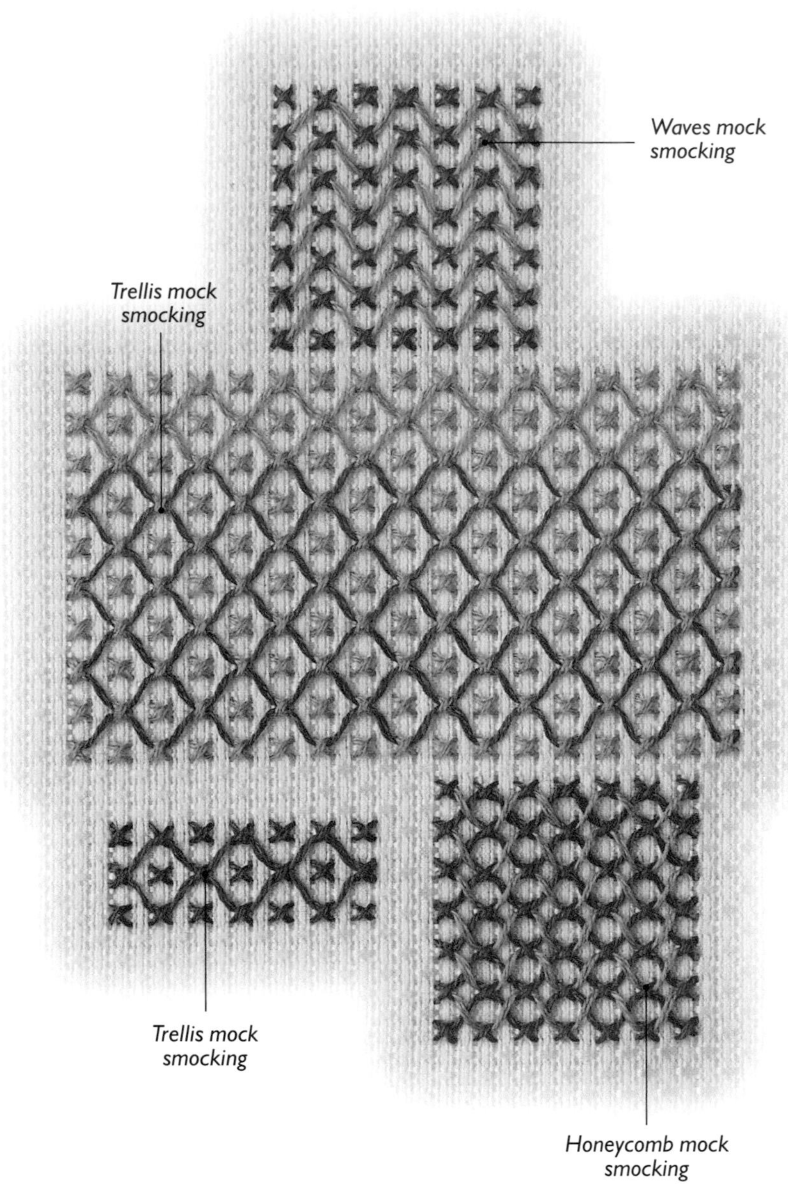

Honeycomb mock smocking

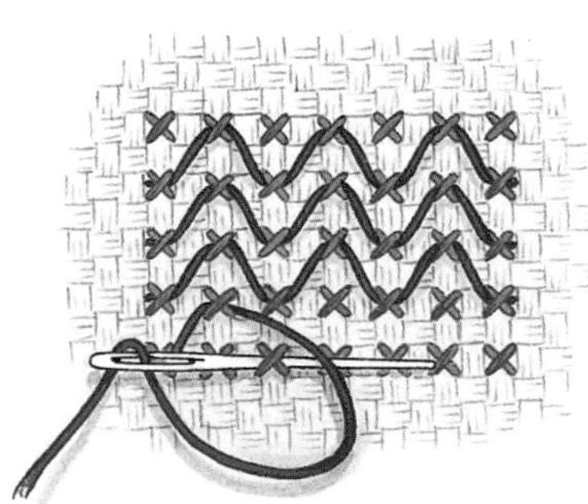

1 Work the required number of foundation rows, as for Waves (page 105). Bring the first lacing thread to the front at the edge of the right-hand cross on the second foundation row. Follow steps **2** and **3** of Waves to work the waves pattern across all the foundation rows. Secure the thread.

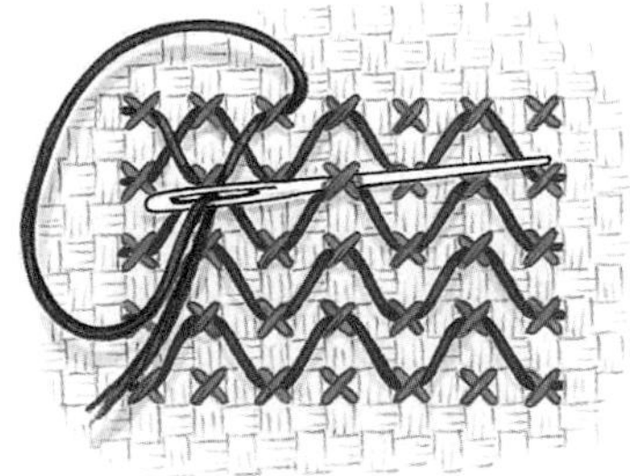

2 Bring the second lacing thread out at the edge of the left-hand cross on the first foundation row. Slip the needle under this cross, then under the next cross on the next row, pulling the thread through carefully. Continue in this way to lace alternate stitches on the first and second rows.

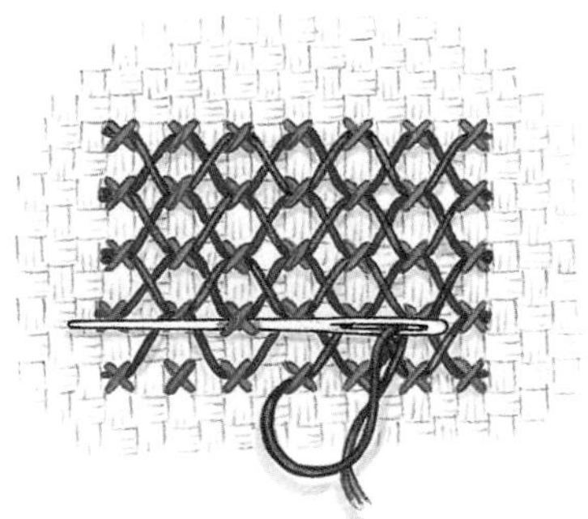

3 At the end of the row, insert the needle at the edge of the last cross on the first row. Bring the needle out one cross down, just below where the first lacing thread emerged. Repeat the lacing in the opposite direction, this time lacing alternate stitches on rows two and three. Continue in this way.

The mock smocking stitches shown here create elaborately laced finishes, and they look very effective worked in narrow bands. For a crisp effect, work them in brilliant cutwork and embroidery thread.

For each stitch, one lacing row requires three foundation rows of spaced cross stitches; each foundation row must have an odd number of crosses. The stitches are shown worked in single blocks over three foundation rows, but they can also be worked as allover patterns over five, seven, or more foundation rows.

You will find more details on mock smocking and advice on suitable fabrics on page 105.

Plain ribbing creates an effect somewhat like a knitted rib.

Box ribbing looks similar to plain ribbing, with a boxier finish.

Diamond pattern creates a series of interlaced diamonds.

Mesh pattern is similar to diamond pattern, but the lacing stitches are shorter.

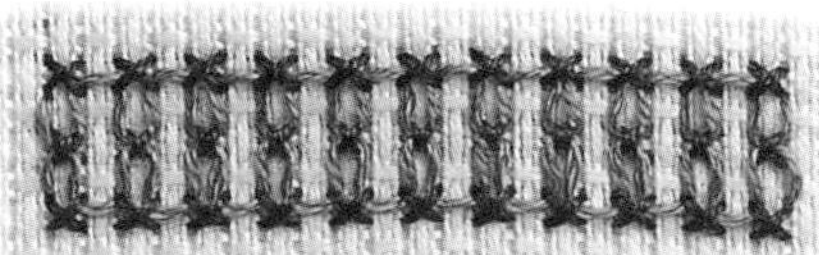

Plain ribbing

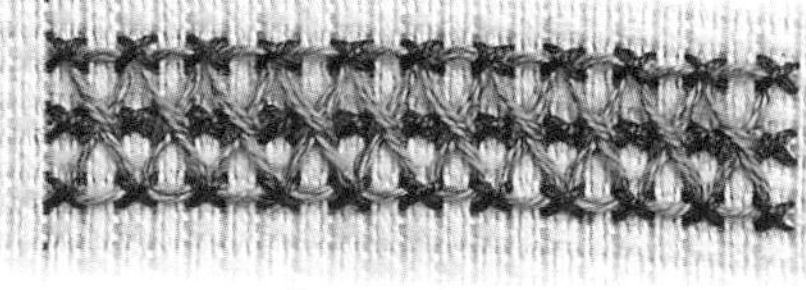

Diamond pattern

Box ribbing

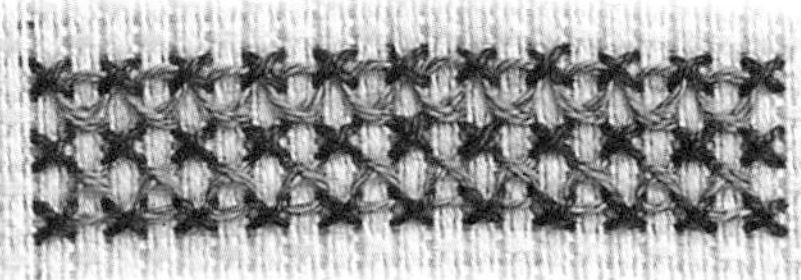

Mesh pattern

Working plain ribbing

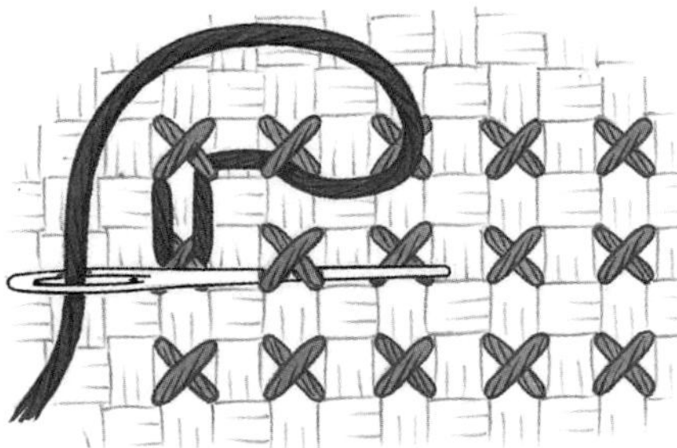

1 Bring the thread out at the bottom left corner of the first cross on the left. Slip the needle under the cross on the row below. Take the needle under the facing lower arms of the first two crosses on the top row. Continue lacing between the top two rows.

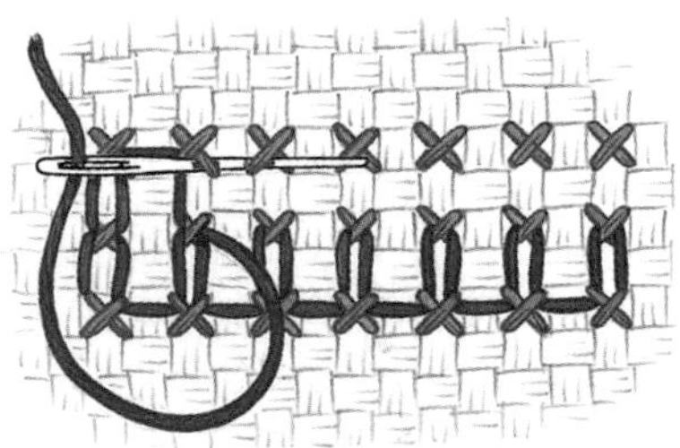

2 At the end of the row, take the thread through to the wrong side at the outer corner of the last cross on the top row. Turn the work; bring the thread out at the outer bottom corner of the left-hand stitch on the top row, and repeat the lacing.

Working box ribbing

1 Bring the thread to the front at the top right corner of the first cross on the left of the second row. Slip the needle under the facing lower arms of the first two crosses on the top row.

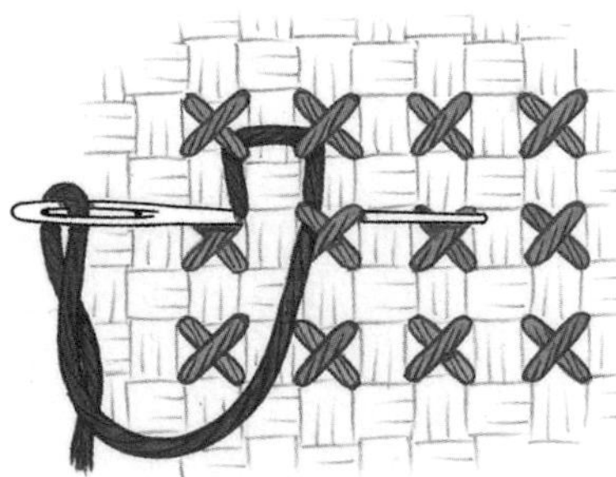

2 Slip the needle under the top left corner of the cross below, take it to the back where it emerged, and bring it through at the top right corner of the second cross on the second row. Repeat along the row.

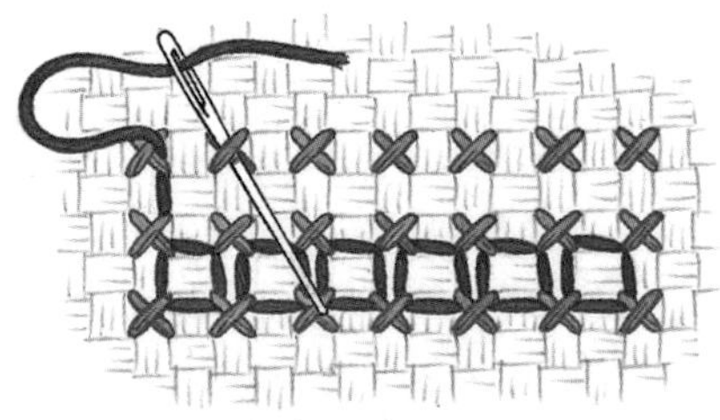

3 At the end of the row, take the thread to the wrong side. Turn the work, bringing the thread out at the top right corner of the first stitch on the second row. Continue lacing along the row.

Working diamond pattern

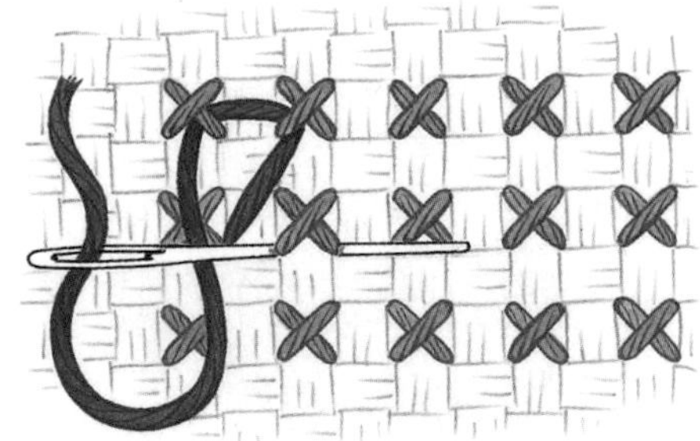

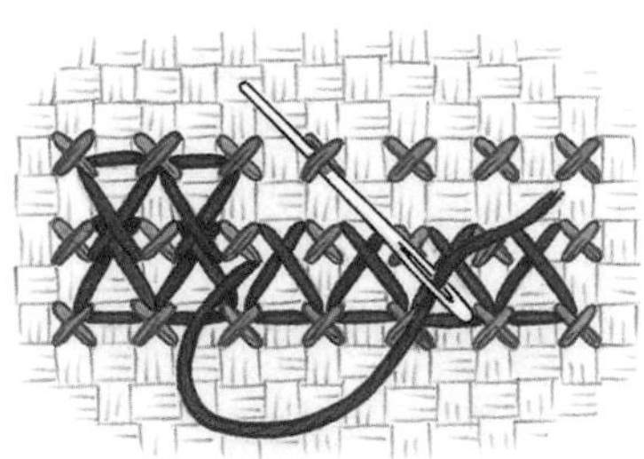

1 Bring the thread to the front at the bottom right corner of the left-hand cross on the second row. Slip the point of the needle from right to left under the facing lower arms of the first two crosses on the top row.

2 Take the needle to the back at the bottom left corner of the next cross on the second row, and bring it through at the bottom right corner of the same cross. Repeat along the row.

3 At the end of the row, take the thread to the wrong side and turn the work, bringing the thread out at the bottom inner corner of the left-hand stitch on the center row. Repeat the lacing along the row.

Working mesh pattern

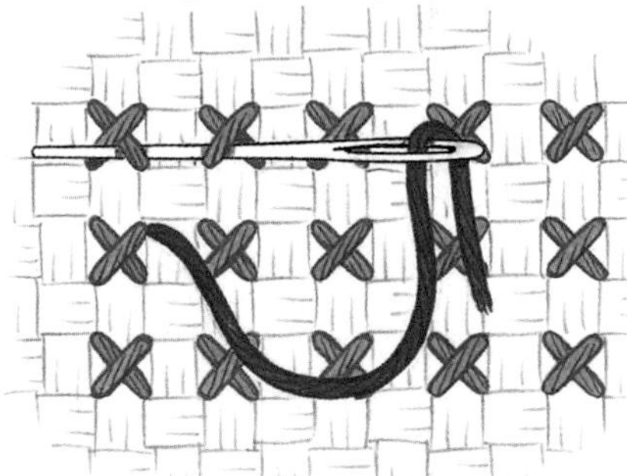

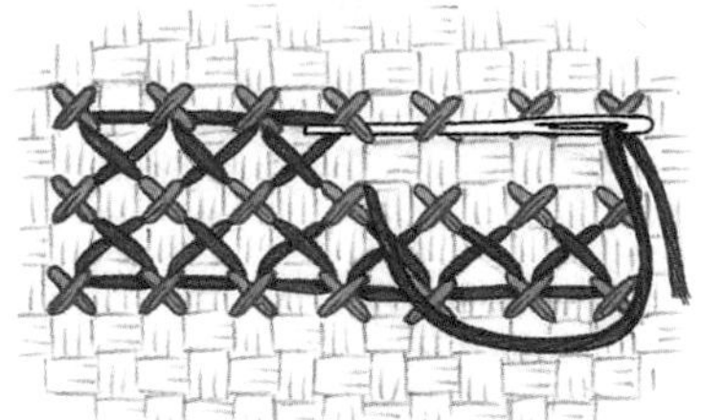

1 Bring the thread out at the top right corner of the left-hand cross on the second row. Slip the point of the needle from right to left under the facing lower arms of the first two crosses on the top row.

2 Take the needle to the back at the top left corner of the second cross on the second row, and bring it through at the top right corner of the same cross. Repeat along the row.

3 At the end of the row, take the thread to the wrong side and turn the work, bringing the thread through at the inner top corner of the left-hand stitch on the center row. Repeat the lacing along the row.

Thread tension Pulling the lacing thread too taut puckers the fabric so that it will not lie flat (top), and leaving it too loose creates unsightly loops (bottom). For the best results, always use an embroidery frame and make sure that the thread lies flat and smooth on the surface of the fabric.

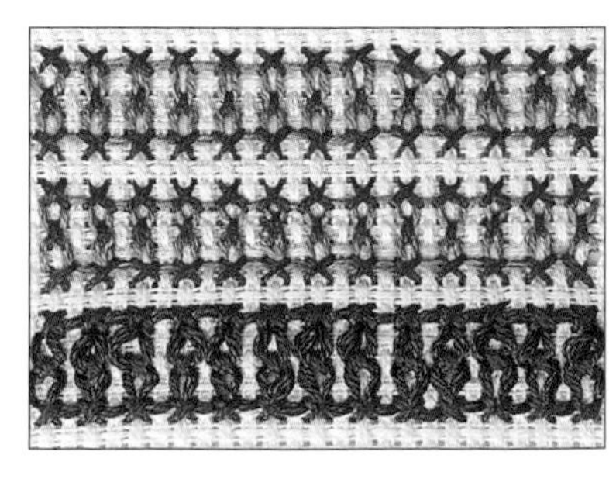

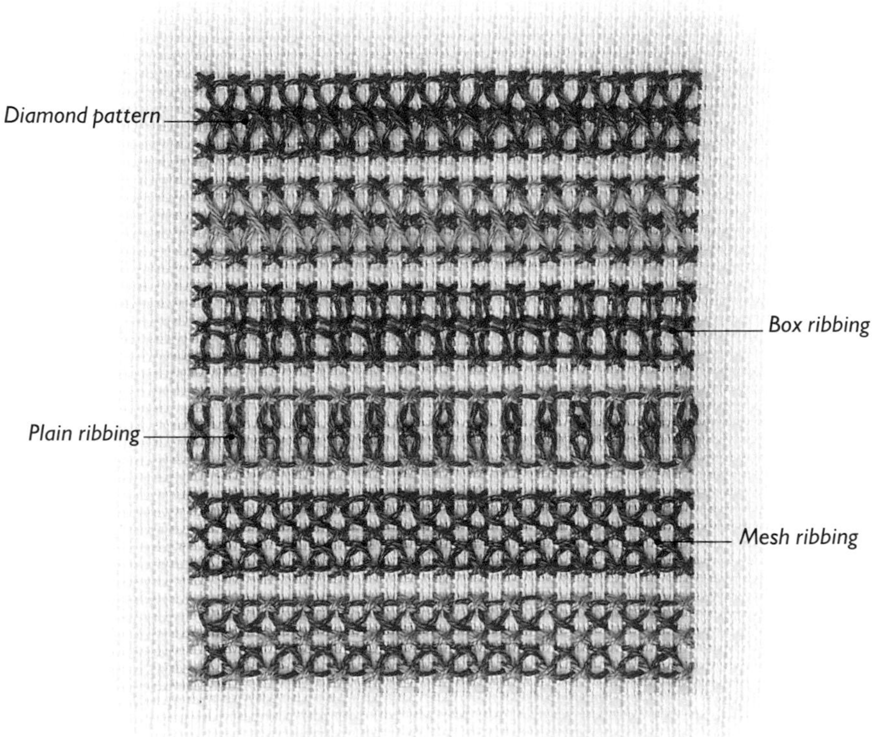

Crib Ducklings

Two little ducklings bob gently as they dangle from yellow satin ribbon. The cute pair rattle as they move and make the perfect gift for a newborn baby.

You Will Need

For each toy:

- 14-count sky blue Aida, 7 x 6¼ in. (18 x 16 cm)
- DMC embroidery floss as listed in the color key
- Matching backing fabric, 7 x 6¼ in. (18 x 16 cm)
- Tapestry needle, size 26
- Polyester toy stuffing
- Embroidery hoop
- Small jingle bell
- 20 in. (50 cm) of ⅝ in.-(15 mm-) wide yellow ribbon
- Sewing needle
- Basting thread
- Matching sewing thread

Color Key

COLORS	SKEINS
White	1
742 Orange-yellow	1
743 Yellow	1
745 Baby yellow	1
762 Pearl gray	1
809 Light blue	1
818 Baby pink	1
3326 Rose pink	1
3807 Blue	1
Backstitch	
415 Light gray	1
742 Orange-yellow	
762 Pearl gray	
971 Bright orange	1
3326 Rose pink	
3807 Blue	

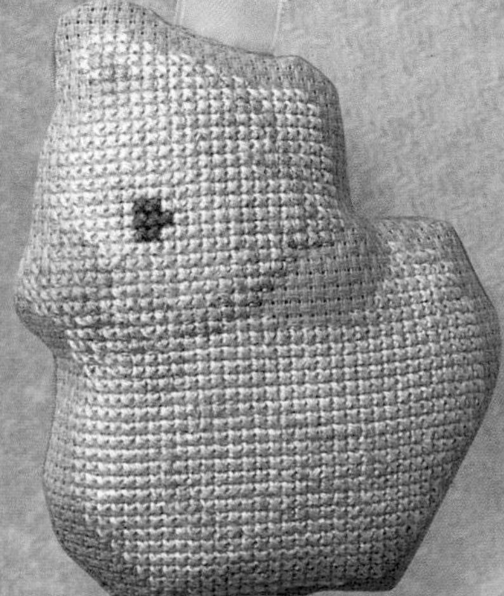

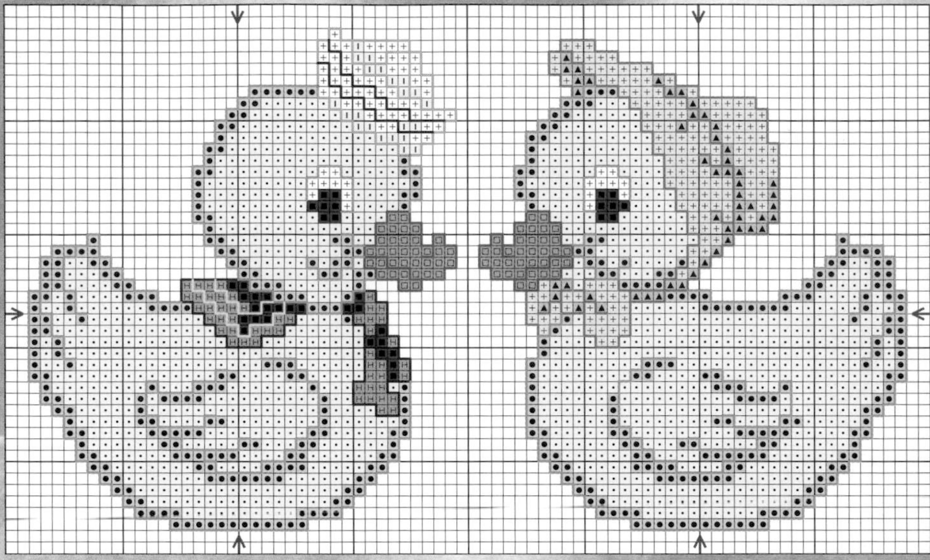

These jingling ducklings, the male in his sailor's hat and the female in her pretty pink bonnet, will bring a smile to any baby's face. The designs are cross-stitched on aida in pastel colors and then made into small crib toys. They can be tied to a baby buggy or crib or simply used to decorate a nursery wall. Each finished toy measures 3½ x 3 in. (9 x 7.5 cm).

Backstitch around the whites of the ducklings' eyes, their cheeks, and their orange beaks to make these features stand out.

Stitching the Designs

Fold the aida in half both ways, and mark the center with basting. Mount the fabric in the hoop.

Stitch each design from the center outward, referring to the appropriate chart and the color key. Leave at least ⅝ in. (1.5 cm) of fabric around each motif. One square on the chart represents one stitch worked over one block of aida. Use two strands of cotton for cross stitch and one strand for backstitch. When you have completed the cross stitch, work the outlines in backstitch.

Remove the fabric from the hoop, and press it with a warm iron.

Assembling the Toys

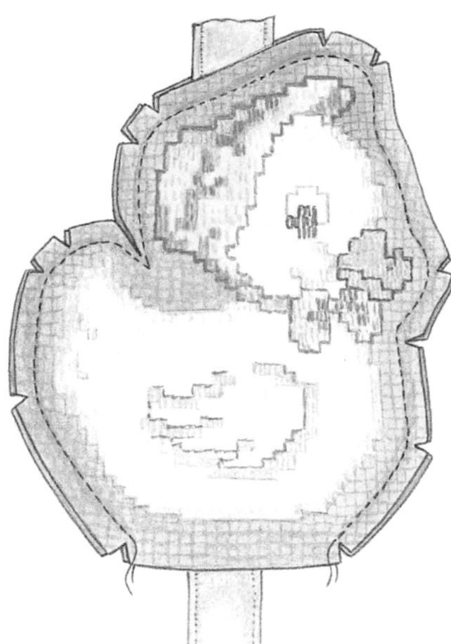

Cut out the duck shapes, leaving a margin of ⅝ in. (1.5 cm) around each design. Using the embroidered pieces as a pattern, cut the shape from the backing fabric.

Place the embroidery on the backing fabric, right sides together. Sandwich the ribbon between the two layers, as shown. Baste around the edges. Stitch the layers together, taking ⅜ in. (1 cm) seams and leaving a 1½ in. (4 cm) gap at the bottom of the design. Remove the basting. Clip the curves, then turn the work right side out.

Gently fill the design with stuffing, inserting the bell into the middle. Don't pack the stuffing too tightly or the bell won't jingle. Slipstitch the gap edges together.

Trailing Leaves

Long intertwining stems tipped with sprays of oval leaves are worked in padded embroidery to embellish a pair of linen pillow covers.

You Will Need

For both pillows:

- Tracing paper and pencil
- Sewing needle and dark basting thread
- Dressmaker's carbon paper
- Crewel needle, size 8
- Large embroidery hoop
- Embroidery scissors

For the white pillow:

- White linen fabric, 71 x 30 in. (180 x 75 cm)
- Firmly woven white cotton backing fabric, 30 in. (75 cm) square
- Beige linen fabric, 36 x 28 in. (92 x 71 cm)
- Pearl cotton, three balls of No. 8 beige
- Embroidery floss, five skeins of beige
- Pillow form, 23½ in. (60 cm) square
- Matching sewing threads

For the natural beige pillow:

- Beige linen fabric, 44 x 18 in. (112 x 46 cm)
- Firmly woven cream cotton backing fabric, 18 in. (46 cm) square
- Pearl cotton, one ball of No. 8 white
- Embroidery floss, one skein of white
- Pillow form, 16 in. (40 cm) square
- Matching sewing thread

The stylized design of stems and leaves is worked in padded satin stitch, using beige on the white linen and white on the beige linen. The larger white pillow features four repeats of the design and is finished with a flanged edge. It is 31 in. (78 cm) square, including the flange, and fits loosely around a 24 in. (60 cm) pillow form. The beige pillow has one repeat and is 16 in. (40 cm) square.

PREPARING THE WHITE LINEN

Cut a 30 in. (75 cm) square of white linen, and overcast the edges. Place the linen and backing fabric squares together with wrong sides facing and edges matching, and baste them together around the edges.

Fold the piece in half both ways and press lightly; then baste along the folds to divide it into quarters. Lay it out linen side up.

TRANSFERRING THE DESIGN

Trace the complete design including the two positioning lines. Lay the tracing in the bottom left quarter, with the lines on the basting. Transfer the design with the carbon paper. Turn the tracing 90 degrees to the right, and repeat to transfer the design in the top left quarter. Repeat in the remaining quarters.

WORKING THE DESIGN

Mount the fabric in the hoop. Using two strands of beige floss, stem-stitch (see page 26) around the edges of the shapes, then fill the centers with light seeding (see page 35).

Next, satin-stitch (see page 27) the shapes using one strand of the beige pearl cotton. Work the leaves from base to tip, and slant the stitches across the length of the stems.

When the design is complete, remove the work from the hoop and steam-press it from the wrong side. Remove all the basting.

ASSEMBLING THE WHITE PILLOW

Cut two 27 x 19½ in. (68 x 49 cm) rectangles of white linen. Press and stitch a ⅝ in. (1.5 cm) double hem along one short edge of each piece; these will be the back pieces.

Trim the embroidery to measure 27 in. (68 cm) square, with the design centered.

Lay out the front and back pieces with the wrong sides together, the raw edges matching, and the hemmed back edges overlapping. Baste the layers together around the outer edges.

Use the beige linen to make and attach a mitered double border with a finished width of 2½ in. (6.5 cm); see page 311. Take ⅝ in. (1.5 cm) seams throughout.

PREPARING THE BEIGE LINEN

Cut an 18 in. (46 cm) square of natural linen. Overcast the edges and baste it to the backing as for the white pillow. Lay the square linen side up. Use the tracing and carbon paper to transfer the design in the center of it, omitting the red shapes. Mount it in the hoop.

WORKING THE DESIGN

Work the design as for the white cushion, but use the white floss for the seeding and the white pearl cotton for the satin stitch.

ASSEMBLING THE BEIGE PILLOW

Trim the embroidery to measure 17 in. (43 cm) square. Use it to make a 15½ in. (40 cm) square pillow cover with an overlapped back, following the instructions given on page 307.

Closely worked satin stitches create the smooth outlines of the curves.

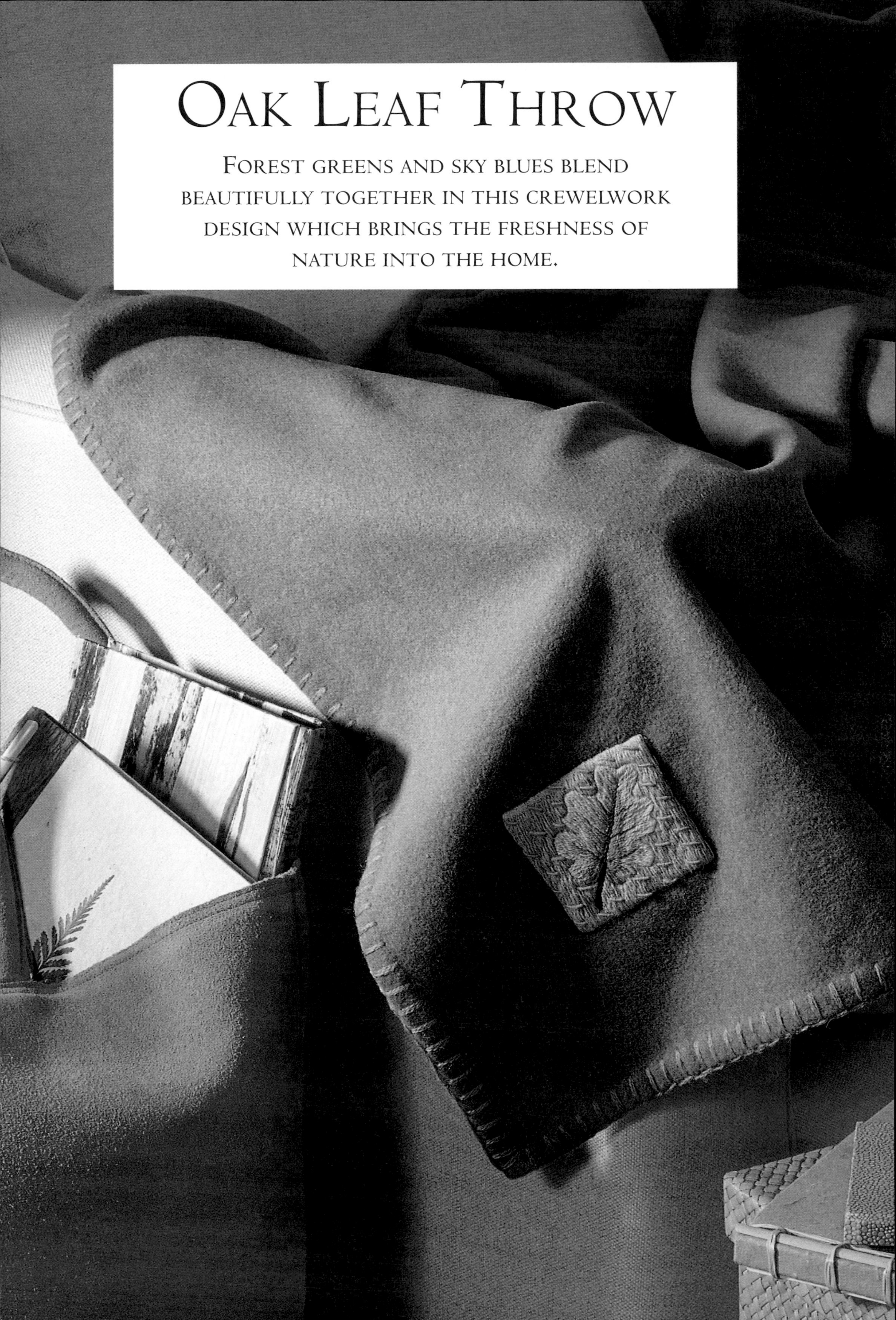

Oak Leaf Throw

Forest greens and sky blues blend beautifully together in this crewelwork design which brings the freshness of nature into the home.

You Will Need

- Blue Polarfleece, the desired size of your throw plus 3 in. (8 cm) all around
- DMC Médicis crewel wool as listed in the color key
- DMC Médicis crewel wool to match the fabric
- Medium-weight unbleached muslin, 10 in. (25 cm) square
- Dressmaking pins
- Sewing needle
- Sewing thread in cream and blue
- Chenille needles, sizes 22 and 26
- Embroidery hoop
- Tracing paper and pencil
- Dressmaker's carbon paper

Color Key

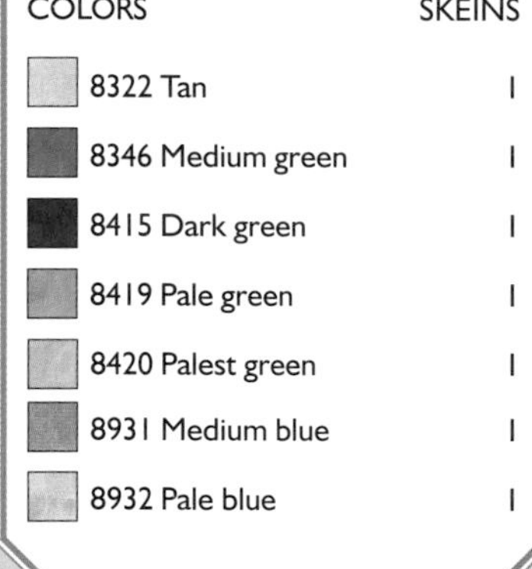

COLORS	SKEINS
8322 Tan	1
8346 Medium green	1
8415 Dark green	1
8419 Pale green	1
8420 Palest green	1
8931 Medium blue	1
8932 Pale blue	1

This crewelwork oak leaf patch makes an attractive embellishment for a throw or lap rug. It is embroidered on unbleached muslin and then slip-stitched onto the throw. Before you start the embroidery, wash the muslin at 140° F. to pre-shrink it.

Make the throw yourself using Polarfleece or other suitable fabric, or buy one ready-made. The design is worked in long and short stitch, bullion knots, and stem stitch and measures about 3 x 2¾ in. (7.5 x 7 cm).

Preparing the Muslin

Trace the design from the diagram below and transfer it onto the center of the muslin with the dressmaker's carbon paper. Mount the fabric in the embroidery hoop.

Working the Design

Embroider the design, referring to the diagram and key for color placement and the photograph for stitch directions. Use one strand in the size 26 needle unless stated otherwise.

Fill the background with long and short stitch (see page 32), leaving a gap for the oak leaf. Work in rows from the center outward, and blend the colors where they meet. Next, use two strands in the size 22 needle to work bullion knots (see page 78) over the background.

Fill the leaf with long and short stitch, beginning at the outer edge and working inward; blend the colors where they meet. Embroider the stalk and central vein with rows of stem stitch (see page 26). To finish, pick out the side veins with a single row of stem stitch.

Finishing

Remove the work from the hoop, and press it gently on the wrong side under a clean press cloth. Trim the muslin ¾ in. (2 cm) outside the stitching. Turn the excess fabric to the back; pin, then sew it in place, using a double length of the cream sewing thread.

Making the Throw

Pin a double ⅝ in. (1.5 cm) hem to the wrong side all around the fabric edges. Thread three strands of the matching crewel wool in the size 22 needle and blanket stitch around the fabric edge to secure the hem in place; make the upright stitches the same depth as the hem. For instructions on working blanket stitch, see page 57.

Applying the Patch

Pin the motif to the throw in the desired position. Slip-stitch in place using the matching sewing thread.

Periwinkles

Crisp blue and white table linen is embroidered with dainty periwinkles for stylish outdoor living.

You Will Need

- Square or rectangular white tablecloth with a blue border
- Matching napkins
- DMC embroidery floss as listed in the color key
- Crewel needle, size 6
- Tracing paper
- Pencil
- Dressmaker's carbon paper
- Embroidery hoop
- Embroidery scissors

Color Key

COLORS

- 794 Light blue
- 987 Dark green
- 989 Light green
- 3807 Dark blue

Fill the petals with long and short stitch, blending the shades of blue where they meet.

The tablecloth is embroidered with a periwinkle border, and the napkins have a single motif. You can buy a ready-made tablecloth or make your own. To make the tablecloth, buy white cotton to size and attach a blue mitered double border with a finished width of 4 in. (10 cm). To make each napkin, cut an 18 in. (45 cm) square of cotton and attach a mitered double border with a finished width of 2 in. (5 cm). For instructions on mitered double borders, see page 311.

The flowers on the tablecloth measure 3⅜ x 1¾ in. (8.5 x 4.5 cm), and the napkin motif measures 2⅛ x 1½ in. (5.5 x 4 cm).

Preparing the tablecloth

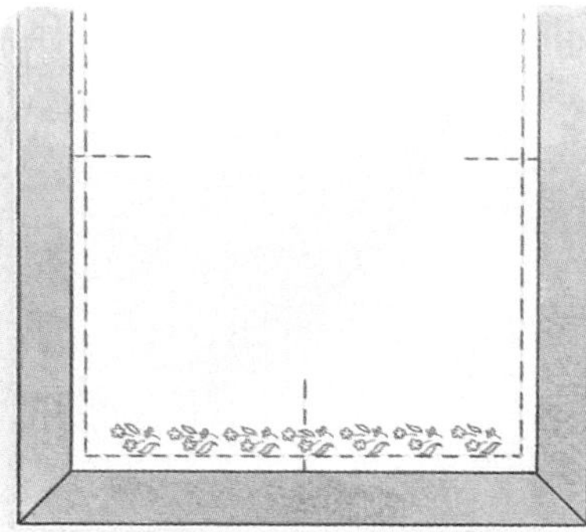

Baste all around the white central panel 1 in. (2.5 cm) in from the edge. Fold the piece in half both ways and work short lines of basting to mark the center of each edge.

Trace the large periwinkle from the diagram (below right), then center the tracing on one edge of the fabric with the base of the lower leaf just above the basting. Transfer it using the carbon paper. Repeat along the edge, working from the center out and leaving ¾ in. (2 cm) between each motif; finish with a complete flower at each end. Mount the fabric in the hoop.

Embroidering the tablecloth

Embroider the flowers, referring to the diagram, the key, and the stitch detail. Use two strands of embroidering floss in your needle, and complete each flower before moving on to the next one.

Fill the petals with long and short stitch (see page 32); use light blue at the center, fading into dark blue at the tips. Work a dark-blue French knot (see page 77) in the center of the open flowers. Use light green to satin-stitch the leaves (see page 27), working outward from the central vein, and to satin-stitch the calyx, slanting the stitches from bottom right to top left. Use dark green to split-stitch the stems and to stem-stitch the veins (see pages 40 and 26).

When the first edge of the tablecloth is complete, transfer the design along the second edge, and embroider the motifs in the same way. Repeat this process all around the tablecloth.

Finally, transfer single flower heads randomly over the tablecloth and embroider them as described above.

Embroidering the napkins

Trace the small periwinkle from the diagram (below left) and transfer it onto one corner of the napkin, 1⅜ in. (3.5 cm) in from the edges. Embroider the motifs as described above.

King of Hearts

A gold crown emblazoned with a single pink heart makes a dazzling emblem for the front of a regal velvet cushion.

You Will Need

- Unbleached muslin, 12 in. (30 cm) square, washed and pressed
- DMC embroidery floss and divisible metallic thread as listed in the color key
- Embroidery hoop
- White felt, 6 in. (15 cm) square
- Chenille needle, size 20
- Crewel needles, sizes 5 and 7
- Tracing paper
- Masking tape
- Dressmaker's carbon paper and pencil
- Matching sewing threads and needle
- 5/8 yd. (50 cm) shocking pink velvet
- 1 5/8 yd. (1.5 m) coordinating cord trim
- Pillow form, 14 x 12 in. (35 x 30 cm)

Color Key

Colors	Skeins
326 Cerise	1
741 Orange	1
743 Pale yellow	1
797 Dark blue	1
814 Russet	1
816 Burgundy	1
900 Deep orange	1
913 Green	1
915 Fuchsia	1
972 Yellow	1
995 Medium blue	1
996 Light blue	1
5282 Gold metallic thread	1

This regal velvet cushion cover has a small oblong panel at its center embroidered with a colorful "king of hearts" motif. The panel is worked in long and short stitch and satin stitch, with French knots and bullion knots adding detail and texture. Metallic gold stem stitches frame the design. Sections of the panel are lightly padded for a three-dimensional effect. The finished cushion measures 14 x 12 in. (35 x 30 cm).

Preparing to stitch

Trace the "king of hearts" design from the picture (below), and transfer it onto the center of the muslin, using the dressmaker's carbon paper and securing it with masking tape. Mount the muslin in the hoop. Unless otherwise instructed, use the size 7 crewel needle and two strands of floss throughout, and work downwards from the top of each section.

Stitching the background

Using long and short stitch (see page 32), start with light blue, blending into medium, then dark blue. Scatter bullion knots diagonally over the top of the embroidery, using three strands of green and the size 5 crewel needle (see page 78).

Adding the padding

Transfer the heart outline four times onto the white felt, and cut out the shapes. Trim three hearts so they decrease in size. Stitch them one by one over the heart shape, starting with the smallest and ending with the largest (see page 30). Pad the base of the crown and the bobbles in the same way with two layers of felt.

Stitching the crown

Work in long and short stitching, start with pale yellow and blending into yellow, then orange. Scatter deep orange French knots (see page 77) over the top using six strands of floss in the chenille needle. Satin-stitch the bobbles and the base using gold thread (see page 27). Stem-stitch around the base and the bobbles with fuchsia (see page 26).

Stitching the heart

Start with burgundy, blending it into cerise, then burgundy again, and finally russet. Stem-stitch around the heart using a single strand of medium blue.

Assembling the cover

Referring to the instructions on page 307, cut the front and back pieces of the cushion from the velvet. Trim the muslin, 1 in. (2.5 cm) outside the embroidery, turn the excess to the back, and baste the panel to the center of the frontpiece. Slip-stitch in place with matching thread. Using six strands of gold thread in the chenille needle, work large stem stitches around the panel. Assemble the cover, and trim it with the cord, as shown on page 308.

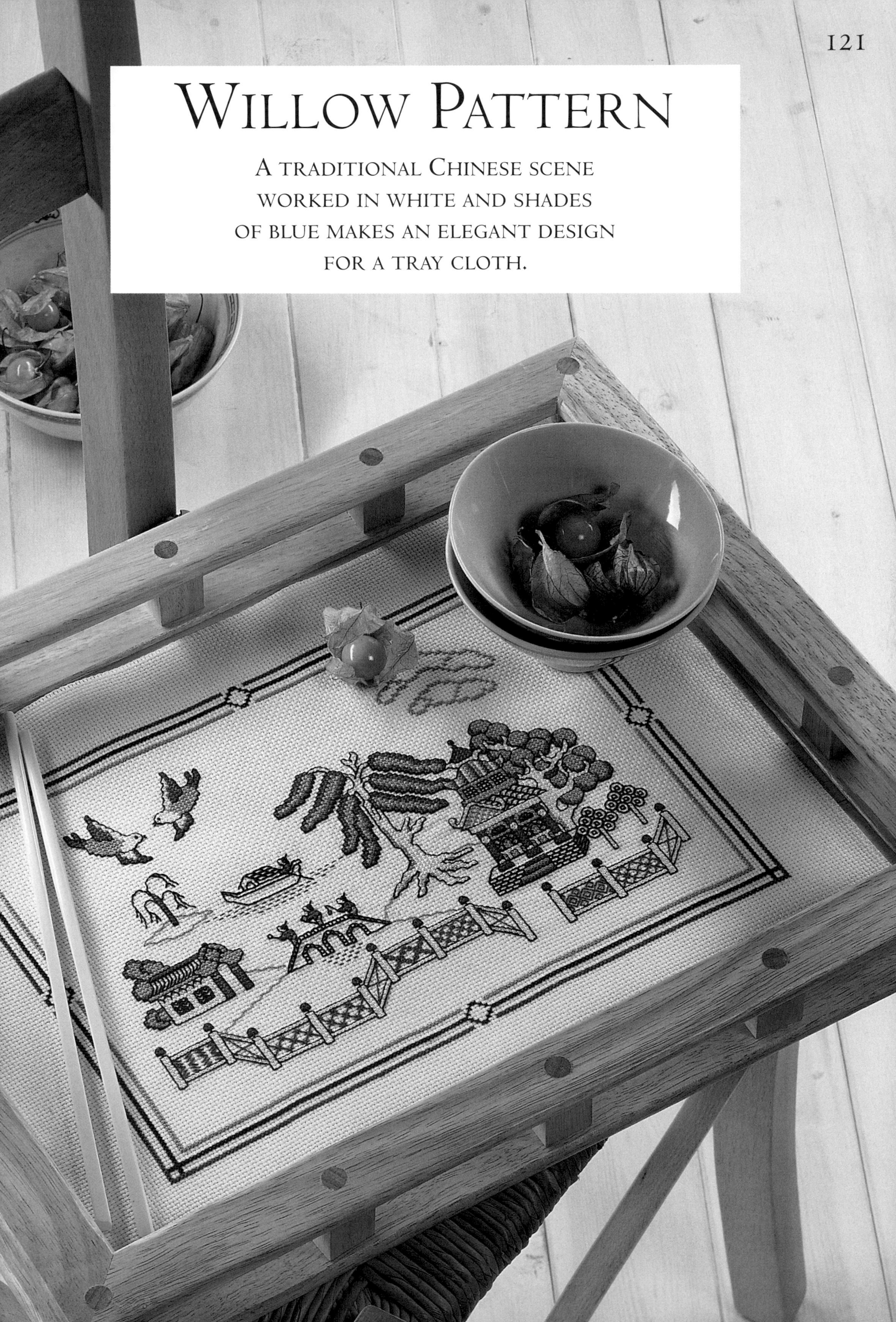

WILLOW PATTERN

A TRADITIONAL CHINESE SCENE WORKED IN WHITE AND SHADES OF BLUE MAKES AN ELEGANT DESIGN FOR A TRAY CLOTH.

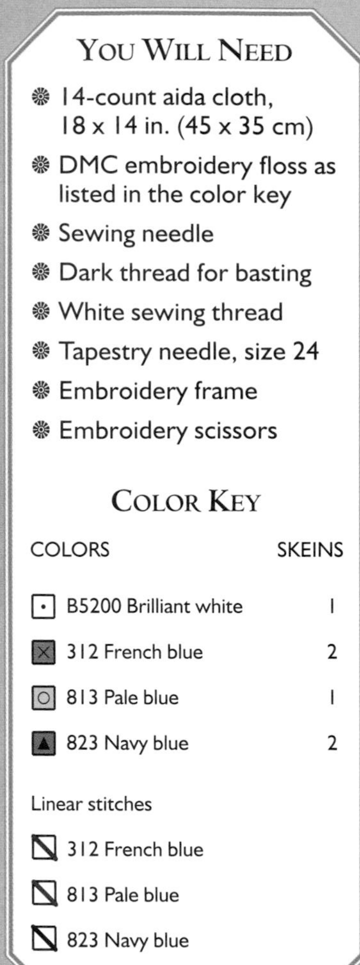

You Will Need

- 14-count aida cloth, 18 x 14 in. (45 x 35 cm)
- DMC embroidery floss as listed in the color key
- Sewing needle
- Dark thread for basting
- White sewing thread
- Tapestry needle, size 24
- Embroidery frame
- Embroidery scissors

Color Key

COLORS	SKEINS
B5200 Brilliant white	1
312 French blue	2
813 Pale blue	1
823 Navy blue	2

Linear stitches

- 312 French blue
- 813 Pale blue
- 823 Navy blue

This cross-stitch sampler is inspired by the traditional willow pattern printed on blue and white ceramics in the 18th century. Supposedly based on a Chinese legend, the pattern depicts a Chinese scene. Although designs vary, willow pattern always features a willow tree, a temple, figures crossing a bridge, a distant island, and two birds hovering above, which symbolize a pair of lovers.

The sampler is worked mainly in cross stitch, backstitch, and fractional stitches. Fly stitch, running stitch, double running stitch and straight stitches add extra detail. The finished stitched area is 12 x 8¼ in. (30 x 21 cm).

For the third fence panel (near left), work two zigzag rows of backstitch over two fabric blocks. Work a cross at each intersection.

Backstitch the outline of the boat and the boatman. Create the ripples of water beneath the boat with running stitch.

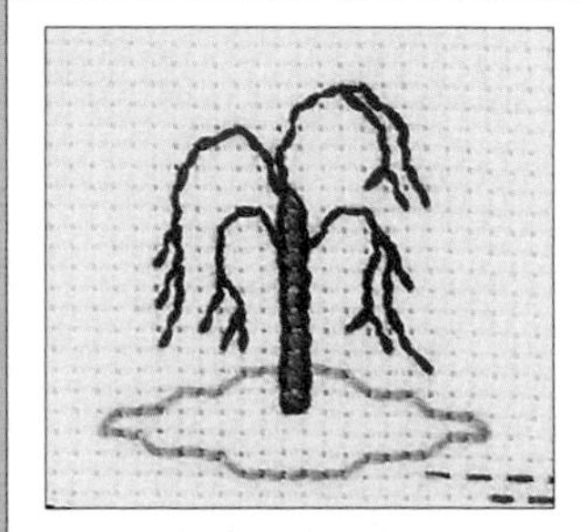

Use double running stitch to work the drooping branches of the willow tree. Backstitch the island outline.

Preparing to stitch

Mark the center of the chart using a pencil and ruler, and use basting to mark the center of the aida cloth. Overcast the raw edges to prevent fraying, and mount the fabric in a hoop or other frame.

Working the design

Work the design in cross stitch, fractional stitches, and backstitch, unless otherwise stated (see pages 43 and 44). Follow the chart and the color key. One square on the chart represents one stitch worked over one block of fabric. Use two strands of floss in the needle throughout.

Working the pictorial motifs

Start with the large tree, the birds, and the clouds. Stitch the boatman and boat, using straight stitches linked with backstitches for the boat roof. Create the ripples of water with running stitch (see pages 25 and 26).

Work the men and the bridge, picking out the brickwork on the bridge with small straight stitches and the ripples of water under the bridge with running stitch.

Stitch the willow tree and the island, using double running stitch for the drooping branches (see page 26).

Next stitch the small house, working the window and roof details with double running stitch, and the trim under the eaves with fly stitches (see page 68).

Stitch the large palace, using rows of backstitch joined with straight stitches for the brick base and single straight stitches for the detail on the arched window. Work the foliage and fruit on the small trees with rings of backstitch, each framing a backstitched square.

Working the fence and border

Stitch the wooden fence posts first, then fill in the panels.

Working from left to right, stitch the first panel in diagonal running stitches worked over two and under one fabric block.

Stitch the third panel with two zigzag rows of backstitch, worked over two fabric blocks. At each intersection work an upright cross (see page 52) over two blocks in each direction. See the photograph on page 122 for more details.

Embroider the fourth panel with straight-stitch stars, radiating the stitches out from the center; work fractional stitches at each corner.

For the seventh panel, work a row of straight-stitch stars across the center, then add a cross stitch between the point of each star in the rows above and below. Backstitch a zigzag line at the top and bottom, outlining the cross stitches as you work; see the photograph above.

Create the flowers on the tenth panel with double running stitch, and work a star in the center.

Finish by working the borders.

Finishing

Take the work out of the frame, and press it gently on the wrong side.

Chinese Influence

The willow pattern was designed in England in about 1780 as a response to the public enthusiasm for all things Chinese. It was printed on ceramics.

Depict the smooth curves of the men's heads, backs, and legs with fractional stitches.

Lattice Shade

A pretty trellis of soft pink flowers and fresh green leaves transforms a lampshade.

You Will Need

- 20 in. (50 cm) square of cream cotton sateen
- Tracing paper and pencil
- Dressmaker's carbon paper
- Soft pencil
- Masking tape
- DMC embroidery floss as listed in the color key
- Crewel needle, size 8
- Sewing thread, needle, and pins
- Fabric adhesive
- Plain candle-style lampshade, 2 in. (5 cm) across the top and 5½ in. (14 cm) across the bottom
- Embroidery frame (optional)

Color Key

COLORS	SKEINS
598 Turquoise blue	1
893 Deep rose pink	1
3708 Light rose pink	1
3364 Green	1

This delicate lampshade design looks quite intricate, yet it's very simple to create using just two embroidery stitches: French knots and chain stitch. The lampshade is just 4 in. (10 cm) high, and can be used on a small wall light or on a chandelier.

Use medium-weight, closely woven fabric, such as cotton, linen, or heavy silk. Make sure that it won't reveal the wrong side of the stitching when the lamp is lit. If you would rather not use an embroidery frame, you can work the piece in the hand on a 20 x 10 in. (50 x 25 cm) fabric piece.

Transferring the Design

Trace the design and the outer cutting line. This includes ½ in. (1.2 cm) seam allowances at the sides and ⅝ in. (1.5 cm) for turning under at top and bottom. Press the fabric and place it right side up

Straight grain

Underlap

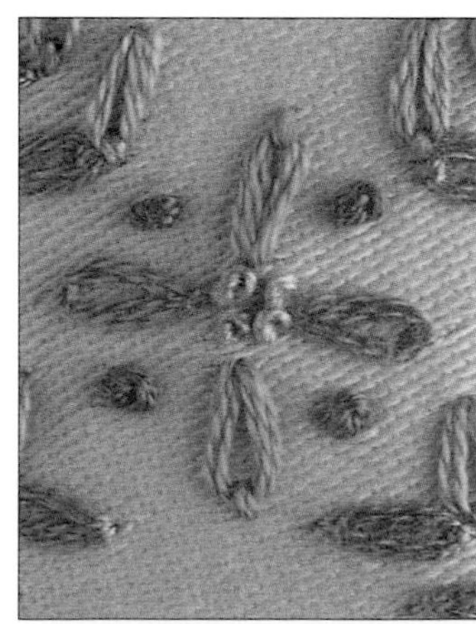

Use light rose pink and four single chain stitches arranged in a star shape to embroider the flower petals. Turquoise blue French knots form the center of the flower.

on a flat surface. Secure the tracing on top with masking tape, making sure the straight grain line follows the straight grain of the fabric. Lift the bottom edge and insert the carbon paper, carbon side down. Go over the outlines with the pencil to transfer the design onto the fabric.

EMBROIDERING THE TRELLIS
Using four strands of deep rose pink floss in the needle and starting at the bottom edge, work French knots upward along each trellis to the second intersection (see page 77). Then complete the rest of the French knots using three strands of floss in the needle. Similarly, work the green leaves in single chain stitches (see page 61), starting with three strands of floss at the bottom. When you reach the intersection, change to two strands.

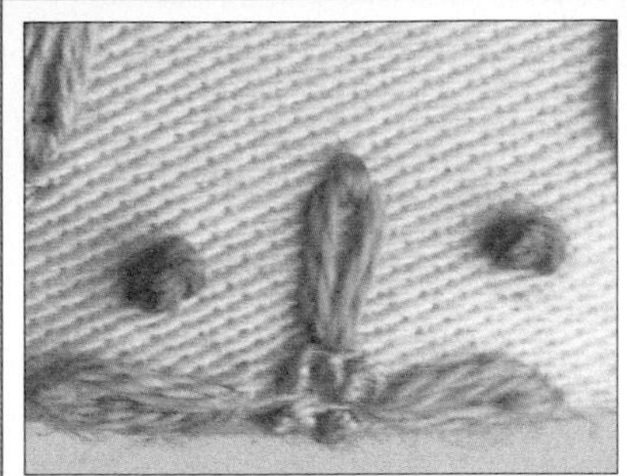

Stitch just three petals and the center of the flower along the lower edge of the lampshade.

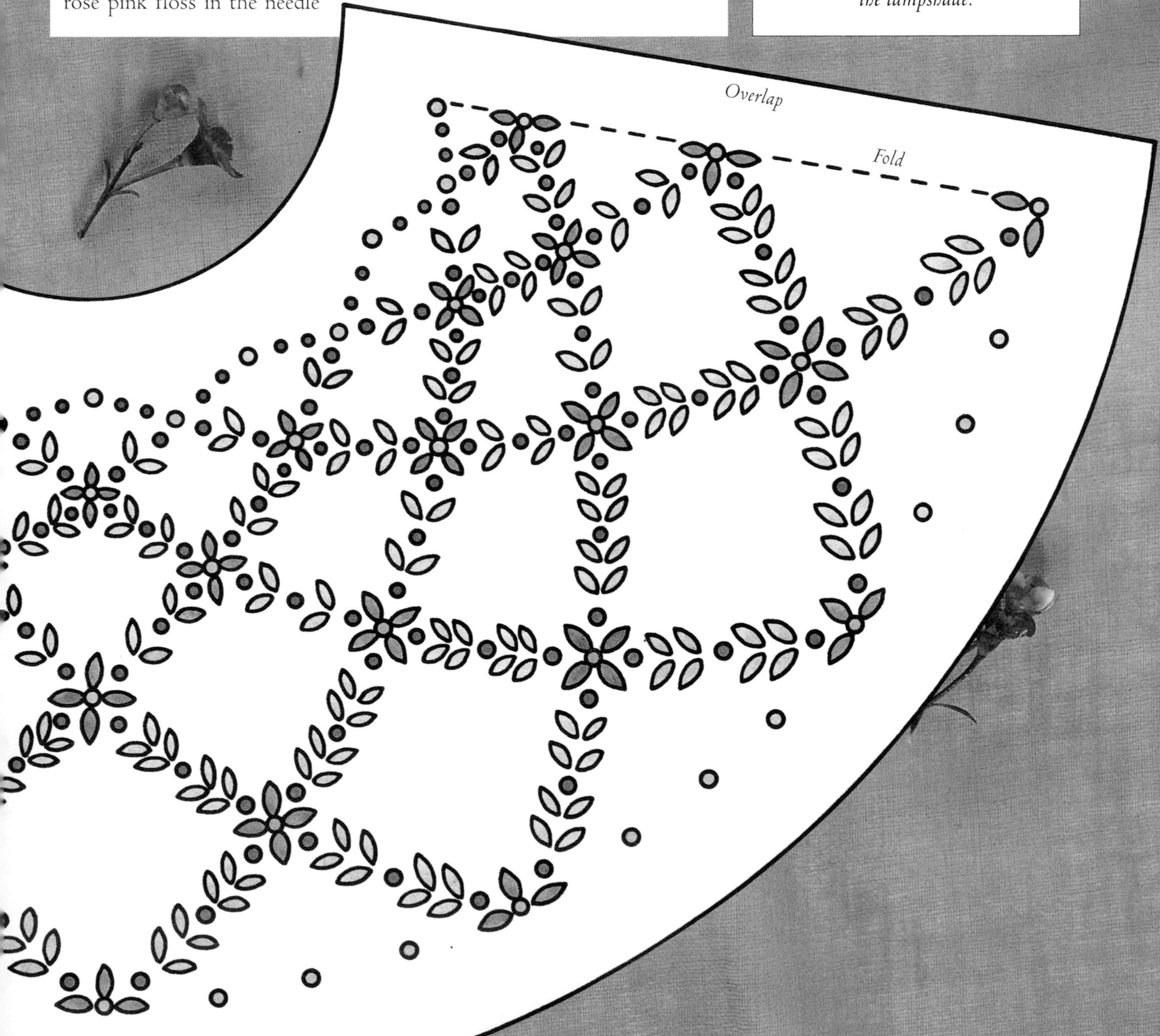

Overlap

Fold

EMBROIDERING THE FLOWERS

With three strands of light rose pink, work the flowers in single chain stitches. Change to two strands of floss at the intersection. Embroider the turquoise blue flower centers with groups of four French knots, using two strands of floss. Work groups of three French knots at the third intersection, and single French knots in the last intersection.

EMBROIDERING THE BORDERS

Using two strands of embroidery floss in the needle, work groups of four French knots in green, then turquoise blue, at the bottom of the shade. Along the top, work groups of three French knots in green.

BLOCKING THE EMBROIDERY

Place the finished embroidery right side down on a well-padded ironing board, and pin it around the edges, gently stretching the fabric smooth and square. Lightly steam-press it on the wrong side, and leave it to cool before removing the pins. Cut it out carefully along the cutting lines.

The leaves are worked in pairs, using individual chain stitches and green floss. They are repeated to create the trellis effect.

COVERING THE LAMPSHADE

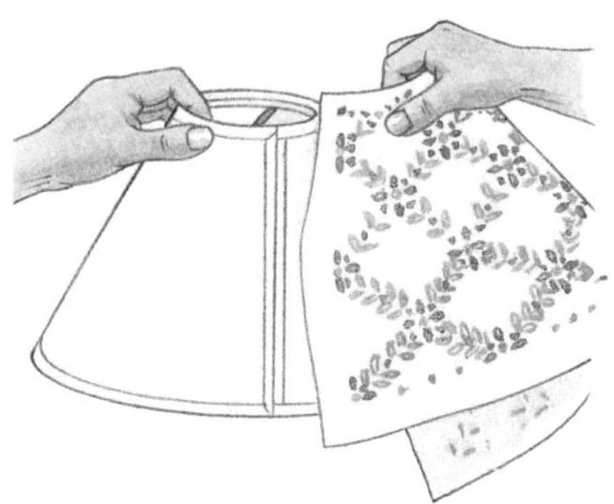

Align the edge marked "underlap" with the seam on the lampshade and secure it temporarily with small pieces of masking tape.

SEWING THE SEAM

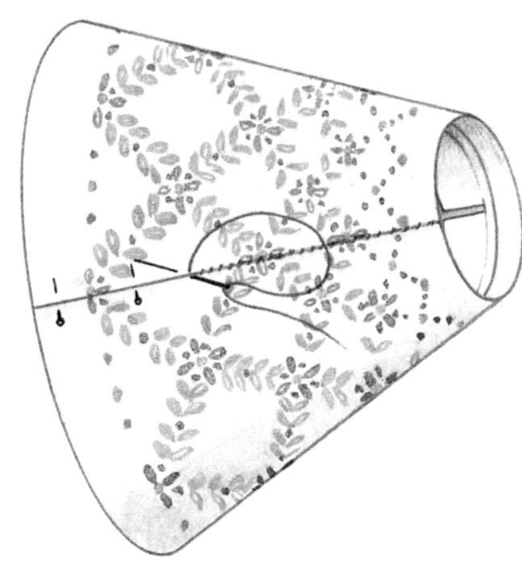

Turn under the edge marked "overlap" and bring it around the lampshade to overlap the secured edge. Pull the fabric firmly, and pin the seam across, leaving the top and bottom edges to extend beyond the lampshade. As you pin, remove the masking tape. Using matching sewing thread, slipstitch the seam.

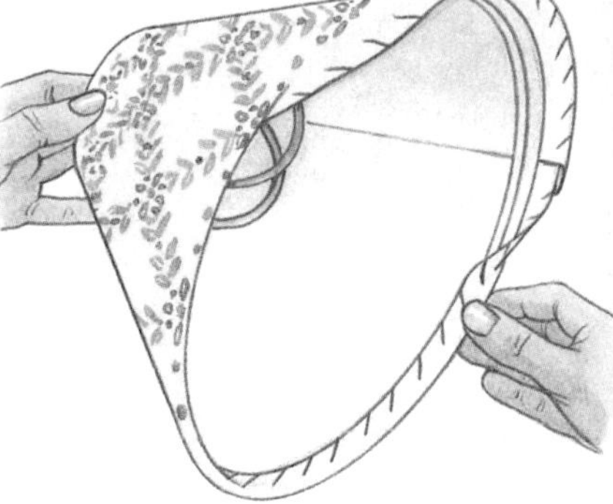

SECURING THE EDGES

At the top and bottom, make snips into the excess fabric about 3/8 in. (1 cm) apart. At the top, cut out small sections where appropriate so that the turned edges will clear the spokes of the shade. Spread a thin layer of the adhesive inside both edges and leave to become tacky. Carefully fold the edges over the edges of the shade, starting with the top edge. As you work, pull the fabric taut.

Wool Slippers

Snug slippers decorated with embroidery, blanket stitch edgings, and jazzy pompoms make chic footwear for children.

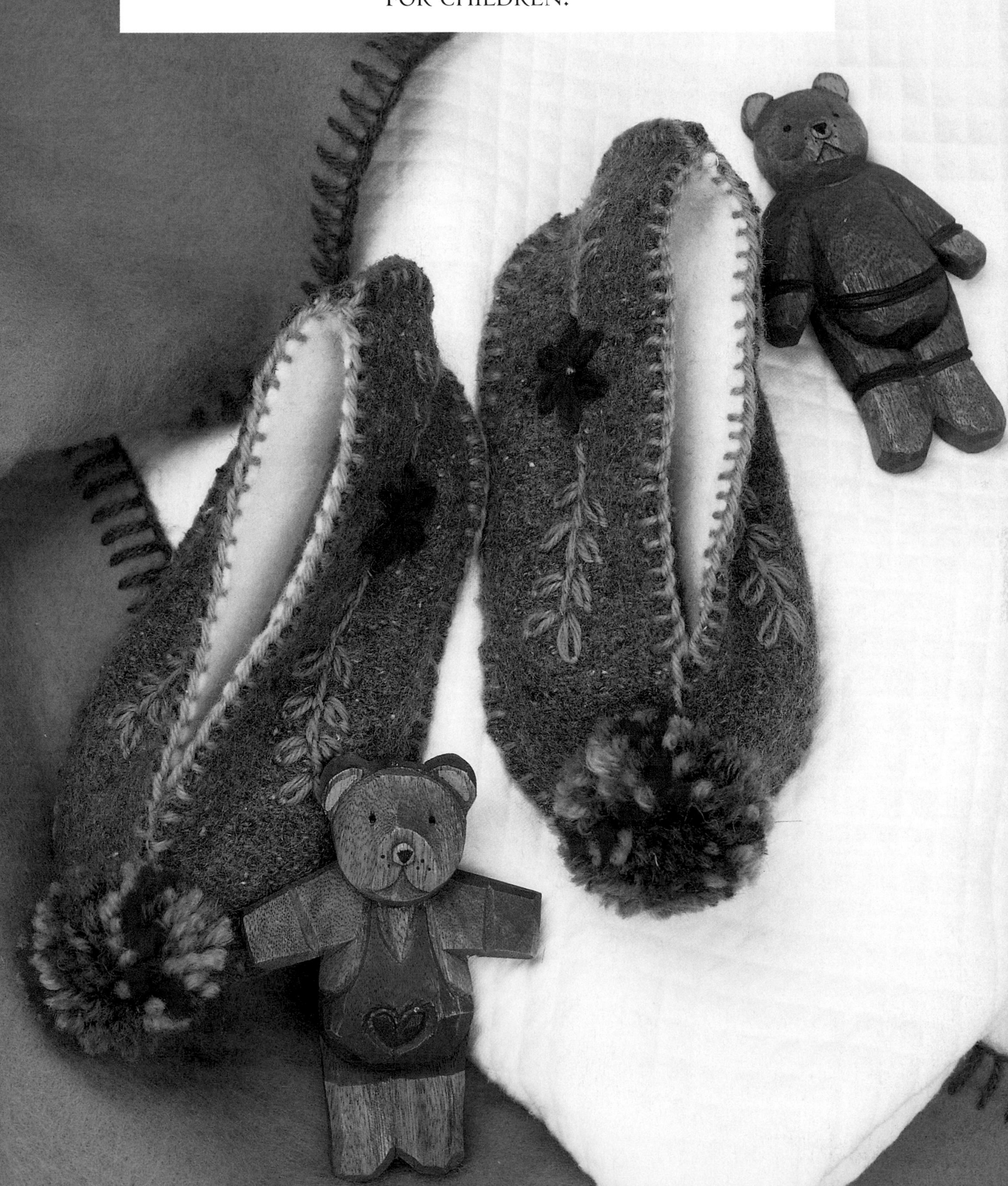

You Will Need

- Gray wool fabric, 20 x 8 in. (50 x 20 cm)
- Cream Polarfleece, 20 x 8 in. (50 x 20 cm)
- Coarse brown wool fabric, 9½ x 8 in. (24 x 20 cm)
- Woven interlining, 17 x 16 in. (44 x 40 cm)
- DMC tapestry yarns as listed in the color key
- Air-erasable marking pen
- Dressmaker's carbon paper and tracing paper
- Chenille needle, size 18
- Sewing needle and matching sewing threads
- Embroidery frame and scissors
- Stiff cardboard

Color Key

COLORS	SKEINS
7138 Rose pink	1
7212 Wine red	1
7323 Light blue-gray	2
7326 Medium blue-gray	2
7376 Grass green	1

Embroider the flower petals in lazy daisy stitch and add a tiny straight stitch in the center.

Little feet will be as warm as toast in these sweet woolen slippers. They have a fleece lining and a hardwearing, quilted sole to protect small feet.

The floral design is embroidered on the uppers in tapestry yarns, using lazy daisy stitch and split stitch. The pompoms are made of medium blue-gray plus yarns left over from the embroidery.

The trace patterns give a choice of sizes for children aged 2–4 years.

Making templates

Trace one upper and its corresponding sole from the patterns provided; include all the seam marks. Cut them out to make tracing paper templates.

Preparing the gray uppers

Use the marking pen to trace around the outline of the upper on the gray wool fabric, drawing in the mark for the toe seam. Turn over the tracing, draw around it again, and mark the top seam. Repeat to mark another pair of uppers on the gray wool fabric for the other slipper. Don't cut out the pieces, because they will be embroidered first.

Use the dressmaker's carbon paper to transfer the floral design onto the center of each of the uppers, turning over the tracing where necessary; use the diagram (above right) as a positioning guide. Mount the gray fabric in the embroidery frame.

Working the design

Embroider the flowers in lazy daisy stitch (see page 62), using wine red on one side of each slipper and rose pink on the other; take care to make each stitch the same size. Emphasize the flower centers with a small straight stitch worked in grass green. Use grass green to create the stems in split stitch (see page 40) and the leaves in lazy daisy stitch.

Carefully cut out all the uppers along the marked lines.

Joining the gray uppers

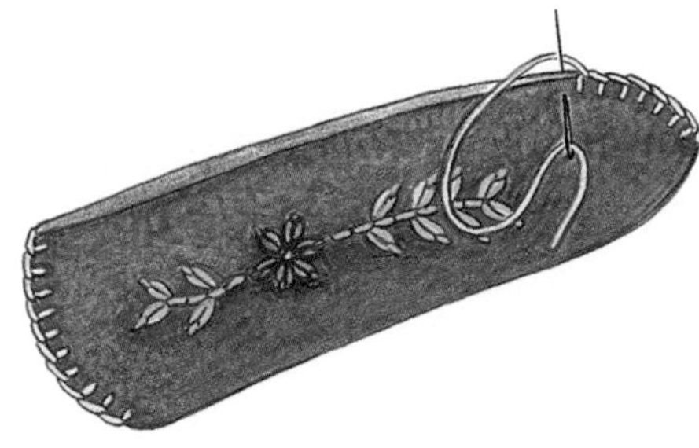

Pin each embroidered pair of uppers together, wrong sides facing. Using light blue-gray tapestry yarn, work blanket stitch along the heel seam (see page 57), then along the toe seam from the tip to the marked line. Space the upright stitches about ¼ in. (5 mm) apart, and make them about ¼ in. (5 mm) long. Fasten off the thread ends securely.

Cutting out the lining pieces

Using the tracing paper templates and the air-erasable marking pen, trace around and cut out two pairs of uppers and two soles from the cream fleece fabric; draw in all the marks for the heel and toe seams as before.

Joining the lining pieces

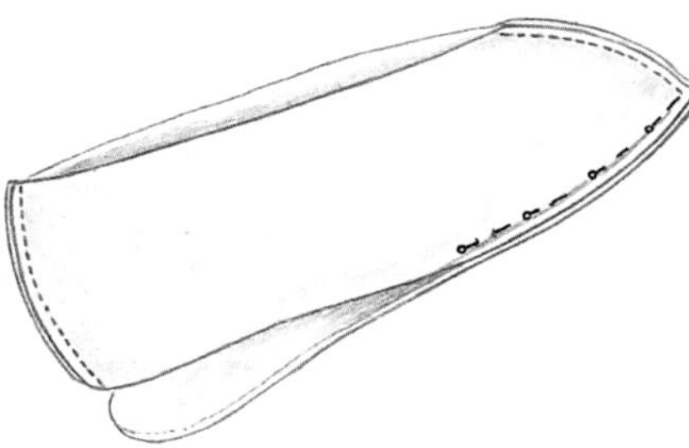

Pin and then baste each pair of cream fleece uppers together, right sides facing. Machine stitch along the heel seam and the toe seam, taking ¼ in. (5 mm) seams. Remove the basting.

Placing right sides together, pin one cream fleece sole to the bottom edge of each pair of cream fleece uppers as shown in the diagram above; match the heel seams and the toe seams to the marked points. Baste in place. Machine stitch all around, taking ¼ in. (5 mm) seams. Remove the basting.

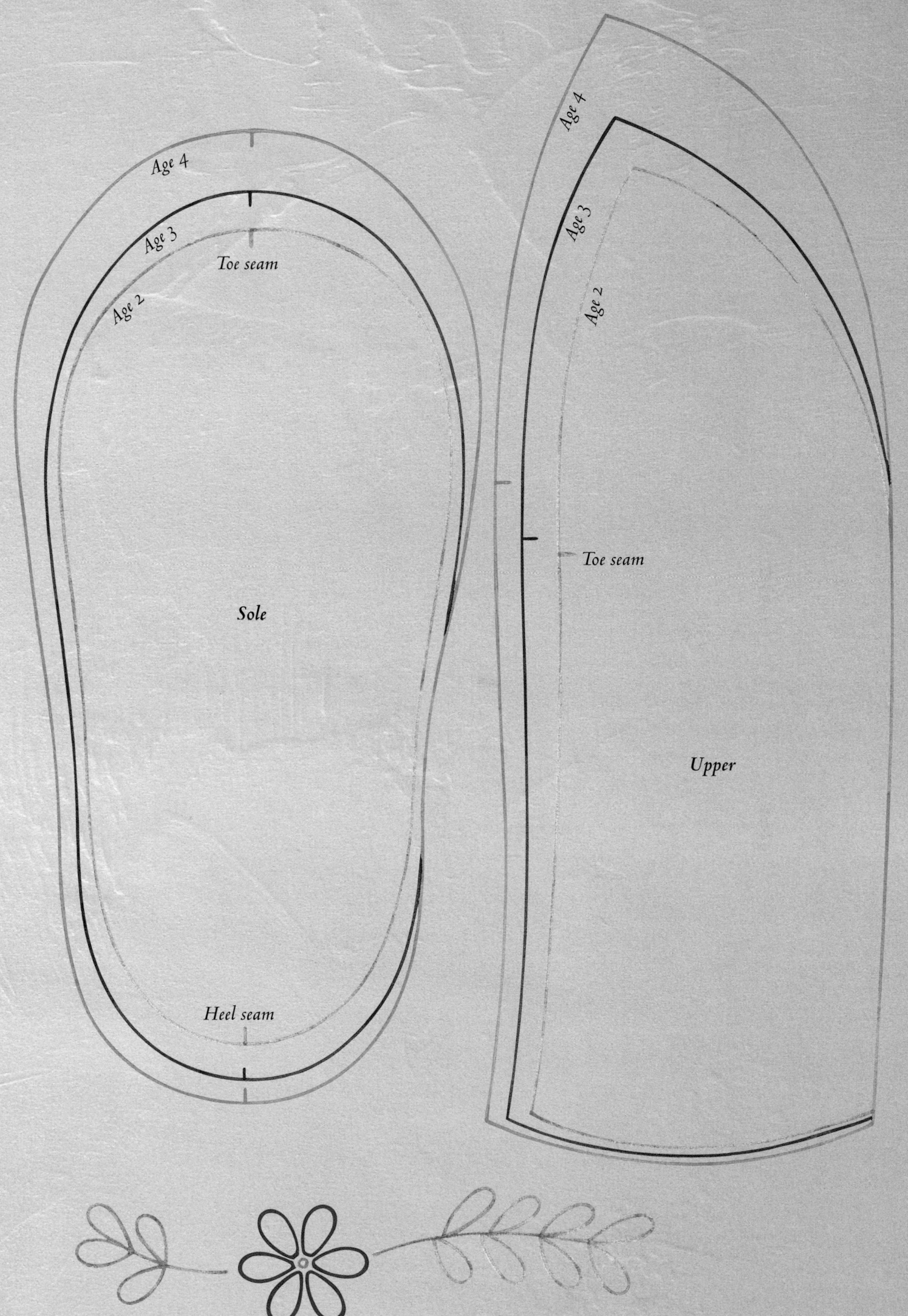
Age 4
Age 3
Toe seam
Age 2
Sole
Heel seam
Age 4
Age 3
Age 2
Toe seam
Upper

Adding the linings

Slip the cream fleece linings inside the embroidered uppers, with wrong sides together, matching the toe and the heel seams. Pin and then baste the pieces together.

Using light blue-gray tapestry yarn, work blanket stitch all around the opening at the top, working the stitches as before.

Preparing the soles

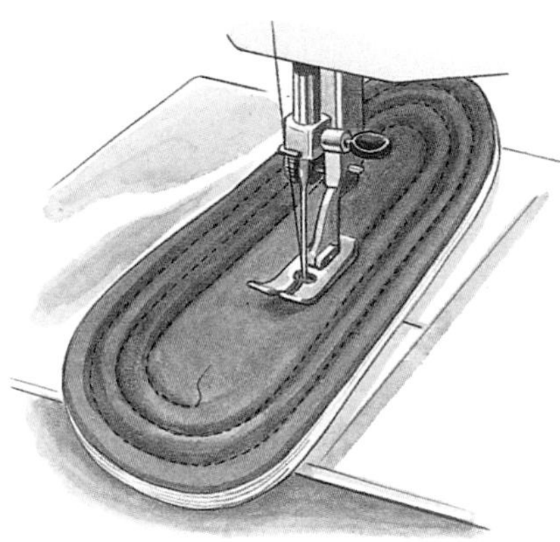

Use the tracing paper template and the air-erasable marking pen to cut out two soles from the coarse brown wool fabric and eight soles from the woven interlining.

Pin four interlining soles to the wrong side of each brown wool sole, then baste the layers together around the outer edge.

Use the brown thread to machine stitch all around each piece ³⁄₈ in. (1 cm) in from the outer edge. Continue to machine stitch smaller and smaller ovals inside the first one, spacing them about ³⁄₈ in. (1 cm) apart, as shown in the diagram above. Remove the basting.

Adding the soles

Pin the soles, interlining side up, to the bottom of the assembled slippers. Use light blue-gray to work blanket stitch all around the edge of the sole, as before.

Adding the pompoms

Make two 1¾ in.- (4.5 cm-) diameter pompoms using medium blue-gray, light blue-gray, and a small length of wine red yarn (for instructions for making pompoms, see page 315.) Sew one to the top of each slipper.

This simple flower and leaf motif has many potential uses. For example, you could embroider it on a little girl's sweater or mittens, using yarn similar to that in the knitting.

Use grass green to split-stitch the stems and work lazy daisy stitches for the leaves.

Wrist Cushion

This jazzy pincushion is made from embroidered felt with a coordinating strap to fasten around the wrist.

You Will Need

Wrist cushion kit, or:

- Bright orange felt, 5½ x 3 in. (14 x 7.5 cm)
- Deep yellow felt, 9½ x 1¼ in. (24 x 3 cm)
- DMC embroidery floss as listed in the color key
- Pencil and ruler
- Scrap of batting
- Crewel needle, size 7
- Embroidery scissors
- Pinking shears
- One snap fastener

Color Key

COLORS	SKEINS
742 Buttercup yellow	1
907 Bright green	1
3804 Deep pink	1

Based on the pincushions worn by professional tailors, this bright and fun sewing accessory fastens around the wrist to keep pins and needles close at hand. It's made from soft felt, so is comfortable to wear, and the cushion top is decorated with simple embroidery, using embroidery floss in three bright colors. For a decorative finish the edges of the cushion and strap are pinked.

The finished pincushion measures 2¾ in. (7 cm) square. The strap is fastened with a snap, so it can be made to fit any size wrist.

Preparing the felt

Cut the orange felt in half to make two 3 in. (7.5 cm) squares. Draw a 1 in. (2.5 cm) square in the center of one of them.

Working the design

Work the design on the marked square using two strands of floss. Refer to the photograph (above left) and the color key.

Begin by working a chain stitch square (see page 61) over the pencil marking, using buttercup yellow. Next, work a square of double featherstitch (see page 68) in bright green ¼ in. (5 mm) outside the chain stitch. To finish, work deep pink French knots (see page 77) at random inside the chain stitch square.

Making the pincushion

Place the two squares together with the embroidery inside and the raw edges matching. Use two strands of deep pink and double running stitch (see page 26) to stitch around three sides, taking ⅜ in. (1 cm) seams. Pad the cushion with batting then stitch the remaining edge closed. Trim the raw edges with the pinking shears.

Attaching the strap

Trim the edges of the yellow felt with the pinking shears. Measure the strip around your wrist, and attach the two halves of the snap on the ends.

Sew the center of the strap to the pincushion, using buttercup yellow and small, neat stitches.

Spanish Country

Bring the rustic simplicity of Spanish peasant cottages into your home with an embroidered curtain and pillow cover.

You Will Need

- Heavyweight decorator fabric in a neutral shade: enough for the pillow (see page 307) and window
- Wool in reddish brown
- Tracing paper
- Pencil
- Dressmaker's carbon paper
- Embroidery hoop
- Chenille needle, size 22
- Materials and equipment to make a curtain in your chosen style
- Pillow form 15 in. (38 cm) square
- Basting and sewing thread

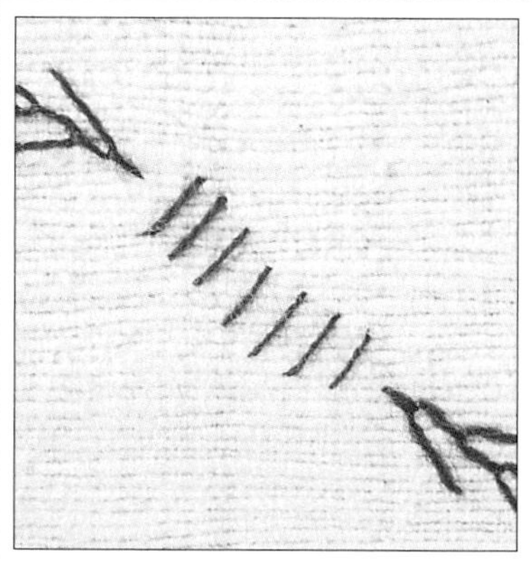

Work parallel straight stitches in the center of the two-tailed swirl.

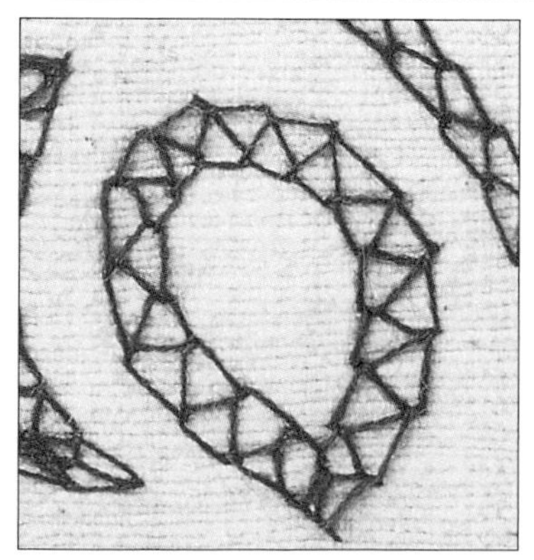

Stitch the central kernels with double chain stitch.

This curtain and pillow were inspired by the simple furnishings traditionally found in Spanish homes. Each piece is made from thick, textured natural fabric embroidered with earthy brown crewel wool using a variety of unusual stitches.

The pillow shown measures 15 in. (38 cm) square, but you can make yours slightly larger or smaller. The curtain is made with a tab heading, so that when drawn it lies flat, or nearly flat, against the window. Make the curtain in any style you like; the important thing is to plan the width carefully so as to accommodate the design (see below).

Preparing the curtain

Use the decorator fabric to make a curtain of the desired size and style. Here the curtain has been cut crosswise from the fabric and the lower (selvage) edge has been left unhemmed to enhance the rustic effect. If you want a hemmed edge, mark the finished lower edge with a line of basting.

Trace the design from the diagram (right). Referring to the photograph (above) for positioning, use the carbon paper to transfer it to the center of the curtain, about 3 in. (8 cm) above the lower edge (when finished). Working outward, repeat to transfer the design across the width of the curtain, finishing with a complete motif at each end; overlap the ends of the motif by about ⅝ in. (1.5 cm) so that the design flows as a continuous border.

WORKING THE DESIGN

Embroider the design using one strand of crewel wool. Do not carry thread across the back of the work. Begin with the top and bottom curves and work them in Cretan stitch (see page 71). Next stitch the vertical two-tailed swirls in Cretan stitch and, in the center of each tail, parallel lines of straight stitches.

Fill the inner kernels with double chain stitch (see page 63). Work the final small curved line in the center of each motif in Scottish Cretan stitch (see page 72).

FINISHING

Steam-press the work on the wrong side. Turn up the hem (if included) and sew it in place.

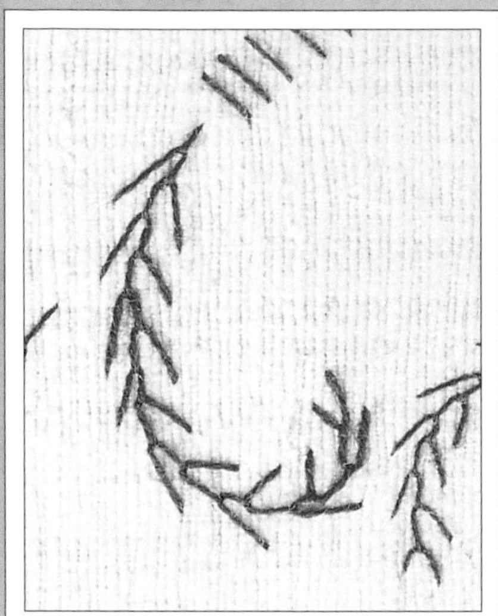

Cretan stitch is used to work the two-tailed swirls and the outer curves.

PREPARING THE PILLOW COVER
Cut a 16 in. (41 cm) square of the decorator fabric. Using the basting thread, baste a 12 in. (30 cm) square in the center to mark the outer edge of the design area.

Trace the top half of the design on page 137 including the two-tailed twirl in the center. Referring to the photograph (above) for positioning, transfer the design to the bottom left-hand corner of the fabric, just inside the basted square. Turn the tracing 90 degrees to the left and repeat to transfer the design to the top left-hand corner. Continue to turn the tracing 90 degrees, transfer the design to the remaining two corners of the basted square.

Mount the fabric in the embroidery hoop.

WORKING THE DESIGN
Work the design in the same way as for the curtain. When it is complete, steam-press it from the wrong side.

ASSEMBLING THE CUSHION
Use the piece to make a 15 in. (38 cm) square pillow cover, referring to the instructions on page 307.

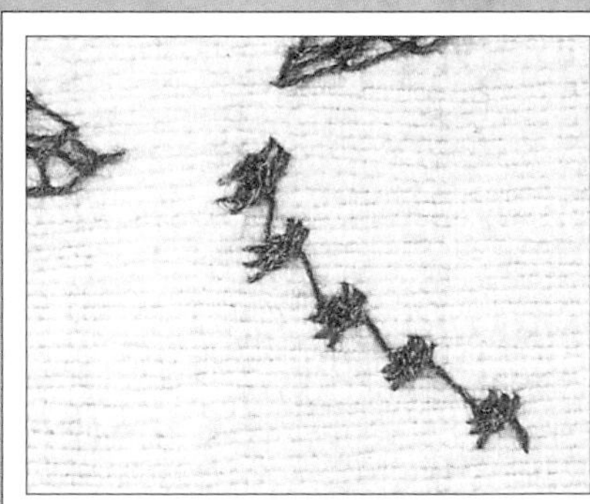

The central curves inside the motifs are worked in Scottish Cretan stitch.

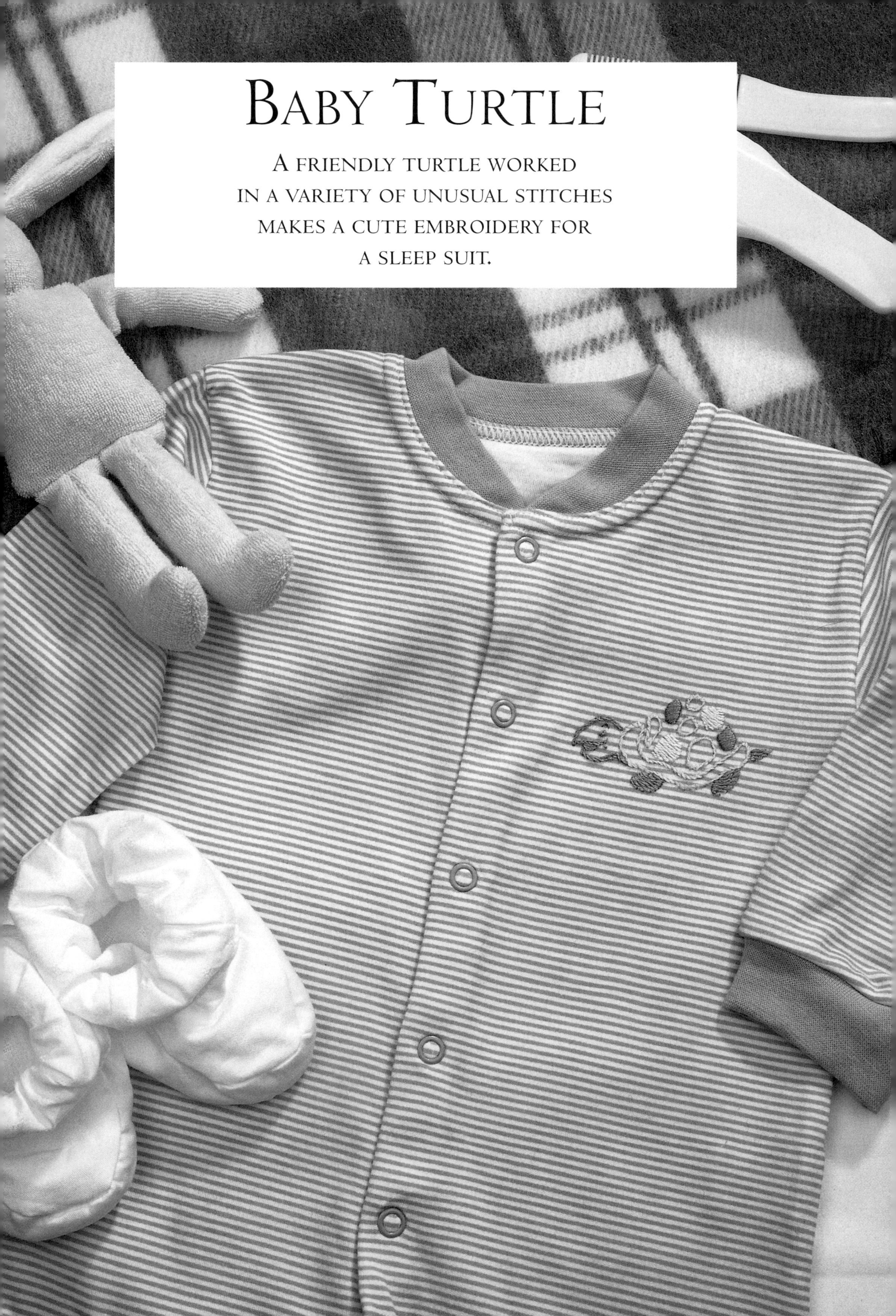

Baby Turtle

A friendly turtle worked in a variety of unusual stitches makes a cute embroidery for a sleep suit.

You Will Need

- Sleep suit or other item of clothing
- DMC embroidery floss as listed in the color key
- Crewel needle, size 7
- Tracing paper
- Pencil
- Dressmaker's carbon paper
- Embroidery hoop
- Embroidery scissors
- Tear-off embroidery backing or lightweight interfacing (optional)

Color Key

COLORS	SKEINS
799 Blue	1
955 Green ice	1
964 Aqua ice	1

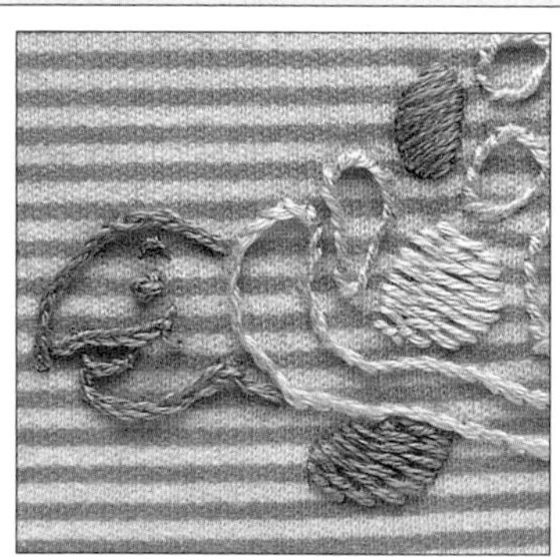

A sideways fly stitch at the end of the mouth suggests the curve of the turtle's cheek.

The turtle uses outline, filling and couching stitches to create a lightweight embroidery with an interesting variety of textures. The finished turtle design measures about $2^{3}/_{4}$ x $1^{1}/_{2}$ in. (7 x 4 cm).

If the item you are stitching is made of a very lightweight fabric, you may wish to stabilize the area first with tear-off embroidery backing or lightweight interfacing. When the stitching is complete, carefully tear or trim away the excess backing. If you are using interfacing, make sure that it won't irritate the baby's skin.

Transferring the Design

Trace the design (below). Transfer it onto the item of clothing using the dressmaker's carbon paper.

Stitching the Turtle

Mount the fabric in the embroidery hoop. Use two strands of floss in the needle throughout and refer to the diagram (below), the key (left), and the pictures here and on page 139 for color placement and stitch direction.

Working the Shell

Pad two patches on the shell with a single layer of diagonal satin stitch, then work another layer of satin stitch over the top, stitching in the opposite direction (see page 30).

Fill two more patches with New England laid stitch (see page 90). Outline the other patches and the ridge at the base of the shell with stem stitch (see page 26).

The Feet, Tail, and Head

Fill the feet and the tail with New England laid stitch, then outline the head and neck with chain stitch (see page 61).

Pick out the eye with a single French knot (see page 77). For the eyebrow, work a small, upside-down fly stitch (see page 68). To finish, work a small, sideways fly stitch at the end of the mouth.

Finishing

Take the work out of the hoop and press it gently on the wrong side, using a damp cloth if appropriate.

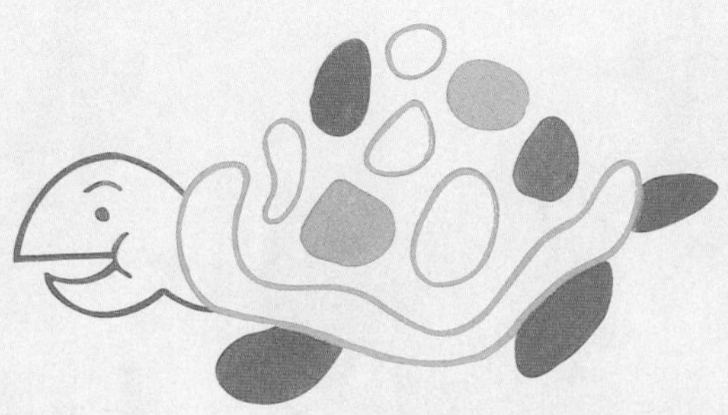

Blackwork Butterfly

This striking butterfly design introduces four new blackwork patterns. Use it to decorate sachets filled with sweet-smelling potpourri.

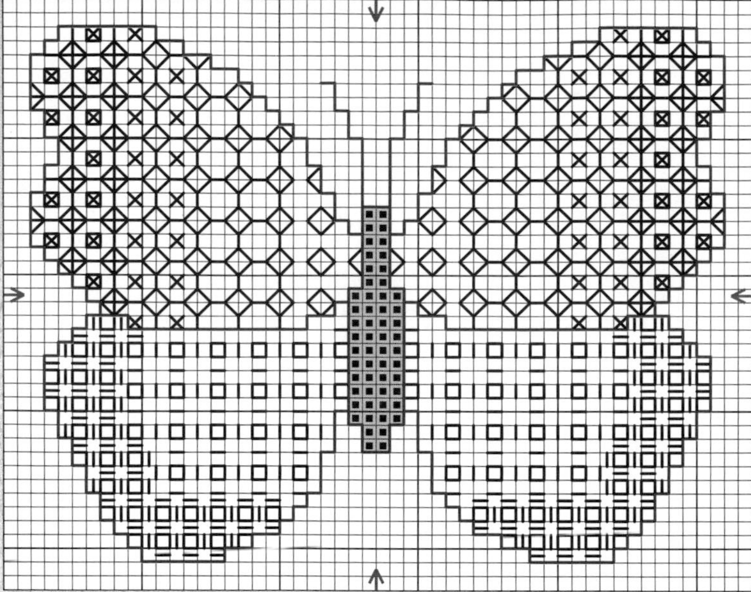

The charming butterfly adorning these two sachets uses blackwork patterns introduced elsewhere in the book. The rectangular sachet measures 4 x 3¾ in. (10 x 8 cm); and the heart sachet, which has a black ribbon hanging loop, measures 5½ in. (14 x 13 cm). If you prefer, you could substitute a single evenweave, perhaps in a pastel color, for the aida cloth used here.

Working the design

Mark the center of the aida with basting and mount it in the hoop.

Work the design from the center out, referring to the chart, the key, and pages 92–94. Make each stitch over one fabric block.

Use three strands to cross-stitch the body and one strand for the patterns on the wings. For the top wings, use patterns five, one, and six; for the lower wings use patterns four and three.

Backstitch using three strands. Take the work out of the hoop, and press gently on the wrong side.

Cutting out the heart

Fold the tracing paper in half and trace the half heart outline, with the fold running between the point at the base and the top indent. Turn the folded tracing over and trace the other half of the heart. Using the tracing as a pattern, cut out the aida and the backing, keeping the design centerd and adding on ⅜ in. (1 cm) all around for seam allowances.

Making the sachets

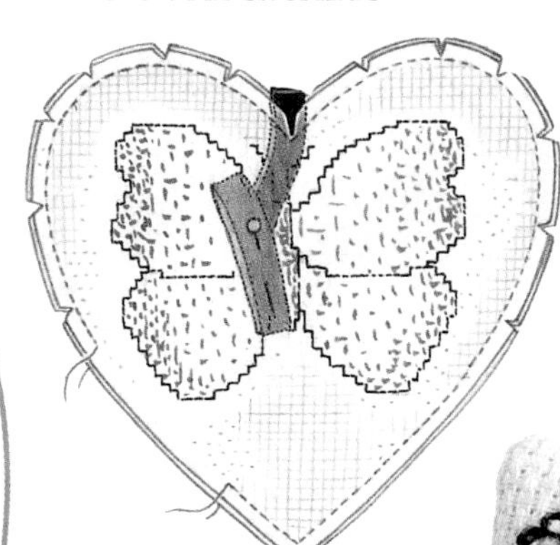

Place the aida and the backing together with right sides facing. If you wish to add a ribbon loop, pin it in place between the two layers before stitching. Taking a ⅜ in. (1 cm) seam, stitch all around, leaving an opening. Trim the seams, snip across the corners or the point, and snip around curves on heart. Turn right side out, and fill with stuffing and a little potpourri. Slip-stitch the opening. Trim with a bow.

You Will Need

Rectangular sachet:

- 14-count cream/aida cloth, 5 x 4 in. (12 x 10 cm)

Heart-shaped sachet:

- 14-count cream/264 aida cloth, 7 in. (18 cm) square
- ½ yd. (40 cm) narrow black velvet ribbon
- Tracing paper and pencil

Both sachets:

- Black embroidery floss, 1 skein
- Backing, same size as aida
- Thread for basting
- Sewing needle
- Tapestry needle, size 26
- Matching sewing thread
- Embroidery scissors
- Embroidery hoop
- Polyester stuffing
- Potpourri

Key

- Cross stitch (use three strands)
- Backstitch (use one strand)
- Backstitch (use three strands)

SHISHA RIBBONS

GIVE PLAIN ACCESSORIES A COLORFUL INDIAN THEME WITH BANDS OF RIBBON DECORATED WITH SHISHA MIRRORS AND SIMPLE EMBROIDERY.

You Will Need

- DMC embroidery floss as listed in the color key, or your own selection of bright colors
- 1 in.- (2.5 cm-) wide black grosgrain ribbon, the required length to decorate the item plus 2 in. (5 cm)
- Tracing paper and pencil
- White dressmaker's carbon paper
- Round Shisha mirrors 5/8 in. (1.5 cm) in diameter; calculate the quantity to decorate the item
- Sewing needle
- Crewel needle, size 8
- Black sewing thread

Color Key

COLORS	SKEINS
333 Purple	1
666 Red	1
702 Bright green	1
740 Deep orange	1
742 Yellow orange	1
797 Blue	1
3770 Cream	2
3804 Fuchsia pink	1

Dress up in style in the summer by adding embroidered ribbons to plain accessories. The embroidery is worked in cream and bright colors on bands of black ribbon, using three stitches. The mirrors are secured with Shisha stitch, and to each side of each mirror the design is worked outward in straight stitch, with the small diamond shapes filled with dainty star filling stitch. The ribbon is sewn to the item once the embroidery is complete. Each repeat is stitched using cream for the straight stitch and a bright color for the Shisha and star filling stitches. The thread quantities given are enough to embroider a 3 yd. (2.7 m) length. The design repeat measures 4½ x 5/8 in. (11.5 x 1.5 cm).

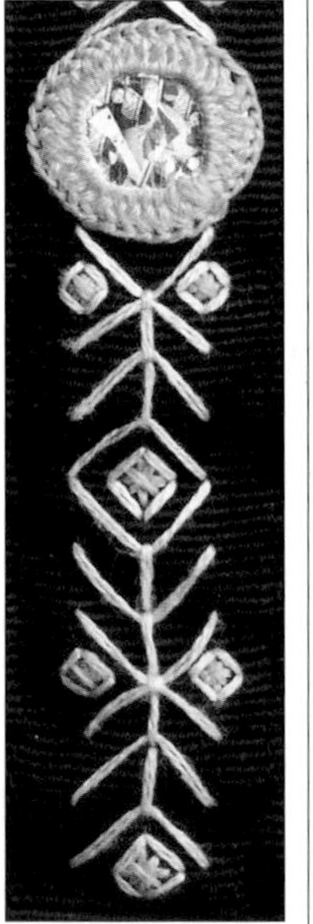

Work the Shisha stitch and star filling stitches using the same bright-colored cotton.

Copying the Design

Trace the design from the diagram (below). Center the tracing on the ribbon, positioning it ¾ in. (2 cm) from one end, then transfer the design using the carbon paper. Repeat along the ribbon, leaving ¼–5/8 in. (5–15 mm) between each repeat and ¾ in. (2 cm) free at each end; the spacing between repeats will depend on the length of ribbon required for the item.

Working the Design

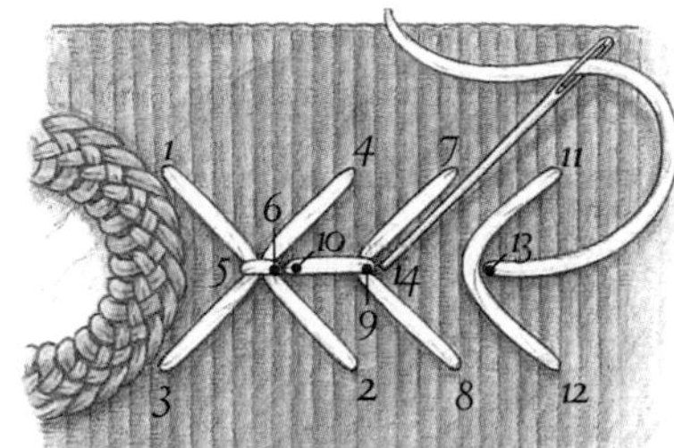

Work the design in Shisha stitch, straight stitch, and star filling stitch using two strands of floss.

Start in the center of the first marked design and attach the mirror using your desired color and Shisha stitch 3 (see page 98). Then, working outward, straight-stitch (see page 25) the design in cream on each side of the mirror, following the number sequence, and add the small diamonds. Finally, fill the small diamonds with star filling stitch (see page 52) using the same color used for the Shisha stitch and working step 1 only of the star. Work each repeat in the same way, using a different color for the Shisha and star filling stitches on each section.

Attaching the Bands

Press the bands lightly. Pin them in place, trim away any excess ribbon, then fold under the raw ends. Baste, then sew the bands in place by machine or by hand, using black sewing thread.

Teddy Pad

The perfect gift for teddy lovers, this miniature bear comes tucked into a pocket on his own presentation pillow.

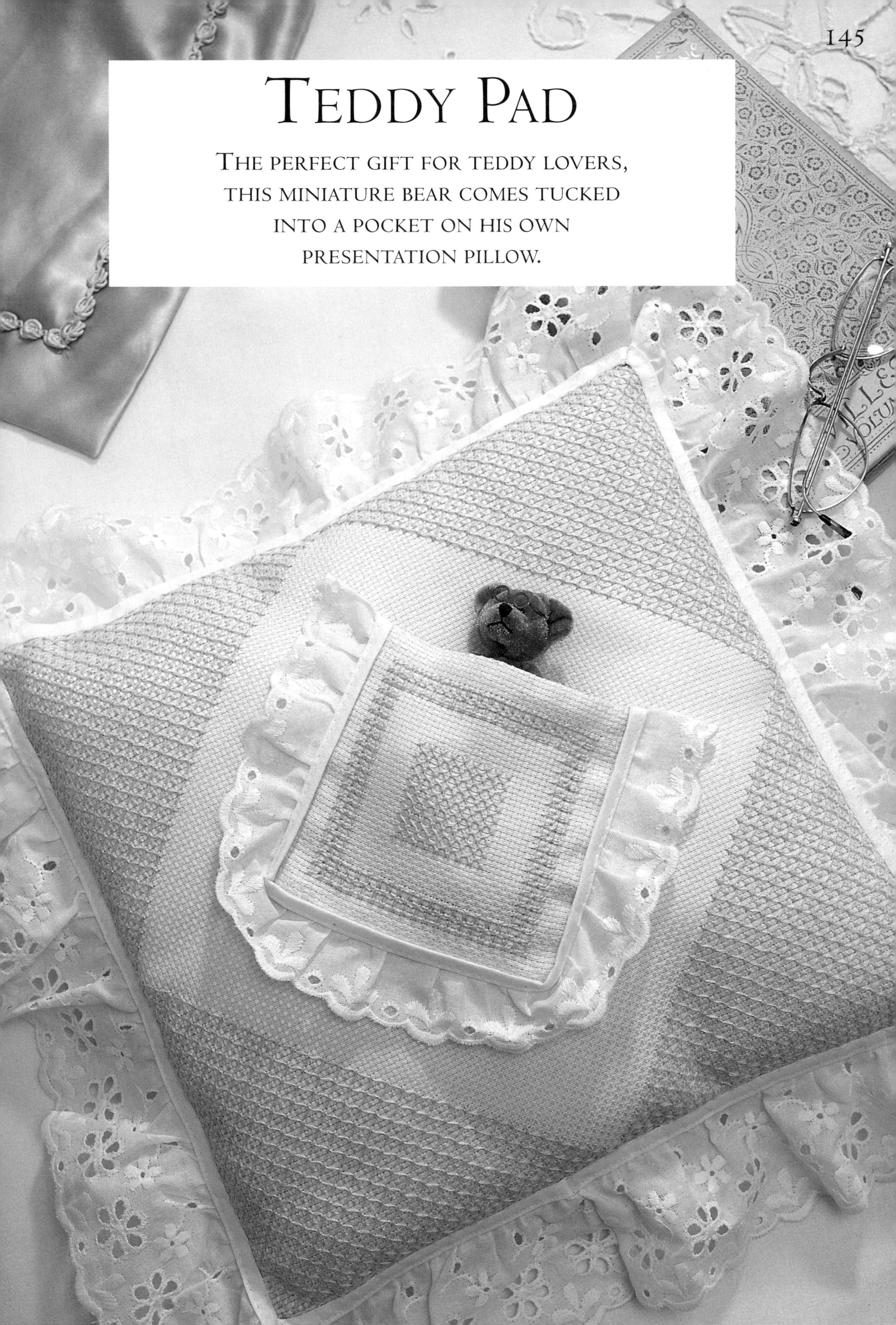

You Will Need

- 14-count cream damask aida, 32 x 12 in. (80 x 30 cm)
- DMC embroidery floss, three skeins of 3774, peach
- Tapestry needle, size 26
- 1½ yd. (1.4 m) of 2¼ in. (6 cm) wide pre-gathered eyelet lace trim to match fabric
- ½ yd. (40 cm) of 1¼ in. (3 cm) wide pre-gathered eyelet lace trim to match fabric
- Cream lining fabric, 32 x 12 in. (80 x 30 cm)
- Sewing needle and thread for basting in two dark colors
- Cream sewing thread
- Embroidery hoop
- Polyester stuffing
- Miniature teddy bear

Cutting Out

From the damask aida: cut two 12 in. (30 cm) squares for the front and back and one 5½ in. (14 cm) square for the pocket
From the lining fabric: cut two 12 in. (30 cm) squares for the front and back and one 4¾ in. (12 cm) square for the pocket.

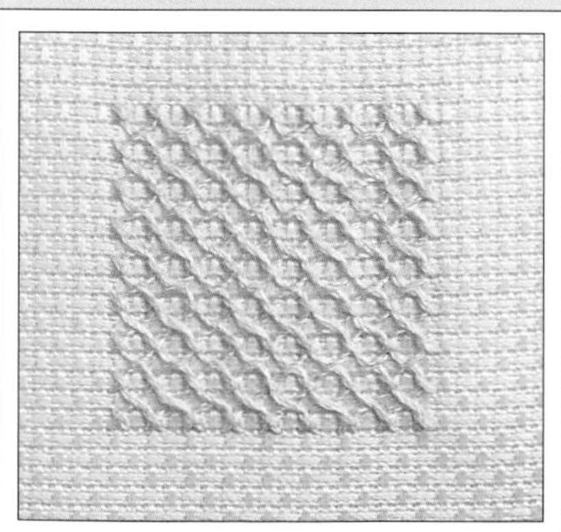

To reveal the sheen of the damask aida, stitch on the matte blocks only.

This sweet bear pad is decorated with mock smocking stitches worked in peach embroidery floss on a softly gleaming background of cream damask aida. Cream-colored eyelet lace finishes the edges of the pillow and its pocket. The pillow measures about 10¼ in. (26 cm) square.

You'll find full instructions for the mock smocking stitches used here on pages 106 and 107.

Preparing the Pillow Front

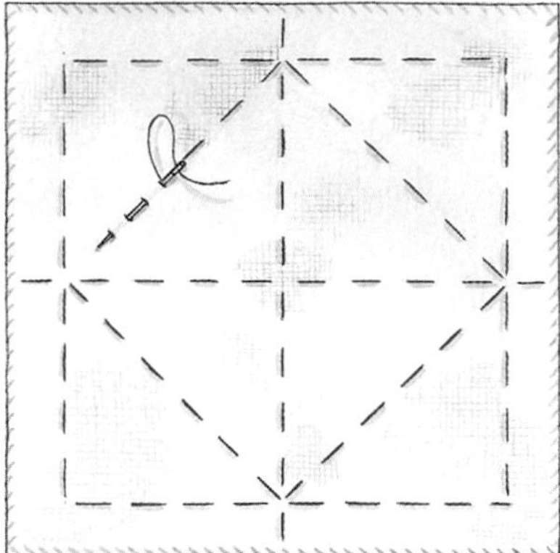

Overcast the edges of one 12 in. (30 cm) damask aida square. Fold it in half both ways to find the center, and mark the nearest matte fabric block with a pin. Work a horizontal and a vertical row of basting, so that the basting lines cross at the block marked by the center pin.

Using the basting thread in the second color, baste a square 133 by 133 fabric blocks; center it around the marked center point and work each basting line between a row of fabric blocks. This square marks the outer edges of the design.

Then join the center points of adjacent sides of the basted square with basted diagonal lines. These lines mark the inner edges of the four corner triangles.

Stitching the Pillow Front

Mount the work in the hoop, and work each stitch over one aida block. Use two strands of floss throughout, and work the stitching on the matte fabric blocks.

Fill the marked corner triangles with trellis mock smocking. Take the work out of the hoop and press it gently on the wrong side.

Stitching the Pocket

Mark the center of the pocket and work the mock smocking as for the pillow front but using honeycomb pattern. Start with the center block: work mock smocking over nine rows of nine stitches each.

Leave a gap of seven aida blocks all around the center block, then work three rows of box ribbing all around it. Take the work out of the hoop and press it gently on the wrong side.

Assembling

Baste the lining pieces to the wrong side of the pillow front and back. Trim the front ⅝ in. (1.5 cm) outside the stitching. Trim the back piece to match.

Trim the pocket piece to measure 4¾ in. (12 cm) square with the stitching centered. Stitch the pocket and its lining together with right sides facing; take a ⅜ in. (1 cm) seam and leave one edge open for turning. Trim the seams and corners, turn right side out, and slipstitch the fourth edge.

Center the pocket diagonally on the front with right sides up. Pin the narrow eyelet lace trim around the sides and bottom, tucking the raw edges neatly under the pocket at the top. Sew the pocket and trim in place by hand.

Stitch the front and back of the pillow together with right sides facing, taking ⅜ in. (1 cm) seams and leaving a gap in one edge. Trim the corners and turn the pocket right side out. Fill it with stuffing, and slip-stitch the gap closed.

Pin the wider eyelet lace trim all around the pillow front, pleating it neatly at the corners so that it lies flat. Sew the trim in place by hand, and then slip the teddy into the pocket.

PARTRIDGES

A VARIETY OF EMBROIDERY STITCHES GIVES THIS PAIR OF PLUMP PARTRIDGES REALISTIC DEPTH AND TEXTURE. THE BIRDS ARE FRAMED BY A RICH FOLIAGE BORDER SET INSIDE BANDS OF GOLD.

You Will Need

- Cream cotton fabric, 10 in. (25 cm) square
- White cotton backing fabric, 10 in. (25 cm) square
- DMC embroidery floss and metallic threads as listed in the color key
- Embroidery hoop, 8 in. (20 cm) in diameter
- Sewing needle
- Dark thread for basting
- Tracing paper and pencil
- Masking tape
- Dressmaker's carbon paper
- Crewel needle, size 7

Color Key

COLORS	SPOOLS/SKEINS
Embroidery floss	
309 Rose red	1
434 Brown	1
783 Golden yellow	1
844 Dark gray	1
900 Flame red	1
907 Grass green	1
988 Green	1
3023 Light gray	1
Metallic threads	
Art. 270 Red	1
Art. 282 Gold	1

This delightful countryside embroidery of two red-legged partridges is richly colored and textured using simple stitches and a combination of embroidery floss and metallic thread.

The plump partridges are filled with a wealth of detail, including their speckled breasts, beady eyes, and bright red beaks and legs. The design is framed inside a border of foliage and couching, which in turn is framed by a trail of footprints. Metallic gold is used extensively in the inner and outer borders and enhances the details on the birds, giving the whole picture a soft luster. The finished picture is 4¼ in. (11 cm) square.

Transferring the Design

Trace the design from the diagram (page 150). Use the masking tape to secure the cream fabric to the work surface, right side up, so that the fabric is taut. Transfer the design to the fabric using the dressmaker's carbon paper.

Adding the Backing

Lay the cream fabric right side down, and place the backing fabric on top. Smooth both layers flat. Pin, then baste the layers together around the outer edge. Mount the fabrics in the hoop with the cream fabric uppermost.

Working the Design

Use two strands of floss or one strand of metallic thread, except for the laid threads in the borders. Refer to the diagram and the color key for color placement, and to the photographs for the direction of the stitches.

Outlining the Birds

Use brown to backstitch (see page 26) a line around each bird from the top of the head down the back to the tip of the wing feathers. Continue around the chest, stopping at the base of the throat. Use brown and encroaching satin stitch (see page 28) to fill in the left-hand bird's cap and the upper part of its back. Repeat for the right-hand bird, filling in the lower part of the wing also.

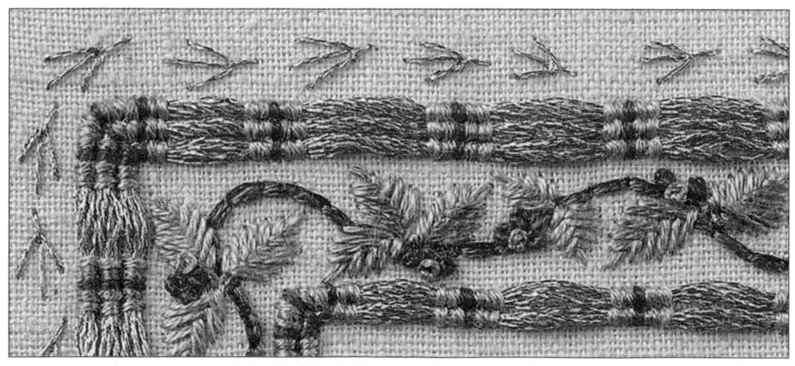

Add the footprints around the outer border with fly stitches; lengthen the anchoring stitch, and work a straight stitch inside the V shape to suggest the center toe. For the foliage border, work the leaves in fishbone stitch, alternating the two shades of green along the stem.

Use dark gray to work two rows of fly stitch on the lower wing; make the V shape long and narrow and the anchoring stitch short. With metallic gold, work a few fly stitches across the upper wing to give it a silky sheen.

Stitching the wings

Using light gray, backstitch around the scalloped shapes at the bottom of the upper wings. Continue using light gray to fill in the upper halves of the wings with encroaching satin stitch; start at the top and work toward the wing tip. Then work the lower edge in the same direction in smooth and even satin stitches (see page 27).

Fill in the middle part of the wings with lines of fly stitches (see page 68) in dark gray, making the V part of the stitch quite long and narrow and keeping the anchoring stitch very short and neat. Scatter a few single fly stitches over the upper wings using metallic gold.

Stitching the chests and tail

Work rows of deep fly stitches in golden yellow over the birds' breasts to produce a linked pattern. Add tiny straight stitches to the upper breasts in golden yellow and brown.

Using dark gray, backstitch around the tail tip, then fill it in with encroaching satin stitch, working from top to tip.

Stitching the feet and beaks

Work the toes in backstitch, then continue backstitching up the outline of the legs. Work satin stitches over the backstitches across the legs to thicken them. Use flame red for the bird on the left and rose red for the bird on the right. Using the same colors, outline the beaks in backstitch and fill them in with satin stitch, as before. Then work a few satin stitches to pick out the eye patches.

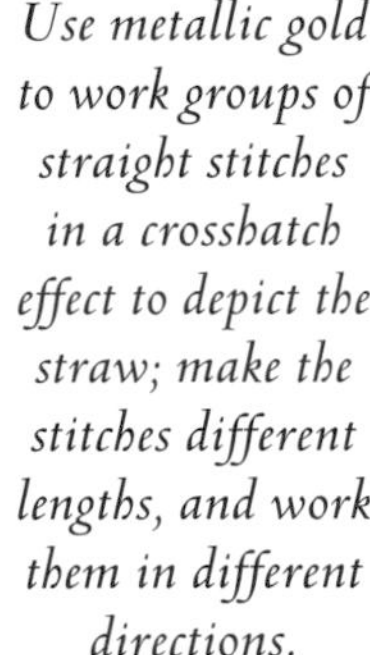

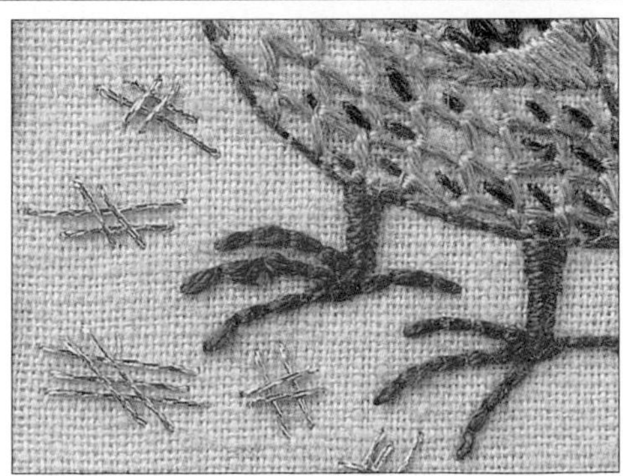

Use metallic gold to work groups of straight stitches in a crosshatch effect to depict the straw; make the stitches different lengths, and work them in different directions.

STITCHING THE FINE DETAILS
Outline the throats, inner edge of the beaks, and around the eyes with dark gray backstitch. Use dark gray to add scattered straight stitches to the speckled area of the upper breasts, gradually changing into encroaching satin stitch for the dark band at the throats. Work a dark gray French knot (see page 77) in the center of each eye.

Work minuscule straight stitches (see page 25) using dark gray and brown thread in the shapes made by the yellow fly stitching. Using one strand of gold, scatter groups of straight stitches in a crosshatch effect around the birds' feet to represent straw; see the photograph on page 149 for details.

Outline the beaks in backstitch, then satin stitch over the backstitches to create a plump, raised outline.

STITCHING THE COUCHED BORDERS
For the inner border, use six strands of metallic gold couched down with rose red at the points marked on the diagram. Add the green and grass green couching on either side. Add a second line in the same way. Repeat for the outer border, but work three lines of couching.

STITCHING THE FOLIAGE BORDER
Work the stems with two lines of backstitch placed close together, one in brown and one in metallic red. Work the leaves in fishbone stitch, alternating the grass green and green floss along the stem. For the berries, work tiny clusters of French knots, in flame red next to the grass green leaves and rose red next to the green leaves. Add a single golden yellow French knot at the center of each cluster.

STITCHING THE FOOTPRINT BORDER
Use metallic gold to work a line of fly stitches around the outer couched band. Complete each footprint by adding a small straight stitch through the V to represent the middle toe.

FINISHING OFF
Remove the work from the hoop. Take the piece to a professional to be mounted and then framed, or frame it yourself following the instructions on pages 305 and 306. If possible, use a ready-made frame, which is significantly less expensive than a made-to-measure one. If the size of the mat opening is slightly bigger than 4½ in. (11.5 cm) square, you can stitch a double set of footprints around the outside of the border to fill the extra space.

Many professional embroiderers prefer to frame their work without glass, to leave the texture visible. If you do use glass, try to place the work where it will be free of reflections.

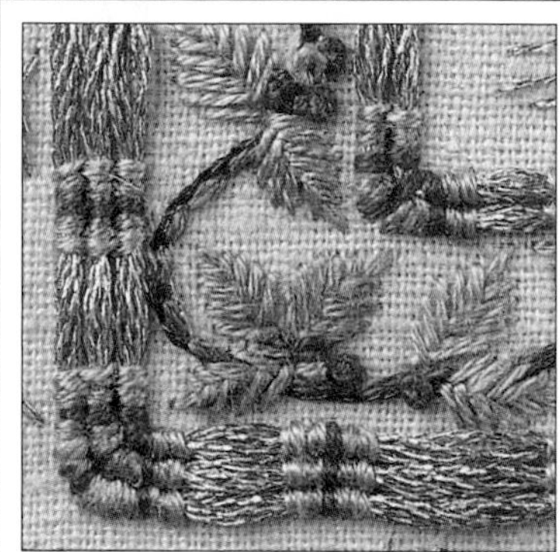

Couch down six strands of metallic gold, using rose red, then work stitches beside the rose red in green and grass green. Follow the trace diagram (below) to produce a mitered effect at each corner.

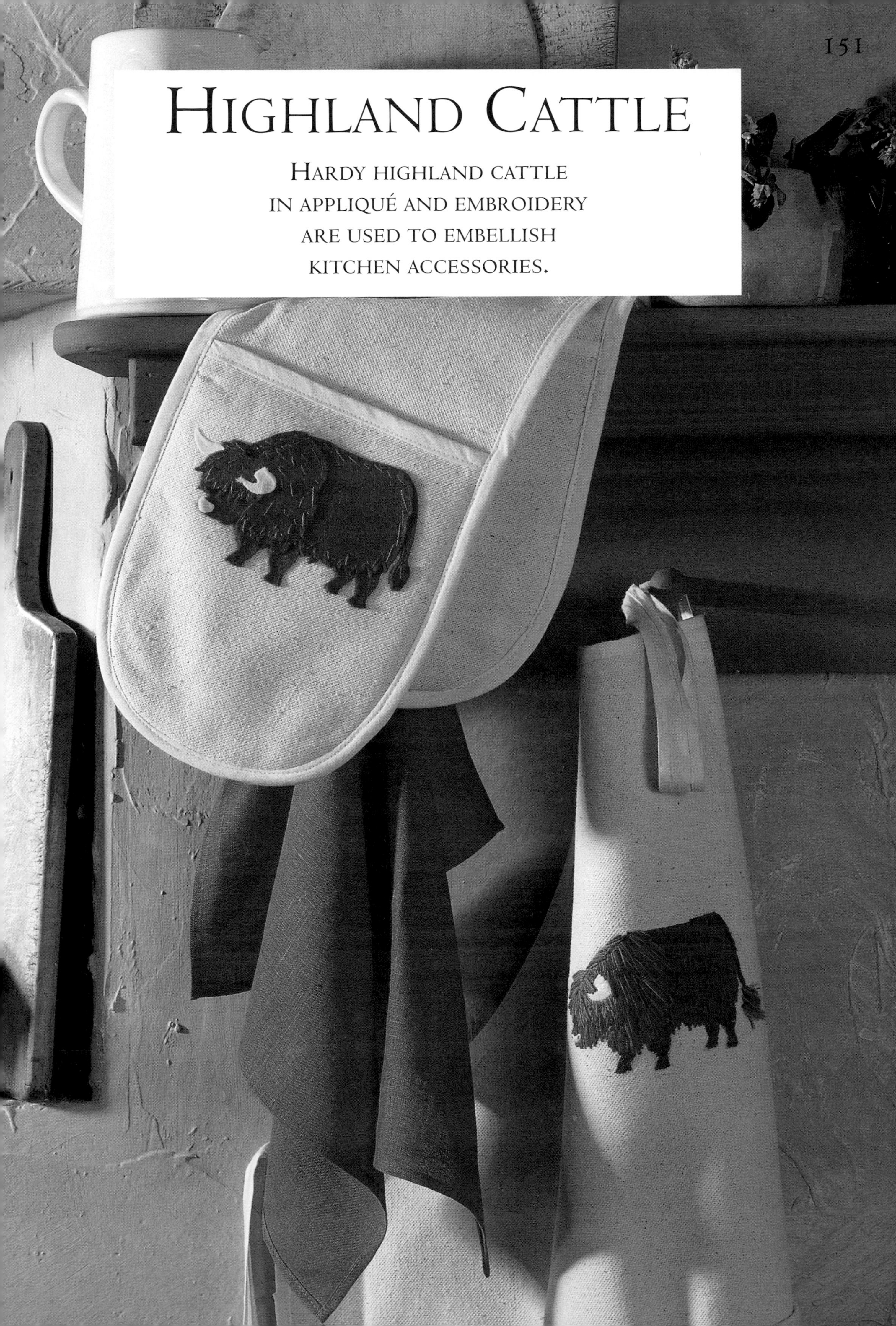

Highland Cattle

Hardy highland cattle in appliqué and embroidery are used to embellish kitchen accessories.

You Will Need

For both items:

- Tracing paper
- Pencil
- Dressmaker's carbon paper
- Embroidery scissors
- Chenille needle, size 26

For embroidered version:

- Apron
- DMC Médicis crewel wools and embroidery floss as listed in the color key
- Chenille needle, size 22
- Embroidery hoop

For appliquéd version:

- Oven gloves
- Felt in brown and white
- Small sharp scissors
- Fabric glue
- DMC Médicis crewel wool in 8176, light chestnut

Color Key

COLORS	SKEINS
Embroidery floss	
White	1
301 Dark tan	1
543 Cream-beige	1
3787 Charcoal gray	1
Médicis wool	
8104 Chestnut	1
8175 Peach	1
8176 Light chestnut	1

The two interpretations of the highland cattle design are used to different effect. The embroidered version emphasizes the animal's long, shaggy winter coat. It is worked using crewel wool and embroidery floss. The colors are blended in the needles for extra realism. The satin stitches and encroaching satin stitches for the coat are longer than usual to create the shaggy effect. The felt version is appliquéd in layers and conveys the creature's bulky form.

The designs shown here could also be used to decorate greeting cards, table linen, and clothing.

Use a heavyweight cotton apron in cream or a pale natural shade and a pair of matching oven gloves. If you cannot find matching oven gloves, you can make your own. Trace the pattern from some existing oven gloves and cut it from suitable fabric and batting. Test the fabric and batting "sandwich" with a hot pan to make sure it is thick enough.

Embroidered version

Preparing the apron

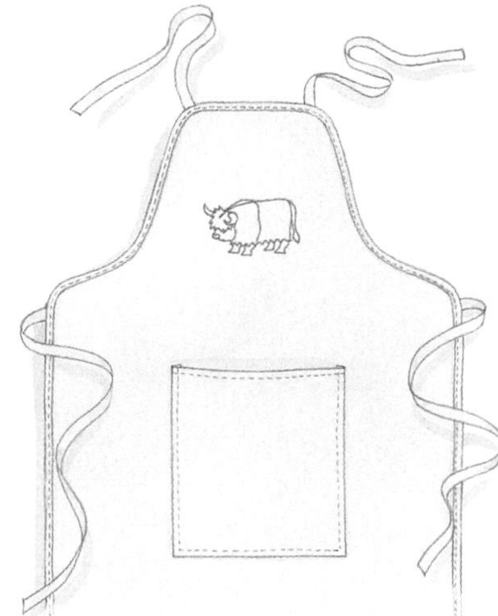

Trace the design from the diagram (below). Lay the apron right side up on the work surface, and transfer the design onto the center of the bib using the carbon paper. Mount the design area in the hoop.

Working the embroidery

Work the design using the size 26 needle unless instructed otherwise.

Fill the legs with one strand of 8104 and long and short stitch (see page 32), slanting the stitches from the top right to the bottom left. Repeat to embroider the tail, but work longer stitches here, slanting them from the top left to the bottom right.

Embroider the body and face with encroaching satin stitch (see page 28); use one strand each of 8104 and 8176 in the needle and work vertically.

Satin-stitch the horns using two strands of white, and the nose using two strands of 543. Pick out the tips of the horns and the nostrils with one strand of 3787 and tiny straight stitches (see page 25).

For the shoulders, use one strand each of 8104, 8175, and 8176 and two strands of 301 in the size 22 needle. Work encroaching satin stitch and angle the stitches to follow the contours of the body. Continue with the size 22 needle to satin-stitch the crown of the head using two strands each of 301, 8175, and 8176; work the stitches in the direction of the coat, fanning them out as shown.

When the body is complete, work three short rows of cut velvet stitch (see page 76) at the bottom of the tail, using one strand each of 8104, 8175, and 8176. Finally, embroider the eye with a French knot (see page 77) using two strands of 3787.

Satin-stitch the crown of the head, radiating the stitches outward where the coat parts.

Work three short rows of cut velvet stitch to make the tufts of hair at the tip of the tail.

FINISHING

Remove the work from the hoop and steam press it gently from the wrong side with a warm iron.

APPLIQUÉD VERSION

CUTTING OUT THE FELT

Trace just the outline of the animal from the trace pattern on page 153. Then trace the following elements of the design separately: the entire animal, omitting the left horn; the body, shoulders, and crown; the left shoulder haunch; the right shoulder haunch; the crown; the end of the tail; the horns; and the nose.

Use the patterns to cut the horns and nose from white felt, extending the left horn where it underlaps the crown; cut all the other pieces from brown felt.

PREPARING THE OVEN GLOVES

Transfer just the outline onto one of the pockets on the oven gloves using the tracing paper and the dressmaker's carbon paper; use the photograph (right) as a positioning guide.

WORKING THE APPLIQUÉ

Work the appliqué in layers, referring to the pattern on page 153 to position the pieces.

To begin, glue the complete animal in place. Next stick the large felt piece consisting of the body, crown, and shoulders on top of it. For the top layer of the appliqué, glue the shoulder haunches and the crown in place, trimming away felt at the base of the large shoulder piece for a triple-layered effect; this is shown in the photograph (right). To finish, glue the horns, nose, and tail end and leave to dry.

WORKING THE EMBROIDERY

Use a single strand of 8176 Médicis wool in the size 26 needle throughout. Work slanting straight stitches around the edge of the crown, on the edge of the body, and on the tip of the tail. Work slanting straight stitches randomly across the shoulders, working the stitches in the direction of the coat.

To finish, work long straight stitches along the top of the crown and between the two shoulder haunches, couching the stitches down at regular intervals.

Trim the bottom of the large shoulder piece to suggest the thick shaggy coat.

Sea Breeze

A jaunty lighthouse encircled by seagulls soaring on the breeze gives a maritime theme to laundry accessories.

You Will Need

- Remnants of striped fabric and red felt
- Blue fabric laundry bag and holdall with removable frames
- DMC embroidery floss as listed in the color key
- Crewel needle, size 5
- Tracing paper
- Pencil
- Dressmaker's carbon paper
- Transfer fusing web
- Embroidery frame
- Embroidery scissors

Color Key

COLORS	SKEINS
Ecru	1
666 Bright red	1
827 Sky blue	1

For the laundry basket, work the fence posts in chain stitch and the rope in double knot stitch.

Created in simple appliqué and a variety of embroidery stitches, these jaunty coastal motifs add a fresh note to a laundry basket and holdall. There's a lighthouse surrounded by seagulls and a pair of sailing dinghies racing in the breeze.

The motifs can be enlarged or reduced to any size using a photocopier. As a guide, the basket here is 25½ in. (65 cm) tall, and the lighthouse has been enlarged to about 400 percent its original size. The holdall motifs have not been altered.

Transferring the design

Remove the frame from inside the laundry basket and lay the fabric flat on the work surface with the side you wish to decorate uppermost.

Enlarge the lighthouse and the seagulls to the correct size for your basket. Trace the lighthouse from the photocopy, and transfer it onto the fabric using the tracing and dressmaker's carbon paper. Repeat to transfer the seagulls, referring to the photograph (below) for positioning.

Working the basket appliqué
Turn the tracing over. On the paper side of the fusing web, trace the lighthouse roof, the viewing balcony, and the top, middle, and bottom sections of the walls; include the door and window outlines and leave at least 3⁄8 in. (1 cm) between each shape. Cut out the shapes roughly.

Fuse the roof and balcony onto the red felt, then fuse the three wall sections onto the wrong side of the striped fabric with the stripes running horizontally. Cut out the shapes accurately and peel off the backing papers.

Position the appliqués on the laundry basket fabric and fuse them in place with a medium iron.

Embroidering the basket
Mount the fabric in the embroidery frame. Work the design using two strands of floss in the needle throughout. Do not carry thread from one area to another across the back of the work because the loose threads may catch on the laundry.

For the grid, couch down diagonal threads with upright cross stitches.

To begin, embroider the waves with sky blue using long stem stitches (see page 26). Next use bright red to work French knots (see page 77) around the roof and viewing balcony; space them about ⅜ in. (1 cm) apart and work them just inside the raw edges. Use ecru for the rest of the embroidery.

Make the grid beneath the roof by laying down thread diagonally and couching it with upright cross stitches (see page 52). For the seagulls work double fly stitch (see page 74). Work blanket stitch (see page 58) around the raw edges of the appliqué wall sections, then stitch the remaining wall outlines with stem stitch. Work the windows and steps in chevron stitch, omitting the areas of window that are edged by the appliqué shapes. Finally, pick out the fence posts with chain stitch (see page 61) and the rope with double knot stitch (see page 82).

FINISHING

Remove the work from the embroidery frame and press it gently from the wrong side. Insert the basket frame.

WORKING THE HOLDALL APPLIQUÉ

Remove the holdall frame and lay out the fabric. Enlarge or reduce the motifs to the correct size for your holdall. Trace the motifs from the photocopy and transfer them onto the fabric referring to the photograph (above) for positioning.

Turn the tracing over and trace the lighthouse walls, the balcony, the roof and the dinghy sails onto the paper side of the fusing web. Cut out the shapes roughly. Fuse the walls on to the wrong side of the striped fabric with the stripes running horizontally, and fuse the roof and balcony onto the red felt. Fuse the dinghy sails onto the wrong side of the striped fabric with the stripes running horizontally, vertically, or diagonally as desired.

Cut out the shapes accurately and bond them to the holdall. Mount the fabric in the frame.

WORKING THE DESIGN

Embroider the lighthouse as before, but work the windows, fence posts, and steps in straight stitches (see page 25); refer to the diagram for positioning.

On the large dinghy sails, use ecru to work evenly spaced running stitches (see page 26) just inside the raw edges. On the small dinghy sails, work cross stitches (see page 44) along the edges. Continue using ecru to outline the hulls with coral stitch (see page 81). Finally, pick out the waves with sky blue and long stem stitches.

Remove the work from the hoop, press, then insert the frame.

Work the dinghy hulls in coral stitch using ecru floss.

Chapter 3

Needlepoint Stitch Library

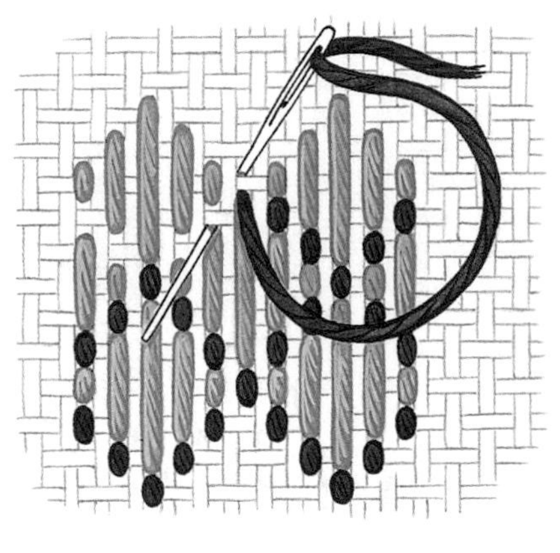

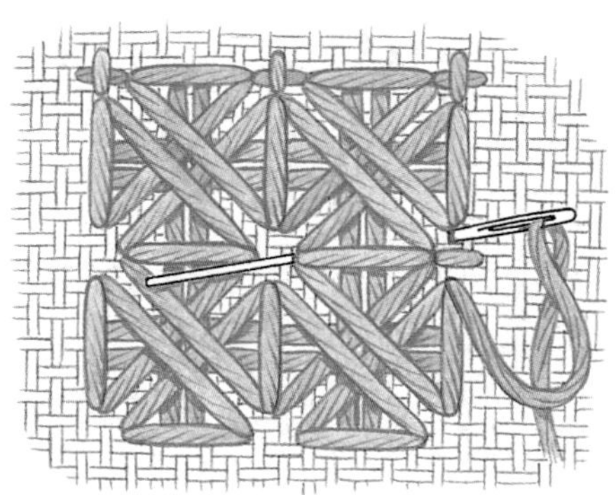

Easy stitches

Half cross stitch and continental tent stitch are two of the most widely used needlepoint stitches. They are small, neat, diagonal stitches which are ideal for detailed designs with an intricate mix of colors. The two stitches look identical from the front, but they are quite different on the back.

Like other needlepoint stitches, half cross stitch and continental tent stitch are worked on canvas, a strong fabric with a regular open mesh of stiffened threads which are easy to count. Canvas comes in a range of different mesh sizes, or gauges; the higher the number, the finer the canvas.

The most popular yarn for needlepoint is tapestry wool, a twisted four-ply yarn. Use tapestry needles, which have large eyes and blunt ends.

Work each stitch in two stabbing movements, up through the canvas then down through the canvas, pulling the thread through each time.

Half cross stitch

Half cross stitch is very quick and easy to work; it is also economical on yarn. It forms a less bulky fabric than other diagonal needlepoint stitches, so it's an ideal choice for items that won't get much wear, such as scatter pillows and pictures. Half cross stitch is worked in horizontal rows and forms small straight stitches on the back of the canvas. Small items can be worked without a frame.

Half cross stitch front

Half cross stitch back

Continental tent stitch

Continental tent stitch forms a hard-wearing, well-padded surface which is durable enough for chair seat covers and stool tops. It is worked in horizontal or vertical rows and forms long, slanting stitches on the back of the canvas. When this technique is used to cover large areas, the diagonal stitches can pull the canvas out of shape. This can be minimized by mounting the canvas in a frame before you start stitching.

Continental tent stitch front

Continental tent stitch back

Starting and fastening off

It is a good idea to test the stitch and yarn you are using on a spare piece of canvas to check that it covers the canvas correctly and that the tension is even.

Work with a length of yarn no more than 15 in. (38 cm) long. A longer length of yarn may become weak and fluffy and fail to cover the canvas properly.

Method A To start, take the needle down a few holes from your starting point, leaving a short tail of yarn at the front. As you work the first row, stitch over the loose yarn, and trim the loose end if necessary. To fasten off, darn the remaining end of the yarn through the back of several stitches.

Method B To start, knot the end of the thread. Take the needle to the back, about 1 in. (2.5 cm) from the start. As you work, stitch over the thread end at the back. When you reach the knot, trim it off. To fasten off, turn the canvas wrong side up, and darn the remaining thread end through the back of several stitches.

Working half cross stitch

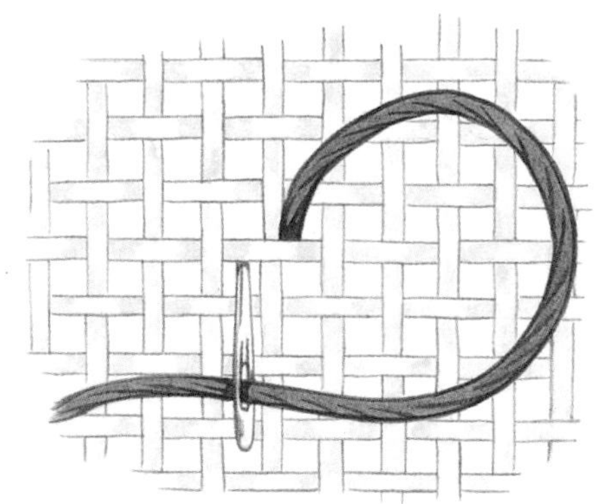

1 Working from right to left, bring the needle out to the front. Insert it one hole to the left and one hole down, and gently pull the yarn through to make a small diagonal stitch on the front of the canvas.

2 Bring the needle out to the front one hole up, then insert it one hole to the left and one down. Continue in this way to the end of the row.

3 To start the second row, bring out the needle one hole down. Working from left to right, insert it one hole up and one to the right; bring it out one hole down. Continue like this to the end of the row. Repeat these two rows to fill the shape.

Working continental tent stitch

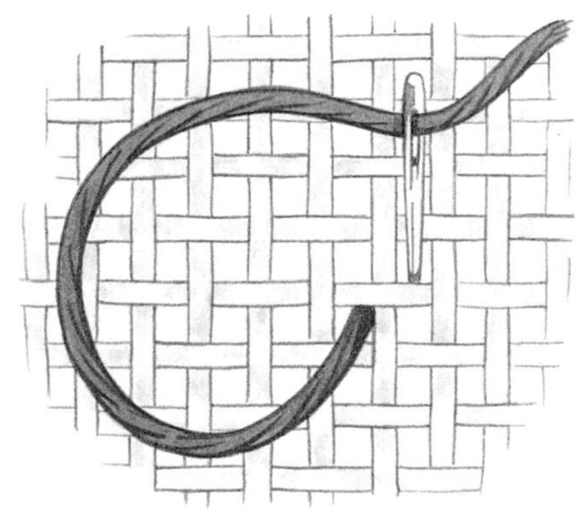

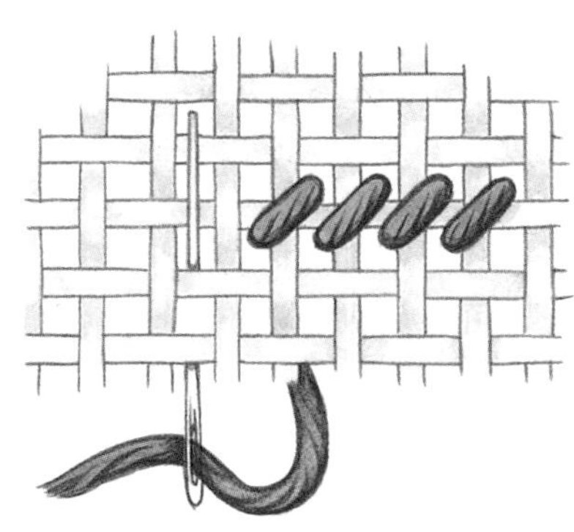

1 Working from right to left, bring the needle out to the front. Insert it one hole up and one hole to the right, then gently pull the yarn through to make a small diagonal stitch.

2 Bring the needle out one hole down and two holes to the left, then make another small upward diagonal stitch. Continue in this way to the end of the row.

3 For the second row, turn the work upside down. Bring the needle out one hole up and repeat steps **1–2**. Repeat steps **1–3** to fill the shape.

Distorted canvas
Tent stitch can pull the canvas badly out of shape if it's worked too tightly. To reduce distortion, mount the canvas in a frame and stitch more loosely.

Speedy stitching

If you are working a very small piece of canvas without a frame, you can speed up your stitching by inserting the needle and bringing it out in one smooth movement. Otherwise, always use a stabbing movement when stitching to avoid distorting the work.

Tent stitch is often used to create natural shaded effects.

Tent stitches

Basketweave tent stitch

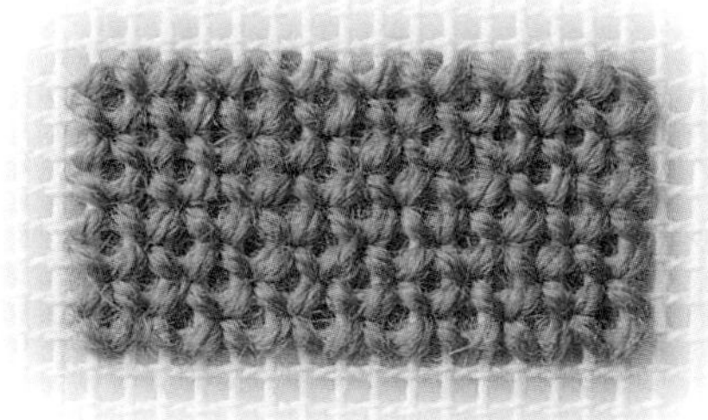

Alternating tent stitch

Threaded alternating tent stitch

Tent stitches cover the canvas well and give a hard-wearing surface. The variations shown here cause little canvas distortion, so they're ideal for filling large shapes and backgrounds.

Basketweave tent stitch looks identical to continental tent stitch at the front, but at the back it looks very different. At the back, the stitches form a vertical-horizontal weave (hence the name). This pulls the canvas evenly in both directions and minimizes distortion, so the stitch is ideal for covering large areas. At the back of continental tent stitch, all the stitches point the same way—over a large area this can distort canvas badly. However, it's very maneuverable, so use it for details and small, solid areas.

Alternating tent stitch is similar to basketweave tent stitch, but the stitches change direction on alternate rows, creating a different texture. It can be worked in one or more thread colors.

Threaded alternating tent stitch is a decorative version of alternating tent stitch in which the stitches are laced with a finer thread.

For details on continental tent stitch and starting and fastening off the thread, see pages 161 and 162.

Working basketweave tent stitch

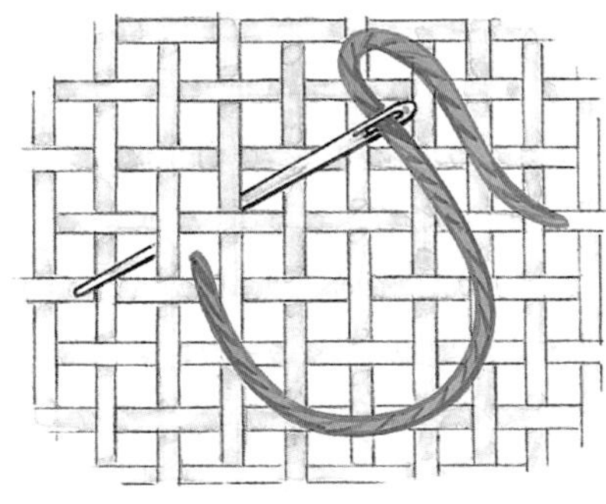

1 Work in diagonal rows. Bring the needle to the front at the top right of the shape. Insert it one hole up and one to the right to work the corner stitch. Bring it to the front two holes to the left and one down, ready to work the first "down" row.

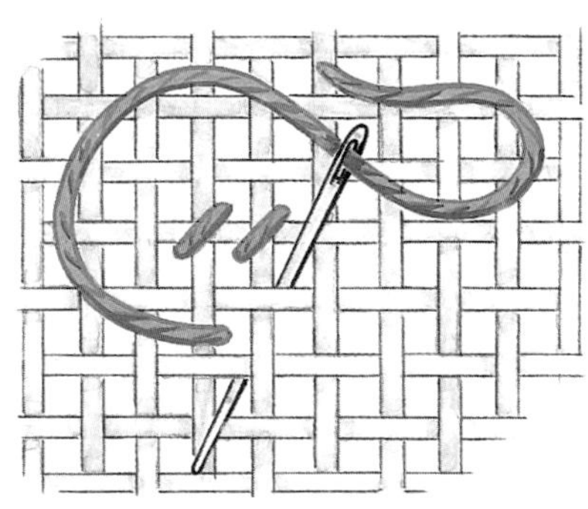

2 Insert the needle one hole up and one to the right. Bring it to the front two holes down. Insert the needle one hole up and one to the right. Bring it to the front again one hole to the left and two down, ready to work the first "up" row.

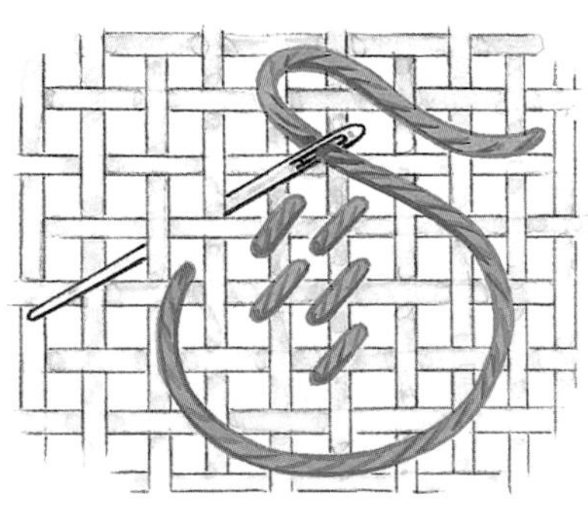

3 Insert the needle one hole up and one to the right. Bring it to the front two holes to the left. Work two more stitches in this way. Bring the needle out one hole down and two to the left at the end of the last stitch, ready to work the next "down" row.

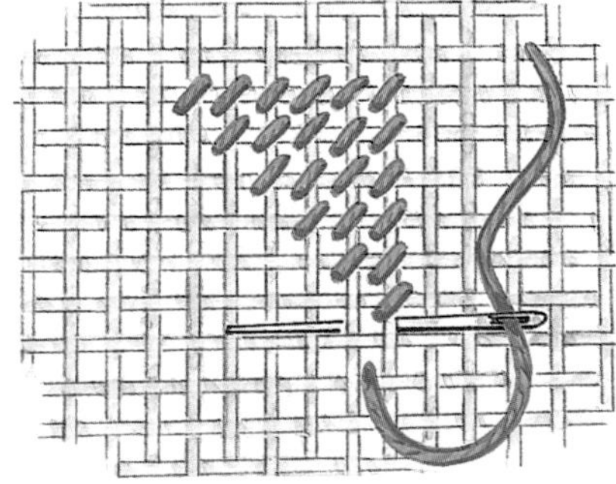

4 Continue in this way, working alternate "down" and "up" rows to fill the shape. Keep the direction of the rows consistent and the thread tension even throughout.

Working alternating tent stitch

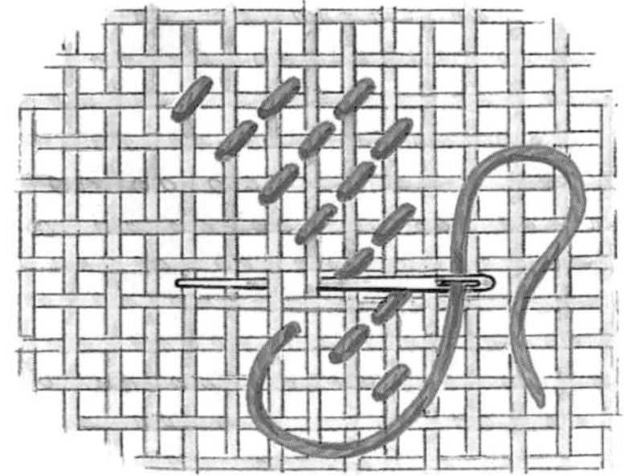

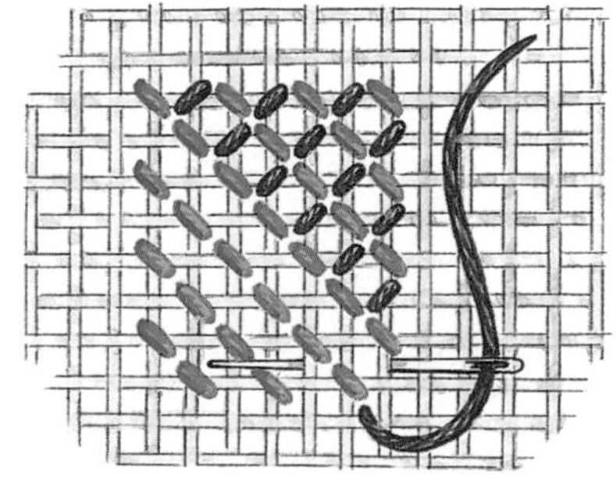

1 Bring the needle to the front at the top right. Work rows of basketweave tent stitch across the shape, following steps **1–4** on the previous page, but arrange the stitches so that every alternate canvas intersection is left unworked.

2 Rotate the canvas 90 degrees to the left . Using the same or a contrasting thread, work rows of basketweave tent stitch, slanting in the opposite direction to the first stitches, to fill the spaces left between the first series of stitches. Keep the thread tension even throughout.

Alternating tent stitch

Working threaded alternating tent stitch

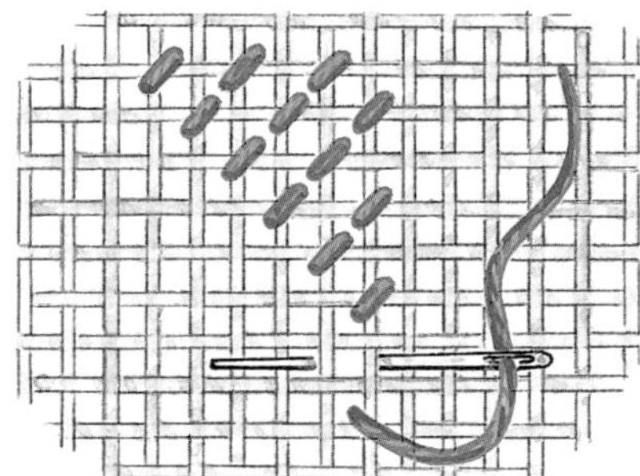

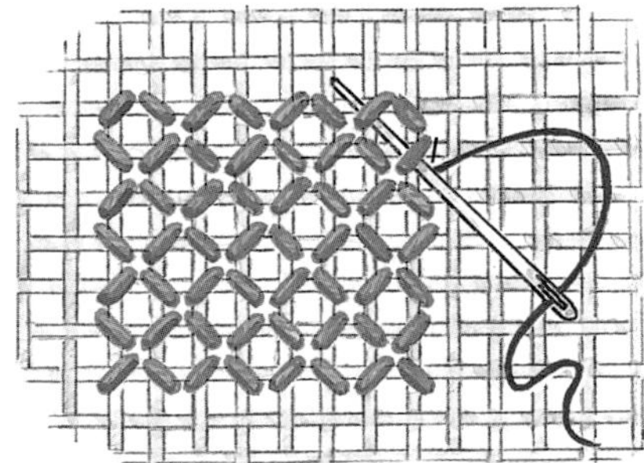

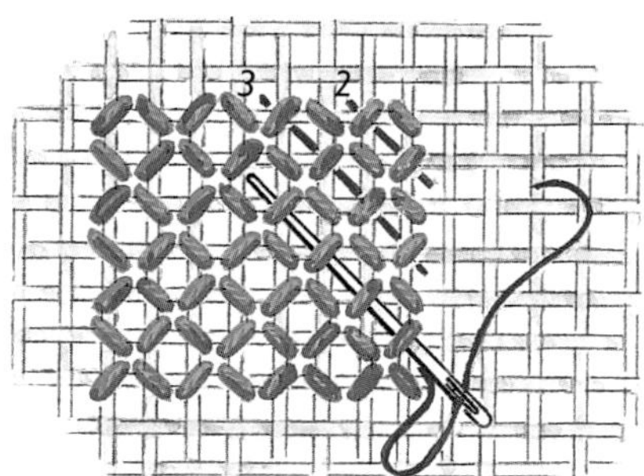

1 Work alternating tent stitch, following steps **1–2** (above) to fill the shape. Keep the tension of the stitches fairly loose throughout to ensure adequate space to accommodate the threading.

2 Thread a fine tapestry needle with a finer thread and secure the thread end on the right-hand edge of the shape. Bring the thread to the front at 1 and take it under all the tent stitches in the first row which slant from top right to bottom left.

3 Take the thread to the back at 2 and bring it to the front at 3. Then take it under the tent stitches that slant from top right to bottom left in the second row. Continue in this way across the shape. Fasten off the thread on the back of the work by weaving it under a few stitches.

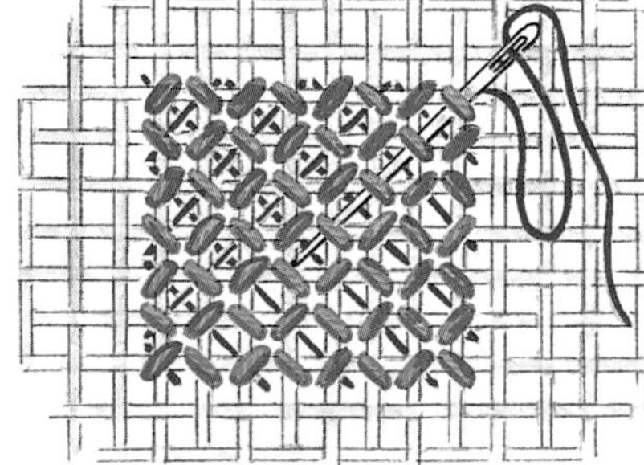

4 Rotate the work 180 degrees and rejoin the second thread at the top left of the shape. Take the thread in diagonal rows under all the tent stitches that slant from top left to bottom right and over the rows worked in steps **2–3**. Then fasten off the thread as before.

Threaded alternating tent stitch

Basketweave tent stitch

Straight stitches

Straight stitches are very easy to work. As a rule, they can span up to eight threads and be placed horizontally or vertically. They can fill any shape, so are ideal for backgrounds, and you can use the different variations to create a range of interesting patterns and textures.

Straight stitch can be worked in either straight rows or diagonal rows to fill regular shapes.

Random straight stitch is used freely to fill any shape. It is usually worked with the design outlines marked out on the canvas, rather than from a chart. Use it for pictures and other items that don't get much wear, as it's not a very durable stitch.

Long stitch makes an attractive pattern of triangles arranged in a double row over five canvas threads.

Brick stitch is worked in interlocking rows and forms a textured filling for shapes and backgrounds.

Straight stitch

Random straight stitch

Long stitch

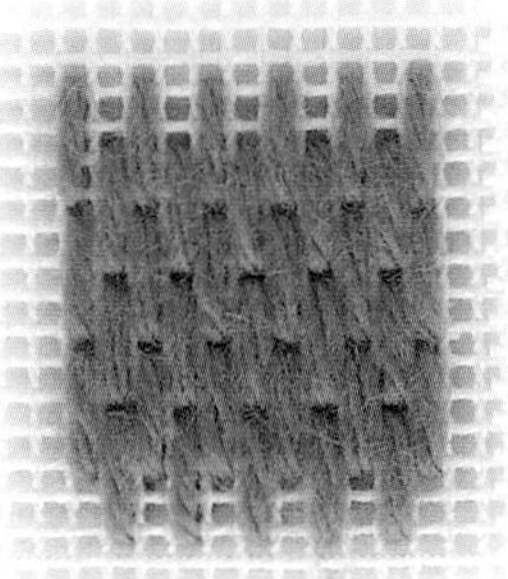

Brick stitch

Working straight rows of straight stitch

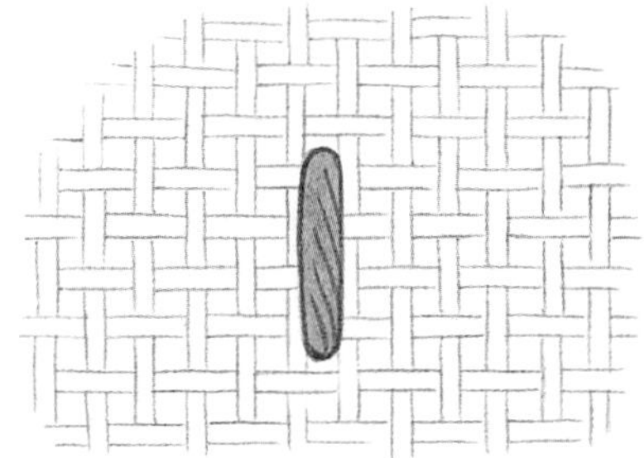

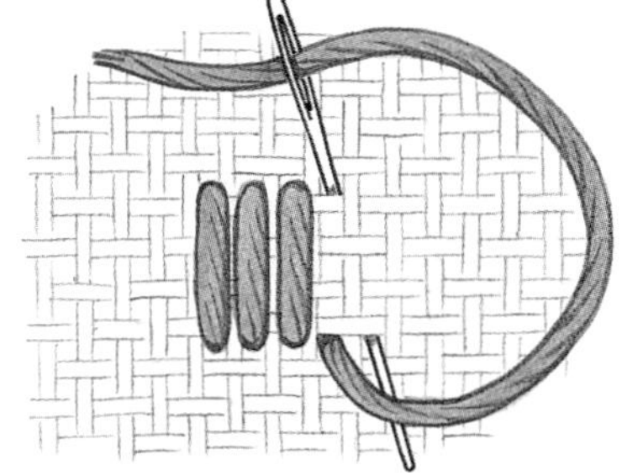

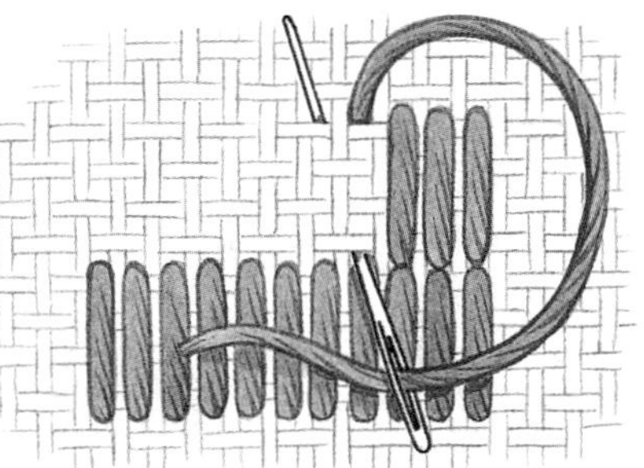

1 Bring the needle out to the front at the bottom left of the shape. Make a stitch straight up or straight along the canvas. It's best to take the stitch over no more than eight canvas threads.

2 Bring the needle out one hole to the right of the previous stitch. Make another straight stitch over the same number of threads. Continue in this way to the end of the row.

3 Work the next row from right to left, but this time work the stitches downward as shown. Continue in this way, working the rows in alternate directions.

Working diagonal rows of straight stitch

1 Make a straight stitch as shown in step **1**, above. Work the next stitch one hole to the right, but start it one hole farther up or down. Continue to the end of the shape.

2 Work the next row in the opposite direction. Continue in this way, keeping all the stitches the same length and alternating the direction of the rows.

Working random straight stitch

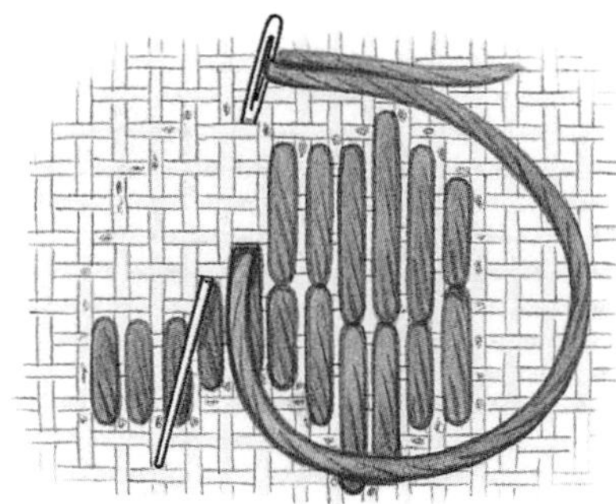

Work vertical or horizontal rows of straight stitches in a free, random way across the shape to be filled. The stitches can vary from quite long to very short. Make sure all the canvas threads are covered.

Filling a rectangle

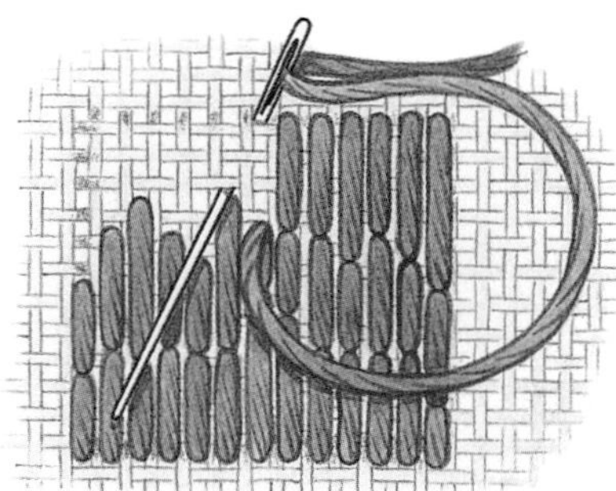

Work rows of random straight stitch across the shape, varying the lengths of the stitches in the top and bottom rows to follow the straight lines marked on the canvas.

Filling a curved shape

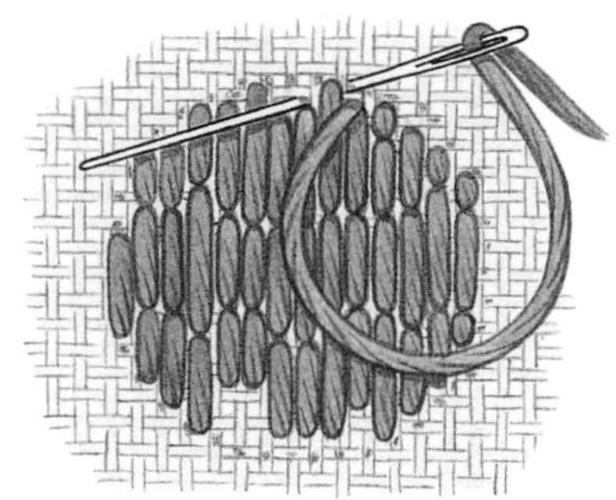

Work rows of random straight stitch, varying the lengths of the outside stitches to follow the curves of the shape. To fill in unworked canvas threads round the outline of the shape, work small individual straight stitches to create a smooth outline.

Working long stitch

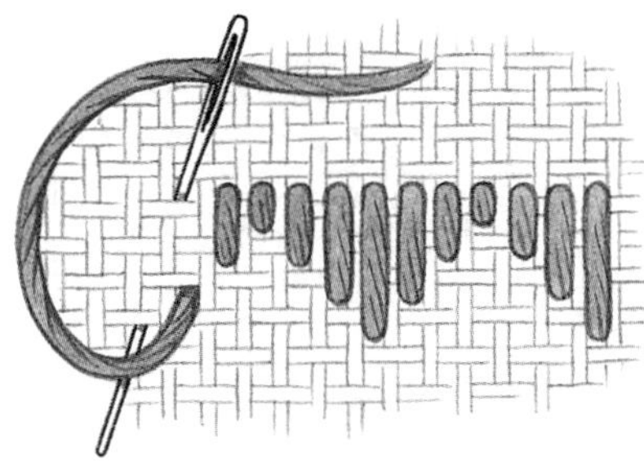

1 Work the first row from right to left, graduating the length of the stitches to make triangular groups.

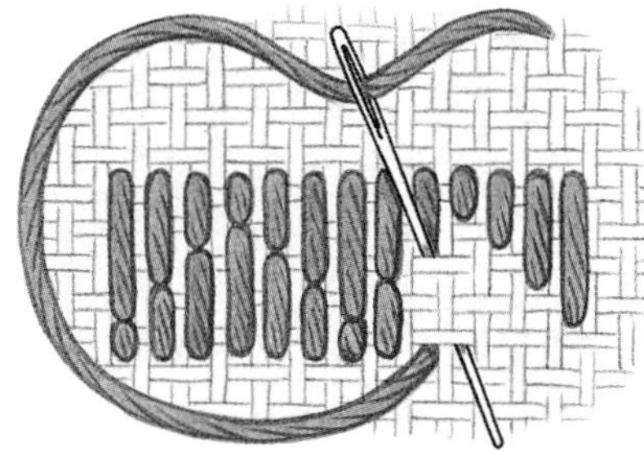

2 Work the second row from left to right, reversing the triangles to fill in the spaces. Continue in this way, alternating the direction of the rows.

WHAT WENT WRONG

A stitch too long
Straight stitches can look very untidy when they span more than eight canvas threads. The tension of the stitching quickly becomes too loose, and individual stitches start to sag, look untidy, and move to one side, revealing the canvas.

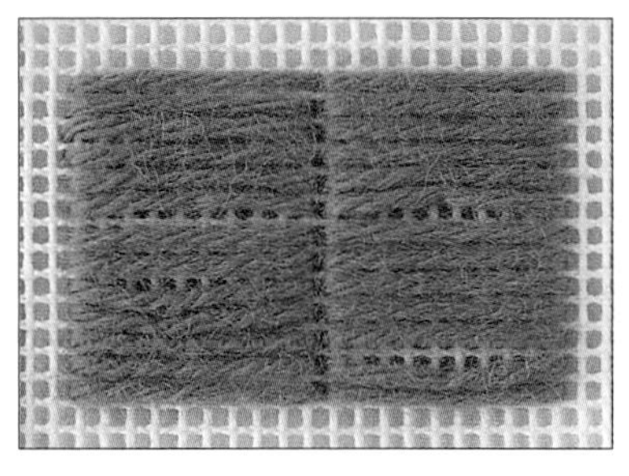

Working brick stitch

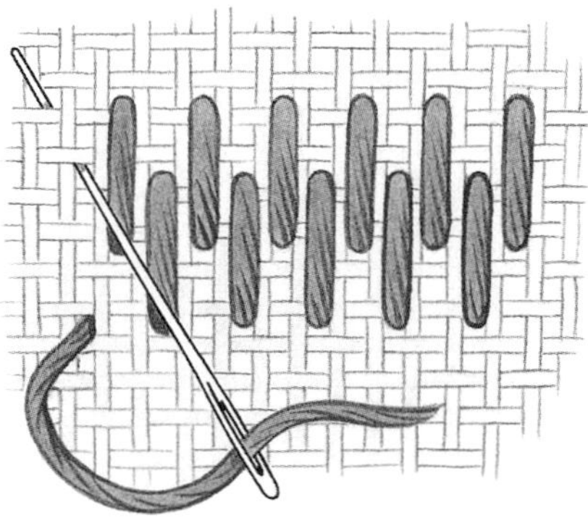

1 Working from right to left at the top of the shape, make a stitch upward over four canvas threads, and the next stitch downward over four threads. Continue in this way.

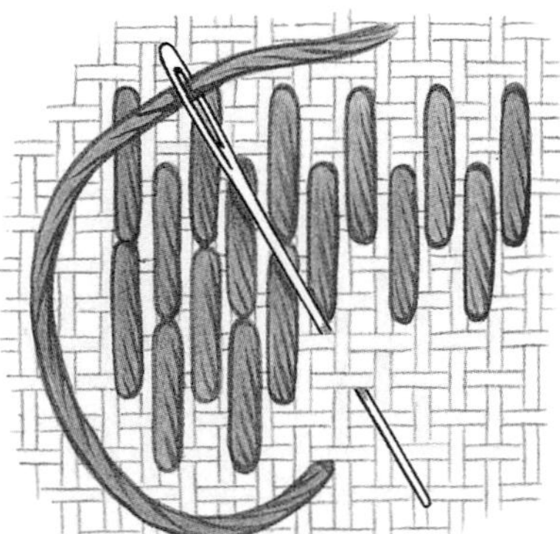

2 Work the next row from left to right, directly below the first row. Place the stitches end to end, each sharing a canvas hole with the one above.

You can use straight stitches to fill straight, curved, or undulating shapes, somewhat like painting with thread on the canvas.

All the stitches in this group create an attractive surface with a regular geometric pattern. They are made by working interlocking rows of vertical straight stitches of varying lengths and are useful for filling large shapes and background areas, as they cover the canvas quickly. You will need to match the weight of the thread carefully with the mesh size of the canvas to ensure that you obtain adequate canvas coverage.

All of the following stitches can be worked in one color, but they also look effective when contrasting threads are used. Twill and double twill stitch look very attractive worked on a fairly fine canvas using a combination of matte yarn and glossy cotton thread for alternate rows. The other stitches look best worked in one type and weight of thread, but you can choose to use two or more colors, depending on the effect you wish to create.

Diamond straight stitch

Twill stitch

Double twill stitch

Parisian stitch

To start and fasten off any of the stitches in this section, refer to page 161.

Diamond straight stitch is worked in spaced blocks. Each block consists of five vertical straight stitches of graduated lengths, with the diamond shapes enclosed by a grid of short vertical stitches.

Twill stitch is worked in diagonal rows and produces patterns which resemble the weave of twill fabric, from which the stitch takes its name.

Double twill stitch is very similar to twill stitch but the stitches vary in length on alternate rows.

Parisian stitch is a similar stitch to brick stitch (see page 166) but uses stitches of different lengths. Here they are worked alternately over six and two canvas threads, but the pattern can also be worked over four and two threads; it can also be worked in two colors.

Working diamond straight stitch

1 Secure the thread and bring the needle through the canvas near the top left of the shape. Work a group of five upward vertical straight stitches over one, three, five, three, and one canvas thread. Repeat across the shape to make a horizontal row, leaving an unworked gap of one thread between each block.

2 Turn at the end of the row, and work a second row of blocks below the first. Fit the blocks on this row between those on the previous row, leaving a gap of one unworked thread between the rows.

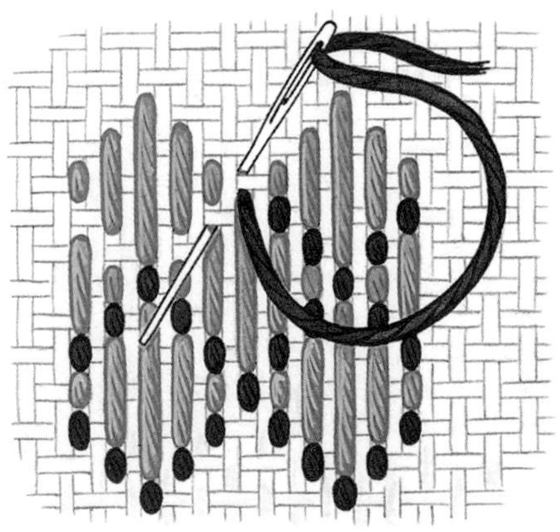

3 When you reach the bottom of the shape, begin working upward. Using the same or a contrasting thread, fill in the gaps between the blocks with short vertical stitches covering one canvas thread.

Working twill stitch

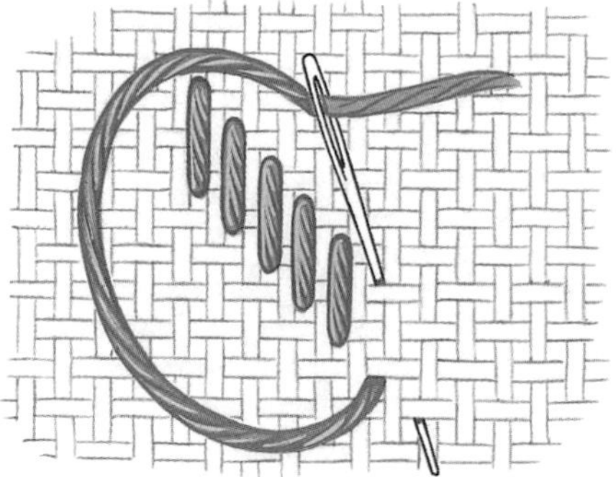

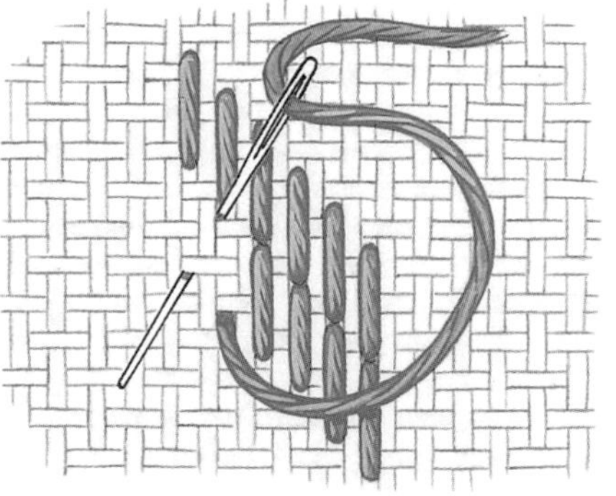

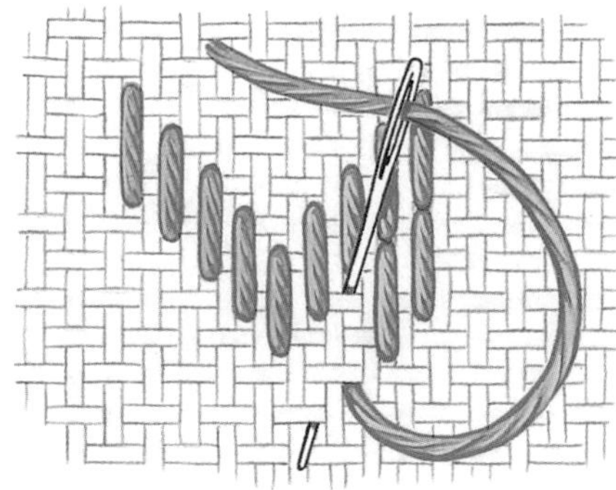

1 Secure the thread and bring the needle through the canvas at the top left of the shape. Work a diagonal row of vertical straight stitches covering three canvas threads. Each stitch should step down from the previous one by one thread.

2 Turn at the end of the row. Work back in the opposite direction with a second diagonal row of stitches of the same size below the first row. Work the next and subsequent rows in the same way.

3 To vary the look of twill stitch, you can change the direction of the rows as shown.

Working double twill stitch

1 Secure the thread and bring the needle through the canvas at the top right of the shape. Work a diagonal row of vertical straight stitches covering four canvas threads. Each stitch should step down from the previous one by one thread.

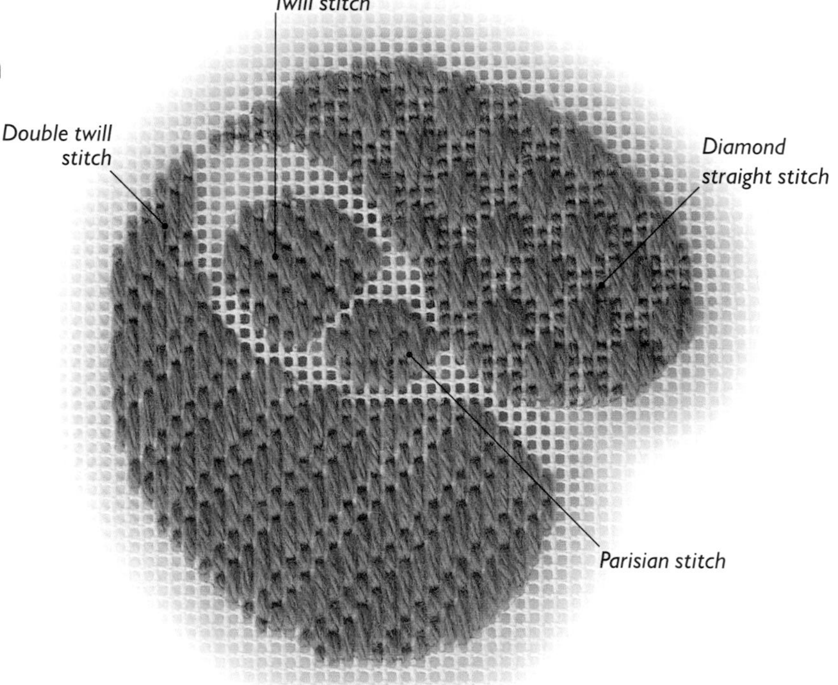

2 Turn at the end of the row and work in the opposite direction. Make a second diagonal row of stitches covering two threads below the first row. Work subsequent rows by alternating these two rows.

Working Parisian stitch

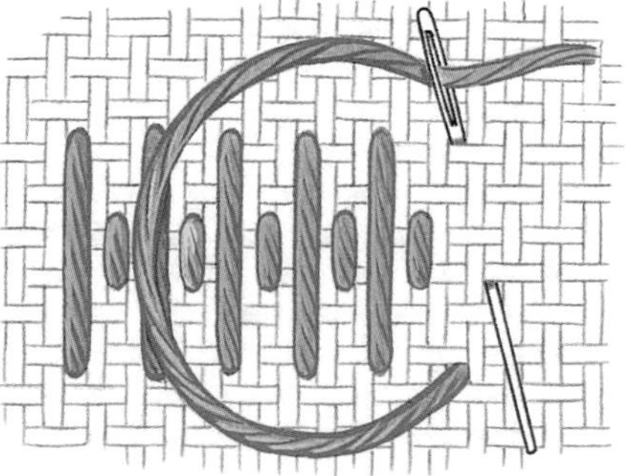

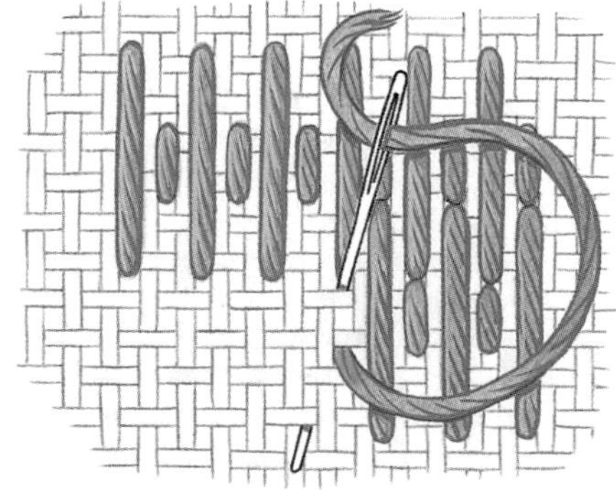

1 Secure the thread and bring the needle through the canvas at the top left of the shape. Work a row of vertical straight stitches alternating long stitches worked over six (or four) canvas threads with short stitches worked over two threads.

2 Turn at the end of the row and work in the opposite direction. Make a second row of stitches of the same size, interlocking them with the stitches on the previous row. Work subsequent rows in the same way.

Hungarian stitches

All the stitches in this section create an attractive surface with a regular geometric pattern. The first two stitches consist of diamond-shaped blocks worked in horizontal rows. The second two combine rows of the diamond-shaped blocks with zigzag rows of vertical straight stitches.

They are all useful for filling large shapes and background areas, as they are very easy to work and will cover the canvas quickly.

The stitches can be worked in a single color, but they can also look effective when contrasting thread colors are used to exaggerate the pattern. As with all straight stitches worked on canvas, match the thread weight you are using carefully with the mesh size of the canvas to ensure adequate coverage.

To start and fasten off any of the stitches in this library, refer to page 161.

Hungarian stitch is easy to work and makes a pretty pattern of small diamond-shaped blocks across the canvas. The pattern looks very attractive worked in two or more contrasting thread colors. Several close shades of the same color will blend attractively across a large area. Alternatively, you can use Hungarian stitch to build up intricate geometric patterns by stitching short rows of diamonds in a wide selection of colors.

Hungarian diamonds are similar in appearance to Hungarian stitch, but the diamonds are larger, creating a bolder pattern.

Hungarian grounding, as its name suggests, is really a background stitch but it also looks good worked on a small scale to fill tiny shapes. It combines rows of Hungarian stitch and of vertical straight stitches ranged in a zigzag pattern. The zigzag can be accentuated by the use of contrasting colors.

Double Hungarian grounding is similar to Hungarian grounding but the zigzag rows lie between double rows of Hungarian stitch.

Hungarian stitch

Hungarian diamonds

Hungarian grounding

Double Hungarian grounding

Working Hungarian stitch

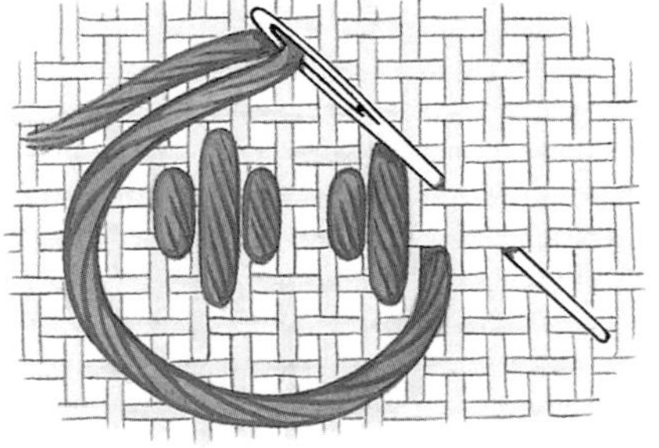

1 Bring the needle to the front at the top left of the shape. Work a diamond-shaped block of three vertical stitches arranged over two, four and two canvas threads. Repeat along the row, leaving two canvas threads between each block.

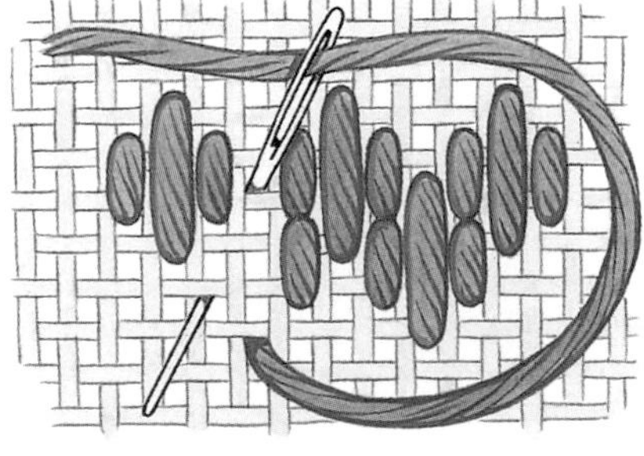

2 Turn at the end of the row and work in the opposite direction. Make a second row of spaced blocks of the same size as the first, interlocking them with the blocks on the previous row, as shown.

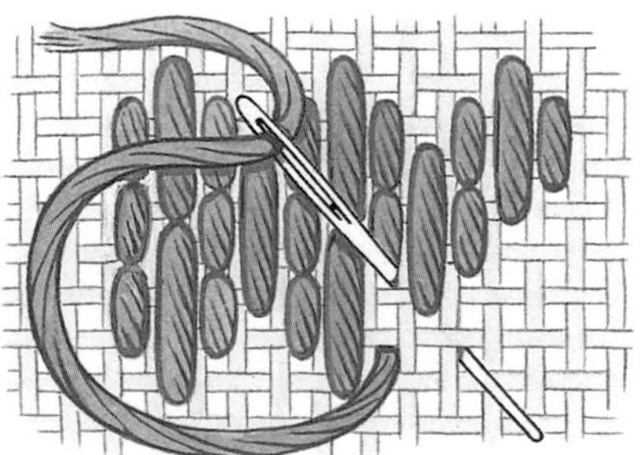

3 Turn at the end of the second row and repeat the first row of blocks, making sure that the long stitches of the blocks on the current row share the same holes as the blocks on the first row. Repeat rows two and three to fill the shape.

Working Hungarian diamonds

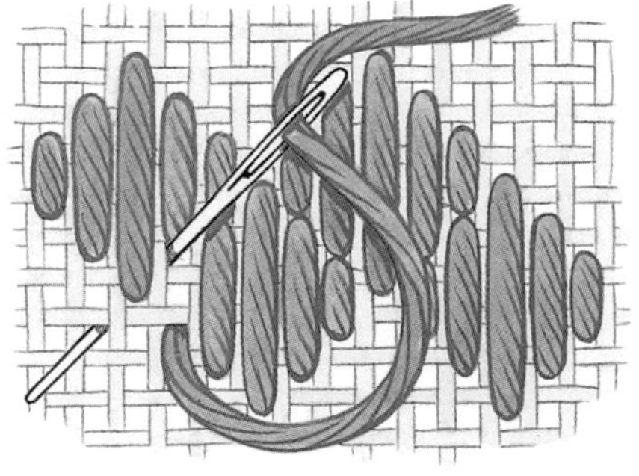

1 Bring the needle to the front at the top left of the shape. Work a diamond-shaped block of five vertical straight stitches arranged over two, four, six, four, and two canvas threads. Repeat along the row, arranging the blocks two canvas threads apart.

2 Turn at the end of the row, and work in the opposite direction. Make a second row of spaced blocks of the same size, interlocking them with the blocks on the previous row, as shown. Repeat these two rows to fill the shape.

Working Hungarian grounding

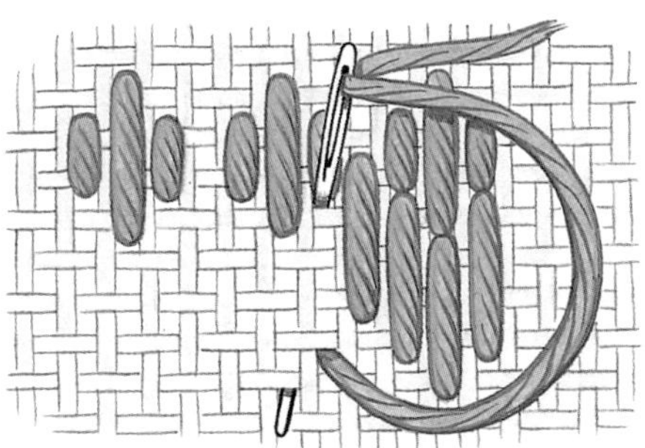

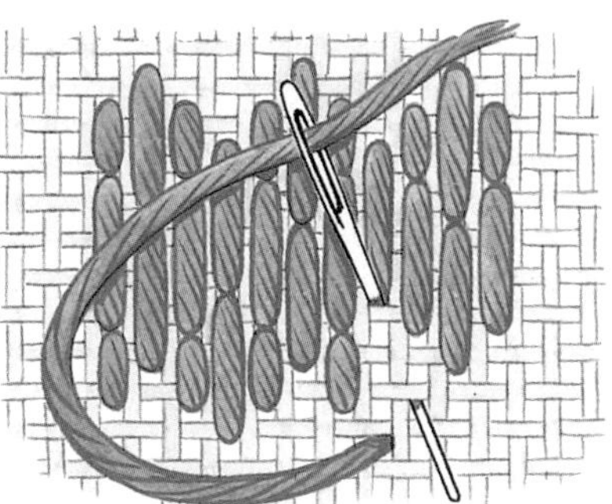

1 Bring the needle to the front at the top left of the shape. Work a row of Hungarian stitch. Turn at the end of the row, and work a zigzag row of vertical straight stitches over four threads, interlocking the top of these stitches with the bottom of the stitches on the previous row, as shown.

2 Turn at the end of the row, and work in the opposite direction. Make a second row of Hungarian stitches, as shown, interlocking the top of the stitches with the bottom of the stitches on the previous row. Repeat the two rows to fill the shape.

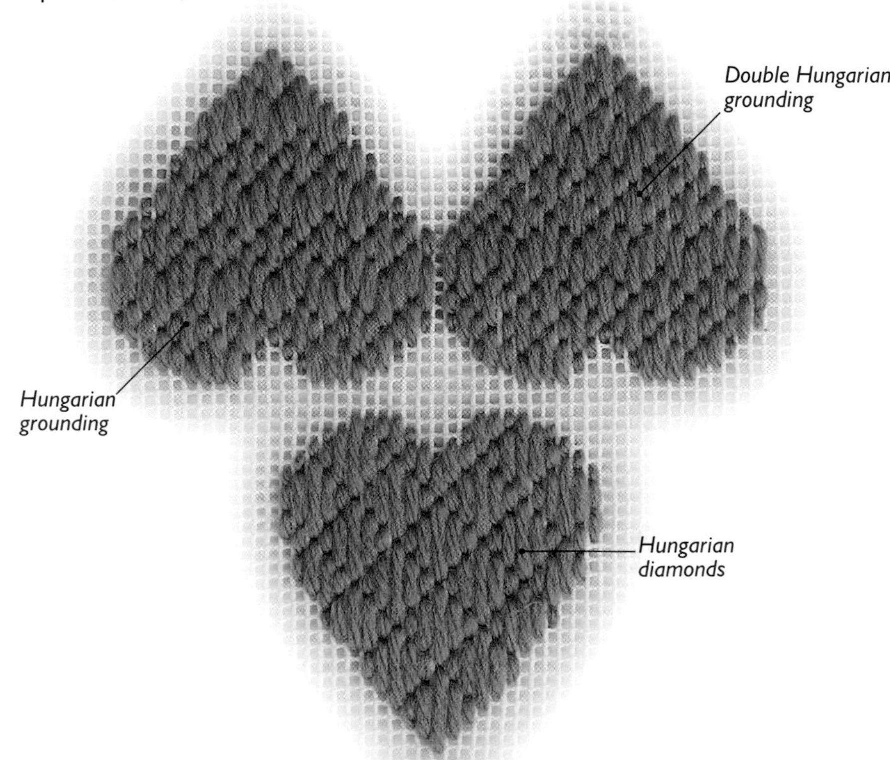

Double Hungarian grounding

1 Bring the needle to the front at the top left of the shape. Work two rows of Hungarian stitch. Turn at the end of the second row and work a zigzag row of vertical straight stitches over four threads, interlocking the top of these stitches with the bottom of the stitches directly above.

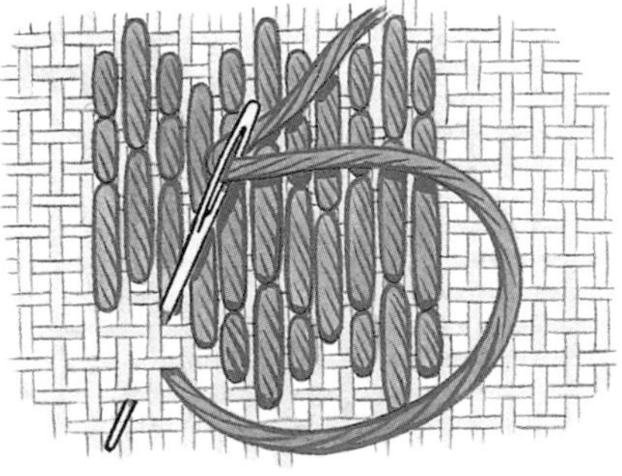

2 Turn at the end of the row and work in the opposite direction. Work a row of Hungarian stitches, interlocking the top of each diamond with the bottom of the vertical stitches, then work a second row directly underneath. Repeat to fill the shape, alternating two rows of Hungarian stitch with one zigzag row.

Slanted stitches

The slanted stitches shown here are all worked on Penelope canvas. This type of canvas is woven from pairs of threads instead of the more usual single thread (or mono) construction.

To start any of these stitches, bring the needle through to the front, leaving a 2 in. (5 cm) thread end at the back. Work your first row, stitching over the loose thread at the back as you go. To fasten off the thread, take the needle to the back and darn in the end under a group of previously worked stitches.

Kilim stitch, also known as knitting stitch, produces a solidly stitched surface and gives good canvas coverage, which makes it ideal for stitching cushion covers, chair seats, and rugs, which get a lot of wear. Persian yarns, in a suitable number of strands, is a good choice for such projects.

Linen stitch produces a neatly woven surface, resembling its namesake fabric.

Rep stitch is a tiny stitch and is good for working very small or detailed designs. It has a ridged texture similar to the woven fabric of the same name.

Web stitch is a form of couching in which long, diagonal stitches across the canvas are held in place by short stitches. It can be used to fill backgrounds and large shapes.

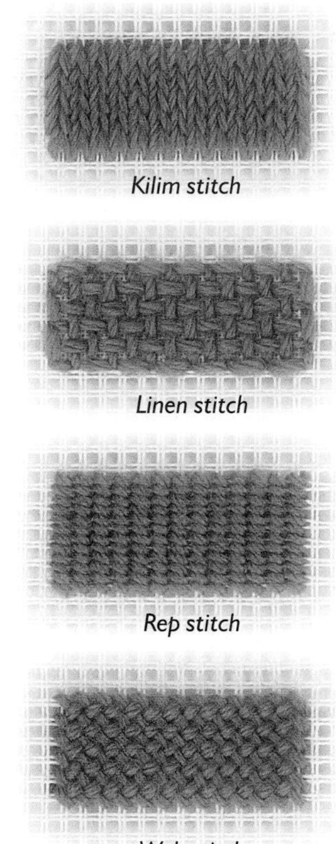

Working kilim stitch

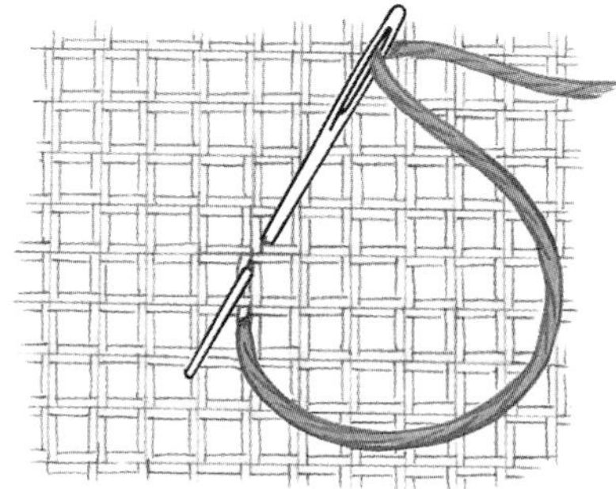

1 Bring the needle to the front between a pair of canvas threads near the bottom right of the shape. Insert it two double threads higher up and one thread to the right. Bring it out one double thread above the point where it previously emerged.

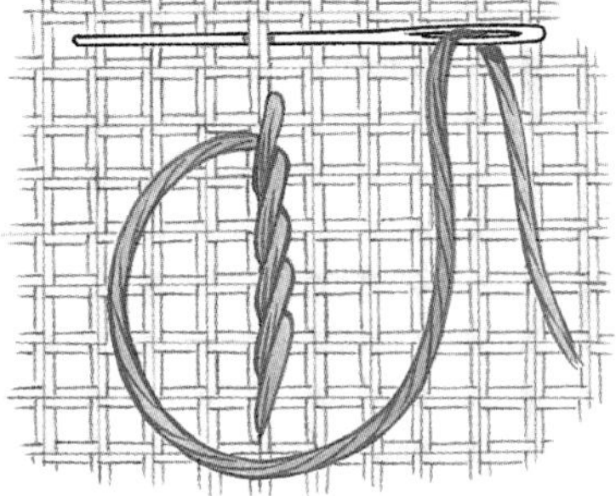

2 Work upward in this way to make the right-hand side of the first row, taking care that the needle goes between the pair of threads to the left. At the top take the needle behind the pair of threads, ready to work the other side of the stitch.

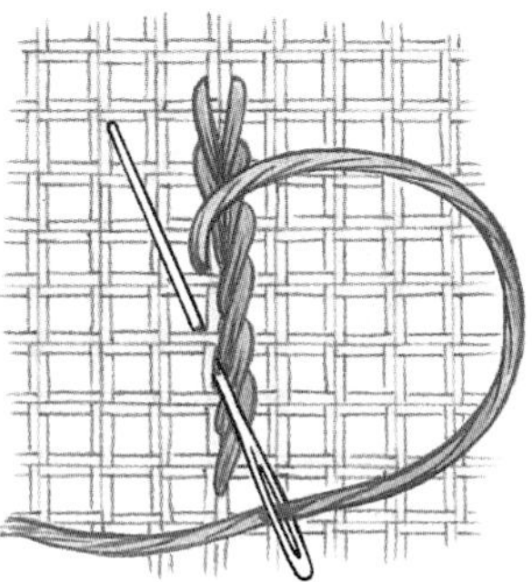

3 Insert the needle two pairs of threads down and one thread to the right to make a diagonal stitch with a reverse slant, then bring the needle through one pair of threads up and one thread to the left. Repeat to complete one row of kilim stitch.

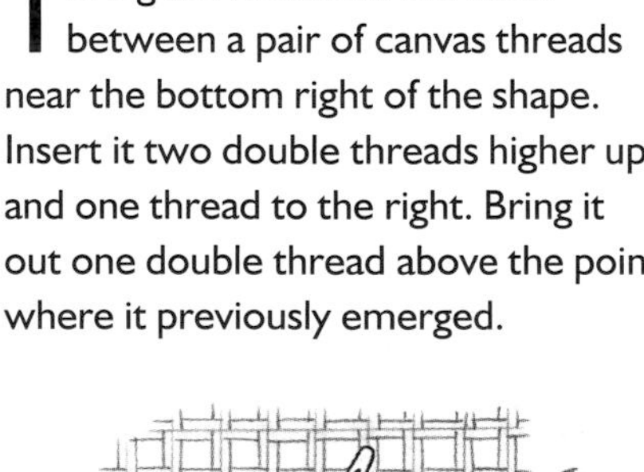

4 Repeat steps **1–3** to work more rows of the stitch, remembering to insert the needle between the pair of threads that run down the center of each finished row.

Working linen stitch

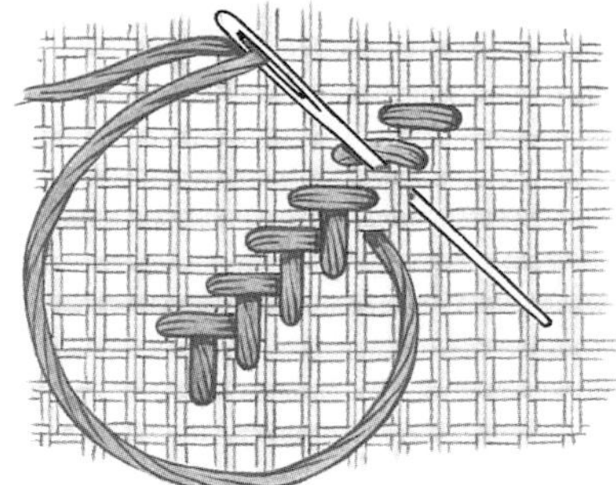

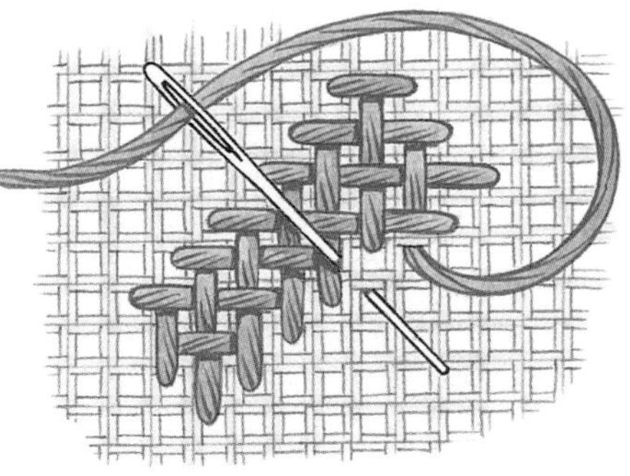

1 Secure the thread and bring the needle through the canvas at the top right of the shape. Work a stepped, diagonal row of horizontal stitches over two pairs of canvas threads. At the bottom of the row, turn and work an interlocking row of vertical stitches over two pairs of threads.

2 Repeat these two rows of interlocking stitches, working diagonally down, then up the canvas, until the shape is filled.

Working rep stitch

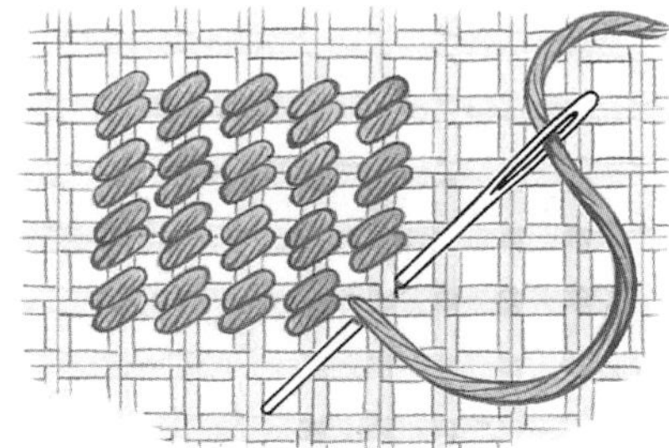

Work rep stitch in the same way as continental tent stitch (see page 162), working the stitches not only into the usual spaces between the pairs of horizontal canvas threads, but also in between the paired threads.

Working web stitch

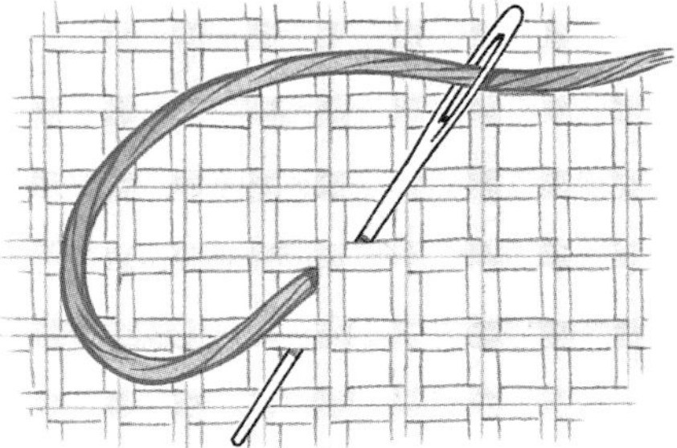

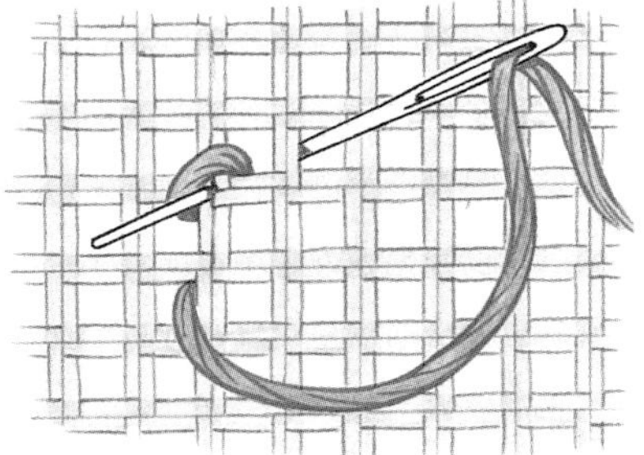

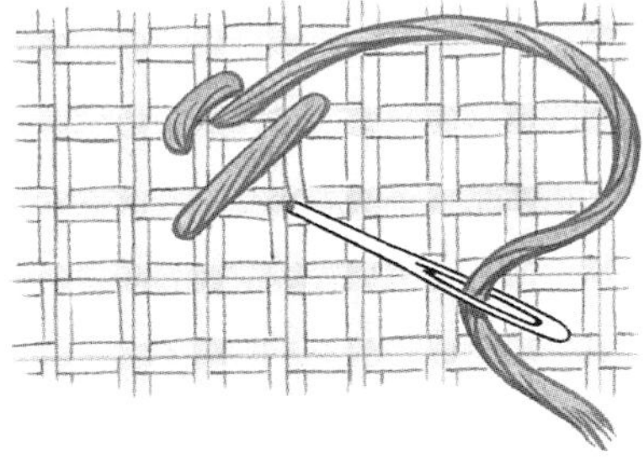

1 Bring the needle to the front at the top left of the shape. Work a diagonal stitch over one canvas intersection, and take the needle under two horizontal and one vertical pair of threads, as shown.

2 Make a second diagonal stitch over two thread intersections, and bring the needle up through the tiny hole in the thread intersection below the top of the first stitch.

3 Make a short securing stitch over the diagonal stitch, inserting the needle in the central hole of the intersection diagonally opposite the first one.

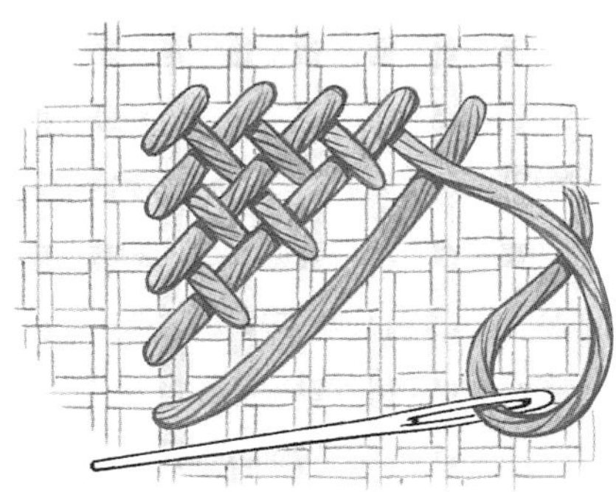

4 Make the next diagonal stitch over three intersections. Repeat step **3** to make a short securing stitch over it. Make another short stitch over it, bringing the needle out through the tiny hole one intersection down and one to the left of the top of the previous securing stitch.

5 Continue in this way, working the long diagonal stitches into the holes between the pairs of canvas threads and the short stitches into the tiny holes at the center of the canvas intersections.

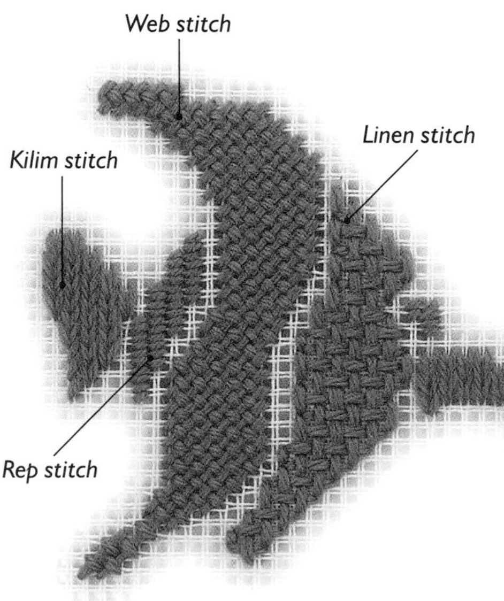

Gobelin stitches

Gobelin stitches are small slanted or straight stitches which create a stitched surface resembling a thickly woven tapestry. They are worked in horizontal rows and are ideal for small, intricate designs and large background areas. The stitches take their name from the Gobelins, a famous family of dyers who settled in Paris in the 15th century. During the 17th century their premises were converted into the famous Gobelins tapestry works.

Gobelin stitches are usually worked in one color, but they can look very effective when contrasting colors are used to stitch alternate rows. You can also create subtly shaded effects with several close tones of the same color. Take care when choosing a thread for straight or plaited Gobelin stitch to cover the canvas, you may need to use a thicker thread than usual. For details on how to start and fasten off any of these stitches, refer to page 161.

Gobelin stitch

Wide Gobelin stitch

Straight Gobelin stitch

Interlocking Gobelin stitch

Plaited Gobelin stitch

Gobelin stitch is a small slanted stitch creating a ribbed effect. It is very easy to work but tends to distort the canvas, so requires a frame (see page 20).

Wide Gobelin stitch looks very similar to Gobelin stitch. It is worked similarly, but the stitches are longer and more slanted.

Straight Gobelin stitch is an upright version of Gobelin stitch. It makes an attractive border around panels worked in other needlepoint stitches.

Interlocking (or encroaching) Gobelin stitch makes a thick, hard-wearing surface. It can be time-consuming to work, as each row overlaps the previous one. For a less closely stitched effect, you can make the stitches longer.

Plaited Gobelin stitch is formed of overlapping, slanting stitches to create an open, plaited surface.

Working Gobelin stitch

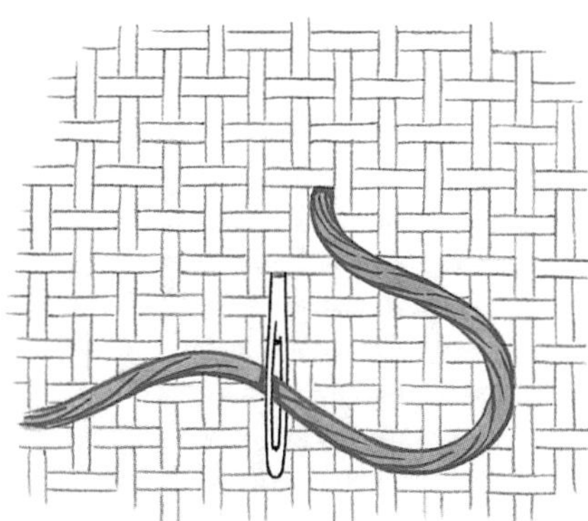

1 Work from left to right. Bring the needle to the front at the top left of the shape. Insert it two holes down and one to the left.

2 Bring the needle through one hole to the right of where it previously emerged, and insert it two holes down and one to the left. Continue in this way along the row.

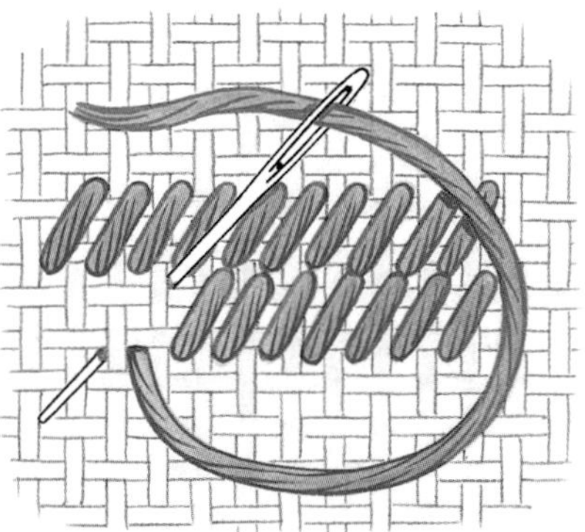

3 At end of row bring the needle out two holes below the base of the last stitch. Work from right to left for the second row. Insert it two holes up and one to the right. Bring it out one hole to the left of where it previously emerged. Continue along the row.

Wide Gobelin stitch

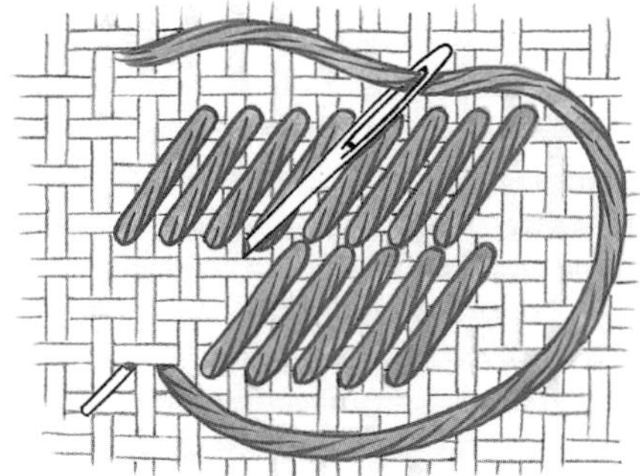

Follow Gobelin stitch steps **1–3** (previous page), but work each stitch over three horizontal threads and two vertical threads.

Straight Gobelin stitch

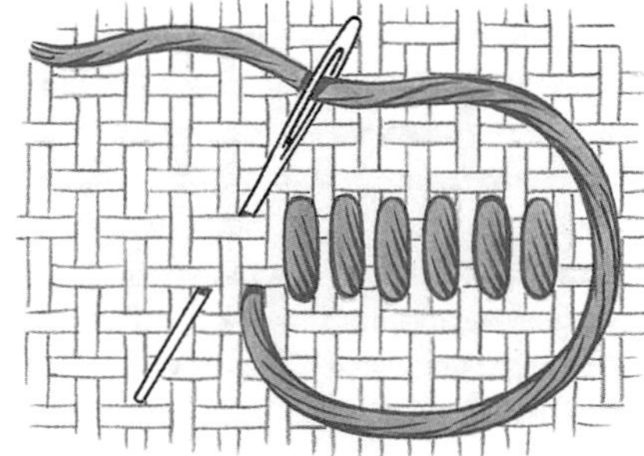

1 Work from right to left. Bring the needle to the front at the top right. Insert it two holes up, then bring it through one hole to the left of the point where it previously emerged. Continue in this way to end of row.

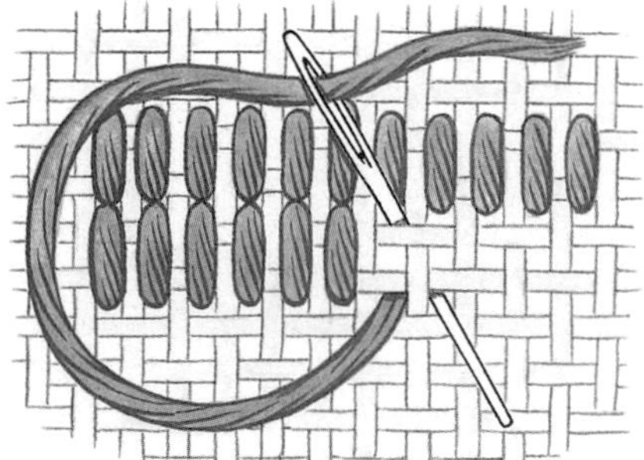

2 Bring the needle out two holes below the base of the last stitch, ready to start the next row. Working from left to right, work a row of vertical stitches underneath the first. Repeat steps **1–2** to fill the shape.

Working interlocking Gobelin stitch

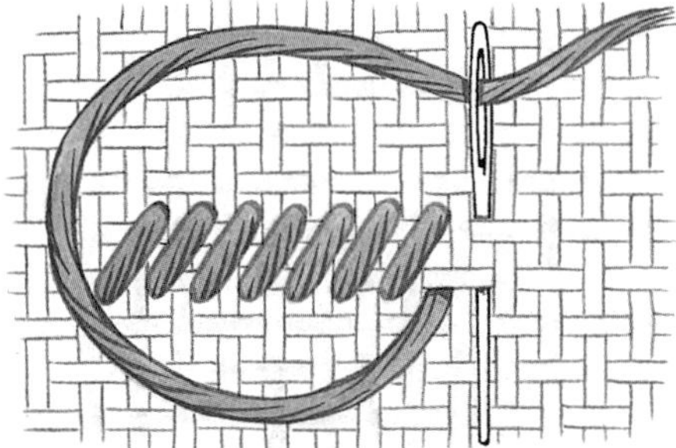

1 Work from left to right. Bring the needle to the front at the top left of the shape. Insert it two holes up and one to the right, then bring the needle through one hole to the right of where it previously emerged. Continue in this way to the end of the row.

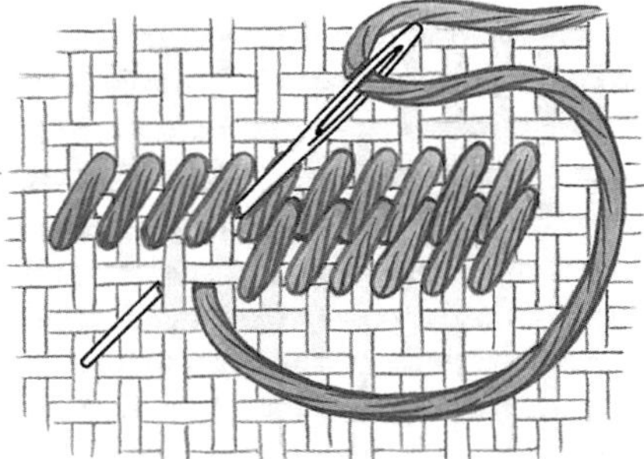

2 Bring the needle through one hole below base of last stitch, ready to work next row. Work from right to left. Insert needle two holes up and one to the right, and bring it through one hole to the left of where it previously emerged. Repeat along row.

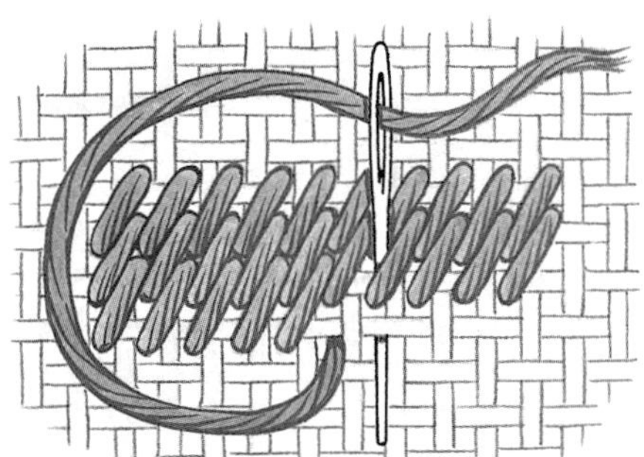

3 Repeat steps **1–2** to fill the shape, inserting the needle between adjacent stitches on the row above so that the rows overlap by one canvas thread.

Working plaited Gobelin stitch

1 Work from left to right. Bring the needle to the front at the top left of the shape. Insert it four holes down and two to the right, and bring it through again two holes to the right of where it previously emerged. Continue in this way along the row.

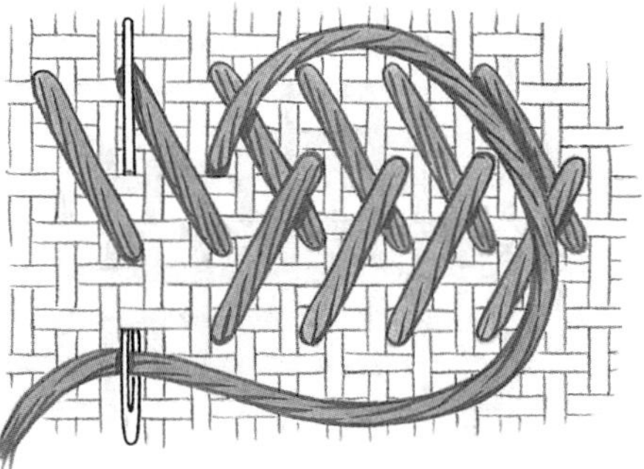

2 At the end of the row, bring needle through two holes above the base of last stitch. Insert it four holes down and two to the left. Then bring it through two holes to the left of where it previously emerged. Continue along the row. Repeat steps **1–2** to fill shape.

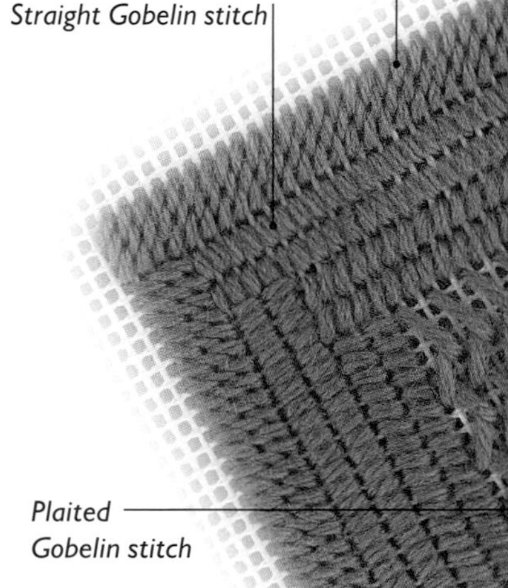

Diagonal stitches

The diagonal stitches shown here make attractive stitched surfaces with regular geometric patterns. They consist of interlocking diagonal rows of slanting straight stitches and are useful for filling large shapes and background areas.

These stitches can be worked in one color, except striped diagonal stitch, which is worked in two colors to create its characteristic striped appearance. They also look effective when contrasting threads are used. Spaced diagonal and framed diagonal stitch, for example, look particularly good with tapestry, Persian or crewel wool used for the main diagonal stitches and floss or pearl cotton for the small stitches.

The other three stitches look best worked in one type and weight of thread, but you can choose two or more colors, depending on the effect you wish to create. Take care to match the weight of your thread to the mesh size to ensure adequate coverage. Try combining several strands of crewel yarn.

For details on starting and finishing any of these stitches, refer to page 161.

Striped diagonal stitch creates a series of bold diagonal stripes across the canvas.

Stepped diagonal stitch has the same sequence as striped diagonal stitch, but the stitches are longer.

Spaced diagonal stitch looks like a series of diagonal ridges, created by working narrow rows of small stitches between blocks of striped diagonal stitch.

Framed diagonal stitch has rows of stepped diagonal stitch framed by large backstitches.

Alternate diagonal stitch makes a pretty, slightly irregular stitched surface. It is created by working rows of stepped diagonal stitch alternated with rows of striped diagonal stitch.

Striped diagonal stitch

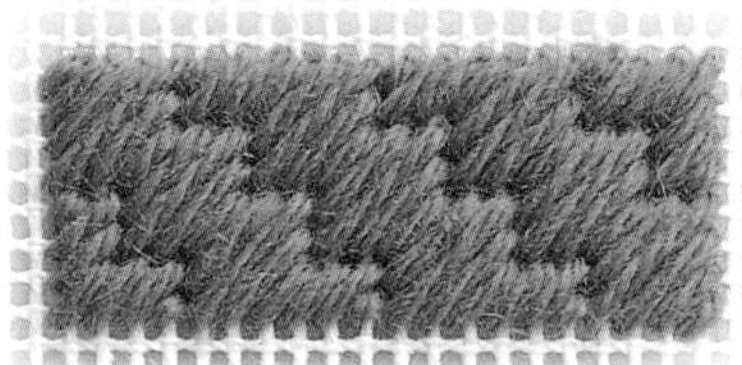

Stepped diagonal stitch

Spaced diagonal stitch

Framed diagonal stitch

Alternate diagonal stitch

Working striped diagonal stitch

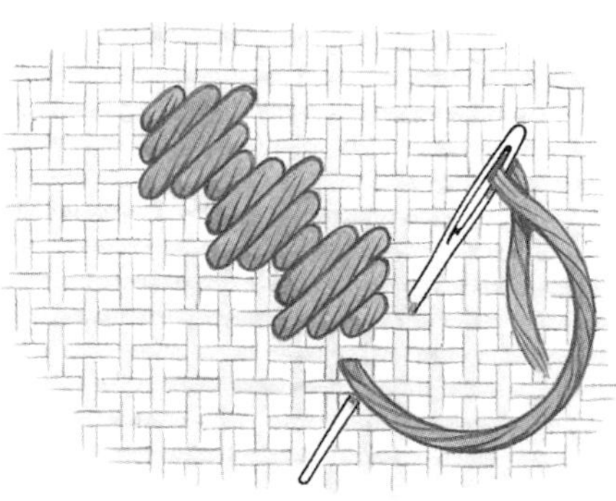

1 Bring the needle to the front at the top left of the shape. Make a block of four slanting stitches worked over one, two, three, and two canvas intersections. Repeat the sequence of stitches to make a diagonal row of blocks across the canvas.

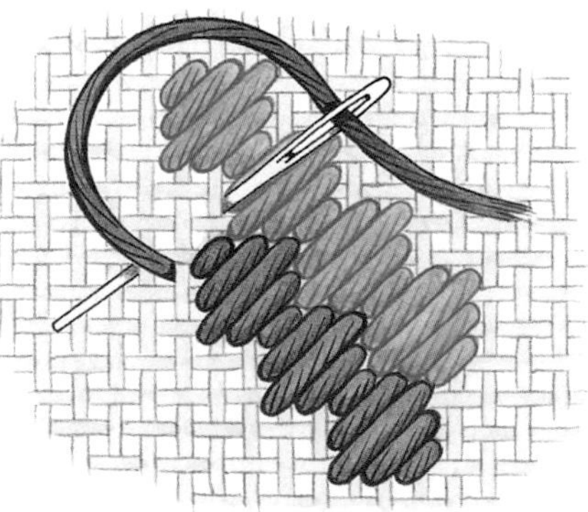

2 Using a second thread color, work in the opposite direction to make a second row of stitches, following the same sequence. Arrange the stitches as shown so that they interlock with the stitches on the previous row. Continue in this way to fill the shape, alternating the colors.

Working stepped diagonal stitch

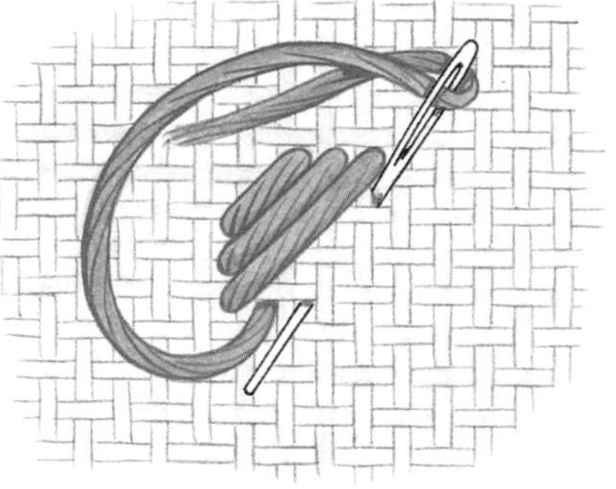

1 Bring the needle to the front at the top left of the shape. Make a block of four slanting stitches worked over two, three, four, and three canvas intersections.

2 Repeat the sequence of stitches to make a diagonal row of blocks across the canvas.

3 Working upward, make a second row of stitches, arranging them to interlock with the stitches on the previous row. Continue in this way, working up and down the canvas.

Working spaced diagonal stitch

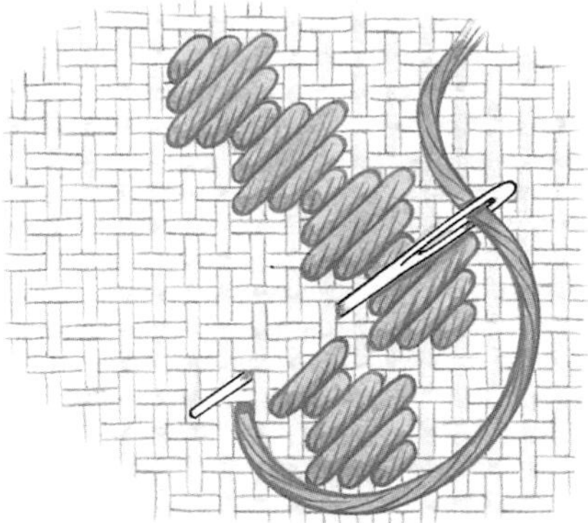

1 Start at the top left. Fill the canvas with rows of striped diagonal stitch, as on the previous page, but space the rows one canvas thread apart and use just one color.

2 Using a second thread, fill the gaps between the rows with stitches worked over one canvas intersection, at a right angle to main stitching. Alternatively, fill with tent stitch, as shown above.

Working framed diagonal stitch

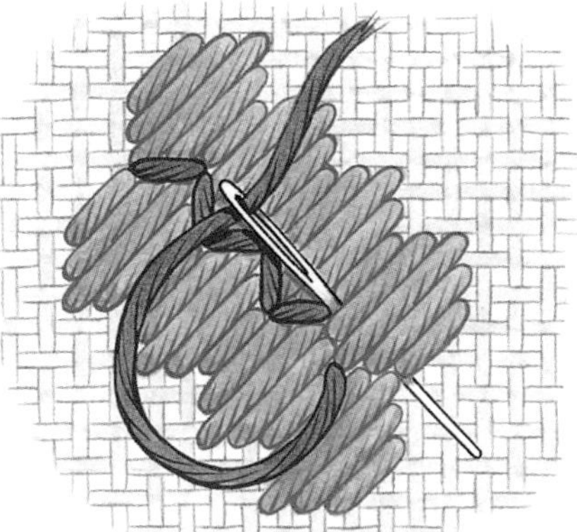

Starting near the top, fill the shape with rows of stepped diagonal stitch. Use a second thread to work backstitch between the rows; follow the stepped outline and work each backstitch over two threads.

Working alternate diagonal stitch

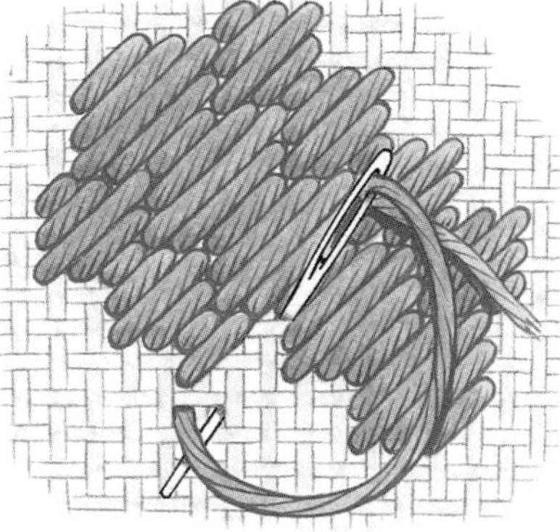

Start near the top left of the shape. Work alternate rows of striped diagonal stitch and stepped diagonal stitch to fill the shape. Use one color of thread throughout and take care to keep the sequence of stitches correct.

Block stitches

The block stitches shown here all create smoothly stitched surfaces, formed by interlocking rows of diagonal stitches, which are worked diagonally. The resulting geometric patterns appear to form steps across the canvas. These stitches cover the canvas quickly, which makes them useful for backgrounds and large shapes.

You can work the stitches in a single color, or use contrasting threads to accentuate the patterns. To start any of these stitches, bring the needle through to the front of the canvas, leaving a short thread end on the back. Work the first row of the stitches, working over the loose thread end. To fasten off, take the needle through to the back and darn in the end under the last few stitches.

Byzantine stitch produces a bold diagonal zigzag.

Cashmere stitch (also known as condensed cashmere, to distinguish it from a simpler version) creates a steeply slanted pattern which resembles densely woven cloth.

Moorish stitch makes an intricate pattern of graduated diagonal stitches and tent stitch.

Jacquard stitch produces a series of wide and narrow zigzags.

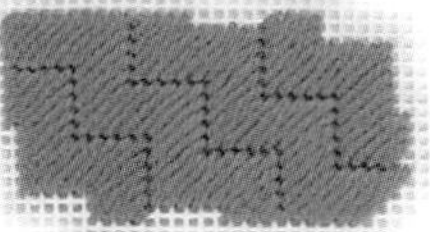

Byzantine stitch

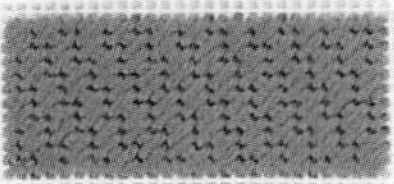

Cashmere stitch

Moorish stitch

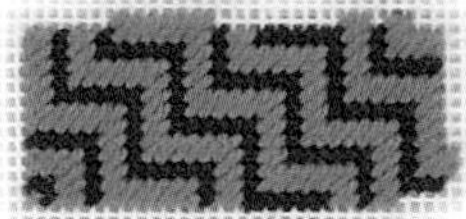

Jacquard stitch

Working Byzantine stitch

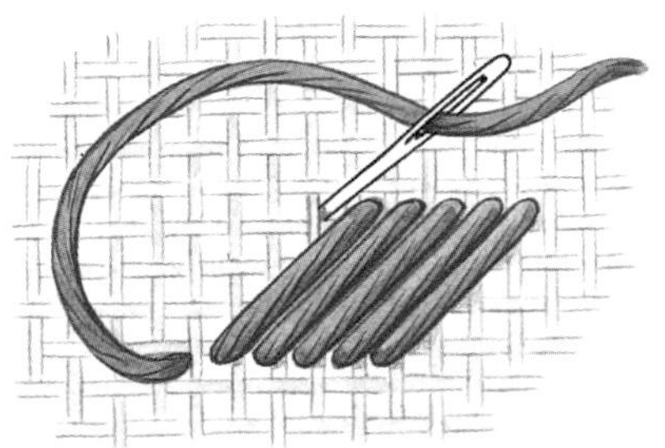

1 Bring the needle to the front at the bottom right, and make a diagonal stitch over four thread intersections. Bring it out one hole to the left of the starting point. Make a second diagonal stitch the same size. Continue in this way to make a horizontal block of six diagonal stitches.

2 Bring the needle through one thread above the base of the previous stitch, and make a diagonal stitch over four thread intersections as before. Continue upward to make a vertical block of six diagonal stitches. The last stitch of the horizontal block is also the first stitch of the vertical block.

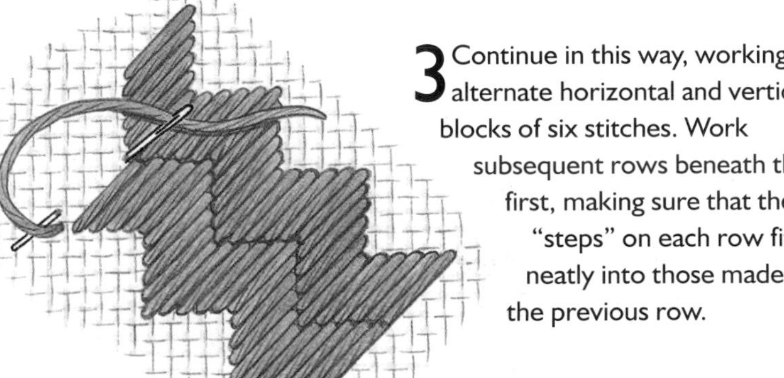

3 Continue in this way, working alternate horizontal and vertical blocks of six stitches. Work subsequent rows beneath the first, making sure that the "steps" on each row fit neatly into those made on the previous row.

Working Cashmere stitch

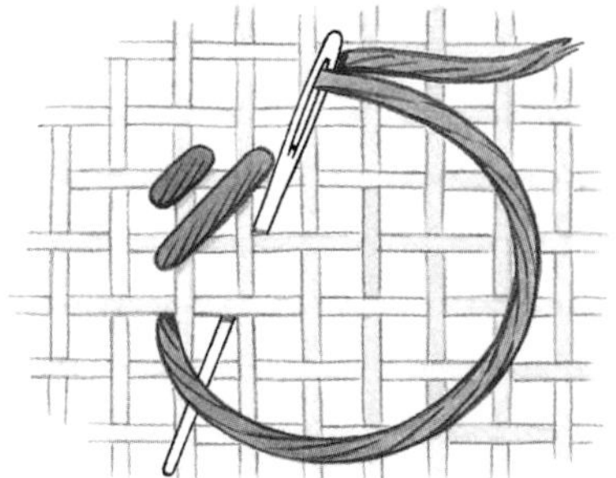

1 At the top left, make a diagonal stitch over one thread intersection. Bring the needle out one hole below your starting point. Work two diagonal stitches over two canvas intersections. Bring the needle out one hole to the right of where it previously emerged.

2 Repeat along the row to work blocks of three stitches. To keep the sequence of stitches correct, at the end of the row, bring the needle to the front at the right of the top diagonal stitch of the previous block, ready to make the first short stitch.

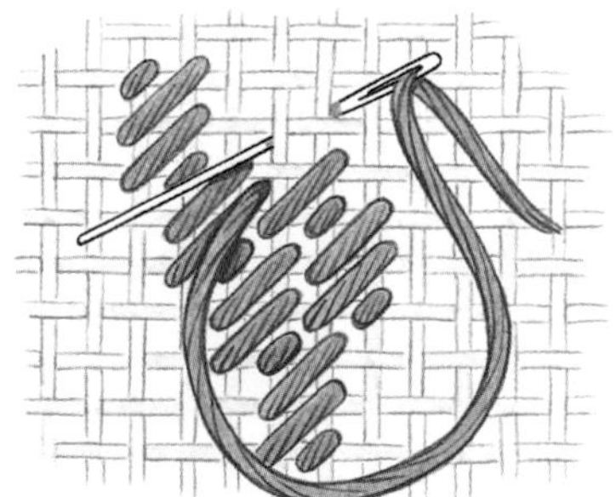

3 Working upward from right to left, work a row of stitches in the same way. Continue to fill the shape, working downward, then upward rows. Make sure that each new row fits into the "steps" of the previous row.

Working Moorish stitch

1 Work from top left to bottom right. Bring the needle to the front at the top of the shape. Work a group of diagonal stitches over one, two, three, and then two canvas intersections. Repeat to make a stepped row across the shape.

2 Work from bottom right to top left. Following the stepped outline of the previous row, work a diagonal row of continental tent stitch to the left of the row (see page 162).

3 Repeat steps **1–2** to fill the shape, making sure that the "steps" on each row fit neatly into those made on the previous row.

Working Jacquard stitch

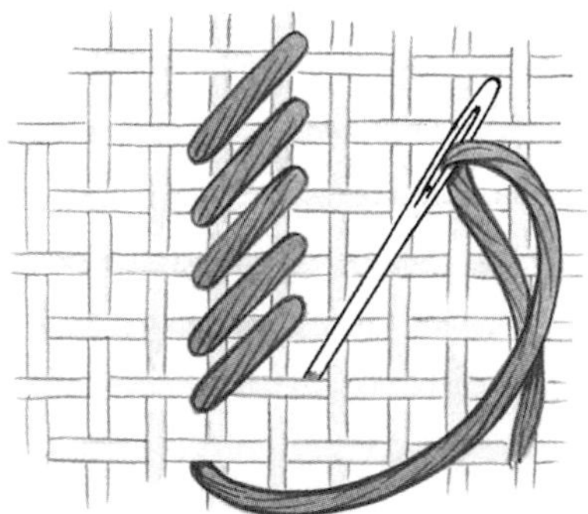

1 Work from top left to bottom right. Bring the needle out to the front at the top of the shape, and make a diagonal stitch over two thread intersections. Repeat to work five more diagonal stitches arranged in a vertical block.

2 Bring the needle out to the front one hole to the right of the base of the previous stitch. Make a diagonal stitch over two thread intersections. Repeat to work four more diagonal stitches in a horizontal block. Note that the last stitch of the vertical block is also the first stitch of the horizontal block.

3 Repeat steps **1–2** until the row is complete. Following the stepped outline of the previous row, work a row of continental tent stitch (see page 162). Make sure that the "steps" on each row fit neatly into those made on the previous row.

The three stitches featured here create small blocks with a regular geometric pattern. They are useful both for filling small shapes and large backgrounds and for working shading and color changes. The stitches can be worked in a single color or in contrasting colors or thread textures—for example, alternating wool and embroidery floss. To start and fasten off the stitches, see page 161. **Mosaic stitch** is particularly attractive when worked in contrasting threads. For multicolored designs, work in blocks, completing each one before moving on to the next. When working in one color, arrange the blocks in horizontal rows, taking two journeys to complete each row.

Reversed mosaic stitch can also be used to work a multicolored design. The real beauty of this stitch, however, lies in the effect of light and shade created by the varying slants of the blocks when stitched with shiny pearl cotton or embroidery floss.

Flat stitch is very similar in structure to reversed mosaic stitch, but occupies three thread intersections instead of two, so that the effect is smoother. Even when worked in crewel wool, it has a glossy appearance.

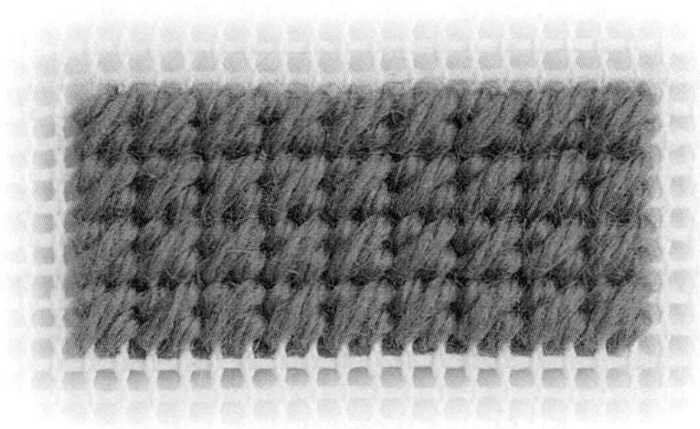

Mosaic stitch

Reversed mosaic stitch

Flat stitch

Working mosaic stitch in one color

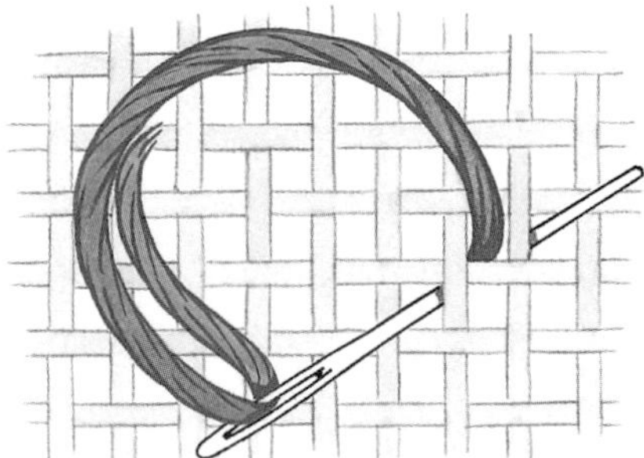

1 Bring the thread to the front at the top left. Take the needle to the back one hole down and one to the left to make a short diagonal stitch. Bring the needle out one hole to the right of where it previously emerged.

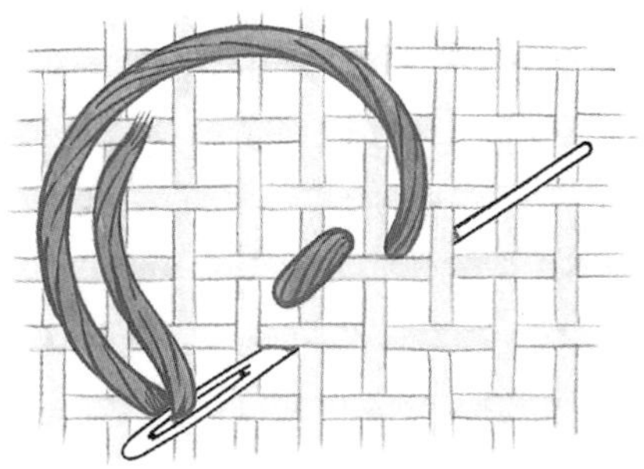

2 Insert the needle one hole below the base of the previous stitch to make a longer diagonal stitch. Continue along the row, making alternate short and long diagonal stitches. Finish with a long stitch.

3 Bring the needle to the front one hole up and two to the right. Insert it one hole down and one to the left. Working from right to left along the row, add the bottom short diagonal stitch to complete each block.

Working mosaic stitch in two or more colors

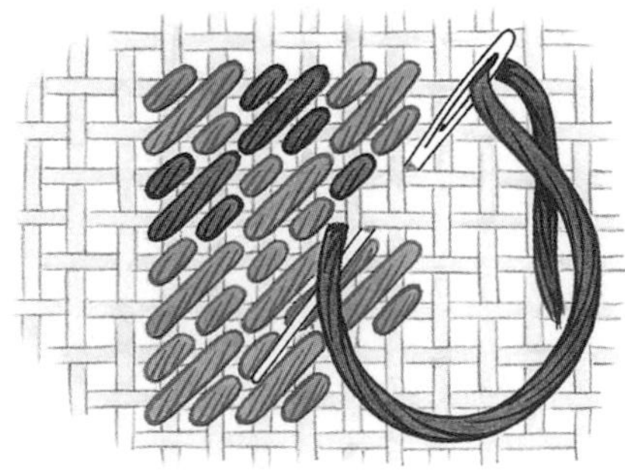

1 Using the main color in the design, work each three-stitch mosaic block individually. For each mosaic block, work a diagonal stitch over one, two, and one vertical and horizontal threads.

2 Choose the next-most common color and work all the stitches in that color. Repeat for each color, finishing with the least-used color.

Working reversed mosaic stitch

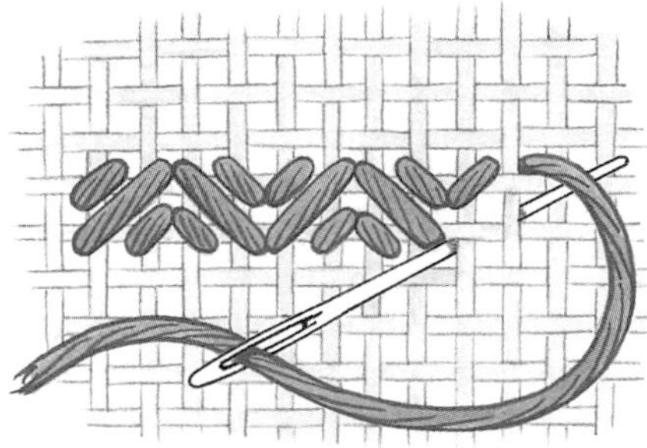

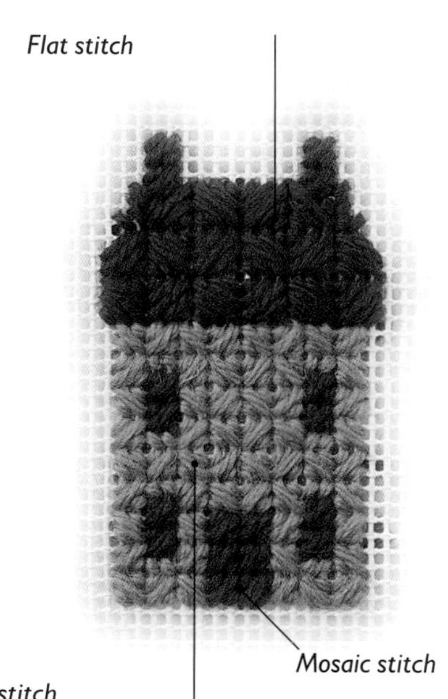

1 Work from left to right along the row, working each three-stitch mosaic block individually and changing the slant of the stitches on alternate mosaic blocks.

2 Working from right to left, work the second row below the first, alternating the slant of the blocks from that on the row above to make a checkerboard pattern. Repeat steps **1–2** to fill the shape.

Working flat stitch

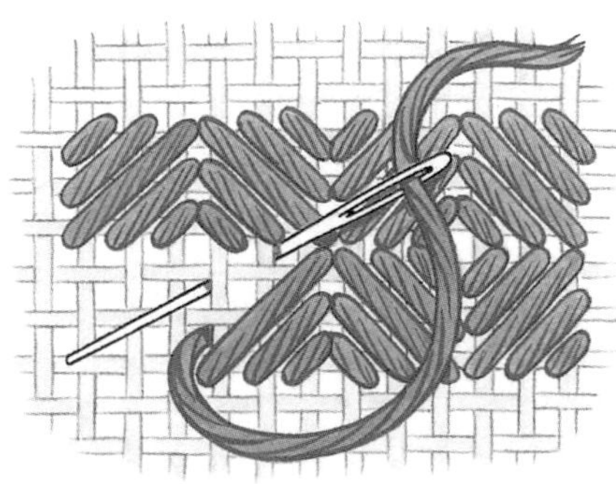

1 Bring the needle to the front at the top left of the shape. Work a group of diagonal stitches over one, two, three, two, and one canvas intersections. Bring the needle to the front one hole to the right and one hole down.

2 Work a second block of diagonal stitches, changing the slant. Repeat steps **1–2** to fill the row.

3 Work the second row below the first, alternating the slant of the blocks from those on the row above to make a checkerboard pattern. Work additional rows in the same way.

The block stitches featured here create attractive, smoothly stitched surfaces with a regular zigzag pattern. They are suitable for filling background areas and large shapes. They look best when worked on a small scale over a large area so that the intricacy of the individual patterns can be seen. For details on starting and fastening off, see page 177.

Block Byzantine stitch is an attractive variation of Byzantine stitch with an interesting mosaic effect. A framework of interlocking zigzag shapes is worked first, then the blocks between the zigzags are filled with diagonal stitches. For full details on Byzantine stitch, refer to page 177.

Milanese stitch forms a series of zigzags on a diagonal. Worked in backstitch, it covers the canvas well on both sides. Milanese stitch can also be worked in two colors to form rows of interlocking triangles and a jagged striped appearance; in this method the stitches are worked in groups of four, over one, two, three, and four intersections to make each triangle.

Extended Milanese stitch looks similar to Milanese stitch, but the four-row sequence of backstitches is worked in a different way to give interlocking zigzags with longer arms.

Block Byzantine stitch

Milanese stitch

Extended Milanese stitch

Working block Byzantine stitch

1 Bring the needle to the front near the top left-hand corner of the shape. Work a zigzag shape in diagonal straight stitches over two canvas intersections, beginning and ending with a short stitch over one canvas intersection.

2 Work a second, identical zigzag shape directly to the right and two threads above the base of the first zigzag. Continue working downward in this way until the row is complete.

3 Work more rows of zigzag below the first; arrange them so that the top of the next row fits directly below the base of the first vertical leg of the zigzag on the row above. Finally, fill the unworked square blocks of canvas with diagonal straight stitches of graduating lengths.

Working Milanese stitch

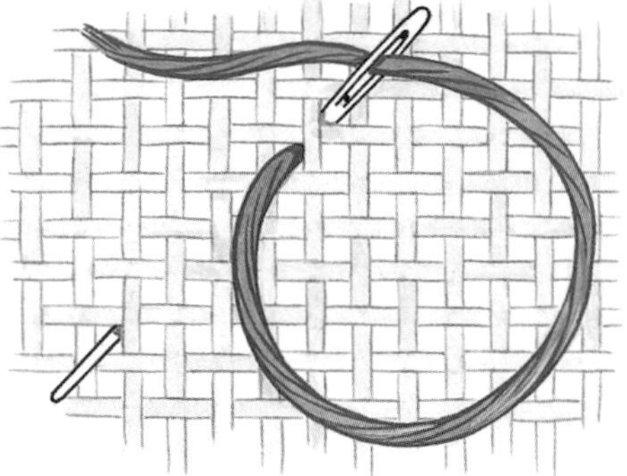

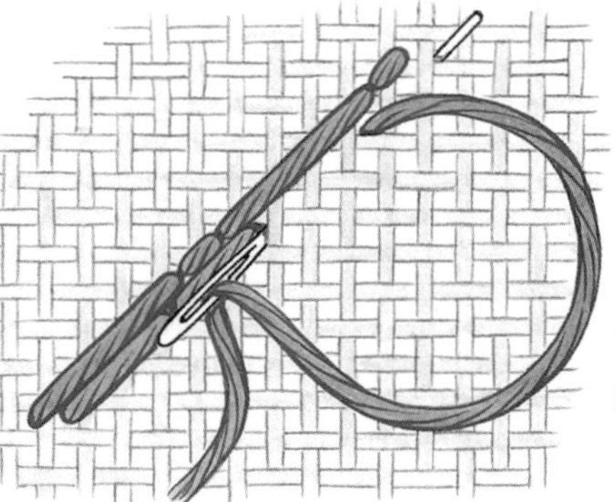

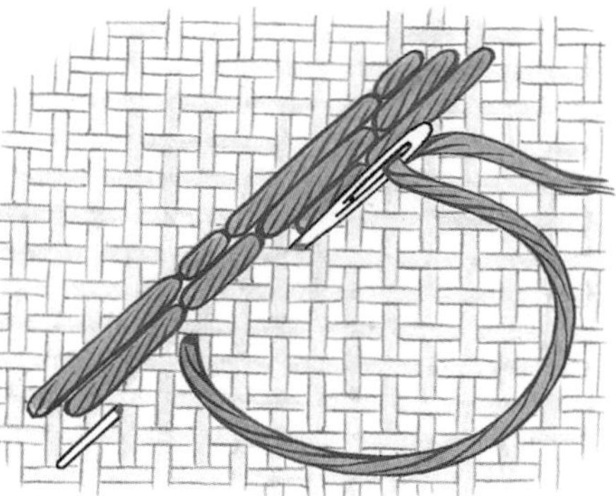

1 Bring the needle to the front near the top right-hand corner of the shape. Work a row of backstitches diagonally across the canvas, working the stitches alternately over one and four canvas intersections.

2 At the end of the row, turn and work a second row of backstitches directly below the first one. This time, work the stitches alternately over two and three canvas intersections.

3 Turn at the end of the row, and work the third row directly below the preceding one. This time, work the backstitches alternately over three and two canvas intersections.

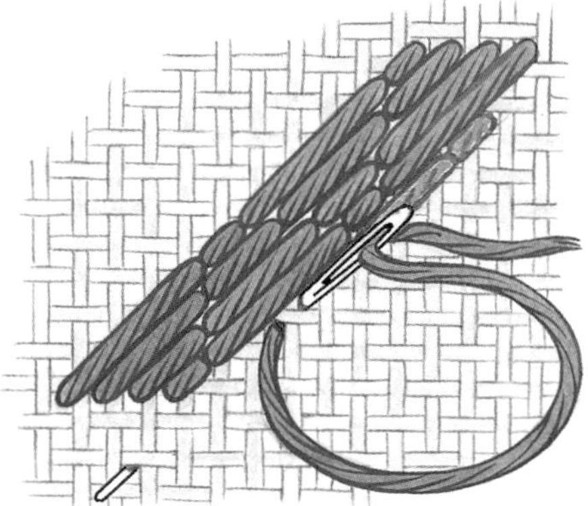

4 Work the fourth and final row of the sequence directly below the preceding one, working the stitches alternately over four and then one intersection. When the four-row sequence is complete, repeat it to fill the shape.

Working extended Milanese stitch

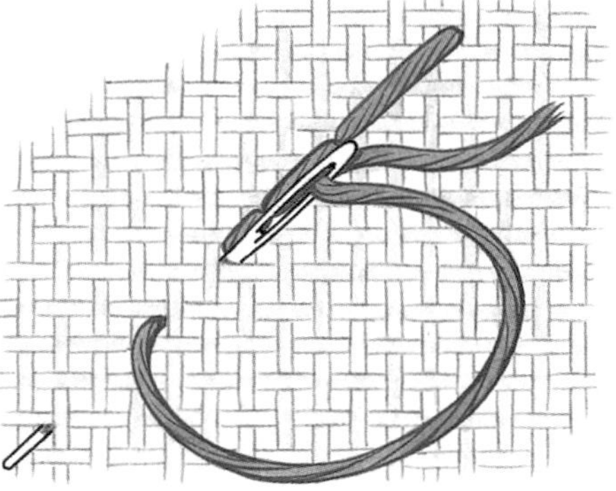

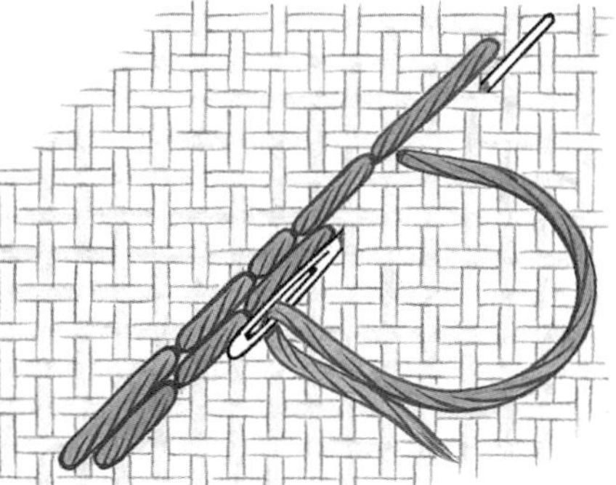

1 Bring the needle to the front near the top right-hand corner of the shape. Work a row of backstitches diagonally across the canvas, working the stitches in a repeating sequence over three, two, one, and two canvas intersections.

2 At the end of the row, turn and work a second row of backstitches directly below the first one. This time, work all the stitches over two canvas intersections.

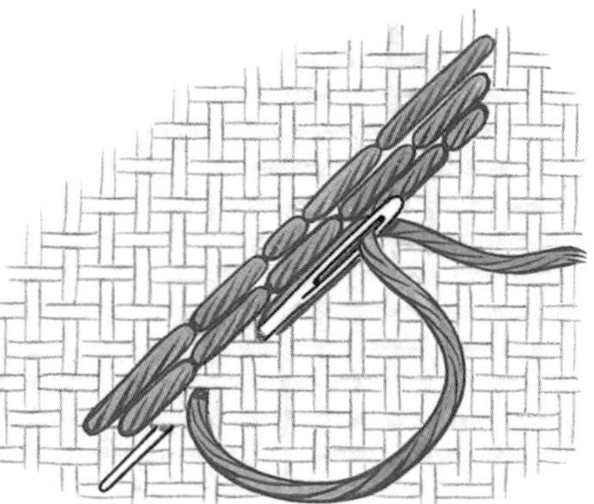

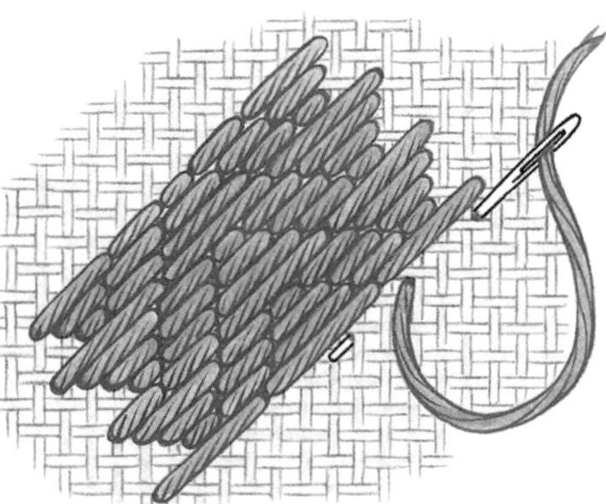

3 Turn at the end of the row and work the third row directly below the preceding one. This time, work the backstitches in a repeating sequence over one, two, three, and two canvas intersections.

4 Work the fourth and final row of the sequence directly below the preceding one, working all the stitches over four intersections. When the four rows are completed, repeat them to fill the shape, taking care to keep the sequence of stitches correct.

Filling stitches

The three filling stitches shown here are worked in similar ways but the effect each stitch creates is quite different. They all consist of diagonal stitches worked in horizontal rows and are ideal for filling shapes and backgrounds and for working color changes.

The stitches can be worked in one color, but they look more striking when contrasting threads are used.

When filling shapes with these stitches, fill gaps of unworked canvas around the edge of the shape with tent stitches for a neat finish. For details on working tent stitch, refer to pages 161–164.

To start and fasten off any of the stitches in this section, refer to page 161.

Oblique Slav stitch creates a smooth surface, with a strongly horizontal character; the stitches are of identical length. This stitch looks good worked in a variegated thread, or you can choose closely harmonizing thread colors to shade a large background.

Nobuko stitch uses two different sizes of diagonal stitch, creating a more broken pattern than oblique Slav stitch. Nobuko stitch is ideal for filling small areas.

Kennan stitch can also be used to work shaded areas, but the real beauty of this stitch lies in the pretty bird's-eye pattern which is created as regular canvas intersections are left unstitched. You can accentuate this attractive effect by using tent stitches and a lighter or darker thread to cover the intersections after the area has been filled with Kennan stitch. Alternatively (if the object does not need to be hard-wearing), you can let the canvas show through.

Oblique Slav stitch

Nobuko stitch

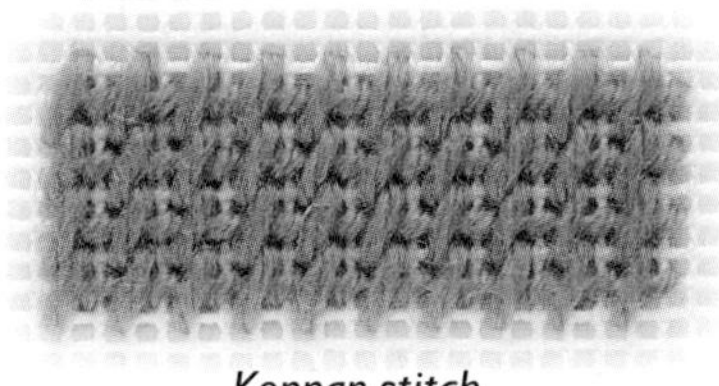

Kennan stitch

Working oblique Slav stitch

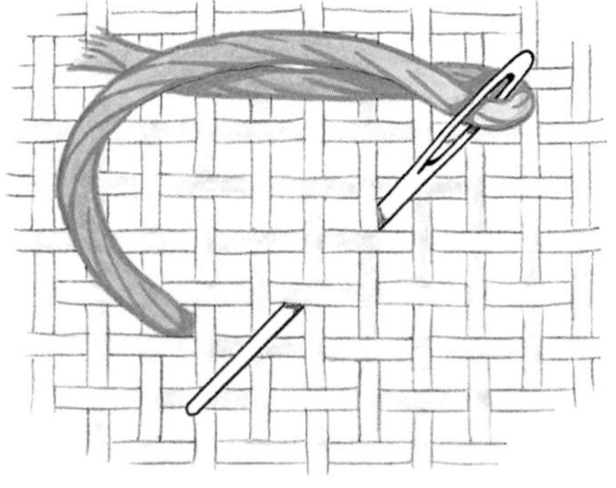

1 Start near the top left of the shape to be filled. Make an upward diagonal stitch over four vertical and two horizontal canvas threads. Bring the needle out two threads to the right of the base of the first stitch, ready to work the next stitch.

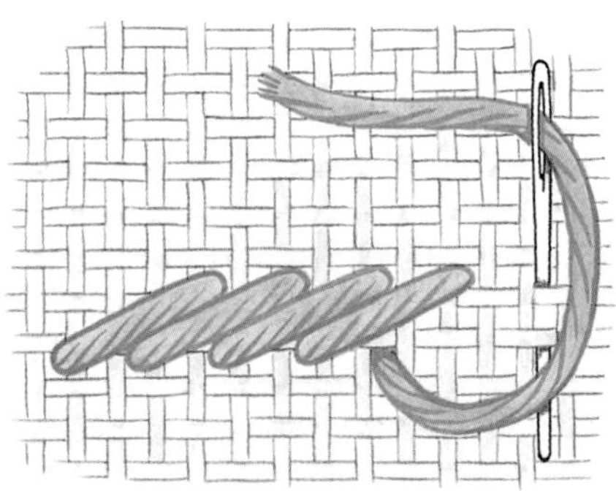

2 Repeat step **1** along the row. To turn at the end of the row, bring the needle out two threads below the top of the last stitch.

3 Work the second row from right to left in the same way, and repeat steps **1** and **2** to fill the shape. You may find it easier to rotate the canvas 180 degrees when working the rows that go from right to left.

Working Nobuko stitch

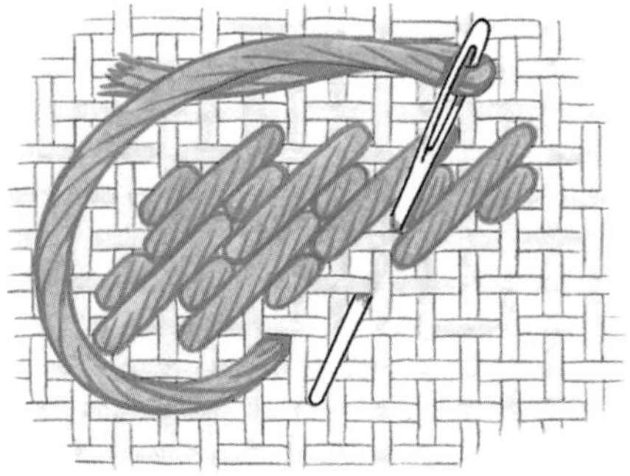

1 Start near the top right. Make a diagonal stitch over one canvas intersection, then bring the needle out one thread below and two to the left of the base of the stitch. Make a diagonal stitch over three canvas intersections; bring the needle out one thread above the base of the stitch.

2 Repeat step 1 along the row. To turn at the end of the row, finish with a short stitch then bring the needle out to the front one thread to the left and one below the base of the last long stitch worked.

3 Work the second row from left to right, alternating the long and short stitches so that they fit between the stitches already worked on the previous row. Repeat these two rows to fill the shape.

Working Kennan stitch

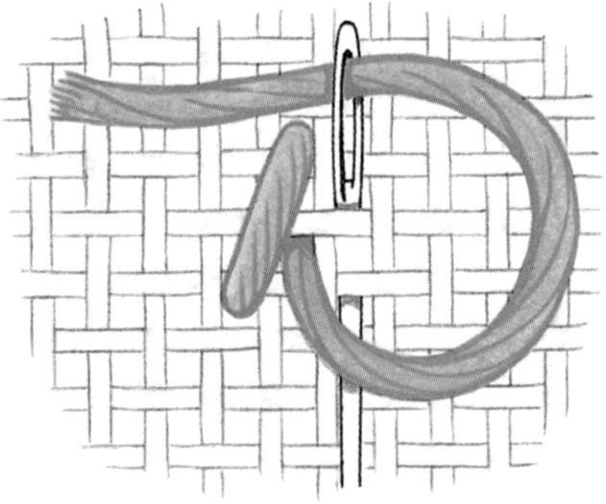

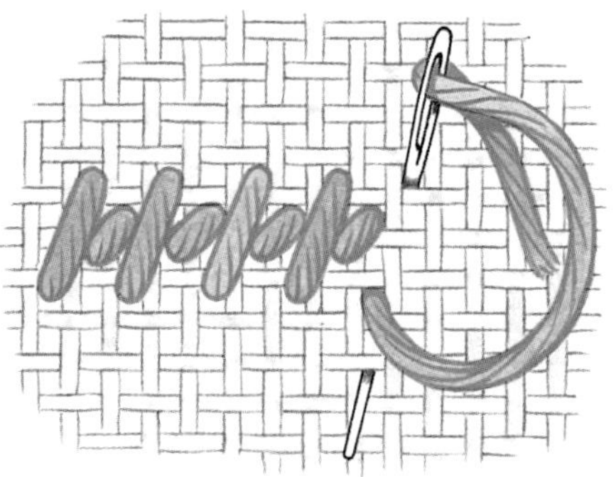

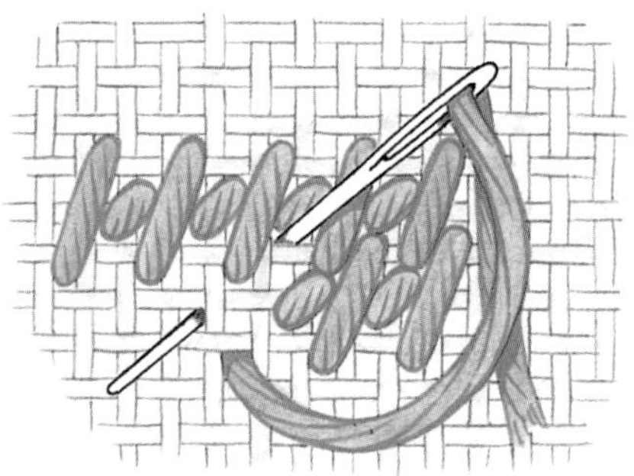

1 Start near the top left. Make a long diagonal stitch from bottom left to top right over three horizontal and one vertical thread, then bring the needle out two threads below. Make a short diagonal stitch over one canvas intersection, and bring the needle out two threads below.

2 Repeat step 1 along the row. To turn at the end of the row, finish with a long stitch, then bring the needle out two threads below the base of the same stitch.

3 Work the second row from right to left, alternating the long and short stitches so that they fit between the stitches already worked on the previous row. Repeat these two rows to fill the shape.

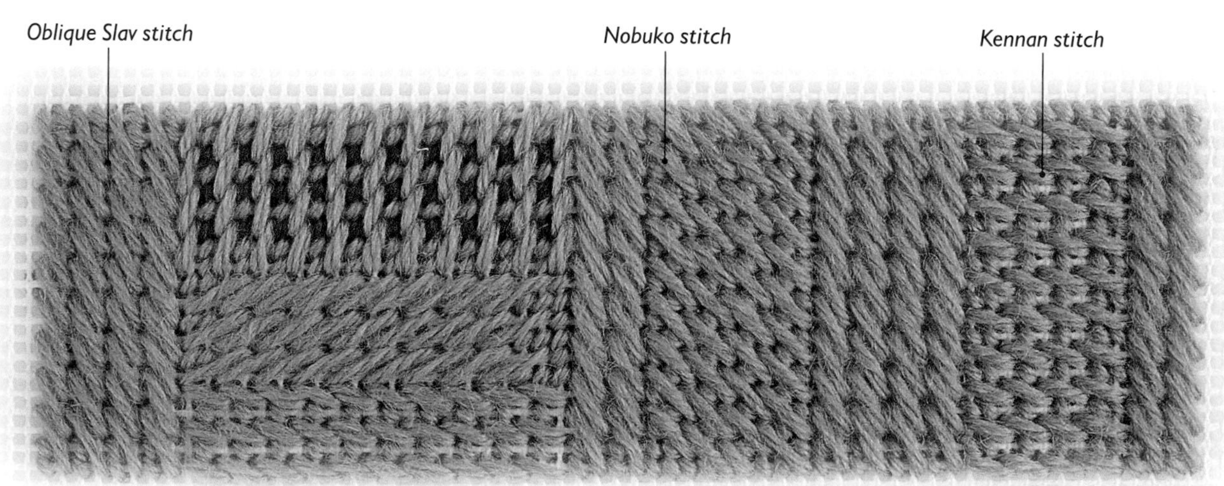

Easy crossed stitches

Cross stitch and its variations are popular needlepoint stitches which give an attractive textured finish. They are quick and easy to work and can be used to fill shapes of any size.

You can work the stitches in any kind of embroidery thread, but tapestry, Persian, and crewel wool give the best results. Match the weight of the thread with the gauge of the canvas to ensure adequate coverage. To prevent the canvas from distorting as you stitch, stretch it tightly across a frame (see page 20).

To start any of these stitches, bring the needle to the front of the canvas at your starting point, leaving a 2 in. (5 cm) tail of thread at the back. Complete the first row of the stitch as usual, but as you work, stitch over the loose thread end to secure it. To fasten off, take the thread to the back and darn it under a few nearby stitches.

Cross stitch forms diagonal crosses and makes hard-wearing, closely worked fabrics, which are ideal for cushion and seat covers.

Rice stitch and **triple rice stitch** are both highly decorative. They are usually worked in two different threads—a thick thread for the foundation crosses and a finer one for the small diagonals worked at the corners of the crosses.

Oblong cross stitch has elongated arms and is used for items not subject to heavy wear, such as pictures.

Upright cross stitch forms upright crosses on the canvas and gives a less dense finish than cross stitch.

Reversed cross stitch combines diagonal rows of cross stitch and upright cross stitch. The foundation layer is worked in one color, then the second layer is worked over the top, using a thread of equal weight in a second color and reversing the pattern.

Cross stitch

Rice stitch

Triple rice stitch

Oblong cross stitch

Upright cross stitch

Reversed cross stitch

Working cross stitch

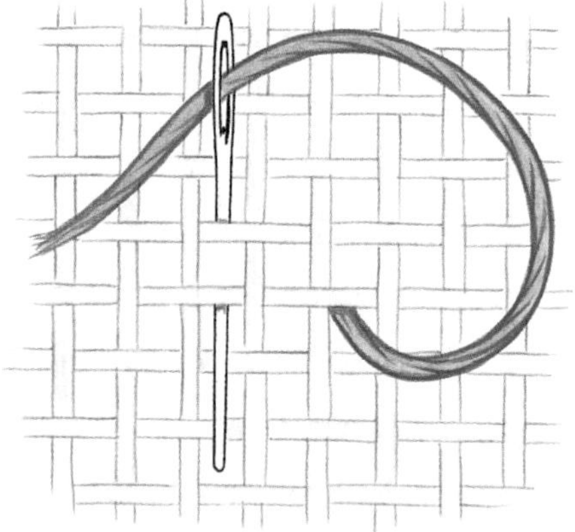

1 Working from right to left, bring the needle to the front at the bottom right. Insert it two holes up and two holes to the left to make a short diagonal stitch. Bring the needle to the front two holes down.

2 Insert the needle two holes up and two holes to the right. Bring it out to the front two holes down and two holes to the left to complete the first stitch. Continue in this way to the end of the row.

3 For the second row, turn the work upside down and repeat steps **1–2**. Repeat steps **1–3** to fill the shape.

Working rice stitch

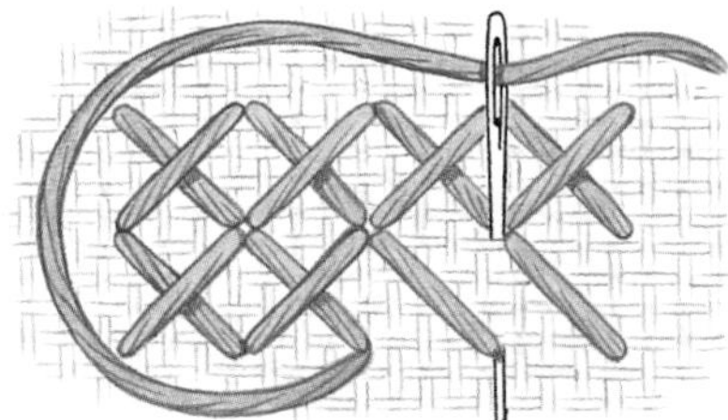

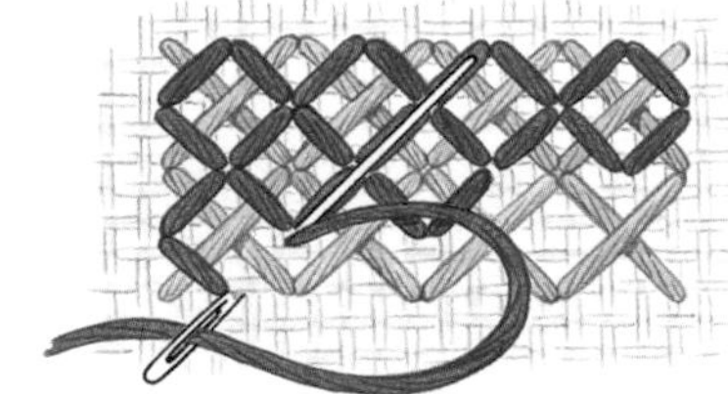

1 Fill the shape with large cross stitches, with each stitch spanning four vertical and horizontal threads. Position each row directly below the preceding one.

2 Using a contrasting thread, work short diagonal stitches over the corners of the crosses, with each stitch spanning two vertical and horizontal threads.

Working triple rice stitch

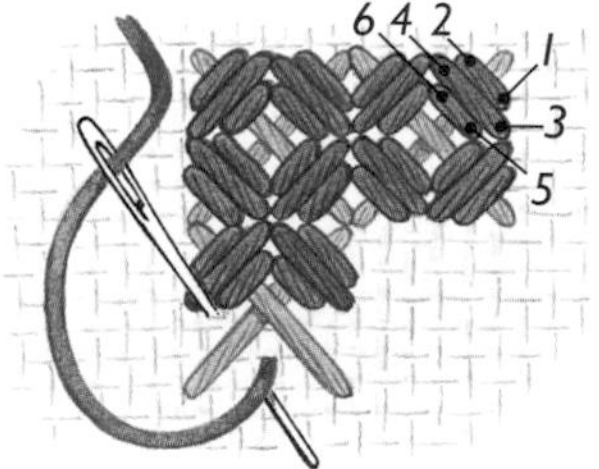

Work cross stitches over six vertical and horizontal threads. Using a second thread, follow the 1–6 sequence to work three graduated diagonal stitches at each corner of each cross.

Working oblong cross stitch

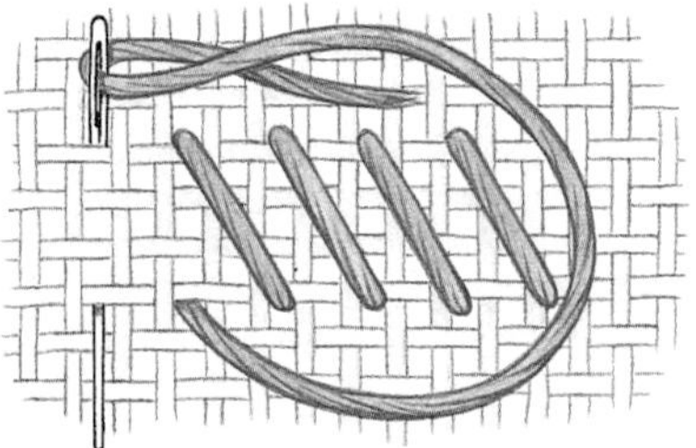

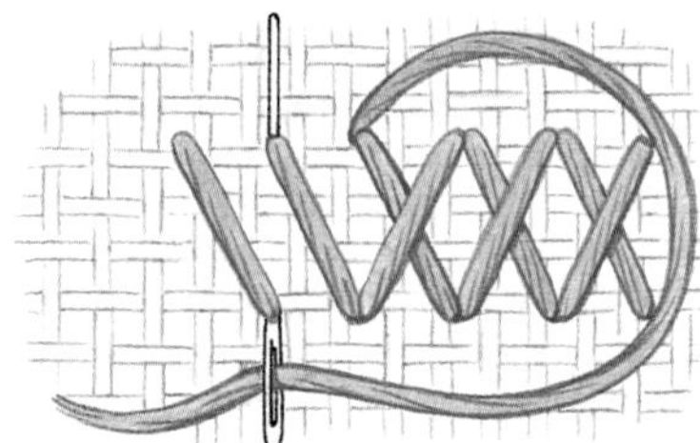

1 Bring the needle to the front at the bottom right. Insert the needle four threads up and two threads to the left. Repeat to work the first arm of the cross stitches along the row.

2 Turn the canvas upside down; take the needle to the back four threads down and two threads to the left. Bring it out four threads up. Repeat along the row to complete the oblong crosses.

Working upright cross stitch

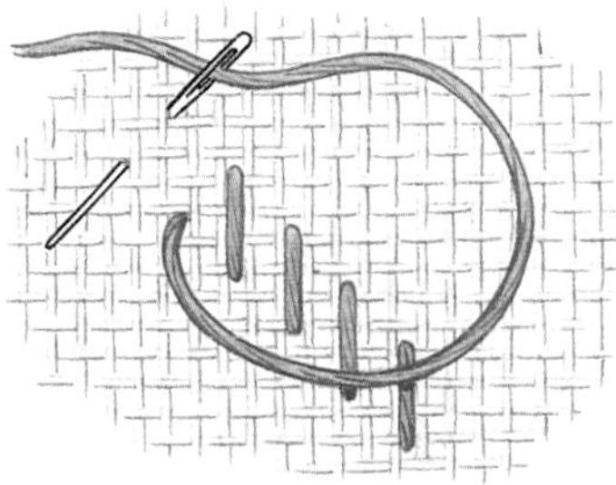

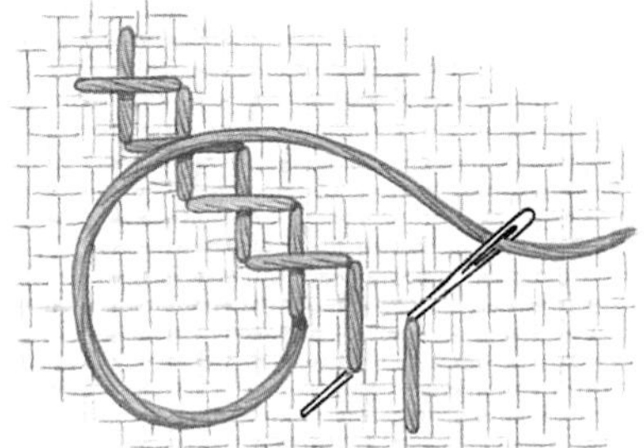

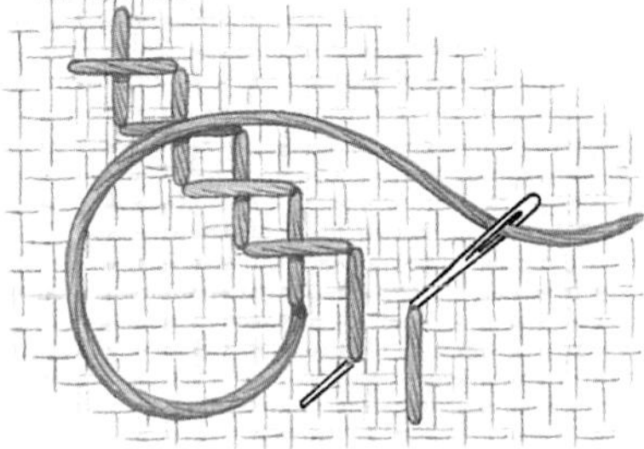

1 Work from the bottom right to the top left. Make a diagonal row of straight stitches over four canvas threads. Separate each stitch by two vertical and two horizontal threads.

2 Work in the opposite direction to complete the stitches. Make horizontal stitches of the same length so that they cross the vertical stitches to make upright crosses.

Working reversed cross stitch

1 Start at the bottom left; make the stitches individually. Work alternate diagonal rows of cross and upright cross stitches over four threads.

2 Using a different-colored thread, repeat step 1, but make upright crosses over the cross stitches, and cross stitches over the upright crosses.

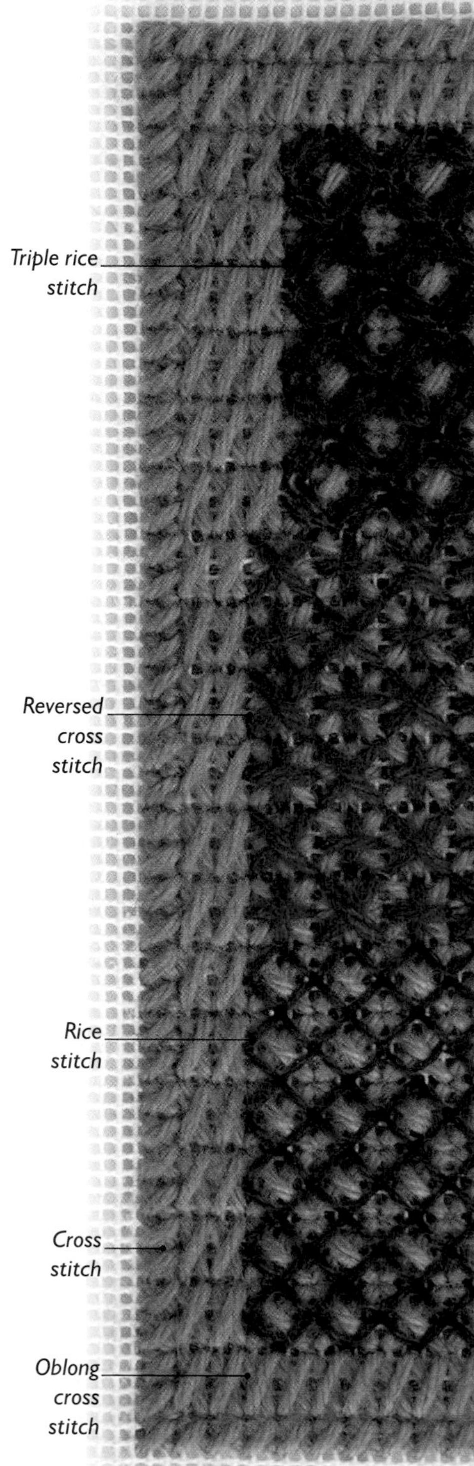

Filling stitches

There are many attractive cross stitch variations for needlepoint. The four featured here create hard-wearing fabrics with subtly textured surfaces and are ideal for covering large areas quickly. For the best results, choose a mono or interlock canvas. (The stitches can also be worked on evenweave fabrics using a fine thread and needle.) To start and fasten off any of these stitches, refer to page 161.

Diagonal cross stitch is worked in diagonal rows. When worked in two or more colors it creates a pretty pattern of diagonal stripes.

Long-armed cross stitch gives a lightly stitched surface with a plaited effect. It can be used to make straight borders or, in multiple rows, to fill a shape.

Underlined stitch is a variation of ordinary cross stitch with a horizontal stitch below each cross.

Italian cross stitch looks similar to underlined stitch, but each cross is framed by straight stitches to give a closely worked surface.

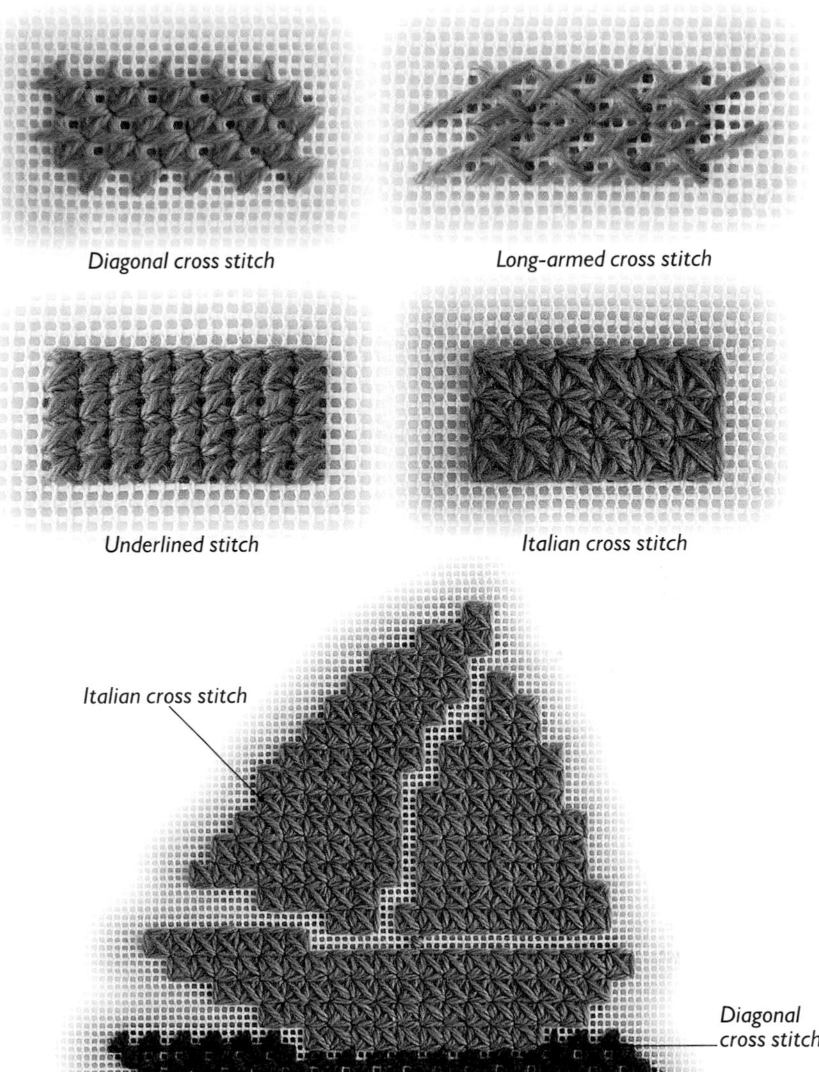

Working diagonal cross stitch

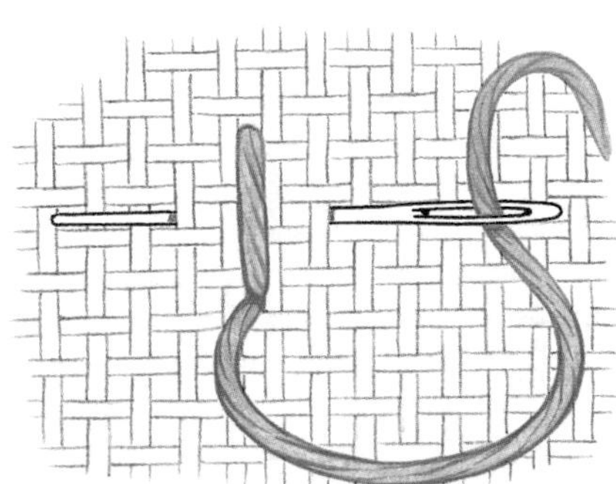

1 Bring the needle out at the bottom right of the area. Insert it four holes up, and bring it out four holes down again. Insert the needle two holes up and two to the right, then bring it out four holes to the left.

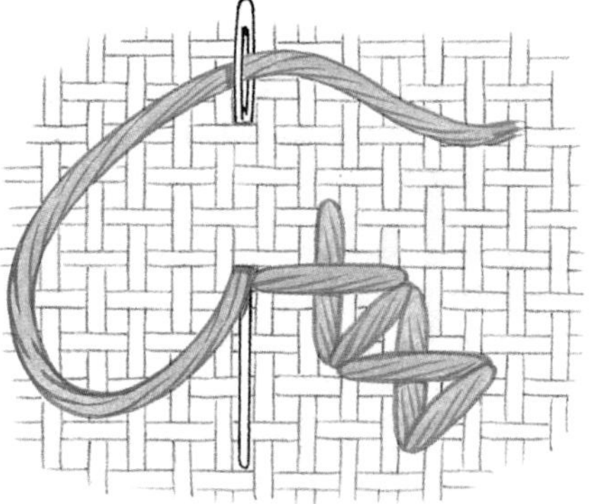

2 Insert the needle four holes to the right to finish the first cross. Then bring it out four holes to the left, ready to start the next one. Continue in this way to the end of the row, then fasten off the thread.

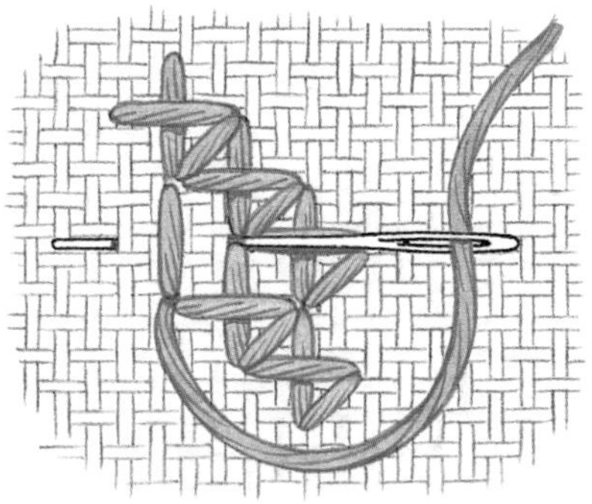

3 To work the next row, bring the needle out four holes below the point where it originally emerged, and repeat steps **1–2**. Repeat steps **1–3** to fill the shape.

Working long-armed cross stitch

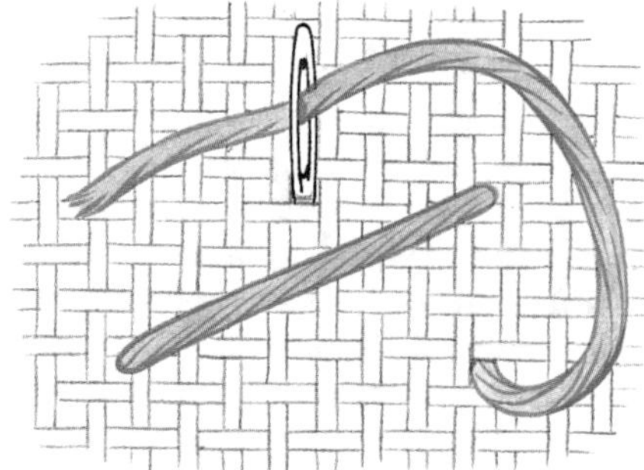

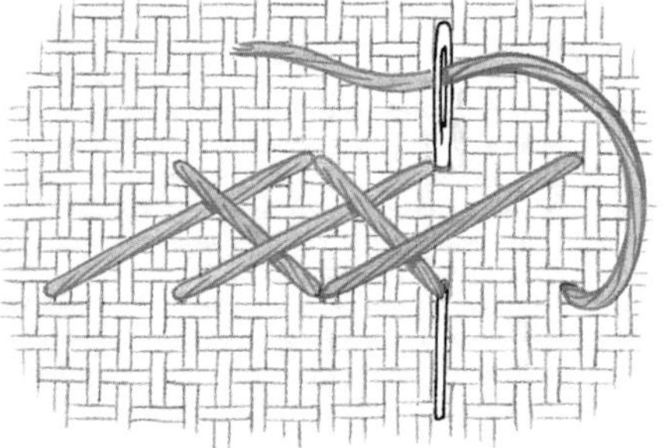

1 Bring the needle out at the left of the shape. Insert it four holes up and eight to the right. Bring the needle out four holes down, and insert it four holes up and four to the left.

2 Bring the needle out four holes down, ready to work the next stitch. Repeat steps **1–2** along the row. For a solid filling, stitch multiple rows, always working from left to right.

Working underlined stitch

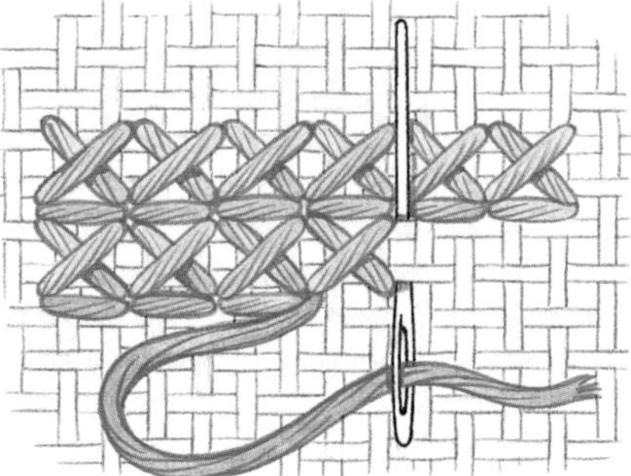

Work cross stitch over two horizontal and two vertical threads. Then work a horizontal stitch over two threads below the cross. Repeat along the row. Work subsequent rows below the first.

Working Italian cross stitch

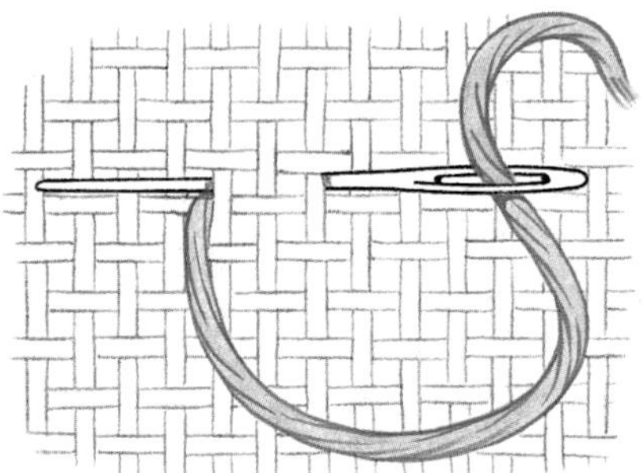

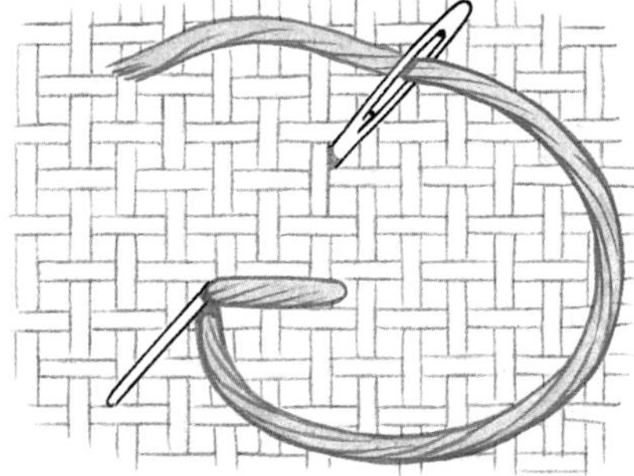

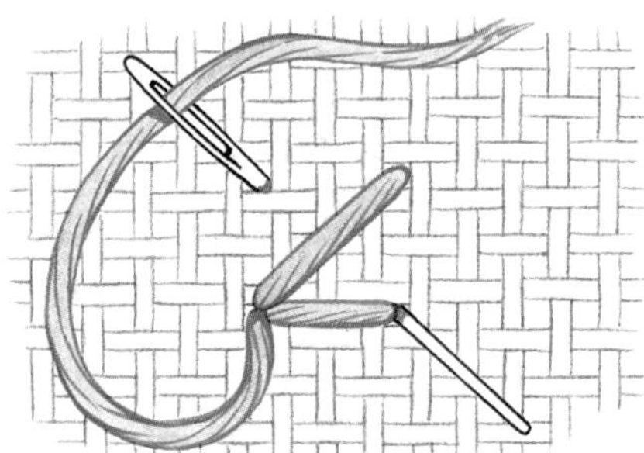

1 Bring the needle to the front at the bottom left of the shape. Insert it three holes to the right, then bring the needle out again at the point where it originally emerged, to make a horizontal stitch.

2 Pull the thread through. Insert the needle three holes up and three to the right to make a diagonal stitch slanting from bottom left to top right. Bring the needle out at the left-hand edge of the horizontal stitch.

3 Pull the thread through. Insert the needle three holes up and bring it to the front at the right-hand edge of the horizontal stitch.

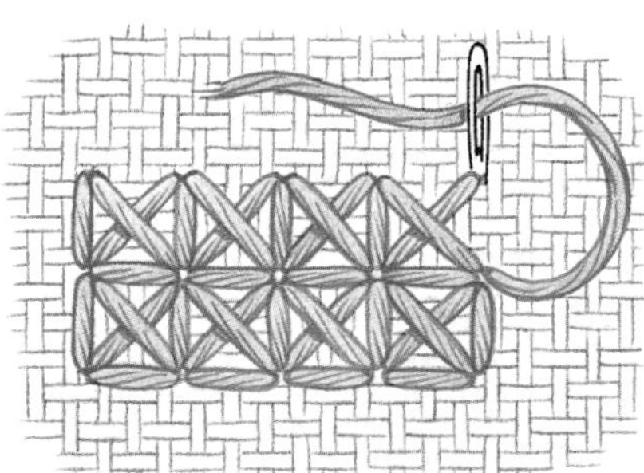

4 Insert the needle three holes up and three to the left to complete one stitch. Repeat steps **1–4** along the row, finishing the right-hand end by working an extra vertical stitch. Work subsequent rows above the first.

5 When all the rows have been worked, add a horizontal stitch spanning three vertical threads directly above each of the crosses on the top row to complete the pattern.

The filling stitches shown are worked in vertical rows to make strongly striped patterns on the canvas (in the case of ridge stitch the stripes are diagonal). They can all be worked in a single color or in a selection of different shades to enhance the striped pattern.

The stitches all create a hard-wearing stitched surface. For the best results, choose either a mono or an interlock canvas—the stitches are less successful when worked on Penelope canvas. Any of the stitches in this section can also be worked on evenweave fabric, using a fine thread.

To start and fasten off any of the stitches in this section, see page 185.

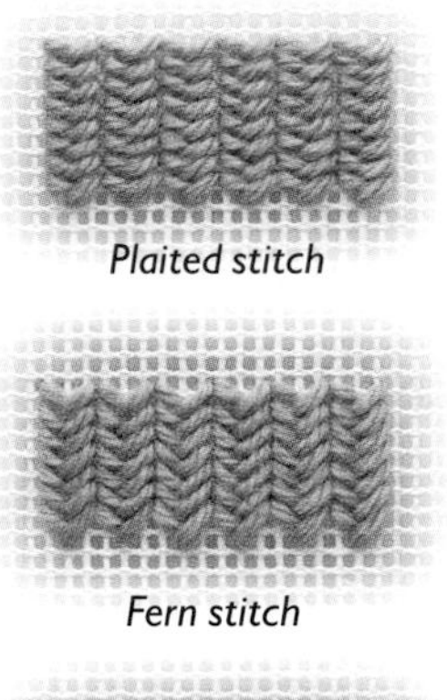

Plaited stitch

Fern stitch

Ridge stitch

Fishbone stitch

Plaited stitch creates a very pretty, densely stitched plaited surface. To give good ground covering, try out a variety of thread weights to find one that suits the stitch and the size of the canvas mesh.

Fern stitch is a close relation of plaited stitch. It is worked in the same way as plaited stitch, but the stitches are deeper.

Ridge stitch has a more textured appearance than plaited stitch and fern stitch. Take care to overlap each row by a single canvas thread and line up the tops of the rows to get the correct appearance.

Fishbone stitch looks somewhat like fishbones. The stitch covers the canvas ground well.

Working plaited stitch

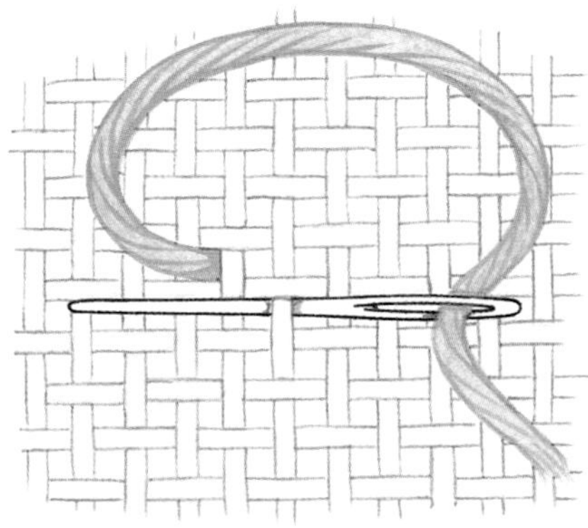

1 Start at the top left. Insert the needle one canvas thread down and two to the right to make a slanted stitch. Bring the needle out one thread to the left.

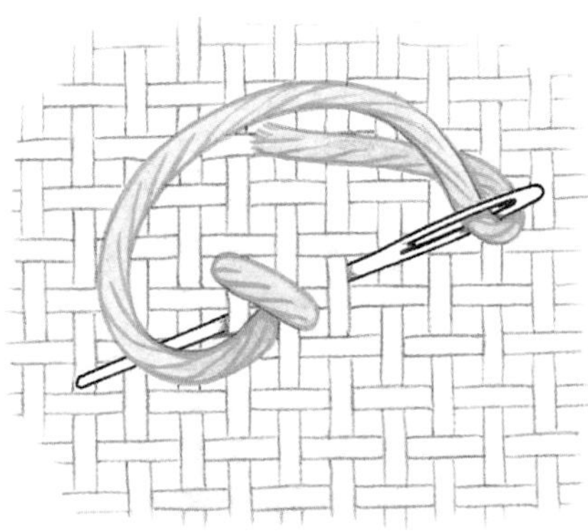

2 Insert the needle one thread higher up and two threads to the right. Bring the needle out one thread below the start of the first stitch, ready to work the next stitch.

3 Repeat steps **1** and **2** along the row. Work the next and subsequent rows to the right of the first row, starting at the top and working down.

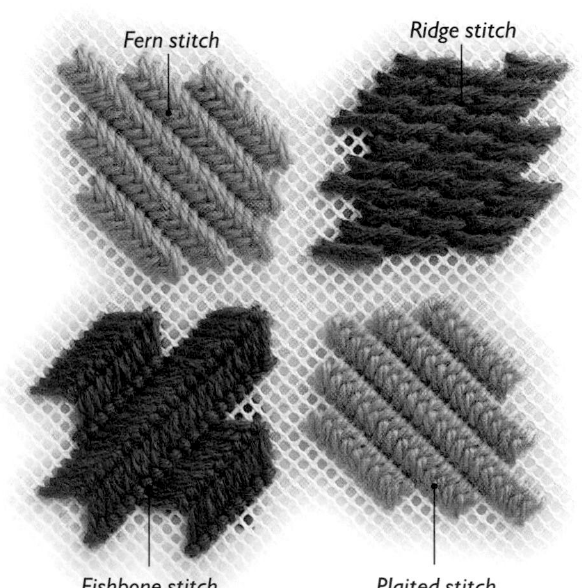

Working fern stitch

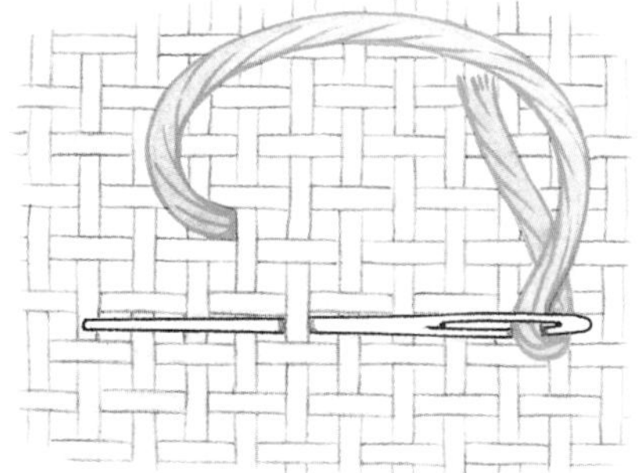

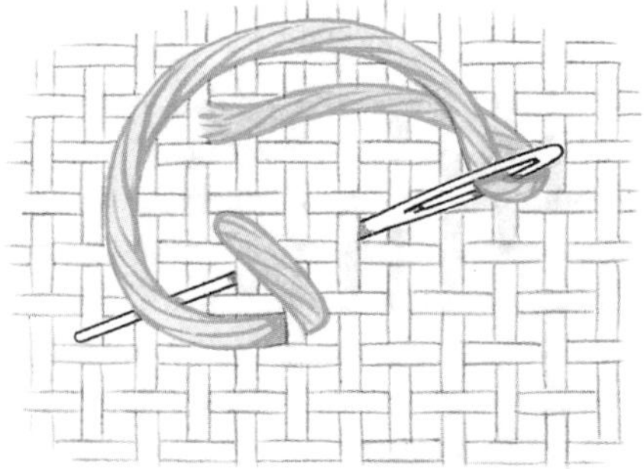

1 Start at the top left. Insert the needle two canvas threads down and two to the right to make a diagonal stitch. Bring the needle out again one thread to the left.

2 Insert the needle two threads up and two threads to the right to complete the first fern stitch. Bring it out three threads to the left and one thread down.

3 Repeat steps **1** and **2** along the row. Work the next and subsequent rows to the right of the first row, starting at the top of each row and working downward.

Working ridge stitch

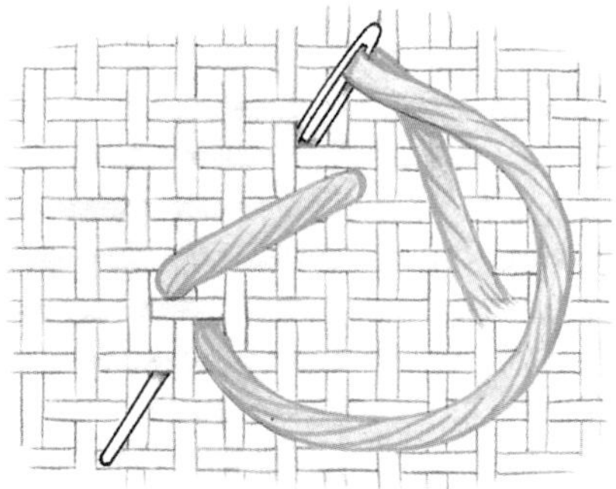

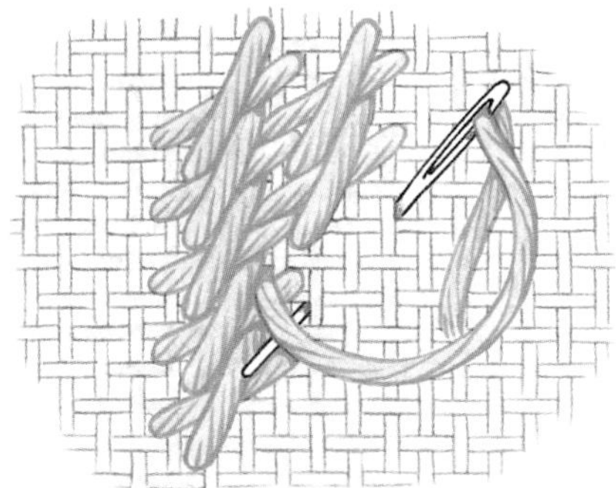

1 Start at the top left. Insert the needle two threads up and four to the right. Make a second diagonal stitch over the top of the first as shown. Bring the needle out again two threads below the starting point, ready to start the next stitch.

2 Repeat the stitches downward along the row. At the end of the row secure the thread. Rejoin the thread at the top right of the row, ready to work the next row.

3 Work the second and subsequent rows in exactly the same way as the first row, overlapping the stitches on the previous row by one vertical canvas thread.

Working fishbone stitch

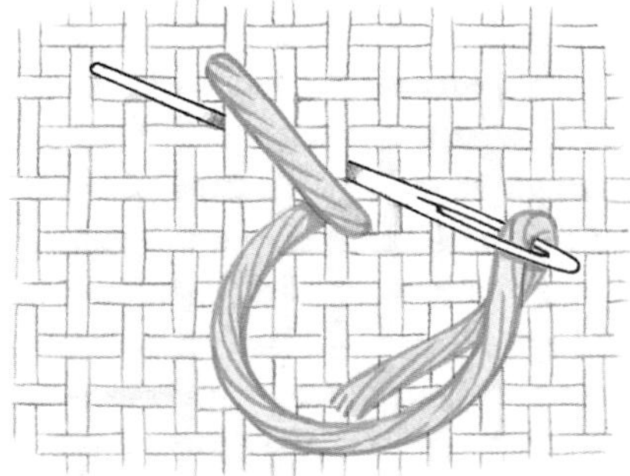

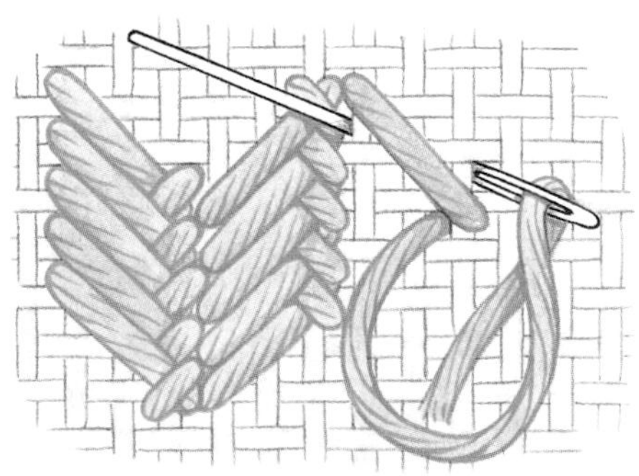

1 Starting at the top left, make a downward diagonal stitch over three canvas intersections. Cross the tip of this stitch with a short upward diagonal stitch over one canvas intersection. Bring the needle out one thread below the start of the diagonal stitch, and repeat along the row.

2 Start the second row at the bottom right of the first. Make an upward diagonal stitch over three canvas intersections. Cross the tip of this stitch with a downward diagonal stitch over one intersection. Bring the needle out one thread above the start of the long diagonal stitch.

3 Continue working upward along the row. When the second row is complete, bring the needle to the front at the top right, ready to start the third row. Repeat steps **1–2** to fill the shape, working downward then upward.

Block stitches

The stitches in this section are all made up of crossed stitches worked over a square block of canvas. The surface the stitches produce is highly textured, and each one creates a strong pattern.

The stitches are ideal for adding interest to large areas of canvas and for filling in backgrounds of abstract designs. They can also be worked in rows to make borders. However, they can be quite dominant, so take care to avoid overshadowing more delicate stitches used nearby.

Worked in a hard-wearing yarn such as Persian wool, the stitches make a very durable fabric suitable for items that are likely to receive a lot of wear, such as chair seat covers, cushion covers, and church kneelers.

Once you have mastered the sequence of the crossing stitches, they are easy to work, but they use up a lot of thread compared to some other crossed stitches.

Double cross stitch

Plaited double cross stitch

Woven cross stitch

To start and fasten off any of the stitches in this section, refer to page 185.

Double cross stitch covers a square block of seven canvas threads. The stitch is framed with long, straight stitches, with tiny upright crosses in the gaps at the corners of the finished blocks.

Plaited double cross stitch is worked in a similar way to double cross stitch, but the individual stitches are interwoven for added interest. It is framed with long straight stitches in the same way as double cross stitch.

Woven cross stitch covers a square block of four canvas threads. It is shown here worked in a single color. For an interesting checkerboard pattern, work the blocks in two harmonizing or contrasting thread colors.

Working double cross stitch

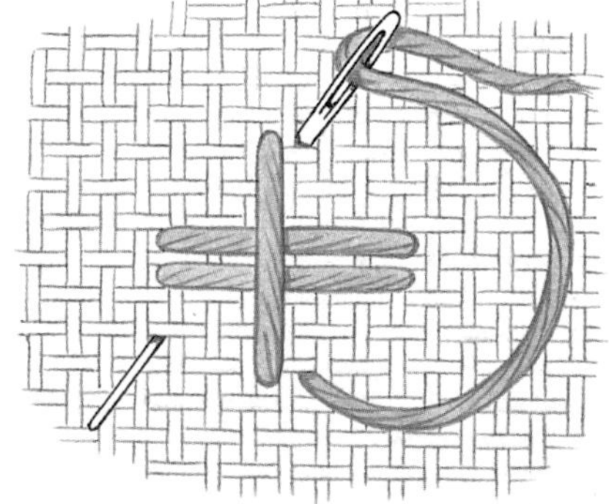

1 Start near the bottom left of the shape to be filled. Work two horizontal stitches over seven canvas threads, then cross these with two vertical stitches of the same length. Bring the needle to the front two threads below the left-hand end of the lower horizontal stitch.

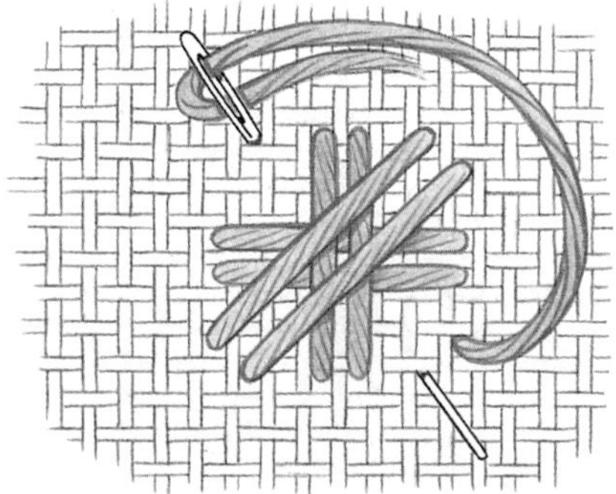

2 Work two slanting stitches across the block, each spanning six canvas threads and slanting from bottom left to top right. Work two more stitches of the same length across the block in the opposite direction.

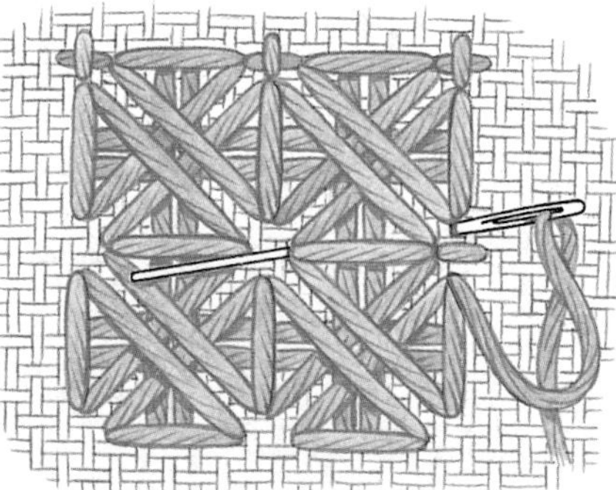

3 Repeat the blocks in horizontal rows, working upward. Arrange them so that the tips of the horizontal stitches touch. To finish, frame each block with straight stitches worked over five canvas threads, then work tiny upright cross stitches over two canvas threads in the gaps at the corners of the blocks.

Working plaited double cross stitch

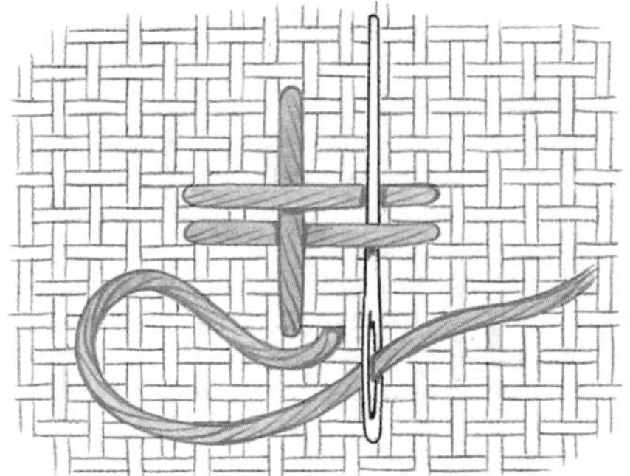

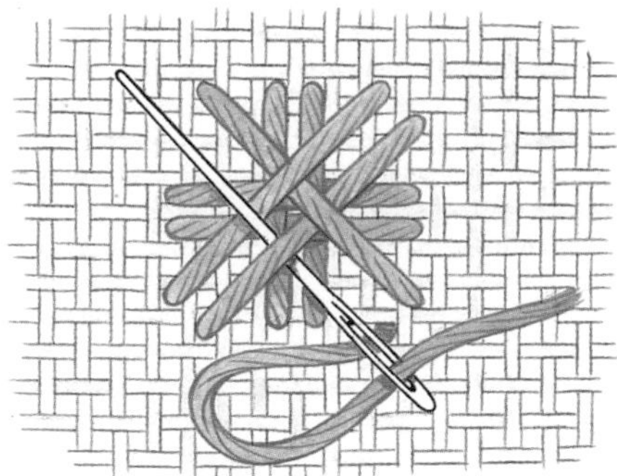

1 Start near the bottom left of the shape to be filled. Work two horizontal stitches over seven canvas threads. Cross them with two vertical stitches as in Double cross stitch, step **1** on page 191, but this time weave the stitches over and under, then under and over the horizontal stitches.

2 Bring the needle to the front again two threads below the left-hand end of the lower horizontal stitch. Work the first two slanting stitches across the block as in Double cross stitch, step **2** on page 191.

3 Work the two remaining slanting stitches as in Double cross stitch, step **2** on page 191, but this time weave the stitches over and under, then under and over each other. To complete the rows, refer to Double cross stitch, step **3** on page 191.

Working woven cross stitch

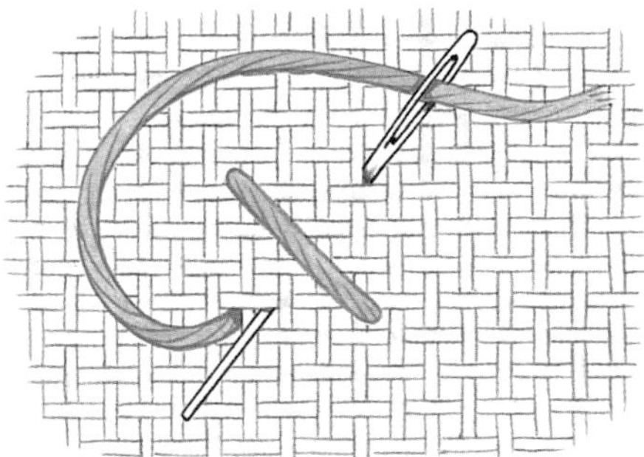

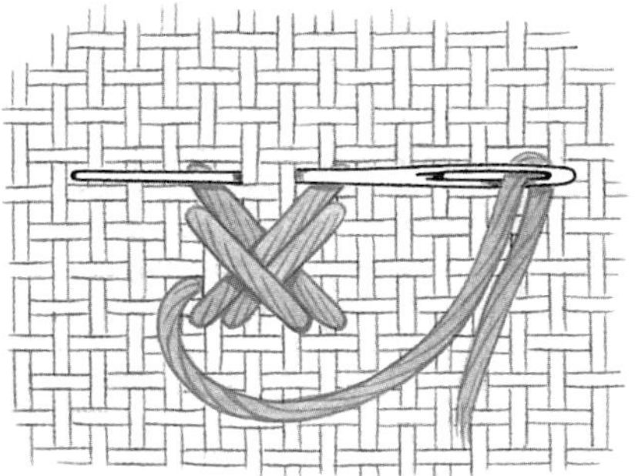

1 Start near the bottom left of the shape to be filled. Work an ordinary cross over a block of four horizontal and four vertical canvas threads, bringing the needle through one thread to the right of the bottom left-hand corner of the block.

2 Insert the needle one thread below the top right-hand corner. Bring it out one thread left of the bottom right-hand corner. Insert the needle one thread below the top left-hand corner and bring it out one thread above the bottom left-hand corner.

3 To make the fifth stitch, insert the needle one thread to the left of the top right-hand corner. Bring the needle out again one thread to the right of the top left-hand corner.

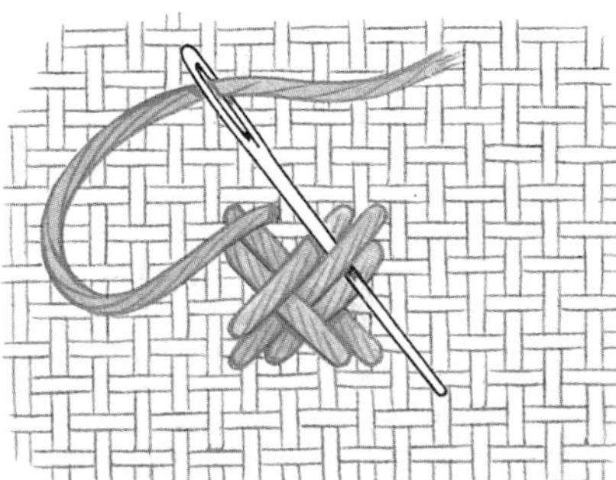

4 To complete the woven cross, slip the needle under the second slanting stitch made, as shown, and insert it one thread above the bottom right-hand corner. Work more blocks in a row from left to right, then work rows directly above the first row.

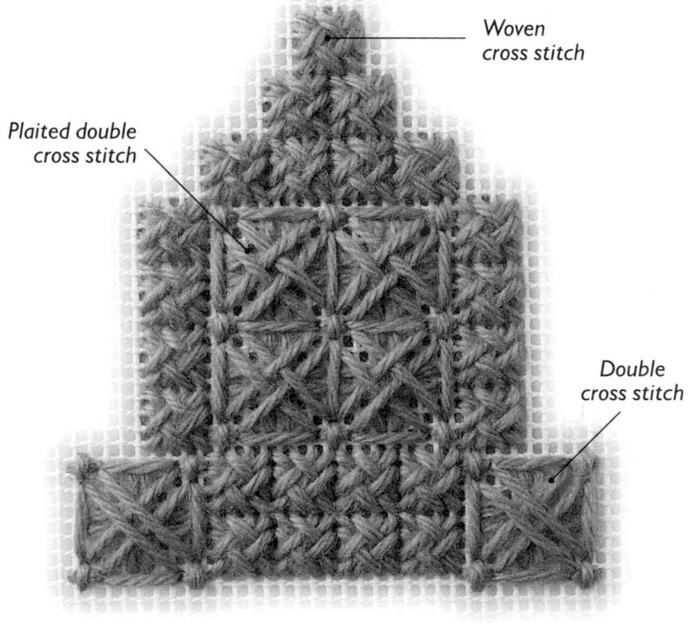

Leviathan stitches

The stitches in this section are all from the same family and take the form of two or more layers of crossing stitches worked over a square or rectangular block of canvas. The surface the stitches produce is very textured, and each one creates a strong pattern.

Worked in a hard-wearing yarn such as Persian wool, the stitches make a durable fabric which is suitable for making into items that receive a lot of wear, such as cushion covers and chair seats. All the stitches are easy to work once you have mastered the sequence of the crossing stitches.

For details on starting and fastening off the thread, refer to page 185.

Leviathan stitch covers a square block of four canvas threads. It consists of an upright cross stitch worked over an ordinary cross stitch, and it looks effective worked in one color or in two contrasting shades of thread to create a checkerboard pattern.

Alternate leviathan stitch is made by arranging rows of leviathan stitches with a half drop of two canvas threads in order to create a less regular pattern.

Elongated leviathan stitch is worked in the same way as leviathan stitch, but it covers a rectangle of two canvas threads by four. This elongated stitch covers the canvas more densely than leviathan stitch.

Double leviathan stitch is the most complicated variation to work, and it also uses the most thread. It covers a square block of four canvas threads, and you should follow the sequence of stitches carefully to ensure that each stitch looks identical. Note that when forming the first cross, the first diagonal is worked from bottom right to top left, unlike the other leviathan stitches.

Leviathan stitch

Alternate leviathan stitch

Elongated leviathan stitch

Double leviathan stitch

Working basic leviathan stitch

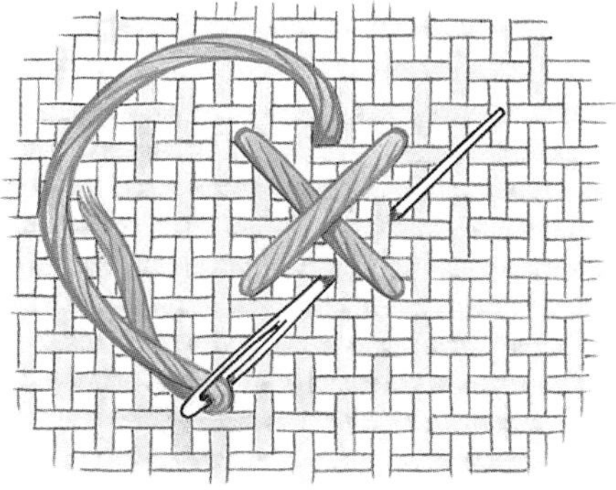

1 Starting at the top left of the shape, work a cross stitch over a block of four horizontal and vertical canvas threads. Bring the needle out at the center top, and insert it four threads below. Bring the needle out halfway up the right-hand side of the block.

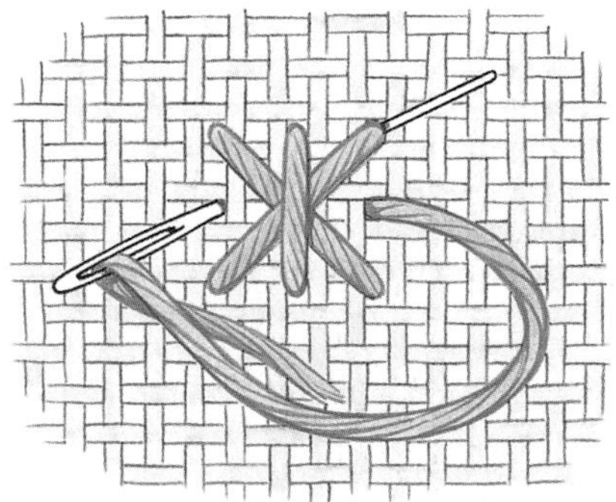

2 Insert the needle at the center left of the block to complete the stitch. Bring it out at the top right-hand corner of the block, ready to make the next leviathan stitch. Continue in this way to complete the row.

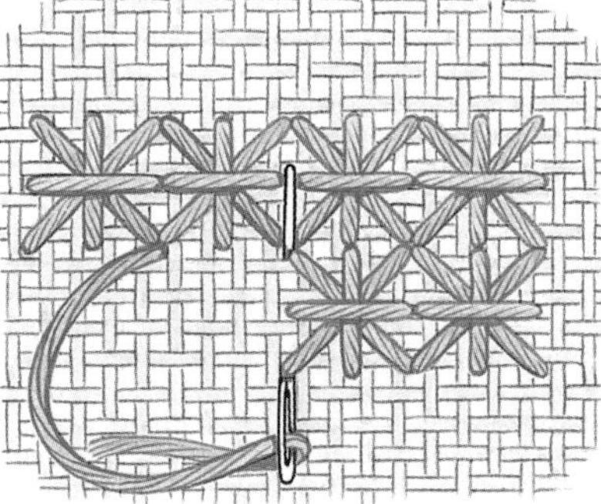

3 Work the next row in the opposite direction directly below the first, so that the top of each stitch shares the same hole as the bottom of the stitch directly above. Form each stitch exactly as before. Continue in this way to fill the shape.

Working alternate leviathan stitch

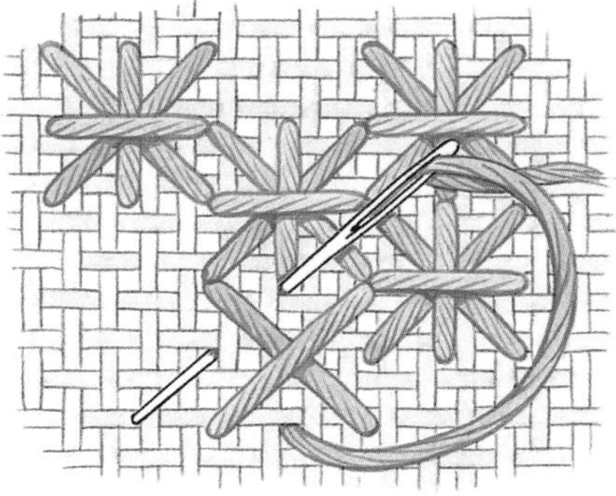

1 Start near the top of the shape. Work a basic leviathan stitch referring to steps **1–3** on the previous page. Begin the next stitch halfway down the right-hand side of the first. Alternate the two blocks along the row.

2 Work the next row in the opposite direction. Form the leviathan stitches in exactly the same way as before, fitting them neatly into the stepped lower edge of the previous row. Continue in this way.

Working elongated leviathan stitch

Start near the top of the shape. Work a row of leviathan stitches, but this time work each stitch over two vertical and four horizontal canvas threads. Work the second and subsequent rows directly below the first row.

Working double leviathan stitch

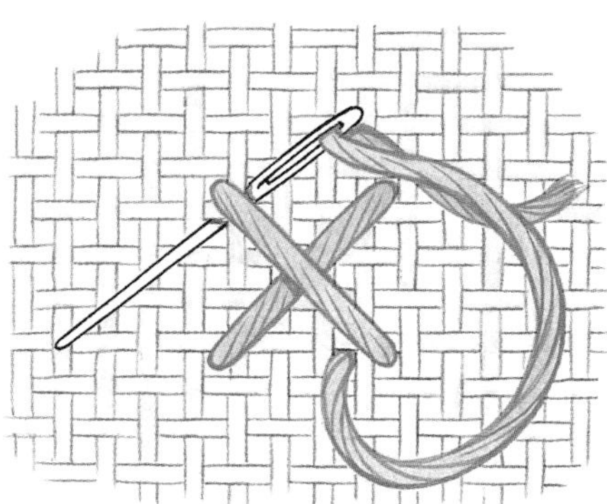

1 Work a cross stitch over a block of four canvas threads, and bring the needle out one thread to the left of the bottom right-hand corner. Insert it one thread to the right of the top left-hand corner, and bring it out again one thread below the top left-hand corner.

2 Pull the thread through. Insert the needle one thread above the bottom right-hand corner of the block, and bring it out one thread to the right of the bottom left-hand corner of the block.

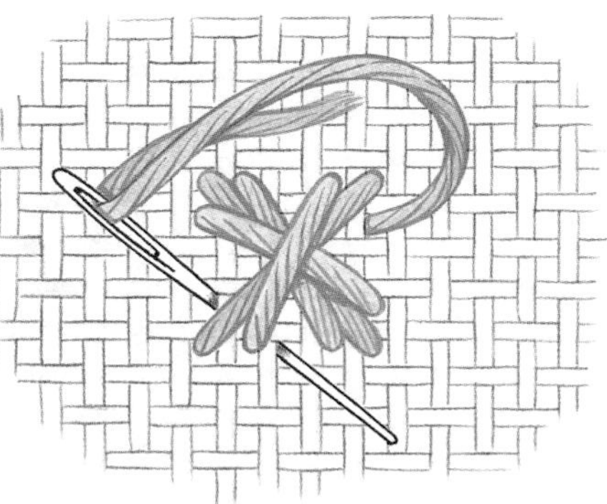

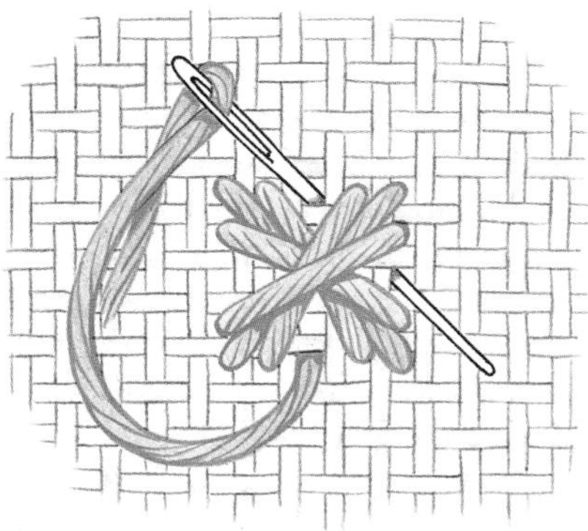

3 Pull the thread through. Insert the needle one thread to the left of the top right-hand corner of the block, and bring it through one thread below the top right-hand corner.

4 Pull the thread through. Insert the needle one thread above the bottom left-hand corner of the block, and bring it out halfway along the bottom of the block.

5 Pull the thread through. To finish the stitch, make one vertical and one horizontal stitch over the block in the same way as in basic leviathan stitch, steps **1–2** on page **193**. Repeat in horizontal rows to fill the shape.

Rhodes stitches

The invention of the British needlepoint designer Mary Rhodes, basic Rhodes stitch forms a textured square-shaped block and has several attractive variations. The stitches are used to fill large shapes and backgrounds and, with the exception of octagonal Rhodes stitch, produce an extremely durable fabric which is ideal for cushion covers, stools, chair seats, and other items subject to wear and tear. Once you have mastered the sequence of stitching, you'll find all Rhodes stitches are very easy to work.

To start off any of the stitches, bring the needle to the front of the canvas close to your starting point, leaving a 2 in. (5 cm) thread end at the back. Work the first few stitches over the thread end to secure it. When the stitching is complete, take the thread to the back and darn it under the last few stitches worked.

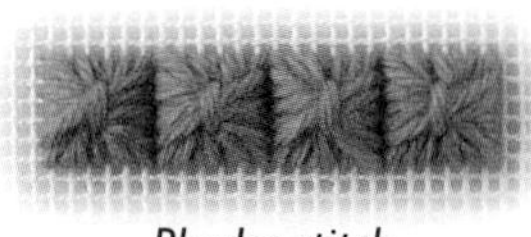

Rhodes stitch

Half Rhodes stitch

Plaited Rhodes stitch

Octagonal Rhodes stitch

Rhodes stitch makes a pretty raised block which can be worked over five, six, or more canvas threads. When working Rhodes stitch over an even number of threads, as shown below, you can tie down the center of the block with a short vertical stitch.

Half Rhodes stitch is a quick and easy variation consisting of vertical rows of half-formed Rhodes-stitch blocks. Stitches on alternate rows are arranged so they interlock with those made on the preceding row to create a novel twisted effect.

Plaited Rhodes stitch is similar in construction to half Rhodes stitch, but the direction of the stitches is changed on alternate rows to give the texture a braided effect.

Octagonal Rhodes stitch is the least hard-wearing of the group and is best reserved for pictures, wall hangings, and other items that won't get much wear.

Working Rhodes stitch

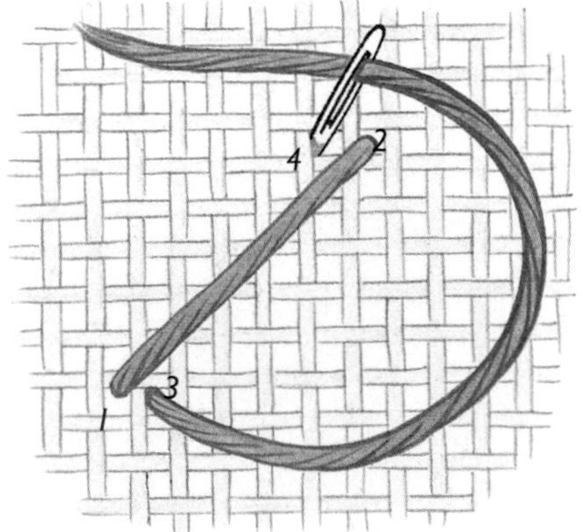

1 Bring the needle to the front at the bottom left at 1. Make a slanting stitch to the right over six horizontal and vertical threads to 2. Bring the needle back to the front one hole to the right of the base of the first stitch at 3. Make a second stitch, inserting the needle one hole to the left of the top of the first stitch at 4.

2 Continue to stitch around in a counterclockwise direction, following the sequence 5–24 to form a square shape with a slightly raised middle created by the overlapping yarn.

3 (Optional) Work a short vertical stitch spanning two threads at the center of the square to secure the crossed stitches. Position the stitch between two central arms of the pattern to avoid splitting the yarn.

Working half Rhodes stitch

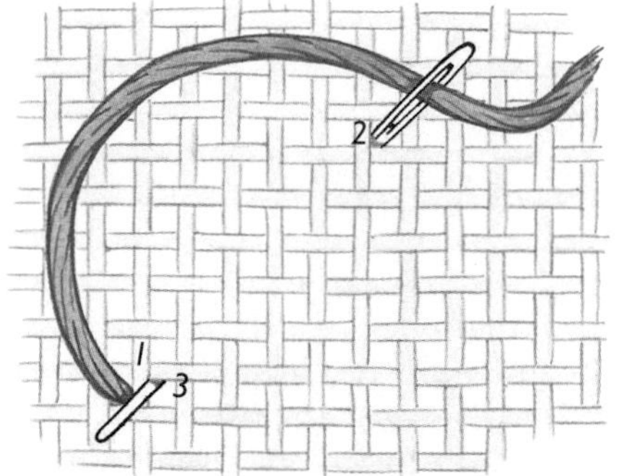

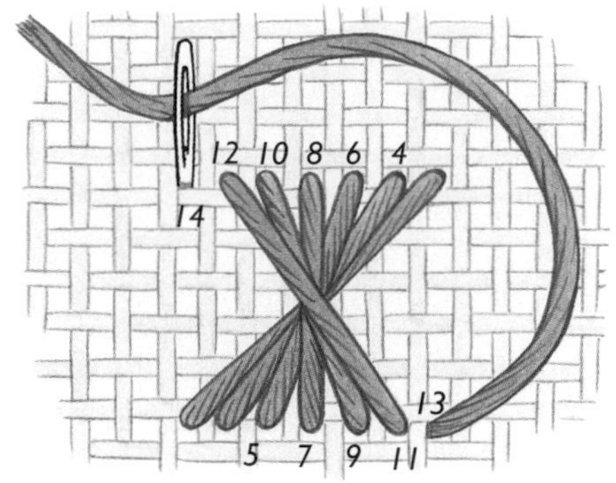

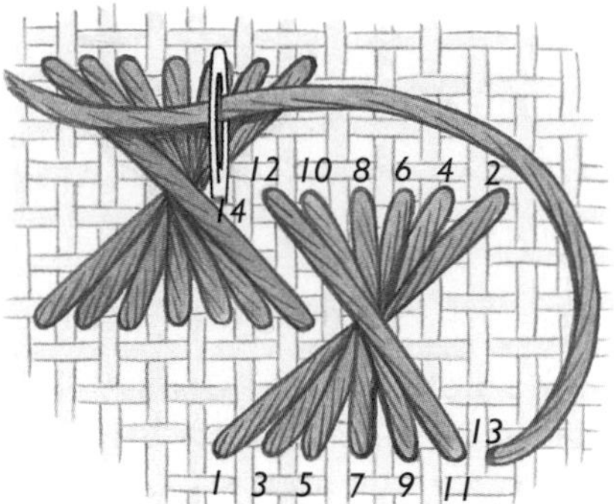

1 Bring the needle to the front at the bottom left at 1. Make a slanting stitch to the right over six horizontal and vertical threads to 2. Bring the needle out at 3, one thread to the right of the base of the first stitch.

2 Following the sequence 4–14, continue in a counterclockwise direction to fill the top and bottom of the square with seven crossing stitches. Work additional blocks of stitches below the first block to make a vertical row.

3 (For clarity, only first block of stitches of previous row is shown.) For next row, bring needle out at 1, three holes below and two holes to left of base of top stitch on previous row. Follow sequence 2–14 to work second block of stitches to interlock with first.

Working plaited Rhodes stitch

Work each stitch in same way as half Rhodes stitch (above), but work over a four-thread square and change the direction of the stitches on alternate rows from counterclockwise to clockwise.

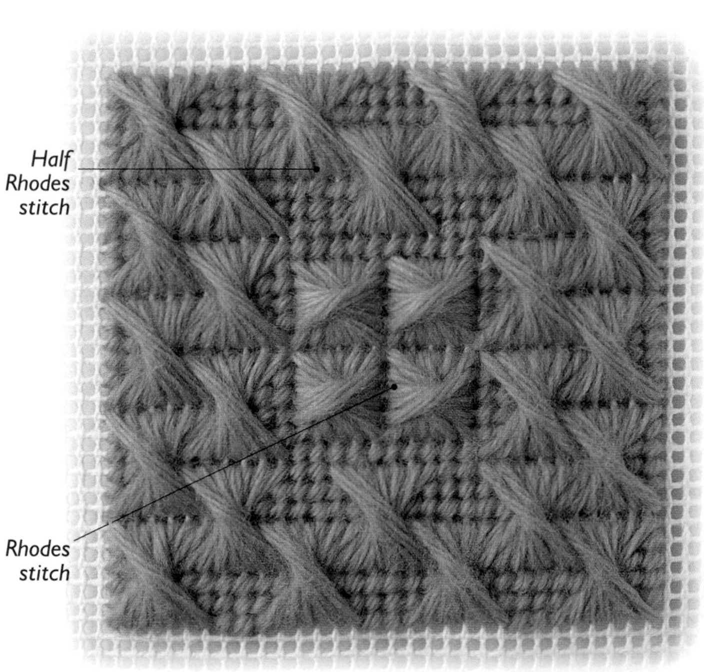

Working octagonal Rhodes stitch

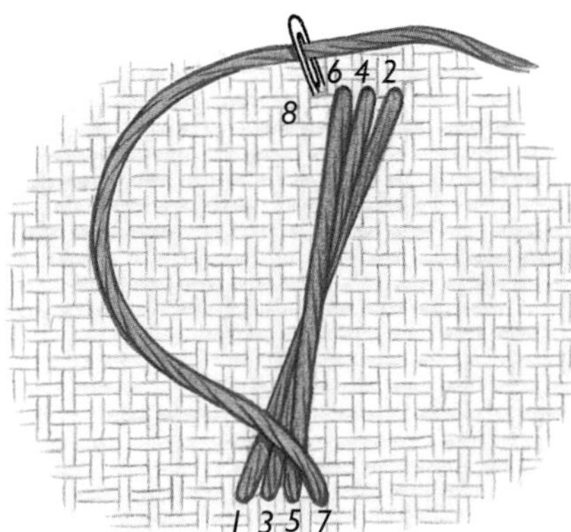

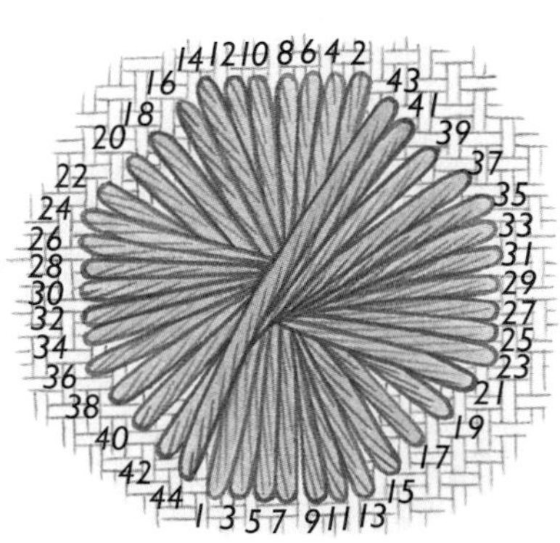

1 Bring needle out at 1 and make a slanting stitch to the right over 16 horizontal and six vertical threads to 2. Bring needle out at 3, and follow the sequence 4–8 for the first four stitches.

2 Working around the octagon in a counterclockwise direction and following the sequence 9–44, work crossing stitches to complete the octagon shape.

3 Repeat steps **1–2** to fill the shape, arranging octagons so that their horizontal and vertical edges meet. Fill in the spaces in between with Rhodes stitch worked on the diagonal.

Victorian crossed stitches

The stitches featured here are all associated with the intricate and highly colored renditions of fruit, flowers, animals, and birds known as Berlin work, which developed during the Victorian period and which is enjoying a revival in popularity. These stitches are used to fill small and large shapes and give a range of interesting textures.

Victorian cross stitch is easy to work. It covers the canvas well and with minimum distortion to create a smooth, hard-wearing surface. The method given below for working the stitch can be used when working from a chart or for stitching a painted canvas. To start this stitch, knot the end of the thread. Leave the knot on the surface of the canvas. As you work the first row, stitch over the thread end at the back. When you reach the knot, trim it off. To fasten off, darn the remaining thread end through the back of several stitches. To start and fasten off the remaining two stitches shown here, refer to page 161.

Victorian tufting creates a thick pile which is ideal for representing both animal fur and birds' plumage. It is a variation of herringbone stitch in which several rows are worked on top of one another. A pile can be formed by cutting the center of the row with scissors. Victorian tufting is a purely decorative stitch suitable only for items that will not need washing.

Velvet stitch creates a smooth, velvety pile which stands out well from a cross-stitched background. To keep the loops of the thread even, slip a pencil or a knitting needle through the loops while working the stitches. When the stitching is complete, the loops can be cut or left intact, depending on the texture you want to create. For the best effect, use soft woolen threads.

Victorian cross stitch

Victorian tufting uncut

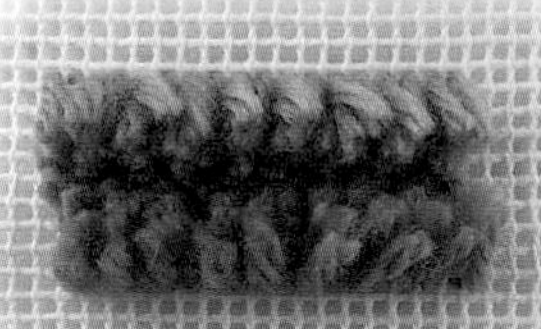
Victorian tufting cut

Velvet stitch uncut

Velvet stitch cut

Working Victorian cross stitch

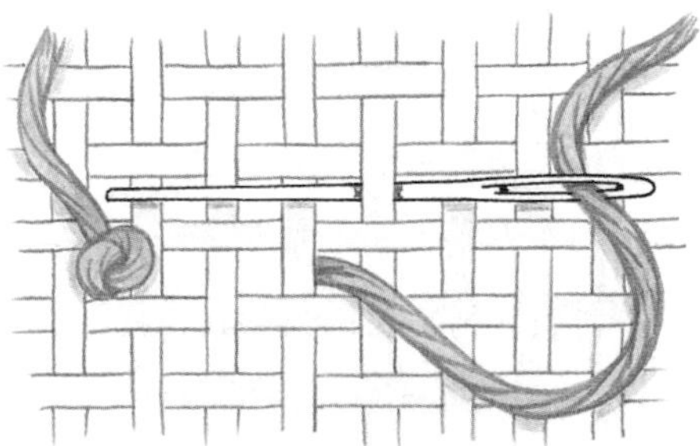

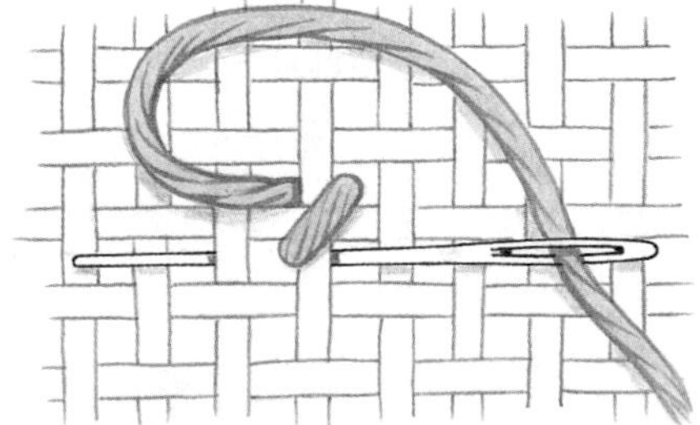

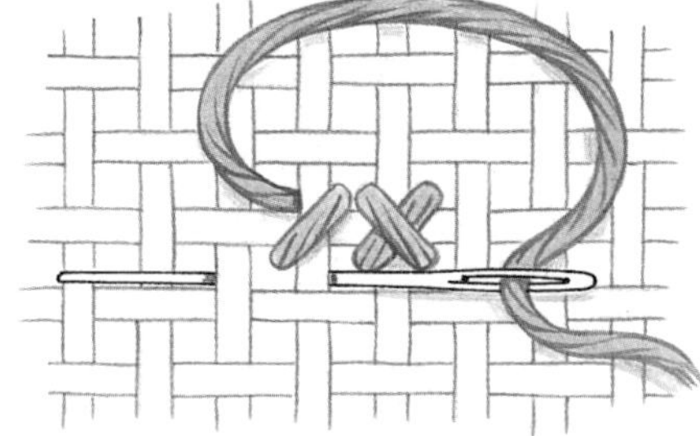

1 Bring the needle to the front one hole in from the right-hand side of the shape. Insert the needle one hole higher up and one hole to the right to make a short diagonal stitch. Bring the needle out one hole to the left.

2 Insert the needle one hole down and one hole to the right to make a second diagonal stitch to cross the first one. Bring the needle through two holes to the left, and pull the thread through, ready to make the next stitch.

3 Insert the needle one hole up and one hole to the right. Bring it out one hole to the left. Insert the needle one hole down and one hole to the right, and bring it out two holes to the left. Continue in this way.

Working Victorian tufting

1 Bring the needle to the front at the left of the shape. Insert it one hole down and two holes to the right. Bring it out one hole to the left. Insert the needle one hole up and two holes to the right. Bring it out one hole to the left. Continue to end of row. Take thread to the back and fasten it off.

2 Bring a length of thread to the front at the left, one hole above previous row. Insert the needle two holes to the right and one below the previous row. Bring it out one hole to the left, and insert it two holes to the right and one hole above the previous row. Continue in this way to the end of the row.

3 Repeat step **2** at least twice, using a new length of thread for each row and making each row of stitches one hole deeper at the top and bottom than those on the preceding row.

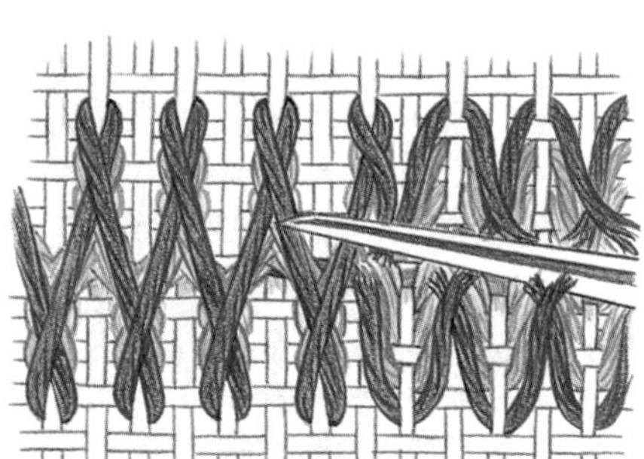

4 When the stitching is complete, carefully cut through the stitches, if desired, right along the center row using a small pair of scissors.

Victorian tufting cut

Working velvet stitch

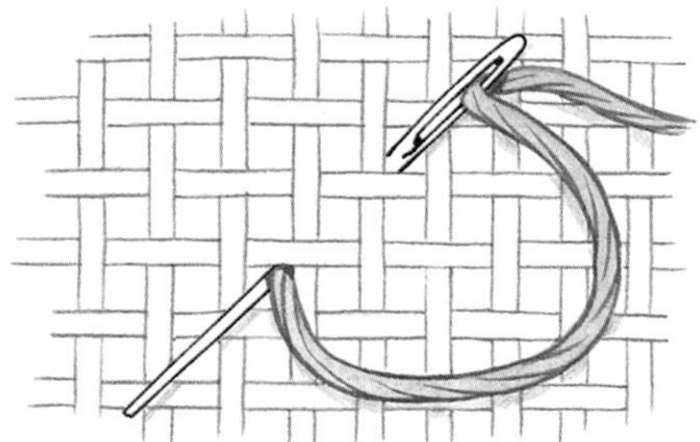

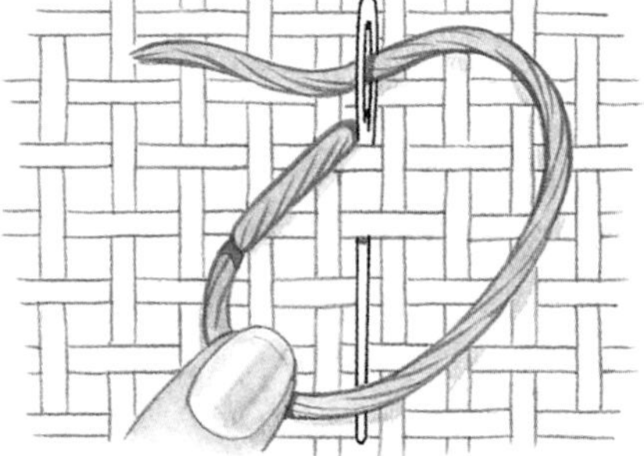

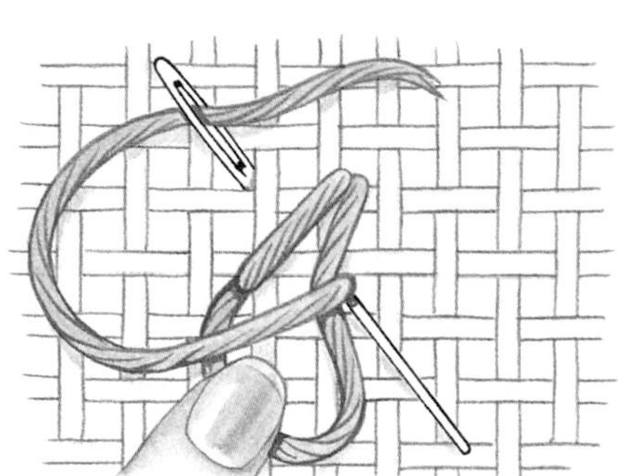

1 Bring the needle to the front at the bottom left of the shape. Insert it two holes up and two to the right. Bring the needle to the front where it originally emerged. Pull the thread through to make a diagonal stitch.

2 Holding the working thread over the needle to make a short loop, make a downward vertical stitch under two canvas threads. Bring the needle through to the front, keeping the loop intact.

3 Make a second diagonal stitch two holes up and two holes to the left, taking the thread over the loop. Bring the needle through at the bottom right of the cross to complete the stitch.

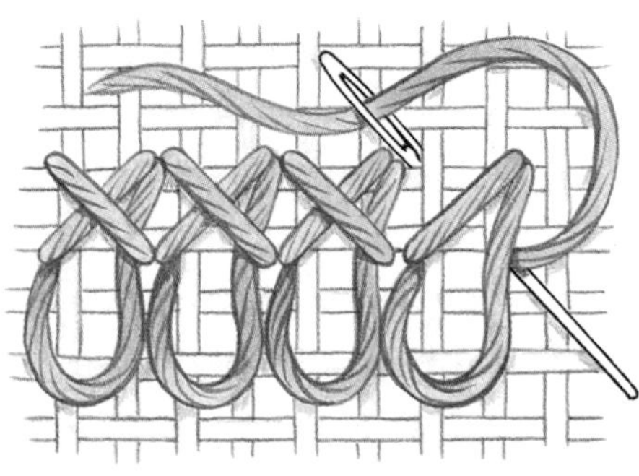

4 Repeat steps **1–3**, to the right of the first stitch, making each loop identical along the row. Work subsequent rows above the first row. If desired, cut the loops with sharp scissors to form the pile.

Velvet stitch uncut

Block stitches

Composite needlepoint stitches are built up in two or more stages to give the finished stitch an interesting surface texture. The stitches featured here are formed by arranging blocks of diagonal straight stitches to create a fascinating play of light and shade over the canvas surface. Three of the stitches have rows or blocks of tent stitch added for contrast. They are used to fill large shapes and make unusual backgrounds.

To start and fasten off any of these stitches, bring the needle to the front, leaving a 2 in. (5 cm) thread end on the back. Work the stitch, covering the loose thread end as you work. Then take the needle to the back and darn it under the last few stitches worked.

Checker stitch

Cushion stitch

Scottish stitch

Crossed corners cushion stitch

Checker stitch is often worked in a single color to make an attractive background, but it can also be worked in two or more colors and types of thread for a bolder look.

Cushion stitch makes a neat, regular pattern of blocks surrounded by a frame of tent stitch. Usually, each block is made up of seven stitches worked over four canvas threads, but you can vary this to make the blocks larger or smaller.

Scottish stitch is worked in exactly the same way as cushion stitch, but looks different, as two colors are used—one for the blocks and a contrasting one for the tent stitch.

Crossed-corners cushion stitch has a crisp, sculpted appearance. It consists of four blocks of diagonal stitches grouped into squares which are then overstitched with triangles.

Working checker stitch

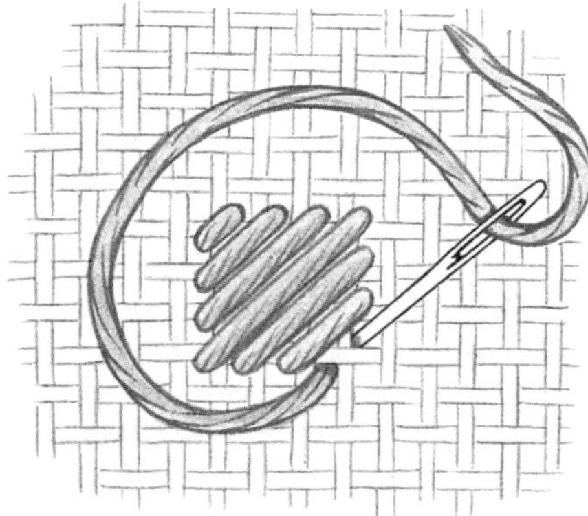

1 Bring the needle to the front at the top left of the shape. Work a block of seven diagonal stitches, slanting upward to the right, over four horizontal and vertical threads.

2 Bring the needle out one hole below and one hole to the right of the base of the last stitch, and work a second, identical block of stitches. Continue in this way, working diagonally across the shape.

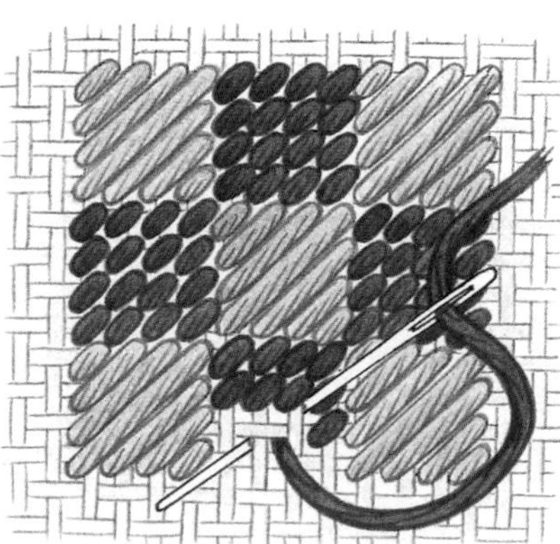

3 Again working in diagonal rows, fill in the gaps with continental tent stitch, referring to page 162.

Working cushion stitch

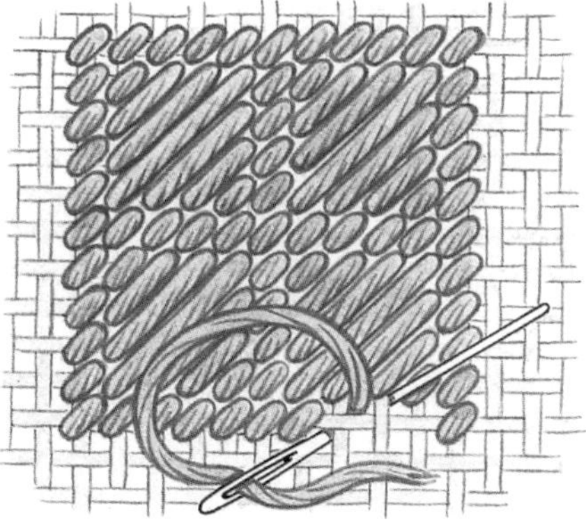

1 Work a block of seven diagonal stitches, following step 1 on the previous page. Work a second block of stitches to the right, leaving one thread between the blocks. Repeat as required to fill the shape.

2 Fill in the gaps between the rows with continental tent stitch (see page 162). When working over a large area, work all the horizontal tent-stitch rows first, then fill in the vertical rows.

Working Scottish stitch

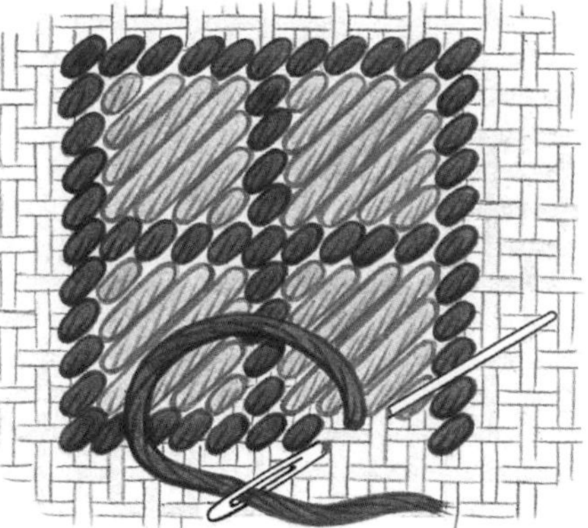

Work in exactly the same way as cushion stitch (left), but use one color of thread to work all the straight-stitch blocks and a contrasting color for the continental tent stitches. Another version of Scottish stitch (or Scotch) stitch omits the tent stitches.

Working crossed-corners cushion stitch

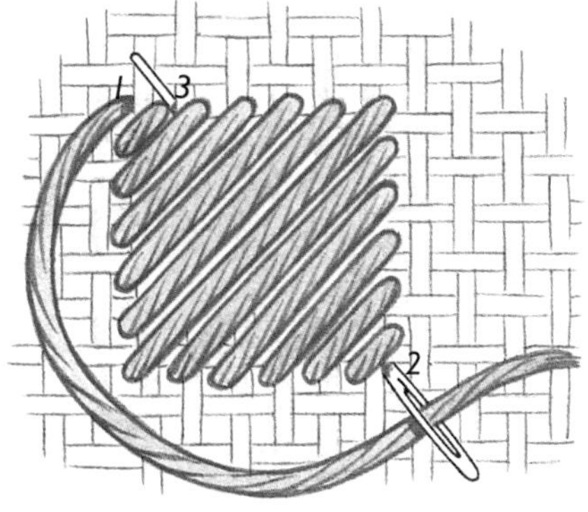

1 Bring the thread to the front at the bottom left of the shape. Work a block of eleven diagonal stitches over six threads, slanted toward top right.

2 Bring the needle to the front, one hole above your starting point at 1. Make a diagonal stitch to the opposite corner at 2 and bring it out at 3.

3 Work a triangular shape of six diagonal stitches over the top of the right half of the square block.

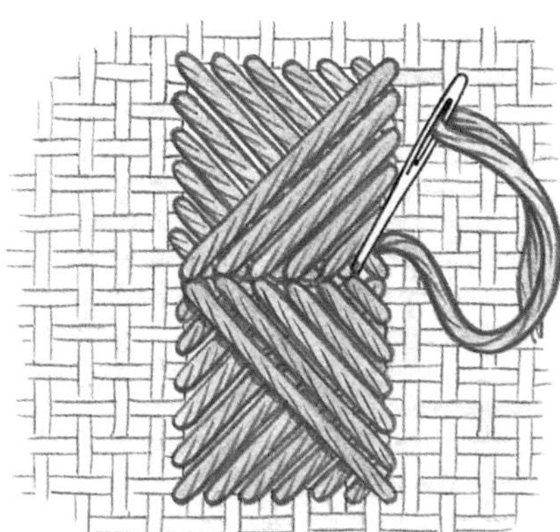

4 Make a second square block of diagonal stitches above the first, but slant the stitches toward the left. Overstitch the bottom right half of the block with a triangular shape.

5 Make two more blocks to the right of the first two to complete one crossed-corners cushion stitch.

Filling stitches

The stitches featured here can all be used to fill areas of any size with attractive textures and patterns. They are built up in two or more journeys, often using two or more thread colors to enhance the pattern.

Stem stitch (also known as canvas stem stitch) looks particularly effective when worked with two different types of thread—a thick one, such as tapestry wool (if appropriate for the mesh size) for the foundation rows, and a thinner one, like a single strand of Persian wool, or brilliant cutwork and embroidery cotton or floss, for the backstitch line running down the center of each row.

Perspective stitch makes a bold, three-dimensional pattern. When it's worked in wool, it is fairly hard-wearing and can be used on stool and chair covers. It is worked in four journeys, usually in two colors. Take care when mixing it with other stitches—the pattern is so dominant that it can overwhelm more subtle stitches.

Rapid stitch is ideal for background areas. It can be worked in either one or two colors—use one color for the foundation crosses and a contrasting color for the V shapes over the top.

Stem stitch

Rapid stitch

Perspective stitch

Working stem stitch

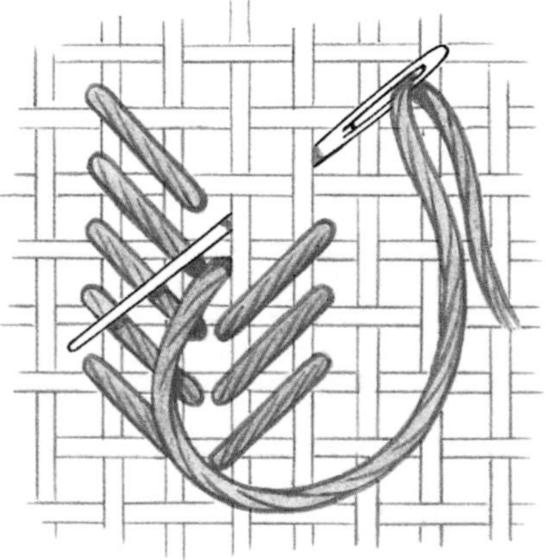

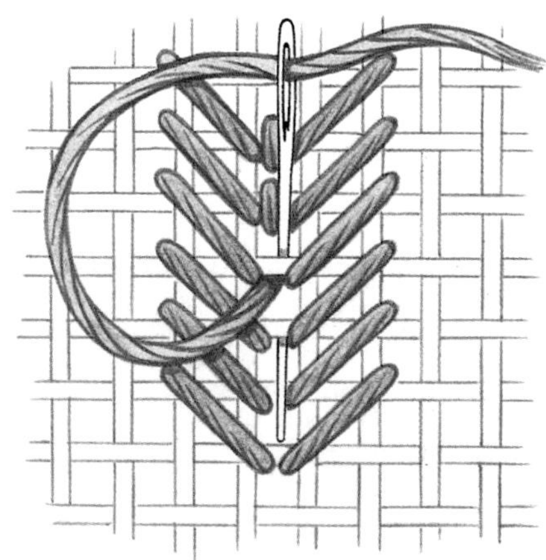

1 Bring the needle through at the top left and work a row of diagonal stitches down the canvas; make each stitch over two canvas intersections and slant the stitches up to the left.

2 At the bottom of the row, bring the needle out at the base of the last stitch worked. Work a second row of diagonal stitches next to the first, slanting the stitches up to the right.

3 Using the same or a contrasting thread, backstitch between the two diagonal rows, working one stitch over every horizontal thread. If using a contrasting thread, add these stitches after completing all the diagonal rows across the shape.

Working perspective stitch

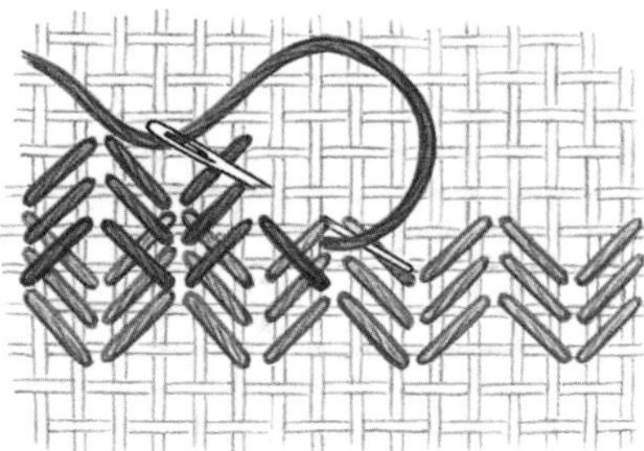

1 Bring the thread to the front at the top left of the shape. Work three diagonal stitches, slanting upward to the right and making each stitch over two canvas intersections.

2 Work a second group of three diagonal stitches to the right of the first group, slanting the stitches downward. Repeat the two groups of stitches across the row. Then, leaving the needle and thread at the back, turn the canvas around.

3 Secure a second thread at the left, and work a group of three diagonal stitches, overlapping the stitches on the first row. Work a second group to the right. Continue in this way across the row. Leave the needle and thread at the back and turn the canvas around.

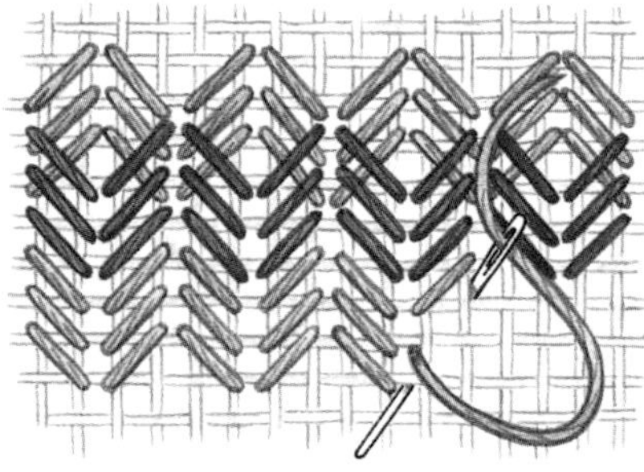

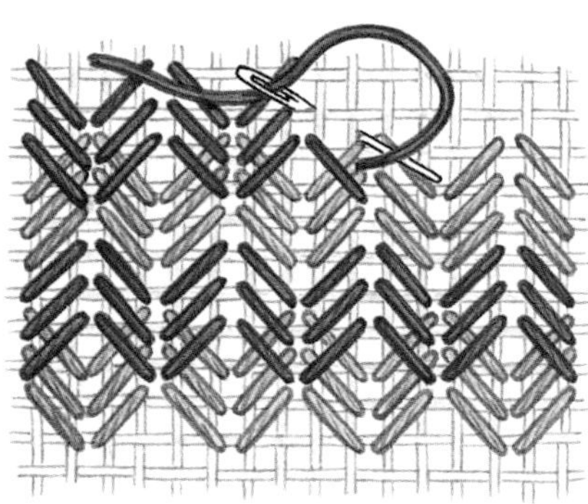

4 Bring the first thread to the front and work groups of three diagonal stitches directly below the preceding row and with the same slant. At the end of the row, leave the needle and thread at the back and turn the canvas.

5 Bring the second thread through. Work groups of three stitches slanting in the opposite direction to the groups on the row just worked. The stitches in this row overlap those underneath. Leave the thread at the back and turn the canvas. Repeat the four journeys to fill the shape.

Working rapid stitch

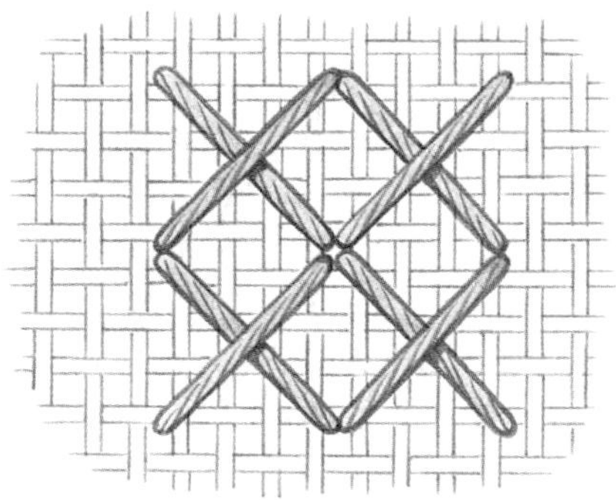

1 Work cross stitch across the area to be filled (see page 185), but make each stitch over four vertical and horizontal threads.

2 Bring a contrasting thread to the front at the top left. Work four diagonal stitches to form two V shapes over each cross stitch.

Radiating filling stitches

The three stitches featured here share a fanlike structure. Although they look rather complex, they are surprisingly straightforward to work. They produce interesting, densely worked effects on the canvas and can be worked in more than one color.

When working any of these stitches, complete each individual stitch before moving on to the next one. Ray stitch and foliage stitch are both block-shaped and should be worked alongside one another in straight horizontal rows. Fan stitches, with their more complex shape, need to be fitted together with care.

To start and fasten off any of these stitches, see page 199.

Foliage stitch makes a delicate leaf-shaped pattern on the canvas and is always worked in horizontal rows from left to right. It makes a good background stitch and looks particularly effective when a variegated thread is used.

Foliage stitch

Ray stitch

Fan stitch

Ray stitch is very attractive and makes a densely worked textured surface. It is very hard-wearing, particularly when worked in a durable yarn such as Persian wool. It is shown here worked with seven stitches over a three-thread block. For faster coverage of the canvas, it can be worked over larger blocks by adding more radiating stitches.

Fan stitch, also known as fantail stitch, creates a strong pattern of large, fan-shaped motifs. It can be used as a filling or as single motifs. Used as a filling, it looks best when the first row is centered within the shape to be filled. It makes an unusual background but needs to be used carefully, as the pattern is so dominant that it can completely overwhelm more subtle stitches.

Working foliage stitch

1 Start at the top left-hand corner of the shape. Work three vertical stitches over four, three, and two threads. Then, at right-angles to these stitches, work three horizontal stitches over two, three, and four threads. Bring the needle out at the bottom left-hand corner of the block.

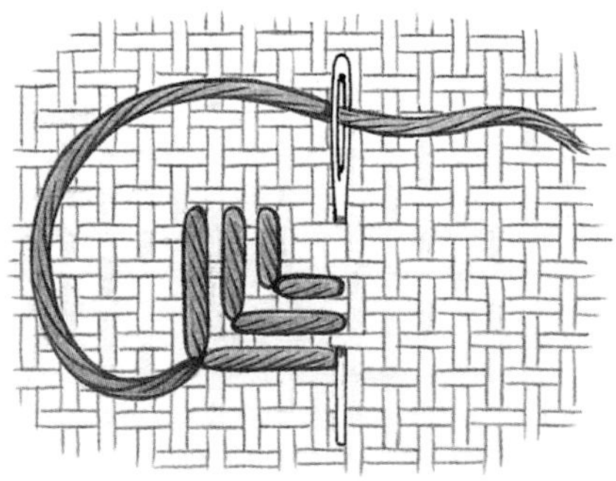

2 Work a long diagonal stitch right across the block to make the central vein of the leaf. Bring the needle through at the bottom right-hand corner of the block, ready to make the next block in the row.

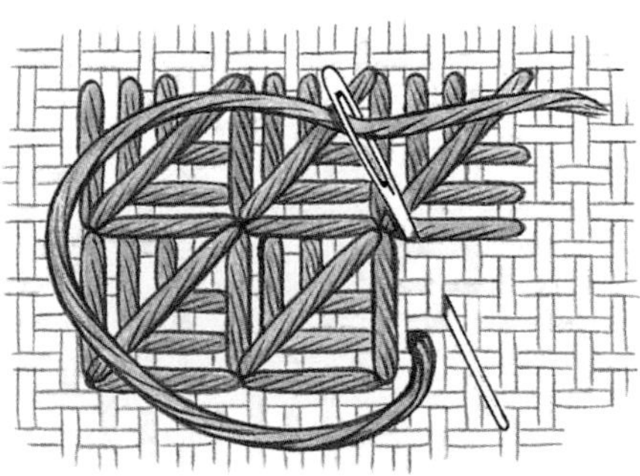

3 Repeat steps **1–2** across the row. At the end of the row, either fasten off the thread on a long row or darn it back under the stitches on the wrong side to bring it into position on the left, ready for the next row.

Working ray stitch

1 Bring the needle out to the front at the top left of the shape to be filled. Working over a three-thread block, make seven straight stitches radiating from the same hole at the bottom left-hand corner of the block. Repeat along the row.

2 At the end of the row, change direction and work the next ray stitch so the seven stitches radiate from the bottom right-hand corner of the block. Repeat along the row, and arrange subsequent rows so the stitches change direction on every row.

3 To achieve a flatter and less textured effect, work all the radiating stitches so they follow the same direction.

Working fan stitch

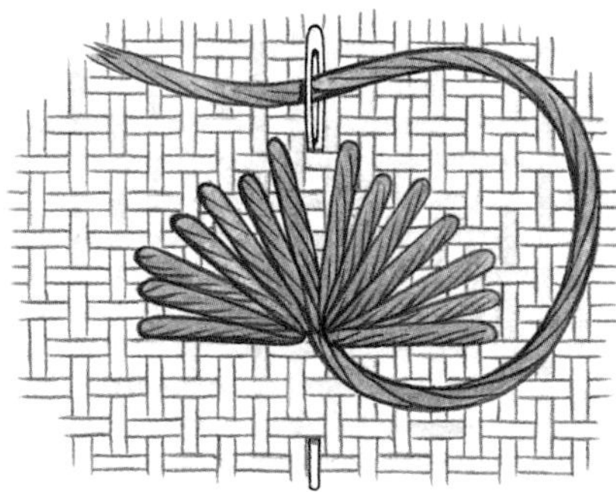

1 Start near the top of the shape in the center. Work the top section of the fan shape, which spans ten vertical and five horizontal canvas threads. Begin at the bottom left and make fifteen straight stitches of graduated lengths radiating from the same hole; finish with the center stitch. Bring the needle out three threads below.

2 Work a group of five radiating stitches spanning four vertical and two horizontal canvas threads. Bring the needle to the front two threads below the base of the group. Finally work a vertical stitch over two threads below the five-stitch group.

3 Work additional fan motifs directly below the first to make a vertical row. At the end of the row, either fasten off the thread on a long row or darn it back under the stitches on the wrong side to bring it into position for the next row.

4 Work additional vertical rows of fan stitch at either side of the central row, arranging them so the bottom stitches of the fan shape share the same hole as the bottom of the upright stitches at the base of each fan.

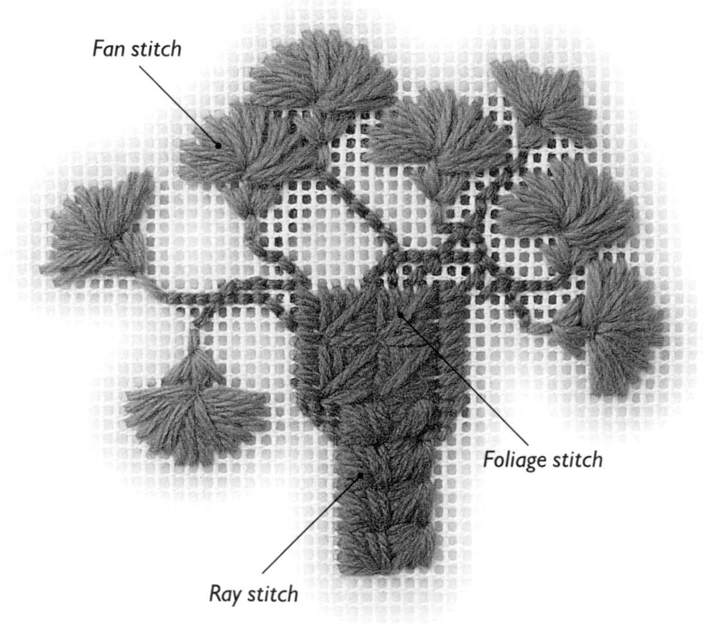

Tied stitches

The composite stitches in this section combine vertical straight stitches with short horizontal ones. The short stitches tie the vertical stitches to the canvas and pull them into a curved shape to make a boldly textured surface.

Most composite stitches are worked over two or more journeys, but each stitch in this collection is finished completely before you move on to work the next one. Although the stitches look quite complex, they are relatively easy to work provided you follow the stitch sequences carefully. When working the vertical stitches, particularly the two outer stitches on rococo and long rococo stitch, make sure that when you pull the thread through, you leave enough "give" to draw the stitches into a smooth curved shape.

All the stitches, particularly the rococo stitches, use a lot of thread but give good canvas coverage.

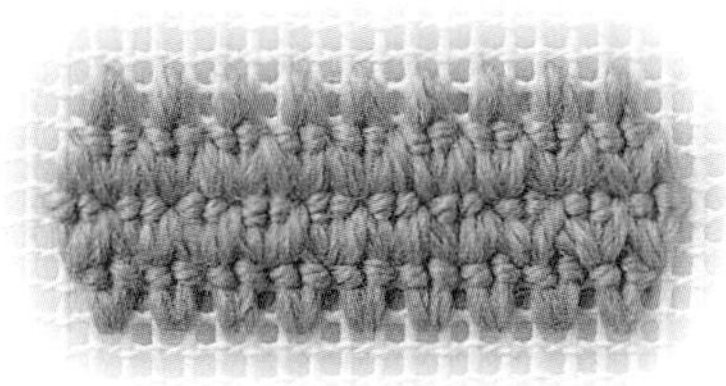

French stitch

Rococo stitch

Long rococo stitch

The stitches are all worked in horizontal rows, with the second and subsequent rows fitting into the spaces left on the lower edge of the previous row.

To start and fasten off these stitches, see page 199.

French stitch is made up of two vertical stitches which are tied down at the center point.

Rococo stitch was very popular in the 18th century. It creates a more textured surface than French stitch, with a larger pattern. The stitches are formed in a similar way but are made up of four vertical stitches instead of two.

Long rococo stitch is also made up of four similar stitches, forming a diamond shape. It is usually worked in two colors to accentuate the pattern.

Working French stitch

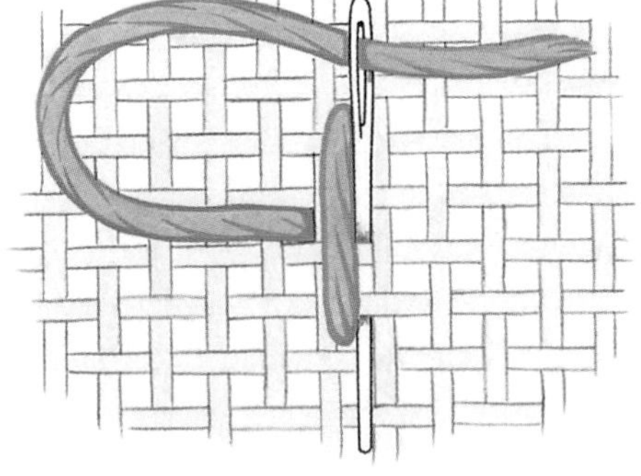

1 Start near the top left. Make a vertical straight stitch over four canvas threads, bring the needle out one thread to the left of the center of this stitch and work a horizontal stitch over one thread. Bring the needle out at the base of the first stitch.

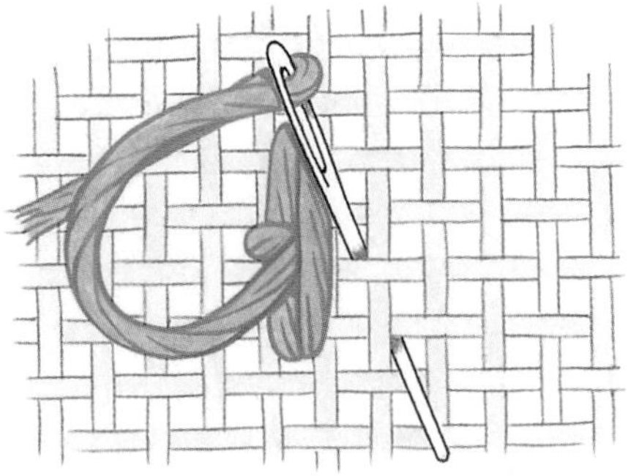

2 Work an identical tied stitch to the right of the first stitch to complete the first French stitch, then bring the needle out again two threads to the right of the base of both stitches, ready to work the next stitch.

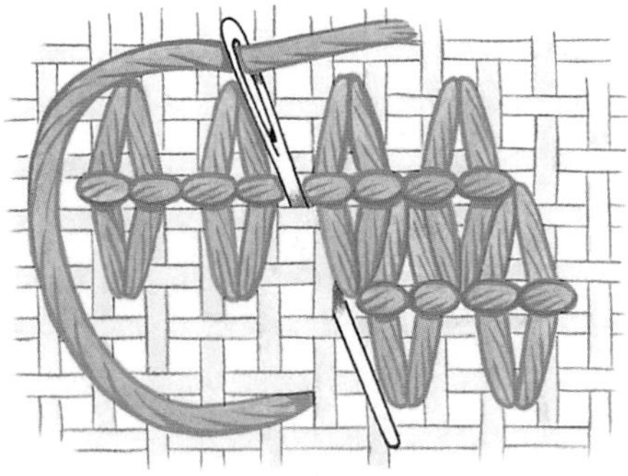

3 Repeat the French stitches along the row, making sure that the tying stitches touch. Work the second and following rows directly below the first row, arranging the stitches so that they fit between those worked on the previous row.

Working rococo stitch

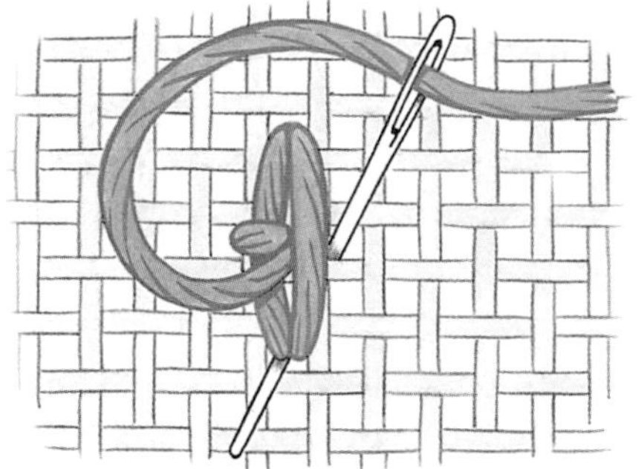

1 Start toward the top left of the shape. Referring to the previous page, make a French stitch over four canvas threads, then bring the needle out at the base of the stitch.

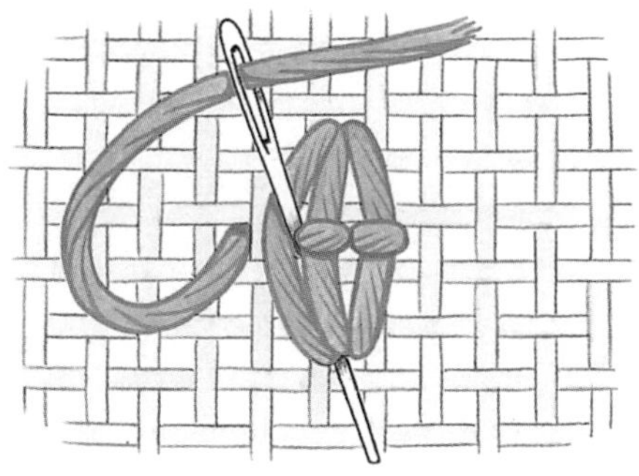

2 Work a third tied stitch to the left of the French stitch, then bring the needle out at the base of the stitch.

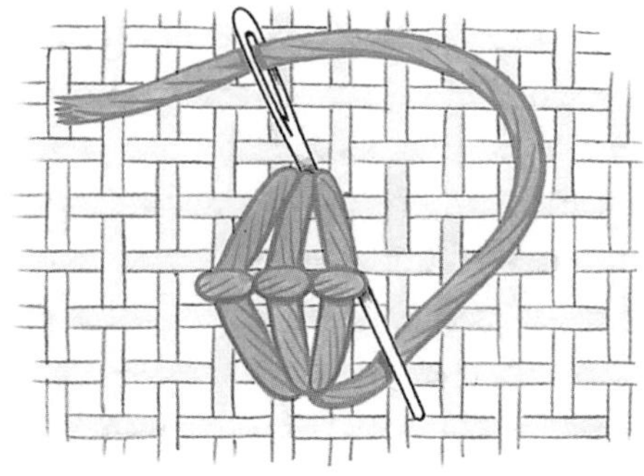

3 Work a fourth tied stitch to the right of the French stitch to complete the first rococo stitch.

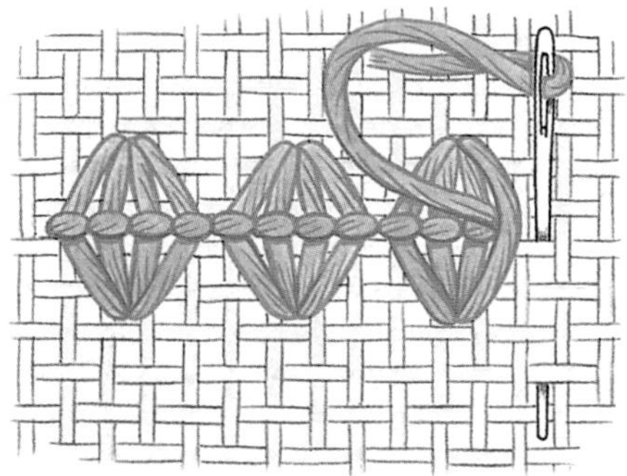

4 Repeat the rococo stitches along the row, spacing the bases of the stitches four threads apart. At the end of the row, bring the needle through four threads below the last tying stitch.

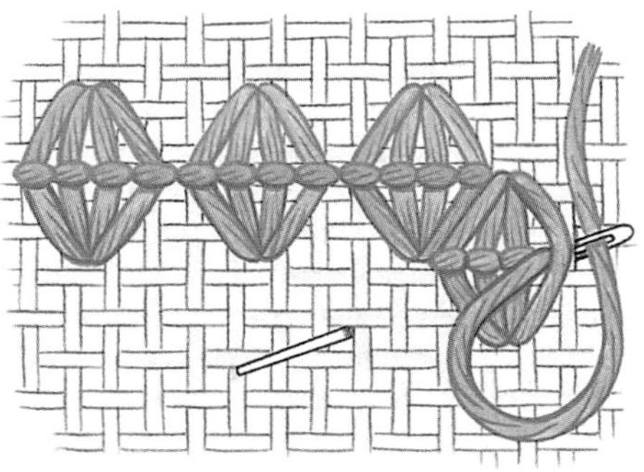

5 Repeat the rococo stitches from right to left along the row, arranging the stitches so they fit between those worked on the previous row. Repeat to fill the shape.

Working long rococo stitch

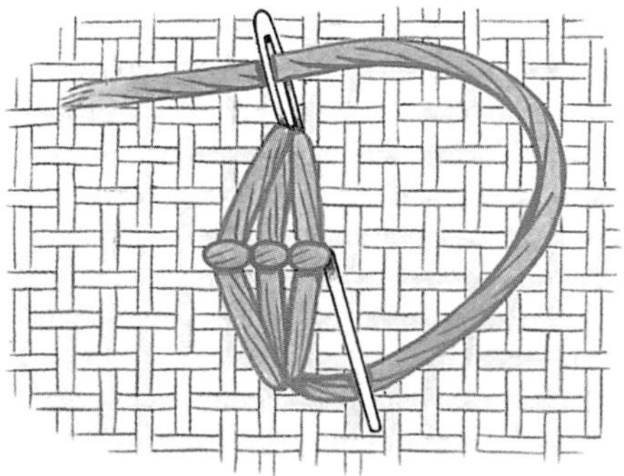

1 Start at the top left of the shape. Referring to the steps above, make a rococo stitch six canvas threads tall. Repeat along the row, leaving a space of four canvas threads between the base of each stitch.

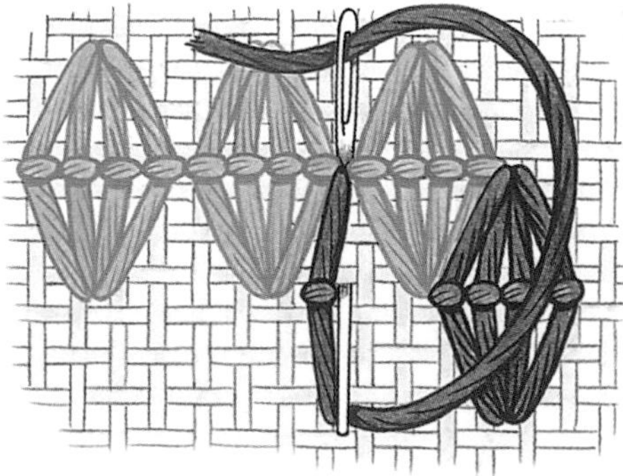

2 At the end of the row, secure the second thread and bring the needle out six threads below the last tying stitch. Repeat the stitches from right to left along the row, as above, then alternate rows worked in the two colors to fill the shape.

Maple Leaves

The rich color palettes of Japanese maple leaves are the inspiration for these gorgeous pincushions and an elegant tieback.

You Will Need

For the tieback:

- 10-count tan Penelope canvas, 28 x 10 in. (70 x 25 cm)
- DMC tapestry wools as listed in the color key
- Tapestry needle, size 20
- Scroll frame
- Lining fabric
- Basting and sewing thread
- Two D-rings

Color Key

COLOR	SKEINS
7002 Dusky pink	1
7057 Mustard	1
7058 Pale mustard	1
7060 Brown	1
7147 Wine red	2
7296 Dark blue	6
7361 Pale yellow-green	2
7363 Yellow-green	1
7376 Moss green	1
7446 Orange-brown	2
7690 Pale blue	1
7746 Cream	1
7758 Old rose	2
7920 Burnt orange	1

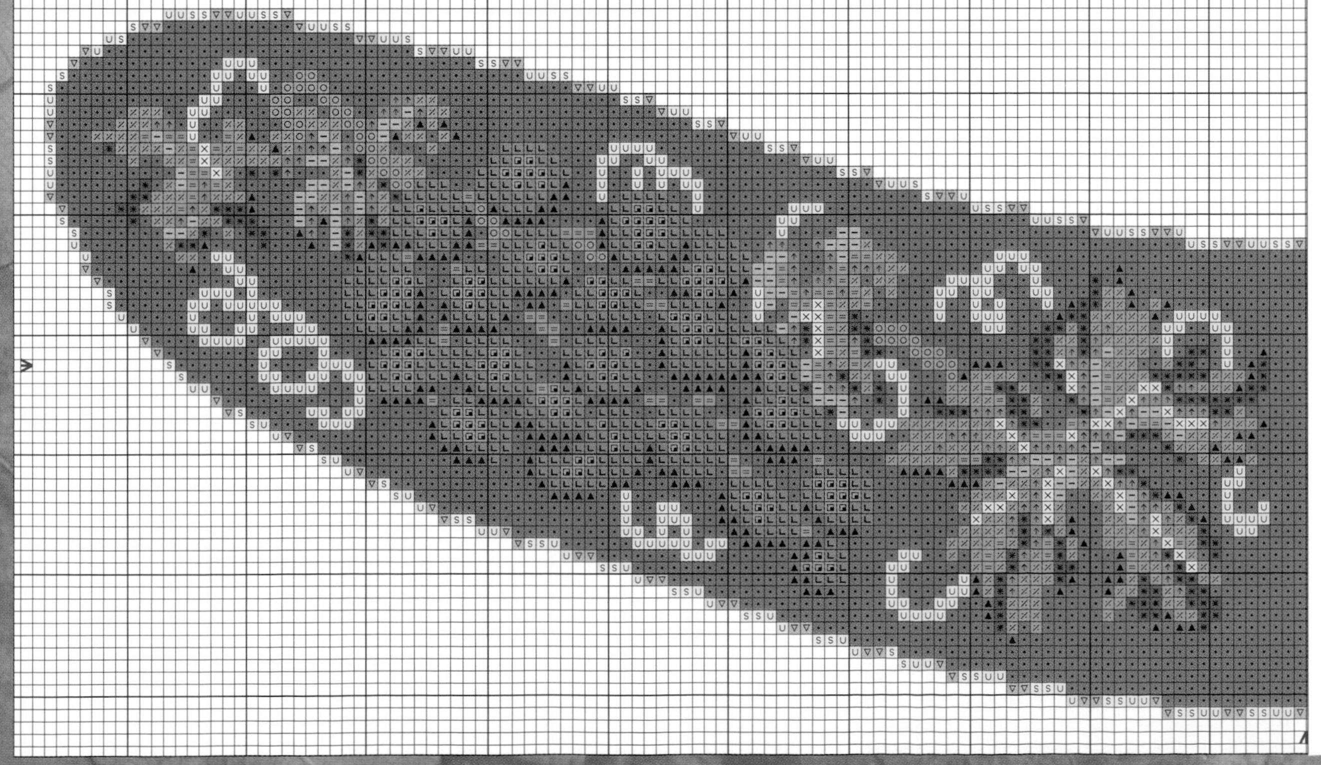

The rich, exotic colors and attractive grape and leaf motif of this needlepoint tieback make it a fitting complement for traditional-style draperies. The design is backed with matching lining fabric and finished with D-rings. The fabric and yarn quantities given here are enough to make one tieback. The finished item is 22 in. (56 cm) long and 4 in. (10 cm) wide.

Preparing the canvas

Referring to pages 19 and 20, mark the center of the canvas with lines of basting; bind the edges with masking tape and mount the canvas in the scroll frame.

Working the design

Work the design using continental tent stitch (see page 162). One square on the chart represents one stitch worked over one pair of canvas threads. Refer to the key for yarn colors.

Starting at the center of the design, stitch the leaf motifs first, using burnt orange, orange-brown and wine red for the outer area, and mustard, pale mustard, moss green, and yellow-green for the centers. Next, work the grape motifs, using wine red and old rose and dusky pink at the centers. Work the small leaf motifs surrounding the grapes, then work the pale yellow-green tendrils. Then fill in the background in dark blue, and finish with the border worked in stripes of cream, pale blue, and pale yellow-green.

Finishing

Take the canvas out of the frame and place it face down on a clean white towel. Steam-press it from the back. If the canvas is very distorted, block it to shape, referring to pages 303 and 304.

Assembling the tieback

Cut a 28 x 10 in. (70 x 25 cm) piece of lining fabric. Place the needlepoint and the fabric together with right sides facing. Baste around the outer edges about 3/8 in. (1 cm) away from the stitching. Machine stitch along the edge of the needlepoint, leaving an opening of about 6 in. (15 cm) along the bottom edge.

Trim the seam allowances to 3/8 in. (1 cm). Snip the seam allowances so they will lie smoothly when the tieback is turned right side out. After turning, slipstitch the opening edges together. At each end, sew a D-ring to the wrong side, about 3/8 in. (1 cm) in from the top edge.

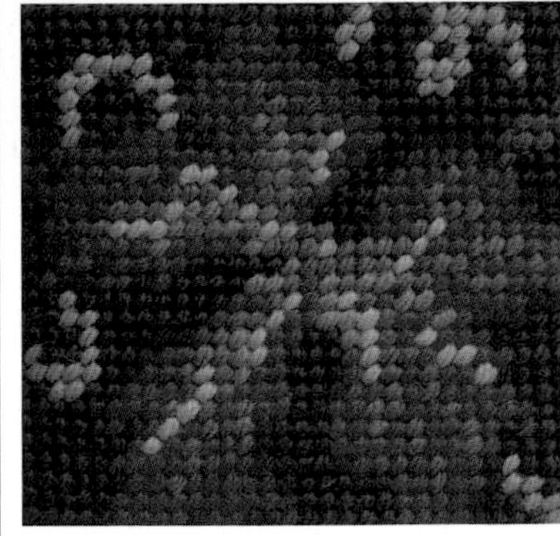

The center of each leaf is worked in mustard and pale mustard, highlighting the moss green veins and complementing the orange-brown and burnt orange outer edges.

To create the effect of light and shadow, the tops of each grape are picked out in dusky pink and the lower edges are worked in wine red.

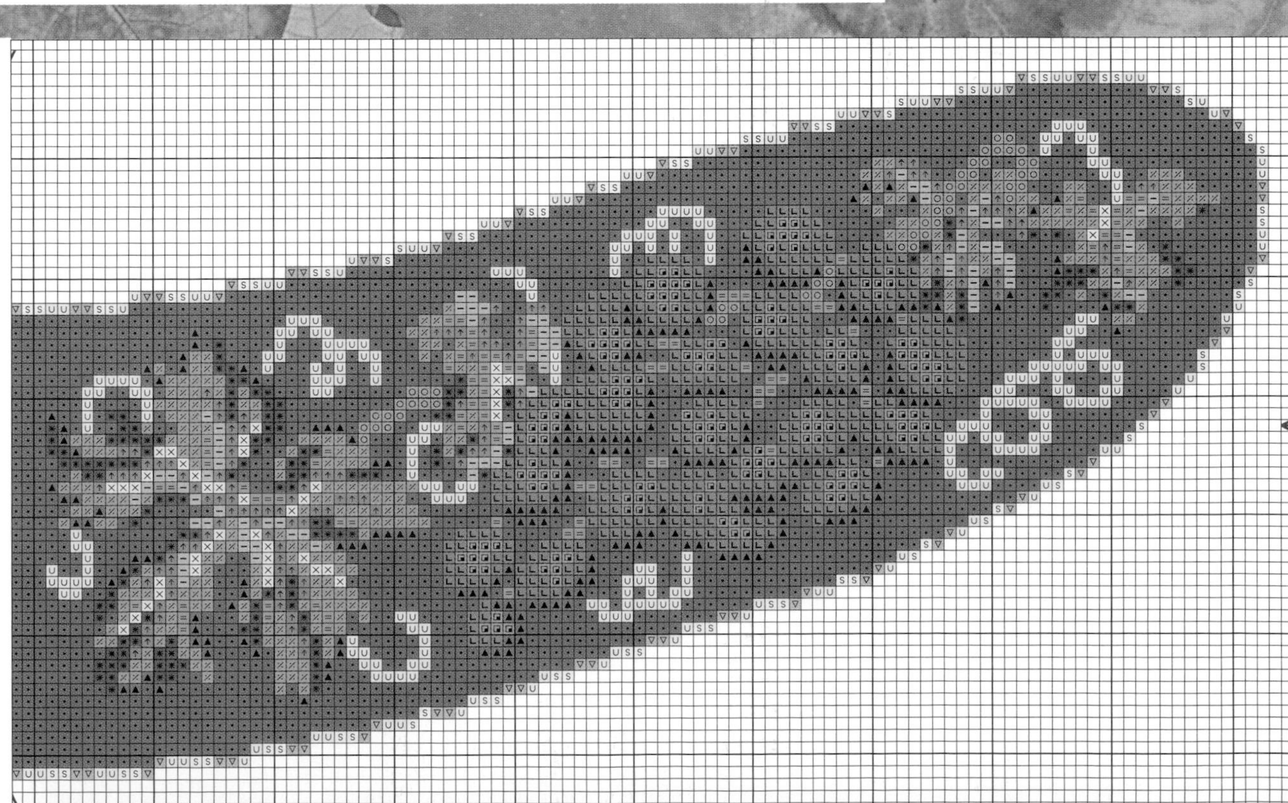

You Will Need

For each pincushion:

- 10-count tan Penelope canvas, 6 in. (15 cm) square
- DMC tapestry wools as listed in the color key
- Backing fabric, 5 in. (13 cm) square
- Sewing needle and matching thread
- Thread for basting
- Stuffing

Blue Color Scheme

Symbol	Color	
–	7057 Mustard	1
×	7058 Pale mustard	1
○	7060 Brown	1
▲	7147 Wine red	1
•	7296 Dark blue	1
U	7361 Pale yellow-green	1
=	7363 Yellow-green	1
↑	7376 Moss green	1
⁄	7446 Orange-brown	1
▽	7690 Pale blue	1
S	7746 Cream	1
✳	7920 Burnt orange	1

Cream Color Scheme

Symbol	Color	
–	7057 Mustard	1
×	7058 Pale mustard	1
○	7060 Brown	1
▲	7147 Wine red	1
U	7361 Pale yellow-green	1
=	7363 Yellow-green	1
↑	7376 Moss green	1
⁄	7446 Orange-brown	1
S	7746 Cream	1
✳	7920 Burnt orange	1

Pincushions

The maple leaf design is so versatile that it can be used over and over again. Here just a single maple leaf, surrounded by a square border, is stitched on canvas and made into a handy pincushion. There are two different color schemes to choose from, each using a selection of yarns from the tieback design. Each pincushion measures 3¾ in. (9.5 cm) square.

Working the Design

Decide which color scheme you wish to stitch. Referring to the appropriate chart and color key, work the design from the center out using continental tent stitch (see page 162). One stitch on the chart represents one stitch worked over one pair of canvas threads. Work the leaf motif first, then the background. Finish by stitching the striped border. To stitch this, work two stitches in each color in rotation all around the outer edge of the background color. (If you have chosen to stitch the cream color scheme, you may prefer to use different colors.)

Stitched inside a cream background, the leaf motif stands out from the needlepoint and is the focus of the design.

Finishing

Block the stitched piece, if necessary (see page 209), or press it gently on the wrong side using a damp cloth and a medium-hot iron. Place the stitched piece and the backing fabric together with right sides facing, and baste around the edges. Machine stitch along the edge of the needlepoint along three sides of the pincushion. Trim the seam to just under ⅜ in. (1 cm) and clip across the corners. Turn the pincushion right side out, and fill it with stuffing. Slipstitch the opening edges together with matching thread.

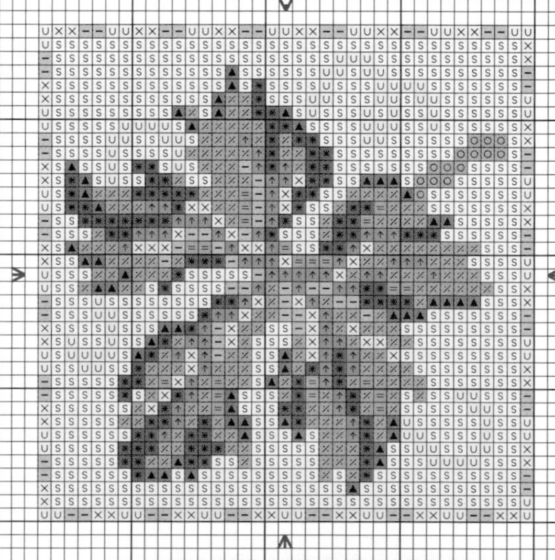

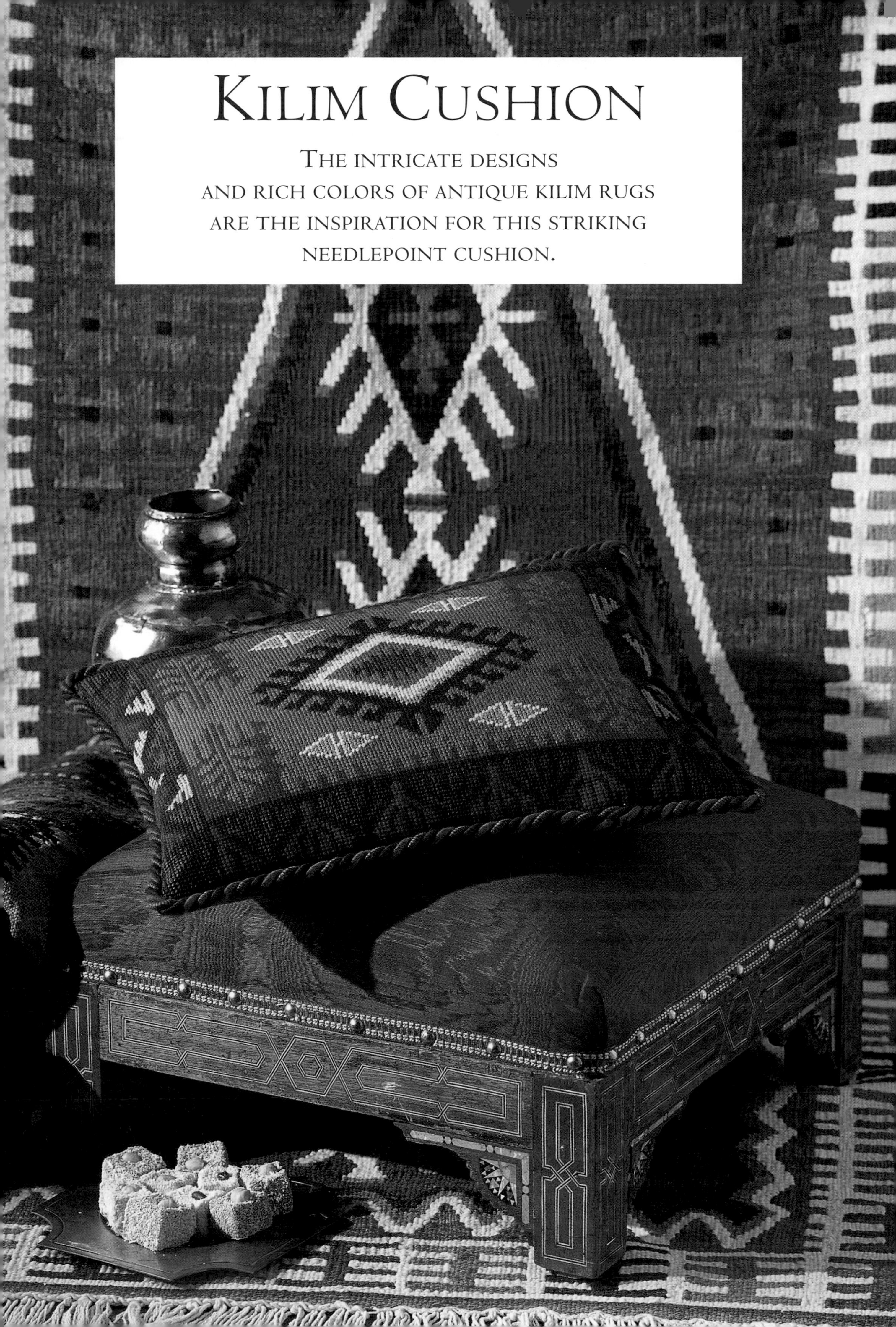

KILIM CUSHION

THE INTRICATE DESIGNS AND RICH COLORS OF ANTIQUE KILIM RUGS ARE THE INSPIRATION FOR THIS STRIKING NEEDLEPOINT CUSHION.

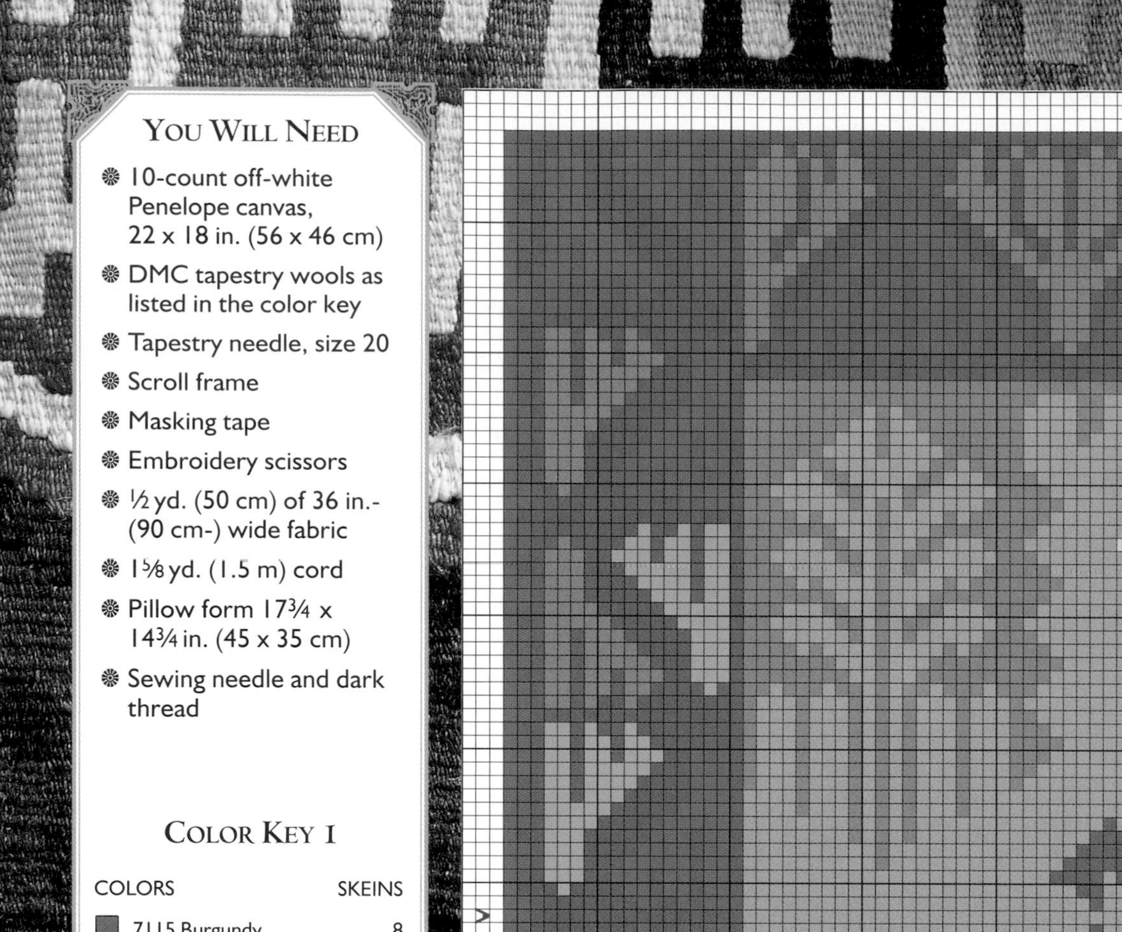

You Will Need

- 10-count off-white Penelope canvas, 22 x 18 in. (56 x 46 cm)
- DMC tapestry wools as listed in the color key
- Tapestry needle, size 20
- Scroll frame
- Masking tape
- Embroidery scissors
- ½ yd. (50 cm) of 36 in.- (90 cm-) wide fabric
- 1⅝ yd. (1.5 m) cord
- Pillow form 17¾ x 14¾ in. (45 x 35 cm)
- Sewing needle and dark thread

Color Key 1

COLORS	SKEINS
7115 Burgundy	8
7184 Terracotta	6
7226 Rose pink	8
7288 Deep sea blue	4
7503 Straw	1
7927 Sea green	2

The rich colors of this needlepoint design, and its two alternative color schemes (see page 214), reflect the muted shades of antique kilim rugs. Backed with matching fabric and trimmed with coordinating two-tone cord, the finished piece makes a lovely cushion cover.

Preparing the canvas

Bind the edges of the canvas with masking tape, then fold it in half both ways to find the center point. Mark with basting stitches. Mount the canvas onto the scroll frame, fixing the center points on each side first, and working outward toward the corners.

Working the design

Work your chosen color scheme using tent stitch throughout (see page 162) and referring to the appropriate chart and the color key. One square on the chart represents one stitch, and the color key shows where the various yarns are used. Starting at the center, work the central motif. For the first color scheme, start with deep sea blue, then rose pink, straw, and sea green. Continue stitching until the diamond shape and burgundy surround are complete. Work the four pairs of small triangles in sea green and straw, the rose pink inner background and the terracotta edging. Then stitch the border motifs in terracotta, sea green, and deep sea blue, and the border background in burgundy to complete the piece. For color schemes two and three, follow the same order of stitching.

Finishing

Take the canvas out of the frame and block it to shape (see page 303). Leave to dry. To assemble the cushion cover, trim the canvas around the needlepoint panel to 1 in. (2.5 cm), then refer to pages 307 and 308 for instructions for completing the cover. Use the needlepoint panel for the front of the cover and matching fabric for the back.

Inspirations

The cushion is inspired by kilim rugs made in Turkey, where each district has its own distinctive patterns. The medallion design comes from villages surrounding Konya, in southern Turkey.

Kilim Color Scheme 2

Color Key 2

COLORS	SKEINS
7377 Dark green	4
7384 Light green	2
7446 Russet	7
7448 Plum red	8
7503 Pale yellow	8

Kilim Color Scheme 3

Color Key 3

COLORS	SKEINS
7127 Brick red	4
7271 Beige	6
7311 Blue	2
7384 Light green	1
7420 Soft lemon	8
7595 Turquoise blue	8

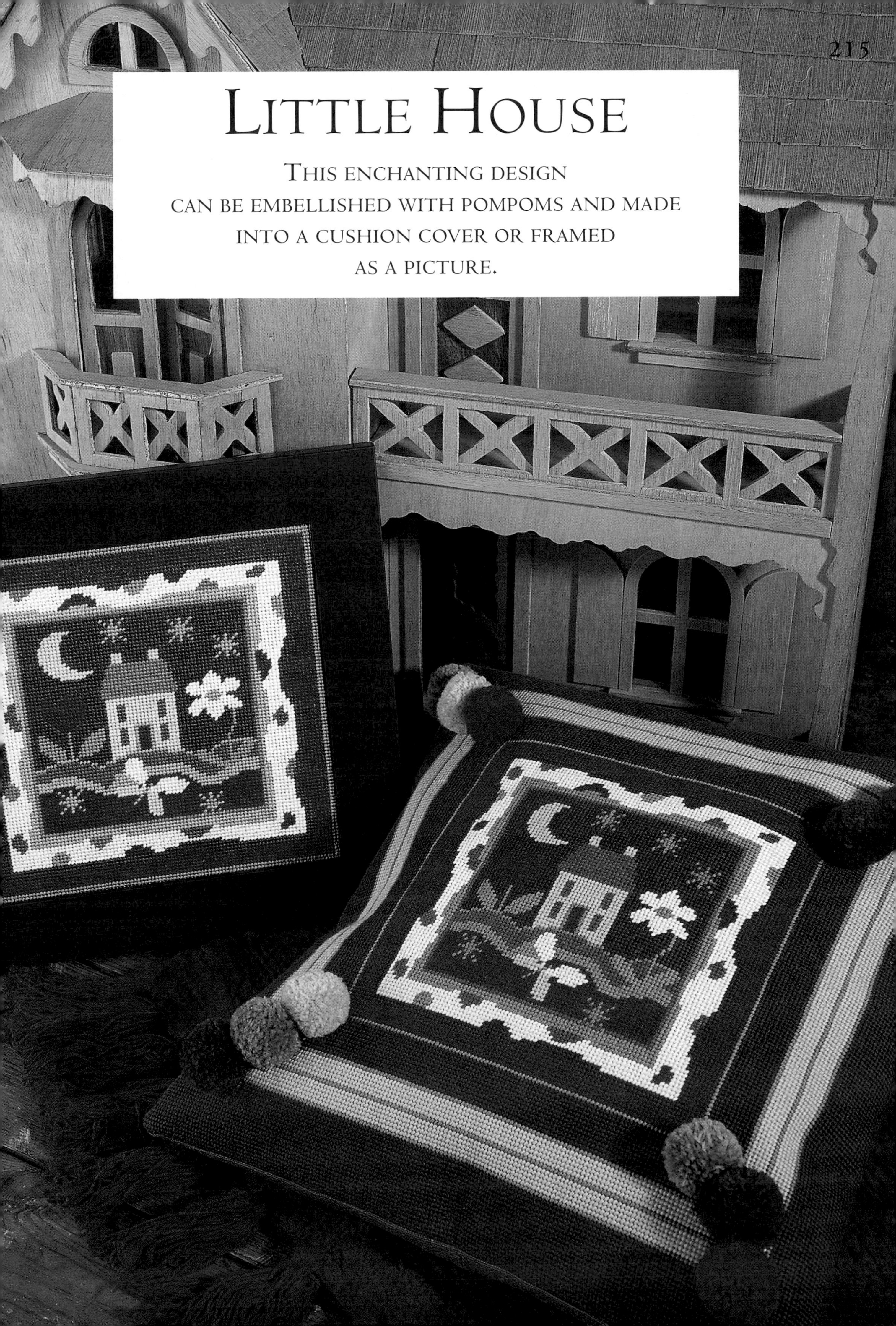

LITTLE HOUSE

THIS ENCHANTING DESIGN CAN BE EMBELLISHED WITH POMPOMS AND MADE INTO A CUSHION COVER OR FRAMED AS A PICTURE.

This fairytale scene of a little house far away on a hill has a childlike simplicity. The house is small, yet surrounding it are giant flowers and an oversized moon and stars. The design is stitched in just a few bright colors to add to its naive charm.

The photograph on page 215 shows the cushion worked in tapestry wool and the picture in pearl cotton. You can work the design in either type of thread, but tapestry wool will produce a softer effect, better suited to a cushion.

The finished cushion cover with its pompoms and striped border is 15 in. (38 cm) square, and the picture is 8 in. (20 cm) square.

Preparing the canvas

Mark the center of the canvas with basting, cover the raw edges with masking tape, then mount the canvas on the frame, following the instructions on page 20.

Embroidering the cushion

Work the design from the center outward, referring to the charts and the appropriate key for your chosen thread. Use basketweave tent stitch throughout (see page 163). One square on the charts represents one stitch worked over one canvas thread.

Follow Chart One to stitch the house, flowers, moon, stars, and butterfly, and to fill in the hill and sky. Work the bands of color around the design, stitching one color at a time; for the cream band, stitch the dots first.

After working Chart One, follow Chart Two (page 218) to stitch the outer borders and the corners; don't stitch the inner green border—this is a positioning guide. Rotate the chart 90 degrees to work each corner, and fill in the areas between, following the repeats.

Chart One

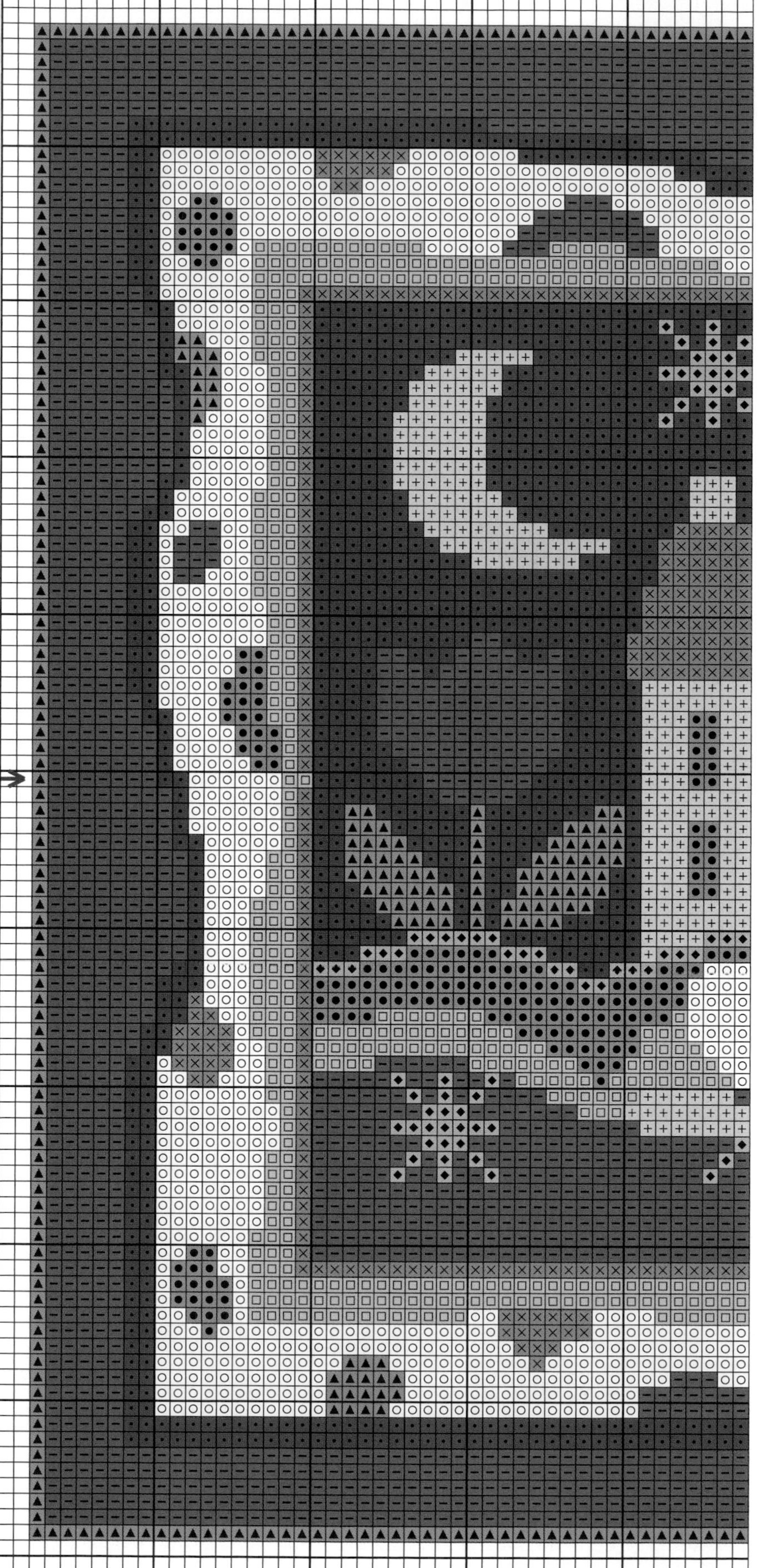

You Will Need

- 12-count white mono canvas, 20 in. (51 cm) square (cushion only)
- DMC tapestry wool as in the key (cushion only)
- ½ yd. (45 cm) of decorator fabric (cushion only)
- Sewing needle and thread
- Thread
- Masking tape
- Scroll frame
- Tapestry needle, size 20
- Pillow form, 15 in. (38 cm) square (cushion only)
- Stiff cardboard for pompoms
- 12 extra skeins of wool for the pompoms (cushion only)

(For picture, see page 218.)

Color Key

COLORS	SKEINS
Tapestry wool	
7026 Mauve	1
7030 Blue	16
7042 Emerald	2
7058 Yellow	4
7342 Green	2
7782 Mustard	1
7905 Cream	2
7920 Red	4
7922 Orange	1
Number 3 pearl cotton (for picture)	
349 Red	2
552 Mauve	1
702 Emerald	1
703 Green	1
725 Yellow	1
745 Cream	1
792 Blue	2
922 Orange	1
977 Mustard	1

Finishing

Steam-press the work gently from the wrong side. If it is distorted block it to shape (see page 303).

Making the pompoms

Using the extra skeins of thread, make twelve 1¼ in. (3 cm) diameter pompoms (see page 315). Neatly trim the pompoms.

Making the cushion cover

Assemble the cushion cover following the instructions on pages 307 and 308. Sew three pompoms in each corner.

Working the picture

You will need materials as for the cushion cover, substituting/adding: 12-count white mono canvas, 13 in. (33 cm) square; DMC no. 3 pearl cotton (see key, page 217); posterboard 8 in. (20 cm) square; heavy-duty thread and needle for lacing.

Work the picture as for the cushion cover, following Chart One and the appropriate key. When complete, stitch an extra row of emerald all around the piece. Frame the design yourself (see pages 305 and 306), or take the piece to a professional framer.

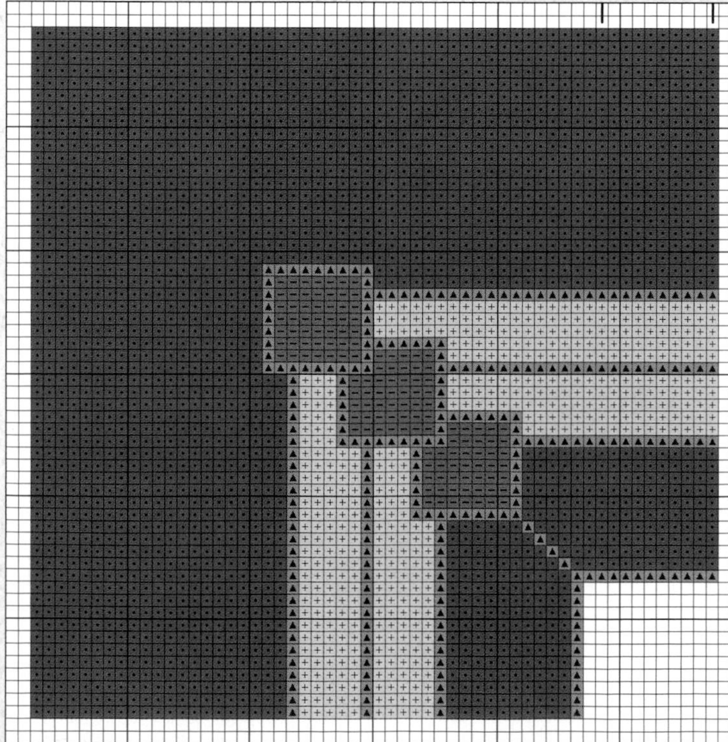

Chart Two

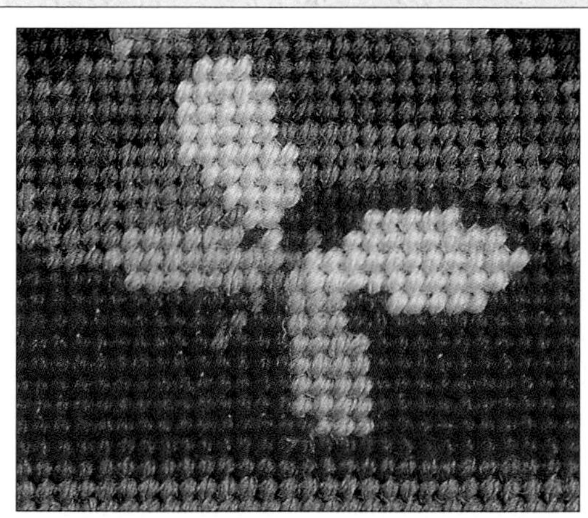

The giant butterfly is stitched using cream for the upper wings and yellow for the lower wings. The body is picked out in mustard.

Summer

This peaceful scene of a harborside village evokes memories of summer vacations and is easily worked in straight stitch.

You Will Need

- 18-count white interlock canvas, 12 in. (30 cm) square
- Tapestry needle, size 22
- DMC embroidery floss as listed in the color key
- Scroll frame
- Indelible embroidery marker
- Masking tape
- Embroidery scissors
- Heavy-duty thread and needle for lacing

Color Key

COLORS	SKEINS
B5200 Brilliant white	2
318 Medium gray	1
319 Dark green	1
336 Navy blue	1
368 Pale green	1
422 Pale gold	1
517 Medium turquoise blue	2
535 Dark gray	1
721 Orange	1
729 Gold	1
742 Yellow	1
775 Pale blue	1
813 Medium blue	1
898 Dark brown	1
993 Jade green	1
3024 Stone	1
3778 Pale terracotta	1
3815 Medium green	1
3830 Terracotta	1

In this summer scene the view is drawn out over a sandy bay fronted by cottages. Boats are sailing, woolly clouds drift overhead, and a large seagull rests on the windowsill. Inside the house a vase of sunflowers adds a splash of color. The picture is given a three-dimensional effect by the open window on the right.

The design is worked almost entirely in straight stitches: a French knot is used to suggest the seagull's eye. Instead of following a chart, the method here is to transfer the design to the canvas with the embroidery marker, then fill in the color areas with vertical, horizontal, or diagonal stitches. The finished picture is about 7 x 6¾ in. (17.5 x 17 cm).

The cheerful sunflowers brighten up the interior of the house. They are worked in 721, 742, 3830, and 898.

Preparing the canvas

Place the design on a work surface and center the canvas over the top of it. (Interlock canvas is required for this project to prevent the long stitches from slipping under the canvas threads.) Use the indelible embroidery marker to trace the outlines onto the canvas.

Bind the edges of the canvas with masking tape to prevent the embroidery floss from catching on the threads. Mount the canvas on the frame (see page 20).

Working the design

Work the design from the center outward using the trace pattern, the photographs, and the key as a guide to placing colors. Use straight stitch (see page 165) for all areas except the seagull's eye; embroider this with a French knot (see page 77). Work with all six strands of floss unless instructed otherwise. To get the best coverage on the canvas, separate the strands of floss and reassemble them; for more details, refer to page 10.

Work all the stitches vertically, with the following exceptions which are worked horizontally: the open window, the vertical sides of the blue window frames, and the vertical sides of the white interior wall, except for the band across the top of the picture where the windows are arched. Make diagonal stitches for the boat stays. Where two colors meet, make sure that the stitches share the same canvas hole.

Stitch beyond the marked outer edge of the picture so that the edges of the stitching will not show when the piece is mounted and framed.

Through the center window

Stitch the boat hulls in 517 and 3830, work the sails in 3778, and stitch the masts in 535; work the diagonal stitches over the straight stitches using just three strands of 535. Fill in the sea with 813. Use 535 and 318 for the pier.

Embroider the eye with a French knot using three strands of 535. Use 729 for the beak and B5200 for the areas of white. Work the patch on the throat, the chest, and the upper wing in 318. Use 535 for the tail.

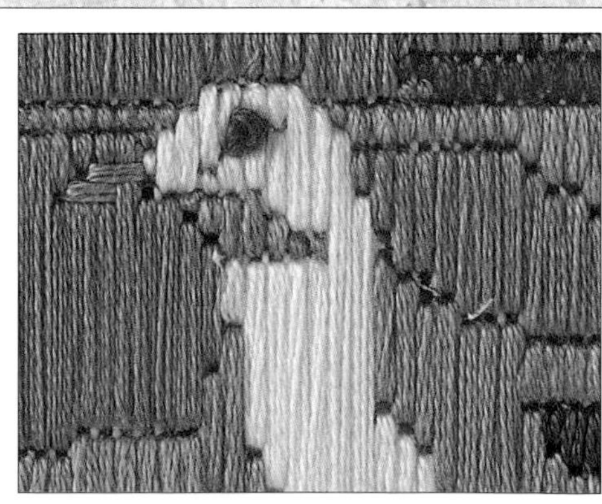

Work the sand in 729 and 422. Use 318, B5200, 729, and 535 for the seagull; make the eye with a French knot and three strands of 535. Work the grass around the bay in 368 and 3815, and the path in 3024. Stitch the balcony in 993. Use 775 and B5200 for the sky.

THROUGH THE LEFT WINDOW
Stitch the sea, sky, grass, sand, path, and balcony as before. Work the white cliff in B5200.

THROUGH THE RIGHT WINDOW
Work the sea, sky, grass, sand, path, and balcony as before. Stitch the open window in 517 and 336. Use 3778 to work the steps leading down the beach. Create the cottages by the sea front in B5200, 535, 775, 422, 3778, 3830, and 318. Use 368 for the hill behind the cottages.

THE INTERIOR
Stitch the sunflower heads in 721, 742, 3830, and 898. Use 319 and 3815 for the leaves. For the pot, use 3830 and 3778. Work the window frames in 517. Finally, fill in the wall with B5200.

FINISHING
Take the completed work off the frame and press it gently from the wrong side. If it is distorted, block it to shape (see page 303). Mount the picture on stiff posterboard (see page 306, steps 5–9), or have this done by a professional framer.

NOTE: If you prefer, you could work this design in tent stitch—though this would, of course, take much longer, and require more thread. Try a small sample to compare the effect this produces.

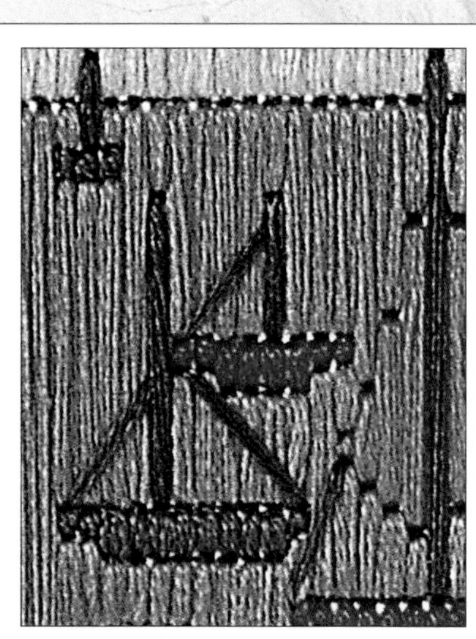

Diagonal stitches in 535 are used to create the boats' stays. Work the stitches over the vertical stitches.

Hunting Scene

A pedigree hunting dog
is depicted in rich,
vibrant colors on this
needlepoint cushion.

You Will Need

- 10-count white mono canvas, 14 in. (35 cm) square
- 12 in. (30 cm) of decorator fabric
- DMC tapestry wools as listed in the color key
- Tapestry needle, size 18
- Sewing needle
- Thread for basting
- Masking tape
- Scroll frame
- Sewing thread to match the fabric
- Pillow form, 10 in. (25 cm) square

Color Key

COLORS	SKEINS
Half cross stitch	
U 7228 Plum	2
● 7288 Deep blue	5
▲ 7303 Dark rust	3
I 7326 Turquoise	1
+ 7360 Rust	1
■ 7408 Dark green	1
– 7494 Tan	3
× 7505 Yellow	1
□ 7724 Beige	5
· 7746 Cream	3
Ⅰ 7833 Golden brown	1
○ 7861 Bright turquoise	1
Gobelin stitch	
⁄ 7303 Dark rust	

This elegant needlepoint design was inspired by an Elizabethan hunting scene. It depicts a stylized dog, perfectly poised, wearing a jewel-encrusted collar. Typical of Elizabethan tapestry and needlepoint, the dog is set in a deep blue background filled with pansies, daffodils, and violas.

The design is worked in half cross stitch and Gobelin stitch and measures 10 in. (25 cm) square. It is shown here made into a cushion to tie to the back of a chair.

Preparing the Canvas

Fold the canvas in half horizontally and vertically and mark the center with two lines of basting. Bind the raw edges with masking tape

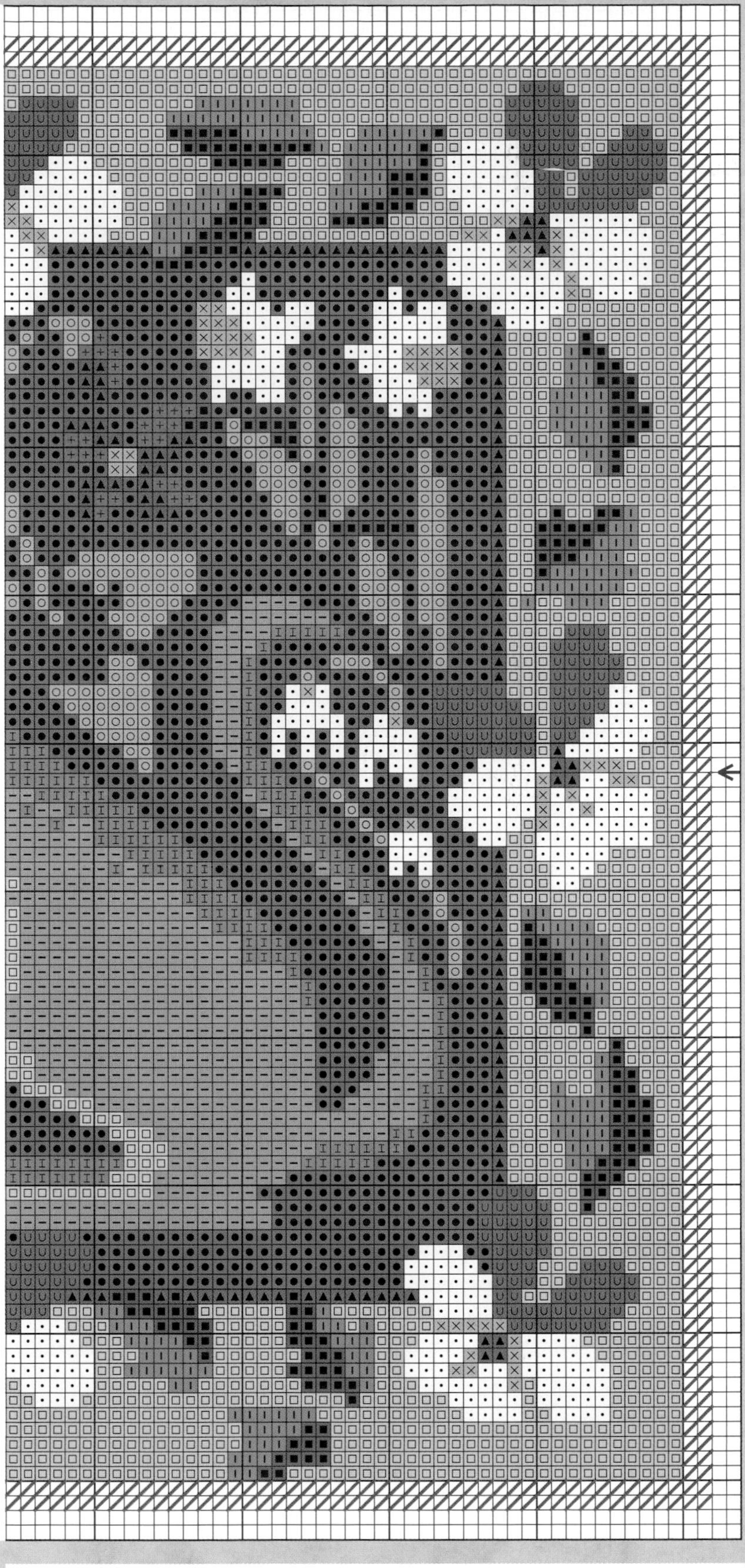

The daffodil petals are stitched in cream, and the trumpets are worked in yellow.

The plum-colored collar is encrusted with amber gemstones.

The beige outer border is decorated with violas and leaves.

and mount the canvas on the frame (see page 20).

WORKING THE DESIGN

Work the design from the center outward in half cross stitch (see page 162), following the chart and the key. One square on the chart represents one stitch worked over one canvas thread.

Begin with the dog. Next stitch the daffodils and pansies surrounding it, then fill in the deep blue background. Stitch the violas and leaves in the beige border, and work the narrow band of deep rust. To complete the design, fill in the areas of beige, then work a row of Gobelin stitch all round using deep rust.

Finishing

Take the work off the frame and steam-press it. If it is distorted block it to shape (see page 303).

Assembling the cushion

Cut four 12 x 3½ in. (30 x 9 cm) strips of decorator fabric for the ties. Fold each one in half lengthwise with the right sides and raw edges matching. Stitch the long edge and one short edge, taking a ⅜ in. (1 cm) seam. Trim the seams, turn right side out and press. Topstitch just inside each edge.

Trim the canvas ⅝ in. (1.5 cm) outside the stitching. Cut a square of the decorator fabric to match.

Lay the needlepoint right side up. With the raw edges matching, pin two ties 1 in. (2.5 cm) in from each edge of the stitching at the top of the canvas. Place the decorator fabric right side down on top, sandwiching the ties in between. Stitch around the top and sides taking a ⅝ in. (1.5 cm) seam. Snip across the corners, turn right side out; press. Insert the pillow form. Slipstitch the open edges.

Flora & Fauna

Charming, naive images of flowers, leaves, birds, snails, and butterflies, arranged in repeating bands, enliven this simple seat pad.

You Will Need

- 12-count tan mono canvas
- DMC tapestry wools as listed in the color key
- Tapestry needle, size 18
- Sewing needle and thread for basting
- Masking tape
- Scroll frame
- Materials to cover a seat pad (see page 309)

Color Key

COLORS	SKEINS
Tent stitch	
Ecru	18
7021 Pale mauve	6
7028 Pale blue	6
7598 Green	3
7599 Pale green	6
7746 Cream	18
7798 Blue	3
7896 Lilac	3
Gobelin stitch	
7021 Pale mauve	
7028 Pale blue	
7599 Pale green	
Cross stitch	
7598 Green	
7798 Blue	
7896 Lilac	

Cool pastel colors are used for this neatly arranged collection of garden plants and creatures—a perfect complement to the simple lines of the chair. Two of the framed motifs, worked in floss, could be used as pictures.

The cover can be made to any size. The skein quantities givem are enough for a $19^1/4$ x $17^3/4$ in. (49 x 45 cm) rectangle.

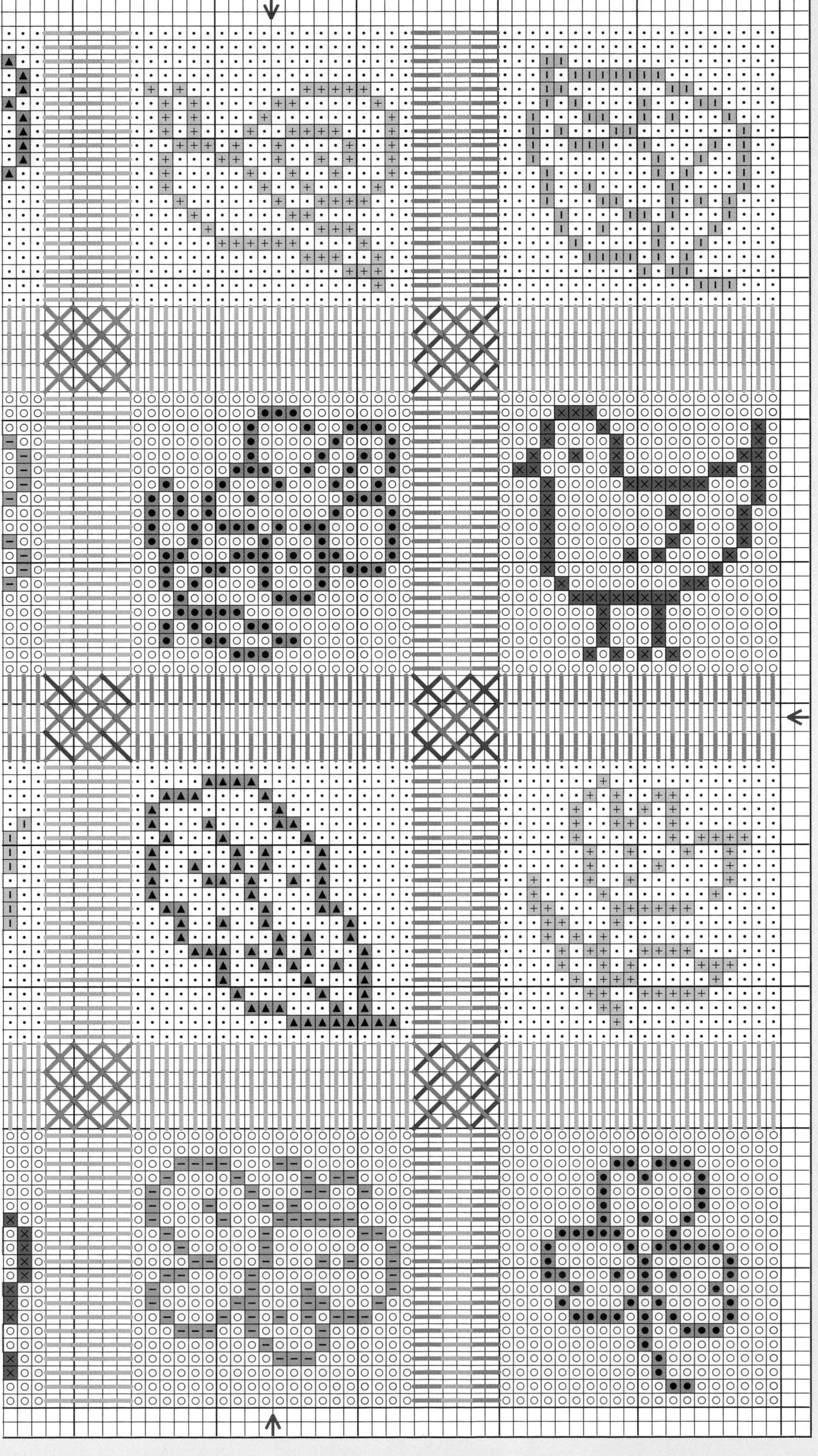

Fill the squares with continental tent stitch; start with the motif and work the background last.

PREPARING THE CANVAS

Cut the canvas to size (see page 310, step 2), adding an extra 2 in. (5 cm) to the total dimension. Mark the center of the canvas with basting, bind the raw edges with masking tape, then mount the canvas on the scroll frame.

WORKING THE DESIGN

Starting at the center, work the horizontal bands of straight Gobelin stitch (see page 174), then the vertical bands, leaving the cross-stitch square at each intersection unworked. Refer to the chart and color key on pages 228 and 229. Work each Gobelin stitch over two canvas threads; work to within 1 in. (2.5 cm) of the canvas edges. Work the stitches fairly loosely—if you pull the yarn too tightly, the canvas will show through.

Next work the sixteen motifs and colored backgrounds as shown on the chart using continental tent stitch (see page 162). One square on the chart represents one stitch worked over one canvas thread. When you have completed the chart, continue in the color sequence set to work motifs of your choice in each square until all of the squares are filled. Avoid carrying long threads across the back of the work, especially dark colors behind pale areas, as they may show through on the right side.

To finish, work the cross stitches at each intersection (see page 188), working each stitch over two canvas threads and working every alternate square in three colors (see chart and photograph to the right).

FINISHING

Take the completed design off the frame and press it lightly from the wrong side. If the piece is distorted, block it to shape (see page 303). Use the piece to cover a seat pad (see pages 309 and 310).

NOTE: To use the motifs individually as pictures, include the Gobelin stitch bands and add a few rows of tent stitch in the background color outside them. Mount the picture on posterboard (see page 306) and insert it in a simple frame.

The cross-stitch intersections are worked alternately in two colors and three colors (shown above).

Peruvian Bag

The Peruvians' love of strong patterns and bright colors is interpreted in needlepoint to display on the front of a denim shoulder bag.

You Will Need

- 15-count white Penelope canvas, 14 x 11 in. (35 x 28 cm)
- DMC embroidery floss as listed in the color key
- ¾ yd. (60 cm) of blue denim
- Tapestry needle, size 24
- Sewing needle
- Thread for basting
- Masking tape
- Scroll frame
- Sewing thread in blue

Color Key

COLORS	SKEINS
Half cross stitch	
304 Dark Christmas red	3
310 Black	3
742 Pale tangerine	2
796 Royal blue	2
907 Pale apple green	2
995 Turquoise	2
Patterned bands	
304 Dark Christmas red	
742 Pale tangerine	
796 Royal blue	
907 Pale apple green	
995 Turquoise	

This dazzling needlepoint panel was inspired by the heavily embroidered borders stitched around Peruvian hats and skirts. For extra color and shine, the design is worked in light-reflecting threads, and the direction of some of the stitching has been changed to create an interplay of patterns. The piece is used to make the front of a denim bag; the bag measures 9 x 6½ in. (23 x 16.5 cm).

You could make a smaller bag by working fewer bands—for example, down to the rows of dark blue below the fourth patterned band.

Preparing the Canvas

Baste a 9 x 6½ in. (23 x 16.5 cm) rectangle in the center of the canvas to mark the edges of the stitched area. Bind the raw edges with the masking tape, then mount the canvas on the frame.

Working the Design

Work the design following the chart (right) and the color key (left). One square on the chart represents one stitch worked over one pair of canvas threads. Use all six strands of floss in the needle, and separate the strands and recombine them to give better coverage; for more details, see page 10. Start at the top of the canvas and work downward, stitching in bands. Work the half cross stitches so that the top stitch slants from bottom right to top left.

Begin by working the top seven rows in half cross stitch (see page 162). Then stitch the first patterned band in Scottish stitch (see page 200), reversing the diagonal stitches for the square blocks.

Stitch another seven rows of half cross stitch, then stitch the second band in stem stitch (see page 201).

Work nine rows of half cross stitch, then fill in the third band with Jacquard stitch (see page 178), working the diagonal stitches over four pairs of canvas threads instead of the two shown in the stitch instructions.

Work seven rows of half cross stitch, and fill the fourth band with rectangles of half cross stitch and squares of flat stitch (see page 180).

Work eight rows of half cross stitch to fill the first sixty rows of the design. Stitch another sixty rows in the same way to finish.

Finishing

Remove the work from the frame and steam-press it gently from the wrong side with a warm iron. If the work is distorted, block it back to shape (see page 303). Trim the canvas ⅝ in. (1.5 cm) outside the stitching.

Jacquard stitch produces a series of wide and narrow zigzags.

The fourth patterned band consists of rectangles of half cross stitch and squares of crossed-corner cushion stitch.

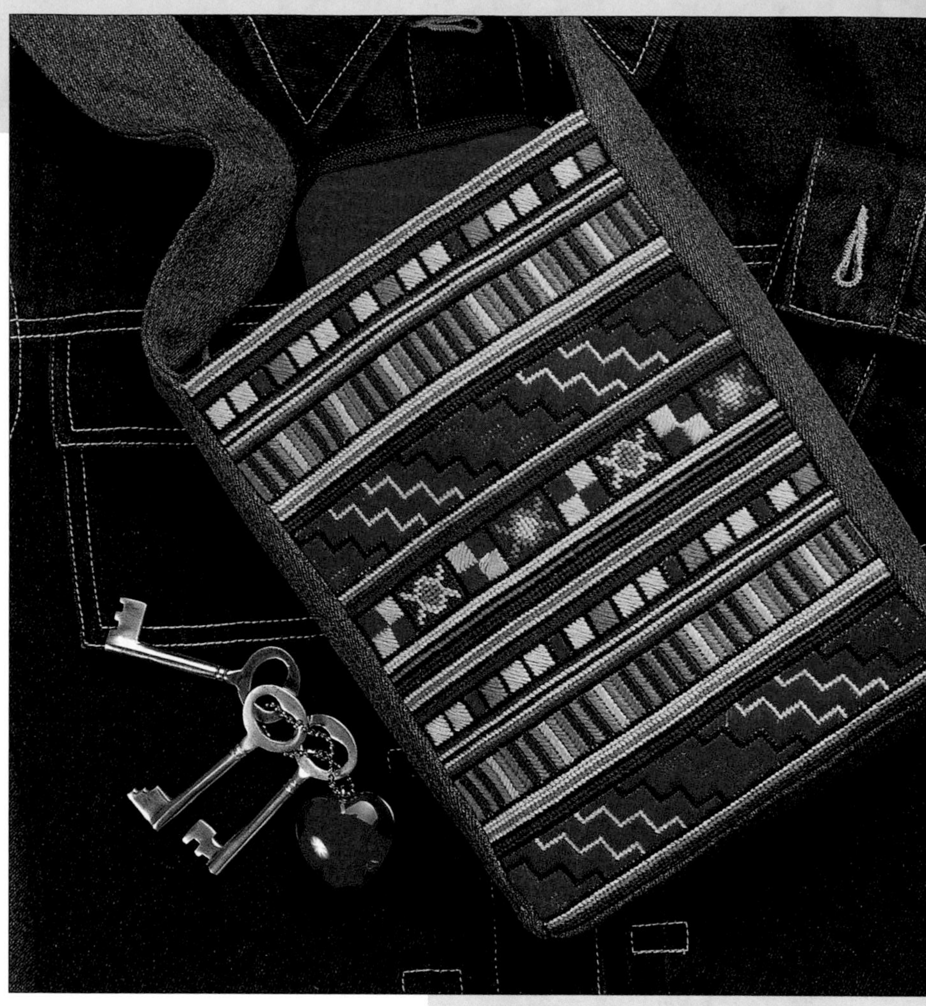

PREPARING THE BAG PIECES

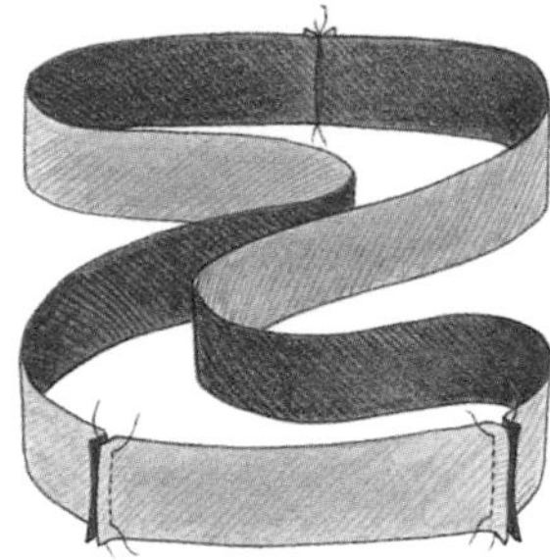

Cut four 29½ x 3¼ in. (75 x 8 cm) strips, two 7¾ x 3¼ in. (19.5 x 8 cm) strips, and three 10¼ x 7¾ in. (26 x 19.5 cm) rectangles from the denim fabric.

Stitch two long denim strips together with right sides facing, along one short end, taking a ⅝ in. (1.5 cm) seam allowance. Stitch the other two short ends to the short ends of a 7¾ in. (19.5 cm) denim strip to make a loop; begin and end the stitching ⅝ in. (1.5 cm) from the edges. Press the seams open.

Next, press under ⅝ in. (1.5 cm) along the top edge of the canvas and along one short edge of a denim rectangle; these pieces will be the bag front and back.

MAKING THE BAG

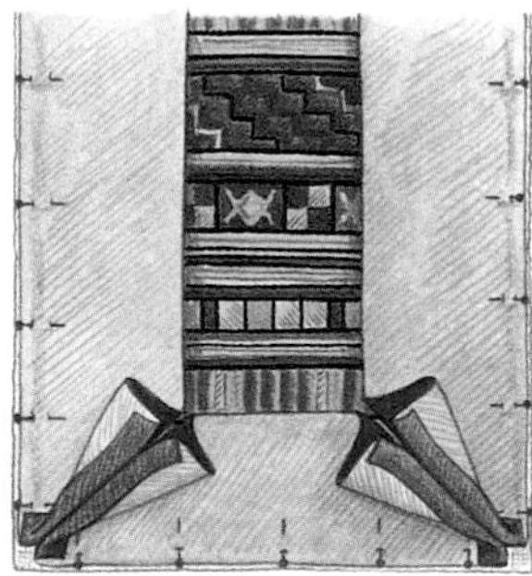

Lay the stitched piece right side up. Pin the denim loop right side down along the bottom and side edges: match the seams on the short section of the loop to the corners of the stitched piece, and open out the seams in the denim to fit it around the corners; stitch.

Repeat to attach the bag back to the other edge of the denim loop.

ADDING THE LINING

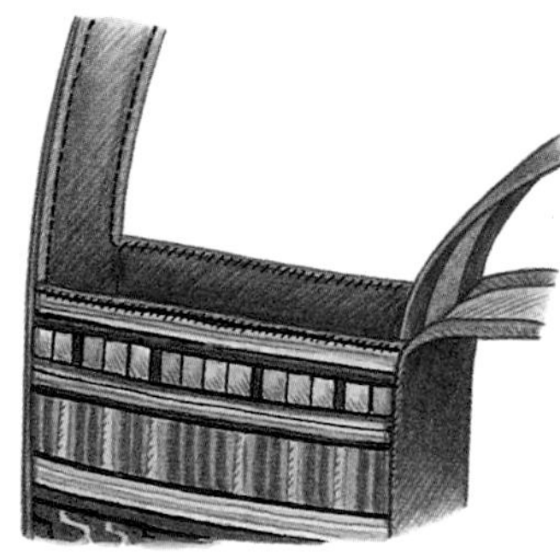

Make a second bag in the same way, using the remaining denim. Press ⅝ in. (1.5 cm) along each long edge of the lining and main bag handle. Turn the lining wrong side out, and slip it into the main bag piece with the wrong sides together. Slip-stitch the lining to the main bag around the top edge.

Machine-stitch the handles together just inside each long edge.

NOTE: For a larger bag, chose a coarser canvas and appropriate thread or yarn.

The columns of stem stitch are worked in turquoise, royal blue, and pale tangerine.

Chapter 4
Special Techniques

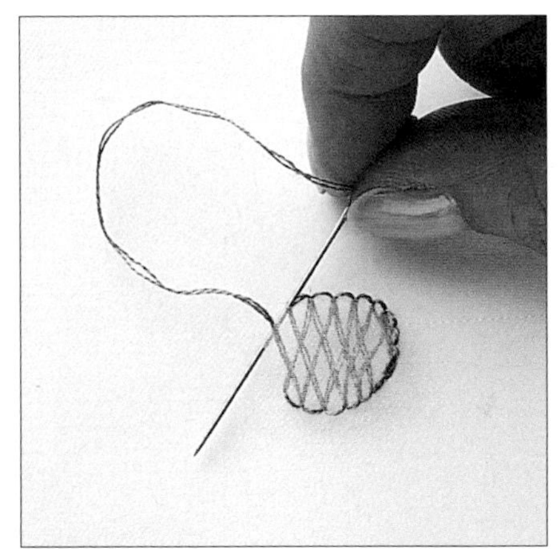

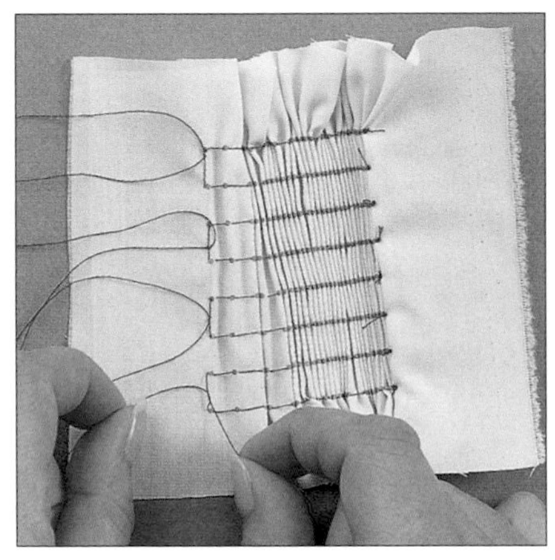

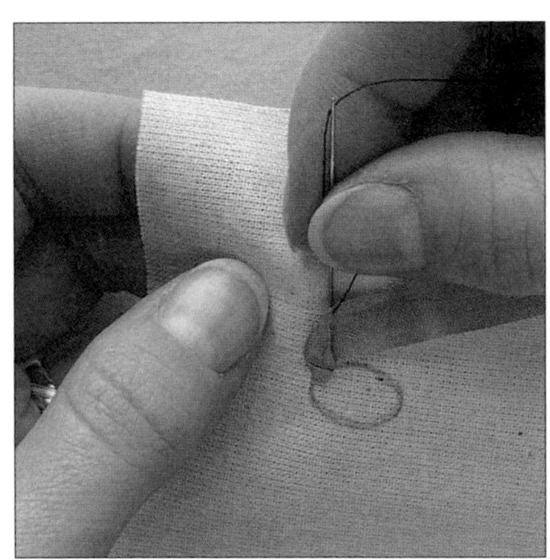

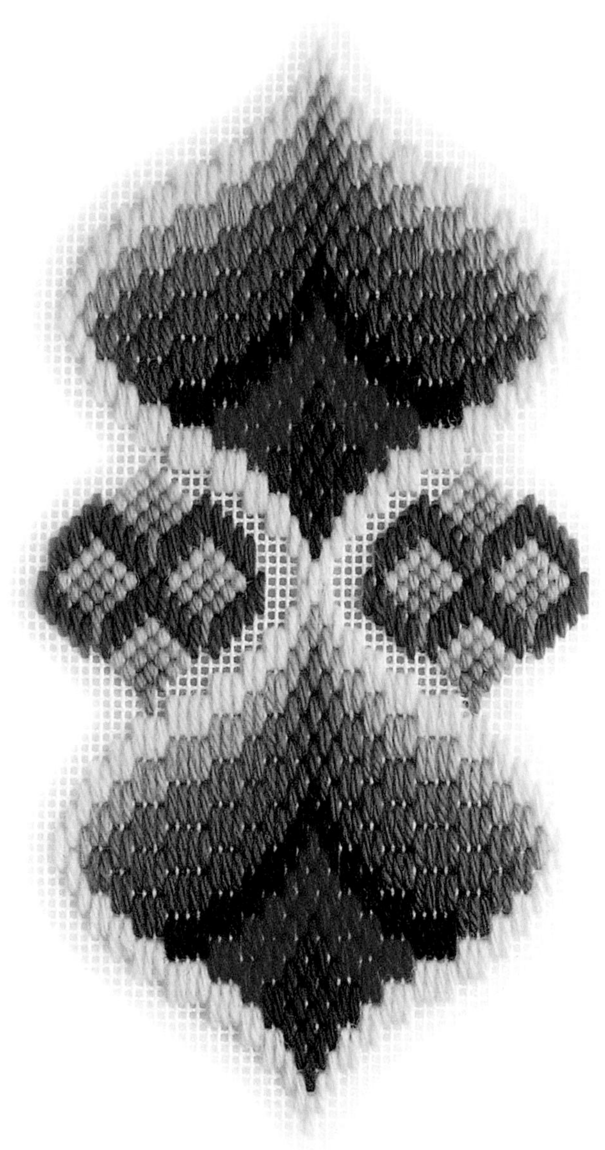

Drawn-thread work

Drawn-thread work is a type of openwork embroidery used to create lacy panels on evenweave fabrics. Horizontal threads are pulled out of the fabric, as shown below, and the remaining vertical threads are held in clusters with needleweaving or hemstitching. The steps on page 238 show how to work simple hemstitching.

Materials

Fabrics and threads Use a good-quality evenweave with threads that are easy to pull out. Make sure the fabric is fairly closely woven so it holds its shape—28 or 32-count evenweave is ideal. Stitch with two or three strands of floss, or use pearl cotton for a bolder look. Baste with a contrasting thread.

Needles and pins Use a tapestry needle to withdraw threads, for basting, and to work the stitches—the blunt point will slide between the threads without catching. A size 22 needle comfortably holds two or three strands of floss or one strand of pearl cotton. Use ordinary dressmaker's pins to secure the hems and sharp embroidery scissors to cut fabric threads.

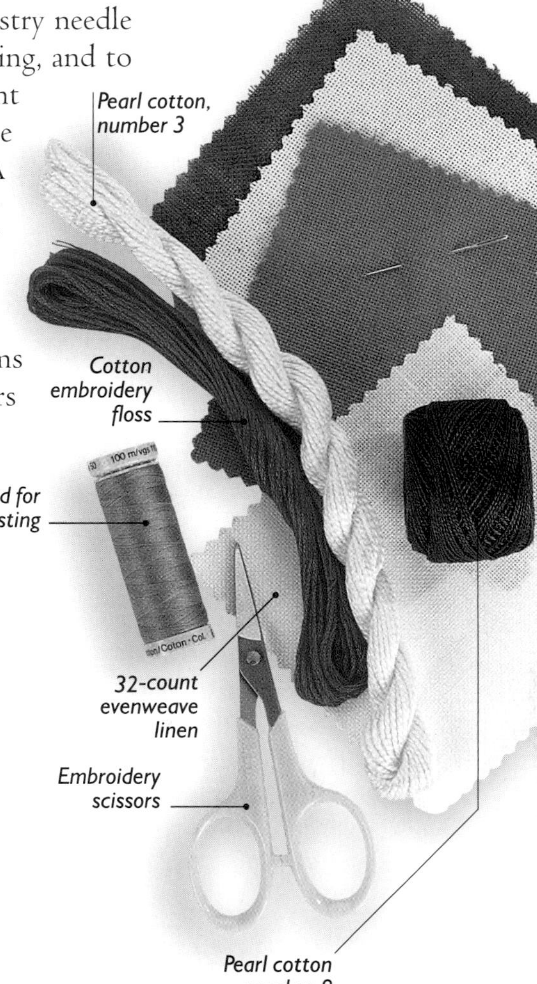

Making a drawn-thread panel

1 Mark the position of the panel with two horizontal rows of basting. Work the basting between two horizontal fabric threads. Mark the center with a vertical row of basting.

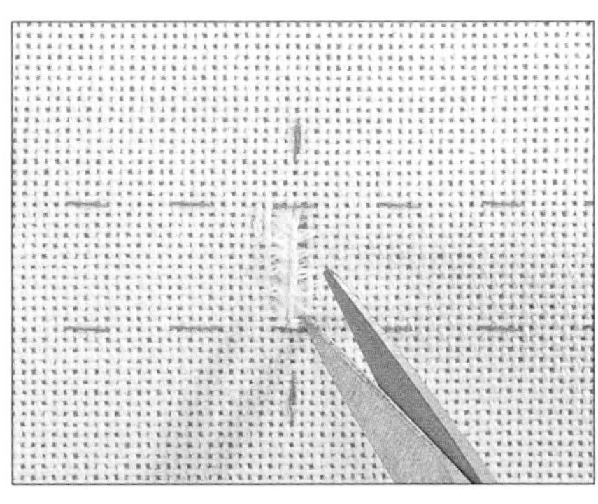

2 Using a small, sharp pair of embroidery scissors, carefully cut through the horizontal fabric threads at the center of the panel.

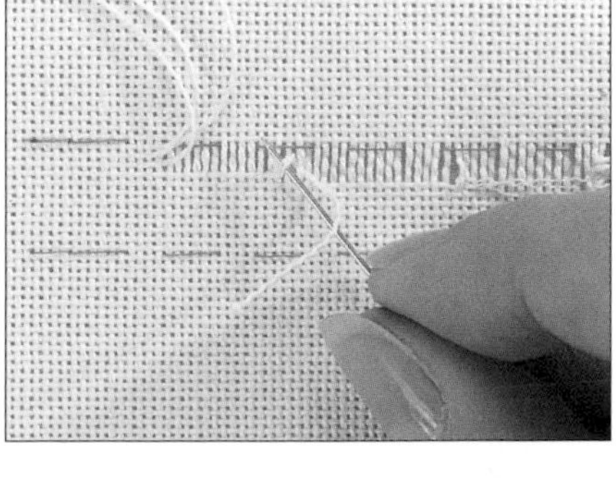

3 Using a tapestry needle, pull out the cut threads up to the panel edges. Leave exactly the right number of vertical threads for your stitching.

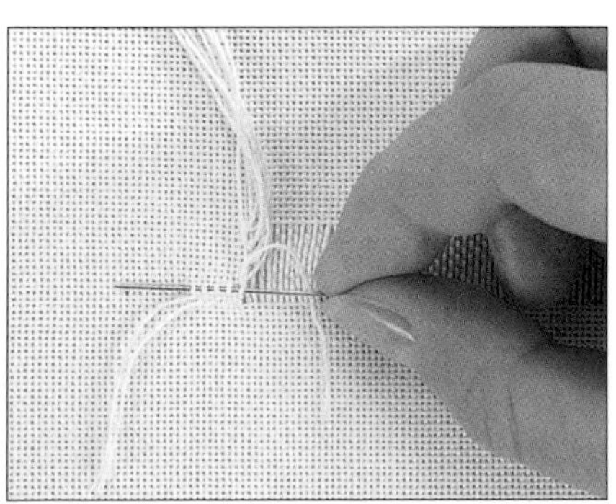

4 At the panel edges, thread the withdrawn threads one by one into the tapestry needle, and weave them back into the wrong side of the fabric.

Drawn-thread border

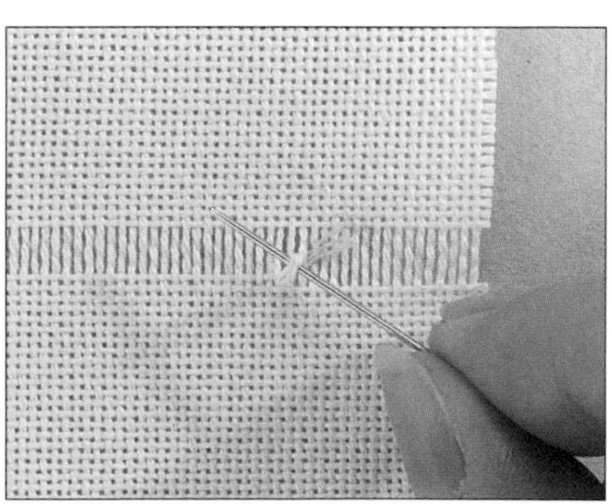

Slip a needle under one thread and gently pull it out right across the fabric. Pull out more threads to make a border of the required depth.

Working single hemstitch

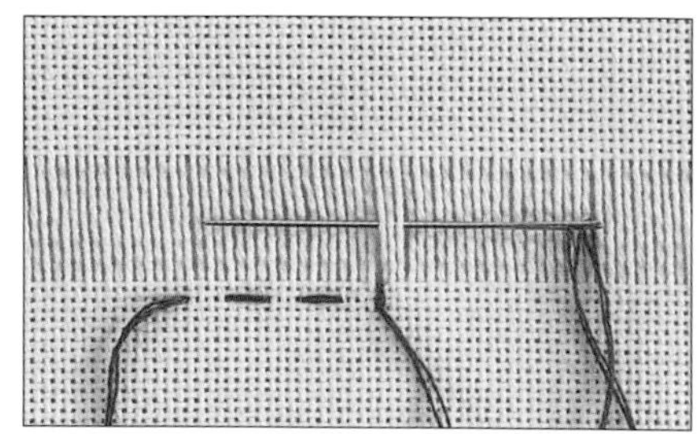

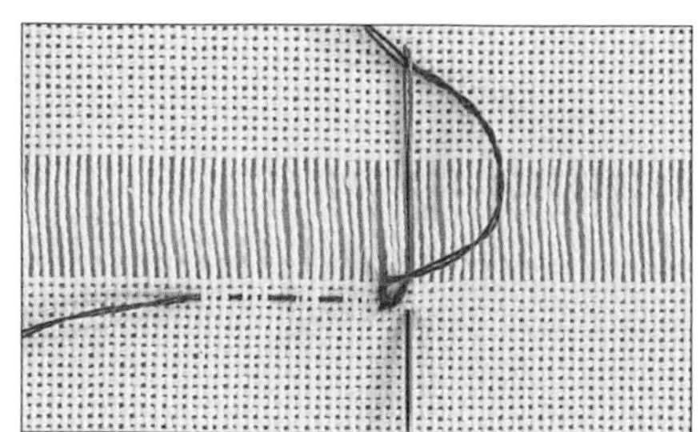

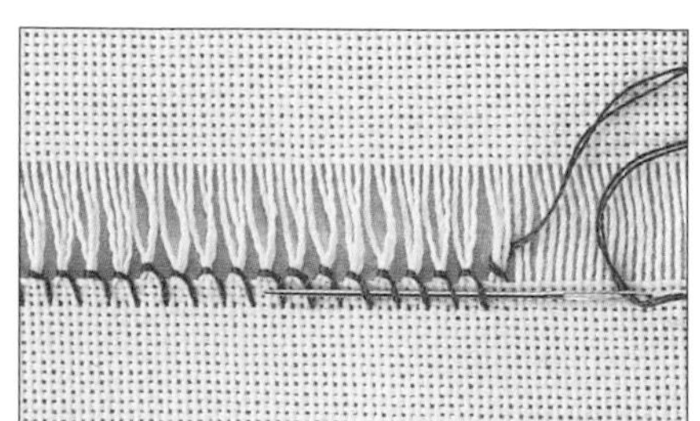

1 Working from the right side, leave a tail of about 4 in. (10 cm), and work a few running stitches up to the left-hand edge. Anchor the thread with a small vertical stitch, then pass the needle under two, three, or more of the vertical strands and pull it through.

2 Make a small vertical stitch under two or three horizontal threads to the right of the cluster. Continue working in this way across the border, keeping the stitches even.

3 At the end of the border, secure the thread under several stitches on the wrong side of the fabric and cut off the end. Pull out the running stitches at the other end of the border and secure in the same way.

Working single hemstitch along a hem

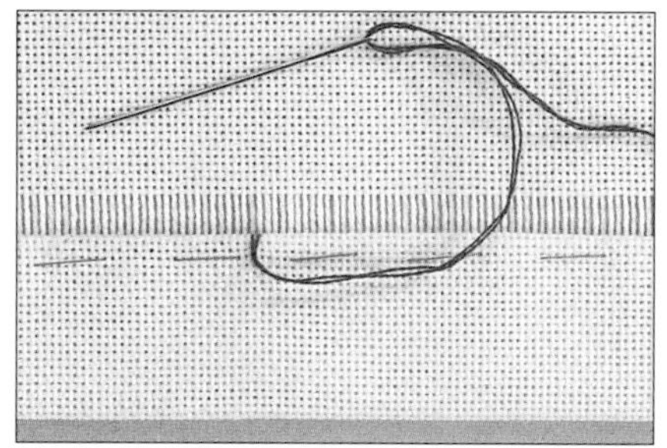

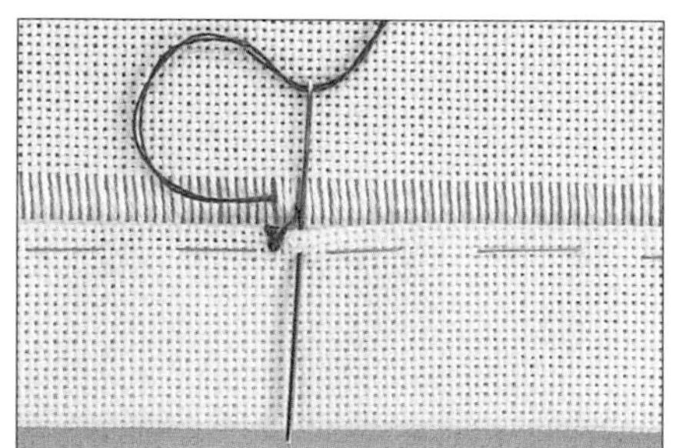

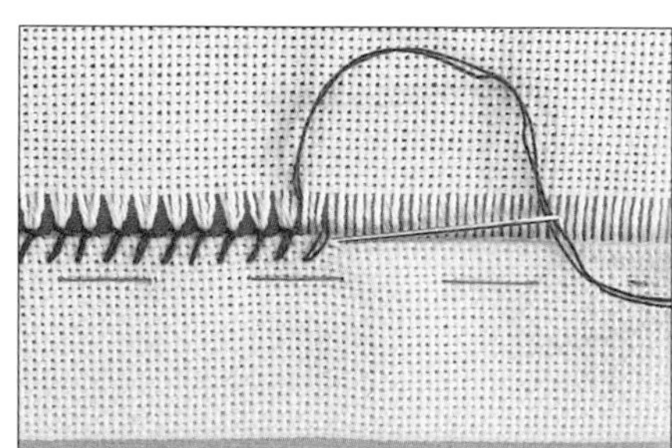

1 Turn up a double hem to the base of the drawn threads and baste. Working from the wrong side, secure the thread end inside the hem fold with a knot. Work a vertical stitch, catching in the hem fold top.

2 Pass the needle under two or more vertical strands and pull it through. Make a vertical stitch under a few horizontal threads to the right, making sure that the needle emerges through the hem fold. Continue in this way.

3 At the end of the border, secure the thread end under the hem fold on the wrong side and cut off the thread end.

Working ladder hemstitch

Ladder stitch is a variation of single hemstitch worked on the upper and lower ends of the vertical threads. Withdraw four or more horizontal threads, then work a row of single hemstitch from left to right along the lower edge of the border. Turn the fabric upside down and hemstitch along the remaining edge, catching the same fabric threads into each cluster to make a ladder pattern.

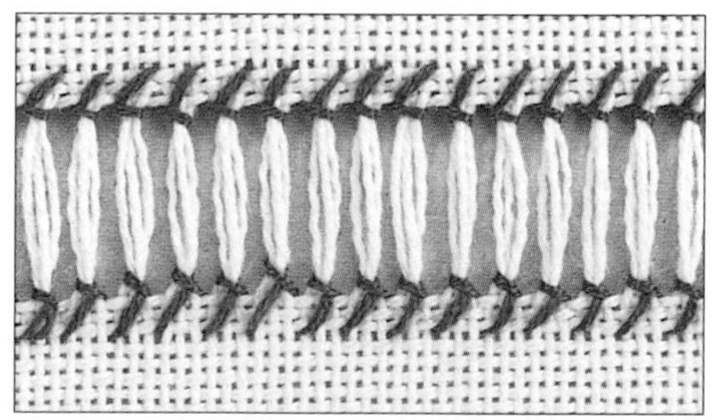

Working trellis hemstitch

Trellis (or serpentine) hemstitch is another variation of single hemstitch. Work a row of single hemstitch along the lower edge of the threads, grouping the threads into clusters of two, four, or any even number. Turn the fabric upside down, and hemstitch along the remaining edge, dividing and regrouping the threads to make a zigzag pattern.

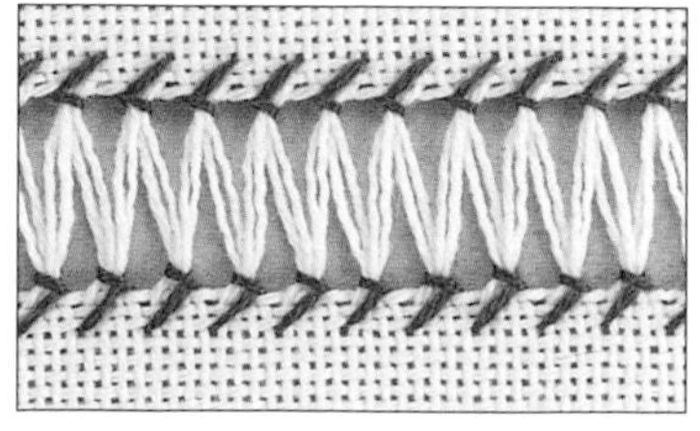

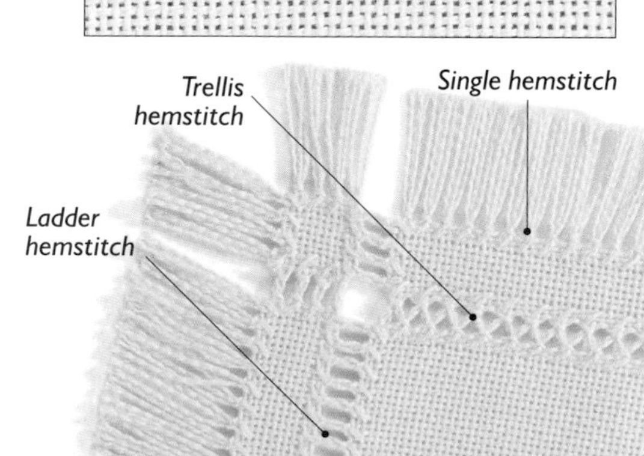

Hardanger

Hardanger embroidery creates crisp, lacy geometric patterns on evenweave fabrics. It is a form of cutwork from the west coast of Norway, and it is traditionally worked in white thread on white linen, but beautiful effects can be achieved using an array of contrasting colors.

In typical Hardanger designs, blocks of satin stitches, called kloster blocks, form the edges of the motifs, and the threads between the blocks are cut and withdrawn. The remaining threads are strengthened with bars, and the open areas are filled with lacy stitches.

Kloster blocks can vary in size; the steps below show five-stitch blocks worked over four vertical and six horizontal threads, but seven stitches over six threads, or four stitches over three threads can also be used.

Two types of bar, and one type of lacy filling stitch are shown. **Woven bars** are worked over and under equal numbers of threads. **Overcast bars** are similar, but the threads are overcast together. **Simple lace filling** can be worked across the open center of four kloster blocks or between woven bars.

Mount the fabric in an embroidery hoop. First work the kloster blocks; then, using sharp-pointed embroidery scissors, carefully cut out the threads to be withdrawn (see page 240) close to the stitching.

To secure the thread, leave a 2 in. (5 cm) tail on the front of the fabric, and make several running stitches close to the position of the first block. At the end, darn in the thread end. Pull out the running stitches and darn in the other thread end.

Fabrics and threads

Specially woven 22-count Hardanger fabric has pairs of threads. It is ideal for this type of embroidery, but you can use any 20–36-count evenweave fabric. The higher the count, the smaller the finished motif.

Pearl cotton or embroidery floss is used for Hardanger. Choose no. 5 pearl cotton for kloster blocks and the finer no. 8 for bars and filling stitches. With floss, use six strands for kloster blocks and three or four for details. Use a tapestry needle to avoid splitting the fabric threads.

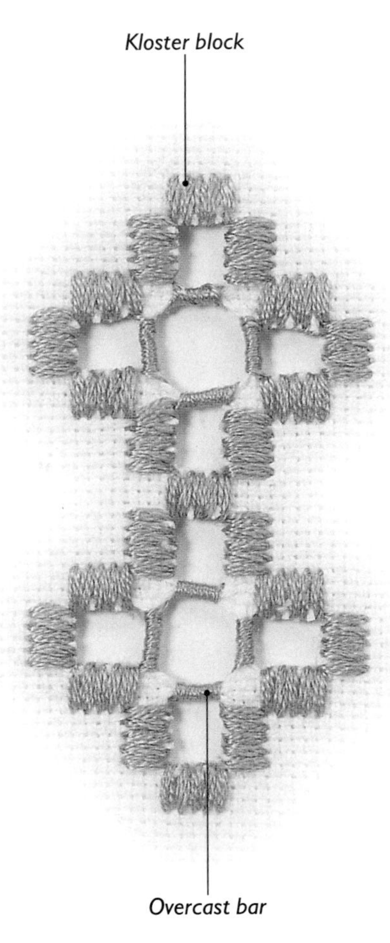

Working a group of four kloster blocks

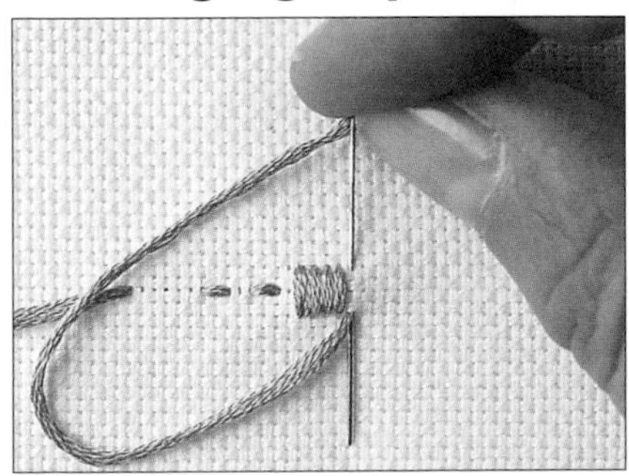

1 Work five vertical satin stitches to make the first kloster block. Bring the needle to the front of the fabric at the base of the last stitch, ready to start the next block.

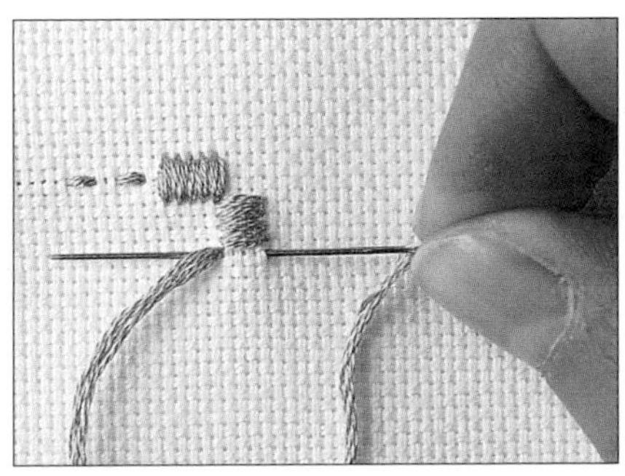

2 Make a block of five horizontal stitches in the new direction, and bring the needle to the front at the left of the last stitch, ready to start the third kloster block.

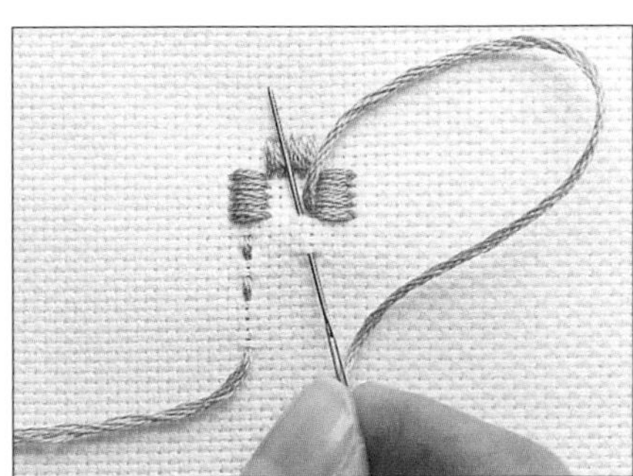

3 Continue in this way, turning the fabric as you go, to work four blocks as shown.

Working stepped kloster blocks

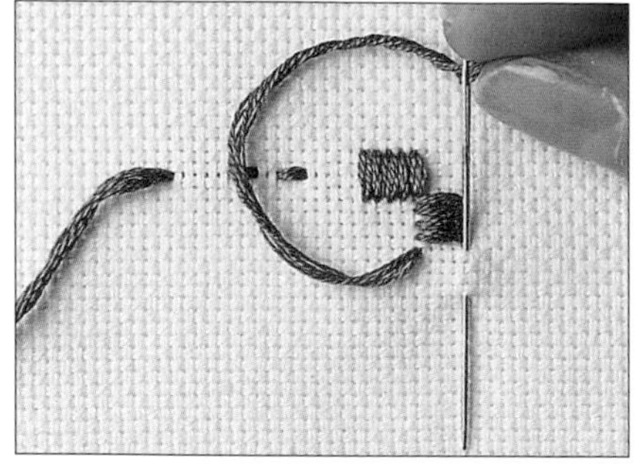

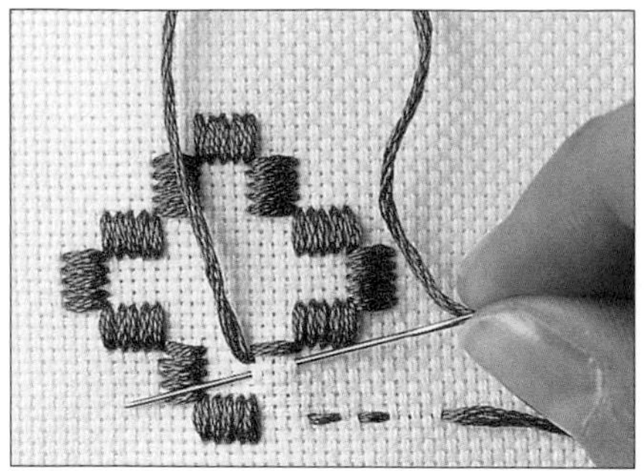

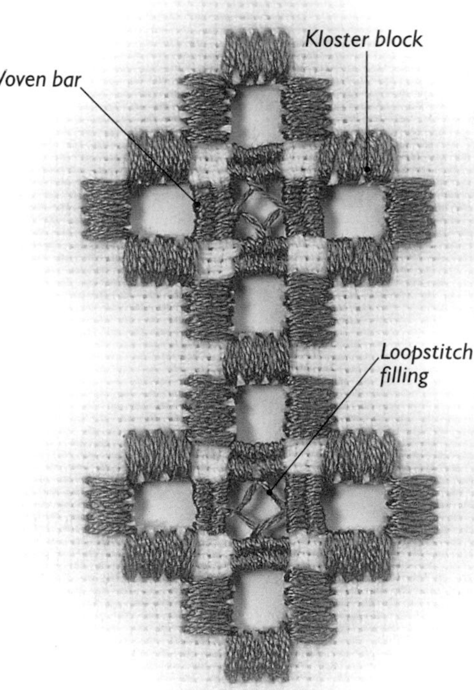

1 Starting at the top, make a block of five vertical stitches, and bring the needle out at the base of the last stitch. Work five horizontal stitches, and bring out the needle four threads below.

2 Repeat the stepped formation of blocks around the edge of the desired shape. Turn the fabric as required to make it easier to work.

Preparing a cut area

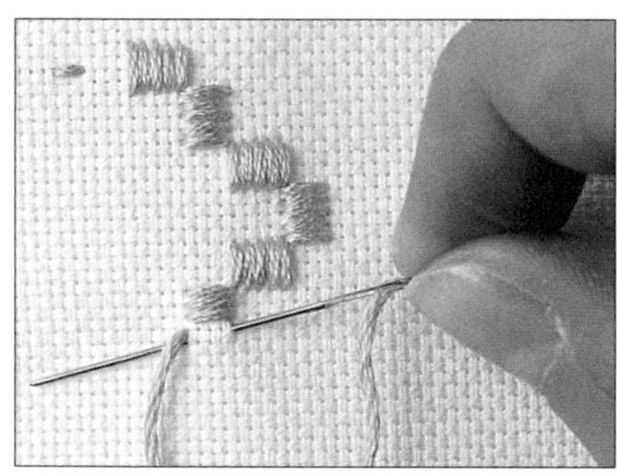

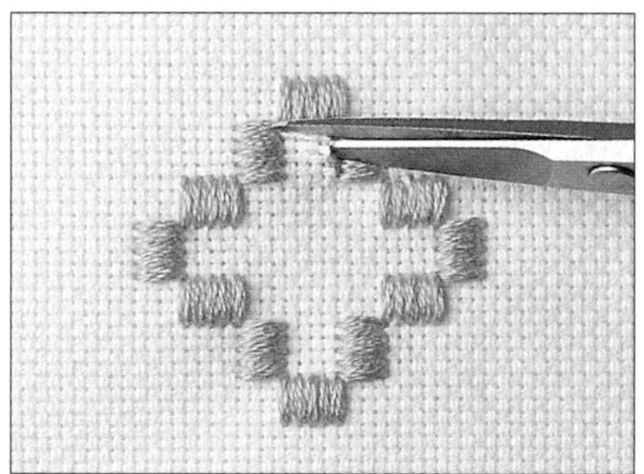

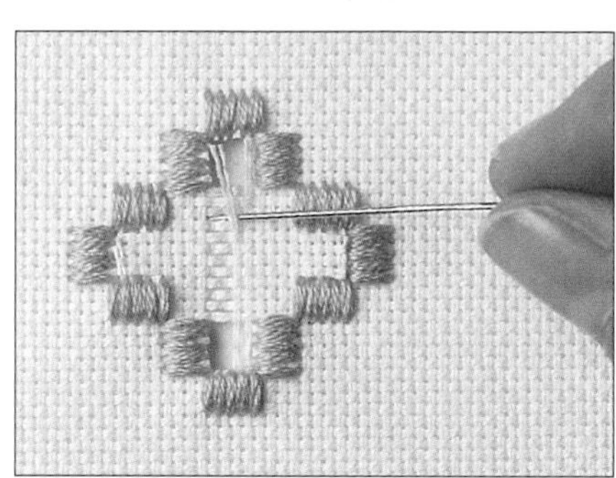

1 Surround the area to be cut with kloster blocks. Arrange the blocks so that each space between them contains the same number of threads as the blocks, and work the corner blocks at right angles to each other.

2 Cut across four fabric threads at the base of each block, using a sharp, pointed pair of scissors and taking care not to snip into the embroidery. Do not cut the threads at the unstitched ends of the blocks.

3 Remove the cut threads from between the blocks; use a tapestry needle or a pair of tweezers to unpick them. Strengthen the remaining bars of four threads by needleweaving or overcasting (below).

Working a woven bar

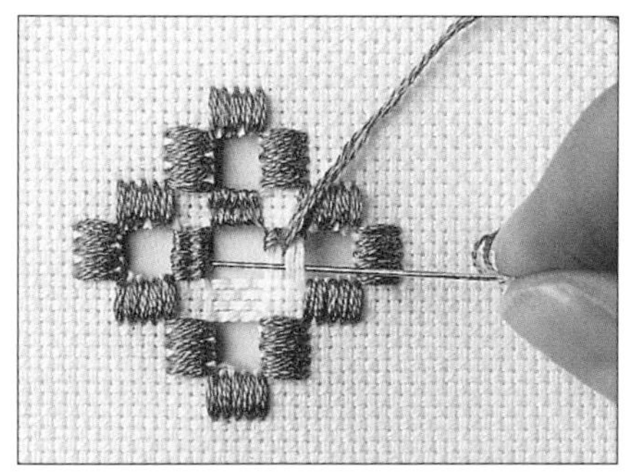

Weave over and under an equal number of threads until each group of threads is completely covered. Take care to hide the working thread behind the fabric when passing the needle from one bar to the next.

Working overcast bars

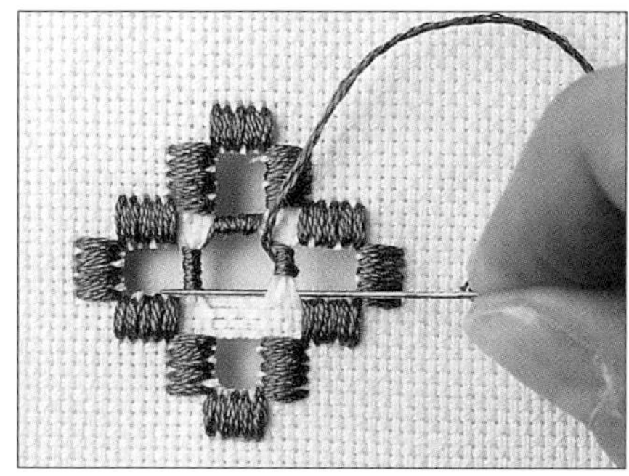

Overcast the loose threads firmly, butting the stitches together to cover the threads completely.

Working loopstitch filling

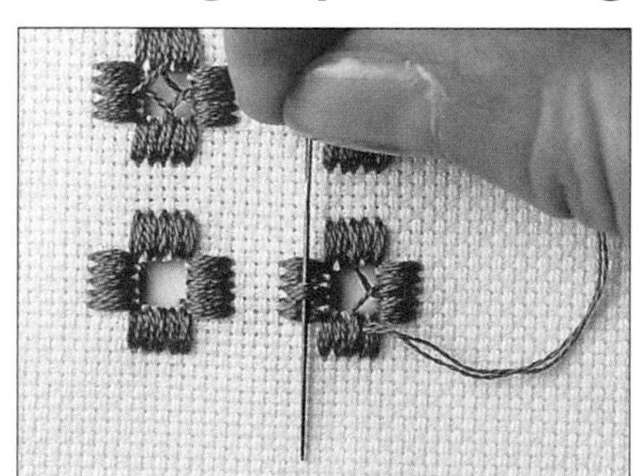

Bring the needle to the front of the fabric, just left of the center stitch of the top block. Take it diagonally across to the center stitch of the right-hand block. Take the needle upward, under the center stitch. Continue working clockwise in this way, making loops on each side of the square.

Once you're familiar with the basic technique of working Hardanger embroidery, as shown in the previous pages, you can begin to add a wider range of decorative touches to your work. The cut-away spaces between kloster blocks and between overcast or woven bars can be filled with a variety of very attractive finishes, including woven wheel (or dove's eye) filling (below) and square filet filling (see page 242).

Some embroiderers prefer to work the bars and fillings without a frame, working over the free index or middle finger. However, beginners will find it easier to control the stitching by using a hoop.

Decorate the fabric around the cut and filled areas with bold motifs and borders worked in satin stitch. The eight-pointed star (overleaf) is a popular motif which can be worked in different sizes. The stars shown here are made up of satin stitches worked over ten fabric threads, but you could work the stitches over eight, six, or four threads. (Note that in this case, the term "fabric thread" refers to a paired thread of Hardanger fabric.)

Satin stitch is also used for borders of rectangular, triangular, or diamond-shaped blocks, repeated in vertical or horizontal rows. A simple triangle border is shown on page 242. To start and fasten off satin stitch, see page 27.

You can finish the raw edges of a piece of Hardanger embroidery in several ways. Turn a hem and secure it with hand stitches; or machine-stitch the hem if the item will need frequent laundering. Hand-embroidered edge finishes, such as buttonhole stitch (see page 242), look pretty on decorative pieces. Before working the buttonhole stitch, withdraw one fabric thread all around the piece to mark the outer edge of the stitching. This ensures that the hem is straight and makes it easier to cut away the surplus fabric without damaging the stitches.

Working woven wheel filling

1 Start at the center of the unstitched square between the top and left-hand kloster blocks. Take a long stitch across to the center of the diagonally opposite unstitched square; come out one thread to the left. Wrap the thread over the stitch until you reach your starting point. Insert the needle and bring it out in the center of the unstitched square between the top and right-hand kloster blocks.

2 Make a long stitch across to the diagonally opposite square as before, then start wrapping the thread around the stitch. When you reach the point where the two long stitches cross, weave the thread over and under the crossing stitches to make a small wheel. Then continue wrapping the thread around the remaining half of the long stitch, and insert the needle at the starting point as before.

Working an eight-pointed star in satin stitch

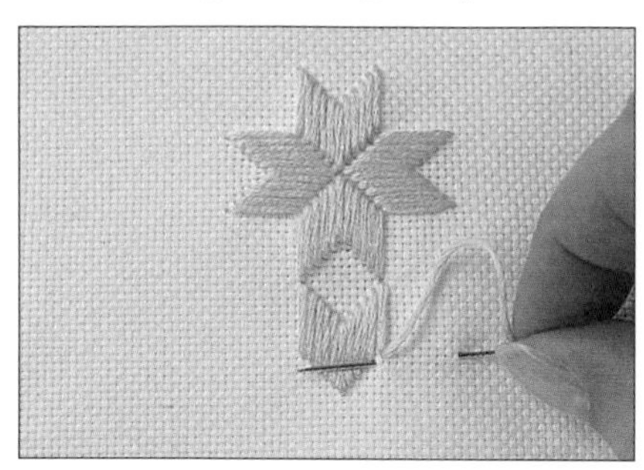

1 Start at the top left. Work a block of six satin stitches over ten fabric threads; step each stitch down by one thread. Repeat, but step upward, to complete the first two points. Bring the needle out at the base of the last stitch. Repeat, but work horizontally to make points three and four.

2 Turn the work upside down and repeat step 1 to work points five, six, seven, and eight. At the end of the last stitch, take the thread through to the back. Then either secure it or weave it through the back of the star until you reach the chosen position to start an adjacent star.

Square filet filling

1 Bring the needle out near the bottom right of the cut square. Working counterclockwise, insert it through the fabric at the top right corner, leaving a thread loop along the cut square. Bring the needle back through the cut square and over the loop; pull the thread gently to tighten.

2 Turning the work as necessary, continue in this way. To work the last stitch, take the needle under the first loop you made and then back through the fabric at the last corner.

Working a triangle border in satin stitch

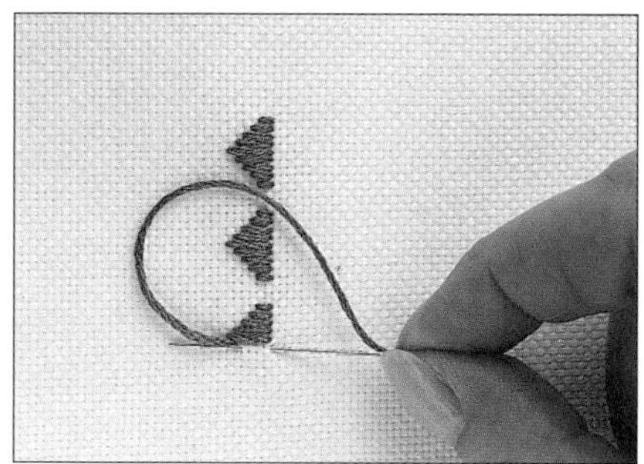

1 Start at the top left of the border. Work a triangular group of horizontal satin stitches. Leave a gap of an odd number of fabric threads, then repeat the triangular shape. Continue until the border is the required length.

2 Work the next row in the opposite direction. Reverse the triangles, arranging them so that the longest stitch of each motif fits into the center of the gap between the triangles worked on the previous row.

Finishing an edge with buttonhole stitch

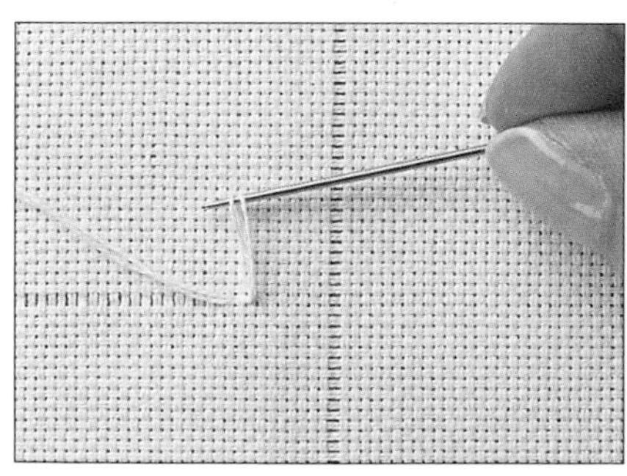

1 Using a tapestry needle, withdraw one pair of threads all around to mark the lower edge of the finished hem. Secure the thread, and bring the needle through at the left in the space left by the withdrawn threads.

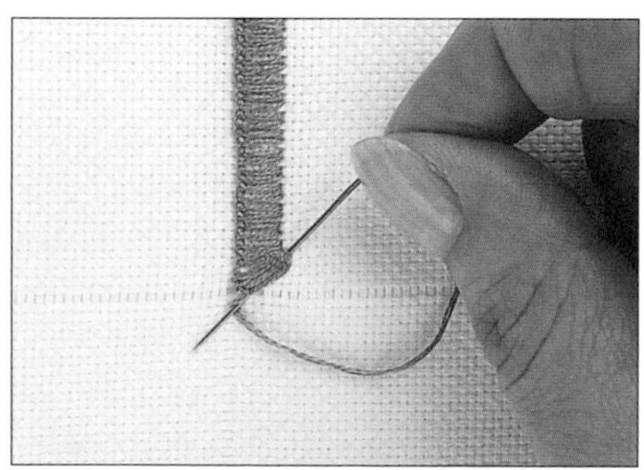

2 Work buttonhole stitches five blocks deep, spaced one block apart. At the corners, space the outer edge of the stitches in the same way, but use the same hole for the inner edge of the stitches.

Eight-pointed star in satin stitch

Triangle border in satin stitch

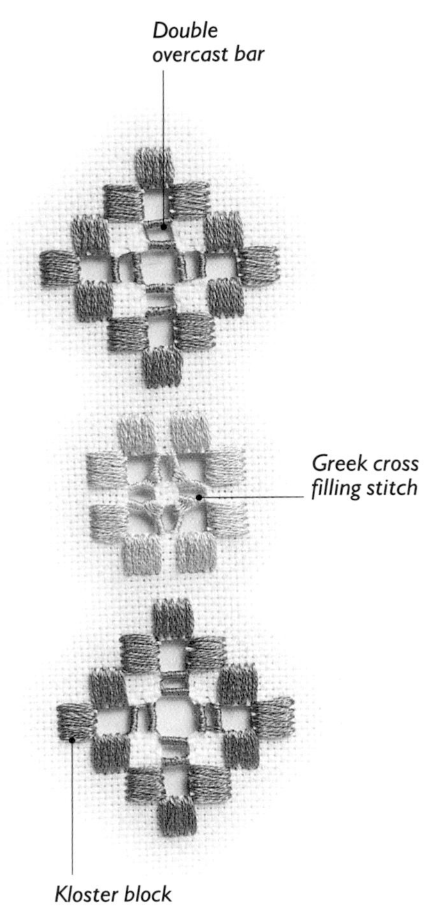

Enlarging your repertoire of Hardanger stitches opens up all sorts of design possibilities. The first techniques shown here describe two more ways to finish groups of threads after cutting away the fabric between kloster blocks. Both involve dividing the thread groups into two sets and then treating each set separately to create lighter, prettier bars than woven or overcast bars.

The first, **Greek cross filling stitch**, creates a delicate arched effect and is ideal for finishing fabric threads arranged in a cross shape. **Double overcast bars** are a bit trickier to work than the single type. Each thread group is worked in two directions; to conceal the working thread between groups, take it to the wrong side and weave it neatly under the nearby kloster blocks until you reach your next starting point.

Cut diamonds (see page 244) can be dotted between larger, more intricate shapes. Four diamond-shaped, satin-stitched blocks are worked around a square of fabric, which can be cut away if desired. The blocks shown have seven stitches, but you can choose any odd number.

Many Hardanger designs are divided into sections, with rows or frames of surface stitching; and **four-sided stitch** (see page 244) is ideal for this purpose. It is easy and can be used in one or more rows to create light or heavy lines.

For more details on Hardanger techniques, refer to the previous pages (239–242) .

Working Greek cross filling stitch

1 Work the kloster blocks and cut and remove the threads. Bring out the second, finer, working thread between a group of fabric threads, dividing them into two equal sets. Work an overcast bar over the upper set, drawing the threads tightly together. Then bring the needle out between the next group of fabric threads, again dividing them into two equal sets.

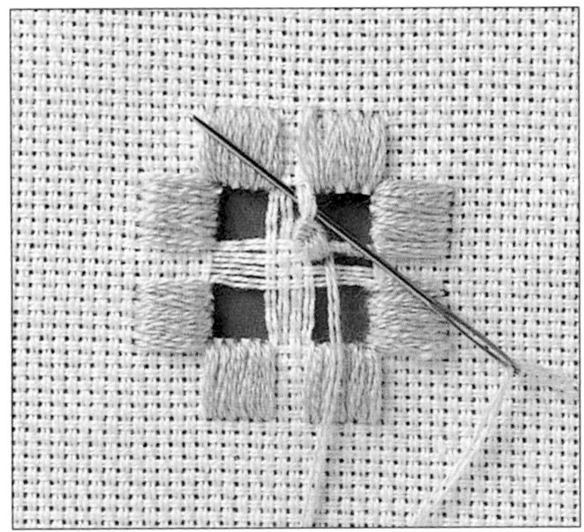

2 Work a short length of woven bar over the overcast bar and the new set of threads; for details on working overcast and woven bars, see page 240. Stop about halfway along the fabric threads.

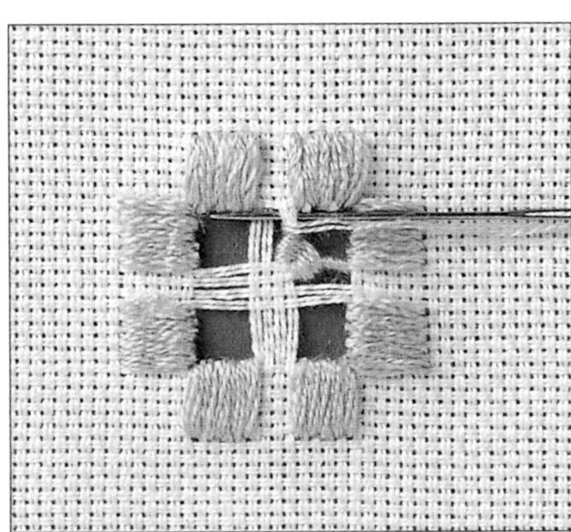

3 Cover the remaining half of the new set of threads with an overcast bar. Continue in this way to work the next section of the cross, keeping the tension of the working thread and the number of stitches consistent. Repeat as required, turning the work as necessary so that you can stitch comfortably.

Working double overcast bars

1 Work the kloster blocks and cut and remove the threads. Bring the new thread to the front, halfway between a group of fabric threads. Work a tight overcast bar over one set of threads (see page 240).

2 When the overcast bar is complete, bring the needle out between the bar and the other set of threads. Work an overcast bar over these threads, making it exactly the same as the previous overcast bar. Repeat as required.

Working a cut diamond

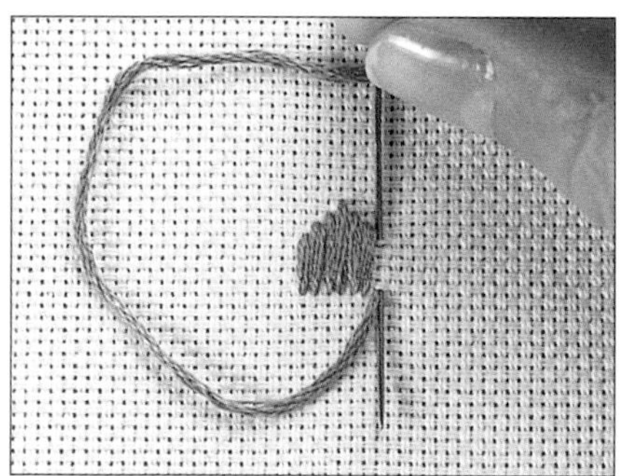

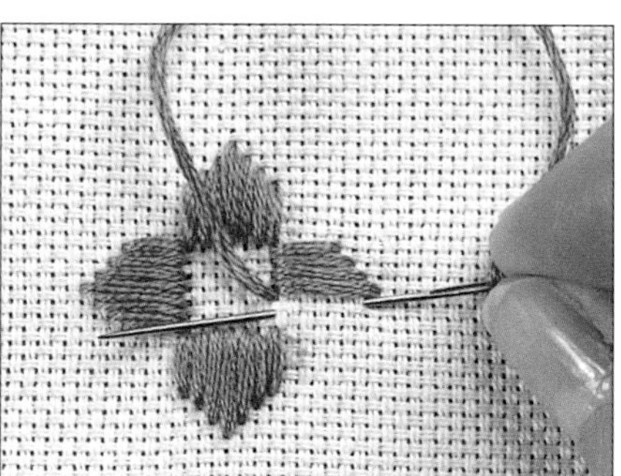

1 Starting at the top left, work a block of seven satin stitches as shown. Work over five, six, seven, then eight, seven, six, then five fabric threads. Bring the needle out at the base of the last stitch, ready to work the next block.

2 Turning the work as necessary, repeat the block to enclose a square of fabric, in the same way as kloster blocks. Secure the working thread. The central square of unstitched fabric can be cut away, if desired.

Working four-sided stitch

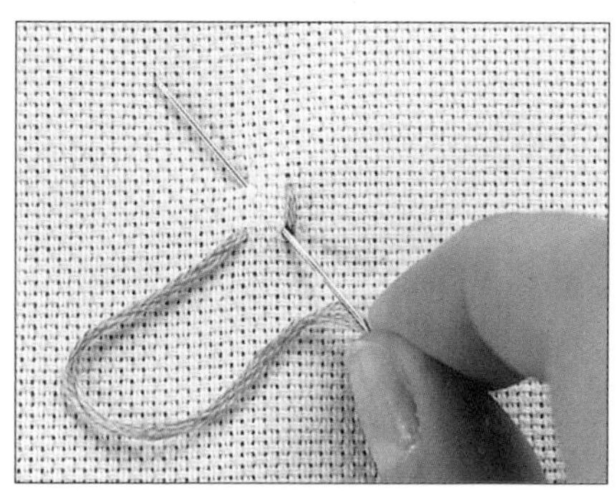

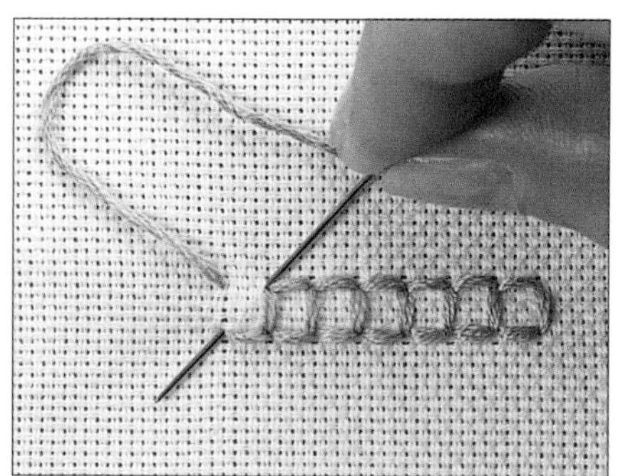

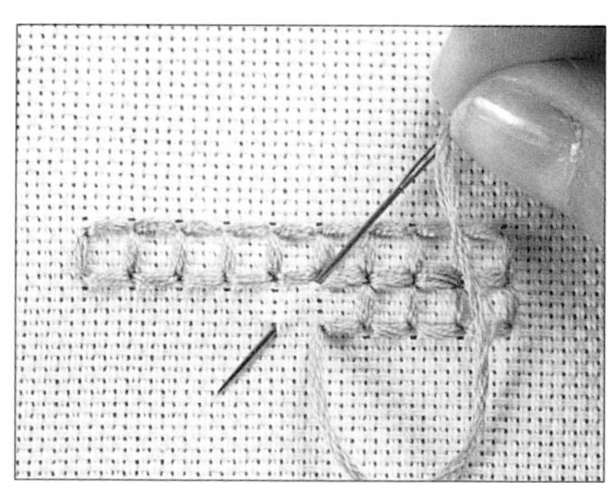

1 Work each stitch over four threads. Start on the right with a vertical stitch, and come out four threads to the left and four threads down. Work a horizontal stitch, and come out four threads to the left of the top of the first stitch.

2 Complete the square with a horizontal stitch, then a vertical stitch. Continue in this way along the row, but omit the first stitch of each square, which is formed by the last stitch of the previous square.

3 For a heavier effect, work a double row of four-sided stitch. Turn the work at the end of the first row and work a second row below the first—where the two rows of stitching meet, a double row of stitches is formed.

Pulled thread work

In pulled thread work the fabric is distorted by pulling the stitches to form a pattern of spaces and holes. The stitches seem to become a part of the fabric creating a range of very attractive bands, borders, and fillings. Here, the stitches have been worked with a loose tension so that you can see clearly how each stitch has been made.

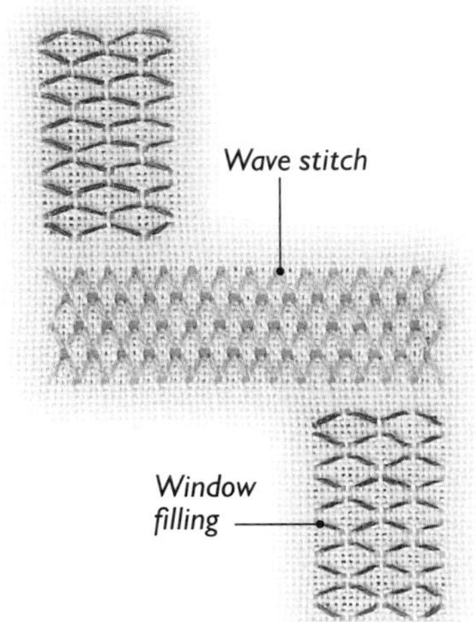

Fabrics and threads

Pulled thread work is traditionally worked with white or cream-colored thread on matching fabric. You can use other colors, but the beauty of the work lies in the resulting texture, not the stitches themselves. The samples here use contrasting thread for clarity.

The fabric should be a fairly loose evenweave, so that the threads can be pulled easily; the more open the weave, the lacier the result. The thread should match the weight of the fabric threads; for evenweave, choose two strands of embroidery floss; for heavier fabric, pearl cotton of an appropriate size would be ideal. Here, the samples are worked on a 28-count evenweave fabric with two strands of floss. Use a tapestry needle to avoid splitting the fabric threads.

Starting to stitch

Mount the fabric in a frame to keep the threads straight while you stitch, but leave it looser than usual so that the threads can move. To secure the thread, leave a 2 in. (5 cm) tail on the front of the fabric and make several loose backstitches close to your starting point. As you work the design, pull each stitch as you work it, keeping the tension consistent. To secure the end of the thread, darn it under several stitches, then pull out the backstitches and darn in the other end.

Basic stitches

The pulled thread work stitches shown here are worked in several different ways. **Wave stitch** and **window filling** are worked horizontally across the fabric; **cobbler filling** is worked over two journeys —the fabric turning between the first and second journeys. **Honeycomb filling** is worked in vertical rows, while **single faggot stitch** and **diagonal drawn filling** are worked in diagonal rows.

Working wave stitch

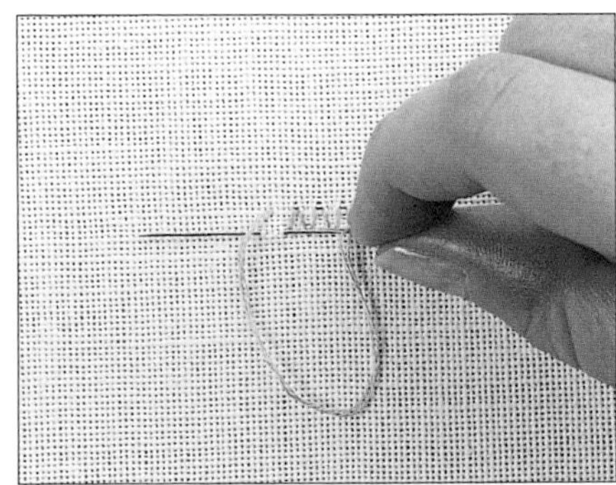

1 Bring the needle out at the top right. Insert it two threads to the right and four threads above and bring it out four threads to the left. Insert it where the thread originally emerged and bring it out four threads to the left. Continue in this way along the row.

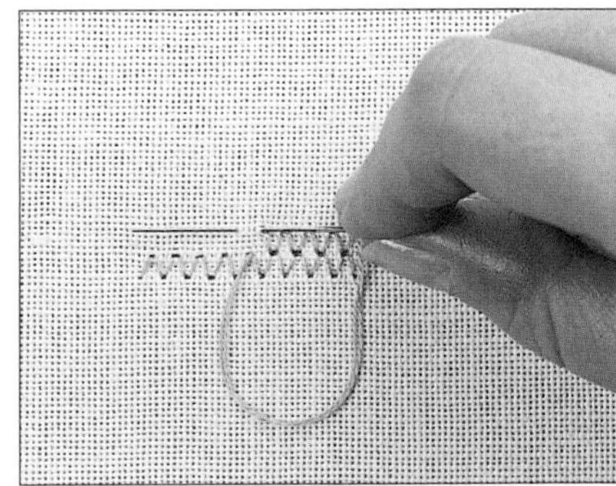

2 At the end of the row, turn the fabric round and work a second row close to the first, so that the bottom of the stitches on this row share the same holes at the top of the stitches on the previous row. Repeat to make a border or fill a shape.

Working window filling

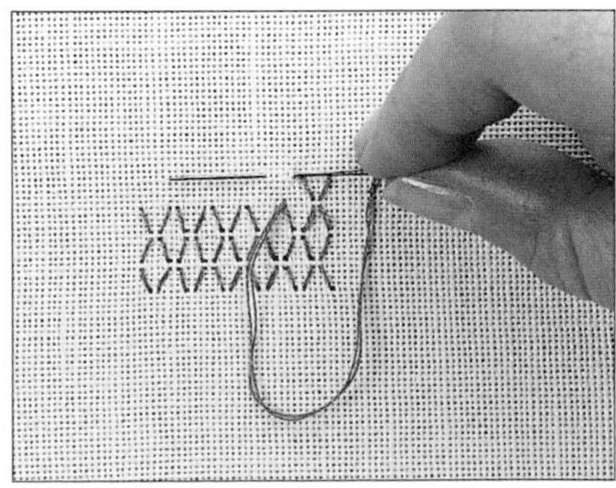

Work this stitch in horizontal rows in the same way as wave stitch (left), but leave one fabric thread between the stitches and also between the rows, as shown.

Working cobbler filling

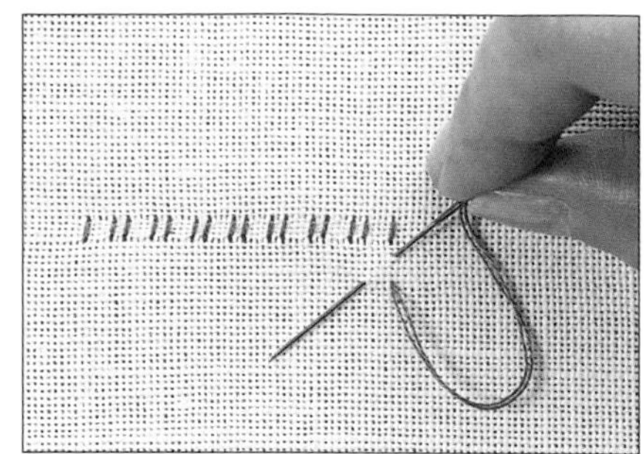

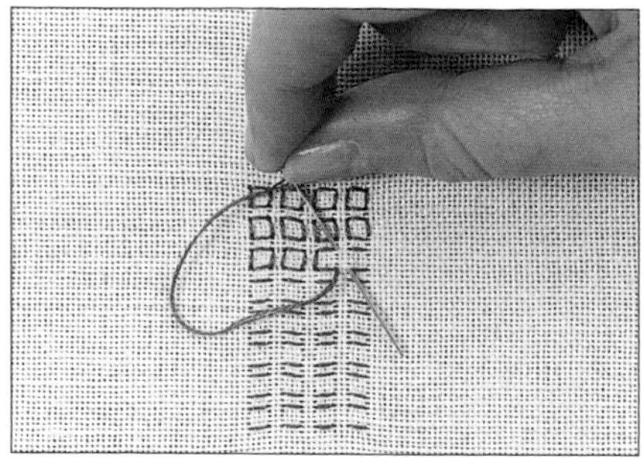

1 Start at the top left with a single upward vertical stitch over four threads. Leave a gap of four threads, then make pairs of vertical stitches, spacing them alternately two, then four threads apart. End the row with a single stitch. Work more rows of stitches two threads apart.

2 When all the vertical stitches are complete, rotate the fabric 90 degrees so the top of the embroidery becomes the side. Repeat the embroidery from the beginning, positioning the stitches worked on this journey so that they complete the series of squares.

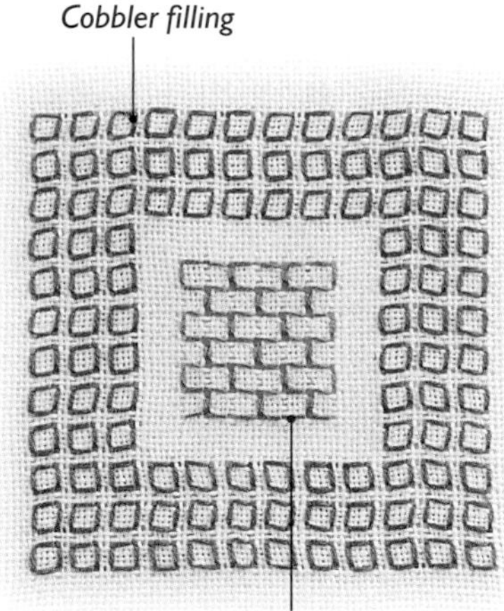

Working honeycomb filling

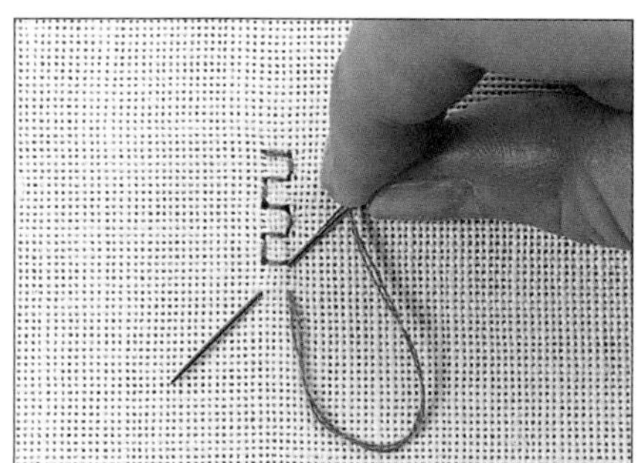

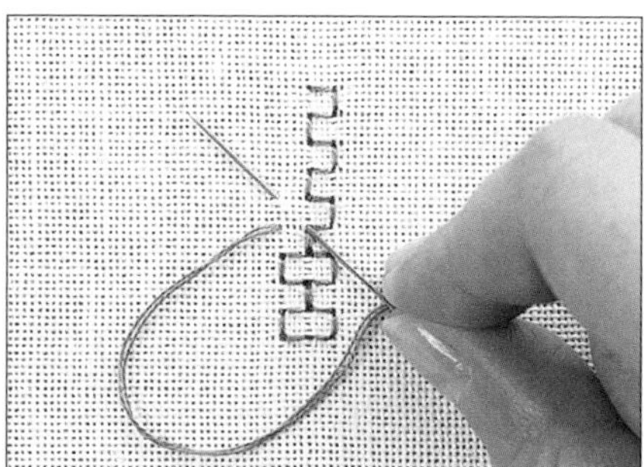

1 Bring the thread out at the top right of the area to be stitched. Insert the needle four threads to the right, and bring it out four below. Insert the needle four threads above and bring it out four to the left and four below. Continue in this way.

2 At the end of the row, turn and work upward so the right-hand side of the stitches made on this row share the same holes as the left-hand side of the stitches worked on the previous row. Repeat to make a border or fill a shape, working alternately upward and downward.

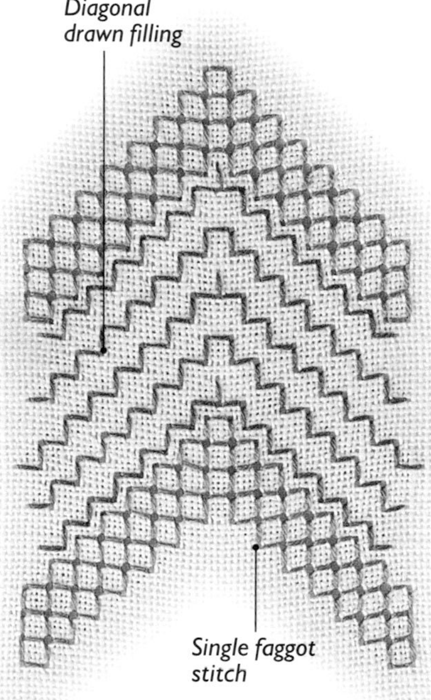

Working single faggot stitch

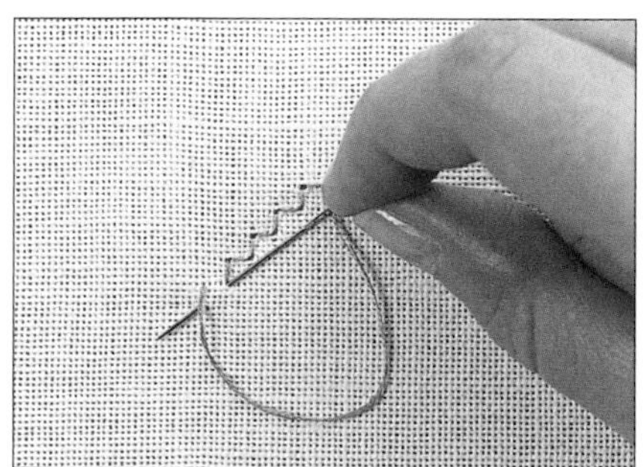

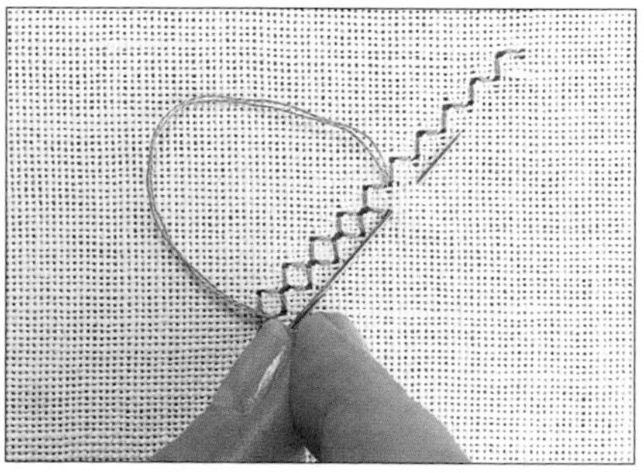

1 Bring the thread out at the top right. Make a series of backstitches over four fabric threads at right angles along the row, keeping the tension of the stitches even. Finish the row with a vertical stitch.

2 Work another vertical stitch, then bring the needle out diagonally to the right. Work a second row of backstitches as before, sharing the same holes, but work upward. Continue in this way to fill the shape.

Working diagonal drawn filling

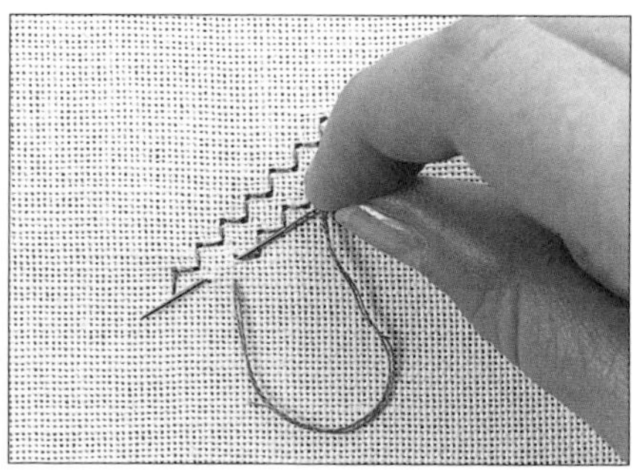

Work in diagonal rows as for single faggot stitch (left), but leave two vertical and two horizontal fabric threads between the rows, as shown.

The stitches described here produce a heavier effect than those shown in the preceding pages. They are all simple variations of satin stitch and are very simple to work once you have seen how the rows are constructed.

Satin stitch is often worked without pulling the stitches, so that its glossy texture can provide a contrast with the openwork. Experiment with these stitches, pulling some of them tightly, some less tightly, and some not at all, to see the different effects that can be produced.

These stitches can be used to create bands and borders or to fill shapes with texture. As with the previous pulled thread stitches, you should use an evenweave fabric with a slightly open weave, so that the threads can be pulled easily as you stitch.

The samples shown here are worked on a 28-count pure linen fabric. When you are pulling the stitches, you may prefer to use a thread slightly thicker than the fabric threads to emphasize the stitched areas. Pull each stitch as you work it, and try to keep the tension consistent throughout the piece of work.

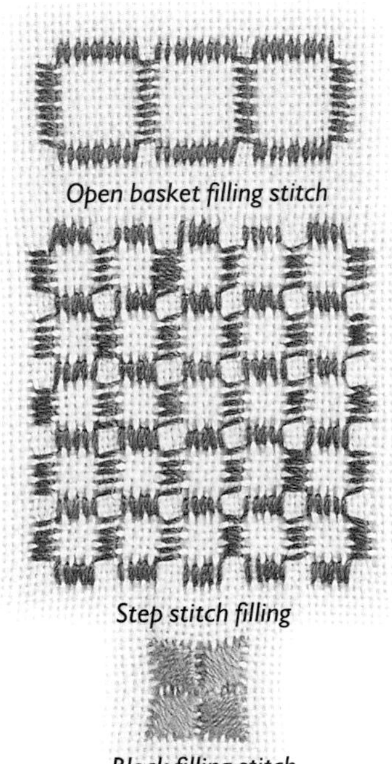

A frame of some kind is essential, in order to keep the fabric threads at the correct tension. For a small motif, a hoop will do; otherwise use a rectangular frame that will accommodate the entire stitched area. An inexpensive alternative to a scroll frame is one that you put together from wooden canvas stretcher, available from art supply stores.

Four of the pulled thread work stitches shown here are worked in horizontal and/or vertical rows and are very similar in construction. Both the **mosaic diamond filling** and **block filling** stitches create solid areas of stitching, whereas the other three stitches—**open basket filling**, **basket filling**, and **step stitch filling**—have a more open appearance as small areas of fabric show between the stitches. The fifth stitch, **step stitch filling**, is worked in diagonal rows.

Working open basket filling

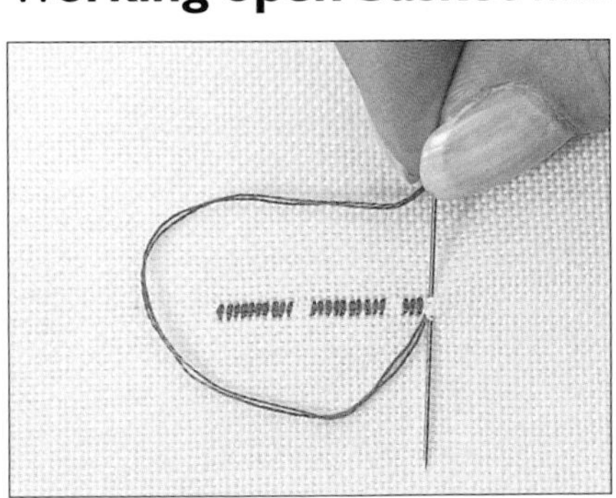

1 Bring the thread to the front at the top left. Work a horizontal block of ten vertical satin stitches over three fabric threads. Work ten more stitch blocks to the right of the first one, separating the blocks by three fabric threads. Continue in this way.

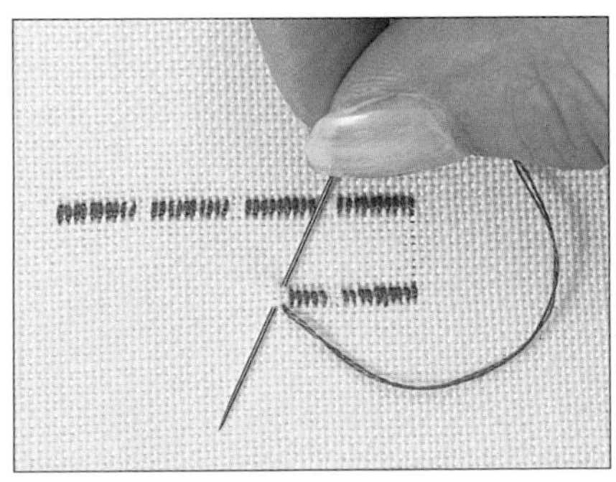

2 At the end of the row, bring the needle through to the front, twelve threads below. Work a second row of identical blocks, nine threads below the first. Continue in this way until the border or shape is filled. Secure the thread end.

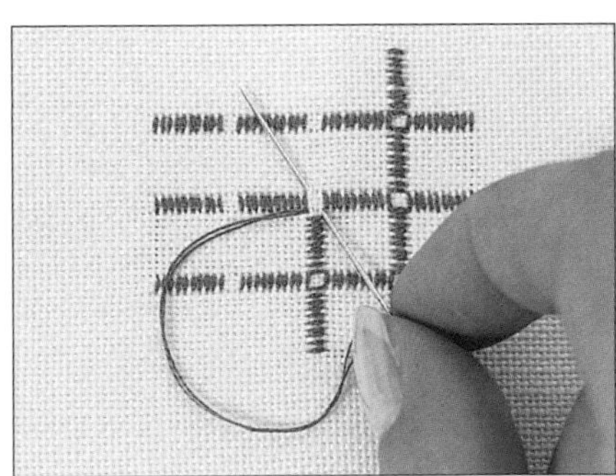

3 Secure the thread nine threads above the left-hand end of the top right-hand block. Work vertical rows of ten stitch blocks to fit between the horizontal blocks already worked.

Working basket filling

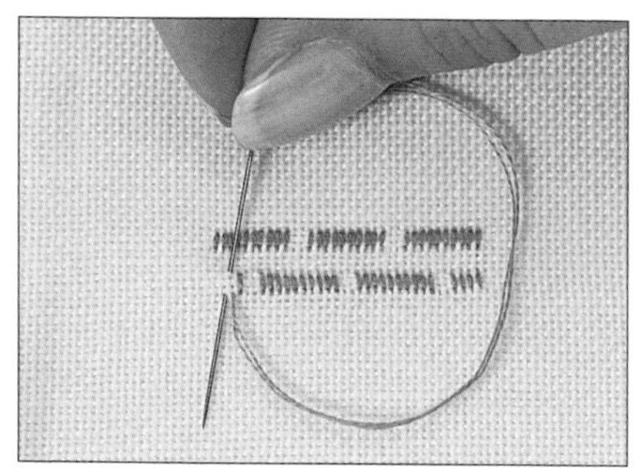

1 Starting at the top left, work the first row of satin-stitch blocks in the same way as open basket filling. On the second and subsequent rows, arrange the blocks so the gaps fall directly beneath the center of the blocks on the previous row.

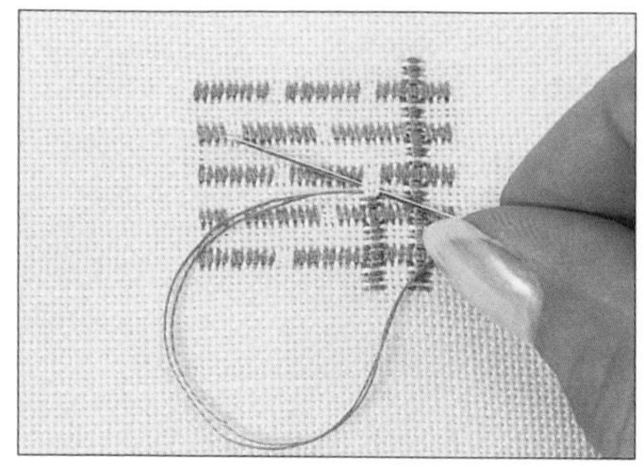

2 Secure the thread three threads above and three threads to the left of the end of the top right-hand block. Work vertical rows of ten-stitch blocks to fill the gaps between the horizontal blocks already worked.

Working block filling

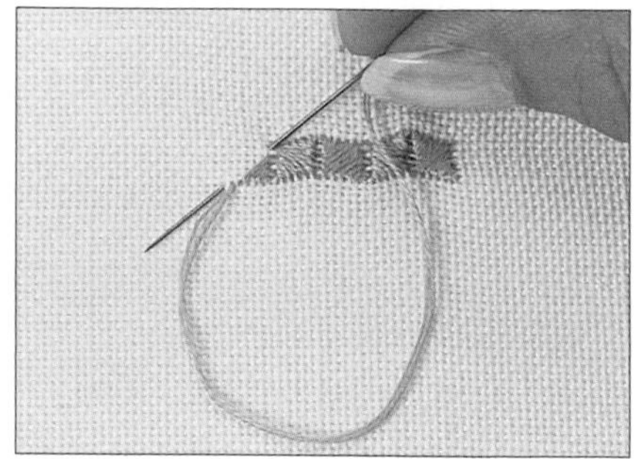

1 Start at the top right and work a square block of diagonal stitches over six fabric threads, slanting from bottom right to top left. Turning the fabric as required, work the next block so the stitches slant in the opposite direction. Repeat along the row.

2 Turn at the end of the row and work further rows of square blocks, arranging the blocks so that the stitches on the next and subsequent rows slant in the opposite direction to those on the previous row. Arrange the rows so that the blocks touch.

Working mosaic diamond filling

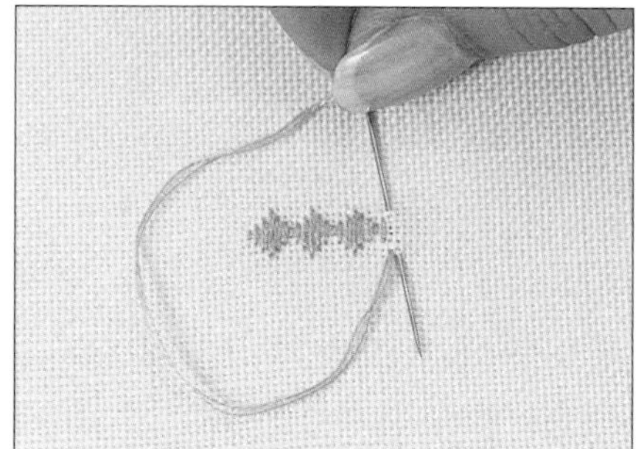

1 Secure the thread at the top left and work a diamond-shaped block of vertical satin stitches, arranging the stitches to cover two, four, six, eight, six, and four fabric threads. Repeat this formation along the row.

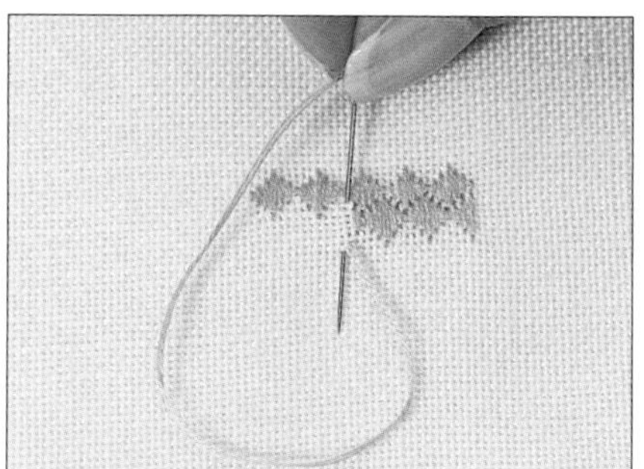

2 Turn at the end of the row and work another row of diamond shapes, so that the shortest stitches on the next and subsequent rows are worked directly under the longest stitches on the previous row. Arrange the rows close together so that the diamond shapes interlock.

Working step stitch filling

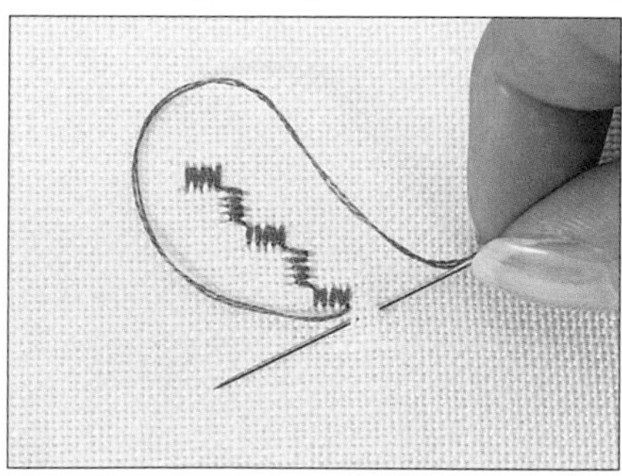

1 Start at the top left and work a horizontal block of five vertical satin stitches over four fabric threads. Bring the needle out at the base of the last stitch and work a vertical block of the same size. Bring the needle out four threads lower down and work another horizontal block. Repeat along the row.

2 At the end of the row, turn and work upward so that the blocks made on this row touch the corners of those made on the previous row. Repeat these two rows to make a border or to fill a shape.

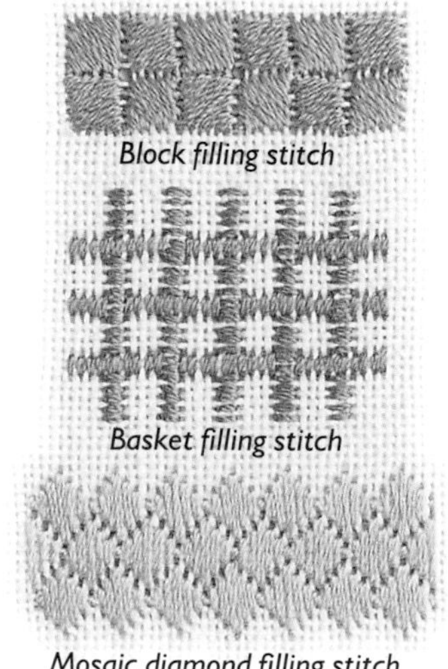

Block filling stitch

Basket filling stitch

Mosaic diamond filling stitch

Shadow work

Shadow work originated in India where it was used to decorate fine, semitransparent fabrics such as gauze, organdy, and muslin. The main areas of shadow-work designs are embroidered on the wrong side of the fabric so that the stitched shapes show through on the right side.

Suitable shapes for shadow work include long, slim petals and leaves, narrow shapes like scrolls of ribbon, and small, rounded shapes. The shapes are filled from the wrong side with a type of herringbone stitch called **shadow stitch** which forms neat outlines of backstitch on the right side of the fabric. Alternatively, you can fill the shapes with **Indian shadow stitch,** which produces long wave-like stitches across the shape on the wrong side and a running-stitch outline on the right side. To make a really neat outline on the right side, you may need to add extra running or backstitches around the shape after filling it.

Pistil stitch is an Australian shadow-work stitch which is used to work the petals of flowers; a French knot can be worked at the tip of each petal.

Add linear details to the right side of the fabric after the shadow work is complete using stem stitch or backstitch (for both see page 26). You can also add tiny solid areas worked in satin stitch (see page 27) for emphasis, and use French knots (see page 77) to add texture to flower centers.

The best types of fabric to use are cotton organdy, silk or polyester georgette and organza, silk Habutai, and lightweight silk crêpe de chine. Always mount the fabric in a frame to help keep the thread tension even.

For most of this work, mount the fabric wrong side up as stitching is usually done on this side.

Cotton embroidery threads can be used for this work, but you may like to try silk thread on silk fabric.

Transferring the design

Draw or trace your design using a heavy black line. Lay the pressed fabric over the design, secure it with strips of masking tape and carefully trace the design with a water-soluble marking pen.

Using a loop start

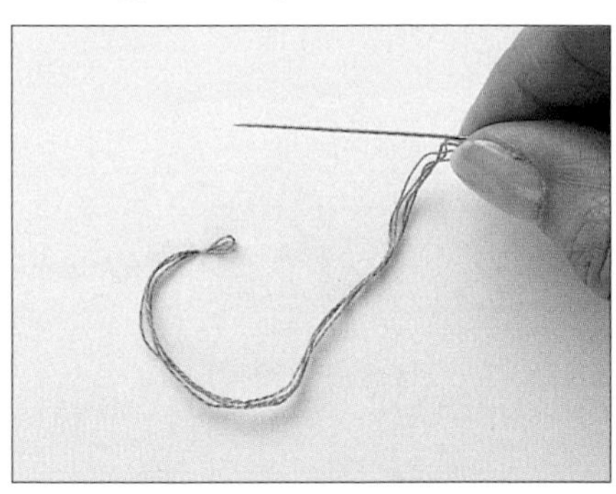

1 Cut a 30 in. (75 cm) length of floss. Withdraw half the number of threads you wish to use, fold them in half, and thread the cut ends through the needle, leaving a loop at the other end. Working from the right side of the fabric, take a tiny stitch through the edge of the shape and pull the thread through until a small loop lies on the surface.

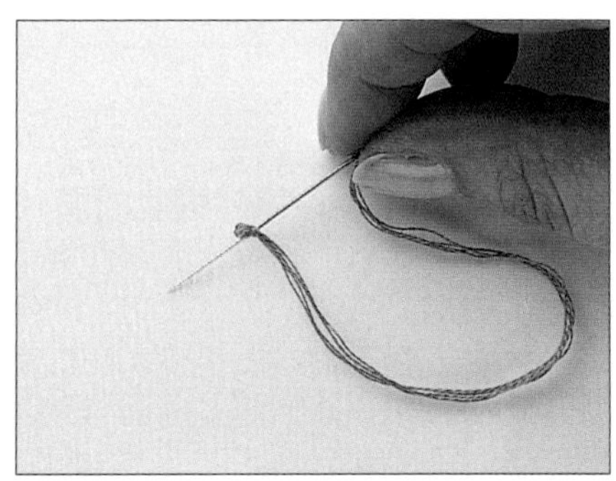

2 Slip the needle through the loop of thread and pull the thread gently. Take the needle back through the fabric where it originally emerged, and tug gently so the loop slips through the hole to the back of the fabric and anchors the thread. Fasten off the other end of the thread by taking it through to the wrong side and darning it neatly under several nearby stitches.

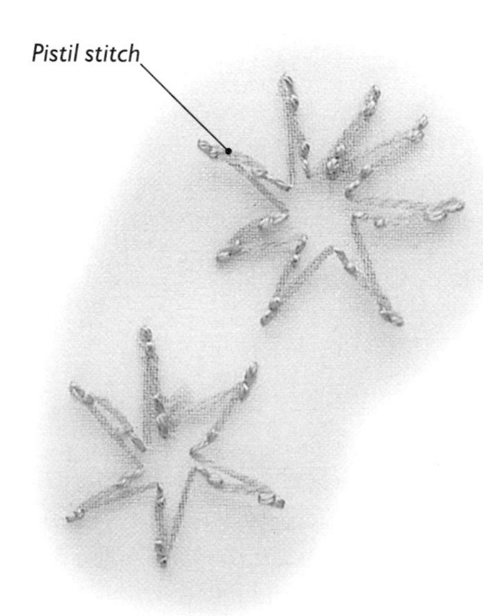

Working basic shadow stitch

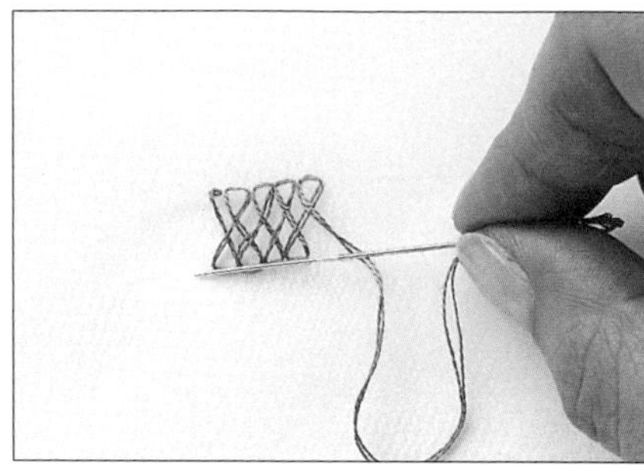

1 Working from left to right on the wrong side of the fabric, make herringbone stitches across the shape. Work evenly, making sure that the diagonals touch at the top and bottom in order to complete the backstitches neatly on the right side of the fabric.

2 To create a really crisp, neat point, bring the thread through at the point and work the shape in graduated lengths of shadow stitch. Make sure that the crossover stitches at the center of the shape are evenly spaced.

Working Indian shadow stitch

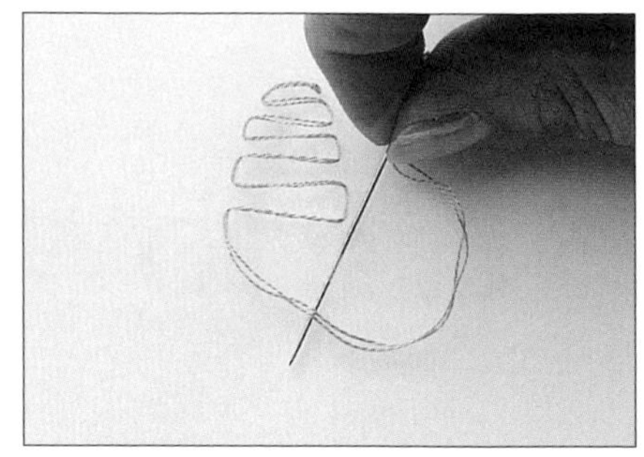

Working from left to right on the wrong side of the fabric, make long zigzag stitches between the opposite outlines of the shape. Work evenly to produce a neat row of running stitches on the right side of the fabric.

Filling rounded shapes with shadow stitch

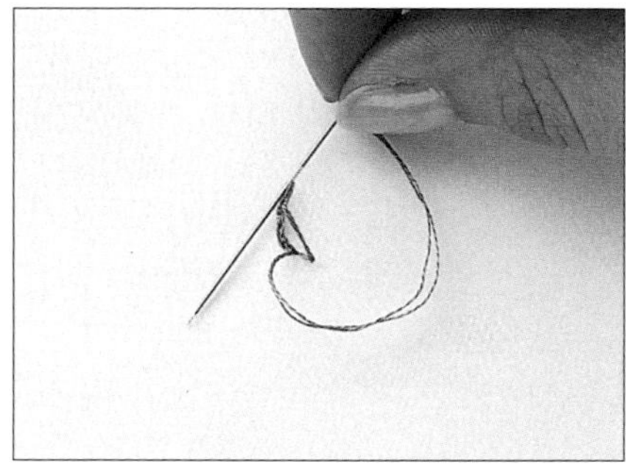

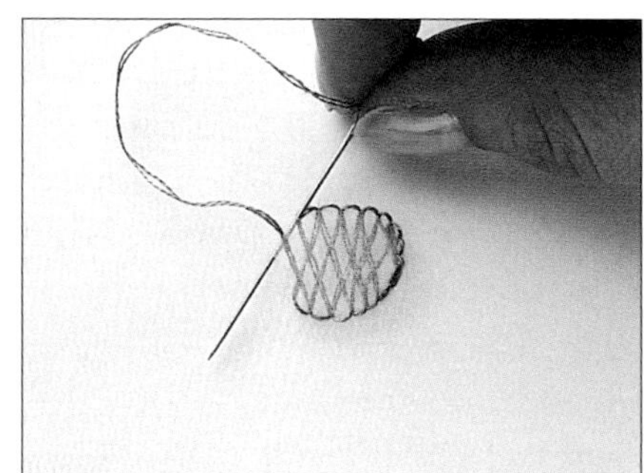

1 Begin by working two or three backstitches around the curve, working from the right side of the fabric. Then turn the fabric over and continue to fill the shape with shadow stitch in the usual way.

2 If the other end of the shape is also rounded, fill the shape in the usual way then turn the fabric right side up and backstitch around the last portion of the curve.

Shadow stitch

Shadow stitch

Stem stitch

Indian shadow stitch

Working pistil stitch

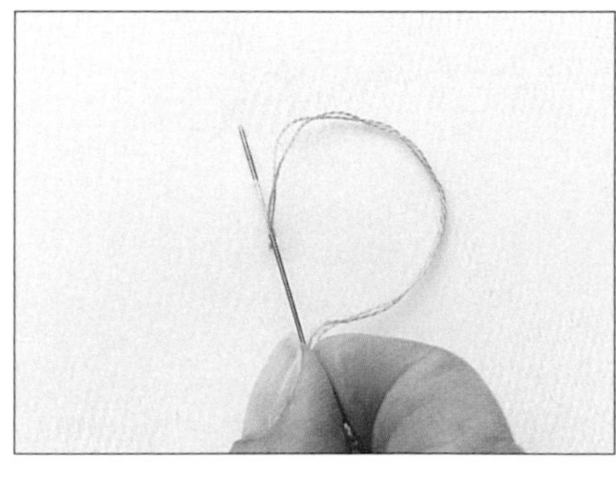

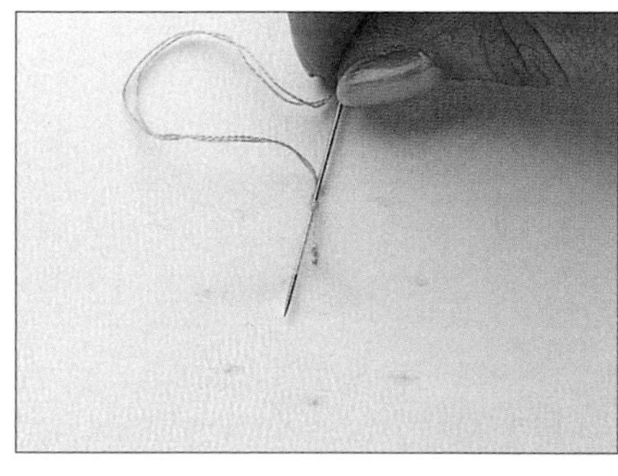

1 Working from the right side of the fabric, work two or three tiny backstitches at the base of the first petal. Take the thread to the back of the fabric, then bring it up just inside the petal tip and work two or three backstitches.

2 Bring the thread out at the base of the next petal to form a diagonal line of thread on the wrong side of the fabric. Repeat to make each petal. To finish, take the thread from the tip of the last petal to the base of the first and secure the thread end.

Insertion stitches

Insertion stitches (also known as fagoting) join fabric pieces with ornate, lacy seams. The technique was developed to join strips of narrow fabric to make large items of household linens, such as sheets and tablecloths. It gradually evolved into a more decorative technique, which was popular during the Victorian era.

Fabrics and threads

Both evenweave and non-evenweave fabrics can be used for insertion stitches. Choose a fairly substantial, closely woven fabric to ensure that the stitches don't pull it out of shape. Use fairly strong thread such as pearl cotton. The thread should be slightly heavier than the fabric, but should pull easily through the weave.

Basic techniques

Before starting, hem the edges to be joined. If the piece is purely decorative, such as a wall hanging, you can simply fold the raw edges under and press the hems in place. The hemmed edges are then basted onto a strip of stiff paper. This makes sure that the gap between the fabric pieces remains the same and also helps the stitches to be worked evenly. Traditionally, brown paper was used, but a better option is graph paper, as the grid will make it easier to position the fabric edges an equal distance apart.

The stitches shown here range from the simplest one, **twisted insertion stitch**, which is worked over a narrow gap of ¼ in. (5 mm) to **interlaced insertion stitch** which can be worked over a gap of up to 1 in. (2.5 cm), depending on the weight of the fabric and thread. **Knotted insertion stitch** is very durable and this stitch can be worked over a gap of ⅜ in. (1 cm). The final stitch, **buttonhole insertion stitch**, is worked over a gap of ¼ in. (5 mm) and is very simple to work.

Insertion stitches were originally developed as a practical way of joining narrow, handwoven strips of fabric. The stitches shown here are, from the top, twisted insertion stitch, knotted insertion stitch, buttonhole insertion stitch, and interlaced insertion stitch.

Preparing the fabric

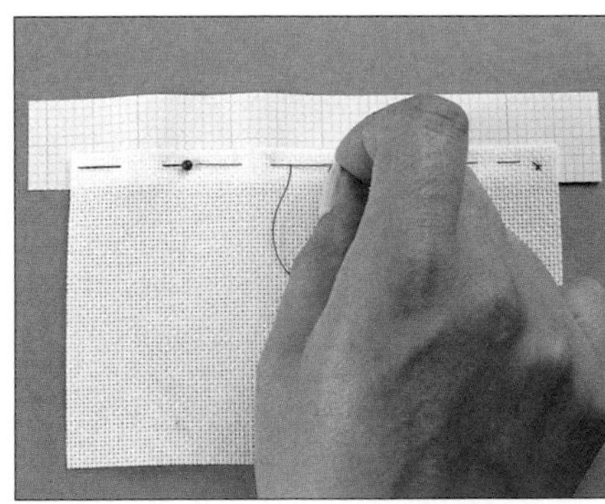

1 Hem each piece of fabric along the edge to be joined, and press the hems. Pin and baste one edge to a long strip of graph paper, keeping the fold straight along one of the grid lines.

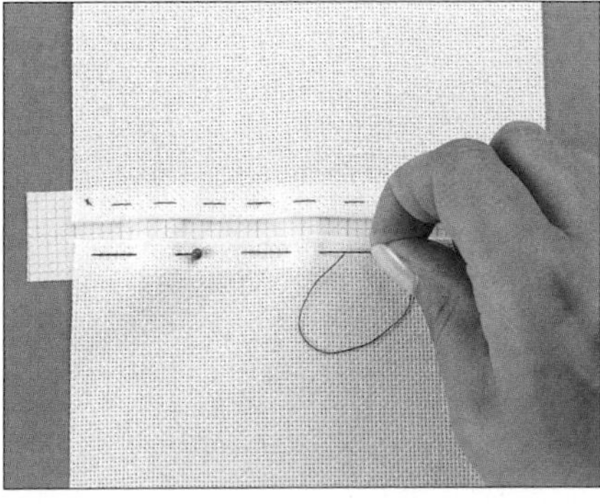

2 Turn the fabric so the graph paper strip faces downward, then tack the second piece of fabric to the paper; align the fold with one of the grid lines as before to ensure that the gap between the edges is even.

Working twisted insertion stitch

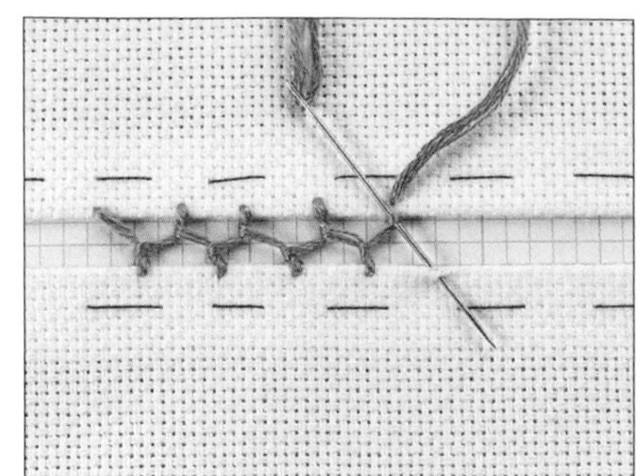

1 Start at the upper left. Take a stitch across to the lower edge, through the fabric from behind. Take the thread across to the upper edge, passing the needle under and over the previous stitch to make the twist. Insert the needle through the upper edge from behind.

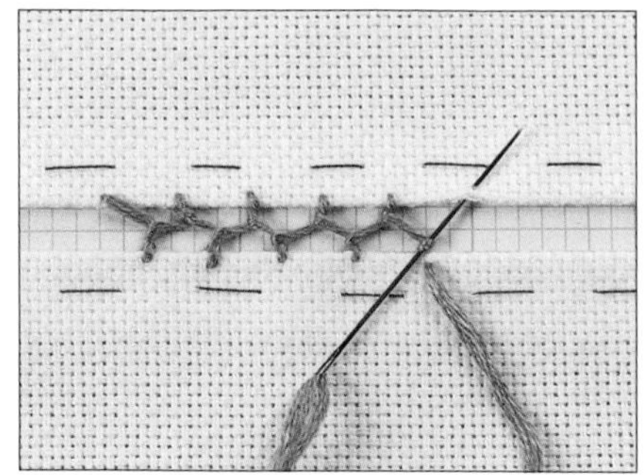

2 Take the thread down to the lower edge, again passing the needle under and over the previous stitch to make a twist. Insert the needle through the lower edge from behind. Continue in this way along the row, then secure the thread under the fold.

Knotted insertion stitch

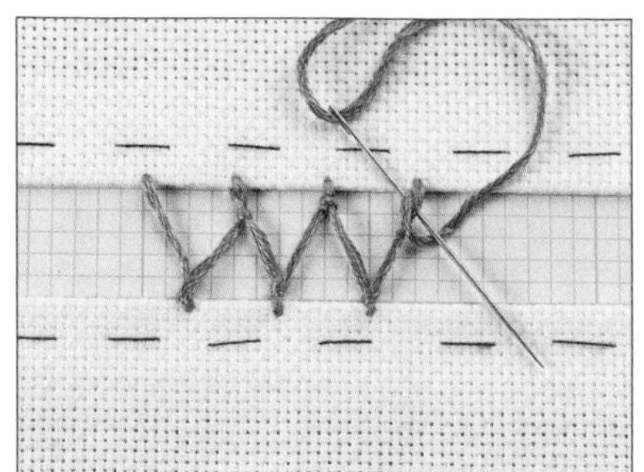

1 Start at the left of the upper edge. Insert the needle through the lower edge from the front. Take a stitch across to the top, and slip the needle under the previous stitch and over the working thread. Pull the needle through to form a small knot.

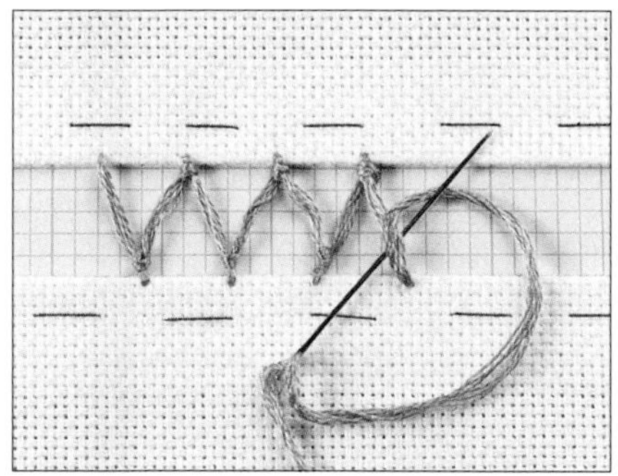

2 Take a stitch down to the lower edge, again taking the needle under the previous stitch and over the working thread to make the knot. Continue in this way along the row.

Working buttonhole insertion stitch

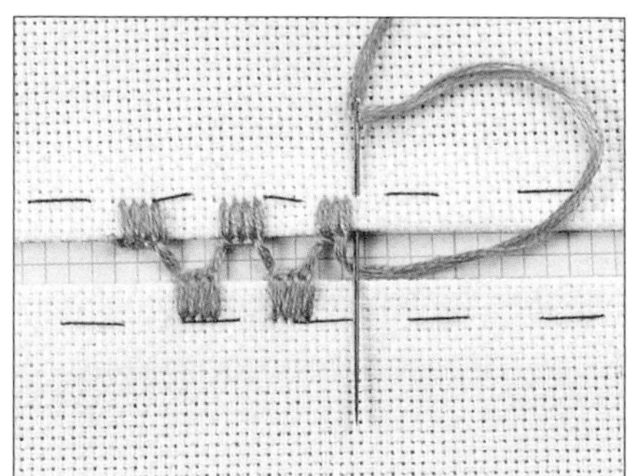

1 Start at the top left. Work a block of four buttonhole stitches into the upper edge (see page 59).

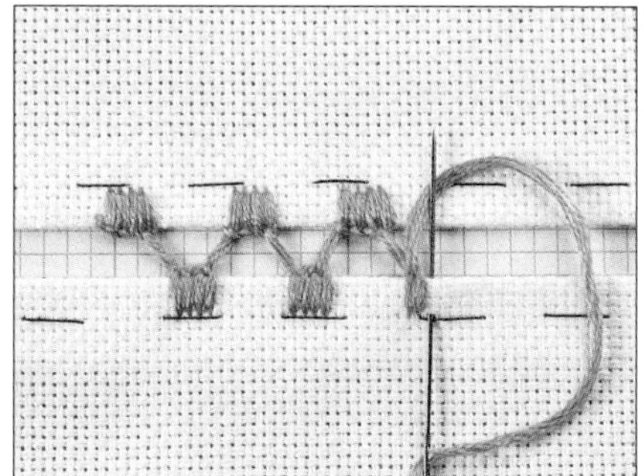

2 Take a stitch down to the lower edge, and make an identical block of buttonhole stitches on this edge. Take a stitch across to the upper edge. Repeat along the row.

Working interlaced insertion stitch

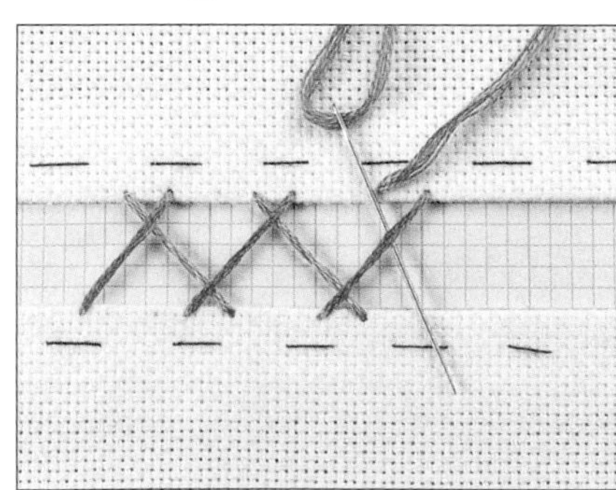

1 Start at the left of the lower edge. Work a row of herringbone stitches (see page 49) between the two edges, slipping the needle under each preceding stitch on the upper edge.

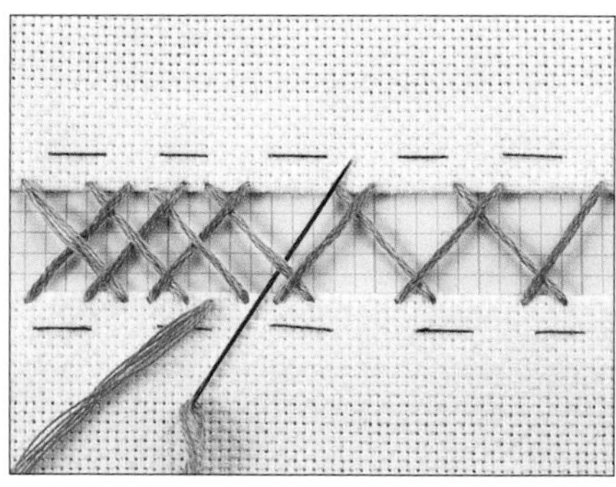

2 Bring the thread out at the top left. Repeat step **1**, but position the stitches between those on the previous row. Slip the needle under each preceding stitch on the top edge and, after working a stitch along the lower edge, slip the needle under the next stitch of the preceding row.

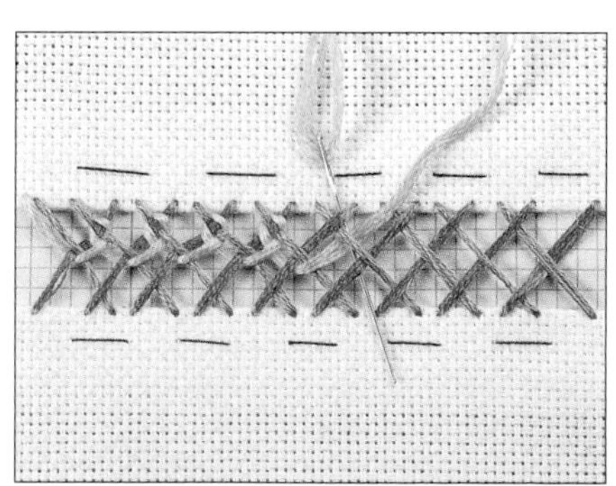

3 Bring the contrasting thread out at the left of the upper edge, close to the first herringbone stitch. Lace it through the stitches along the upper edge and where they cross at the center. Then turn the work and repeat on the other edge.

Smocking

Smocking involves gathering up fabric with decorative stitching. It is used to add fullness and elasticity to children's clothing and to embellish household accessories.

The procedure shown here is very straightforward. The pattern printed on the fabric is used as ready-made guide to position the stitches, and the threads are pulled up to gather the fabric as you stitch. Cable stitch and double cable stitch (below) produce a neat, pleated finish, while honeycomb stitch (overleaf) gives a pretty, crisscrossed look.

Leave a ⅝ in. (1.5 cm) seam allowance around the edge of the smocked panel. Before you start smocking, hem any edges that won't be enclosed in a seam.

Materials

Fabric Use a fabric with a regular pattern, such as gingham checks, or stripes. The stitches are usually spaced ¼-⅝ in. (6-15 mm) apart, so make sure the pattern is an appropriate size. To allow for gathers, buy at least three times the width of the finished piece.

Threads and needles Embroidery floss, pearl cotton and brilliant cutwork and embroidery thread are all ideal for smocking. Split floss into three or four strands, depending on the fabric weight. To emphasize the smocked texture, match the thread color to the fabric; or use a contrasting color to accentuate the stitches. Use a chenille or crewel needle.

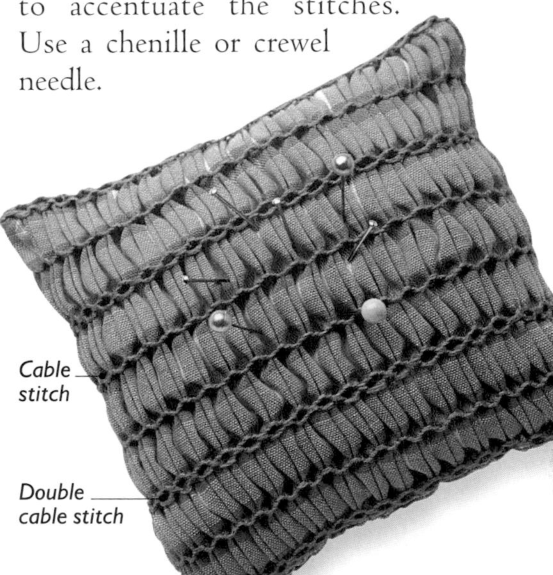

Working cable stitch

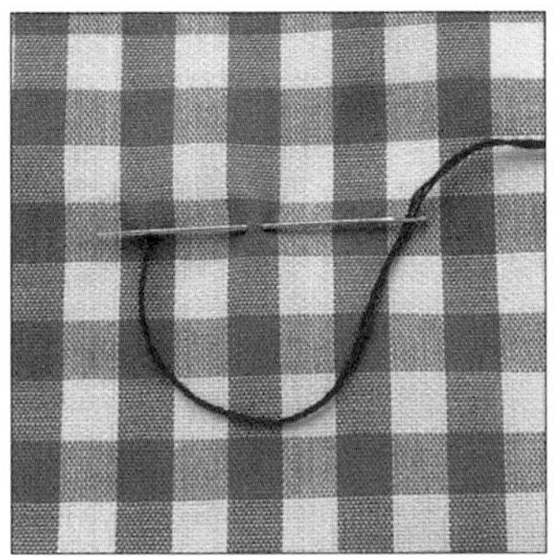

1 Work from left to right. Secure the thread and bring the needle up in the center of the first dark square. With the thread below the needle, work a stitch as shown in the next dark square. Pull up the thread to gather the fabric.

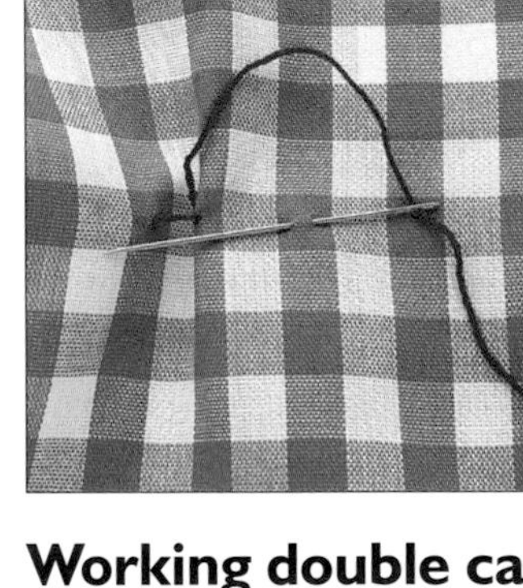

2 With the thread above the needle, work a stitch to the center of the next dark square to the right, pulling up the thread to gather the fabric as before. Continue in this way, placing the thread alternately below and above the needle.

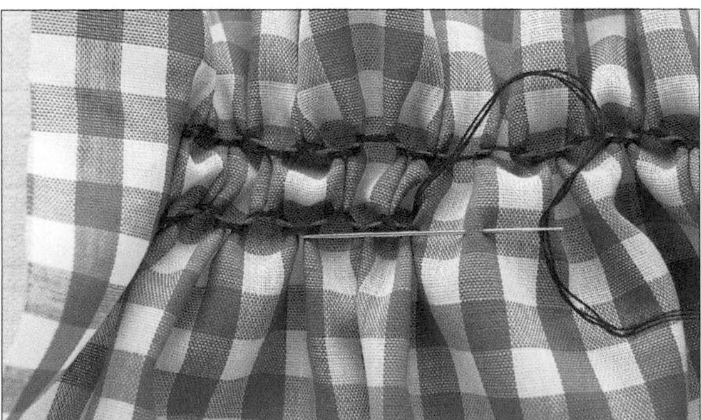

3 To work the next row, repeat steps **1–2**, positioning the stitches across the middle of the next horizontal row of dark squares. Continue in this way.

Working double cable stitch

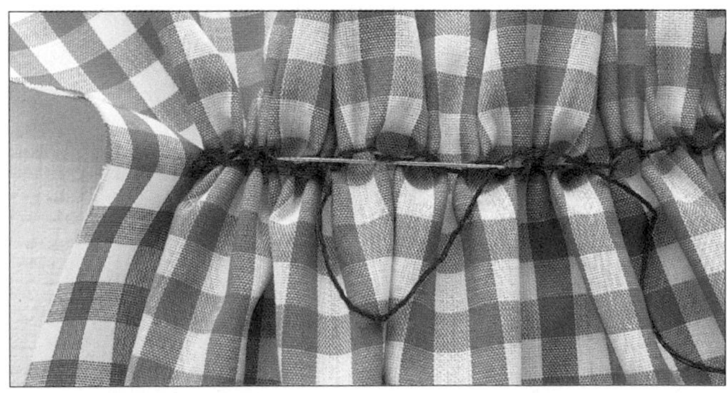

Follow "Working cable stitch," steps **1–2**, positioning pairs of rows directly beneath each other on the same dark square, and positioning the thread alternately above and below the needle to make the loops.

Working honeycomb stitch

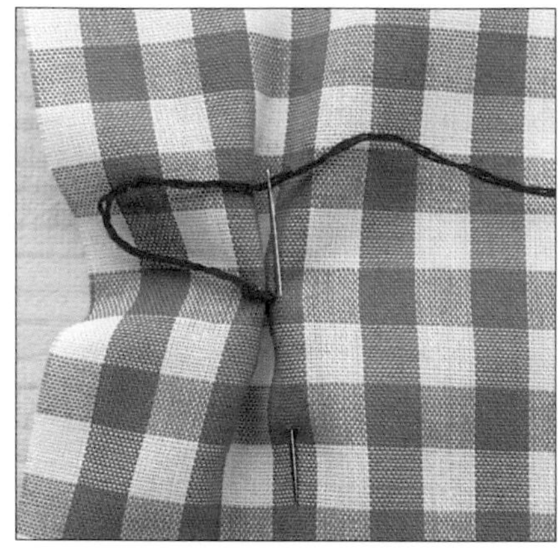

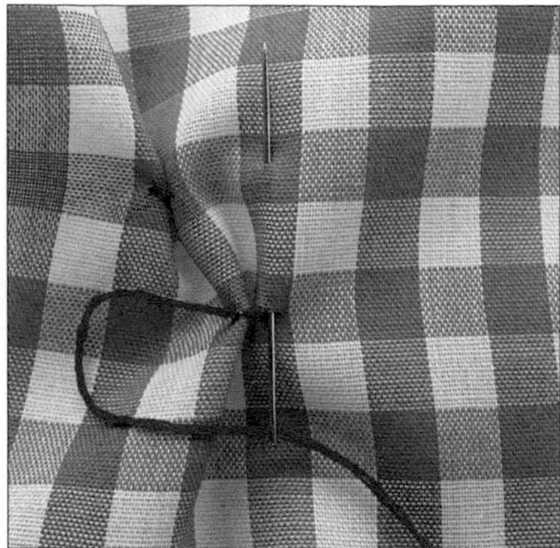

1 Secure the thread on the back of the fabric at the top left. Bring the needle to the front in the center of the first dark square. Take a small stitch from right to left in the center of the next dark square. Then take another stitch in the center of the first stitched square.

2 Pull up the thread to draw the two dark squares together, the enclosing light square between them. Insert the needle again into the center of the second dark square, and bring it out in the center of the dark square directly below it. Keep the thread firm but not taut.

3 Work two stitches from right to left across two parallel dark squares in the second row. Then pull up the thread and bring the needle out in the center of the dark square immediately above the second lower dark square, as shown.

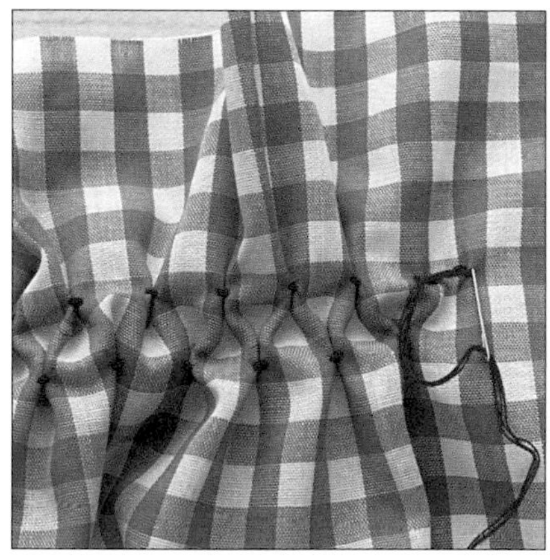

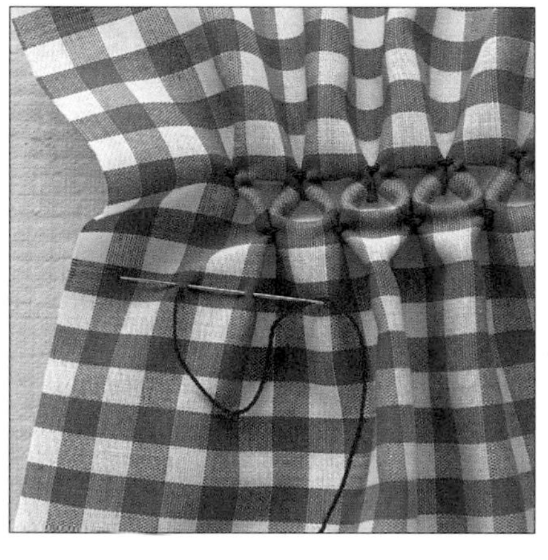

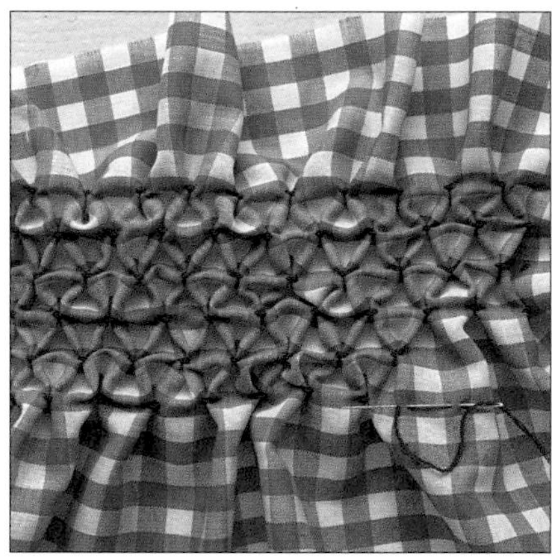

4 Continue along the row, repeating the two stitches up and down the two rows of dark squares. At the end of the pair of rows, take the thread to the back and fasten it off.

5 Secure the thread on the wrong side. Bring the needle up in the third row of dark squares, immediately below your previous starting point. Take a small stitch from right to left in the center of the next dark square to the right. Then take another stitch to the center of the first stitched square.

6 Repeat steps **2–4** to work another pair of rows. Continue in this way.

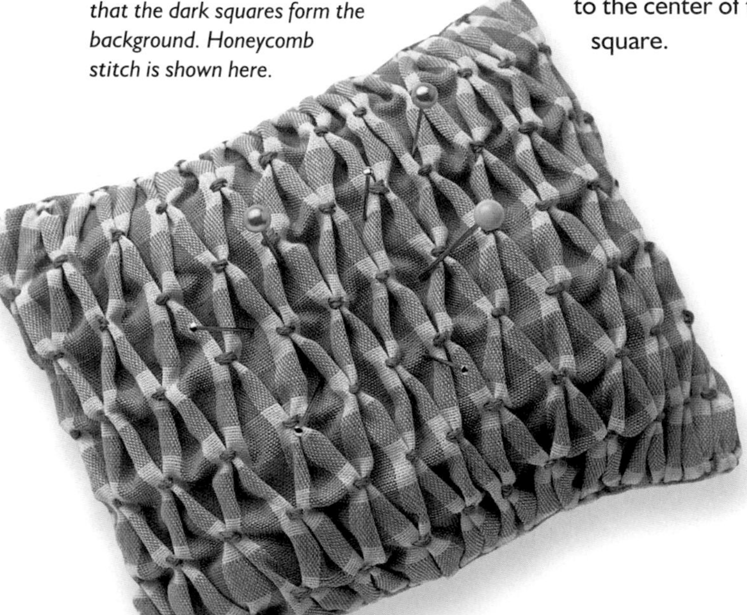

To give your smocking greater depth, stitch the light squares, so that the dark squares form the background. Honeycomb stitch is shown here.

Honeycomb stitch forms a more distinct surface pattern when it is worked on the dark squares of gingham.

The smocking technique shown on the preceding pages is often called "regular" smocking. The stitches are worked directly on the flat fabric, following a grid of some kind. The so-called English smocking method, shown on the following pages, involves gathering the fabric into pleats beforehand and working over these. Although it may appear to be more complicated, it is actually easier to work.

To gather a solid-colored fabric evenly for smocking, you need to transfer a grid of dots onto it, to provide a guide for the gathering stitches. Smocking dot transfers are available from notions departments. The distance between dots and between rows is given on the transfer. As a general rule, choose a transfer with closely spaced dots for a lightweight fabric and a transfer with wider spaces for a heavier fabric. The dots disappear with washing.

On fabrics with a regular pattern, such as checked gingham, the pattern provides a ready-made grid. For further information on smocking on gingham fabric, see pages 253 and 254.

Using smocking dot transfers

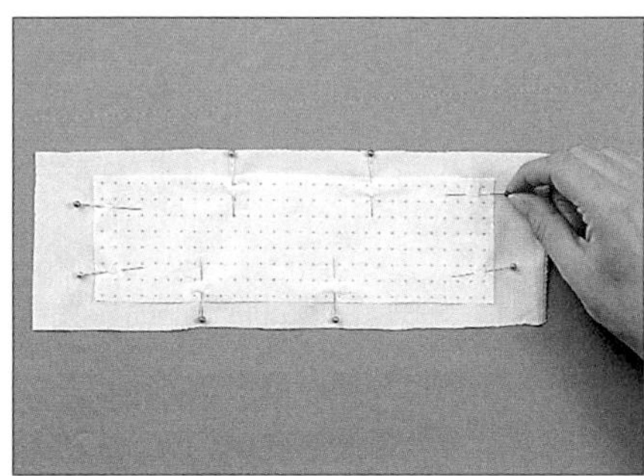

1 Press the fabric and place it right side down on the ironing board. Cut the smocking dot transfer to fit the area of fabric to be smocked, allowing for seam and hem allowances all around as required. Position the transfer printed side down on the fabric. Pin in place.

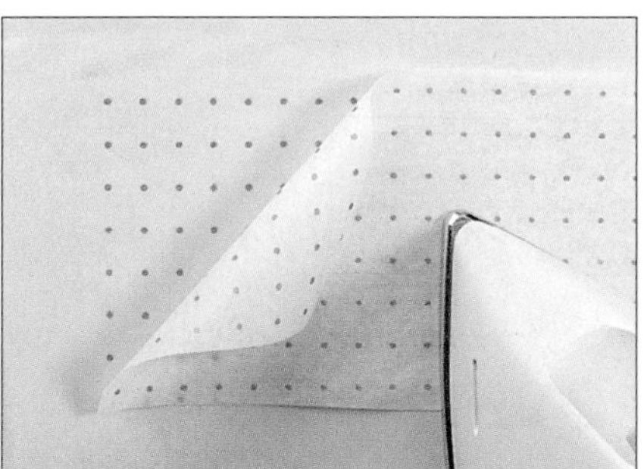

2 Set your iron to a hot setting. Slide the iron lightly and quickly over the transfer, working with a lifting action. Check that all the dots have been transferred, then remove the transfer paper from the fabric.

A baby's romper is given a special touch with a smocked bib worked in stem stitch and wave stitch in coordinating thread colors.

Gathering the fabric

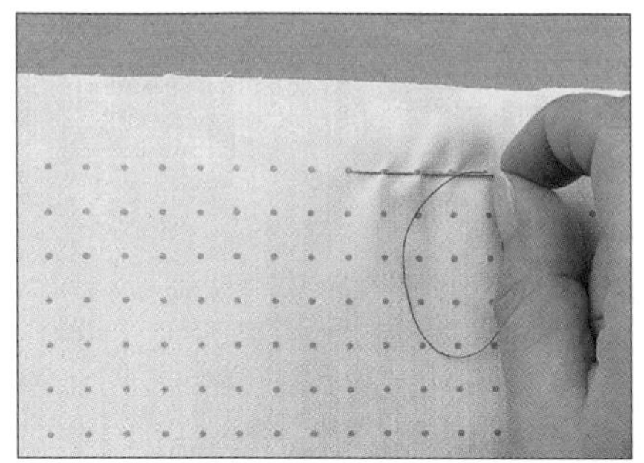

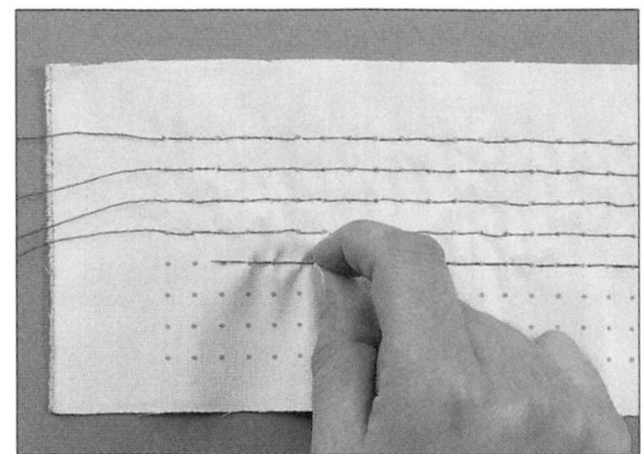

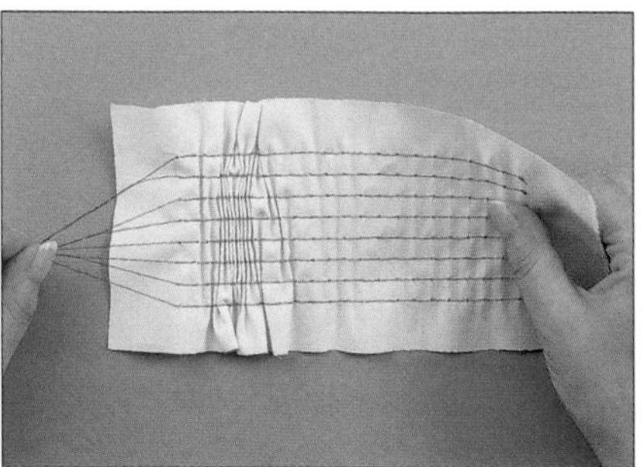

1 Thread a length of strong sewing thread onto a needle, and knot the end. Lay the fabric wrong side up. Working from right to left along the top row of dots, work a line of running stitches, picking up just a few threads as you pass the needle under each dot.

2 When you reach the end of the first row of dots, leave a long thread end. Repeat steps **1** and **2** for each row of dots, working from right to left each time.

3 Pull the thread ends evenly to gather the fabric into parallel pleats. First pull the threads tightly to draw up the pleats, then release them to form the width required for the finished smocked area.

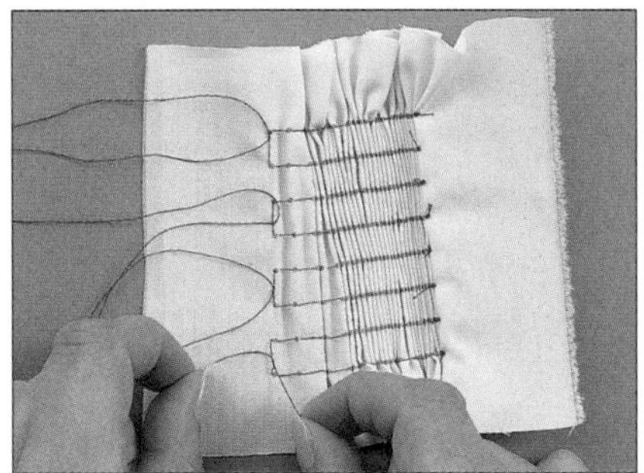

4 Tie the thread ends together in pairs at the left edge of the pleats. Adjust the pleats so they are straight and even. Work the smocking stitches from the right side of the fabric. When the smocking is complete, remove the gathering stitches.

Working stem stitch

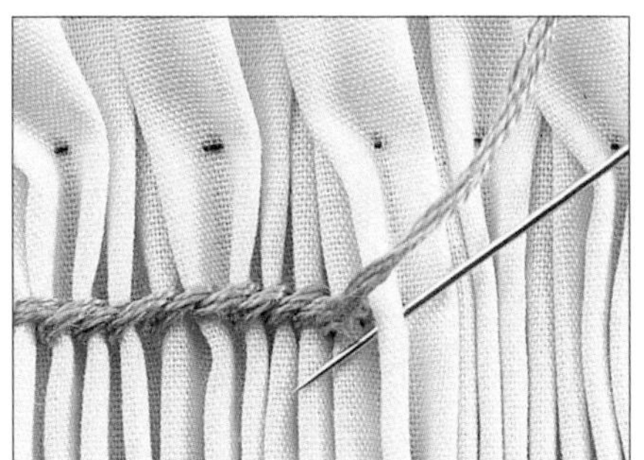

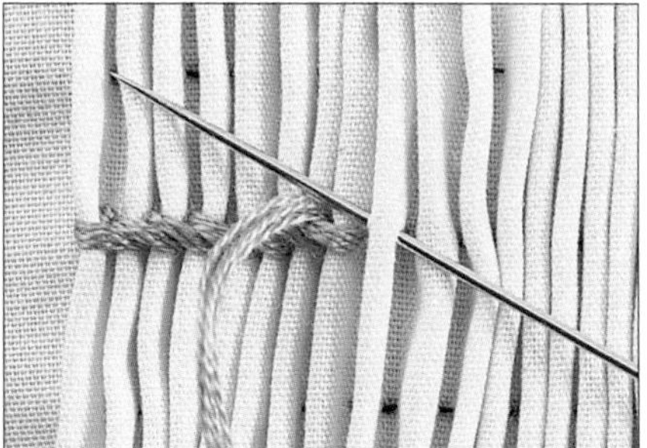

1 Bring the needle to the front at the left of the first pleat on the left. To slant the stitches downward: with the thread above the needle and the needle slanting downward, work a stitch from right to left over the next pleat. Continue in this way.

2 To slant the stitches in the opposite direction: start to the left of the first pleat as in step **1** (left). With the thread below the needle this time, work a stitch from right to left over the next pleat. Continue in this way across the pleats.

Working wave stitch

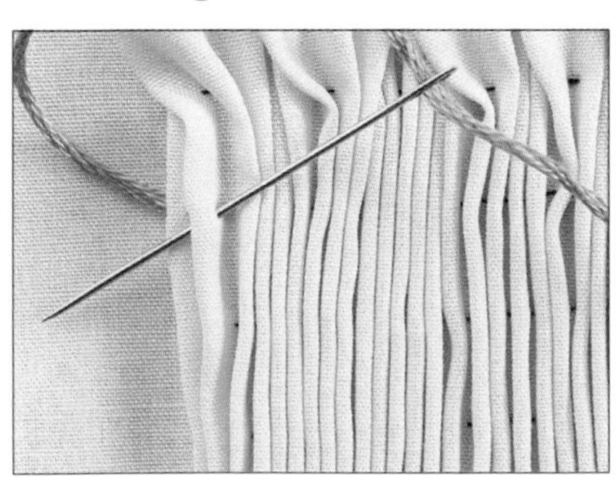

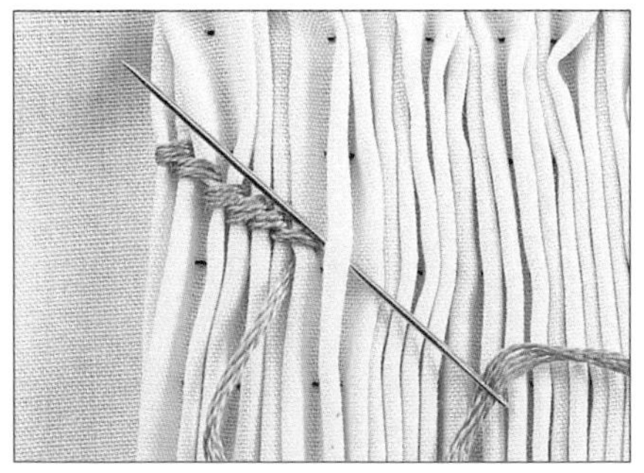

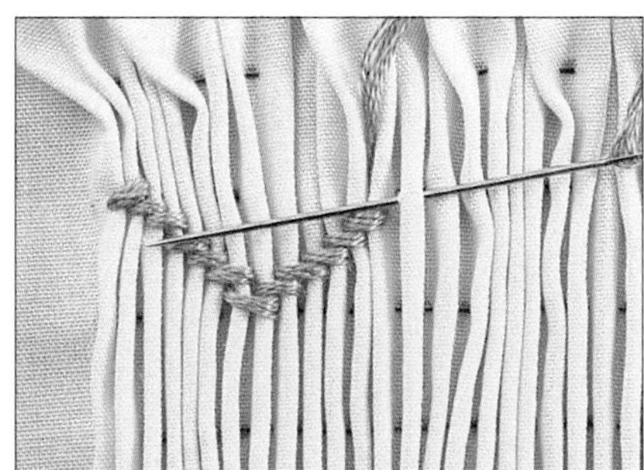

1 Start at the left of the left-hand pleat. With the thread above the needle, take a stitch from right to left over the next pleat, slanting the needle slightly downward. Work six stitches, keeping the thread above the needle and slanting downward with each stitch.

2 On the seventh stitch, take a stitch from right to left over the next pleat, keeping the thread below the needle and slanting the needle slightly upward. Work six stitches in this way, keeping the thread below the needle, and slanting the needle upward with each stitch.

3 On the seventh stitch, take a stitch from right to left over the next pleat, keeping the thread above the needle and slanting the needle slightly downward. Continue in this way to form a wavelike pattern.

Diamond stitch and Vandyke stitch are highly decorative smocking stitches, which you can work in a single row or in a deep band across the fabric. The instructions below show how to work these stitches on pregathered fabric, using the rows of gathering stitches as a guide for spacing. Work the stitches from the right side of the fabric, keeping the needle horizontal and the tension even.

Diamond stitch forms rows of zigzags across the smocked fabric; the diamond shapes are formed where two rows of stitches meet. Work this smocking stitch from left to right along two rows of the gathering stitches. Diamond stitch gives a very elastic finish.

Vandyke stitch is worked from right to left across the fabric, along two rows of gathering stitches. It creates an attractive intricate pattern and gives a moderately elastic finish.

Try working a smocking sampler, using the stitches shown in pages 253–258, and keep this for reference.

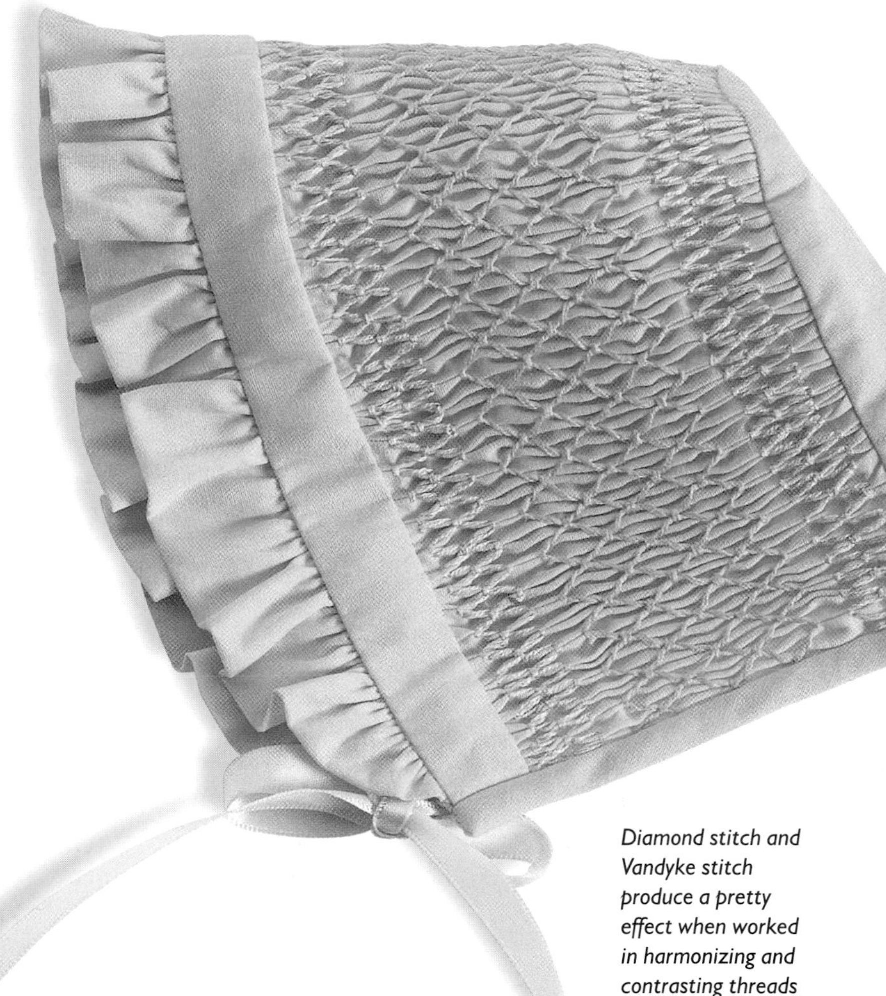

Diamond stitch and Vandyke stitch produce a pretty effect when worked in harmonizing and contrasting threads over a baby's bonnet.

Working diamond stitch

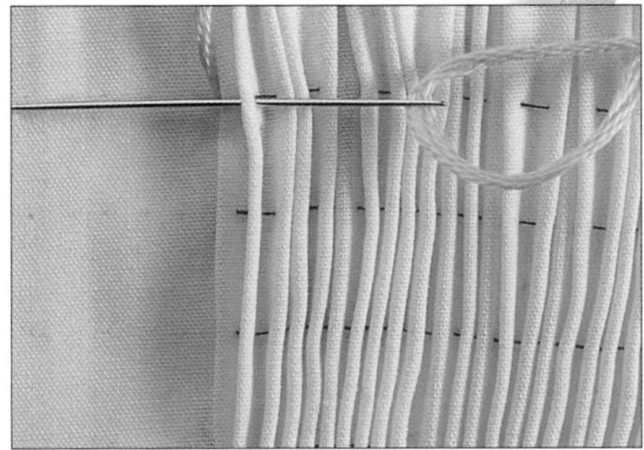

1 Start at the left of the first pleat on the left, level with the upper row of gathering stitches. With the thread above the needle, take a stitch from right to left through the next pleat, keeping the needle horizontal.

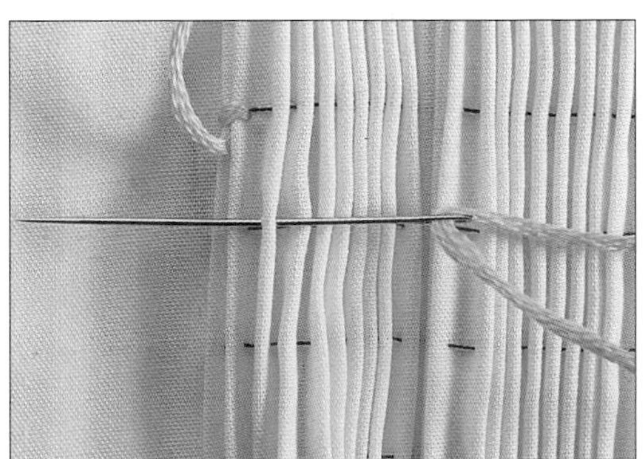

2 Bring the thread down to the lower row of gathering stitches, and take a stitch through the next pleat, keeping the thread above the needle and the needle horizontal.

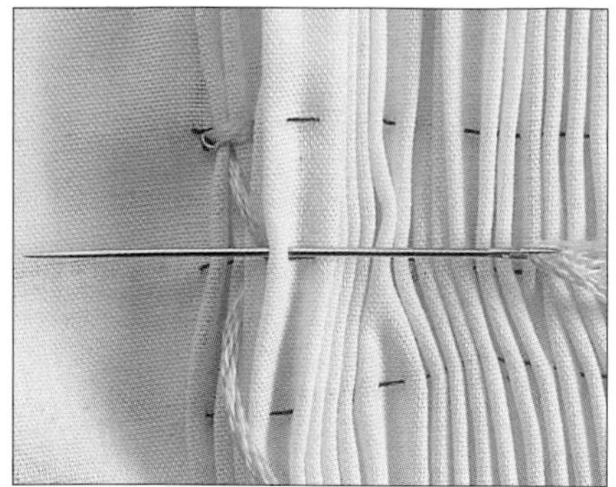

3 With the thread below the needle, take a stitch through the next pleat, keeping the needle horizontal. Keep the thread below the needle, ready to make the next stitch.

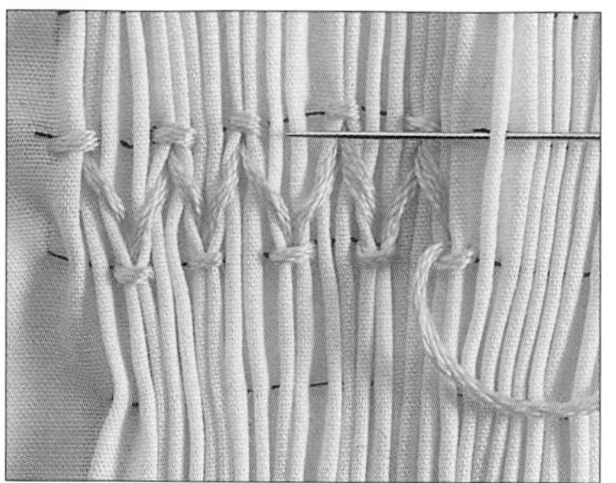

4 Take the needle back up to the upper row of gathering stitches, and take a stitch through the next pleat, keeping the thread below the needle. Repeat steps **1–4** to create a zigzag pattern across the fabric.

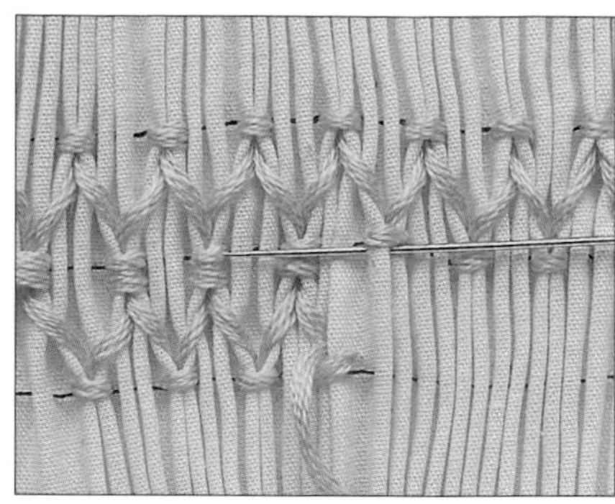

5 To form a diamond pattern, repeat steps **1–4,** producing a mirror-image row of zigzags across the fabric, directly under the first row.

Working Vandyke stitch

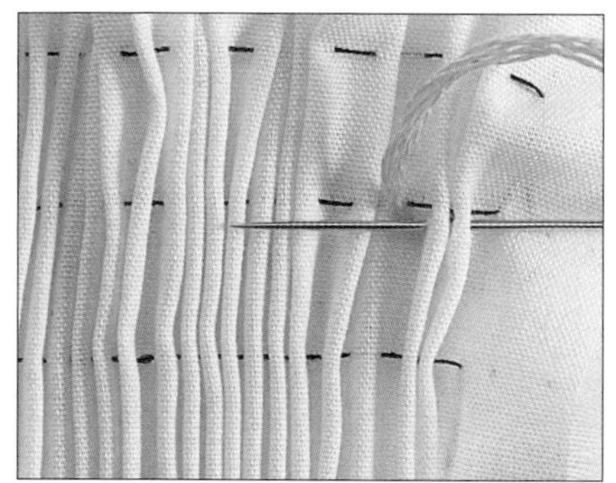

1 Bring the needle to the front at the left of the second pleat from the right, on the upper of the two rows of gathering to be smocked. With the thread above the needle, take a stitch over the first two pleats, keeping the needle horizontal.

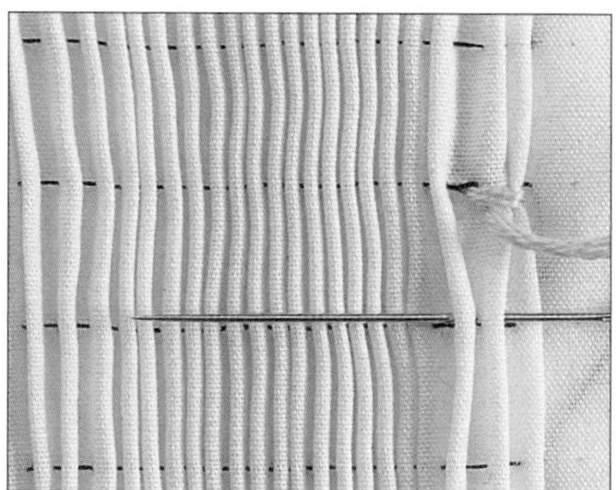

2 Bring the thread down to the lower row of gathering stitches, and take a stitch from right to left through the second and third pleats, keeping the thread above the needle and the needle horizontal.

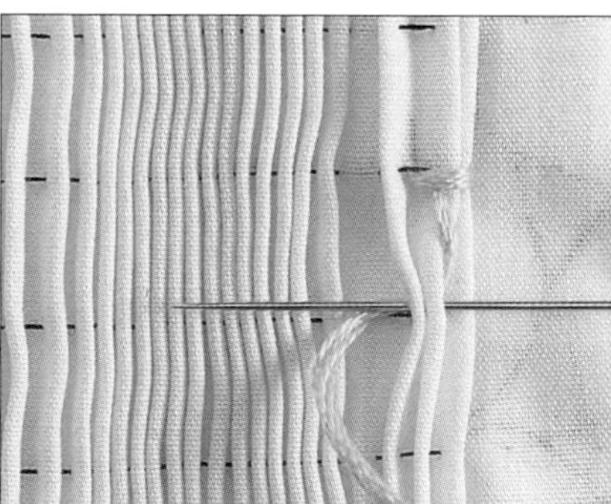

3 With the thread below the needle, take the needle through the second and third pleats again.

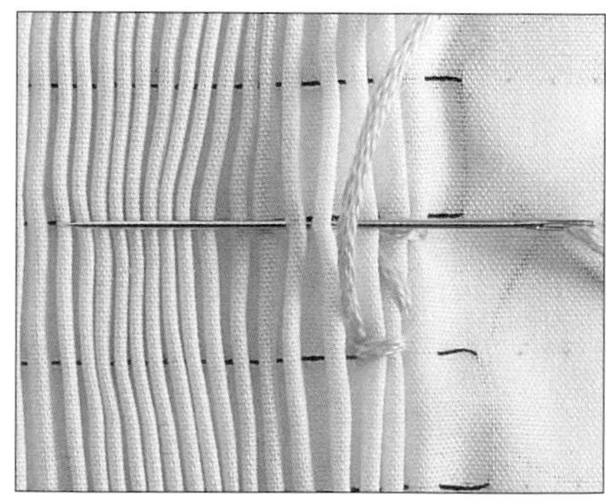

4 Take the thread back to the upper row of gathering stitches, and take a stitch from right to left through the third and fourth pleats; keep the needle horizontal.

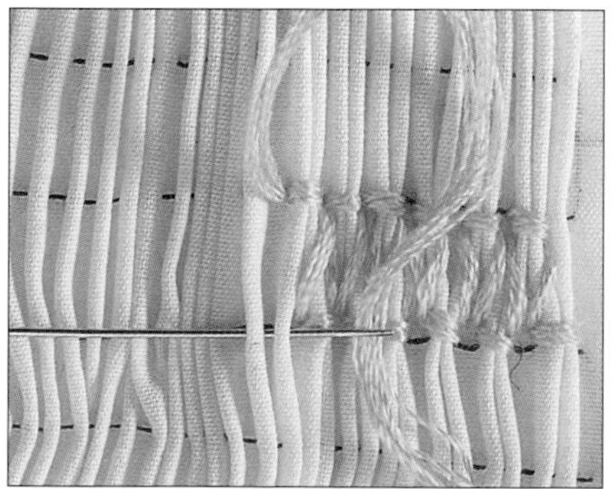

5 With the thread above the needle, take the needle through the third and fourth pleats again. Continue in this way, repeating steps **1–5** across the fabric.

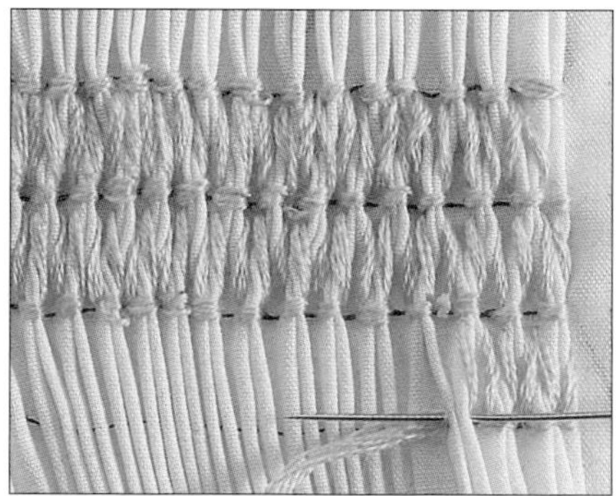

6 To work subsequent rows, repeat steps **1–5** producing a mirror-image row below the previous row, but omit the stitches at the upper edge of each new row; the stitches at the lower edge of the previous row are shared by the next row.

Crewelwork

Basically, crewelwork is any kind of embroidery worked with wool; but the term usually refers to the elaborate, colorful embroidery made in 17th- and 18th-century England and North America. Typical motifs include plants with swirling stems, birds, and animals —usually highly stylized.

The designs are usually worked in both filling and outlining stitches. The thickness of the thread makes them relatively quick to work, and the texture hides minor imperfections.

Popular outlining stitches include chain stitch, backstitch, and stem stitch, while satin stitch and long and short stitch are common fillings. (See the Embroidery Stitch Library.) The steps given here show how to work four traditional crewelwork fillings.

Materials

Threads and fabrics Fine crewel wool is the traditional yarn used, but Persian wool is also suitable, and tapestry wool can be used on coarse fabrics.

The fabric should be quite firmly woven. Evenweave is shown here, as it is useful for spaced lattice fillings; but the traditional choice is a linen twill.

Needles and frames Either a crewel or a chenille needle can be used to stitch the fabric. The choice depends on the thickness of the thread; chenille needles have larger eyes and come in larger sizes. For working lacing stitches over laid threads, use a tapestry needle.

Always use a hoop or other embroidery frame for crewelwork.

Working cloud filling stitch

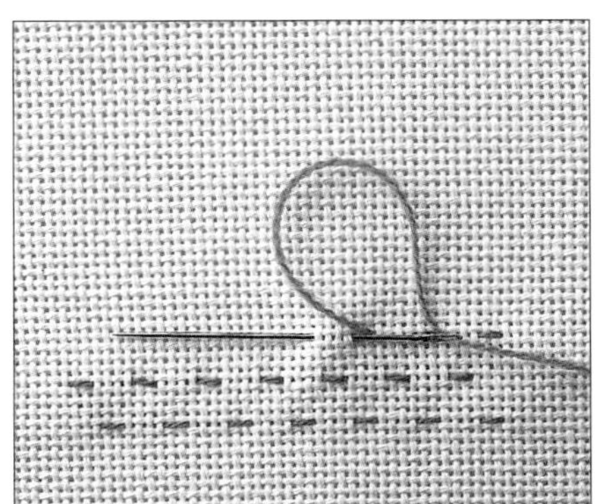

1 Using a crewel or chenille needle, cover the area to be filled with small horizontal running stitches, spacing the stitches alternately in rows.

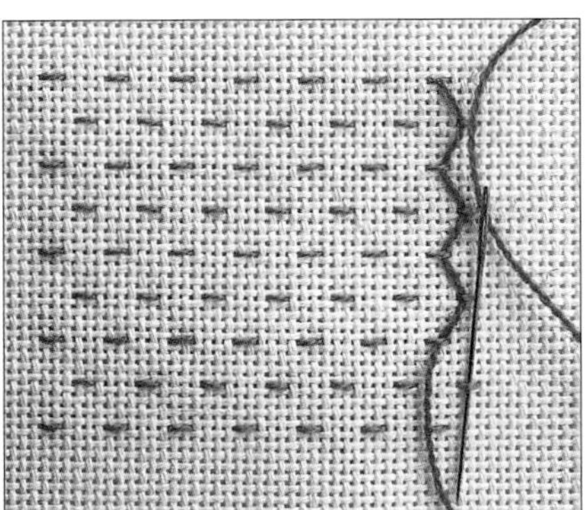

2 Thread a tapestry needle with a contrasting or matching thread and bring it up just below the stitch at the top right. Working downward, weave the thread through the first two rows of horizontal stitches, without entering the fabric. Insert the needle just above the stitch at the bottom right.

3 Bring the needle out again close to where you inserted it, and pull the thread through gently. Then, working upward, weave the thread through the horizontal stitches on the second and third rows, to form diamond shapes, as shown. Continue in this way across the shape.

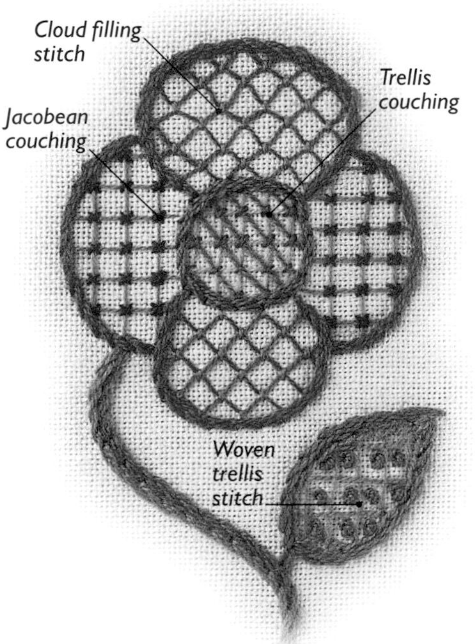

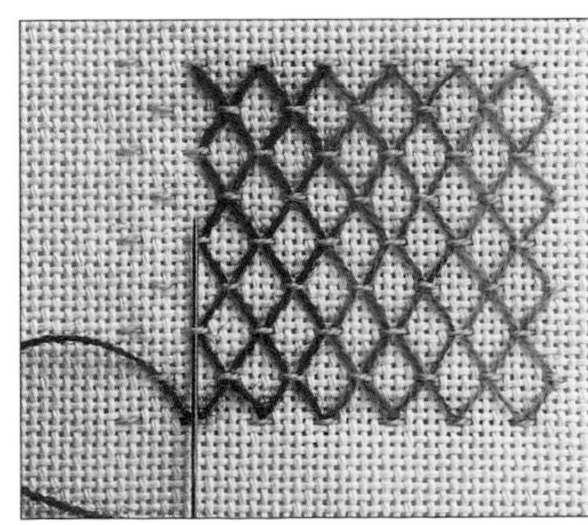

Cloud filling stitch looks particularly attractive when worked in graduated bands of color. You can also add French knots (see page 77) to enhance the tactile quality of the work.

Jacobean couching

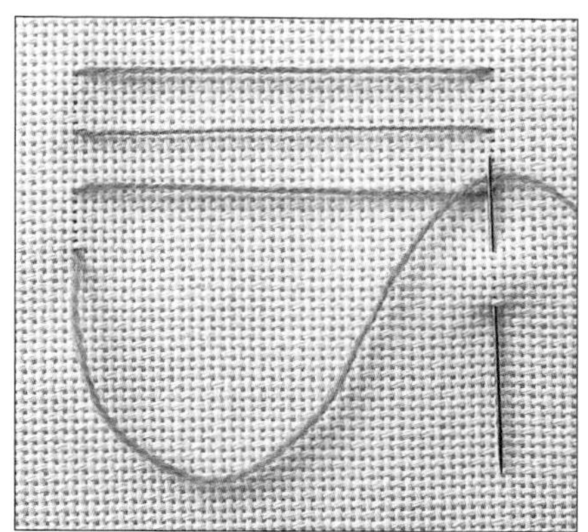

1 Using a crewel or chenille needle and the yarn of your choice, cover the area to be filled with evenly spaced, long horizontal stitches.

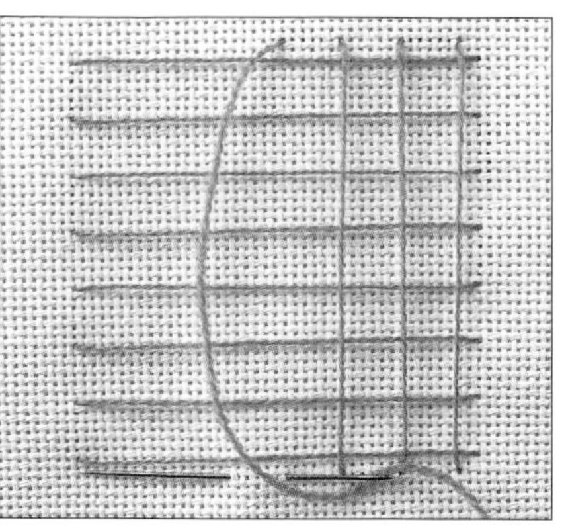

2 Using the same needle and thread, work evenly spaced, long vertical stitches over the top to form a lattice effect.

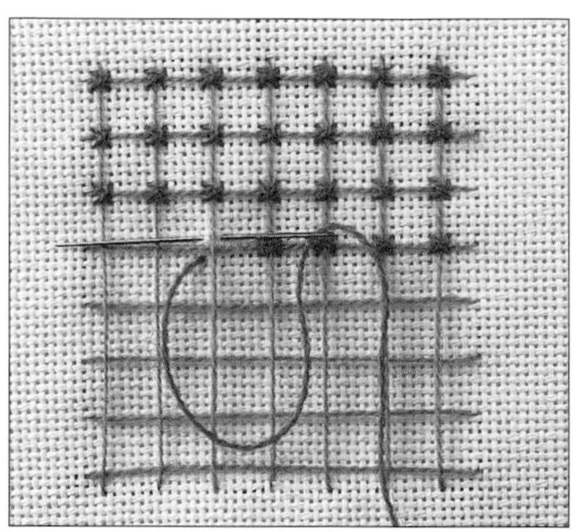

3 Using a matching or contrasting yarn, work a tiny cross stitch (see page 44) over each intersection, through the fabric, thus tying down the laid threads.

Trellis couching

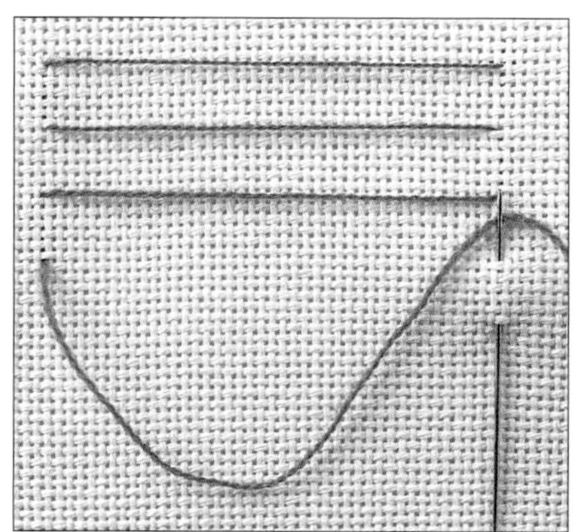

1 Following steps **1–2** (above), cover the area to be filled with evenly spaced, long horizontal and then long vertical stitches.

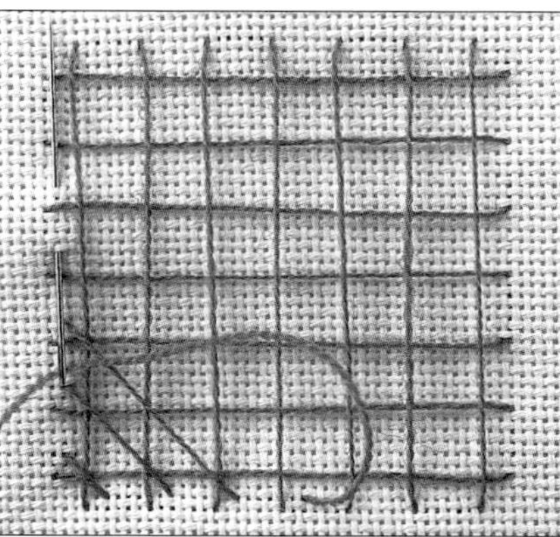

2 Using a matching or contrasting thread, work evenly spaced, long diagonal stitches, positioning them so that they cross the intersections of the horizontal and vertical stitches.

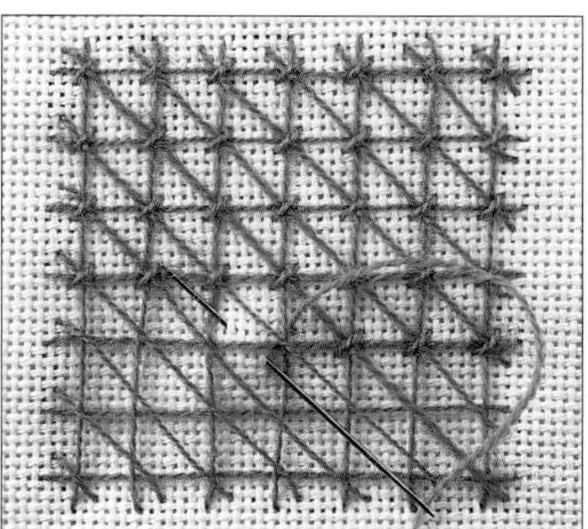

3 Using a matching or contrasting thread, anchor the horizontal, vertical, and diagonal stitches to the fabric with small diagonal stitches.

Working woven trellis stitch

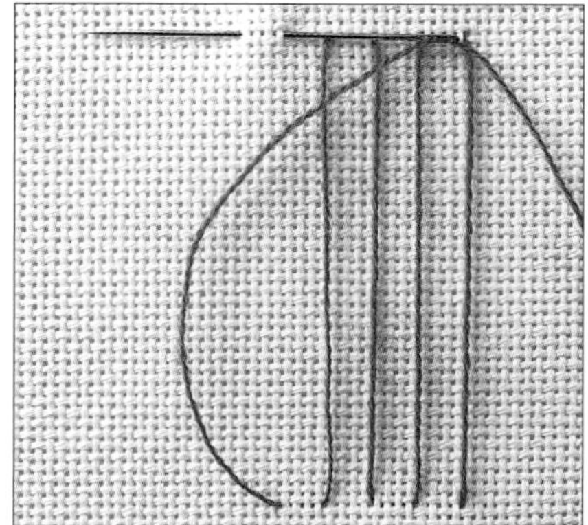

1 Using a crewel or chenille needle and the thread of your choice, cover the area to be filled with evenly spaced, long vertical stitches.

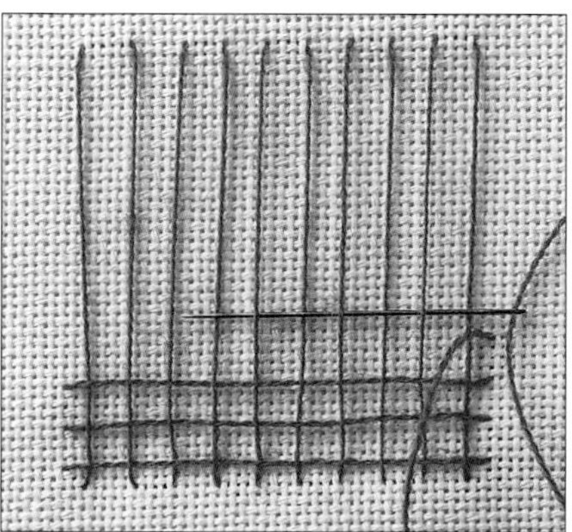

2 Weave a matching or contrasting thread horizontally across the vertical threads, taking care to space the rows at regular intervals.

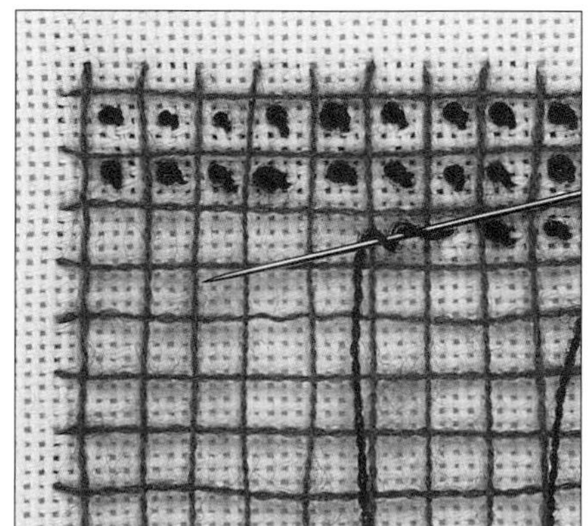

3 In the center of each square, use a matching or contrasting thread to work a French knot (see page 77).

Ribbon embroidery

Ribbon embroidery is the art of creating designs with ribbon. It can be used to add a personal touch to many items around the home; to make samplers; and to embellish clothing. The technique is ideal for forming floral designs, as the ribbon has a natural tendency to twist and curl. It also suits abstract designs that require a raised, textured finish.

The instructions below explain how to lock the ribbon onto the needle and how to secure it when the stitching is complete. Locking ribbon onto the needle lets you get maximum use from each length of ribbon. A step-by-step guide to popular ribbon embroidery stitches is given on page 262. Ribbon stitch and its variations create dainty flowers and leaves; loop stitch is used to make bolder, raised blooms.

Materials

Threads Silk ribbon gives the best results, as it is made specially for embroidery. It comes in a wide range of colors, in widths ranging from ⅛ to 1¼ in. (3 to 32 mm). Rich velvet, delicate organza, and polyester satin ribbons also give impressive results. To prevent wear on the ribbon, use lengths no longer than 10 in. (25 cm). Embroidery floss and pearl cotton are used as a basis for some stitches.

Fabrics Unbleached muslin is ideal for beginners. Also try finer cotton, linen, taffeta, velvet, and silk. Check that the fabric is shrink resistant. If the item is to be washed, the fabric must be preshrunk.

Needles Use a needle with an eye large enough to take the ribbon and to make a hole in the fabric that will allow the ribbon to pass through it without friction. A size 18 chenille needle is suitable for most projects.

Miscellaneous You also need an embroidery frame large enough for the stitched area, tailor's chalk or an air-erasable marking pen, pins, embroidery scissors and small beads.

Locking on and fastening off

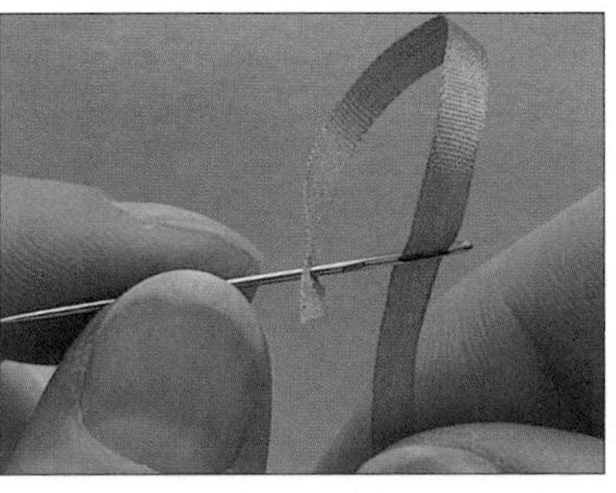

1 Thread the ribbon through the needle eye, then insert the needle point ¼ in. (5 mm) from the ribbon end. Gently pull on the long end to lock the ribbon on the needle. Tie a knot at the other end.

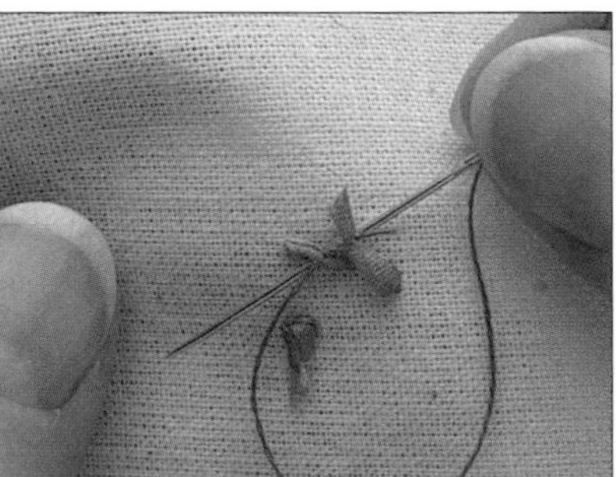

2 When you've finished stitching or come to the end of a ribbon length, weave the ribbon through a few stitches on the back of the fabric. Alternatively, anchor it to a stitch using sewing thread.

Working ribbon stitch

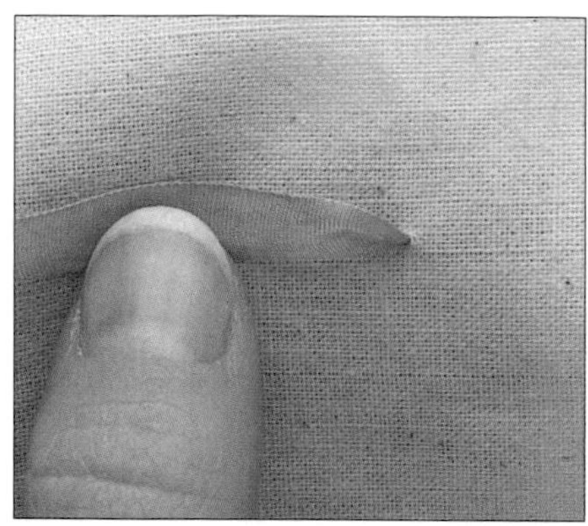

1 Bring the needle up at your starting point. Smooth the ribbon down on the fabric in the direction you wish to make your stitch.

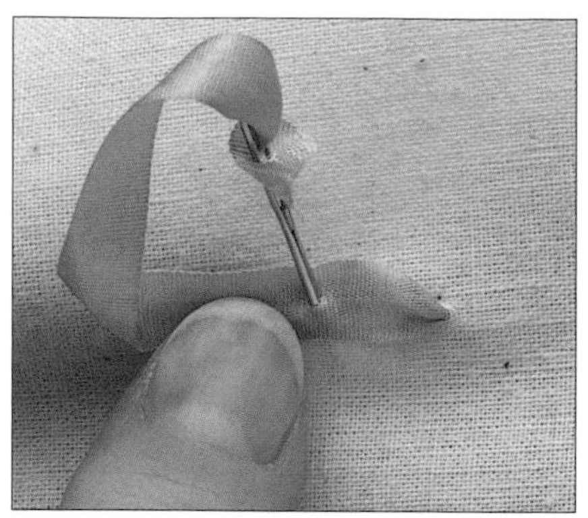

2 At the point where you wish to make your stitch, take the needle through to the back of the fabric, piercing the ribbon.

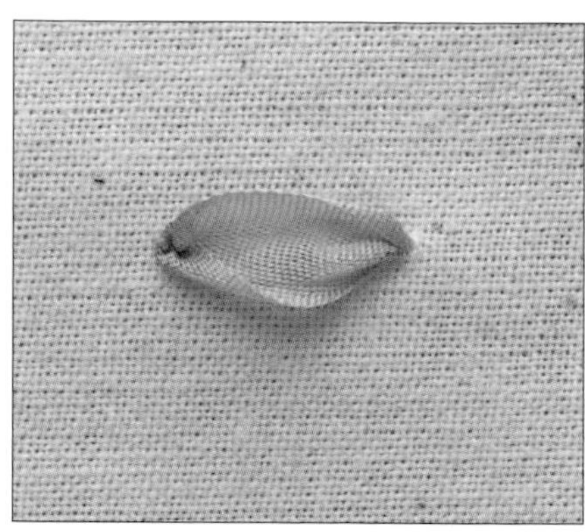

3 Gently pull the ribbon through the fabric so that it forms an oval shape on the surface. Continue in this way.

Working ribbon stitch variations

Side ribbon stitch Repeat step **1** for ribbon stitch. Then, instead of piercing the ribbon in the center, pierce it to the left or right. Pull the ribbon through for an interesting curved effect.

Back-to-back ribbon stitch Follow steps **1–3** to work one ribbon stitch. Starting at the base of the first stitch, work a second ribbon stitch as close as possible to the first.

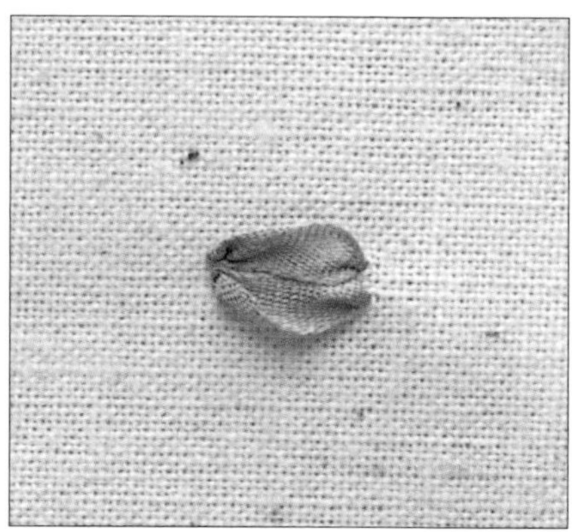

Back-to-back side ribbon stitch Work one side ribbon stitch, referring to the instructions on this page. Then, starting at the base of the first, work another stitch close to the first.

Working loop stitch

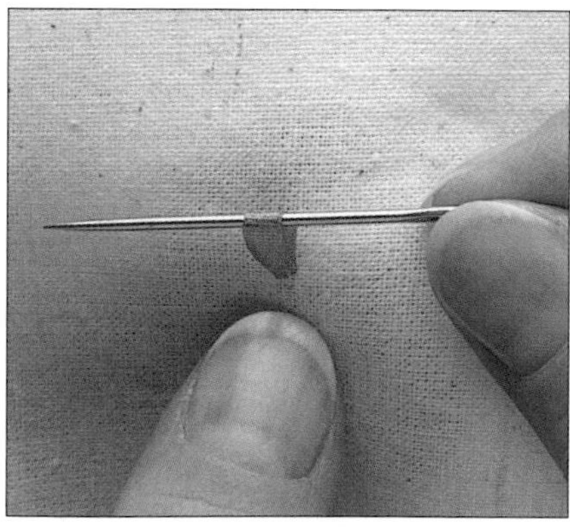

1 Bring needle up at the starting point. Depending on the size needed, form the loop over another needle or pencil. Take the needle back down into fabric, close to start of next stitch. Slide pencil or second needle out of the loop.

2 Hold the first loop with your thumb and forefinger, then bring needle out at the start of the next stitch. Repeat, working around in a circle to make a flower. Do not let the ribbon twist, and keep each petal the same length.

3 To make the petals stand out in a circle, finish each bloom by sewing a few beads at the center. Alternatively, work a few French knots (see page 77) at the center.

Ribbon embroidery is a satisfying and rewarding technique—you can build up beautiful designs quickly and you don't need a very high level of precision.

To begin with, plan your design in advance and work from that plan. With a little experience, you'll be able to adopt a free-style approach, letting the design build up as you stitch.

The steps below and overleaf show how to work two pretty blooms and an elegant bow. Refer to page 121 for instructions on locking on and securing your ribbon at the start of each motif, and anchoring it when you've finished stitching.

Spider's web roses are perfect for clothes and items that need laundering, as the ribbon is attached securely to the fabric.

Large ruffled flowers create a pretty frilled effect and look good in fairly large designs, scattered singly or clustered in groups.

Bows add a stylish finishing touch.

Working spider's web roses

1 Thread a crewel needle with pearl cotton or two strands of embroidery floss in a color to match your ribbon. Work a single straight stitch, then add four more, positioning them to form a spider's web.

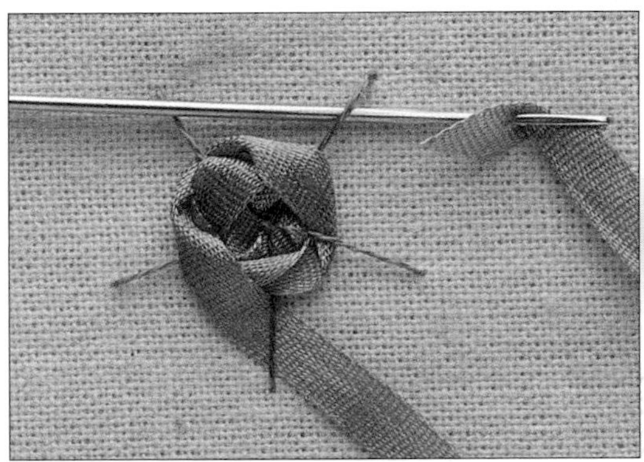

2 Thread a ⅛ in.- (3 mm-) wide ribbon into a size 18 chenille needle. Lock the ribbon onto the needle and knot the end. Come up to the front of the fabric at the center of the web. Weave the ribbon under and over the thread, working outward around the web.

3 Continue working in this way until you reach the outside of the web. Don't worry if the ribbon twists—the twists add to the effect. Take the ribbon through to the back and secure it.

Spider's web roses look particularly effective worked in two or three different-colored ribbons. Work around the web two or three times with each color.

Large ruffled flower

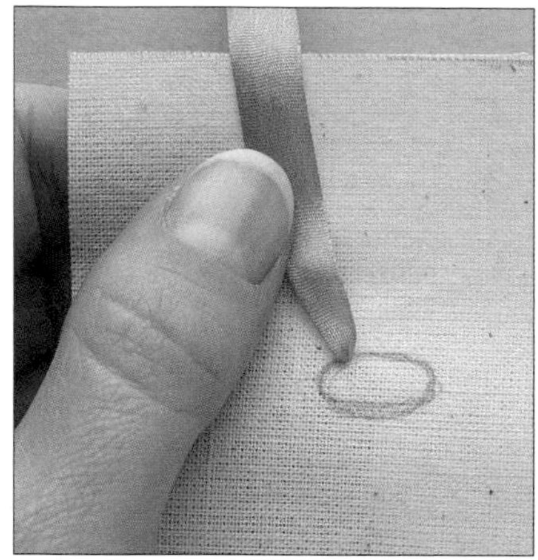

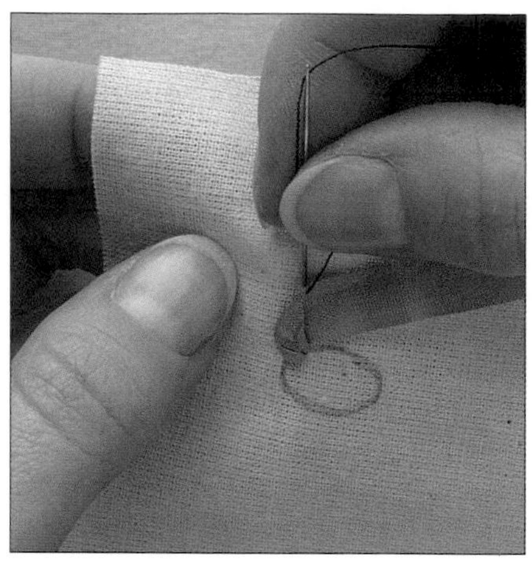

1 Using an air-erasable marking pen, draw a ⅜ in.- (1 cm-) long oval. Lock a ¼ in.- (7 mm-) wide ribbon onto a size 18 chenille needle, and knot the end. Bring the needle through to the front on the marked line.

2 Smooth down the ribbon in the direction of your stitch. Turn the ribbon under at a right angle, and secure the tip with a tiny straight stitch worked in a matching thread.

3 Fold the ribbon back down, and take your needle down to the back, next to the point where you came up. Work around the oval forming more petals in this way.

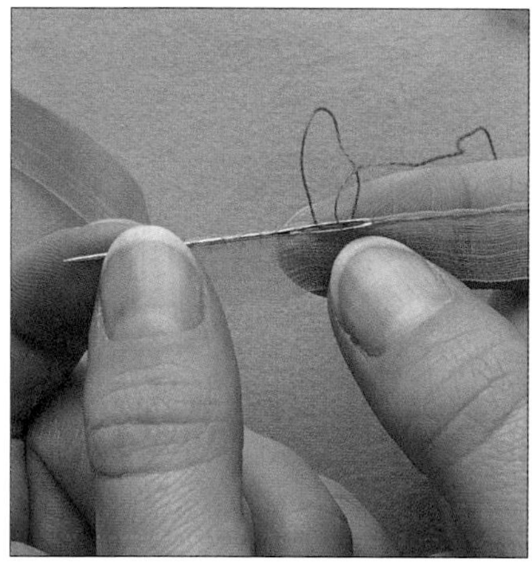

4 Cut 11 in. (28 cm) of ⅜ in.- (1 cm-) wide organza ribbon and the same length of matching sewing thread. Knot the ribbon end. Using the thread and a sewing needle, work running stitch (see page 26) along one long ribbon edge.

5 Thread the stitched ribbon into a size 18 chenille needle, and bring it to the front at the center. Draw up the thread to gather a short length of the ribbon at the center. Stitch it down using another thread.

6 Gather some more ribbon, wrap it around into a spiral, and stitch it down at intervals. Carry on until there is about ¾ in. (2 cm) of ribbon left. Take the ribbon to the back and fasten it off.

Ribbon bow

Decide on the length of your bow and cut a piece of ribbon to this length. Lay the ribbon onto the fabric in a bow shape. Using two strands of matching floss and a crewel needle, attach the ribbon to the fabric at regular intervals with French knots (see page 77). Take the ends of the ribbon to the back of the fabric and secure them.

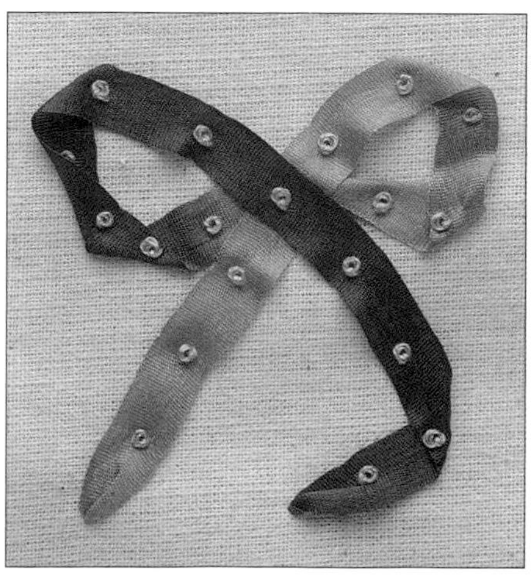

Beading

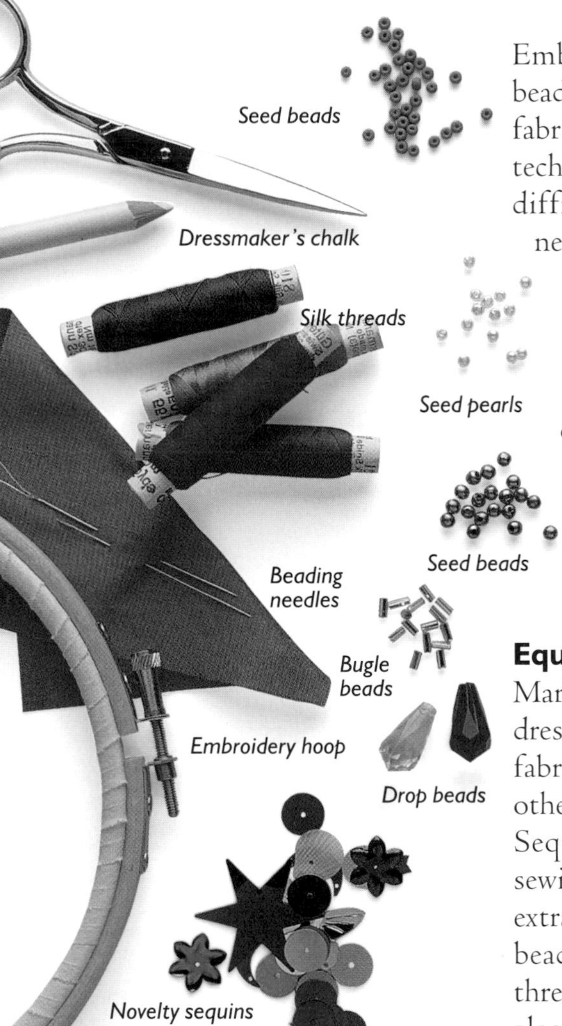

Embellishing embroidery with beads and sequins can turn a plain fabric into something special. The techniques involved are not at all difficult, but they do demand neatness and accuracy.

You can create flowing lines by couching—stitching a row of threaded beads to the surface of the fabric—or by overlapping sequins. You can also anchor single beads, and secure sequins with a tiny bead or with decorative stitching in a sunburst shape.

Equipment

Mark the design on the fabric with dressmaker's chalk, and mount the fabric in an embroidery hoop or other frame to prevent puckering. Sequins can be sewn on with a sewing needle, but you'll need an extra long, fine beading needle for beads. Use any ordinary sewing thread or fine silk thread. You can also use embroidery threads to attach large sequins.

Choosing beads and sequins

Beads and sequins are sold in all shapes and sizes in notions departments, bead shops, and by mail order. Most are sold in small packs, but you can also buy large display beads individually.

Rocailles or **seed beads** are tiny round beads.

Seed pearls are tiny imitation pearls or real, pierced pearls.

Square rocailles are seed beads with square holes.

Bugles are long, cylindrical beads.

Drop beads are shaped to hang from a point at the top. For embroidery, use drop beads with a hole that runs across the tip, rather than down the length, so that they dangle.

Faceted beads have numerous tiny faces (facets) to reflect light.

Flat sequins are completely flat.

Concave sequins are smooth or faceted with a curved surface.

Novelty sequins come in a huge variety of shapes, such as squares, stars, and moons.

Couching beads

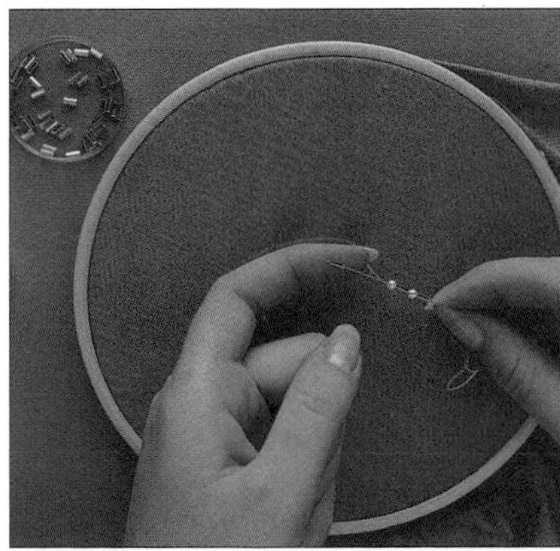

1 Secure a length of sewing thread with a couple of backstitches at the back of the fabric. Bring the thread to the front at the starting point and thread on the beads.

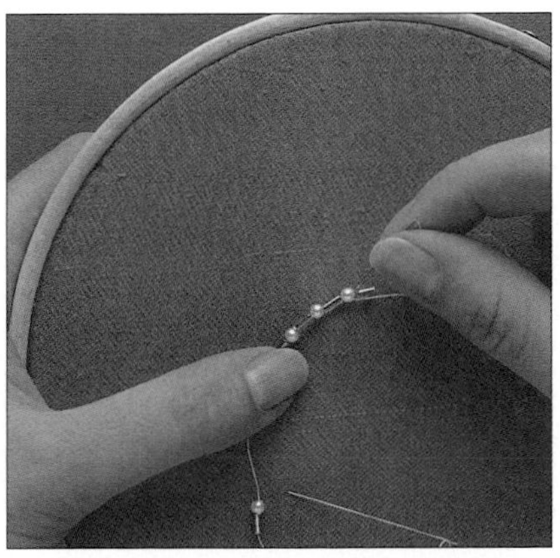

2 Secure another thread at the starting point. Lay the string of beads over the design line. With the second thread, stitch over the thread between the first two beads.

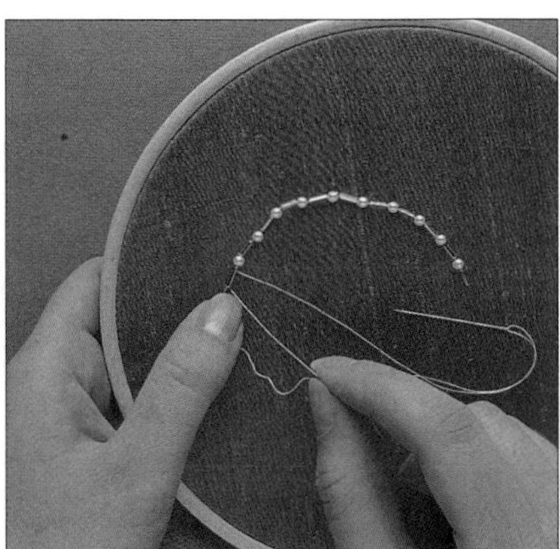

3 Continue stitching over the thread between the beads. Thread on more beads as you work. Secure both threads at the end with a couple of tiny backstitches at the back of the fabric.

Single beads

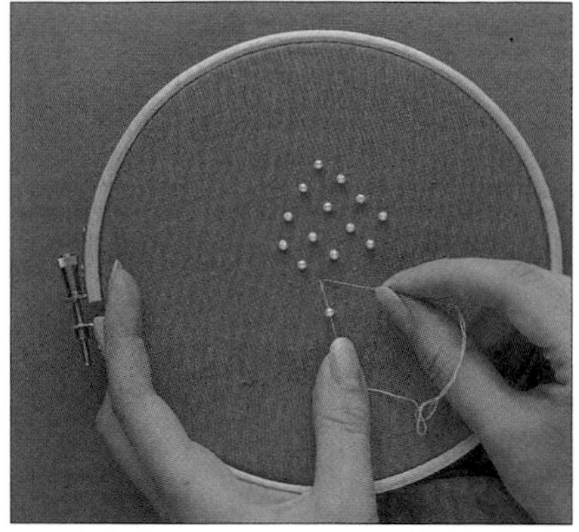

Bring the needle to the front. Thread it through the bead, then take the needle back into the fabric, so that the bead lies flat against the fabric.

This glittering crown is outlined with couched beads and overlapping sequins. Individual sequins and beads, and beaded sequins suggest priceless jewels.

Sunburst sequins

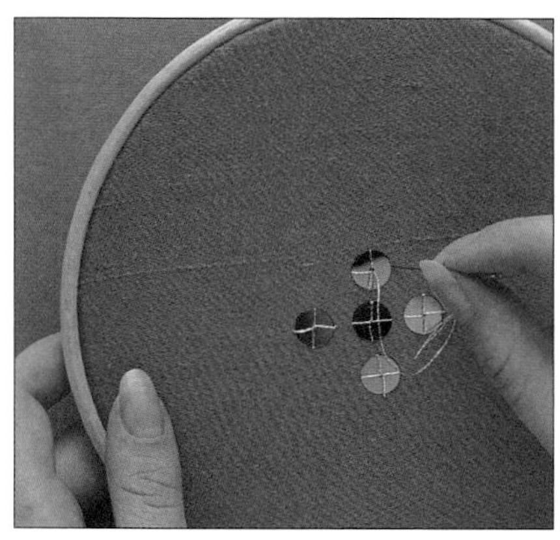

Bring the needle up through the center of the sequin, and insert it at the top of the sequin. Bring the needle back up through the center, and make three or four more stitches in a sunburst shape.

Overlapping sequins

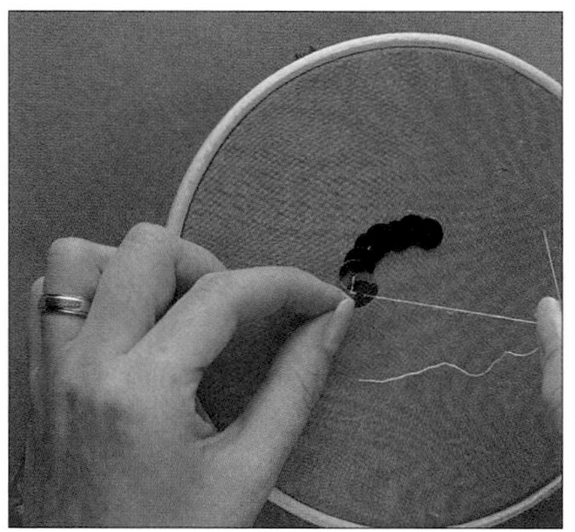

1 Secure the thread on the wrong side. Bring the needle up through the center of a sequin, and insert it immediately below the sequin.

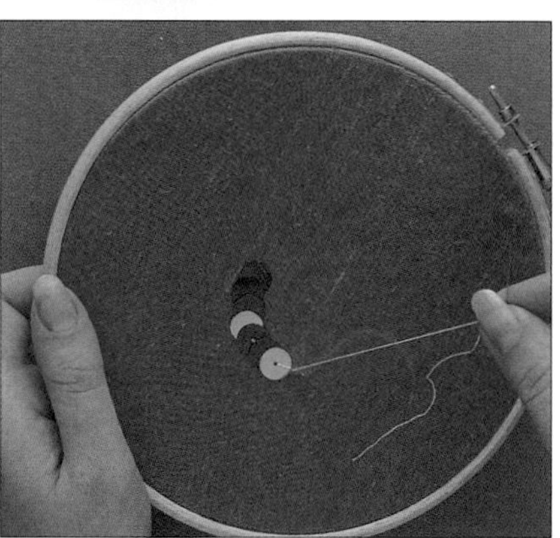

2 Bring the needle out again, very close to where it entered the fabric. Thread on the next sequin and insert the needle close below the edge as in step **1**. Continue in this way.

Securing sequins with a small bead

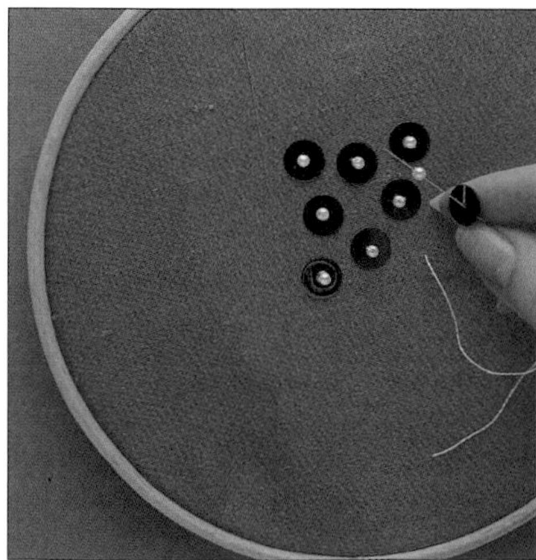

1 Secure the thread and bring the needle to the front. Thread on a sequin and a bead. Ease the sequin down so that it lies flat on the fabric.

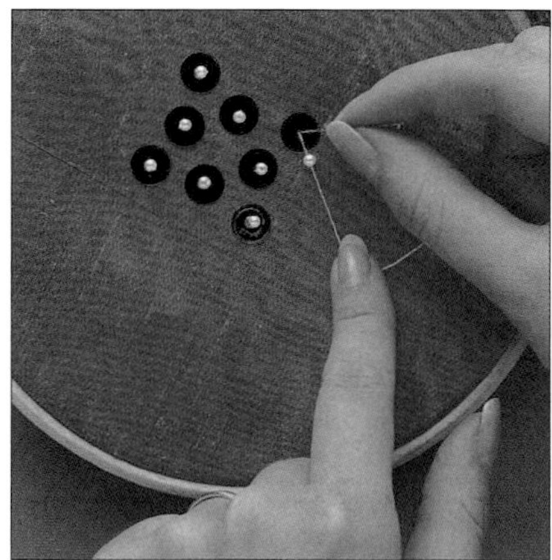

2 Take the needle back through the sequin, and pull the thread through gently from the back, so that the bead sits firmly on the sequin.

WHAT WENT WRONG

Loose beads

Always fasten off the yarn after completing each beaded or sequinned area. Otherwise, loose threads can slip to the front of the fabric and spoil the look of your work—you may even lose some of the beads or sequins.

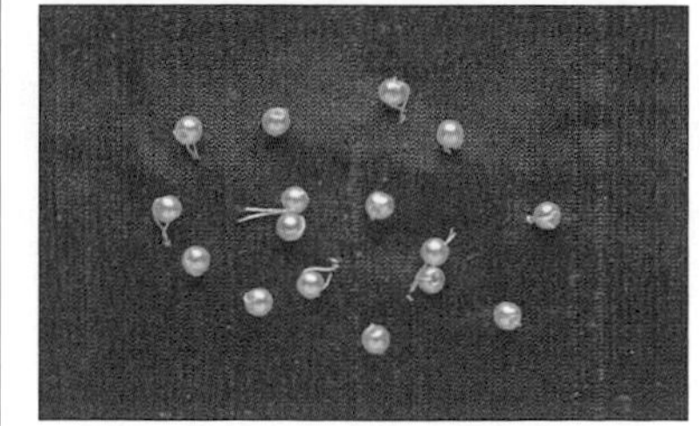

Secured onto canvas with continental tent stitch, glittering glass seed beads suggest the pitted surface of a lemon.

Adding beads and baubles to counted cross stitch and needlepoint designs is a quick and easy way to give texture and sparkle to your projects. You can cover an entire area with beads for a rich and opulent look, or create interesting textures and patterns by positioning the beads individually.

The techniques involved are quite straightforward, whether you are applying small or large beads. The steps below explain how to add beads to canvas using half cross stitch and continental tent stitch; the steps overleaf show how to add beads to aida cloth using cross stitch, half cross stitch, and backstitch.

The right materials

For a flat, even finish, match the bead to the fabric or canvas count. Seed beads fit 14-count aida and canvas; small rocaille beads fit 11-count. Apply larger beads to alternate stitches, or space them farther apart.

Small beads have tiny holes, so use the finest crewel or tapestry needle. For bigger beads, use a correspondingly larger needle. Use embroidery floss on aida cloth and Persian or crewel yarn on canvas.

Beading on canvas

Beaded half cross stitch Work horizontal rows of half cross stitch (see page 162), applying one bead with every stitch.

Beaded continental tent stitch Work continental tent stitch (see page 162) over the canvas, applying one bead with every stitch. Take care to fasten off the beginning and end of the thread securely.

Applying large beads Referring to Beaded continental tent stitch (left), use continental tent stitch to apply beads larger than the canvas mesh, applying the beads with alternate stitches. If you prefer, apply the beads with beaded half cross stitch.

Beading on aida

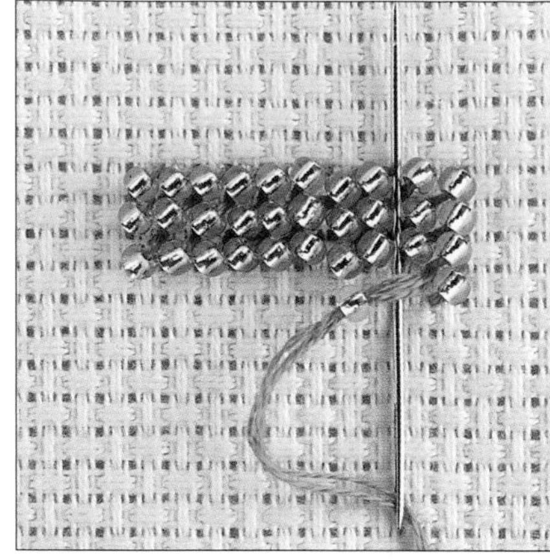

Beaded half cross stitch Bring the thread out to the front, thread on a bead, then insert the needle one hole down and one to the left, pushing the bead down the thread so it lies against the fabric. Bring the needle out one hole up, ready to start the next stitch. Continue in this way.

Beaded cross stitch Work a row of upward diagonal stitches (see page 44), working the stitches in either direction (consistently). Then complete the crosses with downward diagonals, applying the beads as you go. Follow the same technique to work individual cross stitches.

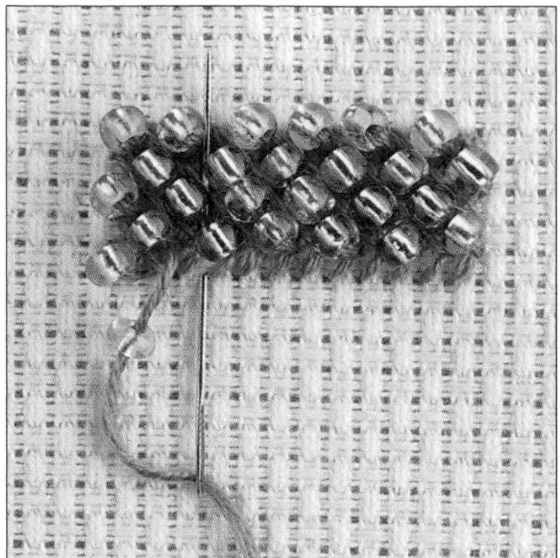

Applying large beads to aida Use this method to apply beads that are larger than the fabric count. Work beaded cross stitch as shown (left), but apply the beads to alternate stitches, instead of every stitch.

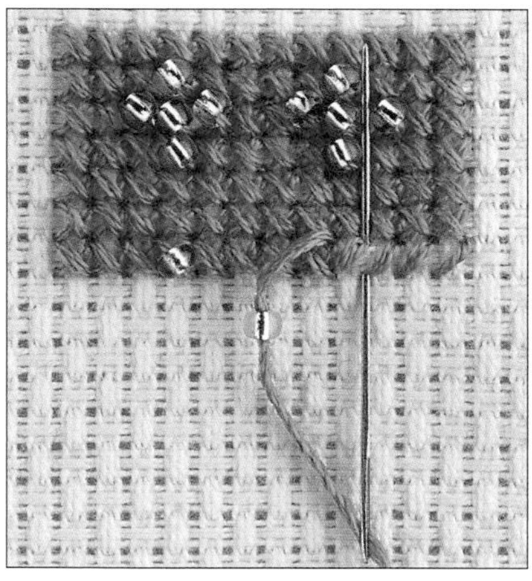

Repeat pattern Work the shape in cross stitch (see page 44), applying beads to the top diagonals of groups of stitches and positioning these at regular intervals.

Beaded backstitch Use a dark thread and beads that match or are slightly smaller than the fabric count. Outline the design with backstitch (see page 26), applying one bead with every stitch. Take care to work with an even tension.

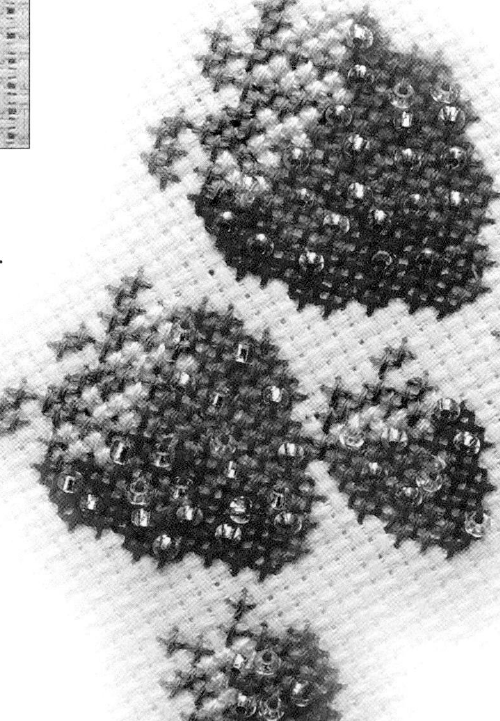

Small glass seed beads, sprinkled over the surface of each strawberry, suggest pips embedded in the dimpled skin. The fruits are cross-stitched on aida.

WHAT WENT WRONG

Bunched beads

Oversize beads obscure the stitching, making it difficult to see where to insert the needle, and the end result can be an overcrowded surface. For ease of stitching, and a flat, smooth finish, either match the beads to the fabric count or canvas mesh, or space out larger beads carefully.

Tramé

Tramé (from the French word *trame,* meaning "weft") involves padding the canvas with long stitches before working a needlepoint design. The design is worked over these threads, creating a thick and durable surface—the tramé also helps to prevent the canvas from showing. Tramé is useful for items that receive a lot of wear, such as rugs, floor cushions, and chair seat covers.

Many stitches can be traméed successfully, including half cross stitch, continental tent stitch, and Gobelin stitches. When the stitch spans only one horizontal canvas thread—as does half cross stitch—it's best to use Penelope canvas and work the tramé in the narrow spaces between pairs of threads. For larger stitches spanning two to four canvas threads, use mono or interlock canvas and work the tramé between two threads.

As a general rule, use the same thread for the tramé and the main stitching. On small areas up to ten threads wide and on designs with many small color changes, work the tramé at the same time as the main stitch. To tramé a large area in one color, work all the rows of tramé across the area first, then work the main stitching. Always mount your canvas on a scroll frame.

The steps below show how to work tramé on Penelope canvas and on mono canvas. On page 270 are instructions on working mitered corners and cross shapes in straight traméed Gobelin stitch to add extra detail to your projects.

Tramé on Penelope canvas

1 To tramé over a short distance, secure the thread and bring the needle up at the left-hand side between a pair of threads. Make a long stitch from left to right, inserting the needle through the same pair of threads.

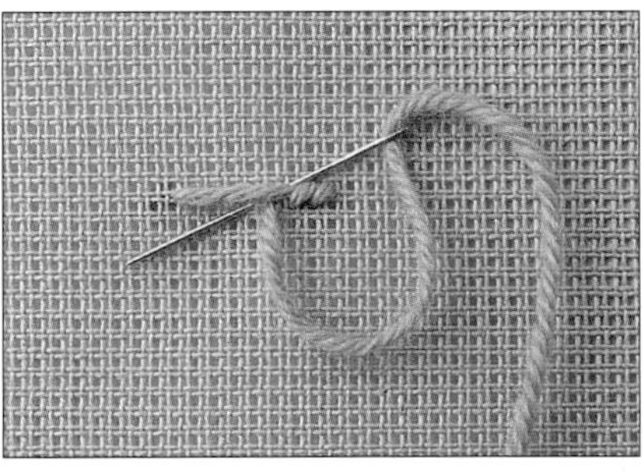

2 Bring the needle out at the end of the traméed line in the larger space between the pairs of threads, ready to work your chosen stitch. Using the larger holes, work the stitch over the tramé.

To tramé over a longer distance, work long stitches, following step **1** (left), but bring the needle through the canvas to split the previous stitch. Then work your chosen stitch over the tramé as in step **2** (left).

Tramé on mono or interlock canvas

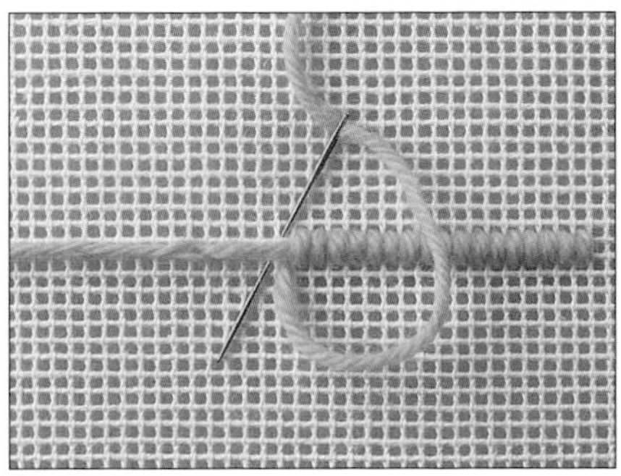

Tramé small or large areas, using the method shown above, but work each row of tramé along the center of the number of threads you'll be working your stitches over.

Some commercially made canvases come with tramé already worked on them. The designs are usually worked in half cross stitch.

Mitered corners in traméed straight Gobelin stitch

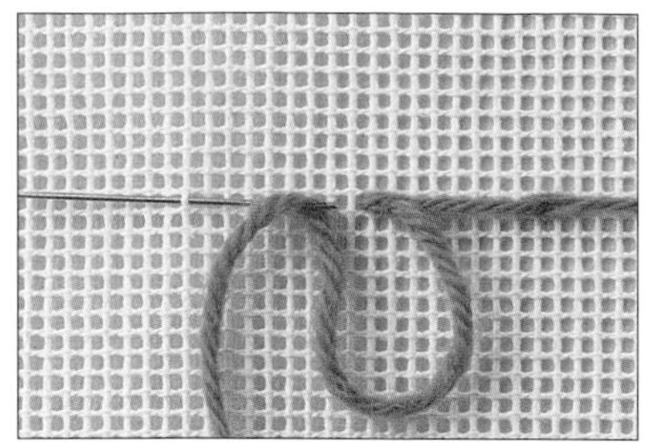

1 Stitch the first row of tramé along one side of the border, as shown. Finish the tramé two threads from the end of the border, then bring the needle to the front one hole to the left.

2 Make a backstitch over the vertical thread to the right, bringing the needle out one hole below and to the left. Insert it one hole above and bring it up again one hole down. Continue to tramé, turning following corners in the same way.

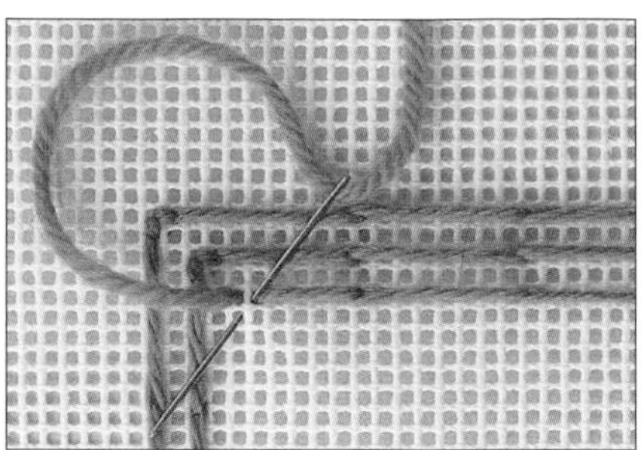

3 Work more rows of tramé, following steps **1–2** (left) to fill the desired depth of border, spacing the rows two canvas threads apart.

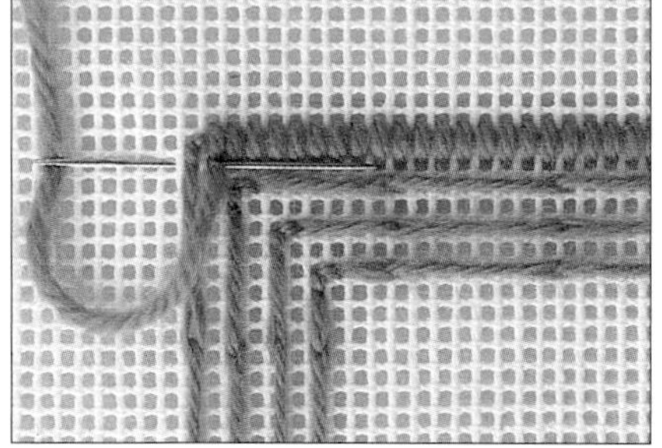

4 Stitching toward the corner, work the outer row of straight Gobelin stitches (see page 174). When you reach the inner hole at the corner, work a stitch at right angles to the previous one, and bring the needle back up through the same hole.

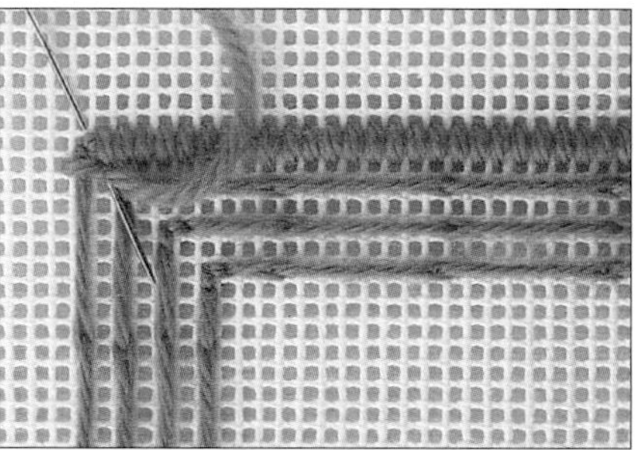

5 Work two more stitches slanting from the inner corner hole to the two holes on either side of the outer corner hole. Bring the needle to the front again through the hole at the inner corner, ready to work the outer corner stitch.

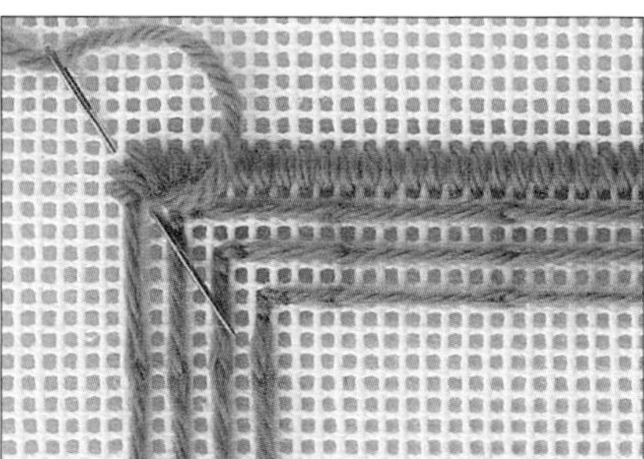

6 Work the outer corner stitch to link the inner and outer corner holes. Bring the needle through to the front again, ready to continue working straight Gobelin stitch along the next side. Repeat steps **4–6** along the remaining traméed rows.

Cross shapes in traméed straight Gobelin stitch

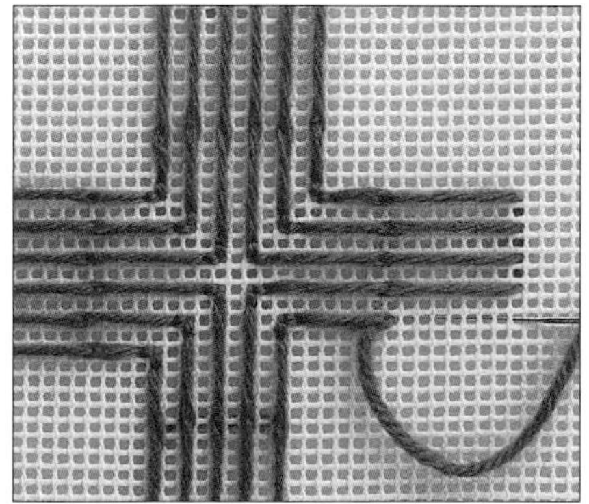

1 Form the cross by working four mitered corners in tramé. Arrange the corners so that the points face toward the center of the cross. Space the points two threads apart.

2 Work rows of straight Gobelin stitch over the cross (see page 174). To stitch the corners follow steps **4–6** above.

Traméed straight Gobelin stitch gives a durable, thick surface. Arranged in a cross shape, mitered corners add interest to a design.

Bargello

Bargello, also known as Florentine work or Hungarian point, uses rows of straight, vertical stitches arranged in step formations to form zigzags or curves shading from light to dark. The technique has been known for hundreds of years and enjoyed its height of popularity across Europe during the 16th and 17th centuries. It spread to the American Colonies during this period, and some finely worked examples of this form of needlepoint have survived.

Use a mono interlock canvas and either tapestry wool or several strands of Persian or crewel yarn. Choose a slightly thicker thread (or more strands) than you would normally use on the canvas; and mount the canvas in a frame to reduce distortion.

Two working methods are shown here, and both can be used to work any of the stitch patterns. The second produces a harder-wearing surface but uses more thread. Three popular Bargello patterns are shown: curve pattern (below), flame pattern, and the simple zigzag pattern (for both, see page 272).

Working the stitches

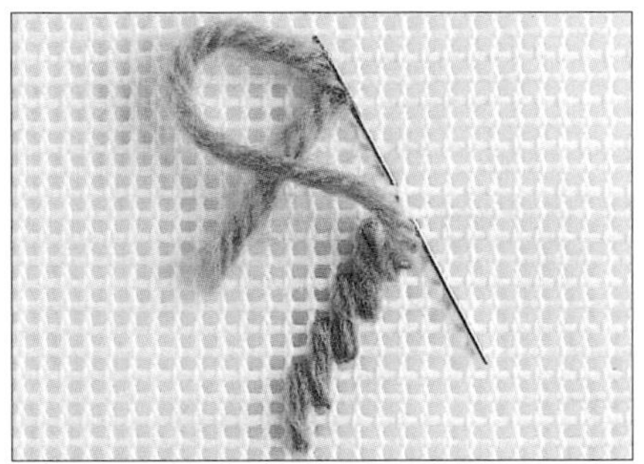

1 **Method 1** Work the left-hand face of the peak upward with the needle pointing down.

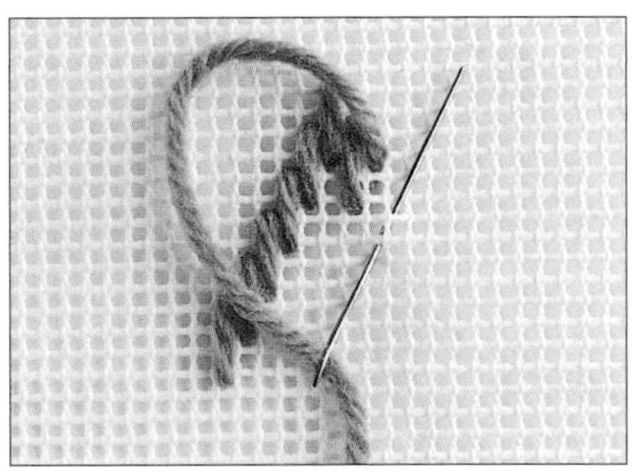

2 Work the right-hand face of the peak with the needle pointing up. Alternate steps **1** and **2** along the row.

3 **Method 2** Work both the left- and right-hand faces of the peak with the needle pointing down.

Working the curve pattern

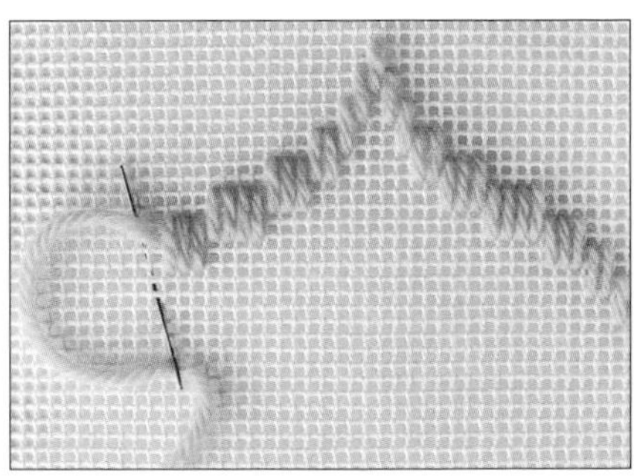

1 Working from the center to the right, make three vertical stitches over four threads with a two-thread step. Then work blocks of two, three, four, three, and two stitches, again with a two-thread step. Repeat in mirror image, then repeat the full sequence to the end of the row. Work a mirror image on the opposite side, as shown.

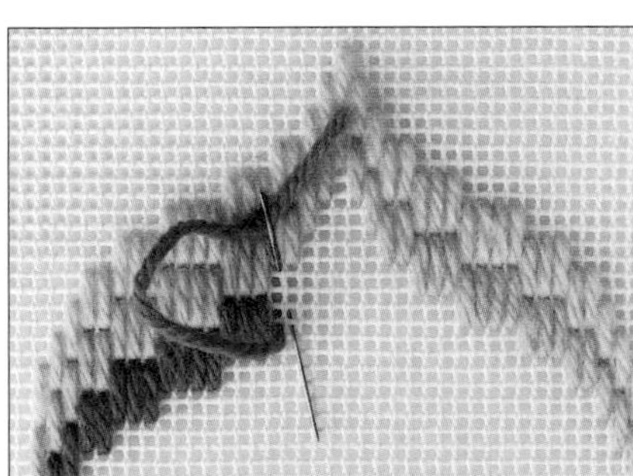

2 Working below the first row, make identical rows of stitches, using each color in your established sequence. Start at the left and repeat the stitch sequence of the row above. Work more repeats in the same color sequence. Fill any unworked areas using the same color sequence and shorter stitches as necessary.

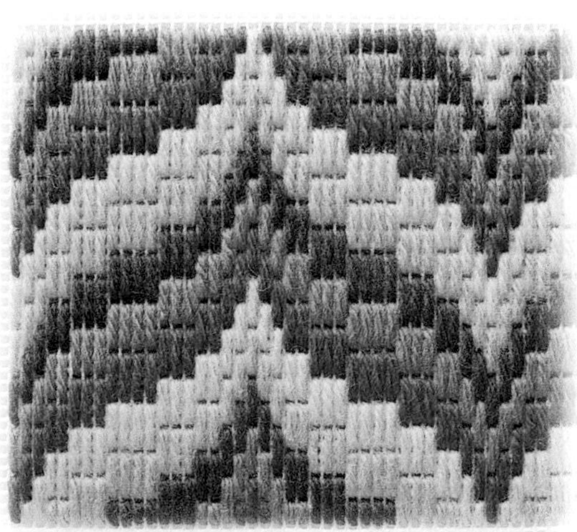

The curve pattern includes stitches worked in blocks, creating a curved look. To accentuate this effect, your color sequence should include one row in a very dark or strongly contrasting color.

Working the flame pattern

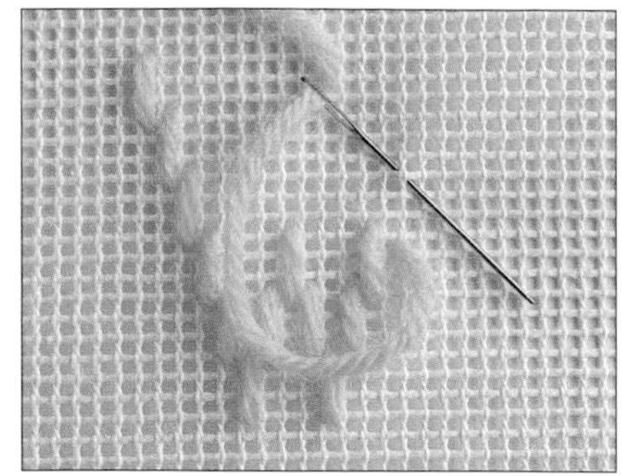

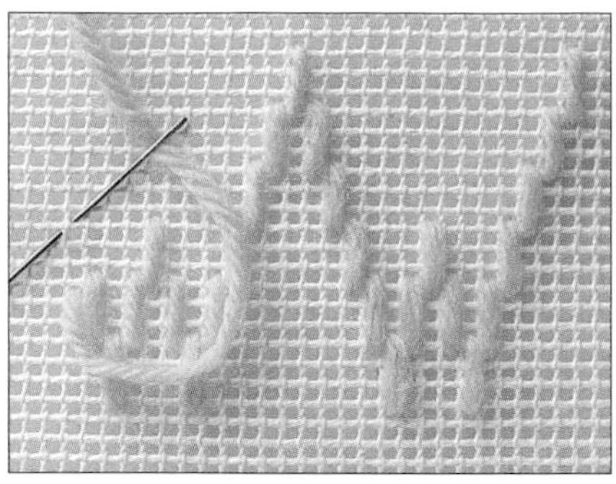

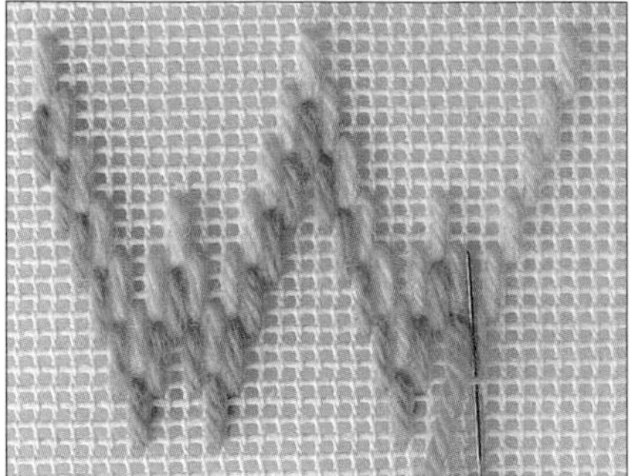

1 Start near the center. Working toward the right, make six vertical stitches over four threads, with a one-thread step. Work a short peak of two more stitches upward and two stitches downward, then work five more stitches upward. Repeat this sequence to the end of the row.

2 Rejoin the same thread near the top of the first peak at the center of the canvas. Working toward the left, work a mirror image of the right-hand half of the row on the left-hand side of the canvas.

3 Starting at the left, work identical rows below the first in each color in your chosen color sequence. After the sequence is complete, work repeats below the first. Fill any unworked areas using the same color sequence and shorter stitches as necessary.

Working the zigzag pattern

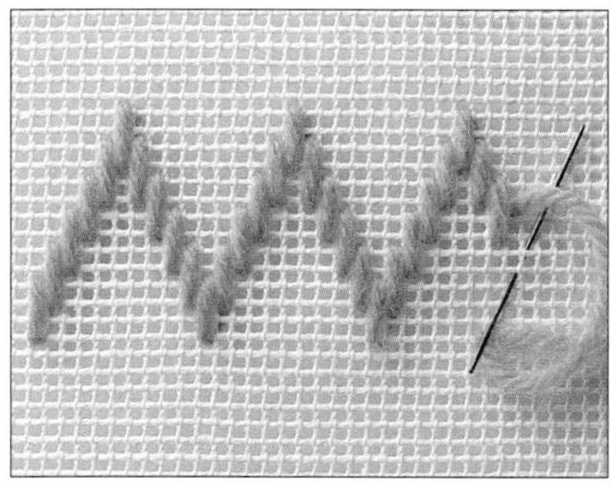

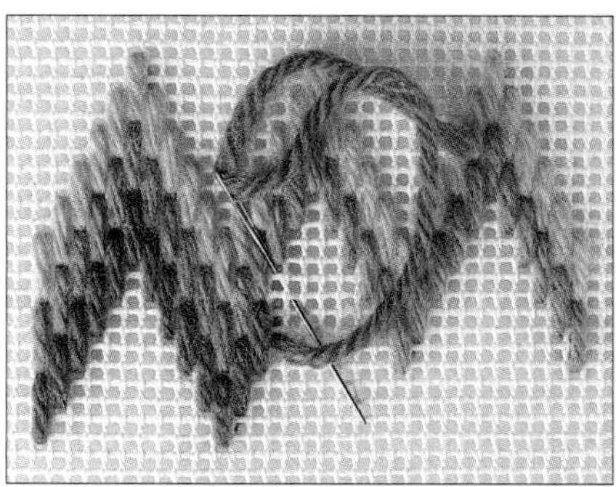

1 Start at the left. Work six vertical stitches over four threads with a two-thread upward step. Then work five vertical stitches over four threads with a two-thread downward step. These nine stitches form one repeat of the pattern. Repeat along the row.

2 Working downward below the first row, make identical rows of stitches using each color in your chosen color sequence and shading from light to dark.

3 After the sequence is complete, work more repeats below the first, following the sequence carefully until the shape is filled.

4 Fill any areas of unworked canvas along the top and bottom edges of the shape by working stitches in the same color sequence; work shorter stitches as necessary to completely fill all the gaps.

The zigzag pattern is easy to work, with peaks of identical size and a nine-stitch repeat.

In the flame pattern, each stitch is worked over four threads with an upward or downward step of one thread.

The allover patterns shown here are simple variations of basic Bargello designs. A diamond-shaped framework of straight stitches is worked over the canvas, using one color, and the areas within the framework are filled with pattern.

The beauty of allover Bargello patterns depends to a large extent on the selection of colors used, so that the shading of the areas between the framework varies from light to dark in a subtle way.

When working allover Bargello designs, begin by stitching the main diamond framework over the entire area, as shown below. Marking the center of the canvas with basting will help to position the design. Note that the stitch at the right-hand point of each diamond serves as the first stitch on the next diamond. Although stitching the framework requires a lot of counting to keep the pattern correct, it is much easier to stitch the rest of the pattern once the diamonds are in place. When the framework is complete, you can fill it with the patterns provided here.

The first pattern shown is the shaded diamond pattern, which is worked in slanting rows of four colors, shading from light to dark. The second pattern looks like a candle flame and is usually worked in yellow, orange, and red. The last section shows how to create different effects by combining two patterns and by altering the color sequence of a pattern.

For more information on Bargello, see pages 271 and 272.

Working a basic diamond-shaped framework

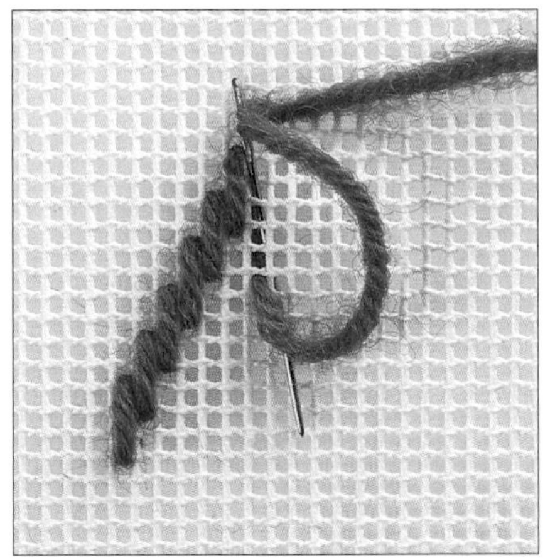

1 Start just left of the center of the canvas. Working toward the right, make six vertical stitches over four canvas threads, taking a two-thread step upward each time. Then work four vertical stitches, taking a two-thread step down each time. These ten stitches form the top half of the center diamond.

2 Bring the needle to the front four threads below the last stitch. Working toward the left, make five vertical stitches over four canvas threads, taking a two-thread step down each time. Work four more vertical stitches, taking a two-thread step upward each time to complete the bottom of the center diamond.

3 Keeping the diamond shapes correct, work additional diamonds to each side of the center diamond, as shown, to fill the width of the shape. Work more rows above and below the first to complete the framework.

Working a shaded diamond pattern

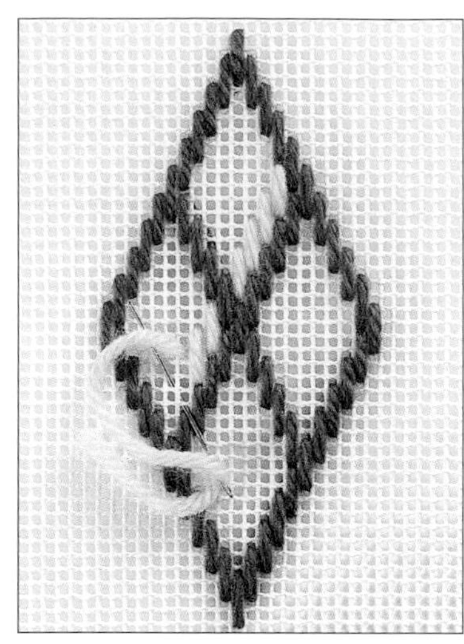

1 Choose five shades of one color. Use the darkest shade to cover the canvas with the basic diamond-shaped framework. Using the lightest color, work four stitches over four threads, following the inside of the lower right-hand face of each diamond.

2 Work three more identical rows of stitches inside each diamond, using the three remaining shades of thread; follow the color sequence from light to dark.

Working two patterns

Try using a neutral color to stitch the diamond-shaped framework, then alternate two patterns inside the diamond, keeping the same color combination throughout the design. Here, candle flame pattern and shaded diamond pattern alternate.

Changing the pattern

You can also create different filling patterns inside the diamond-shaped framework by altering the sequence of the colors. Try using the lightest colors for the framework of the candle flame pattern and then reversing the positions of the filling colors inside the diamonds.

Working a candle flame

1 Using red yarn, cover the canvas with the framework. To make the wick of the candle, use black thread, working a single stitch over four canvas threads at the base of each diamond.

2 Work three bright red stitches over four canvas threads, with an upward or downward step of one or two threads each time, to surround the top of each black candle wick.

3 To complete the candle flame motif, work five orange stitches above the bright red ones, then seven yellow stitches above the orange ones.

Here are two more allover patterns to add to your repertoire of Bargello—the pomegranate design and Persian flower garden.

The pomegranate design is a classic Bargello pattern worked inside a framework of cream or another light color. The framework is created with straight stitches in a similar way to the diamond framework (see pages 273), but here the stitches are used to create a shapely curved outline. Note that the stitch at the right side of each pomegranate shape serves as the first stitch on the next pomegranate.

The top part of the pomegranate filling consists of several curved lines shading from putty-color to black. After the shaded area has been worked, two rows of a bright color, such as scarlet, are added, then the rest of the shape is filled with a darker thread in a contrasting color such as purple (as used in this example) or bottle green.

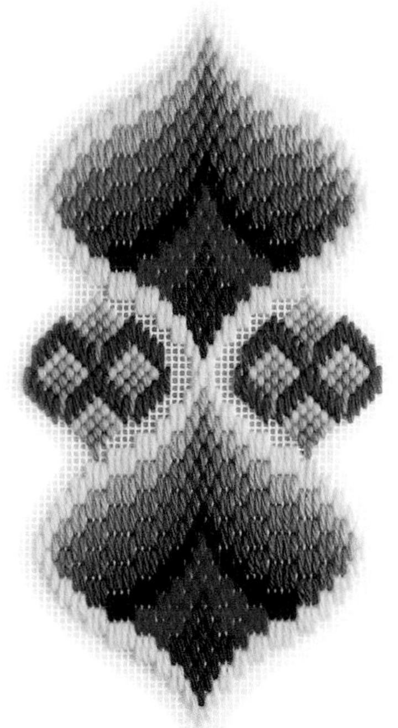

The second allover pattern shown, Persian flower garden, has a framework of small diamonds filled with tree shapes. As usual, the framework is stitched first, but instead of starting at the center of the canvas and working outward, work in horizontal rows starting at the top of the canvas. Use either a light or dark shade of blue for the framework, then fill in the tree shapes with two shades of green and a typical flower color such as yellow, lavender, or pale pink.

As before, use a mono interlock thread canvas for this work. For more information on Bargello needlepoint, see pages 271–274.

Working a basic pomegranate framework

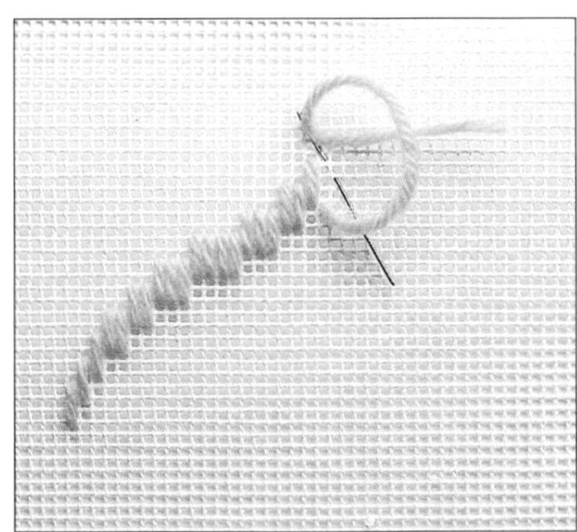

1 Start just to the left of the center of the canvas. Working toward the right, make a sequence of blocks of vertical stitches (one, one, one, two, two, three, four, three, two, two, one, one, one) over four canvas threads. Take a two-thread upward step between each block.

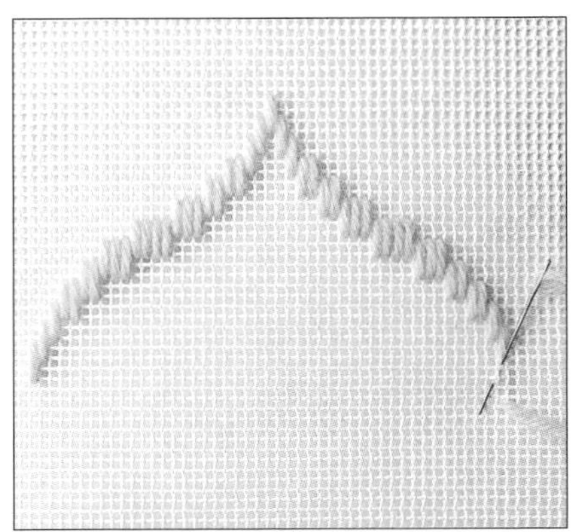

2 Repeat the sequence downward in mirror image, omitting the first and the last single-stitch steps. Bring the needle out four threads below the last stitch, and repeat the sequence again, but this time work downward toward the left.

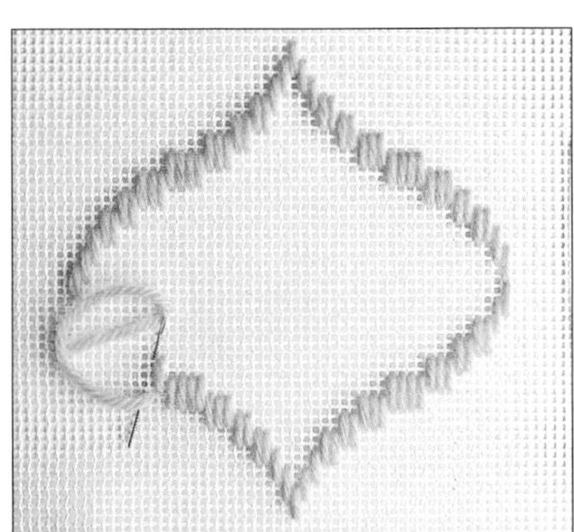

3 Repeat the sequence upward in mirror image, working toward the left and omitting the last single stitch. Work additional pomegranate shapes at each side of the center shape to make a row across the canvas. Repeat above and below the first row until the framework is complete.

Filling the pomegranate framework

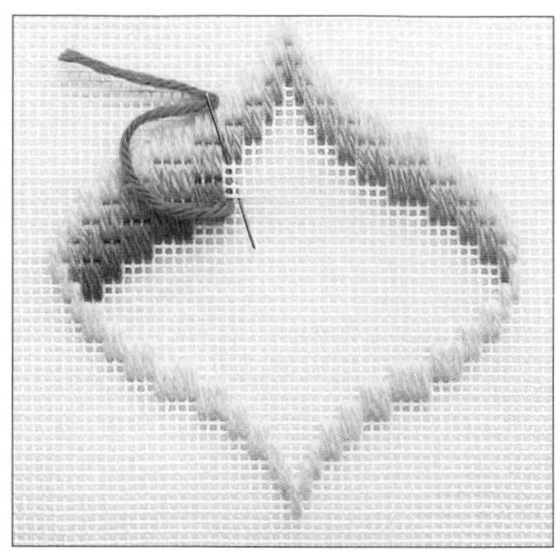

1 After working the framework in a light shade, choose four other colors, shading from light to dark to fill the shape. Following the established sequence, use the lightest to work a row of identical stitches along the top.

2 Secure the next thread below the left-hand end of the previous row. Following the sequence in the row above, work a row of identical stitches below the previous row, as shown.

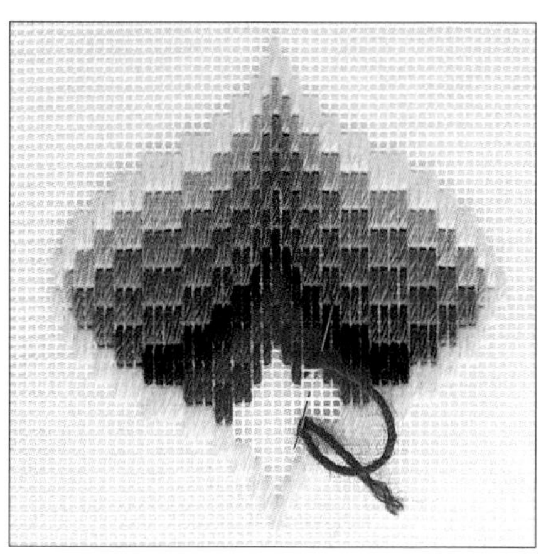

Pomegranate design

Persian flower garden design

3 Repeat with the last two colors in the sequence, then use the black thread to work a row of identical stitches below the previous row.

4 Next, work two rows of identical stitches in red. Secure the darker contrasting thread and fill in the remaining canvas in the same way.

Working the Persian flower garden pattern

1 Using blue, make an arrowhead shape of nine vertical stitches over four canvas threads. Repeat, leaving two threads between each shape. Work another row below the first, then repeat the two rows to fill the shape.

2 Secure the darker green thread inside the top left-hand diamond. Work a vertical stitch over four threads at the base to form the tree trunk, then work three short vertical stitches over two threads above the long stitch. Repeat in each diamond.

3 Secure the lighter green thread inside the left-hand top diamond. Work a row of stitches over two threads above the darker green stitches, then repeat with the final flower color to complete the tree.

TABLE RUNNER

CRISP WHITE STITCHING
ON A BLUE LINEN TABLE RUNNER
GIVES A MODERN TWIST TO THE TRADITIONAL
ART OF DRAWN-THREAD WORK.

You Will Need

- 32-count medium-blue evenweave linen, 29 x 12½ in. (74 x 32 cm)
- Two skeins of embroidery floss in white
- Tapestry needle, size 24
- Contrasting thread for basting
- Sewing needle
- Sharp scissors

PREPARATION

Neaten the edges of the fabric by pulling away any loose threads. Press the fabric gently with a hot steam iron, and allow it to dry. To mark the outer edge of the fringe, withdraw one fabric thread, ⅜ in. (1 cm) in from each raw edge.

Use a combination of satin stitch and three types of hemstitch to create this simple drawn-thread work design on a linen table runner. The finished runner measures 29¼ x 11¾ in. (72 x 30 cm).

Withdrawing the threads

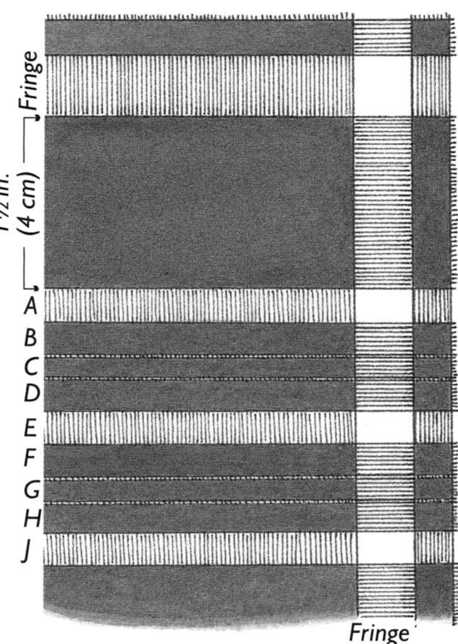

For the fringe, withdraw 14 threads *inside* the single withdrawn thread on each edge. This leaves an outer margin of fabric to protect the fringe. The fabric will be trimmed off later.

For the withdrawn-thread border, work inward from the fringe on each short edge. Leave 1½ in. (4 cm) of fabric, withdraw eight threads (A). Leave eight threads (B), withdraw one. Leave six threads (C), withdraw one. Leave eight threads (D), withdraw eight (E). Leave eight threads (F), withdraw one. Leave six threads (G), withdraw one. Leave eight threads (H), withdraw eight (J).

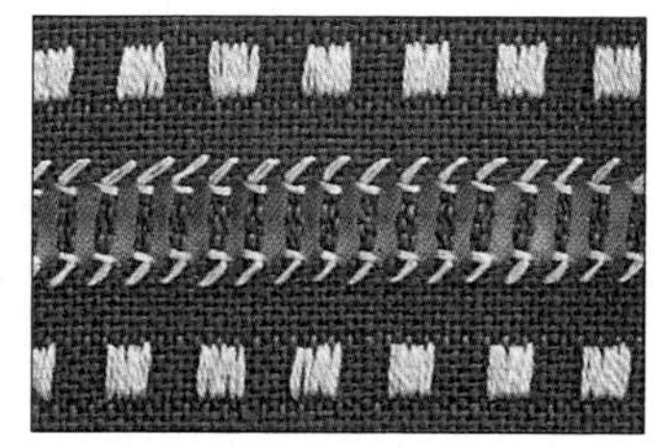

At each end of the table runner, the satin-stitched blocks separate the central band of ladder hemstitch from the two bands of trellis hemstitch, providing a bold contrast of texture.

Satin-stitching the blocks

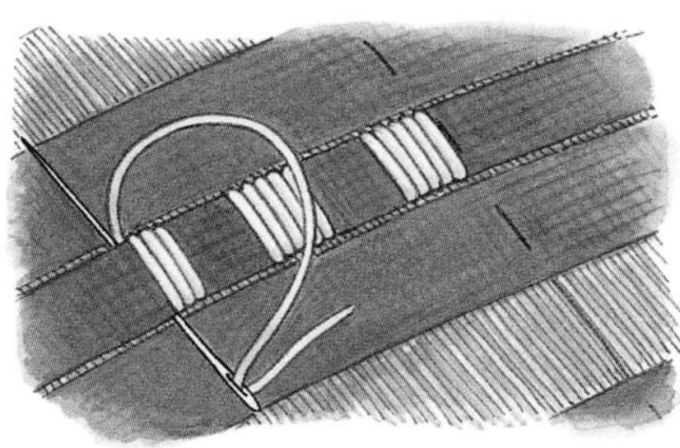

Baste down the center of the fabric between one pair of threads. With two strands of floss, work outward from the center along the bands of six intact threads between the single withdrawn threads. Work blocks of five satin stitches (see page 27), leaving six threads between each block.

Working the hemstitching

Use two strands of floss and work from the right side of the fabric. Work a row of ladder hemstitching (see page 238) along the central band of eight withdrawn threads. Group four vertical threads together and make each stitch over three horizontal threads. Leave two or three unworked threads at each end.

Work trellis hemstitch (see page 238) across the remaining bands of eight withdrawn threads. Leave two or three unworked threads at each end. Make the stitches the same size as the ladder hemstitch.

Hemstitching the edges

Starting at the center of one long edge, work single hemstitch around the *inner* edge of the fringe, using two strands of floss. Make two or three overcast stitches over the unworked threads at the ends of the stitched bands, then continue hemstitching.

Finishing

Press the embroidery with a warm iron on the wrong side over a well padded surface. Using a sharp pair of scissors, cut away the surplus fabric.

LINEN EDGINGS

THE FRESH SIMPLICITY OF TRADITIONAL COUNTRY-STYLE FURNISHINGS TAKES ON A NEW ELEGANCE WITH CRISP SCALLOPED LINEN EDGINGS.

You Will Need

- 32-count antique white evenweave linen
- No. 8 pearl cotton in ecru
- Tapestry needle, size 26
- Embroidery hoop
- Small, sharp scissors
- Sewing needle
- Thread for basting
- Sewing thread to match the linen
- Sew 'n' Stick Velcro
- Graph paper
- Pins

Create the scallop-shaped border with blocks of buttonhole stitch.

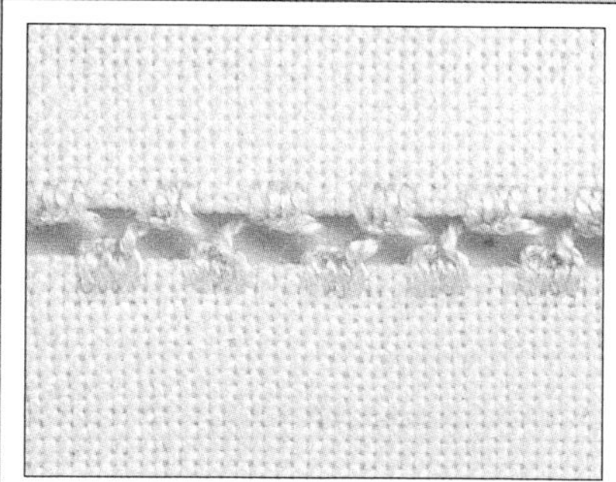

Join the windowsill cover pieces with insertion buttonhole stitch.

The valance, windowsill cover, and shelf edging are made from crisp linen embellished with scallop-shaped borders. The borders are worked in buttonhole stitch, and on the valance and shelf edging alternate scallops are finished with simple flowers; these are created in kloster blocks and straight stitches.

The valance and shelf edging are made from one linen piece. The windowsill cover is made from two pieces joined together with insertion buttonhole stitch. All the items can be made to any size. The valance is fixed in place with Sew 'n' Stick Velcro so it needs to be secured to an existing valance shelf.

Preparing the valance

Measure the width of the valance shelf (**A**), and decide on the desired depth of the new valance (**B**). Cut a piece of linen **A** by **B** adding on 1 in. (2.5 cm) all around. Overcast the raw edges to prevent them from fraying. Mount the fabric in the embroidery hoop.

Working the scalloped edge

Work the design in the pearl cotton and buttonhole stitch (see page 59). Refer to the chart (below) and the stitching instructions that follow. One square on the chart represents one stitch worked over one linen thread. The lower part of each stitch should cover one or two threads as indicated on the chart, and each upright should cover four threads.

Start 1 in. (2.5 cm) in from the left edge and 1½ in. (4 cm) above the bottom. Work a block of four vertical stitches. Working downward, stitch a block of four horizontal stitches, work a corner block of three diagonal stitches worked into the same hole as the last horizontal stitch, then work four vertical stitches, working the first stitch into the same hole as the corner. Refer to the chart to continue working blocks of horizontal, diagonal, and vertical stitches to create the scallop shape.

Repeat along the width of the linen to the required length, finishing with a complete scallop and four vertical stitches.

Working the flowers

Embroider the flowers in alternate scallops with the top of the flowers about 1 in. (2.5 cm) above the base of the scallop.

For the flowerhead, work a group of four kloster blocks (see page 239), but with each block containing four, not five, stitches. Cut away the threads as shown on

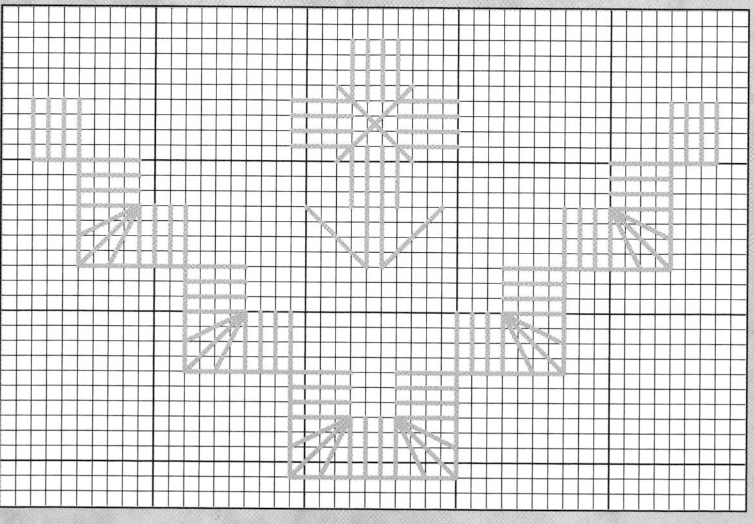

page 240, then work two diagonal straight stitches across the center to create a cross. Embroider the stalk with two parallel straight stitches (see page 25), working each stitch over four linen threads. Add the leaves with diagonal straight stitches.

Finishing

Remove the work from the hoop and steam-press it gently from the wrong side with a warm iron.

Making the valance

Trim the short edges of the linen ⅝ in. (1.5 cm) outside the stitching; press and stitch double ¼ in. (5 mm) hems. At the top, press and stitch a double ⅝ in. (1.5 cm) hem.

Using the scissors, carefully cut away the linen below the stitching to create the scallop-shaped border.

Stick one side of the Velcro around the valance shelf and stitch the other to the back of the linen.

The windowsill edging

Measure the width and depth of the windowsill. Cut a piece of linen to this size, adding on ⅝ in. (1.5 cm) all around. Turn and press double ¼ in. (5 mm) hems all around.

Cut a second piece of linen 4¼ in. (11 cm) deep by the width of the windowsill plus 2 in. (5 cm). Overcast the raw edges to prevent them from fraying and mount the fabric in the embroidery hoop.

Working the scalloped edge

Work the design in buttonhole stitch in the same way as for the valance; omit the flowers. Remove the work from the hoop and steam-press it gently from the wrong side.

Hem the short edges and shape the bottom as before. On the top edge, press and stitch a double ¼ in. (5 mm) hem.

Making the windowsill cover

Prepare the linen pieces to work insertion embroidery following steps **1** and **2** on page 251.

Use the ecru pearl cotton and buttonhole insertion stitch to join the pieces together; follow the instructions on page 252.

Preparing the shelf edging

Measure the width of the shelf (**A**), the depth (**B**), and the desired drop of the edging (**C**). Cut a piece of linen **A** by **B** plus **C** adding on 1 in. (2.5 cm) all around for hemming. Overcast the raw edges.

Making the shelf edging

Embroider the scalloped border in the same way as for the valance.

Hem the edges and the shelf edging in the same way as for the pelmet.

NOTE: If you prefer, you could use 22-count Hardanger fabric and no. 5 pearl cotton. Calculate the widths from the fabric count, and position the scallops symmetrically.

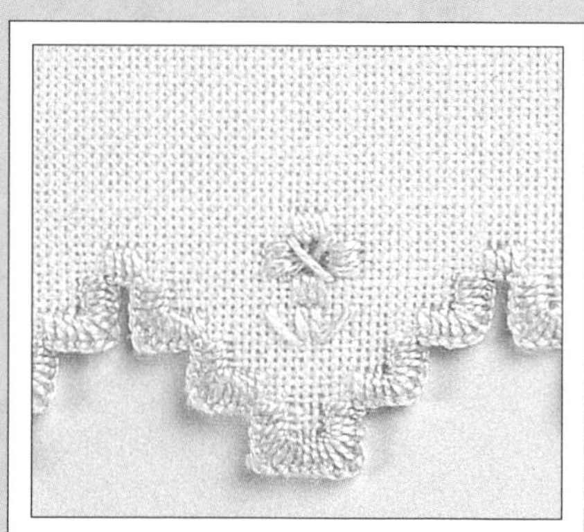

Decorate alternate scallops with simple stylized flowers.

Regency Footstool

Ornate scrolls, fleurs-de-lys, and floral motifs are framed in borders on a Regency-style footstool.

You Will Need

- Furnishing fabric in pale gold, a piece to cover your footstool pad plus 4 in. (10 cm) all around
- DMC Médicis crewel wools as listed in the color key
- Chenille needle, size 24
- Tracing paper and pencil
- Dressmaker's carbon paper
- Ruler
- Embroidery frame
- Embroidery scissors
- Square or rectangular footstool
- Staple gun and staples

Color Key

COLORS	SKEINS
8101 Deep pink	1
8324 Deep old gold	1
8325 Medium old gold	2
8326 Pale old gold	1

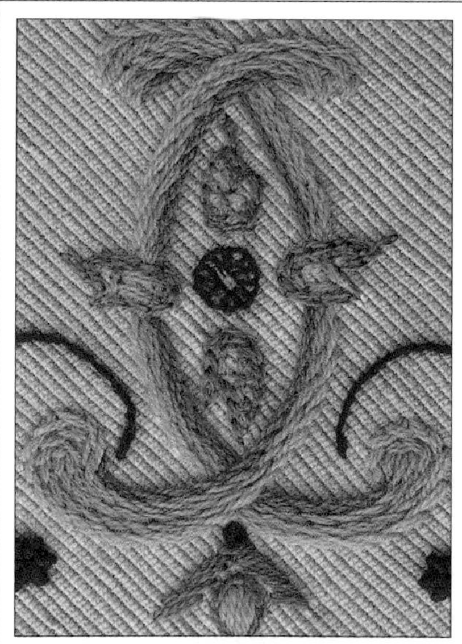

The stem-stitched scrolls blend from pale to deep old gold.

This handsome footstool is embroidered in a style evoking the early 19th-century Regency period in Britain. The design is made up of intertwining scrolls set in borders, and incorporates stylized fleurs-de-lys and scattered floral motifs.

The embroidery is worked in crewel yarn using three shades of old gold and deep pink. It fits an 11 in.- (28 cm-) square footstool pad, but you could adapt it to fit any square or rectangular pad.

Preparing the fabric

Measure the surface of the pad, and baste a square or rectangle of this size on the center of the fabric.

Trace the design and transfer it to the fabric. If your pad has an 11 in. (28 cm) square surface, center the design inside the basting. If your pad is a different size, transfer one corner at a time inside the basting, with the point of the fleur-de-lys 3⁄8 in. (1 cm) in from each corner. Join the borders using the pencil, carbon paper, and ruler. Mount the fabric in the frame.

Working the design

Embroider the design, referring to the photographs for color placement and stitch direction. Use one strand of the yarn unless otherwise instructed.

Begin with the interlocking scrolls, embroidering them in closely worked rows of stem stitch (see page 26) using two strands. Outline the four acorn shapes with chain stitch (see page 61) and fill them with Jacobean couching (see page 260) using two strands for the laid thread. Work the flower in the center of the scrolls in blanket stitch (see page 58). Use two strands and

French knots (see page 77) to work the dots at the base and tip of the scrolls.

Next work the leaves and buds between the scrolls and the outer border: use two strands of yarn to satin stitch (see page 27) the leaves and the buds; outline the buds with split stitch (see page 40). Work the deep pink flowers on either side of the buds with two strands and ribbed spider's web stitch (see page 104).

Embroider the inner border in split stitch and double chain stitch (see page 63). Work the outer border in rows of stem stitch in the same way as for the scrolls.

To complete the design, work the outer corner motifs: create the circle at the base of the fleur-de-lys with spider's web stitch (see page 103); use two strands to satin-stitch the curving band; outline the fleur-de-lys with two strands and whipped backstitch (see page 100), then fill it with open Cretan stitch (see page 72).

Finishing

Press the piece gently from the wrong side; or, for an extra-neat finish, block the work, right side up, as described on pages 303 and 304. Unscrew the stool top and center the work over the pad. Pull the edges smoothly and firmly to the underside, keeping the design centered. On the underside, pleat the fabric at the corners, and trim away any excess bulk. Staple the fabric to the underside of the pad.

Note: This design could also be used for a throw pillow. Use a pillow form slightly larger than the cover, and fasten the back opening (see page 307) with a few buttons.

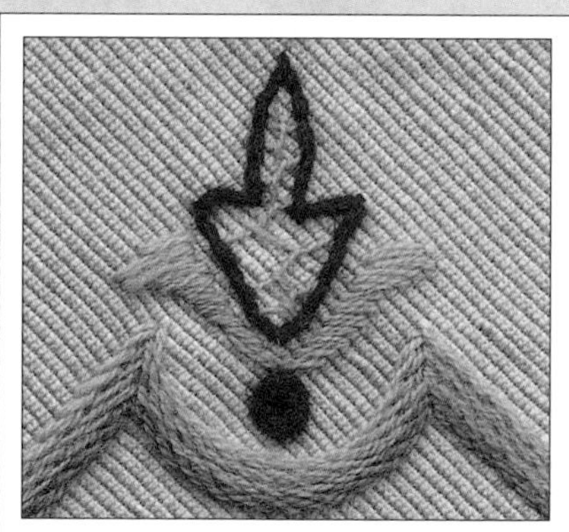

Fill the fleur-de-lys with open Cretan stitch.

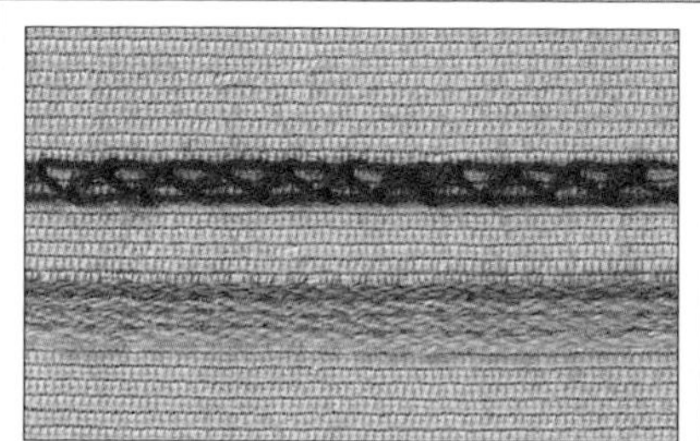

Work the inner border in split stitch and double chain stitch.

Ribbon Bouquet

A bouquet of dainty silk ribbon flowers and ferns, tied with a trailing bow, forms an exquisite corner motif on a soft cream woolen throw.

You Will Need

- Cream wool throw or blanket
- Tracing paper
- Pencil
- Dressmaker's carbon paper
- Masking tape
- Embroidery hoop
- Chenille needle
- Crewel needle, size 8
- Beading needle
- 12 gold seed beads and matching thread
- DMC embroidery floss as listed in the color key
- 1 yd. (90 cm) of ⅛ in.- (3 mm-) wide light pink silk ribbon
- 1 yd. (90 cm) of ⅛ in.- (3 mm-) wide medium pink silk ribbon
- ⅞ yd. (80 cm) of ⅛ in.- (3 mm-) wide dark lilac silk ribbon
- ⅞ yd. (80 cm) of ⅛ in.- (3 mm-) wide pale lilac silk ribbon
- 1 yd. (90 cm) of ⅛ in.- (3 mm-) wide gold silk ribbon
- 1 yd. (90 cm) of ¼ in.- (5 mm-) wide dusty pink silk ribbon
- 1 yd. (90 cm) of ¼ in.- (5 mm-) wide burgundy silk ribbon
- ⅞ yd. (80 cm) of ¼ in.- (5 mm-) wide dark green silk ribbon
- 2¼ yd. (2 m) of ⅛ in.- (3 mm-) wide light green silk ribbon
- ¾ yd. (70 cm) of ⅜ in.- (1 cm-) wide cream organza ribbon

Color Key

COLORS	SKEINS
Ecru	1
223 Pink	1
561 Dark green	1
902 Burgundy	1
966 Pale green	1
3815 Medium green	1

This elegant bouquet is worked in ribbon embroidery, creating a sumptuous effect on a soft woolen throw. Gleaming silk and organza ribbons are used to create the flowers and the foliage, while the stems are worked in embroidery floss. The bouquet of rosebuds, spider's web roses, ruffle flowers, loop flowers, and arching ferns is tied with a flowing ribbon bow, anchored with French knots. You could continue the theme and work just part of the design to decorate a smaller item, such as a pillow cover or a tray cloth, in order to have matching accessories.

The finished design measures 9½ x 8 in. (24 x 20 cm). For more information on ribbon embroidery, refer to pages 261–264.

Transferring the Design

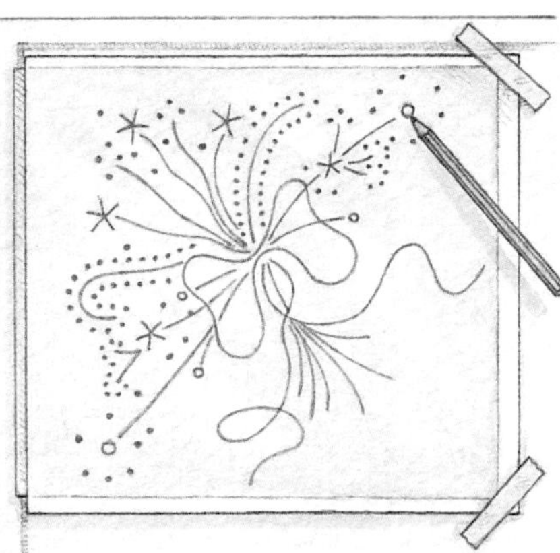

Trace the stems and bow from the photograph (right), and mark the positions of the flowers and buds. Place the tracing paper face up on one corner of the throw and secure it at the top with masking tape. Slip the dressmaker's carbon paper underneath the tracing.

Pressing quite hard on the pencil, trace over the outlines of the stems and bow again to transfer them to the fabric. Make small dots to mark the positions of the leaves and buds, tiny spider's webs to mark the positions of the roses, ovals to mark the ruffle flowers, and little circles to mark the positions of the loop flowers. Mount the fabric in the embroidery hoop.

Embroidering the Lilac Buds

Using the dark lilac narrow silk ribbon, work two back-to-back side ribbon stitches (see page 262), fastening off at the back of the work. Then, with the pale lilac narrow ribbon, work two side ribbon stitches one to either side of the darker lilac petals, finishing off at the back.

Side ribbon stitches and two colors of narrow ribbon create the tiny silk petals of the dainty lilac buds.

Working the Gold Flowers

Using the gold silk ribbon, work the petals of each flower in loop stitch (see page 262). Wrap the ribbon around a pencil to ensure that each petal is the same length, taking care not to twist the ribbon as you stitch it down. Use the beading needle and the gold sewing thread to sew four gold seed beads at the center of each of the flowers (see page 266).

Even loops of gold ribbon make up the three-dimensional petals of the gold flowers. Miniature matching beads form the realistic centers.

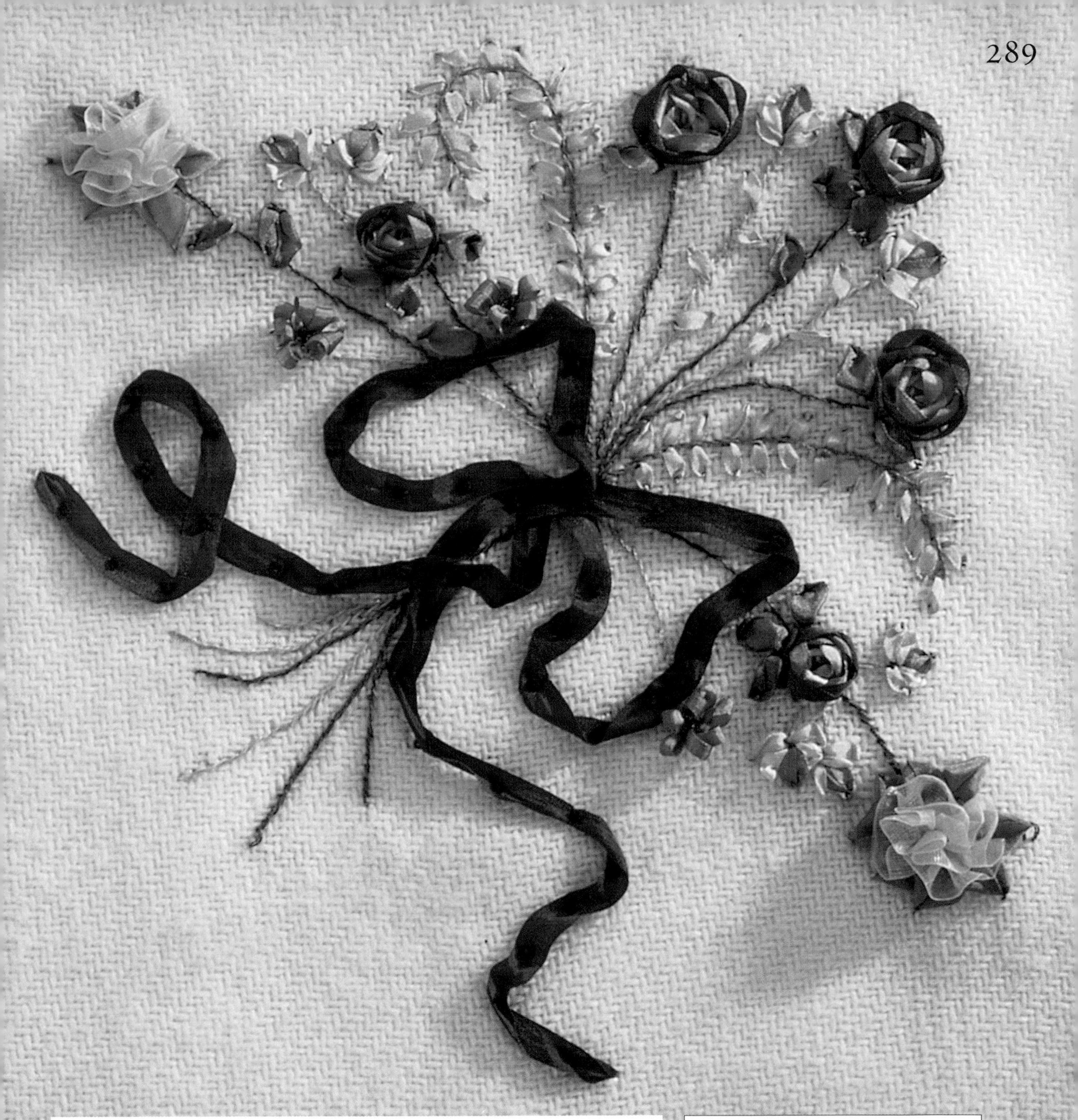

EMBROIDERING THE ROSES

Using two strands of pink floss in the needle, work ¾ in.- (2 cm-) wide webs for the spider's web roses at the marked positions (see page 263). Thread an 8 in. (20 cm) length of narrow light pink ribbon in the chenille needle, and come up through the fabric at the center of the web. Work around the web three times, leaving any ribbon twists in place, and finish off on the back of the work. Using the narrow medium pink ribbon, start where you fastened off the light pink, and work around the web twice. Fasten off, then work around the web three times with the dark pink narrow ribbon, fastening off as before.

WORKING THE FLOWER STEMS

Stem-stitch (see page 26) the stems of the spider's web roses and the ruffle flowers in two strands of dark green floss. With two strands of pale green floss, stem-stitch the stems of the lilac rosebuds and the gold loop stitch flowers.

Weave three shades of pink ribbon through a web of pink floss to form the exquisite spider's web roses.

WORKING THE LARGE RUFFLE FLOWERS
Using the ¼ in. (5 mm) dusty pink ribbon, work the outer petals. Secure the tip of each petal using a single strand of pink floss. Form the ruffled center from an 11 in. (28 cm) length of cream organza ribbon, gathering it up with one strand of ecru floss.

EMBROIDERING THE FERNS
Using the medium green thread, stem-stitch the fern stems. Work the fern leaves in ribbon stitch, using the light green narrow ribbon. Set the leaves in opposite pairs, one on each side of the stem.

WORKING THE LEAVES
Refer to the photographs above and on the previous page. Work the leaves for the spider's web roses in the ¼ in. (5 mm) dark green ribbon, using ribbon stitch and side ribbon stitch (see page 262). Use the same ribbon to work two back-to-back ribbon stitches for the lower leaf on the stem of the left-hand ruffle flower. Work the leaf above it using side ribbon stitch. Work the leaves for the lilac buds in side ribbon stitch and the light green narrow ribbon. Position one on each side of each bud and along the stem as shown.

STITCHING THE BOW
Lay the ribbon on the fabric, following the tracing. Secure it to the fabric using two strands of burgundy floss and French knots (see page 77). At the ends of the bow tails, take the ends of the ribbon to the back of the fabric and fasten them down.

The bow is worked in a length of burgundy ribbon studded with matching French knots, which secure the ribbon in place and decorate it.

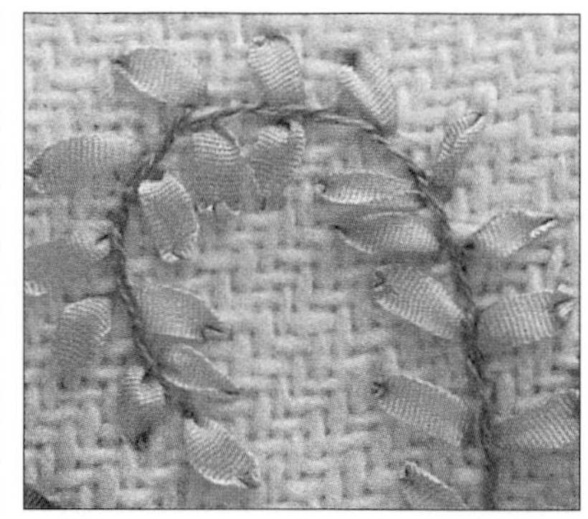

Curved lines of stem stitch create a realistic-looking fern stem in medium green floss. Lining the stem are many pairs of lifelike leaves. Use the light green narrow ribbon and work it in ribbon stitch to form the leaves, taking great care to make them all the same size.

The pointed petals of the ruffle flowers look highly effective, yet are simple to achieve. The ribbon is stitched as for a standard petal, then secured with a strand of pink floss. The ruffle is formed by gathering a length of cream organza ribbon into a frothy rosette.

You can work just a section of this enchanting bouquet to decorate a small area, such as a corner of a tablecloth or pillow cover, as shown below.

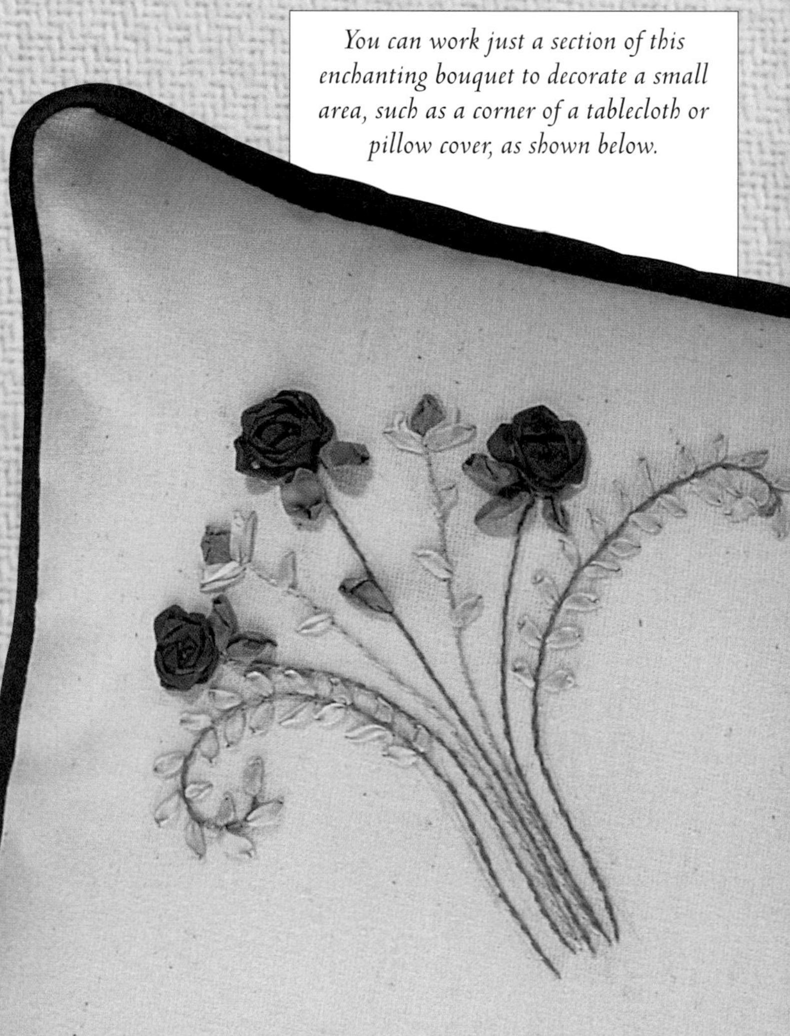

Silver Spirals

Decorative silver spirals worked in metallic embroidery and beading embellish a crushed velvet scarf and evening bag.

You Will Need

For both items:

- Gray crushed velvet: two 40 x 14 in. (102 x 35 cm) pieces for the scarf, two 12 in. (30 cm) squares for the bag
- Gray lining fabric: two 40 x 14 in. (102 x 35 cm) pieces for the scarf, two 12 in. (30 cm) squares for the bag
- Metallic silver organza: two 14 in. (35 cm) squares for the scarf, one 12 in. (30 cm) square for the bag
- Six skeins of DMC stranded metallic thread in 5283 silver
- Tracing paper and pencil
- Dressmaker's carbon paper
- Embroidery hoop
- Chenille needle, size 18
- Beading needle
- Sewing needle
- Thread for basting
- Sewing thread in gray
- Silver bugle beads and rocaille beads
- Scissors
- Three silver tassels
- 1⅜ yd. (1.2 m) of gray cord trim for the bag handle

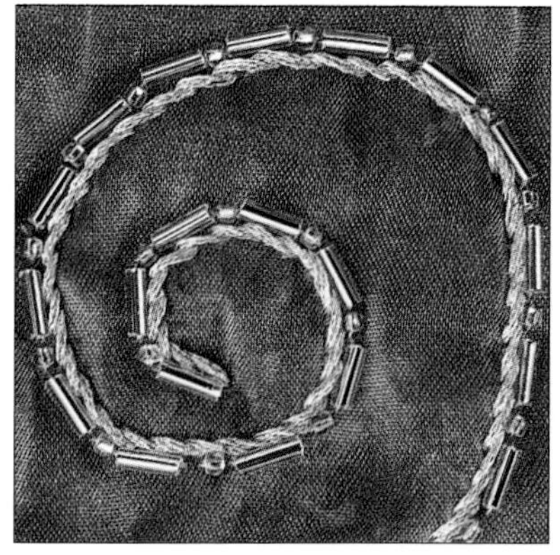

Alternate the two types of bead around the outer edges of the large spirals.

In this elegant design for a scarf and an evening bag, silver organza is laid over crushed gray velvet and embellished with bold silver spirals. The spirals are stem-stitched using metallic silver thread, then the outer curves of the large spirals are highlighted with bugle beads and rocailles.

Both the scarf and bag are fully lined, and each item is finished with sparkly silver tassels. The scarf measures 37 x 12 in. (94 x 30 cm)—excluding the tassels—and the bag is about 8 in. (20 cm) wide and 8 in. (20 cm) deep.

Preparing the pattern

Use a photocopier to enlarge the shape template (above right) to twice its original size (200%). Fold the tracing paper in half and lay it on the enlargement, matching the fold to the broken line. Trace the enlargement, and cut out the tracing to make a pattern.

Lay the pattern over the spirals (below right). Transfer the spirals as desired inside the pattern; use the photograph as a guide.

Preparing the scarf pieces

Place the velvet scarf pieces together, right sides facing and with raw edges matching. Stitch across one short end, taking ⅝ in. (1.5 cm) seam allowance. Repeat with the scarf lining pieces. Press the seams open.

Use the carbon paper to transfer the pattern, centering it onto each organza square. Press in the seam allowance along the top edge; trim it to measure ¼ in. (5 mm).

Place one organza square at each end of the velvet, right sides upward, with pressed edges inward and raw edges matching. Pin and baste the layers together; mount one end in the hoop.

Working the design

Work one end of the scarf at a time. Stem-stitch (see page 26)

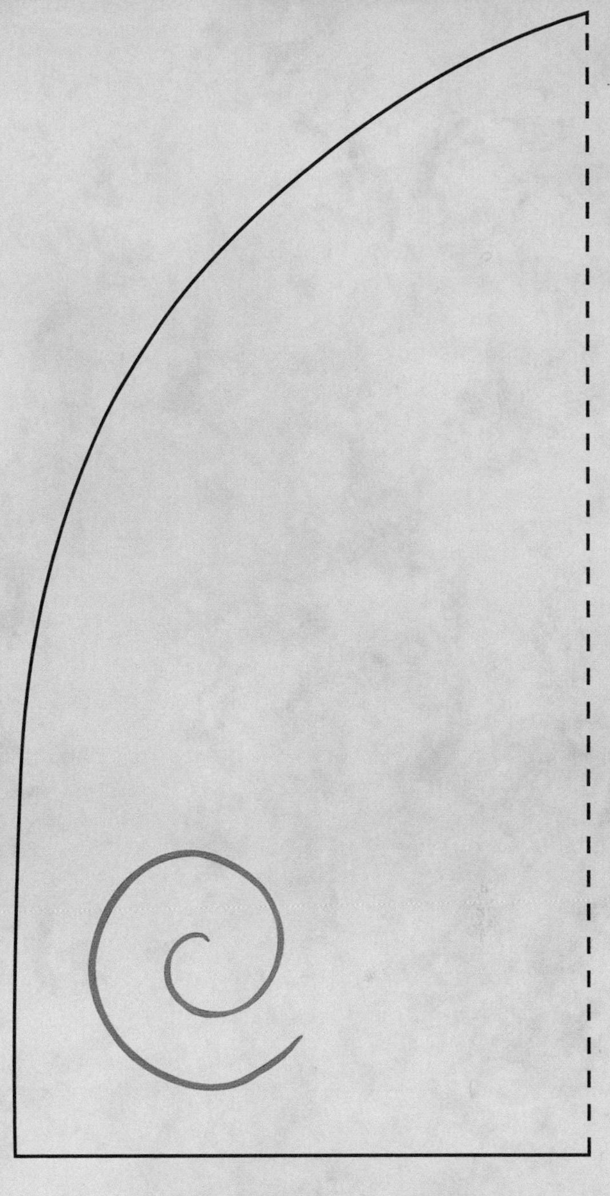

the spirals, using the chenille needle and all six strands of the metallic thread. Next, use the beading needle and the gray sewing thread to add beads around the outer edge of the large spirals; alternate bugle beads and rocailles, and stitch through them twice to hold them in place. When the stitching is complete, remove the work from the hoop.

Secure the pressed edges of the organza to the velvet, using the gray sewing thread and a tiny running stitch (see page 26). When both ends are complete, press the scarf on the wrong side with a cool iron.

Shaping the scarf

Remove the basting, then trim the layers 1 in. (2.5 cm) outside the outline to shape the ends. Cut the lining fabric to match.

Making the scarf

Placing the right sides together and matching the raw edges, pin the lining and velvet together. Baste, then stitch all around taking a 1 in. (2.5 cm) seam and leaving a gap in one long edge for turning. Clip into the curves and cut across the points to reduce bulk. Turn right side out and press. Slipstitch the edges of the gap together.

Work a line of beads over the pressed inner edges of the organza in the same way as for the spirals. To finish, sew a tassel to each point; make your own tassels as shown on page 313, or buy them ready-made.

Working the bag

Use a photocopier to reduce the pattern by 30%. Trace the photocopy, then transfer the design onto the organza as described above. Baste the organza to the right side of one velvet square, and mount the fabric in the hoop.

Work the spirals as on the scarf.

Making the bag

Trim both velvet squares 1 in. (2.5 cm) outside the outline to shape the bag pieces. Placing the right sides together and matching the raw edges, stitch the pieces together, taking a 1 in. (2.5 cm) seam and leaving the top open. Trim and clip the seams, and cut across the point as above. Turn the bag right side out. Baste each end of the cord inside the bag on the seams to form the handle.

Make the lining as for the bag, but make it ¼ in. (5 mm) smaller and leave a gap in one side.

Put the bag inside the lining with the right sides together. Stitch around the top taking a 1 in. (2.5 cm) seam. Turn the bag right side out and slipstitch the edges of the gap together.

Work a line of alternate bugle and rocaille beads along the top of the bag front. To finish, sew a tassel to the bottom of the bag.

Work a line of bugle and rocaille beads over the pressed edges of the organza. For the spirals, use six strands of thread.

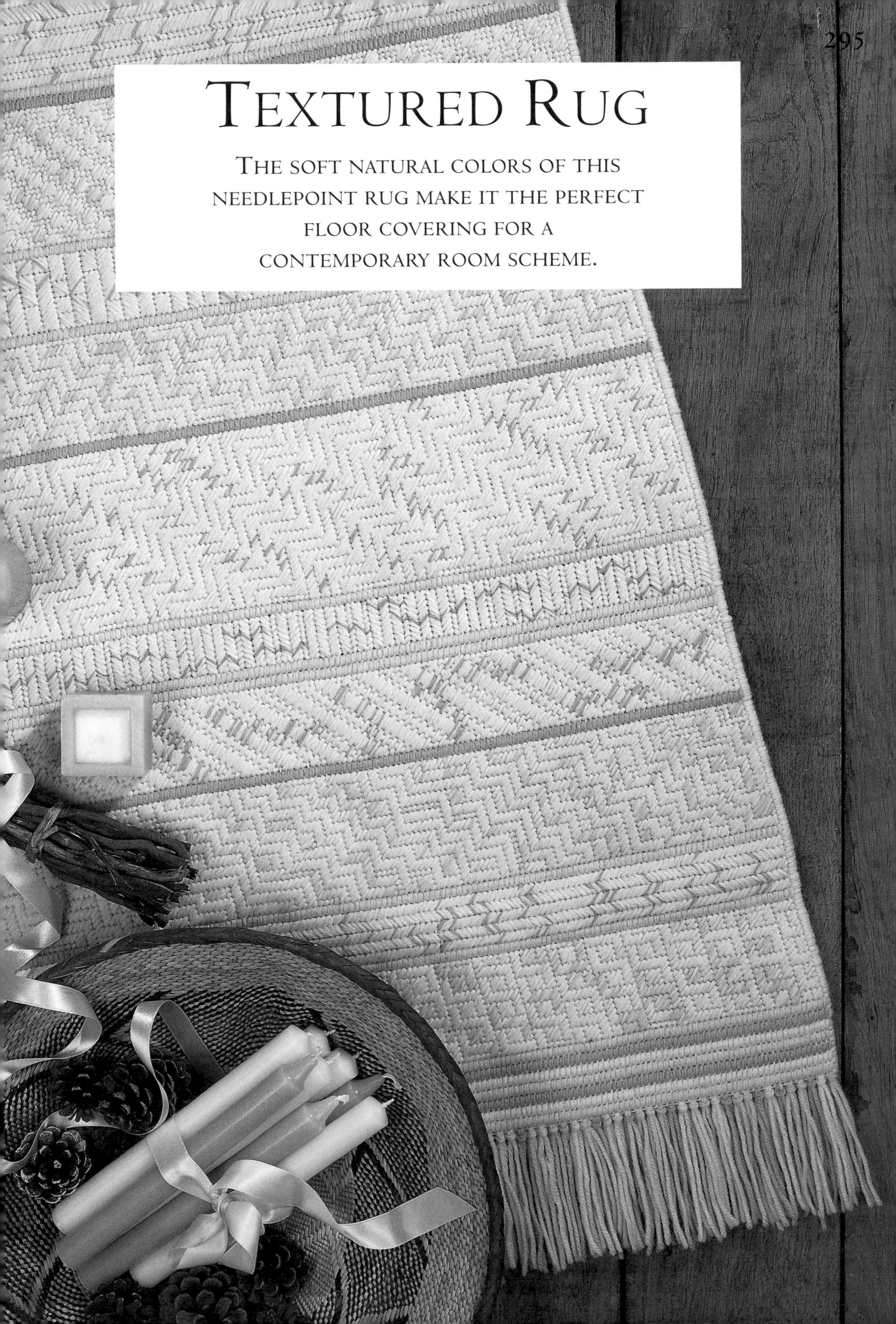

Textured Rug

The soft natural colors of this needlepoint rug make it the perfect floor covering for a contemporary room scheme.

You Will Need

- 8-count white interlock canvas, 47 x 31½ in. (120 x 80 cm)
- Heavyweight backing fabric
- DMC tapestry yarns as listed in the color key
- Tapestry needle, size 18
- Medium-sized crochet hook
- Large standing scroll frame
- Large chenille needle and heavy-duty thread
- Masking tape

Color Key

COLORS	HANKS
Ecru	25
7746 Cream	6
7453 Pale tan	3

COLORS	SKEINS
7162 Beige	3
7171 Oyster	3
7917 Peach	3

For the fourth band, work rows of varying diagonal straight stitches.

Work blocks of diagonal stitches for the sixth band, changing the direction of the stitches in the rows.

This lovely rug is made up of bands of needlepoint finished at each end with a generous fringe. The bands, separated by rows of straight Gobelin stitch, are filled with richly textured stitches, enhanced by the neutral color scheme. All the bands are worked in ecru, with short lengths of other colors randomly blended in; for the blending use one strand of ecru and one of the other color.

You'll find instructions on all the stitches in the Needlepoint Stitch Library. The finished rug works up to about 48 x 27 in. (122 x 68 cm), including the fringe.

Preparing to Stitch

Baste two parallel lines 27 in. (68 cm) apart down the center of the canvas to mark the width of the rug. Bind the raw edges of the canvas with tape, and attach it to the frame as shown on page 20. Mount the top section of the canvas on the frame.

Stitching the Rug

Start 2 in. (5 cm) from the top of the canvas. Work the design, referring to the chart and stitching instructions. One square on the chart equals one stitch worked over one canvas thread. Use two strands of yarn throughout. For the tramé straight Gobelin stitches (see page 269 for the tramé, page 174 for straight Gobelin stitch), use two strands of the same color, referring to the picture on page 295; work the textured bands in ecru, blending in other colors at random. The textured bands are numbered on the chart. Work from the top of the canvas down, and finish each section before unlacing and moving the canvas.

Working the Borders

Work tramé straight Gobelin stitch in ecru along the long sides of the canvas just inside the basting. Use the same color for the tramé as for the stitches. Work as far as you can without moving the canvas into a new frame position; continue the borders later when you move the canvas.

Next, work the first seven rows of tramé straight Gobelin stitch; vary the colors to create stripes. When these rows are complete, refer to the chart to stitch the rows of tramé straight Gobelin stitch that divide the textured bands.

Working the Top Section

Work the first band in Jacquard stitch (see page 178). Work the second band in stem stitch (see page 201; but omit the backstitch). Use Milanese stitch (see page 182) for the third band.

For the fourth band, work diagonal straight stitches over one, two or three canvas threads and alternate the stitch direction; this is shown clearly in the photograph. Work the fifth band in Moorish stitch (see page 178).

For the sixth band, work vertical blocks of diagonal straight stitches, working the stitches mainly over three canvas threads. Change the stitch direction within the vertical rows and between the rows; refer to the photograph (bottom left).

Working the Bottom Section

Use Byzantine stitch (see page 177) for the seventh band, but stitch blocks of five diagonal stitches worked over two canvas threads.

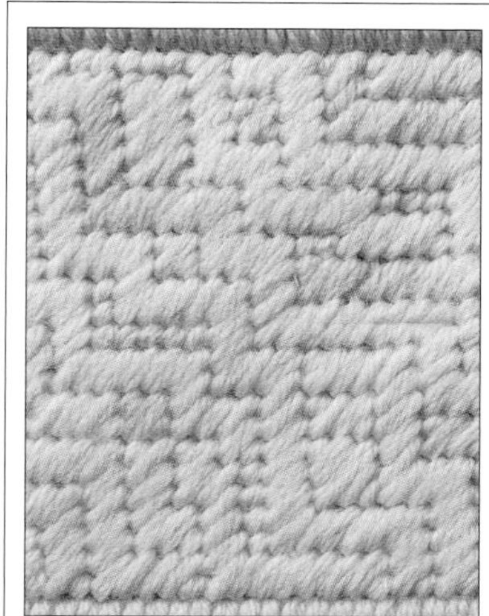

Fill the eleventh band with zigzag rows of diagonal stitches worked over two canvas threads; fill the gaps with smaller or larger stitches.

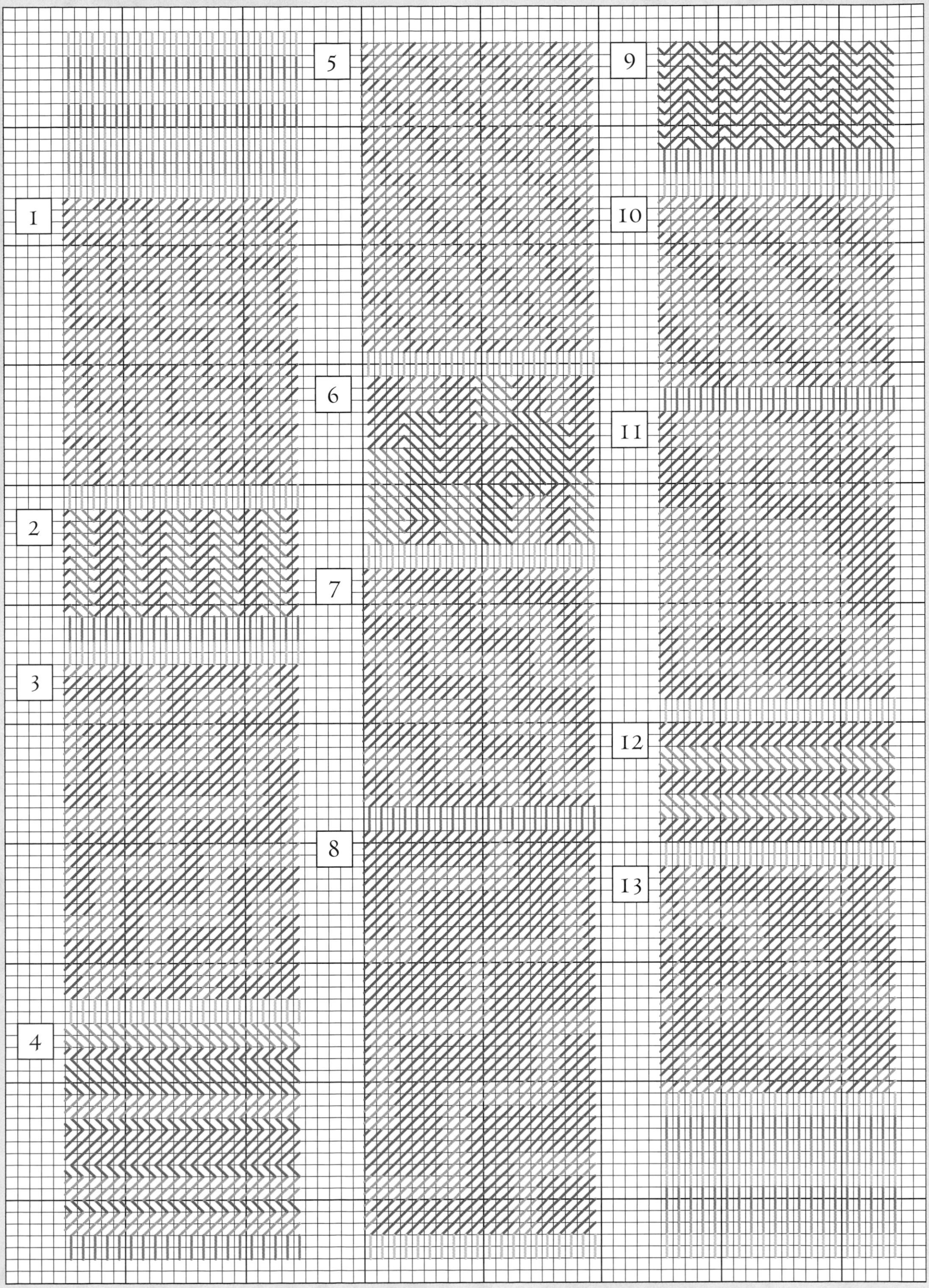

5

9

1

10

6

11

2

7

3

12

8

13

4

Work the eighth band in extended Milanese stitch (see page 182).

For the ninth band, again work rows of stem stitch but work the rows randomly over one or two canvas threads; see the photograph (top right).

Work the tenth band in a variation of mosaic stitch (see page 179), alternating blocks of stitches worked over one, two, and one canvas threads with blocks worked over two, three, and two canvas threads. See the photograph (right).

For the eleventh band, work random zigzags of diagonal stitches over two threads, filling in the gaps with smaller or larger stitches; see the photograph on page 296.

Work the twelfth band as for the fourth band, but work the stitches over two canvas threads. Stitch the last band in block Byzantine stitch (see page 181).

To finish, work seven more rows of tramé straight Gobelin stitch.

Finishing

Remove the work from the frame and press gently from the wrong side. If necessary, block it to shape, as described on pages 303 and 304.

Trimming the canvas

Trim the canvas to within 1¼ in. (3 cm) of the stitching. Press the unstitched canvas to the wrong side, leaving one row of holes at each short end to work the fringe. Miter the corners and secure the edges in place with herringbone stitch (see page 49), using the chenille needle and heavy-duty thread.

Working the fringe

Cut two 8 in. (20 cm) lengths of yarn. Place them together and fold them in half. Insert the crochet hook from back to front through the folded edge of the canvas. Hook the loops over the hook and pull them through to the back. Pull the ends through the loop and tighten. Continue in this way to fringe each short end of the rug, looping two threads through each canvas hole.

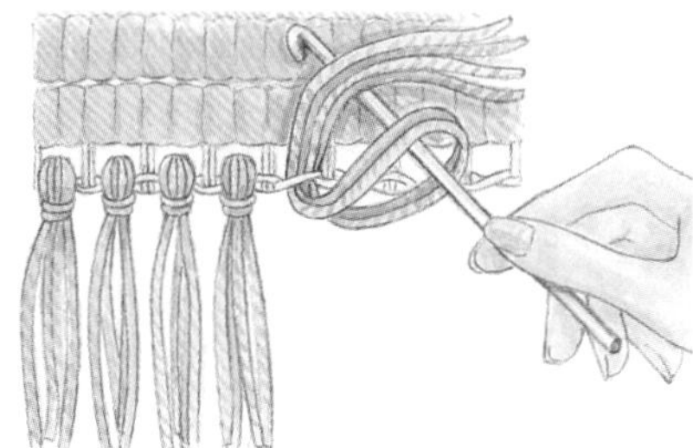

Attaching the backing

Cut the backing fabric to the same size as the stitched canvas, adding an extra ¾ in. (2 cm) to all four edges for turning under. Press the ¾ in. (2 cm) to the wrong side. Placing the wrong sides together, slipstitch the backing fabric to the canvas.

NOTE: This design can easily be varied. You can make it shorter by omitting some of the bands or reducing their depth; longer, by adding or extending them. You could substitute one or more preferred stitch patterns; you could use different colors.

For the ninth band, work rows of stem stitch in a random pattern over one or two canvas threads.

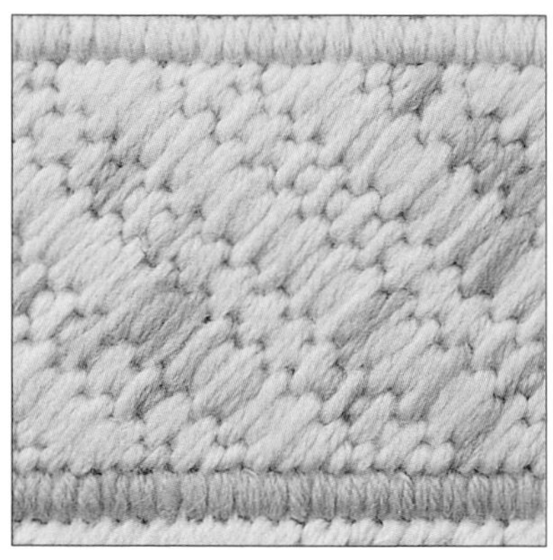

Work the tenth band in mosaic stitch variation, alternating blocks worked over one, two, and one thread, with blocks worked over two, three, and two.

Florentine Footstool

The gentle waves of Bargello in sea greens, blues, and grays soften the lines of this footstool.

You Will Need

- 12-count white single thread interlock canvas, 16 x 12 in. (40 x 30 cm)
- DMC tapestry wool as listed in the color key
- Tapestry needle, size 18
- Dark thread for basting
- Sewing needle
- Masking tape
- Scroll frame
- Embroidery scissors
- Footstool with removable pad, 13½ x 10 in. (34 x 25 cm)
- Tacks and hammer or staple gun

Color Key

COLORS	SKEINS
7287 Gray	3
7542 Sea green	3
7595 Turquoise	3
7597 Pale turquoise	3
7604 Pale sea green	3

On this handsome footstool cover, soft tapestry wool in watery shades of turquoise, sea green, and misty gray complement the fluid lines of the Bargello pattern to perfection.

The finished size of the stitched area is 13½ x 10 in. (34 x 25 cm), to cover a footstool pad of the same size. However, you can adapt the instructions for a stool with either a smaller or a larger pad.

Preparing the Canvas

Bind the canvas edges with masking tape. Baste a 13½ x 10 in. (34 x 25 cm) rectangle in the center of the canvas, and mark the center with two lines of basting. Mount it on the frame.

Working the Design

Stitch the design, referring to the photographs (right and above) and color key (above), following the instructions on page 271. Work across the canvas in horizontal rows using Stitch Method 1, starting at the top of the canvas and working down to the bottom.

For the first row, start at the top center of the canvas with the turquoise, and work out to the right, and then in mirror image to the left. Work the row below in pale turquoise, from left to right. Repeat, to work subsequent rows from left to right, using sea green, pale sea green, then gray. Repeat the colors in the sequence until the rectangle is completely covered.

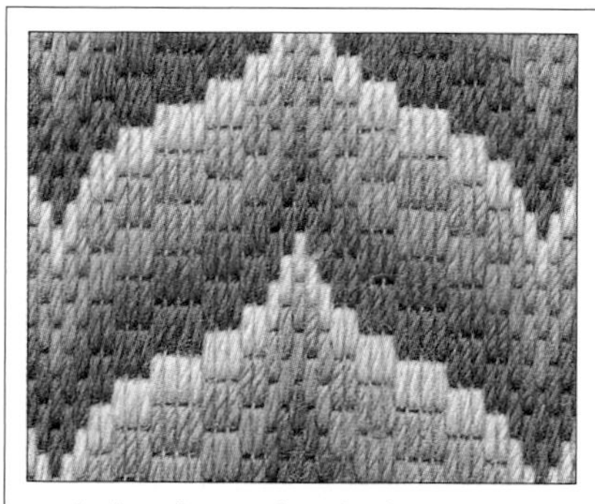

The bands of color shade from dark to light, accentuating the design.

Fill any unworked areas using the same color sequence and shorter stitches as necessary.

Finishing

Take the finished piece off the frame and press it from the wrong side. If the work is badly distorted, block it as described on pages 303 and 304.

Covering the Footstool Pad

Trim the canvas 1¼ in. (3 cm) from the stitching. Use the canvas to cover the footstool pad, following the instructions for a removable seat pad on pages 309 and 310. Replace the pad in the footstool.

Chapter 5
Finishing & Making Up

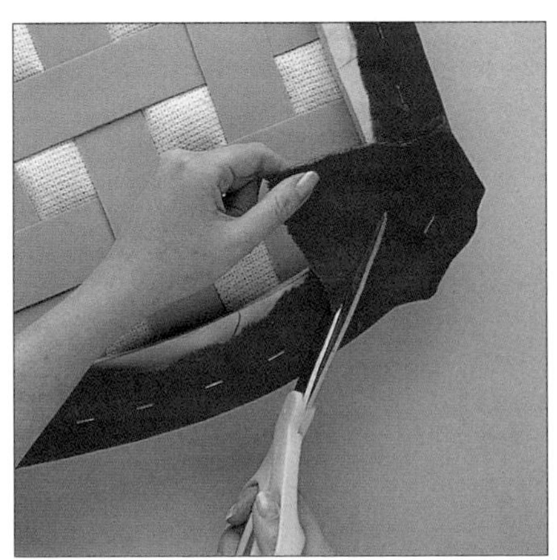

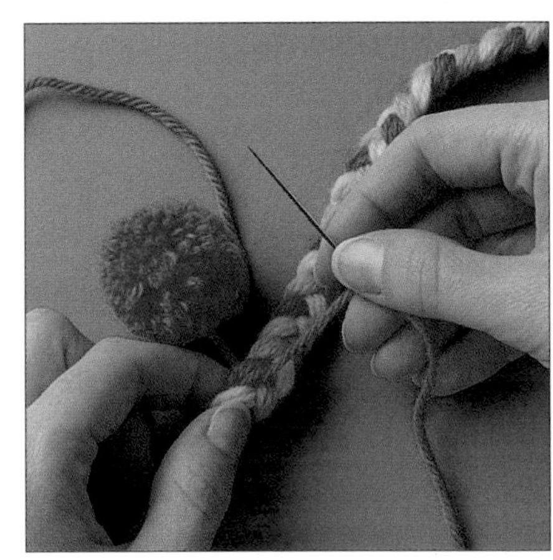

Blocking needlepoint

Even if you use a frame, many needlepoint stitches—especially popular diagonal stitches such as continental tent and half cross stitch—tend to distort the canvas, no matter how carefully you stitch. Blocking your finished work will straighten the canvas and leave the stitching looking fresh and smooth.

To block the work, dampen it, then place it on a board marked with a grid of lines. Using the grid as a guide, stretch the work back into shape, secure it with tacks, and leave it to dry fully, which can take several days. As it dries, the canvas "sets" in the correct shape.

Always leave the needlepoint to dry at room temperature, away from direct heat or sunlight, which can fade thread colors. Make sure the piece is bone-dry before you take it off the block, or it may become distorted again.

Block your needlepoint face down, unless the design is heavily textured—in this case, place it face up on the blocking board to avoid flattening the stitches.

This method can also be used for blocking highly textured pieces of surface embroidery, such as crewelwork, for which pressing is inadequate.

For the blocking board, use a piece of unstained, unpainted wood at least ¾ in. (2 cm) thick.

You Will Need

- Softwood board, at least ¾ in. (2 cm) thick and 2 in. (5 cm) larger all around than the canvas
- Ruler
- Fine black waterproof marking pen
- Sheet of thick, clear plastic
- Staple gun and staples
- Spray bottle
- Rust proof finish nails or tacks
- Hammer
- Pincers
- Triangle (optional)

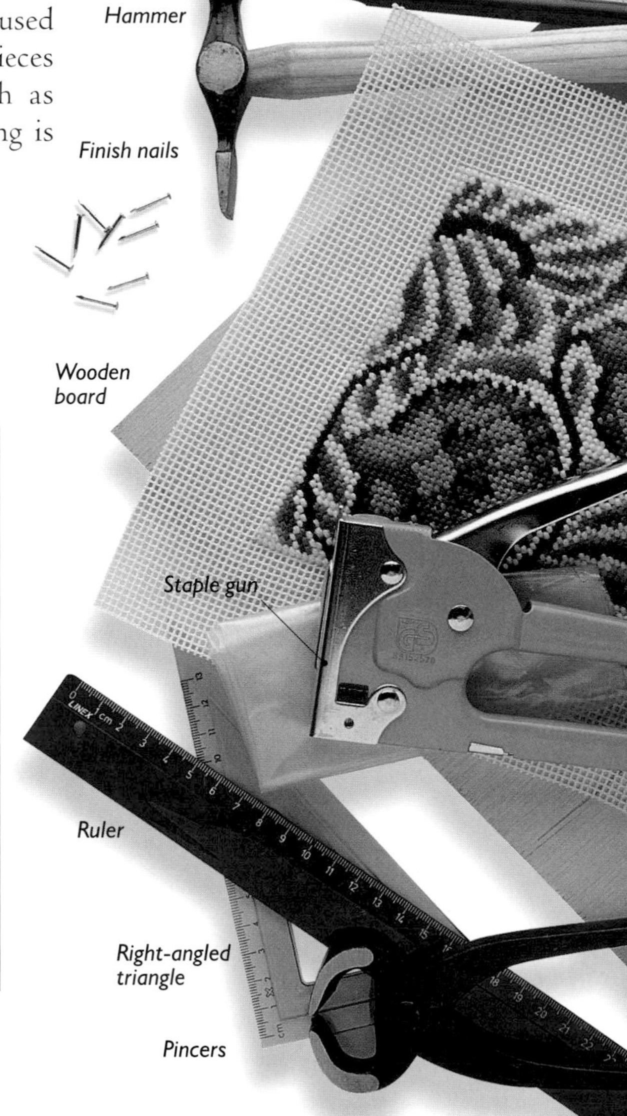

Making the blocking board

1 Using the waterproof marking pen, steel ruler, and triangle, mark a grid of lines on the board at a right angle to the edges. Position the lines about 1 in. (2.5 cm) apart. Allow to dry thoroughly.

2 Cut a piece of plastic about 2 in. (5 cm) larger all around than the board. Cover the board with the plastic, securing the surplus with staples on the wrong side and turning in the corners neatly.

Blocking needlepoint

1 Trim the unworked canvas around the stitching to 2 in. (5 cm). Spray the canvas with cool, clean water to moisten it lightly. Then center the dampened canvas face down on the blocking board.

2 With the top of the stitching along one horizontal line, lightly hammer a nail into the unworked canvas at the center top. Ease the canvas downward, aligning the threads vertically. Hammer in a nail at the center bottom.

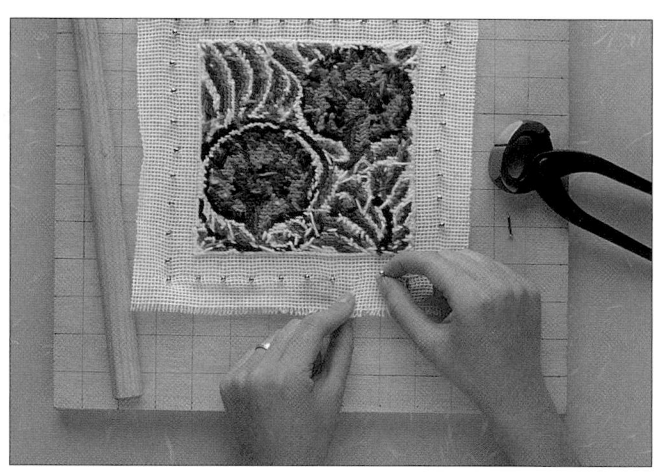

3 Hammer in a nail at the center of each remaining side of the canvas, using the grid or a triangle to ensure that the vertical canvas threads are at a right angle to the horizontal threads. Hammer the nails in lightly in case you need to adjust them later.

4 Working out from the center of each edge, insert nails every ¾ in. (2 cm), gently stretching the canvas as you go. Check that the edges line up with the grid, and adjust if necessary. Allow to dry thoroughly. Use pincers to remove the nails.

QUICK BLOCKING

If the distortion is only slight, steam-press on the wrong side, gently easing the work into shape.

Continental tent stitch tends to distort the canvas (below) because the diagonal stitches pull the threads out of alignment. Blocking restores it to shape (right).

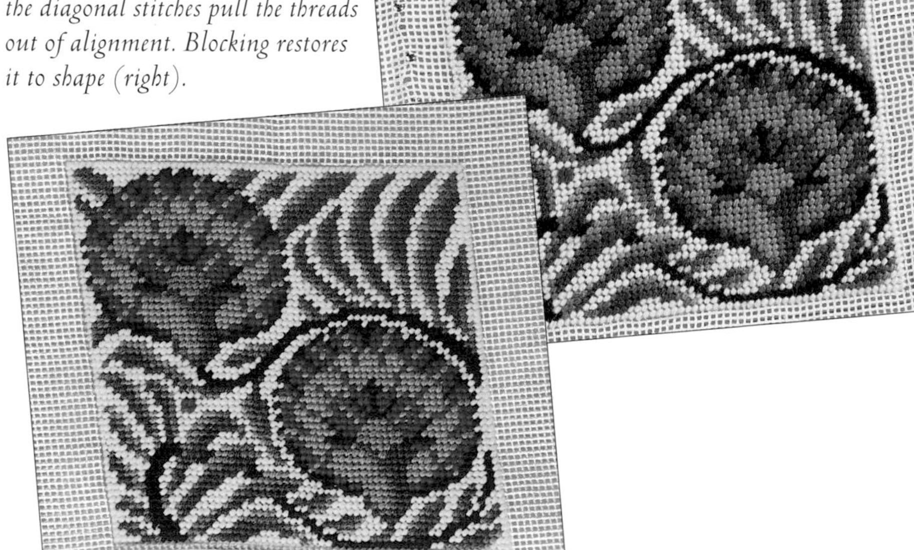

Framing a design

Framed needlecraft designs look their best with an inner frame, known as a mat. The mat sets off the work and stops it from touching the glass.

Choose a frame and mat board in colors that enhance the work or coordinate with your room scheme. A wide mat looks better than a thin one. Use only acid-free (archival) mat board to prevent damage to the work.

The aperture on the mat can have a straight or bevelled edge—a straight edge is cut at 90 degrees to the surface; a beveled edge is cut at 45 degrees (see page 306). A straight edge is cut with a utility knife and ruler. For a beveled edge, you'll need a bevel mat cutter—a metal ruler with a cutter that runs along a track.

Even if you plan to have the work professionally framed, you can do the initial mounting yourself, as shown in steps 5–9, page 306, and thus save some money.

Mounting a design

1 Check that the design fits the frame with a fairly even border all around. The border should be at least 2 in. (5 cm) wide, depending on the size of the design. For the best effect, the lower border should be at least ½ in. (1.2 cm) deeper than the others.

2 Remove the backing board from the frame and place it on the mat board to use as a template. Draw around it on the mat board, then cut out the mat with a sharp utility knife and a metal ruler on a cutting mat.

3 Place strips of mat board around the design to decide on the crop; put the frame on top to decide how wide to make the mat. When you are satisfied, measure the width of the cropped design. Deduct this from the width of the backing board. Each side edge of the mat will be half the remainder in width. Repeat with the height of the design, but make the lower border ½ in. (1.2 cm) deeper than the upper border. Using these measurements, mark the aperture position on back of the cut mat board.

YOU WILL NEED

- Ready-made frame
- Acid-free mat board
- Utility knife
- Metal ruler
- Cutting mat
- Bevel mat cutter (optional)
- Pencil and pins
- Masking tape
- Strong thread for lacing
- Sturdy needle for lacing

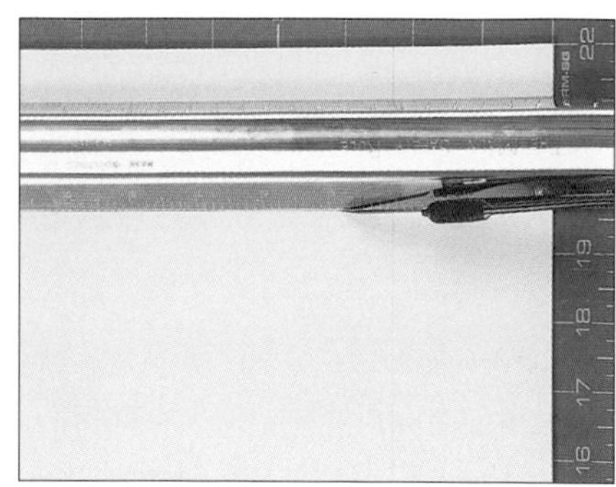

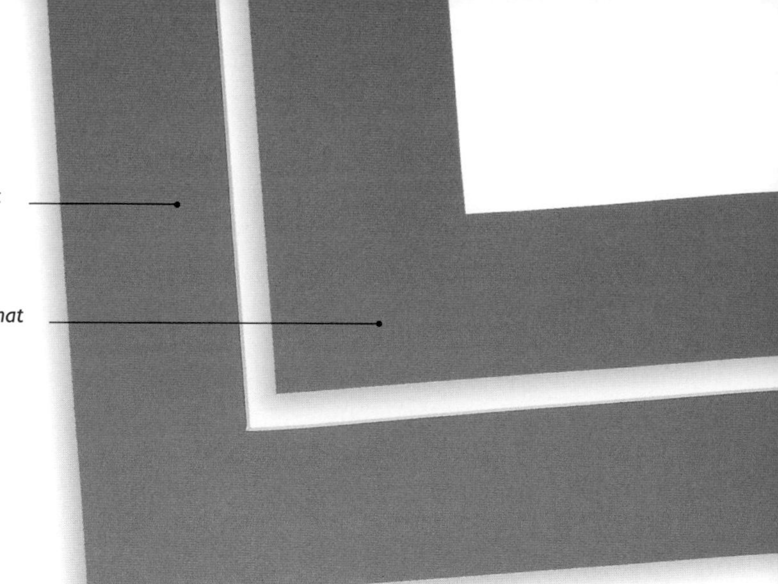

4a For a straight aperture edge, score along the aperture lines, using a utility knife and metal ruler, until you cut through the board.

4b For a beveled edge, mark a second set of lines on the cut mat board, 1 in. (2.5 cm) inside the lines showing the position of the aperture. Place the bevel mat cutter and ruler on the pencil lines, and cut along the outer lines, following the manufacturer's instructions.

5 Cut a piece of mat board larger than the aperture on your mat but small enough for the edges of the fabric to wrap over onto the back. Measure and mark the center of each edge of the mat board, then join up opposite marks to form a cross. Mark the center of each edge of the design with a pin or basting.

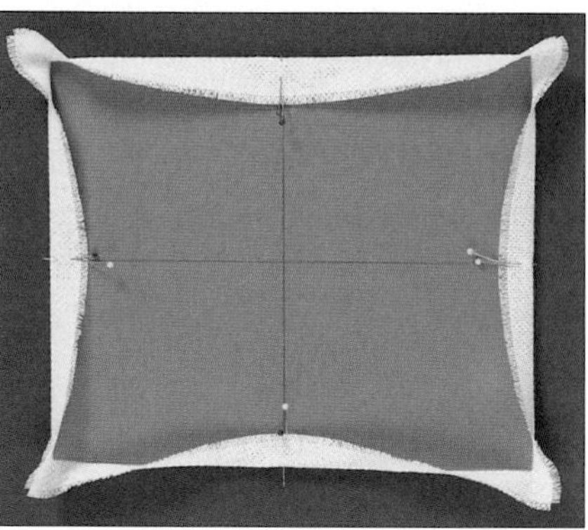

6 Lay the board, wrong side down, over the back of the fabric matching the center marks. Use pins to secure the center of each edge of the fabric to the corresponding edge of the board. Remove the marker pins.

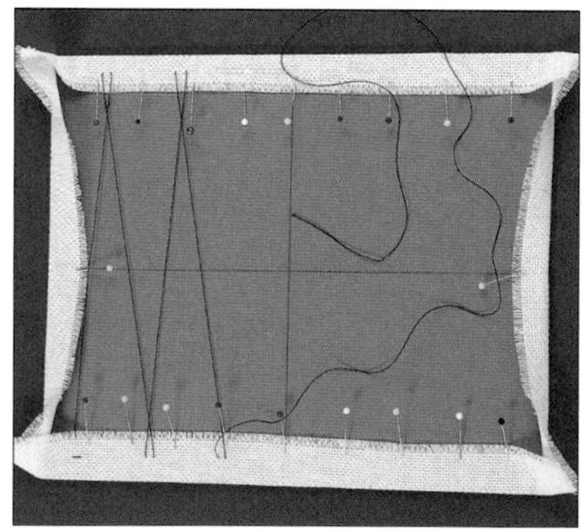

7 Pin one long edge of the fabric to the back of the board at regular intervals. Pin the opposite edge in the same way. Thread a long length of strong thread onto a sturdy needle and lace from one side to the other, starting at the bottom left-hand corner. Keep the thread taut and knot on additional lengths as necessary.

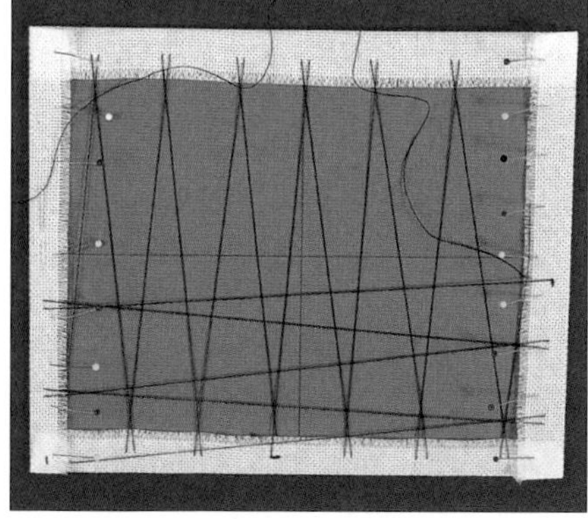

8 Rotate the board 90 degrees, and lace the short edges of the fabric in the same way. Fold in the fabric neatly at the corners to prevent bulges, and make sure it is smooth and taut on the right side. Remove the pins after working the lacing.

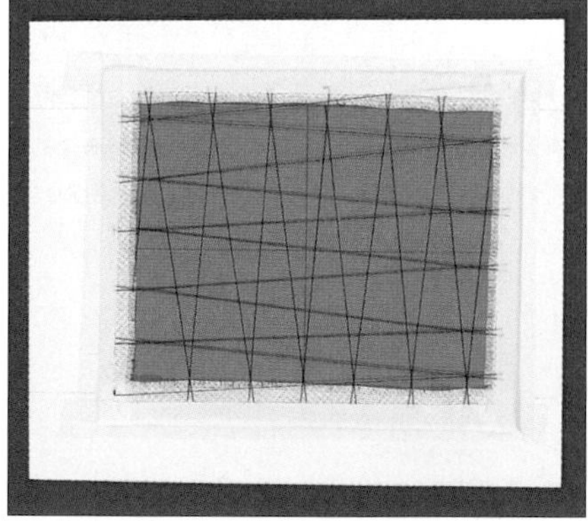

9 Place the design face up, and position the mat on top. Holding both securely, turn them over and tape the mounted design firmly to the back of the mat with masking tape. Place the mat and embroidery in the frame and replace the backing board. Tape the edges of the backing board to the edges of the frame.

Pillow covers

The easiest type of pillow cover to make is a simple square or rectangular shape with an overlapped back opening. You can cut both the front and back pieces from fabric, as shown below, or you can use the front to display a piece of embroidery, such as a needlepoint panel.

If the embroidered piece is small, stitch it to the front before assembling the cushion. Larger pieces can form the whole cushion front, so you'll only need fabric for the back piece. Instructions for both styles are given on page 308.

To hold the pillow form firmly in place, the pillow cover needs a generous overlap at the back. The steps below explain how to make a cover with a 4½ in. (12 cm) wide overlap, which suits pillows up to 14 in. (35 cm) square. For larger pillows, the overlap needs to be at least 6 in. (15 cm), so cut the back piece 8½ in. (22 cm) wider than the front.

To ensure that the pillow cover holds its shape when it is in use, position the back overlap on a rectangular cover so that it runs widthwise (parallel to the two shorter sides).

Use fabrics that are closely woven, crease-resistant, and durable. Strong decorator fabrics made of cotton and linen blends are ideal.

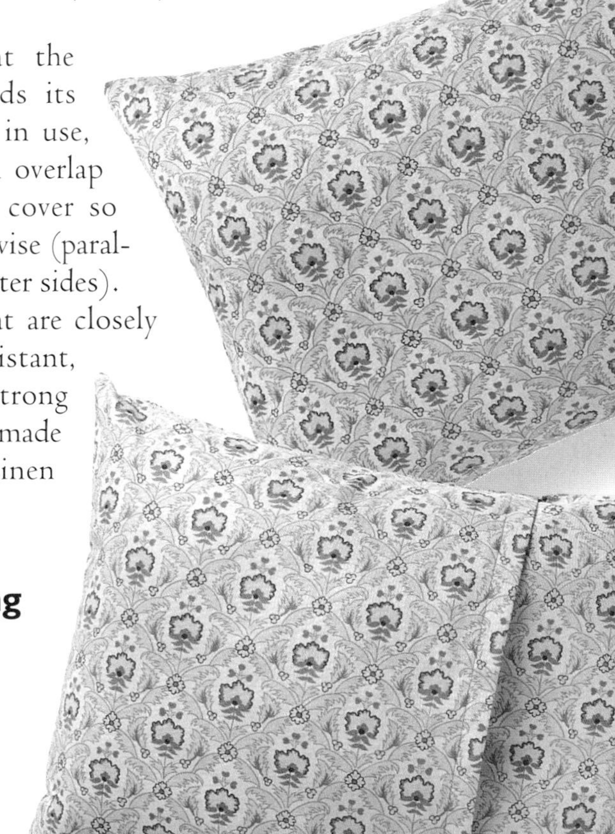

Making a cushion with an overlapped opening

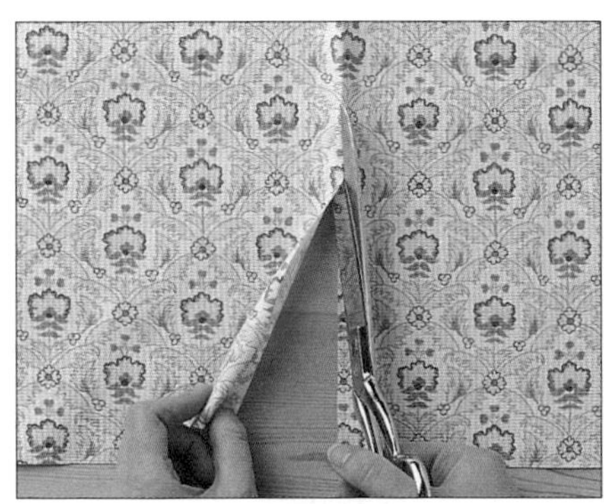

1 Cut the fabric for the front piece ⅝ in. (1.5 cm) larger all around than the finished cover. Cut the fabric for the back piece 7 in. (18 cm) wider than the front. Cut the back piece in half widthwise.

2 Turn, press, and machine-stitch a ⅝ in. (1.5 cm) double hem along the center edge of each back piece.

3 Placing right sides together, pin the back pieces to the front. Make sure that the raw edges match all around and that the hemmed center back edges overlap by about 4½ in. (12 cm).

4 Stitch around the outer edges, with ⅝ in. (1.5 cm) seam allowances. Stitch twice across each end of overlap. Trim the corners of seam allowances diagonally. Turn the cover right side out and insert pillow form.

Making a cover with a needlepoint panel and braid trim

1 Trim the canvas or fabric around the needlepoint to leave an unstitched border a little narrower than the width of the braid trim.

2 Cut out the cover front following step 1 on page 307. Center the needlepoint on the right side of cover front and slip-stitch in place all around.

3 Machine- or hand-sew the trim over the raw edges of needlepoint. Cut out the back piece and assemble the cover, steps **1–4**, page 307.

Making a cover with a needlepoint front and cord trim

1 Block the needlepoint (see page 303), then trim the canvas edges to 1 in. (2.5 cm). Cut the back of the cover as on page 307**,** step **1**, but allow a 1 in. (2.5 cm) seam allowance. Press and stitch a 5/8 in. (1.5 cm) double hem on center edge of each back piece.

2 Placing right sides together, pin back pieces to needlepoint, overlapping hemmed edges at center. Working on the needlepoint side and using a zipper foot, stitch around twice, close to the needlepoint. Leave a 1 in. (2.5 cm) opening in the lower edge. Trim seams to 5/8 in. (1.5 cm).

3 Cut across corners to reduce bulk, and turn cover right side out. Push one end of cord through opening in seam. Slip-stitch cord along seamline, all around the edge. Insert other end of cord into seam opening and slip-stitch in place. Insert pillow form.

For cushions with a needlepoint front, stitch a cord trim over the seam to conceal any canvas threads.

The neatest way to attach the braid is to cu it so that it extends to the sides of the cover.

Covering seat pads

Replacing the covers on dining chairs is an easy process. The steps on page 310 show you how to put a new cover on any removable seat pad—including traditional types with webbing strips stretched across a frame, and modern styles with a solid wooden base.

Most seat pads are softened with a foam pad and a layer of batting—sometimes the batting is protected by a layer of unbleached muslin or burlap. The new fabric cover is stretched over the top, and simply stapled to the underside with a staple gun—though you could use tacks and a hammer if you don't have a staple gun.

Before you start, make sure the seat pad is easy to remove. Drop-in seat pads can be simply pushed out of the frame, while other types may need to be unscrewed first.

Choosing the fabric

Fabric cover Choose a closely woven, medium-weight fabric. If you are using a piece of needlepoint, the stitched area should be large enough to cover both the top and sides of the pad. Leave a margin of unworked canvas around the stitching of at least 2 in. (5 cm).

Base cloth Unbleached muslin, drapery lining fabric or burlap are all suitable.

YOU WILL NEED

- Chair with removable seat pad
- Fabric for the seat cover
- Lining fabric for base
- Tape measure
- Screwdriver and pliers, or staple remover
- Scissors
- Staple gun and staples

When a seat cover looks shabby or grubby, it's time to replace it. Simply take off the old cover, then wrap a new piece of fabric over the top of the pad and staple it to the underside.

SEWING BOX

REPLACING THE PADDING

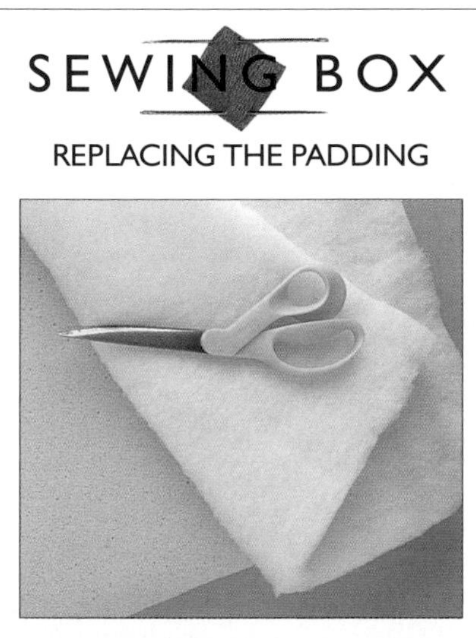

If the seat has lost its bounce, ask a foam supplier to cut you a new piece of foam. Glue it on to the base with white glue and cover with thick polyester batting, then add the fabric cover.

Re-covering a removable seat pad

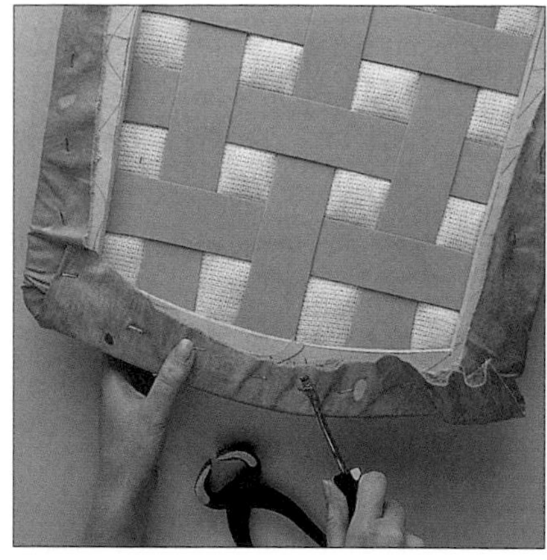

1 Remove the seat pad and place it wrong side up on the work surface. Pry out the staples or tacks with a screwdriver and pliers, or use a staple remover. Take off the backing cloth. Remove the fabric cover in the same way.

2 Measure the width of the seat from one base edge to the opposite base edge (**A**). Measure the depth from the front base edge to the back base edge (**B**). Cut a piece of fabric measuring **A** plus 2 in. (5 cm) by **B** plus 2 in. (5 cm).

3 Center the seat pad on the wrong side of the fabric. Staple the fabric to the center back. Working outward from the center, add more staples, spacing them about 1½ in. (4 cm) apart. Stop 2 in. (5 cm) from the corners.

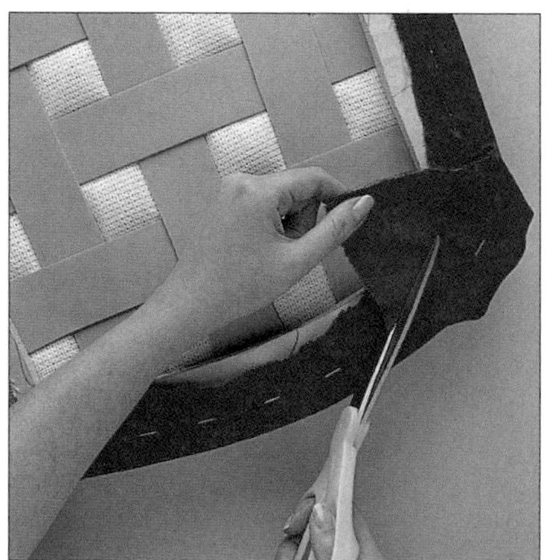

4 Turn the pad around, and pull the fabric tightly to the front edge. Staple it in place from the center outward. Repeat to secure the sides.

5 At each corner, pull the fabric tightly to the back, and staple in place. Trim off the point with scissors.

Re-covering the seat pad gives dining and bedroom chairs a bright new look. You can use a piece of embroidery or needlepoint, or a fabric chosen to match your room scheme.

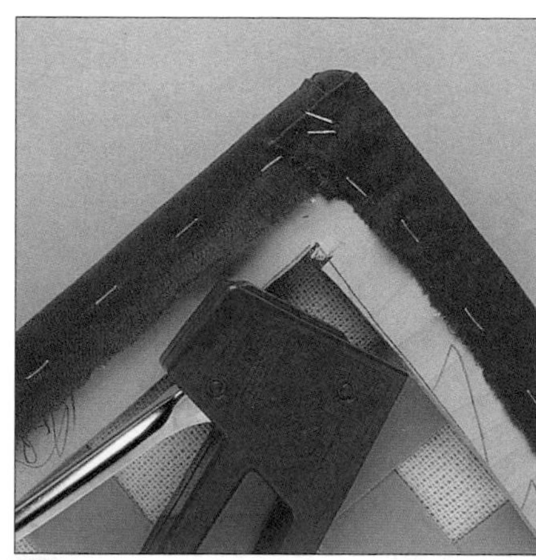

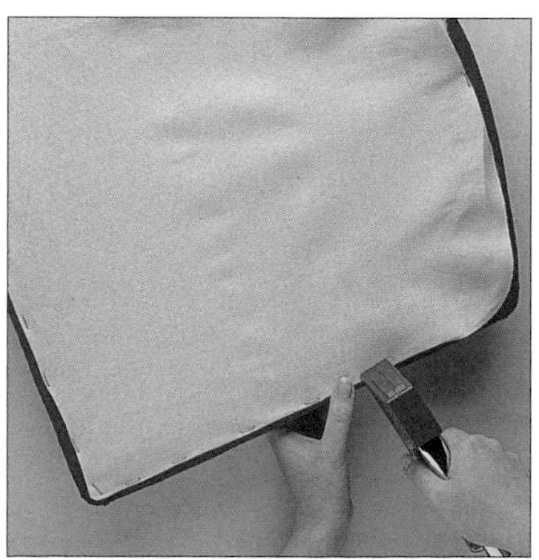

6 Fold the tucks of fabric over the corner and staple them down.

7 Cut a piece of base cloth slightly larger than the base. Lay it on the underside, turning under the edges so that they conceal the raw edges and staples. Staple it in place.

Mitered double borders

A mitered double border is made up of four border strips stitched to the edges of a square or rectangular panel and joined together diagonally at the corners. This style of border gives a professional finish to scatter pillows and other soft furnishings and is perfect for framing quilted and patchwork panels. It also makes an effective mount for embroidery and needlepoint designs.

There are a number of different ways of attaching mitered borders. Here, the four border strips are cut separately in a double width. The strips are joined together, then stitched to the front of the item. The border is folded to the back of the item, then neatly slipstitched in place, so that the item is fully reversible.

Making a neat miter can be quite tricky, but the end results are well worth the effort involved. The key to successful miters is to accurately measure and mark the positions of the seams, particularly at corners, and to stitch on the borders precisely. It's best to match the weight of the border fabric to that of the central panel and to practice the mitering techniques on fabric remnants before tackling your main project.

The instructions given here use a seam allowance of ⅝ in. (1.5 cm). For an accurate result, it is important to use the same seam allowance throughout.

Mitered double borders give a professional finish to reversible soft furnishings.

Preparing the border strips

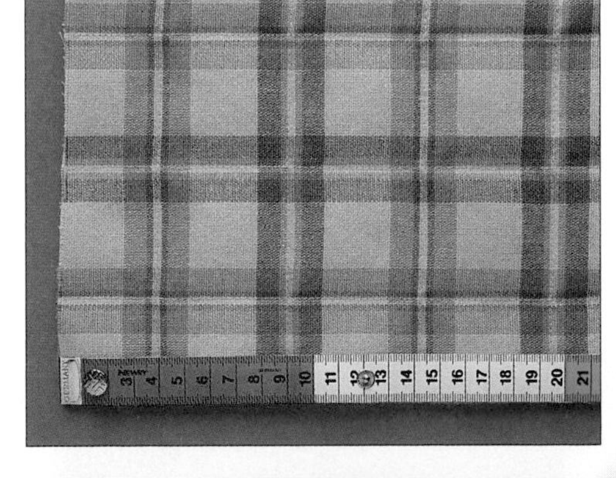

1 Decide on the finished width of your border. Double this measurement and add on twice the seam allowance (**A**).

For a square panel: Measure the length of the edge of the panel and add on twice the finished border width and twice the seam allowance (**B**). Cut four strips **A** by **B**.

For a rectangular panel: Measure the length of one long edge, and add on twice the finished border width and twice the seam allowance (**C**). Cut two strips **A** by **C**. Measure the length of one short edge, and add on twice the finished border width and twice the seam allowance (**D**). Cut two strips **A** by **D**.

2 Press each of the strips in half lengthwise, right sides together, with a medium-hot iron.

Mix and match border and panel fabrics to create colorful coordinating table linen.

Making the border

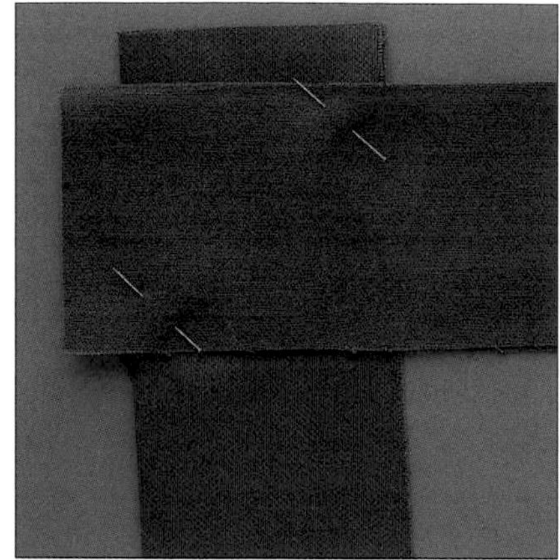

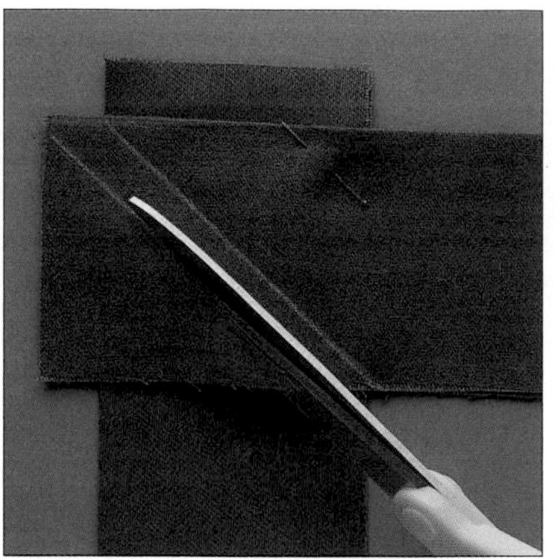

1 Lay two pressed strips at right angles to each other, overlapping them at the top and the side by the width of the seam allowance. Pin the pieces together.

2 Mark the seam position with a line at 45 degrees from the points where the border strips intersect. Add and mark on the seam allowance. Cut along seam allowance. Turn strips over and repeat to mark and cut the second strip.

3 Remove the pins and unfold the strips, wrong side up. Measure the seamline on the unmarked section, and draw it as shown.

4 Place the two strips together with right sides facing and raw edges matching. Pin and stitch along the marked seamline to within ⅝ in. (1.5 cm) of each end. Trim the point. Repeat steps **1–4** to join the second pair of strips.

5 Refold the stitched strips into a border shape, right sides together. Position the four remaining unstitched ends together, overlapping them by the width of the seam allowance, and pin. Repeat steps **2–5** to miter the two remaining corners.

Attaching the border

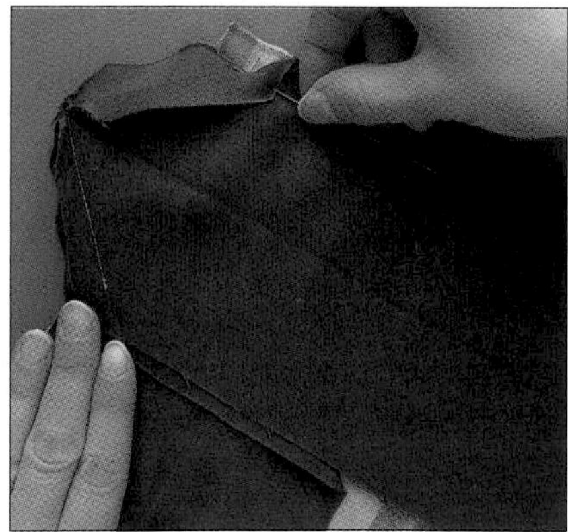

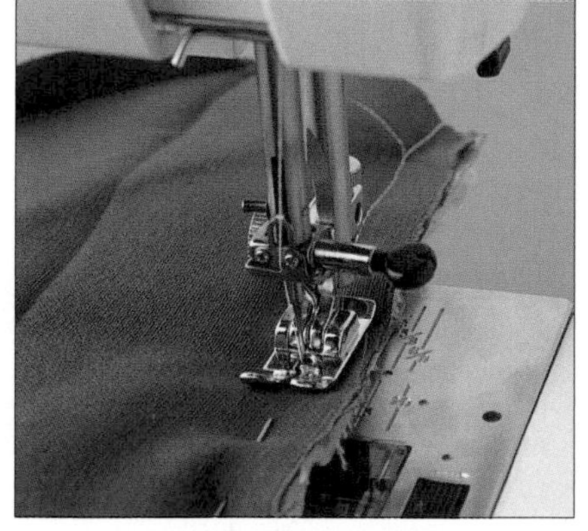

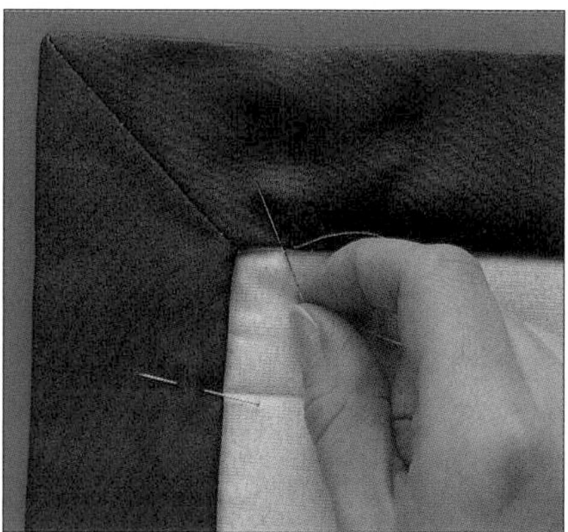

1 Pin the stitched border to the central panel with right sides facing and edges matching. Align the points where the mitered seams finish exactly with the corners of the panel.

2 Machine-stitch along the seam allowance, stopping and starting at each corner. Take care to reinsert the needle close to the point where it came out.

3 Fold the border right side out, pushing the corners into a point. On the wrong side, pin in the seam allowance. Slip-stitch the border in place.

Tassels & cord trims

Tassels and twisted cord trims are ideal for decorating many items throughout the home—from embroidered pillows and drapery tiebacks to valances, shades and light pulls. You can buy a wide selection of ready-made tassels and cords in a range of standard widths, but it's well worth making your own. The techniques are very simple, and you can make the cord or tassel to exactly the right color and size for your decor.

The steps below show how to make a simple tassel of any size. The steps on page 314 show how to make a plush, round-headed tassel and how to make a twisted cord trim. The cord can be as fine or as thick as you like. Finer cords can be used to edge items such as cushions, footstools, and book covers, while thick cords can be used to make sumptuous, tassel-trimmed tiebacks.

Materials

Yarn and needles Tassels and cord trims can be made from almost any type of yarn: knitting or tapestry yarn, embroidery threads, chenille, and even raffia work well. You'll also need a tapestry needle with an appropriate-sized eye.

Molds and cardboard Tassels are constructed by wrapping yarn around a shape. Use firm cardboard for simple tassels. For round-headed tassels, use a suitably sized form with a central hole, such as a craft ball or an empty thread spool.

Ornaments Thread on trinkets and beads to add extra interest to tassels.

Making a simple tassel

1 Cut a piece of stiff cardboard the desired length of the tassel and about 2 in. (5 cm) wide. Wrap the yarn evenly around the card to the desired thickness. Thread a length of yarn onto a tapestry needle. Slip it under the tops of the loops and tie them loosely together. Ease the loops off the card.

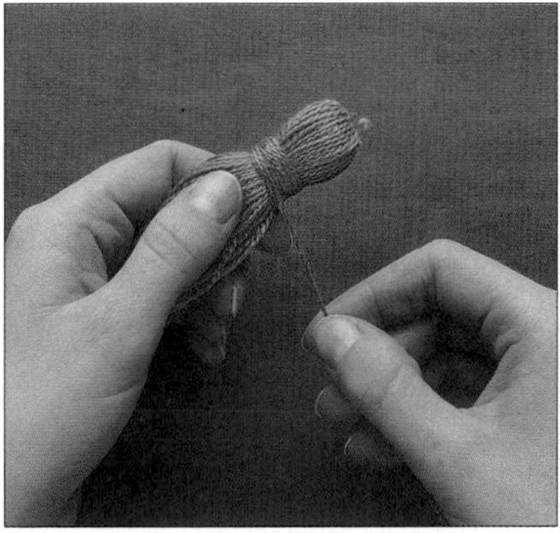

2 Cut a length of yarn about 30 in. (80 cm) long. Knot it around the tassel, about one-third of the way down from the top. Wrap the end of the yarn firmly around the tassel, covering the knot.

3 Thread the loose end of the yarn onto the tapestry needle, and take it into the center of the tassel, down into the tail. Then cut through the loops at the bottom of the tassel and trim them neatly.

Making a round-headed tassel

You Will Need

- Yarn in one or two colors
- Paper or polystyrene craft ball, 2 in. (5 cm) in diameter
- Pointed scissors or utility knife
- Tweezers
- Tapestry needle
- Cardboard rectangle, 6 x 4 in. (15 x 10 cm)
- Small wooden or plastic bead

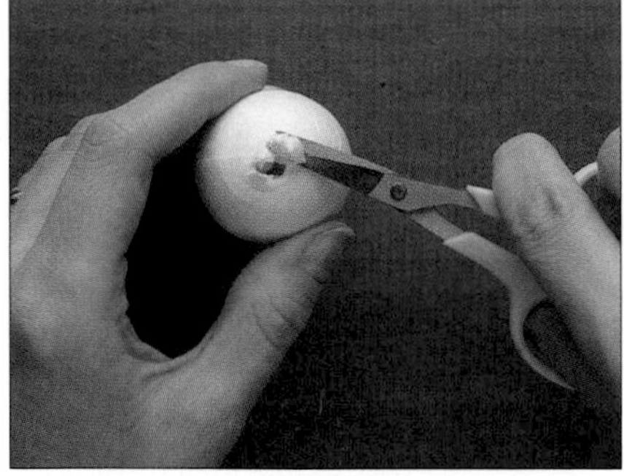

1 Using pointed scissors or a utility knife, cut a hole about ⅝ in. (1.5 cm) in diameter through the center of the craft ball. Trim off any rough edges, then use the tweezers to remove the waste material.

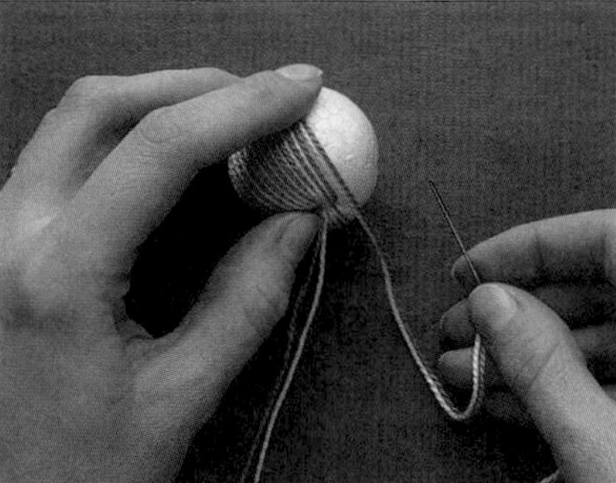

2 Thread two or three 2 yd. (2 m) lengths of yarn onto the needle. Take it through the hole in the ball, leaving 6 in. (15 cm) tails of yarn at the base. Wrap the yarn around the ball to cover it. Add more yarn as needed.

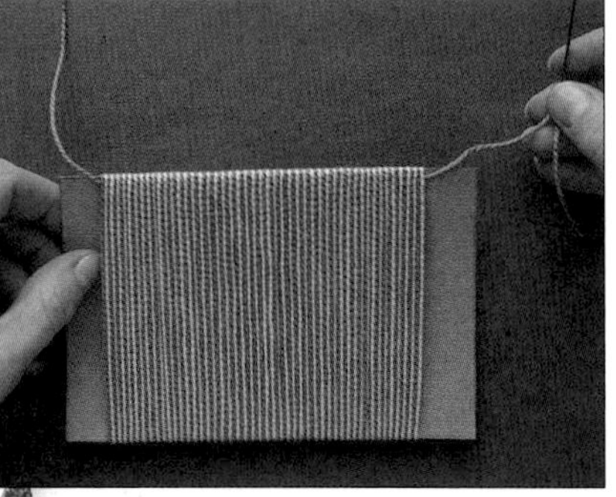

3 Wrap yarn evenly around the narrow width of the card until you have the desired thickness of the tassel tail. Thread the needle with a length of yarn, then slip it under the loops at the top of the card.

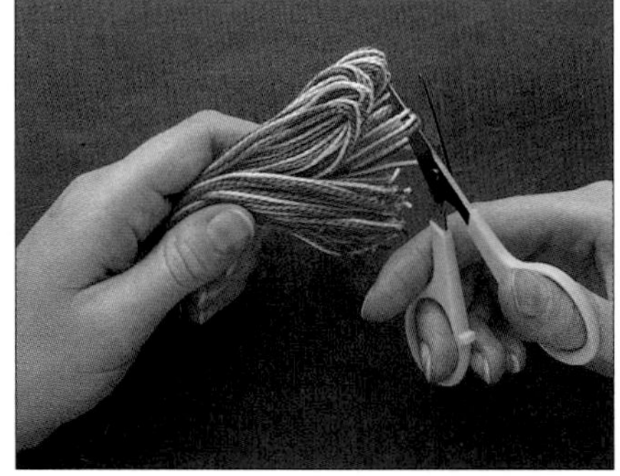

4 Ease the loops off the card, and tie the thread around them. Sew the loose ends of the yarn into the middle of the tail. Cut through the loops at the base of the tail and trim them neatly.

5 Thread the tails of yarn at the bottom of the ball onto the needle. Push the needle into the center of the tassel tail, pulling the yarn through firmly to bring the tassel and ball close together. To secure the yarn, knot it around the bead.

Round-headed tassels look particularly striking when made up of yarns in two or more different colors.

To secure a length of twisted cord to a tassel top, simply sew it neatly in place using the same thread.

Making a twisted cord trim

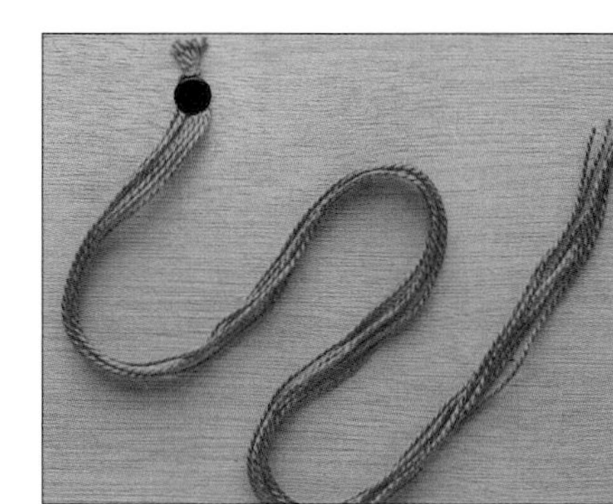

1 Cut lengths of yarn three times the desired length of the cord, and knot the ends together. Use a thumbtack to pin them to a work board or the back of a chair, or hang them from a sturdy hook.

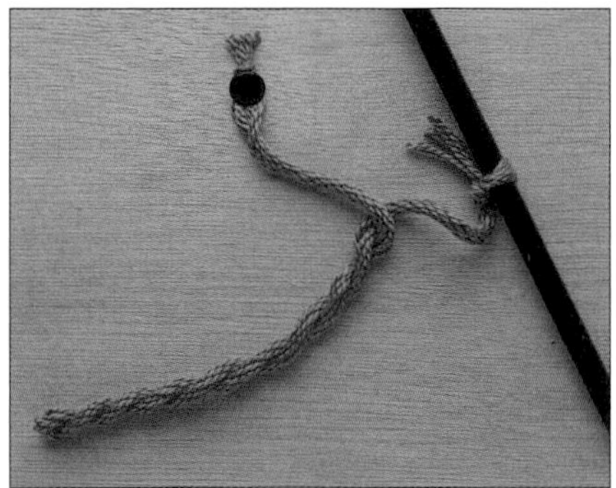

2 Tie the thread ends around a pencil. Rotate the pencil in one direction until the threads are very firmly twisted. Fold the twisted threads in half, and allow the strands to twist around each other. Run your hand down the threads to even out the twists. Knot and trim the ends.

Pompoms & fringe

Pompoms and fringe are ideal for embellishing all sorts of household accessories. You can add single pompoms to cushion corners or dangle them from tiebacks or valances. Pompom fringe—pompoms strung onto a length of cord—look delightful bobbing down the leading edge of a drapery or around the base of a lampshade, and plain fringe adds a cozy finishing touch to throws and pillow covers. You can buy pompoms in needlecraft stores, and pompom fringe and plain fringe from furnishing and notions departments, but it's easy and fun to make your own from remnants of yarn, as shown in the steps below and on page 316.

Making pompoms

1 Using a compass, draw a circle the desired size of the pompom on cardboard. Then, inside it, draw a smaller circle, about a third of the diameter of the outer one. Cut along both marked lines to make a ring. Use this as a template to make second ring the same size.

2 Thread a long length of yarn into a tapestry or yarn needle. Holding the card rings together, wind the yarn tightly around them. Continue until the ring is completely covered and the hole in the center is filled; add in extra lengths of yarn as you work, if necessary.

3 Push the blades of a pair of scissors between the two rings, and cut the yarn around the outer edges; keep the blades of the scissors between the rings so that you cut the yarn evenly. Then slip a length of yarn between the rings and tie it tightly around the cut yarn. Pull off the card rings and fluff out the pompom. Trim off any straggly ends, but leave the tied yarn long for attaching the pompom.

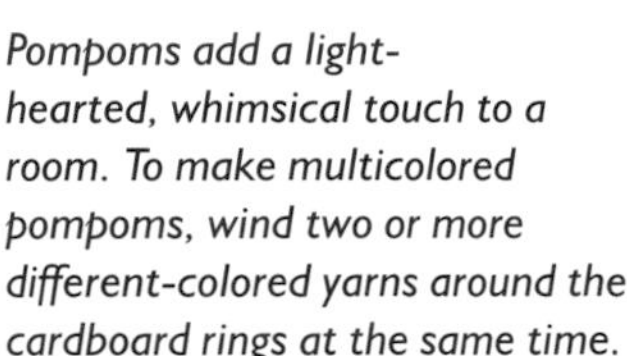

Pompoms add a lighthearted, whimsical touch to a room. To make multicolored pompoms, wind two or more different-colored yarns around the cardboard rings at the same time.

Making a pompom fringe

1 Cut three bunches of yarn, twice the length of the desired fringe, and knot them together at one end. Pin the knotted end to a firm surface, and braid the three bunches together. Knot them together at the other end.

Pompom fringe made from leftover yarns is an economical way to brighten up plain pillow covers, throws, and other informal soft furnishings.

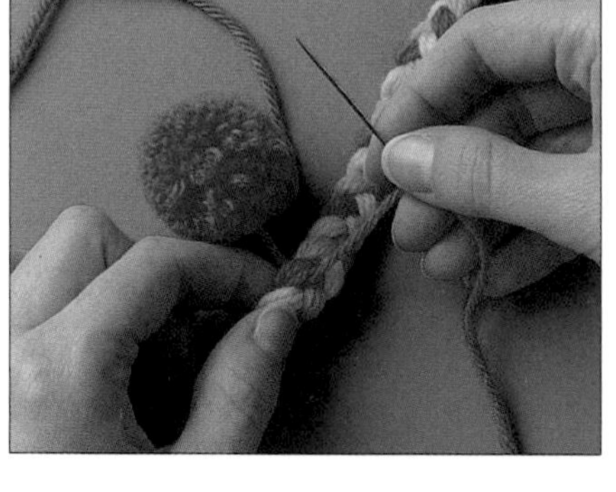

2 Work out how many pompoms you need for the cord—remember that the pompoms should be evenly spaced along the cord. Make this number of pompoms, following steps **1–3** on page 315.

3 Take a pompom and thread one end of the attaching yarn onto a tapestry or yarn needle. Thread the yarn through the braid and remove the needle. Neatly knot the two ends of the attaching yarn behind the braid. Repeat to hang all the pompoms.

4 Trim the loose ends from the knots, including those on the ends of the braided cord. Sew the fringe in place, or glue it with fabric adhesive.

Making a plain fringe

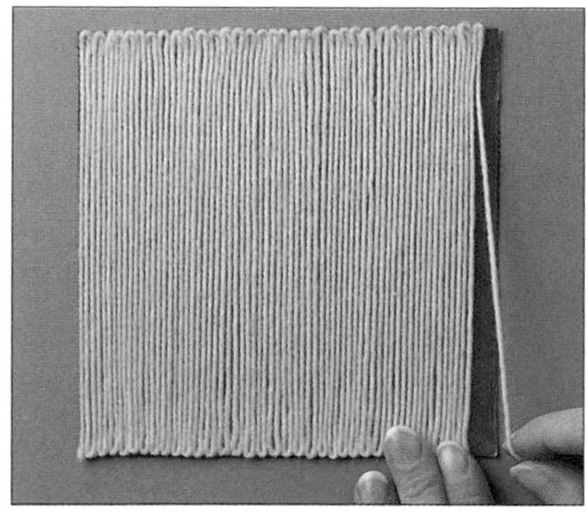

1 Cut a piece of cardboard twice the desired depth, plus ¾ in. (2 cm), of the fringe. Stick double-sided tape across the top and bottom. Fold the yarn in a zigzag pattern, pressing it onto the tape. Cut horizontally across the center of the card, behind the yarn.

2 Fold out the two sections of cardboard. Set the machine to a short straight stitch, and stitch two parallel rows, ¾ in. (2 cm) apart, down the center of the yarn. Stitch carefully, making sure that all the yarn is secured.

3 Cut across the yarn, between the stitched rows, to give two lengths of fringe. Cut through the center of loops, then smooth out the fringe. To attach it, insert the stitched edge into the seam allowance of the item, raw edges together, and machine stitch. To finish, trim the ends evenly.

Index

Page numbers in *italics* refer to illustrations

K

L

M

N

O

P

R

S

Acknowledgements

Photography:
Edward J Allwright, Jon Bouchier, Paul Bricknell, Julien Busselle, Alan Duns, David Garcia, Christine Hanscombe, Peter Marshall, Rob Mitchell Photography, Gloria Nicol, Lizzie Orme, Steven Pam, Russell Sadur, Lucinda Symons, Steve Tanner, Adrian Taylor, Shona Wood.
Photo on page 314(t) from Marie Claire Idées (Gilles de Chabaneix).

Illustrations:
Maria Diaz, Jan Eaton, Terry Evans, Sally Holmes, Coral Mula.

Project Design:
Pages 111–114, 215–218, 223–226 designed by Lesley Teare